ARISTARCHUS OF SAMOS

THE ANCIENT COPERNICUS

BY

Sir Thomas Heath

DOVER PUBLICATIONS, INC.
NEW YORK

Published in Canada by General Publishing Company,
Ltd., 30 Lesmill Road, Don Mills, Toronto, Ontario.
Published in the United Kingdom by Constable and
Company, Ltd., 10 Orange Street, London WC2H 7EG.

This Dover edition, first published in 1981, is an unabridged and unaltered republication of the work originally
published in 1913 by the Clarendon Press, Oxford, under
the title, *Aristarchus of Samos, The Ancient Copernicus, A
History of Greek Astronomy to Aristarchus Together with
Aristarchus's Treatise on the Sizes and Distances of the
Sun and Moon, A New Greek Text with Translation and
Notes.* The present edition is published by special arrangement with Oxford University Press.

International Standard Book Number: 0-486-24188-2
Library of Congress Catalog Card Number: 81-66916

Manufactured in the United States of America
Dover Publications, Inc.
180 Varick Street
New York, N.Y. 10014

PREFACE

THIS work owes its inception to a desire expressed to me by my old schoolfellow Professor H. H. Turner for a translation of Aristarchus's extant work *On the sizes and distances of the Sun and Moon*. Incidentally Professor Turner asked whether any light could be thrown on the grossly excessive estimate of 2° for the angular diameter of the sun and moon which is one of the fundamental assumptions at the beginning of the book. I remembered that Archimedes distinctly says in his *Psammites* or *Sand-reckoner* that Aristarchus was the first to discover that the apparent diameter of the sun is about 1/720th part of the complete circle described by it in the daily rotation, or, in other words, that the angular diameter is about $\frac{1}{2}$°, which is very near the truth. The difference suggested that the treatise of Aristarchus which we possess was an early work; but it was still necessary to search the history of Greek astronomy for any estimates by older astronomers that might be on record, with a view to tracing, if possible, the origin of the figure of 2°.

Again, our treatise does not contain any suggestion of any but the geocentric view of the universe, whereas Archimedes tells us that Aristarchus wrote a book of hypotheses, one of which was that the sun and the fixed stars remain unmoved and that the earth revolves round the sun in the circumference of a circle. Now Archimedes was a younger contemporary of Aristarchus; he must have seen the book of hypotheses in question, and we could have no better evidence for attributing to Aristarchus the first enunciation of the Copernican hypothesis. The matter might have rested there but for the fact that in recent years (1898) Schiaparelli, an authority always to be mentioned with profound respect, has maintained that it was not after all Aristarchus, but Heraclides of Pontus, who first put forward the heliocentric hypothesis. Schiaparelli, whose two papers *Le sfere omocentriche di Eudosso, di Callippo e di Aristotele* and *I precursori di Copernico nell' antichità* are classics, showed in the latter paper that Heraclides discovered that the planets Venus and Mercury revolve round the sun, like satellites, as well as that the earth rotates about its own axis in about twenty-four hours. In his later paper of 1898 (*Origine del sistema planetario eliocentrico presso i Greci*) Schiaparelli went further and suggested that Heraclides must have arrived at the same conclusion about the superior planets as about Venus and Mercury, and would therefore hold that all alike revolved round the sun, while the sun with the planets moving in their orbits about it revolved bodily round the earth as centre in a year; in other words, according to Schiaparelli, Heraclides was probably the inventor of the system known as that of Tycho Brahe, or was acquainted with it and adopted it if it was invented by some contemporary and not by himself. So far it may be admitted that Schiaparelli has made out a plausible case; but when, in the same paper, he goes further and credits Heraclides with having originated the Copernican hypothesis also, he takes up much more doubtful ground. At the same time it was clear that his arguments were entitled to the most careful consideration, and this again necessitated research in the earlier history of Greek astronomy with the view of tracing every step in the progress towards the true Copernican theory. The first to substitute another centre for the earth in the celestial system were the Pythagoreans, who made the earth, like the sun, moon, and planets, revolve round the central fire; and, when once my study of the subject had been carried back so far, it seemed to me that the most fitting introduction to Aristarchus would be a sketch of the whole history of Greek astronomy up to his time. As regards the newest claim made by Schiaparelli on behalf of Heraclides of Pontus, I hope I have shown that the case is not made out, and that there is still no reason to doubt the unanimous testimony of antiquity that Aristarchus was the real originator of the Copernican hypothesis.

In the century following Copernicus no doubt was felt as to

identifying Aristarchus with the latter hypothesis. Libert Fromond, Professor of Theology at the University of Louvain, who tried to refute it, called his work *Anti-Aristarchus* (Antwerp, 1631). In 1644 Roberval took up the cudgels for Copernicus in a book the full title of which is *Aristarchi Samii de mundi systemate partibus et motibus eiusdem libellus. Adiectae sunt Æ. P. de Roberval, Mathem. Scient. in Collegio Regio Franciae Professoris, notae in eundem libellum.* It does not appear that experts were ever deceived by this title, although Baillet (*Jugemens des Savans*) complained of such disguises and would have had Roberval call his work *Aristarchus Gallus*, 'the French Aristarchus,' after the manner of Vieta's *Apollonius Gallus* and Snellius's *Eratosthenes Batavus.* But there was every excuse for Roberval. The times were dangerous. Only eleven years before seven Cardinals had forced Galilei to abjure his 'errors and heresies'; what wonder then that Roberval should take the precaution of publishing his views under another name?

Voltaire, as is well known, went sadly wrong over Aristarchus (*Dictionnaire Philosophique*, s. v. 'Système'). He said that Aristarchus 'is so obscure that Wallis was obliged to annotate him from one end to the other, in the effort to make him intelligible', and further that it was very doubtful whether the book attributed to Aristarchus was really by him. Voltaire (misled, it is true, by a wrong reading in a passage of Plutarch, *De facie in orbe lunae*, c. 6) goes on to question whether Aristarchus had ever propounded the heliocentric hypothesis; and it is clear that the treatise which he regarded as suspect was Roberval's book, and that he confused this with the genuine work edited by Wallis. Nor could he have looked at the latter treatise in any but a very superficial way, or he would have seen that it is not in the least obscure, and that the commentary of Wallis is no more elaborate than would ordinarily be expected of an editor bringing out for the first time, with the aid of MSS. not of the best, a Greek text and translation of a mathematical treatise in which a number of geometrical propositions are assumed without proof and therefore require some elucidation.

There is no doubt whatever of the genuineness of the work. Pappus makes substantial extracts from the beginning of it and quotes the main results. Apart from its astronomical content, it is of the greatest interest for its geometry. Thoroughly classical in form and language, as befits the period between Euclid and Archimedes, it is the first extant specimen of pure geometry used with a *trigonometrical* object, and in this respect is a sort of forerunner of Archimedes' *Measurement of a Circle*. I need therefore make no apology for offering to the public a new Greek text with translation and the necessary notes.

In conclusion I desire to express my best acknowledgements to the authorities of the Vatican Library for their kindness in allowing me to have a photograph of the best MS. of Aristarchus which forms part of the magnificent Codex Vaticanus Graecus 204 of the tenth century, and to Father Hagen of the Vatican Observatory for his assistance in the matter.

T. L. H.

CONTENTS

PART I

GREEK ASTRONOMY TO ARISTARCHUS OF SAMOS

PART II

ARISTARCHUS ON THE SIZES AND DISTANCES OF THE SUN AND MOON

CORRIGENDUM

P. 179, lines 26 and 31. It appears that προχωρήσεις, not προσχωρήσεις, is the correct reading in *Timaeus* 40 C. The meaning of προχωρήσεις is of course 'forward movements', but the change to this reading does not make it any the more necessary to take ἐπανακυκλήσεις in the sense of retrogradations ; on the contrary, a 'forward movement' and a 'returning of the circle upon itself' are quite natural expressions for the different stages of one simple circular motion. Cf. also *Republic* 617 B, where ἐπανακυκλούμενον is used of the 'counter-revolution' of the planet Mars ; what is meant is a simple circular revolution in a sense contrary to that of the fixed stars, and there is no suggestion of retrogradations.

PART I

GREEK ASTRONOMY TO ARISTARCHUS OF SAMOS

I

SOURCES OF THE HISTORY

THE history of Greek astronomy in its beginnings is part of the history of Greek philosophy, for it was the first philosophers, Ionian, Eleatic, Pythagorean, who were the first astronomers. Now only very few of the works of the great original thinkers of Greece have survived. We possess the whole of Plato and, say, half of Aristotle, namely, those of his writings which were intended for the use of his school, but not those which, mainly composed in the form of dialogues, were in a more popular style. But the whole of the pre-Socratic philosophy is one single expanse of ruins;[1] so is the Socratic philosophy itself, except for what we can learn of it from Plato and Xenophon.

But accounts of the life and doctrine of philosophers begin to appear quite early in ancient Greek literature (cf. Xenophon, who was born between 430 and 425 B.C.); and very valuable are the allusions in Plato and Aristotle to the doctrines of earlier philosophers; those in Plato are not very numerous, but he had the power of entering into the thoughts of other men and, in stating the views of early philosophers, he does not, as a rule, read into their words meanings which they do not convey. Aristotle, on the other hand, while making historical surveys of the doctrines of his predecessors a regular preliminary to the statement of his own, discusses them too much from the point of view of his own system; often even misrepresenting them for the purpose of making a controversial point or finding support for some particular thesis.

From Aristotle's time a whole literature on the subject of the older philosophy sprang up, partly critical, partly historical. This

---

[1] Gomperz, *Griechische Denker*, i³, p. 419.

again has perished except for a large number of fragments. Most important for our purpose are the notices in the *Doxographi Graeci*, collected and edited by Diels.[1] The main source from which these retailers of the opinions of philosophers drew, directly or indirectly, was the great work of Theophrastus, the successor of Aristotle, entitled *Physical Opinions* (Φυσικῶν δοξῶν $\overline{\iota\eta}$). It would appear that it was Theophrastus's plan to trace the progress of physics from Thales to Plato in separate chapters dealing severally with the leading topics. First the leading views were set forth on broad lines, in groups, according to the affinity of the doctrine, after which the differences between individual philosophers within the same group were carefully noted. In the First Book, however, dealing with the Principles, Theophrastus adopted the order of the various schools, Ionians, Eleatics, Atomists, &c., down to Plato, although he did not hesitate to connect Diogenes of Apollonia and Archelaus with the earlier physicists, out of their chronological order; chronological order was indeed, throughout, less regarded than the connexion and due arrangement of subjects. This work of Theophrastus was naturally the chief hunting-ground for those who collected the ' opinions' of philosophers. There was, however, another main stream of tradition besides the doxographic; this was in the different form of biographies of the philosophers. The first to write a book of ' successions' (διαδοχαί) of the philosophers was Sotion (towards the end of the third century B.C.); others who wrote ' successions' were a certain Antisthenes (probably Antisthenes of Rhodes, second century B.C.), Sosicrates, and Alexander Polyhistor. These works gave little in the way of doxography, but were made readable by the incorporation of anecdotes and apophthegms, mostly unauthentic. The work of Sotion and the 'Lives of Famous Men' by Satyrus (about 160 B.C.) were epitomized by Heraclides Lembus. Another writer of biographies was the Peripatetic Hermippus of Smyrna, known as the Callimachean, who wrote about Pythagoras in at least two Books, and is quoted by Josephus as a careful student of all history.[2] Our chief storehouse of biographical details derived from these and all other available sources is the great compilation which goes by the

---

[1] *Doxographi Graeci*, ed. Diels, Berlin, G. Reimer, 1879.
[2] *Doxographi Graeci* (henceforth generally quoted as *D. G.*), p. 151.

name of Diogenes Laertius (more properly Laertius Diogenes). It is a compilation made in the most haphazard way, without the exercise of any historical sense or critical faculty. But its value for us is enormous because the compiler had access to the whole collection of biographies which accumulated from Sotion's time to the first third of the third century A. D. (when Diogenes wrote), and consequently we have in him the whole residuum of this literature which reached such dimensions in the period.

In order to show at a glance the conclusions of Diels as to the relation of the various representatives of the doxographic and biographic traditions to one another and to the original sources I append a genealogical table [1]:

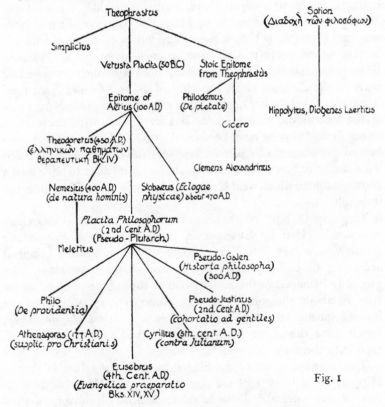

Fig. I

---

[1] Cf. Günther in Windelband, *Gesch. der alten Philosophie* (Iwan von Müller's *Handbuch der klassischen Altertumswissenschaft*, Band v. I), 1894, p. 275.

Only a few remarks need be added. 'Vetusta Placita' is the name given by Diels to a collection which has disappeared, but may be inferred to have existed. It adhered very closely to Theophrastus, though it was not quite free from admixture of other elements. It was probably divided into the following main sections: I. De principiis; II. De mundo; III. De sublimibus; IV. De terrestribus; V. De anima; VI. De corpore. The date is inferred from the facts that the latest philosophers mentioned in it were Posidonius and Asclepiades, and that Varro used it. The existence of the collection of Aëtius (*De placitis*, περὶ ἀρεσκόντων) is attested by Theodoretus (Bishop of Cyrus), who mentions it as accessible, and who certainly used it, since his extracts are more complete and trustworthy than those of the *Placita Philosophorum* and Stobaeus. The compiler of the *Placita* was not Plutarch, but an insignificant writer of about the middle of the second century A. D., who palmed them off as Plutarch. Diels prints the *Placita* in parallel columns with the corresponding parts of the *Eclogae*, under the title of *Aëtii Placita*; quotations from the other writers who give extracts are added in notes at the foot of the page. So far as Cicero deals with the earliest Greek philosophy, he must be classed with the doxographers; both he and Philodemus (*De pietate*, περὶ εὐσεβείας, fragments of which were discovered on a roll at Herculaneum) seem alike to have used a common source which went back to a Stoic epitome of Theophrastus, now lost.

The greater part of the fragment of the Pseudo-Plutarchian στρωματεῖς given by Eusebius in Book I. 8 of the *Praeparatio Evangelica* comes from an epitome of Theophrastus, arranged according to philosophers. The author of the *Stromateis*, who probably belonged to the same period as the author of the *Placita*, that is, about the middle of the second century A. D., confined himself mostly to the sections *de principio, de mundo, de astris*; hence some things are here better preserved than elsewhere; cf. especially the notice about Anaximander.

The most important of the biographical doxographies is that of Hippolytus in Book I of the *Refutation of all Heresies* (the sub-title of the particular Book is φιλοσοφούμενα), probably written between 223 and 235 A.D. It is derived from two sources. The

one was a biographical compendium of the διαδοχή type, shorter
and even more untrustworthy than Diogenes Laertius, but containing excerpts from Aristoxenus, Sotion, Heraclides Lembus,
and Apollodorus.   The other was an epitome of Theophrastus.
Hippolytus's plan was to take the philosophers in order and then
to pick out from the successive sections of the epitome of Theophrastus the views of each philosopher on each topic, and insert
them in their order under the particular philosopher.   So carefully
was this done that the divisions of the work of Theophrastus can
practically be restored.[1] Hippolytus began with the idea of dealing
with the chief philosophers only, as Thales, Pythagoras, Empedocles,
Heraclitus. For these he had available only the inferior (biographical)
source.   The second source, the epitome of Theophrastus, then
came into his hands, and, beginning with Anaximander, he proceeded
to make a most precious collection of opinions.

Another of our authorities is Achilles (not Tatius), who wrote
an Introduction to the *Phaenomena* of Aratus.[2]   Achilles' date is
uncertain, but he probably lived not earlier than the end of the
second century A.D., and not much later. The foundation of
Achilles' commentary was a Stoic compendium of astronomy,
probably by Eudorus, which in its turn was extracted from a work
by Diodorus of Alexandria, a pupil of Posidonius.   But Achilles
drew from other sources as well, including the Pseudo-Plutarchian
Placita; he did not hesitate to alter his extracts from the latter,
and to mix alien matter with them.

The opinions noted by the *Doxographi* are largely incorporated
in Diels' later work *Die Fragmente der Vorsokratiker*.[3]

For the earlier period from Thales to Empedocles, Tannery gives
a translation of the doxographic data and the fragments in his
work *Pour l'histoire de la science hellène, de Thalès à Empédocle*,
Paris, 1887; taking account as it does of all the material, this work is
the best and most suggestive of the modern studies of the astronomy
of the period.   Equally based on the *Doxographi*, Max Sartorius's
dissertation *Die Entwicklung der Astronomie bei den Griechen bis*

---

[1] Diels, *Doxographi Graeci*, p. 153.
[2] Excerpts from this are preserved in Cod. Laurentian. xxviii. 44, and are
included in the *Uranologium* of Petavius, 1630, pp. 121–64, &c.
[3] Second edition in two vols. (the second in two parts), Berlin, 1906–10.

Anaxagoras und Empedokles (Halle, 1883) is a very ʽconcise and useful account. Naturally all or nearly all the material is also to be found in the monumental work of Zeller and in Professor Burnet's *Early Greek Philosophy* (second edition, 1908); and picturesque, if sometimes too highly coloured, references to the astronomy of the ancient philosophers are a feature of vol. i of Gomperz's *Griechische Denker* (third edition, 1911).

Eudemus of Rhodes (about 330 B.C.), a pupil of Aristotle, wrote a History of Astronomy (as he did a History of Geometry), which is lost, but was the source of a number of notices in other writers. In particular, the very valuable account of Eudoxus's and Callippus's systems of concentric spheres which Simplicius gives in his Commentary on Aristotle's *De caelo* is taken from Eudemus through Sosigenes as intermediary. A few notices from Eudemus's work are also found in the astronomical portion of Theon of Smyrna's *Expositio rerum mathematicarum ad legendum Platonem utilium,*[1] which also draws on two other sources, Dercyllides and Adrastus. The former was a Platonist with Pythagorean leanings, who wrote a book on Plato's philosophy. His date was earlier than the time of Tiberius, perhaps earlier than Varro's. Adrastus, a Peripatetic of about the middle of the second century A.D., wrote historical and lexicographical essays on Aristotle; he also wrote a commentary on the *Timaeus* of Plato, which is quoted by Proclus as well as by Theon of Smyrna.

[1] Edited by E. Hiller (Teubner, 1878).

II

HOMER AND HESIOD

WE take as our starting-point the conceptions of the structure
of the world which are to be found in the earliest literary monuments
of Greece, that is to say, the Homeric poems and the works of
Hesiod. In their fundamental conceptions Homer and Hesiod
agree. The earth is a flat circular disc; this is not stated in so
many words, but only on this assumption could Poseidon from
the mountains of Solym in Pisidia see Odysseus at Scheria on the
further side of Greece, or Helios at his rising and setting descry
his cattle on the island of Thrinakia. Round this flat disc, on the
horizon, runs the river Oceanus, encircling the earth and flowing
back into itself (ἀψόρροος); from this all other waters take their
rise, that is, the waters of Oceanus pass through subterranean
channels and appear as the springs and sources of other rivers.
Over the flat earth is the vault of heaven, like a sort of hemispherical dome exactly covering it; hence it is that the Aethiopians
dwelling in the extreme east and west are burnt black by the sun.
Below the earth is Tartarus, covered by the earth and forming
a sort of vault symmetrical with the heaven; Hades is supposed
to be beneath the surface of the earth, as far from the height of
the heaven above as from the depth of Tartarus below, i.e. presumably in the hollow of the earth's disc. The dimensions of the
heaven and earth are only indirectly indicated; Hephaestus cast
down from Olympus falls for a whole day till sundown; on the
other hand, according to Hesiod, an iron anvil would take nine
days to pass from the heaven to the earth, and again nine days
from the earth to Tartarus. The vault of heaven remains for ever
in one position, unmoved; the sun, moon, and stars move round
under it, rising from Oceanus in the east and plunging into it again
in the west. We are not told what happens to the heavenly bodies

between their setting and rising; they cannot pass round under the earth because Tartarus is never lit up by the sun; possibly they are supposed to float round Oceanus, past the north, to the points where they next rise in the east, but it is only later writers who represent Helios as sleeping and being carried round on the water on a golden bed or in a golden bowl.[1]

Coming now to the indications of actual knowledge of astronomical facts to be found in the poems, we observe in Hesiod a considerable advance as compared with Homer. Homer mentions, in addition to the sun and moon, the Morning Star, the Evening Star, the Pleiades, the Hyades, Orion, the Great Bear ('which is also called by the name of the Wain, and which turns round on the same spot and watches Orion; it alone is without lot in Oceanus's bath'[2]),

---

[1] Athenaeus, *Deipnosoph.* xi. 38–9.

[2] It seems that some of the seven principal stars of the Great Bear do now set in the Mediterranean, e.g., in places further south in latitude than Rhodes (lat. 36°), γ, the hind foot, as well as η, the tip of the tail, and at Alexandria all the seven stars except α, the head. But this was not so in Homer's time. In proof of this, Sir George Greenhill (in a lecture delivered in 1910 to the Hellenic Travellers' Club) refers to calculations made by Dr. J. B. Pearson of the effect of Precession in the interval since 750 B.C., a date taken 'without prejudice' (*Proceedings of the Cambridge Philosophical Society*, 1877 and 1881), and to the results obtained in a paper by J. Gallenmüller, *Der Fixsternhimmel jetzt und in Homers Zeiten mit zwei Sternkarten* (Regensburg, 1884/85). Gallenmüller's charts are for the years 900 B.C. and A.D. 1855 respectively, and the chart for 900 B.C. shows that the N.P.D. of both β, the fore-foot, and η, the tip of the tail, was then about 25°. But we also find convincing evidence in the original writings of the Greek astronomers. Hipparchus (*In Arati et Eudoxi phaenomena commentariorum libri tres*, ed. Manitius, 1894, p. 114. 9–10) observes that Eudoxus [say, in 380 B.C., or 520 years later than the date to which Gallenmüller's chart refers] made the fore-foot (β) about 24°, and the hind-foot (γ) about 25°, distant from the north pole. This was perhaps not very accurate; for Hipparchus says (ibid., p. 30. 2–8), 'As regards the north pole, Eudoxus is in error in stating that "there is a certain star which always remains in the same spot, and this star is the pole of the universe"; for in reality there is no star at all at the pole, but there is an empty space there, with, however, three stars near to it [probably α and κ of Draco and β of the Little Bear], and the point at the pole makes with these three stars a figure which is very nearly square, as Pytheas of Massalia stated.' (Pytheas, the great explorer of the northern seas, was a contemporary of Aristotle, and perhaps some forty years later than Eudoxus.) But, as Hipparchus himself (writing in this case not later than 134 B.C.) makes the angular radius of the 'always-visible circle' 37° at Athens and 36° at Rhodes (ibid., pp. 112. 16 and 114. 24–6), it is evident that in Eudoxus's time the whole of the Great Bear remained well above the horizon. A passage of Proclus (*Hypotyposis*, c. 7, §§ 45–8, p. 234, ed. Manitius) is not without interest in this connexion. He is trying to controvert the theory of astronomers that the fixed stars themselves have a movement about the pole of the ecliptic (as distinct from the pole of the universe) of about 1° in 100 years

Sirius ('the star which rises in late summer . . . which is called among men "Orion's dog"; bright it shines forth, yet is a baleful sign, for it brings to suffering mortals much fiery heat'), the 'late-setting Boötes' (the 'ploughman' driving the Wain, i. e. Arcturus, as Hesiod was the first to call it). Since the Great Bear is said to be the *only* constellation which never sets, we may perhaps assume that the stars and constellations above named are all that were definitely recognized at the time, or at least that the Bear was the only constellation recognized in the northern sky. There is little more that can be called astronomy in Homer. There are vague uses of astronomical phenomena for the purpose of fixing localities or marking times of day or night; as regards the day, the morning twilight, the rising and setting of the sun, midday, and the onset of night are distinguished; the night is divided into three thirds. Aristotle was inclined to explain Helios's seven herds of cattle and sheep respectively containing 50 head in each herd (i. e. 350 in all of each sort) as a rough representation of the number of days in a year. Calypso directed Odysseus to sail in such a way as to keep the Great Bear always on his left. One passage,[1] relating to the island called Syrie, 'which is above Ortygia where are the turnings ($\tau\rho o\pi a\ell$) of the sun', is supposed by some to refer to the *solstices*, but there is no confirmation of this by any other passage, and it seems safer to take 'turning' to mean the turn which the sun takes at setting, when of course he begins his return journey (travelling round Oceanus or otherwise) to the place of his

---

(this is Ptolemy's estimate). ' How is it ', says Proclus, 'that the Bears, which have always been visible above the horizon through countless ages, still remain so, if they move by one degree in 100 years about the pole of the zodiac, which is different from the world-pole ; for, if they had moved so many degrees as this would imply, they should now no longer graze ($\pi a\rho a\xi\acute{\epsilon}\epsilon\iota\nu$) the horizon but should partly set ' ! This passage, written (say) 840 years after Eudoxus's location of β and γ of the Great Bear, shows that the Great Bear was then much nearer to setting than it was in Eudoxus's time, and the fact should have made Proclus speak with greater caution. [The star which Eudoxus took as marking the north pole has commonly been supposed to be β of the Little Bear; but Manitius (*Hipparchi in Arati et Eudoxi phaen. comment.*, 1894, p. 306), as the result of studying a 'Precession-globe' designed by Prof. Haas of Vienna, considers that it was certainly a different star, namely, 'Draconis 16,' which occupies a position determined as the intersection of (1) a perpendicular from our Polar Star to the straight line joining κ and λ of Draco and (2) the line joining γ and β of the Little Bear and produced beyond β.]

[1] *Odyssey* xv. 403–4.

rising, in which case the island would simply be situated on the
western horizon where the sun *sets*.[1]

Hesiod mentions practically the same stars as Homer, the
Pleiades, the Hyades, Orion, Sirius, and Arcturus. But, as might
be expected, he makes much more use than Homer does of celestial
phenomena for the purpose of determining times and seasons in the
year. Thus, e. g., he marked the time for sowing at the beginning
of winter by the setting of the Pleiades in the early twilight, or
again by the early setting of the Hyades or Orion, which means
the 3rd, 7th, or 15th November in the Julian calendar according to
the particular stars taken;[2] the time for harvest he fixed by the
early rising of the Pleiades, which means the Julian 19th of May;[3]
threshing-time he marked by the early rising of Orion (Julian 9th
of July), vintage-time by the early rising of Arcturus (Julian 18th
of September), and so on.[4] With Hesiod, Spring begins with the
late rising of Arcturus; this would in his time and climate be the
24th February of the Julian calendar, or 57 days after the winter
solstice, which in his time would be the 29th December. He himself makes Spring begin 60 days after the winter solstice; he may
be intentionally stating a round figure, but, if he made an error of

---

[1] Martin has discussed the question at considerable length ('Comment
Homère s'orientait' in *Mémoires de l'Académie des Inscriptions et Belles-
Lettres*, xxix, Pt. 2, 1879, pp. 1–28). He strongly holds that τροπαὶ ἠελίοιο can
only mean the *solstice*, that by this we must also understand the *summer*
solstice, and that the expression ὅθι τροπαὶ ἠελίοιο must therefore be in the
direction of the place on the horizon where the sun sets at the summer solstice,
i.e. west-north-west. Martin's ground is his firm conviction that τροπαὶ ἠελίοιο
has *never*, in any Greek poet or prose writer, any other than the technical
meaning of 'solstice'. This is, however, an assumption not susceptible of proof;
and Martin is not very successful in his search for confirmation of his view.
Identifying Ortygia with Delos, and Syrie with Syra or Syros, he admits that
the southern part of Syra is due west of the southern part of Delos; only the
northern portion of Syra stretches further north than the northern portion of
Delos; therefore, geographically, either west or west-north-west would describe
the direction of Syra relatively to Ortygia well enough. Of the Greek commentators, Aristarchus of Samothrace and Herodian of Alexandria take τροπαὶ
to mean 'setting' simply; Martin is driven therefore to make the most he can
of Hesychius who (s. v. Ὀρτυγίη) gives as an explanation τοῦτο δέ ἐστιν ὅπου αἱ
δύσεις ἄρχονται, 'This is where the settings commence', which Martin interprets
as meaning 'where the sun sets *at the commencement of the Greek year*', which
was about the time of the summer solstice; but this is a great deal to get o·t
of 'commencement of setting'.

[2] Ideler, *Handbuch der mathematischen und technischen Chronologie*, 1825,
i, pp. 242, 246.

[3] Ibid. p. 242.   [4] Ibid. pp. 246, 247.

three days, it would not be surprising, seeing that in his time there were no available means for accurately observing the times of the solstices. His early summer ($\theta\acute{\epsilon}\rho os$), as distinct from late summer ($\acute{o}\pi\acute{\omega}\rho a$), he makes, in like manner, end 50 days after the summer solstice. Thus he was acquainted with the solstices, but he says nothing about the equinoxes, and only remarks in one place that in late summer the days become shorter and the nights longer. From the last part of the *Works and Days* we see that Hesiod had an approximate notion of the moon's period; he puts it at 30 days, and divides the month into three periods of ten days each.[1]

Hesiod was also credited with having written a poem under the title of 'Astronomy'. A few fragments of such a poem are preserved;[2] Athenaeus, however, doubted whether it was Hesiod's work, for he quotes 'the author of the poem "Astronomy" which is attributed to Hesiod' as always speaking of Peleiades. Pliny observes that 'Hesiod (for an Astrology is also handed down under his name) stated that the matutinal setting of the Vergiliae [Pleiades] took place at the autumnal equinox, whereas Thales made the time 25 days from the equinox'.[3] The poem was thought to be Alexandrine, but has recently been shown to be old; perhaps, if we may judge by the passage of Pliny, it may be anterior to Thales.

[1] Sartorius, op. cit., p. 16; Ideler, i, p. 257.
[2] Diels, *Vorsokratiker*, ii². 1, 1907, pp. 499, 500.
[3] Pliny, *N. H.* xviii, c. 25, § 213 ; Diels, loc. cit.

III

THALES

Such astronomy as we find in Homer and Hesiod was of the merely practical kind, which uses the celestial recurrences for the regulation of daily life; but, as the author of the *Epinomis* says, 'the true astronomer will not be the man who cultivates astronomy in the manner of Hesiod and any other writers of that type, concerning himself only with such things as settings and risings, but the man who will investigate the seven revolutions included in the eight revolutions and each describing the same circular orbit [i. e. the separate motions of the sun, moon, and the five planets combined with the eighth motion, that of the sphere of the fixed stars, or the daily rotation], which speculations can never be easily mastered by the ordinary person but demand extraordinary powers'. The history of Greek astronomy in the sense of astronomy proper, the astronomy which seeks to explain the heavenly phenomena and their causes, begins with Thales.

Thales of Miletus lived probably from about 624 to 547 B.C. (though according to Apollodorus he was born in 640/39). According to Herodotus, his ancestry was Phoenician; his mother was Greek, to judge by her name Cleobuline, while his father's name, Examyes, is Carian, so that he was of mixed descent. In 582/1 B.C. he was declared one of the Seven Wise Men, and indeed his versatility was extraordinary; statesman, engineer, mathematician and astronomer, he was an acute business man in addition, if we may believe the story that, wishing to show that it was easy to get rich, he took the opportunity of a year in which he foresaw that there would be a great crop of olives to get control of all the oil-presses in Miletus and Chios in advance, paying a low rental when there was no one to bid against him, and then, when the accommodation was urgently wanted, charging as much as he liked for it, with the result that he made a large profit.[1] For his many-sided culture he

[1] Aristotle, *Politics* i. 11. 9, 1259 a 6-17.

was indebted in great measure to what he learnt on long journeys which he took, to Egypt in particular ; it was in Egypt that he saw in operation the elementary methods of solving problems in practical geometry which inspired him with the idea of making geometry a deductive science depending on general propositions ; and he doubtless assimilated much of the astronomical knowledge which had been accumulated there as the result of observations recorded through long centuries.

Thales' claim to a place in the history of scientific astronomy depends almost entirely on one achievement attributed to him, that of predicting an eclipse of the sun. There is no trustworthy evidence of any other discoveries, or even of any observations, made by him, although one would like to believe the story, quoted by Plato,[1] that, when he was star-gazing and fell into a well in consequence, he was rallied 'by a clever and pretty maid-servant from Thrace'[2] for being so 'eager to know what goes on in the heavens when he could not see what was in front of him, nay, at his very feet'.

But did Thales predict a solar eclipse? The story is entirely rejected by Martin.[3] He points out that, while the references to the prediction do not exactly agree, it is in fact necessary, if the occurrence of a solar eclipse at any specified place on the earth's surface is to be predicted with any prospect of success, to know more of the elements of astronomy than Thales could have known, and in particular to allow for parallax, which was not done until much later, and then only approximately, by Hipparchus. Further, if the prophecy had rested on any scientific basis, it is incredible that the basis should not have been known and been used by later Ionian philosophers for making other similar predictions, whereas we hear of none such in Greece for two hundred years. Indeed, only one other supposed prediction of the same kind is referred to. Plutarch[4] relates that, when Plato was on a visit to Sicily and staying with Dionysius, Helicon of Cyzicus, a friend of Plato's, foretold a solar eclipse (apparently that which took place on 12th May,

---

[1] *Theaetetus* 174 A ; cf. Hippolytus, *Refut.* i. 1. 4 (*D. G.* p. 555. 9–12).

[2] There is another version not so attractive, according to which [Diog. Laert. i. 34], being taken out of the house by an old woman to look at the stars, he fell into a hole and was reproached by her in similar terms. This version might suggest that it was the old woman who was the astronomer rather than Thales.

[3] *Revue Archéologique*, ix, 1864, pp. 181 sq. [4] *Life of Dion*, c. 19, p. 966 A.

361 B. C.),[1] and, when this took place as predicted, the tyrant was filled with admiration and made Helicon a present of a talent of silver. This story is, however, not confirmed by any other evidence, and the necessary calculations would have been scarcely less impossible for Helicon than for Thales. Martin's view is that both Thales and Helicon merely explained the cause of solar eclipses and asserted the necessity of their recurrence within certain limits of time, and that these explanations were turned by tradition into predictions. In regard to Thales, Martin relies largely on the wording of a passage in Theon of Smyrna, where he purports to quote Eudemus; 'Eudemus', he says, 'relates in his Astronomies that ... Thales was the first to *discover* (εὗρε πρῶτος understood) *the eclipse of the sun* and the fact that the sun's period with respect to the solstices is not always the same',[2] and the natural meaning of the first part of the sentence is that Thales discovered the explanation and the cause of a solar eclipse. It is true that Diogenes Laertius says that 'Thales appears, according to some, to have been the first to study astronomy and to predict both solar eclipses and solstices, as Eudemus says in his History of Astronomy',[3] and Diogenes must be quoting from the same passage as Theon ; but it is pretty clear, as Martin says, that he copied it inaccurately and himself inserted the word (προειπεῖν) referring to *predictions* ; indeed the word 'predict' does not go well with 'solstices', and is suspect for this reason. Nor does any one credit Thales with having predicted more than one eclipse. No doubt the original passage spoke of 'eclipses' and 'solstices' in the plural and used some word like 'discover' (Theon's word), not the word 'predict'. And I think Martin may reasonably argue from the passage of Diogenes that the words 'according to some' are Eudemus's words, not his own, and therefore may be held to show that the truth of the tradition was not beyond doubt.[4]

---

[1] Boll, art. 'Finsternisse' in Pauly-Wissowa's *Real-Encyclopädie der classischen Altertumswissenschaft*, vi. 2, 1909, pp. 2356–7; Ginzel, *Handbuch der mathematischen und technischen Chronologie*, vol. ii, 1911, p. 527.

[2] Theon of Smyrna, ed. Hiller, p. 198. 14–18.

[3] Diog. L. i. 23 (*Vorsokratiker*, i², p. 3. 19–21).

[4] There is, however, yet another account purporting to be based on Eudemus. Clement of Alexandria (*Stromat.* i. 65) says : 'Eudemus observes in his History of Astronomy that Thales predicted the eclipse of the sun which took place at the time when the Medes and the Lydians engaged in battle, the king of the

Nevertheless, as Tannery observes,[1] Martin's argument can hardly satisfy us so far as it relates to Thales. The evidence that Thales actually predicted a solar eclipse is as conclusive as we could expect for an event belonging to such remote times, for Diogenes Laertius quotes Xenophanes as well as Herodotus as having admired Thales' achievement, and Xenophanes was almost contemporary with Thales. We must therefore accept the fact as historic, and it remains to inquire in what sense or form, and on what ground, he made his prediction. The accounts of it vary. Herodotus says[2] that the Lydians and the Medes continued their war, and 'when, in the sixth year, they encountered one another, it fell out that, after they had joined battle, the day suddenly turned into night. Now that this transformation of day (into night) would occur was foretold to the Ionians by Thales of Miletus, who fixed as the limit of time this very year in which the change actually took place.'[3] The prediction was therefore at best a rough one,

Medes being Cyaxares, the father of Astyages, and Alyattes, the son of Croesus, being the king of the Lydians; and the time was about the 50th Olympiad [580–577].' The last sentence was evidently taken from Tatian 41; but, if the rest of the passage correctly quotes Eudemus, it would appear that there must have been two passages in Eudemus dealing with the subject.

[1] Tannery, *Pour l'histoire de la science hellène*, p. 56.

[2] Herodotus, i. 74.

[3] Other references are as follows: Cicero, *De Divinatione* i. 49. 112, observes that Thales was said to have been the first to predict an eclipse of the sun, which eclipse took place in the reign of Astyages; Pliny, *N.H.* ii, c. 12, § 53, 'Among the Greeks Thales first investigated (the cause of the eclipse) in the fourth year of the 48th Olympiad [585/4 B.C.], having predicted an eclipse of the sun which took place in the reign of Alyattes in the year 170 A.U.C.'; Eusebius, *Chron.* (*Hieron.*), under year of Abraham 1433, 'An eclipse of the sun, the occurrence of which Thales had predicted: a battle between Alyattes and Astyages'. The eclipse so foretold is now most generally taken to be that which took place on the (Julian) 28th May, 585. A difficulty formerly felt in regard to this date seems now to have been removed. Herodotus (followed by Clement) says that the eclipse took place during a battle between Alyattes and Cyaxares. Now, on the usual assumption, based on Herodotus's chronological data, that Cyaxares reigned from about 635 to 595, the eclipse of 585 B.C. must have taken place during the reign of his son; and perhaps it was the knowledge of this fact which made Eusebius say that the battle was between Alyattes and Astyages. But it appears that Herodotus's reckoning was affected by an error on his part in taking the fall of the Median kingdom to be coincident with Cyrus's accession to the throne of Persia, and that Cyaxares really reigned from 624 to 584, and Astyages from 584 to 550 B.C. (Ed. Meyer in Pauly-Wissowa's *Real-Encyclopädie*, ii, 1896, p. 1865, &c.); hence the eclipse of 585 B.C. would after all come in Cyaxares' reign. Of two more solar eclipses which took place in the reign of Cyaxares one is ruled out, that of 597 B.C., because it took place at sunrise, which would not agree with Herodotus's story. The other was on 30th September, 610, and, as regards this, Bailly and Oltmanns showed that it was not total on the

since it only specified that the eclipse would occur within a certain year; and the true explanation seems to be that it was a prediction of the same kind as had long been in vogue with the Chaldaeans. That they had a system enabling them to foretell pretty accurately the eclipses of the moon is clear from the fact that some of the eclipses said by Ptolemy[1] to have been observed in Babylon were so partial that they could hardly have been noticed if the observers had not been to some extent prepared for them. Three of the eclipses mentioned took place during eighteen months in the years 721 and 720. It is probable that the Chaldaeans arrived at this method of approximately predicting the times at which lunar eclipses would occur by means of the period of 223 lunations, which was doubtless discovered as the result of long-continued observations. This period is mentioned by Ptolemy[2] as having been discovered by astronomers 'still more ancient' than those whom he calls 'the ancients'.[3] Now, while this method would serve well enough for lunar eclipses, it would very often fail for solar eclipses, because no account was taken of parallax. An excellent illustration of the way in which the system worked is on record; it is taken from a translation of an Assyrian cuneiform inscription, the relevant words being the following:

1. To the king my lord, thy servant Abil-istar.
2. May there be peace to the king my lord. May Nebo and Merodach
3. to the king my lord be favourable. Length of days,
4. health of body and joy of heart may the great gods

presumed field of battle (in Cappadocia), though it would be total in Armenia (Martin, *Revue Archéologique*, ix, 1864, pp. 183, 190). Tannery, however (*Pour l'histoire de la science hellène*, p. 38), holds that the latter eclipse was that associated with Thales. The latest authorities (Boll, art. 'Finsternisse', in Pauly-Wissowa's *Real-Encyclopädie*, vi. 2, 1909, pp. 2353-4, and Ginzel, *Spezieller Kanon der Sonnen- und Mondfinsternisse* and *Handbuch der mathematischen und technischen Chronologie*, vol. ii, 1911, p. 525) adhere to the date 28th May, 585.

[1] Ptolemy, *Syntaxis* iv, c. 6 sq.
[2] Ptolemy, *Syntaxis* iv, c. 2, p. 270, 1 sq., ed. Heiberg.
[3] Suidas understands the Chaldaean name for this period to have been *saros*, but this seems to be a mistake. According to Syncellus (*Chronographia*, p. 17, A–B), Berosus expressed his periods in *sars*, *ners*, and *sosses*, a *sar* being 3,600 years, while *ner* meant 600 years, and *soss* 60 years; but we learn that the same words were also used to denote the same numbers of days respectively (Syncellus, p. 32 C). Nor were they used of years and days only; in fact *sar*, *ner*, and *soss* were collective *numerals* simply, like our words 'gross', 'score', &c. (Cantor, *Gesch. d. Mathematik*, i³, p. 36).
[4] See George Smith, *Assyrian Discoveries*, p. 409.

5. to the king my lord grant.   Concerning the eclipse of the
   moon
6. of which the king my lord sent to me; in the cities of
   Akkad,
7. Borsippa, and Nipur, observations
8. they made and then in the city of Akkad
9. we saw part . . . .
10. The observation was made and the eclipse took place.

   •   •   •   •   •   •   •

17. And when for the eclipse of the sun we made
18. an observation, the observation was made and it did not take
    place.
19. That which I saw with my eyes to the king my lord
20. I send.   This eclipse of the moon
21. which did happen concerns the countries
22. with their god all.   Over Syria
23. it closes, the country of Phoenicia,
24. of the Hittites, of the people of Chaldaea,
25. but to the king my lord it sends peace, and according to
26. the observation, not the extending
27. of misfortune to the king my lord
28. may there be.

It would seem, as Tannery says,[1] that these clever people knew
how to turn their ignorance to account as well as their knowledge.
For them it was apparently of less consequence that their predictions should come true than that they should not let an eclipse take
place without their having predicted it.[2]

As it is with Egypt that legend associates Thales, it is natural
to ask whether the Egyptians too were acquainted with the period
of 223 lunations.   We have no direct proof; but Diodorus Siculus
says that the priests of Thebes predicted eclipses quite as well as
the Chaldeans,[3] and it is quite possible that the former had learnt
from the latter the period and the notions on which the successful
prediction of eclipses depended.   It is not, however, essential to
suppose that Thales got the information from the Egyptians; he
may have obtained it more directly.   Lydia was an outpost of

---

[1] Tannery, op. cit., p. 57.
[2] Delambre (*Hist. de l'astronomie ancienne*, i, p. 351) quotes a story that in
China, in 2159 B.C., the astronomers Hi and Ho were put to death, *according
to law*, in consequence of an eclipse of the sun occurring which they had not
foretold.
[3] Cf. Diodorus, i, c. 50; ii, c. 30.

Assyrio-Babylonian culture ; this is established by (among other things) the fact of the Assyrian protectorate over the kings Gyges and Ardys (attested by cuneiform inscriptions) ; and 'no doubt the inquisitive Ionians who visited the gorgeous capital Sardes, situated in their immediate neighbourhood, there first became acquainted with the elements of Babylonian science '.[1]

If there happened to be a number of *possible* solar eclipses in the year which (according to Herodotus) Thales fixed, he was not taking an undue risk; but it was great luck that it should have been total.[2]

Perhaps I have delayed too long over the story of the eclipse ; but it furnishes a convenient starting-point for a consideration of the claim of Thales to be credited with the multitude of other discoveries in astronomy attributed to him by the *Doxographi* and others. First, did he know the cause of eclipses ? Aëtius says that he thought the sun was made of an earthy substance,[3] like the moon, and was the first to declare that the sun is eclipsed when the moon comes in a direct line below it, the image of the moon then appeaiing on the sun's disc as on a mirror ;[4] and again he says that Thales, as well as Anaxagoras, Plato, Aristotle, and the Stoics, in accord with the mathematicians, held that the moon is eclipsed by reason of its falling into the shadow made by the earth when the earth is between the two heavenly bodies.[5] But, as regards the eclipse of the moon, Thales could not have given this explanation, because he held that the earth floated on the water ;[6] from which it may also be inferred that he, like his successors down to Anaxagoras inclusive, thought the earth to be a disc or a short cylinder. And if he had given the true explanation of the solar eclipse, it is impossible that all the succeeding Ionian philosophers should have exhausted their imaginations in other fanciful explanations such as we find recorded.[7]

We may assume that Thales would regard the sun and the moon as discs like the earth, or perhaps as hollow bowls which could

---

[1] Gomperz, *Griechische Denker*, i³, p. 421.   [2] Tannery, op. cit., p. 60.
[3] Aët. ii. 20. 9 (*D. G.* p. 349).   [4] Aët. ii. 24. 1 (*D. G.* pp. 353, 354).
[5] Aët. ii. 29. 6 (*D. G.* p. 360).
[6] Theophrastus apud Simpl. *in Phys.* p. 23. 24 (*D. G.* p. 475; *Vors.* i², p. 9. 22); cf. Aristotle, *Metaph.* A. 3, 983 b 21 ; *De caelo* ii. 13, 294 a 28.
[7] Tannery, op. cit., p. 56.

turn so as to show a dark side.[1] We must reject the statements
of Aëtius that he was the first to hold that the moon is lit up by
the sun, and that it seems to suffer its obscurations each month
when it approaches the sun, because the sun illuminates it from
one side only.[2] For it was Anaxagoras who first gave the true
scientific doctrine that the moon is itself opaque but is lit up by
the sun, and that this is the explanation no less of the moon's
phases than of eclipses of the sun and moon; when we read
in Theon of Smyrna that, according to Eudemus's History of
Astronomy, these discoveries were due to Anaximenes,[3] this would
seem to be an error, because the *Doxographi* say nothing of any
explanations of eclipses by Anaximenes,[4] while on the other hand
Aëtius does attribute to him the view that the moon was made
of fire,[5] just as the sun and stars are made of fire.[6]

We must reject, so far as Thales is concerned, the traditions that
'Thales, the Stoics, and their schools, made the earth spherical',[7]
and that 'the school of Thales put the earth in the centre'.[8]
For (1) we have seen that Thales made the earth a circular or
cylindrical disc floating on the water like a log[9] or a cork; and (2),
so far as we can judge of his conception of the universe, he would
appear to have regarded it as a mass of water (that on which the
earth floats) with the heavens superposed in the form of a *hemisphere*
and also bounded by the primeval water. It follows from this
conception that for Thales the sun, moon, and stars did not, between
their setting and rising again, continue their circular path *below* the
earth, but (as with Anaximenes later) laterally round the earth.

Tannery [10] compares Thales' view of the world with that found
in the ancient Egyptian papyri. In the beginning existed the *Nū*,
a primordial liquid mass in the limitless depths of which floated
the germs of things. When the sun began to shine, the earth was
flattened out and the waters separated into two masses. The one
gave rise to the rivers and the ocean; the other, suspended above,
formed the vault of heaven, *the waters above*, on which the stars

---

[1] Tannery, op. cit., p. 70.   [2] Aët. ii. 28. 5; 29. 6 (*D. G.* p. 358. 19; p. 360. 16).
[3] Theon of Smyrna, p. 198. 19-199. 2.
[4] Tannery, op. cit., pp. 56, 153.   [5] Aët. ii. 25. 2 (*D. G.* p. 356. 1).
[6] Aët. ii. 20. 2 (*D. G.* p. 348. 8); Hippol. *Refut.* i. 7. 4 (*D. G.* p. 561. 3).
[7] Aët. iii. 10. 1 (*D. G.* p. 376. 22).   [8] Aët. iii. 11. 1 (*D. G.* p. 377. 7).
[9] Aristotle, *De caelo* ii. 13, 294 a 30.   [10] Tannery, op. cit., p. 71.

and the gods, borne by an eternal current, began to float. The sun, standing upright in his sacred barque which had endured millions of years, glides slowly, conducted by an army of secondary gods, the planets and the fixed stars. The assumption of an upper and lower ocean is also old-Babylonian (cf. the division in Gen. i. 7 of the waters which were under the firmament from the waters which were above the firmament).

In a passage quoted by Theon of Smyrna, Eudemus attributed to Thales the discovery of 'the fact that the period of the sun with respect to the solstices is not always the same'.[1] The expression is ambiguous, but it must apparently mean the inequality of the length of the four astronomical seasons, that is, the four parts of the tropical year [2] as divided by the solstices and the equinoxes. Eudemus referred presumably to the two written works by Thales *On the Solstice* and *On the Equinox*,[3] which again would seem to be referred to in a later passage of Diogenes Laertius: 'Lobon of Argos says that his written works extend to 200 verses'. Now Hesiod, in the *Works and Days*, advises the commencement of certain operations, such as sowing, reaping, and threshing, when particular constellations rise or set in the morning, and he uses the solstices as fixed periods, but does not mention the equinoxes. Tannery [4] thinks, therefore, that Thales' work supplemented Hesiod's by the addition of other data and, in particular, fixed the equinoxes in the same way as Hesiod had fixed the solstices. The inequality of the intervals between the equinoxes and the solstices in one year would thus be apparent. This explanation agrees with the remark of Pliny that Thales fixed the matutinal setting of the Pleiades on the 25th day from the autumnal equinox.[5] All this knowledge Thales probably derived from the Egyptians or the Babylonians. The Babylonians, and doubtless the Egyptians also,

---

[1] Theon of Smyrna, p. 198. 17 (Θαλῆς εὗρε πρῶτος) . . . τὴν κατὰ τὰς τροπὰς αὐτοῦ περίοδον, ὡς οὐκ ἴση ἀεὶ συμβαίνει.

[2] The 'tropical year' is the time required by the sun to return to the same position with reference to the equinoctial points, while the 'sidereal year' is the time taken to return to the same position with reference to the fixed stars.

[3] Diog. L. i. 23 (*Vors.* i², p. 3. 18).

[4] Tannery, op. cit., p. 66.

[5] Pliny, *N. H.* xviii, c. 25, § 213 (*Vors.* i², p. 9. 44). This datum points to Egypt as the source of Thales' information, for the fact only holds good for Egypt and not for Greece (Zeller, i⁵, p. 184; cf. Tannery, op. cit., p. 67).

were certainly capable of determining more or less roughly the solstices and the equinoxes; and they would doubtless do this by means of the *gnomon*, the use of which, with that of the *polos*, the Greeks are said to have learnt from the Babylonians.[1]

Thales equally learnt from the Egyptians his division of the year into 365 days;[2] it is possible also that he followed their arrangement of months of 30 days each, instead of the practice already in his time adopted in Greece of reckoning by lunar months.

The *Doxographi* associate Thales with Pythagoras and his school as having divided the whole sphere of the heaven by five circles, the arctic which is always visible, the summer-tropical, the equatorial, the winter-tropical, and the antarctic which is always invisible; it is added that the so-called zodiac circle passes obliquely to the three middle circles, touching all three, while the meridian circle, which goes from north to south, is at right angles to all the five circles.[3] But, if Thales had any notion of these circles, it must have been of the vaguest; the antarctic circle in particular presupposes the spherical form for the earth, which was not the form which Thales gave it. Moreover, the division into zones is elsewhere specifically attributed to Parmenides and Pythagoras; and, indeed, Parmenides and Pythagoras were the first to be in a position to take this step,[4] as they were the first to hold that the earth is spherical in shape. Again, Eudemus is quoted[5] as distinctly attributing the discovery of the 'cincture of the zodiac (circle)' to Oenopides, who was at least a century later than Thales.

Diogenes Laertius says that, according to some authorities, Thales was the first to declare the apparent size of the sun (and the moon) to be 1/720th part of the circle described by it.[6] The version of this story given by Apuleius is worth quoting for a human touch which it contains:

[1] Herodotus, ii. 109.
[2] Herodotus (ii. 4) says that the Egyptians were the first of men to discover the year, and that they divided it into twelve parts, 'therein adopting a wiser system (as it seems to me) than the Greeks, who have to put in an intercalary month every third year, in order to keep the seasons right, whereas the Egyptians give their twelve months thirty days each and add five every year outside the number (of twelve times 30)'. As regards Thales, cf. Diog. L. i. 27 and 24 (*Vors.* i², pp. 3. 27; 4. 9).   [3] Aët. ii. 12. 1 (*D. G.* p. 340. 11 sq.).
[4] As to Parmenides cf. Aët. iii. 11. 4 (*D. G.* p. 377. 18–20).
[5] Theon of Smyrna, p. 198. 14.
[6] Diog. L. i. 24 (*Vorsokratiker*, i², p. 3. 25).

'The same Thales in his declining years devised a marvellous calculation about the sun, which I have not only learnt but verified by experiment, showing how often the sun measures by its own size the circle which it describes. Thales is said to have communicated this discovery soon after it was made to Mandrolytus of Priene, who was greatly delighted with this new and unexpected information and asked Thales to say how much by way of fee he required to be paid to him for so important a piece of knowledge. "I shall be sufficiently paid", replied the sage, "if, when you set to work to tell people what you have learnt from me, you will not take credit for it yourself but will name me, rather than another, as the discoverer."' [1]

Seeing that in Thales' system the sun and moon did not pass under the earth and describe a complete circle, he could hardly have stated the result in the precise form in which Diogenes gives it. If, however, he stated its equivalent in some other way, it is again pretty certain that he learnt it from the Egyptians or Babylonians. Cleomedes,[2] indeed, says that, by means of a water-clock, we can compare the water which flows out during the time that it takes the sun when rising to get just clear of the horizon with the amount which flows out in the whole day and night; in this way we get a ratio of 1 to 750; and he adds that this method is said to have been first devised by the Egyptians. Again, it has been suggested[3] that the Babylonians had already, some sixteen centuries before Christ, observed that the sun takes 1/30th of an hour to rise. This would, on the assumption of 24 hours for a whole day and night, give for the sun's apparent diameter 1/720th of its circle, the same excellent approximation as that attributed to Thales. But there is the difficulty that, when the Babylonians spoke of 1/30th of an hour in an equinoctial day as being the 'measure' (ὅρος) of the sun's course, they presumably meant 1/30th of their *double*-hour, of which there are 12 in a day and night, so that, even if we assume that the measurement of the sun's apparent diameter was what they meant by ὅρος, the equivalent

[1] Apuleius, *Flor.* 18 (*Vors.* i², p. 10. 3–11).
[2] Cleomedes, *De motu circulari corporum caelestium* ii. 1, pp. 136. 25–138. 6, ed. Ziegler.
[3] Hultsch, *Poseidonios über die Grösse und Entfernung der Sonne*, 1897, pp. 41, 42. Hultsch quotes Achilles, *Isagoge in Arati phaen.* 18 (*Uranolog.* Petavii, Paris, 1630, p. 137); Brandis, *Münz-, Mass- und Gewichtswesen in Vorderasien*, p. 17 sq. ; Bilfinger, *Die babylonische Doppelstunde*, Stuttgart, 1888, p. 21 sq. The passage of Achilles is quoted *in extenso* by Bilfinger, p. 21.

would be 1°, not ½° as Hultsch supposes.[1] However, it is difficult to
believe that Thales could have made the estimate of 1/720th of
the sun's circle known to the Greeks; if he had, it would be very
strange that it should have been mentioned by no one earlier than
Archimedes, and that Aristarchus should in the first instance have
used the grossly excessive value of 2° which he gives as the angular
diameter of the sun and moon in his treatise *On the sizes and
distances of the sun and moon*, and should have been left to discover the value of ½° for himself as Archimedes says he did.[2]

A few more details of Thales' astronomy are handed down. He
said of the Hyades that there are two, one north and the other
south.[3] According to Callimachus,[4] he observed the Little Bear;
'he was said to have used as a standard [i. e. for finding the pole]
the small stars of the Wain, that being the method by which
Phoenician navigators steer their course.'   According to Aratus[5]
the Greeks sailed by the Great Bear, the Phoenicians by the Little
Bear. Consequently it would seem that Thales advised the Greeks
to follow the Phoenician plan in preference to their own. This use
of the Little Bear was probably noted in the handbook under the
title of *Nautical Astronomy* attributed by some to Thales, and
by others to Phocus of Samos,[6] which was no doubt intended to
improve upon the Astronomy in poetical form attributed to Hesiod,
as in its turn it was followed by the *Astrology* of Cleostratus.[7]

---

[1] An estimate amounting to 1° is actually on record in Cleomedes (*De motu
circulari*, ii. 3, p. 172. 25, Ziegler), who says that 'the size of the sun and moon
alike appears to our perception as 12 *dactyli*'. Though this way of describing
the angle follows the Babylonian method of expressing angular distances
between stars in terms of the *ell* ($\pi\hat{\eta}\chi\upsilon\varsigma$) consisting of 24 *dactyli* and equivalent
to 2°, it does not follow that the estimate itself is Babylonian. For the same
system of expressing angles may have been used by Pytheas and was certainly
used by Hipparchus (cf. Strabo, ii. 1. 18, p. 75 Cas., *Hipparchi in Arati et Eudoxi
phaenomena comment*. ii. 5. 1, p. 186. 11, Manit., and Ptolemy, *Syntaxis* vii. 1,
vol. ii, pp. 4-8, Heib.).

[2] Archimedes, ed. Heiberg, vol. ii, p. 248. 19; *The Works of Archimedes*, ed.
Heath, p. 223.

[3] *Schol. Arat.* 172, p. 369. 24 (*Vors.* ii. 1², p. 652).

[4] In Diog. L. i. 23 (*Vors.* i², p. 3. 14; cf. ii. 2, p. v).

[5] Aratus, lines 27, 37-39; cf. Ovid, *Tristia* iv. 3. 1-2:
' Magna minorque ferae, quarum regis altera Graias,
            Altera Sidonias, utraque sicca, rates';
Theo in Arati phaen. 27. 39: Scholiast on Plat. *Rep.* 600 A.

[6] Diog. L. i, p. 23; Simpl. *in Phys.* p. 23. 29; Plutarch, *Pyth. or.* 18, 402 F (*Vors.*
i², pp. 3. 12; 11. 7, 13).   [7] Diels, *Vors.* ii. 1², p. 652; cf. pp. 499, 502.

IV

ANAXIMANDER

ANAXIMANDER of Miletus (born probably in 611/10, died soon after 547/6 B.C.), son of Praxiades, was a fellow citizen of Thales, with whom he was doubtless associated as a friend if not as a pupil. A remarkably original thinker, Anaximander may be regarded as the father or founder of Greek, and therefore of western, philosophy. He was the first Greek philosopher, so far as is known, who ventured to put forward his views in a formal written treatise.[1] This was a work *About Nature*,[2] though possibly that title was given to it, not by Anaximander himself, but only by later writers.[3] The amount of thought which went to its composition and the maturity of the views stated in it are indicated by the fact that it was not till the age of 64 that he gave it to the world.[4] The work itself is lost, except for a few lines amounting in no case to a complete sentence.

Anaximander boldly maintained that the earth is in the centre of the universe, suspended freely and without support,[5] whereas Thales regarded it as resting on the water, and Anaximenes as supported by the air. It remains in its position, says Anaximander, because it is at an equal distance from all the rest (of the heavenly bodies).[6] Aristotle expands the explanation thus:[7] 'for that which is located in the centre and is similarly situated with reference to the extremities can no more suitably move up than

---

[1] Themistius, *Orationes*, 36, p. 317 C (*Vors.* i², p. 12. 43).
[2] Ibid. ; Suidas, *s. v.*
[3] Zeller, *Philosophie der Griechen*, i⁵, p. 197.
[4] Diog. L. ii. 2 (*Vors.* i², p. 12. 7–10).
[5] Hippol. *Refut.* i. 6. 3 (*D. G.* p. 559. 22 ; *Vors.* i², p. 14. 5).
[6] Ibid. ; cf. Plato's similar view in *Phaedo* 108 E–109 A.
[7] *De caelo* ii. 13, 295 b 10–16. It is true that Eudemus (in Theon of Smyrna, p. 198. 18) is quoted as saying that Anaximander held that 'the earth is suspended freely and *moves* (κινεῖται) about the centre of the universe'; but there must clearly be some mistake here ; perhaps κινεῖται should be κεῖται ('lies').

down or laterally, and it is impossible that it should move in opposite directions (at the same time), so that it must necessarily remain at rest.' Aristotle admits that the hypothesis is daring and brilliant, but argues that it is not true : one of his grounds is amusing, namely, that on this showing a hungry and thirsty man with food and wine disposed at equal distances all round him would have to starve because there would be no reason for him to stretch his hand in one direction rather than another [1] (presumably the first occurrence of the well-known dilemma familiar to the schoolmen as the ' Ass of Buridan ').

According to Anaximander, the earth has the shape of a cylinder, round, ' like a stone pillar ' ; [2] one of its two plane faces is that on which we stand, the other is opposite ; [3] its depth, moreover, is one-third of its breadth. [4]

Still more original is Anaximander's conception of the origin and substance of the sun, moon, and stars, and of their motion. As there is considerable difference of opinion upon the details of the system, it will be well, first of all, to quote the original authorities, beginning with the accounts of the cosmogony.

' Anaximander of Miletus, son of Praxiades, who was the successor and pupil of Thales, said that the first principle (i.e. material cause) and element of existing things is the Infinite, and he was the first to introduce this name for the first principle. He maintains that it is neither water nor any other of the so-called elements, but another sort of substance, which is infinite, and from which all the heavens and the worlds in them are produced ; and into that from which existent things arise they pass away once more, " as is ordained ; for they must pay the penalty and make reparation to one another for the injustice they have committed, according to the sequence of time ", as he says in these somewhat poetical terms.' [5]

---

[1] Aristotle, *De caelo* ii. 13, 295 b 32.

[2] Hippol. *Refut.* i. 6. 3 (*D. G.* p. 559. 24; *Vors.* i², p. 14. 6); Aët. iii. 10. 2 (*D. G.* p. 376; *Vors.* i², p. 16. 34).

[3] Hippol., loc. cit.

[4] Ps. Plut. *Stromat.* 2 (*D. G.* p. 579. 12; *Vors.* i², p. 13. 34).

[5] Simplicius, *in Phys.* p. 24. 13 (*Vors.* i², p. 13. 2-9). The passage is from Theophrastus's *Phys. Opin.*, and the words in inverted commas at all events are Anaximander's own. I follow Burnet (*Early Greek Philosophy*, p. 54) in making the quotation begin at ' as is ordained '; Diels includes in it the words just preceding 'and into that from which . . . .'

'Anaximander said that the Infinite contains the whole cause of the generation and destruction of the All; it is from the Infinite that the heavens are separated off, and generally all the worlds, which are infinite in number. He declared that destruction and, long before that, generation came about for all the worlds, which arise in endless cycles from infinitely distant ages.'[1]

'He says that this substance [the Infinite] is eternal and ageless, and embraces all the worlds. And in speaking of time he has in mind the separate (periods covered by the) three states of coming into being, existence, and passing away.'[2]

'Besides this (Infinite) he says there is an eternal motion, in the course of which the heavens are found to come into being.'[3]

'Anaximander says eternal motion is a principle older than the moist, and it is by this eternal motion that some things are generated and others destroyed.'[4]

'He says that (the first principle or material cause) is boundless, in order that the process of coming into being which is set up may not suffer any check.'[5]

'Anaximander was the first to assume the Infinite as first principle in order that he may have it available for his new births without stint.'[6]

'Anaximander . . . said that the world is perishable.'[7]

'Those who assumed that the worlds are infinite in number, as did Anaximander, Leucippus, Democritus, and, in later days, Epicurus, assumed that they also came into being and passed away, *ad infinitum*, there being always some worlds coming into being and others passing away; and they maintained that motion is eternal; for without motion there is no coming into being or passing away.'[8]

'Anaximander says that that which is capable of begetting the hot and the cold out of the eternal was separated off during the coming into being of our world, and from the flame thus produced a sort of sphere was made which grew round the air about the earth as the bark round the tree; then this sphere was torn off and

---

[1] Ps. Plut. *Stromat.* 2 (*D. G.* p. 579 ; *Vors.* i², p. 13. 29 sq.). This passage again is from Theophrastus.

[2] Hippol. *Refut.* i. 6. 1 (*D. G.* p. 559 ; *Vors.* i², pp. 13. 44–14. 2).

[3] Ibid. i. 6. 2.

[4] Hermias, *Irris.* 10 (*D. G.* p. 653 ; *Vors.* i², p. 14. 21).

[5] Aët. i. 3. 3 (*D. G.* p. 277 ; *Vors.* i², p. 14. 29).

[6] Simplicius on *De caelo*, p. 615. 13 (*Vors.* i², p. 15. 24). In this passage Simplicius calls Anaximander a 'fellow citizen and friend' of Thales (Θαλοῦ πολίτης καὶ ἑταῖρος) ; these appear to be the terms used by Theophrastus, to judge by Cicero's equivalent 'popularis et sodalis' (*Acad. pr.* ii. 37. 118).

[7] Aët. ii. 4. 6 (*D. G.* p. 331 ; *Vors.* i², p. 15. 33).

[8] Simplicius, *in Phys.* p. 1121. 5 (*Vors.* i², p. 15. 34–8).

became enclosed in certain circles or rings, and thus were formed the sun, the moon, and the stars.'[1]

'The stars are produced as a circle of fire, separated off from the fire in the universe and enclosed by air. They have as vents certain pipe-shaped passages at which the stars are seen; it follows that it is when the vents are stopped up that eclipses take place.'[2]

'The stars are compressed portions of air, in the shape of wheels, filled with fire, and they emit flames at some point from small openings.'[3]

'The moon sometimes appears as waxing, sometimes as waning, to an extent corresponding to the closing or opening of the passages.'[4]

Further particulars are given of the circles of the sun and moon, including the first speculation about their sizes:

'The sun is a circle 28 times the size of the earth; it is like a wheel of a chariot the rim of which is hollow and full of fire, and lets the fire shine out at a certain point in it through an opening like the tube of a blow-pipe; such is the sun.'[5]

'The stars are borne by the circles and the spheres on which each (of them) stands.'[6]

---

[1] Ps. Plut. *Stromat.* loc. cit.

[2] Hippol. *Refut.* i. 6. 4 (*D. G.* pp. 559, 560; *Vors.* i², p. 14. 8).

[3] Aët. ii. 13. 7 (*D. G.* p. 342; *Vors.* i², p. 15. 39).

[4] Hippol., loc. cit.

[5] Aët. ii. 20. 1 (*D. G.* p. 348; *Vors.* i², p. 16. 8).

[6] Aët. ii. 16. 5 (*D. G.* p. 345; *Vors.* i², p. 15. 43). This sentence presents difficulties. It occurs in a collection of passages headed 'Concerning the motion of stars', and reads thus: Ἀναξίμανδρος ὑπὸ τῶν κύκλων καὶ τῶν σφαιρῶν, ἐφ' ὧν ἕκαστος βέβηκε, φέρεσθαι. If ἕκαστος means ἕκαστος τῶν ἀστέρων, each *of the stars*, the expression ἐφ' ὧν ἕκαστος βέβηκε, 'on which each of them stands' or 'is fixed', is certainly altogether inappropriate to Anaximander's system; it suggests Anaximenes' system of stars 'fixed like nails on a crystal sphere'; I am therefore somewhat inclined to suspect, with Neuhäuser (*Anaximander Milesius*, p. 362 note), that the words ἐφ' ὧν ἕκαστος βέβηκε (if not καὶ τῶν σφαιρῶν also) are wrongly transferred from later theories to that of Anaximander. It occurred to me whether ἕκαστος could be ἕκαστος τῶν κύκλων, 'each *of the circles*'; for it would be possible, I think, to regard the circles as 'standing' or 'being fixed' on (imaginary) spheres in order to enable them to revolve about the axis of such spheres, it being difficult to suppose a wheel to revolve about its centre when it has no spokes to connect the centre with the circumference.

Diels ('Ueber Anaximanders Kosmos' in *Archiv für Gesch. d. Philosophie*, x, 1897, p. 229) suggests that we may infer from the word 'spheres' here used that the rings are not separate for each star, but that the fixed stars shine through vents on *one* ring (which is therefore a sphere); the planets with their different motions would naturally be separate from this. I doubt, however, whether this is correct, since *all* the rings are supposed to be like wheels; they are certainly not spheres. But no doubt the Milky Way may be one ring from which

'The circle of the sun is 27 times as large ⟨as the earth and that⟩ of the moon ⟨is 19 times as large as the earth⟩.'[1]

'The sun is equal to the earth, and the circle from which the sun gets its vent and by which it is borne round is 27 times the size of the earth.'[2]

'The eclipses of the sun occur through the opening by which the fire finds vent being shut up.'[3]

'The moon is a circle 19 times as large as the earth; it is similar to a chariot-wheel the rim of which is hollow and full of fire, like the circle of the sun, and it is placed obliquely like the other; it has one vent like the tube of a blowpipe; the eclipses of the moon depend on the turnings of the wheel.'[4]

'The moon is eclipsed when the opening in the rim of the wheel is stopped up.'[5]

'The sun is placed highest of all, after it the moon, and under them the fixed stars and the planets.'[6]

We are now in a position to make some comments. First, what is the nature of the eternal motion which is an older principle than water and by which some things are generated and others destroyed? Teichmüller held it to be circular revolution of the Infinite, which he supposed to be a sphere, about its axis;[7] Tannery adopted the same view.[8] Zeller[9] rejects this for several reasons. There is no evidence that Anaximander conceived the spherical envelope of fire to be separated off by revolution of the Infinite and spread out over the surface of its mass; the spherical envelope lay, not round the Infinite, but round the atmosphere of the earth, and it was only the world, when separated off, which revolved; it is the world too, not the Infinite, which stretches at equal distances, and therefore in the shape of a sphere, round the earth as centre. Lastly, a spherical Infinite is in itself a gross and glaring contradiction, which we could not attribute to Anaximander without

a multitude of stars flame forth at different vents: this may indeed be the idea from which the whole theory started (Tannery, op. cit., p. 91; Burnet, *Early Greek Philosophy*, p. 69).

[1] Hippol., *Refut.* i. 6. 5 (*D. G.* p. 560; *Vors.* i², p. 14. 12, and ii. I², p. 653).
[2] Aët. ii. 21. 1 (*D. G.* p. 351; *Vors.* i², p. 16. 11).
[3] Aët. ii. 24. 2 (*D. G.* p. 354; *Vors.* i², p. 16. 13).
[4] Aët. ii. 25. 1 (*D. G.* p. 355; *Vors.* i², p. 16. 15).
[5] Aët. ii. 29. 1 (*D. G.* p. 359; *Vors.* i². p. 16. 19).
[6] Aët. ii. 15. 6 (*D. G.* p. 345; *Vors.* i², p. 15. 41).
[7] Teichmüller, *Studien zur Gesch. der Begriffe*, Berlin, 1874, pp. 25 sqq.
[8] Tannery, op. cit., pp. 88 sqq.
[9] Zeller, i⁵, p. 221.

direct evidence. Tannery[1] gets over the latter difficulty by the assumption that the Infinite was not something infinitely extended *in space* but *qualitatively indeterminate* only, and in fact finite in extension. This is rather an unnatural interpretation, especially in view of what we are told of the 'infinite worlds' which arise from the Infinite substance. The idea here seems to be that the Infinite is a boundless stock from which the waste of existence is continually made good.[2] With regard to the 'infinite worlds' Zeller[3] held that they were an infinity of successive worlds, not an unlimited number of worlds existing, or which may exist, at the same time, though of course all are perishable; but in order to sustain this view Zeller was obliged to reject a good deal of the evidence. Burnet[4] has examined the evidence afresh, and adopts the other view. In particular, he observes that it would be very unnatural to understand the statement that the Boundless 'encompasses the worlds' of worlds succeeding one another in time; for on this view there is at a given time only one world to 'encompass'. Again, when Cicero says Anaximander's opinion was that there were gods who came into being, rising and setting at long intervals, and that these were the 'innumerable worlds'[5] (cf. Aëtius's statement that, according to Anaximander, the 'innumerable heavens' were gods[6]), it is more natural to take the long intervals as intervals of space than as intervals of time;[7] and, whether this is so or not, we are distinctly told in a passage of Stobaeus that 'of those who declared the worlds to be infinite in number, Anaximander said that they were at equal distances from one another', a passage which certainly comes from Aëtius.[8] Neu- häuser,[9] too, maintains that Anaximander asserted the infinity of worlds in two senses, holding both that there are innumerable worlds co-existing at one time and separated by equal distances, and that these worlds are for ever, at certain (long) intervals of

[1] Tannery, op. cit., pp. 146, 147.
[2] Burnet, *Early Greek Philosophy*, p. 55.
[3] Zeller, i[5], pp. 229-36.
[4] Burnet, *Early Greek Philosophy*, pp. 62-6.
[5] Cicero, *De nat. deor.* i. 10. 25 (*Vors.* i[2], p. 15. 27).
[6] Aët. i. 7. 12 (*D. G.* p. 302; *Vors.* i[2], p. 15. 26).
[7] Probably, as Burnet says, Cicero found διαστήμασιν in his Epicurean source.
[8] Aët. ii. 1. 8 (*D. G.* p. 329; *Vors.* i[2], p. 15. 32).
[9] Neubäuser, *Anaximander Milesius*, pp. 327-35.

time,[1] passing away into the primordial Infinite, and others continually succeeding to their places.[2]

The eternal motion of the Infinite would appear to have been
the 'separating-out of opposites',[3] but in what way this operated
is not clear. The term suggests some process of shaking and
sifting as in a sieve.[4] Neuhäuser[5] holds that it is not spatial
motion at all, but motion in another of the four Aristotelian senses,
namely *generation*, which takes the form of the 'separating-out of
opposites', condensation and rarefaction incidentally playing a part
in the process.

As regards the motion by which the actual condition of the
world was brought about (the earth in the centre in the form of
a flat cylinder, the sun, moon, and stars at different distances from
the earth, and the heavenly bodies revolving about the axis of the
universe), Neuhäuser[6] maintains that it was the motion of a vortex
such as was assumed by Anaxagoras, the earth being formed in
the centre by virtue of the tendency of the heaviest of the things
whirled round in a vortex to collect in the centre. But there is
no evidence of the assumption of a vortex by Anaximander;
Neuhäuser relies on a single passage of Aristotle, which however
does not justify the inference drawn from it.[7]

---

[1] κατὰ τὴν τοῦ χρόνου τάξιν, Simpl. *in Phys.* p. 24. 20 (*Vors.* i², p. 13. 9).
[2] Cf. Simpl. *in Phys.* p. 1121. 5 (*Vors.* i², p. 15. 34-8, quoted above, p. 26).
[3] οἱ δὲ ἐκ τοῦ ἑνὸς ἐνούσας τὰς ἐναντιότητας ἐκκρίνεσθαι, ὥσπερ Ἀναξίμανδρός φησι,
Aristotle, *Phys.* i. 4, 187 a 20.
[4] Burnet, *Early Greek Philosophy*, p. 61.
[5] Neuhäuser, *Anaximander Milesius*, pp. 305-15.
[6] Neuhäuser, *Anaximander Milesius*, pp. 409-21.
[7] The passage is Aristotle, *De caelo* ii. 13, 295 a 9 sqq. It is there stated that
'if the earth, as things are, is kept *by force* where it is, it must also have come
together (by force) through being carried towards the centre by reason of the
whirling motion; for this is the cause assumed by everybody on the ground of
what happens in fluids and with reference to the air, where the bigger and the
heavier things are always carried towards the middle of the vortex. Hence it is
that all who describe the coming into being of the heaven say that the earth came
together at the centre; but the cause of its remaining fixed is still the subject
of speculation. Some hold...' Now Neuhäuser paraphrases the passage thus:
'All philosophers who hold that the world was generated or brought into being
maintain that the earth is not only kept *by force* in the middle of the world, but
was, at the beginning, also brought together by force. For all assign as the
efficient cause of the concentration of the earth in the middle of the world a
vortex (δίνη), arguing from what happens in vortices in water or air.' It is clear
that Aristotle says no such thing. He says that the philosophers referred to
assert that the earth comes together at the centre, but not that they hold that it
is kept there *by force*; indeed he expressly says later (295 b 10-16) that Anaxi-

We come now to Anaximander's theory of the sun, moon, and stars. The idea of the formation of tubes of compressed air within which the fire of each star is shut up except for the one opening is not unlike Laplace's hypothesis with reference to the origin of Saturn's rings.[1] A question arises as to how, if rings constituting the stars are nearer than the circles of the sun and moon, they fail to obstruct the light of the latter. Tannery[2] suggests that, while of course the envelopes of air need not be opaque, the rarefied fluid within the hoops, although called by the name of fire, may also be transparent, and not be seen as flame except on emerging at the opening. The idea that the stars are like gas-jets, as it were, burning at holes in transparent tubes made of compressed air is a sufficiently original conception.

But the question next arises, in what position do the circles, wheels, or hoops carrying the sun, moon, and stars respectively revolve about the earth? Zeller and Tannery speak of them as 'concentric', their centres being presumably the same as the centre of the earth; and there is nothing in the texts to suggest any other supposition. The hoops carrying the sun and moon 'lie obliquely', this being no doubt an attempt to explain, in addition to the daily rotation, the annual movement of the sun and the monthly movement of the moon. Tannery raises the question of the heights ('hauteurs') of these particular hoops, by which he seems to mean their *breadths* as they would be seen (if visible) from the centre. Thus, if the bore of the sun's tube were not circular but *flattened* (like a hoop), in the surface which it presents towards the earth, to several times the breadth of the sun's disc, it might be possible to explain the annual motion of the sun by supposing the opening through which the sun is seen to change its position continually on the surface of the hoop. But there is nothing in the texts to support this. Zeller[3] feels difficulty in accepting the sizes of the hoops as given, on the supposition that the earth is the centre.

mander regarded the earth as remaining at the centre *without* any force to keep it there. Again 'everybody' is not 'all philosophers', but 'people in general'. Lastly, the tendency of the heavier things in a vortex to collect at the centre might easily suggest that the earth had come together in the centre because it was *heavy*, without its being supposed that a vortex was the only thing that could cause it to come together.

[1] Tannery, op. cit., p. 88.   [2] Ibid. p. 92.
[3] Zeller, i⁵, pp. 224, 225.

For we are told that the sun's circle or wheel is 27 or 28 times the size of the earth, while the sun itself is the same size as the earth; this would mean that the apparent diameter of the sun's disc would be a fraction of the whole circumference of the ring represented by $1/28\pi$, that is, the angular diameter would be about $360°/88$, or a little over $4°$, which is eight times too large, and would be too great an exaggeration to pass muster even in those times. Zeller therefore wonders whether perhaps the sun's circle should be 27 times the moon's circle, which would make it 513 times the size of the earth. But the texts, when combined, are against this, and further it would make the apparent diameter of the sun much too small. According to Anaximander, the sun itself is of the same size as the earth; therefore, assuming d to be the diameter of the sun's disc and also the diameter of the earth, the circumference of the sun's hoop would be $513\pi d$, so that the apparent diameter of the sun would be about 1/1600th part of its circle, or less than half what it really is. Teichmüller[1] and Neuhäuser[2] try to increase the size of the sun's hoop $3\cdot1416$ times, apparently by taking the diameter of the hoop to be 28 times the *circumference* of the earth, 'because the measurement clearly depended on an unrolling'; but this is hardly admissible; the texts must clearly be comparing like with like. Sartorius[3] feels the same difficulty, and has a very interesting hypothesis designed to include provision for the sun's motion in the ecliptic as well as the diurnal rotation. He bases himself on a passage of Aristotle which, according to a statement of Alexander Aphrodisiensis made on the authority of Theophrastus, refers to Anaximander's system.

Aristotle speaks of those who explain the sea by saying that

'at first all the space about the earth was moist, and then, as it was dried up by the sun, one portion evaporated and set up winds and the turnings (τροπαί) of the sun and moon, while the remainder formed the sea';[4]

[1] Teichmüller, *Studien zur Geschichte der Begriffe*, 1874, pp. 16, 17.
[2] Neuhäuser, *Anaximander Milesius*, p. 371.
[3] Sartorius, *Die Entwicklung der Astronomie bei den Griechen bis Anaxagoras und Empedokles*, pp. 29, 30.
[4] Aristotle, *Meteorologica* ii. 1, 353 b 6–9. A note of Alexander (*in Meteor.* p. 67. 3; see *D.G.* p. 494; *Vors.* i², p. 16. 45) explains the passage thus: 'For, the space round the earth being moist, part of the moisture is then evaporated by the sun, and from this arise winds and the turnings of the sun and moon, the

and again he says in another place :

'The same absurdity also confronts those who say that the earth, too, was originally moist, and that, when the portion of the world immediately surrounding the earth was warmed by the sun, air was produced and the whole heaven was thus increased, and that this is how winds were caused and the turnings of the heaven brought about.'[1]

It is on these passages that Zeller[2] grounds his view that the heavens are moved by these winds (πνεύματα) and not by the eternal rotational movement of the Infinite about its axis assumed by Teichmüller and Tannery; accordingly, Zeller cannot admit that the word τροπαί in these passages is used in its technical sense of 'solstices'.[3] Sartorius, however, clearly takes the τροπαί to refer specially to the solstices (so does Neuhäuser[4]), and he shows how the motions of the sun could be represented by two different but simultaneous revolutions of the sun's wheel or hoop. Suppose the wheel to move bodily in such a way that (1) its centre describes a circle in the plane of the equator, the centre of which is the centre of the earth, while (2) the plane of the wheel is always at right angles to the plane of the aforesaid circle, and always touches its circumference; lastly, suppose the wheel to turn about

---

meaning being that it is by reason of these vapours and exhalations that the sun and moon execute their turnings, since they turn in the regions where they receive abundant supplies of this moisture ; but the part of the moisture which is left in the hollow places (of the earth) is the sea.'

[1] Aristotle, *Meteorologica* ii. 2, 355 a 21.   [2] Zeller, i[5], p. 223.

[3] Zeller (i[5], pp. 223, 224) has a note on the meanings of the word τροπή. Even in Aristotle it does not mean 'solstice' exclusively, because he speaks of 'τροπαί of the stars' (*De caelo* ii. 14, 296 b 4), 'τροπαί of the sun *and moon*' (*Meteor.* ii. 1, 353 b 8), and 'τροπαί *of the heaven*' (according to the natural meaning of τὰς τροπὰς αὐτοῦ, 355 a 25). It is true that τροπαί could be used of the moon in a sense sufficiently parallel to its use for the solstices, for, as Dreyer says (*Planetary Systems*, p. 17, note 1), the inclination of the lunar orbit to that of the sun is so small (5°) that the phenomena of 'turning-back' of sun and moon are very similar. But the use of the word by Aristotle with reference to the *stars* and the *heaven* shows that it need not mean anything more than the 'turnings' or revolutions of the different heavenly bodies. Zeller's view is, I think, strongly supported by a passage in which Anaximenes is made to speak of *stars* 'executing their turnings' (τροπὰς ποιεῖσθαι Aët. ii. 23. 1, *D. G.* p. 352) and the passage in which Anaximander himself is made to say that the eclipses of the moon depend on 'the turnings (τροπάς) of its *wheel*' (Aët. ii. 25. 1, *D. G.* p. 355 b 22).

[4] Neuhäuser, op. cit., p. 403.

its own centre at such speed that the opening representing the sun completes one revolution about the centre of the wheel in a year, and suppose the centre of the wheel to describe the circle in the plane of the equator at uniform speed in one day.

In the figure appended, E represents the earth, the C's are positions of the centre of the sun's hoop or wheel;

S_1 represents the sun's position at the vernal equinox;

S_2 ,,   ,,   ,,   ,,   summer solstice;

S_3 ,,   ,,   ,,   ,,   autumnal equinox;

S_4 ,,   ,,   ,,   ,,   winter solstice.

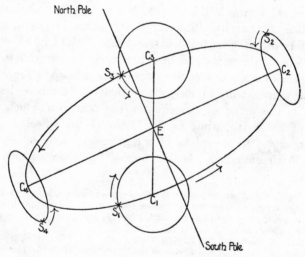

Fig. 2.

At the winter solstice the sun is south of the equator, at the summer solstice north of it, and the diameter of the wheel corresponds to an angle at E which is double of the obliquity of the ecliptic, say $47°$. Now, as the diameter of the sun's wheel is 28 times the diameter of the earth, i.e. of the sun itself (which is the same size as the earth), the angular diameter of the sun at E will be about $47°/28$ or $1°41'$. This is still far enough from the real approximate value $\frac{1}{2}°$, but it is much nearer than the $4°$ obtained from the hypothesis of a hoop with its centre at the centre of the earth.

Let us consider what would be the distance of the sun from the earth on the assumption that the sun's diameter (supposed to be equal to that of the earth) subtends at E an angle of $1\frac{2}{3}°$. If d be the diameter of the earth, and D the distance of the sun from the earth, we shall have approximately

$$360\,d/1\tfrac{2}{3} = 2\pi D,$$

or $\qquad D = 34\cdot4$ times the diameter of the earth.

But Sartorius's hypothesis is nothing more than an ingenious guess, as the texts give no colour to the idea that Anaximander

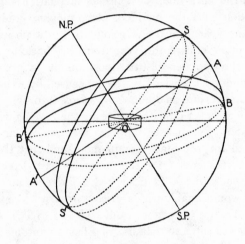

Fig. 3.

intended to assign a double motion to the sun, nor is there anything to suggest that the hoops of the sun and moon moved in any different way from those of the stars, except that they were both 'placed obliquely'.

The hypothesis of concentric rings with centres at the centre of the earth seems therefore to be the simplest.

Neuhäuser,[1] in his attempted explanation of Anaximander's theory of the sun's motion, contrives to give to τροπαὶ ἡλίου the technical meaning of solstices, while keeping the ring concentric with the earth. The flat cylinder (centre O) is the earth, $N.P.$ and $S.P.$ are the north and south poles, the equator is the circle about AA' as

[1] Neuhäuser, pp. 405–8 and Fig. 2 at end.

diameter and perpendicular to the plane of the paper. Neuhäuser then supposes the plane of the sun's circle or hoop to be differently inclined to the circle of the equator at different times of the year, making with it at the summer solstice and at the winter solstice angles equal to the obliquity of the ecliptic in the manner shown in the figure, where the circle on AA' as diameter in the plane of the paper is the meridian circle and SS' is the diameter of the sun's ring at the summer solstice, BB' the diameter of the sun's ring at the winter solstice. Between the extreme positions at the solstices the plane of the sun's hoop changes its inclination slightly day by day, its section with the meridian plane moving gradually during one half of the year from the position SS' to the position BB', and during the other half of the year from BB' back to SS'. As it approaches the summer-solstitial position, it is prevented from swinging further by the winds, which are caused by exhalations, and which by their pressure on the sun's ring force it to swing back again. The exhalations and winds only arise in the regions where there is abundant water. Neuhäuser supposes that Anaximander had the Mediterranean and the Black Sea in mind, and that their positions sufficiently ' correspond ' (?) to the summer-solstitial position SS' to enable the winds to act as described. There is no sea in such a position as would enable winds arising from it to repel the sun's ring in the reverse direction from BB' to SS'; consequently Neuhäuser has to suppose that the ring has an automatic tendency to swing towards the position SS' and that it begins to go back from BB', of itself, as soon as the force of the wind which repelled it from SS' ceases to operate. There is, however, no evidence in the texts to confirm in its details this explanation of the working of Anaximander's system ; on the contrary, there seems to be positive evidence against it in the phrase ' *lying* obliquely ', used of the hoops of the sun and moon, which suggests that the hoops remain at *fixed* inclinations to the plane of the equator instead of oscillating, as Neuhäuser's theory requires, between two extreme positions relatively to the equator.

In any case Anaximander's system represented an enormous advance in comparison with those of the other Ionian philosophers in that it made the sun, moon, and stars describe circles, passing right under the earth (which was freely suspended in the middle), instead of moving laterally round from the place of setting to the place of rising again.

We are told by Simplicius that

'Anaximander was the first to broach the subject of sizes and distances; this we learn from Eudemus, who however refers to the Pythagoreans the first statement of the order (of the planets) in space.'[1]

This brings us back to the question of the sizes of the hoops of the sun and moon as given by Anaximander. We observe that in one passage the sun's circle is said to be 28 times as large as the earth, while in another the circle 'from which it gets its vent' is 27 times as large as the earth. Now, on the hypothesis of concentric rings, we, being in the centre, of course see the *inner* circumference at the place where the sun shines through, the sun's light falling, like a spoke of the wheel, towards the centre. The words, then, used in the second passage, referring to the circle *from which* the sun *gets its vent*, suggest that the '27 times' refers to the inner circumference of the wheel, while the '28 times' refers to the outer;[2] the breadth therefore of the sun's wheel measured in the direction from centre to circumference is equal to once the diameter of the earth. A like consideration suggests that it is the *outer* circumference of the moon's hoop which is 19 times the size of the earth, and that the *inner* circumference is 18 times the size of the earth; nothing is said in our texts about the size of the moon itself. Nor are we told the size of the hoops from which the stars shine, but, as they are in Anaximander's view nearer to the earth

---

[1] Simplicius on *De caelo*, p. 471. 4, ed. Heib. (*Vors.* i², p. 15. 47). Simplicius adds: 'Now the sizes and distances of the sun and moon as determined up to now were ascertained (by calculations) starting from (observations of) eclipses, and the discovery of these things might reasonably be supposed to go back as far as Anaximander.' If by 'these things' Simplicius means the use of the phenomena of eclipses for the purpose of calculating the sizes and distances of the sun and moon, his suggestion is clearly inadmissible. On Anaximander's theory eclipses of the sun and moon were caused by the stopping-up of the vents in their respective wheels through which the fire shone out; moreover, the moon was itself bright and was not an opaque body receiving its light from the sun, notwithstanding the statement of Diogenes Laertius (ii. 1; *Vors.* i², pp. 11. 40–12. 1) to the contrary; it is clear, therefore, that Anaximander's estimates of sizes and distances rested on no such basis as the observation of eclipses afforded to later astronomers.

[2] Diels, 'Über Anaximanders Kosmos' in *Archiv für Gesch. d. Philosophie*, x, 1897, p. 231; cf. Tannery, p. 91.

than the sun and moon are, it is perhaps a fair inference that he
would assume for a third hoop or ring containing stars an inner
circumference representing 9 times the diameter of the earth ; the
three rings would then have inner circumferences of 9, 18, 27,
being multiples of 9 in arithmetical progression, while 9 is the
square of 3 ; this is appropriate also to the proportion of 1 : 3
between the depth of the disc representing the earth and the
diameter of one of its faces.   These figures suggest that they were
not arrived at by any calculation based on geometrical constructions, but that we have merely an illustration of the ancient cult of
the sacred numbers 3 and 9.[1]   3 is the sacred number in Homer,
9 in Theognis, 9 being the second power of 3.   The cult of 3 and
its multiples 9 and 27 is found among the Aryans, then among
the Finns and Tartars, and next among the Etruscans (the Semites
connected similar ideas with 6 and 7).   Therefore Anaximander's
figures really say little more than what the Indians tell us, namely
that three Vishnu-steps reach from earth to heaven.

The story that Anaximander was the first to discover the
gnomon[2] (or sun-dial with a vertical needle) is incorrect, for
Herodotos says that the Greeks learnt the use of the *gnomon*
and the *polos* from the Babylonians.[3]   Anaximander may, however,
have been the first to 'introduce'[4] or make known the gnomon in
Greece, and to show on it 'the solstices, the times, the seasons, and
the equinox'.[5]   He is said to have set it up in Sparta.[6]   He is
also credited with constructing a sphere to represent the heavens,[7]
as was Thales before him.[8]

But Anaximander has yet another claim to undying fame.   He
was the first who ventured to draw a map of the inhabited earth.[9]
The Egyptians had drawn maps before, but only of particular dis-
tricts ;[10] Anaximander boldly planned out the whole world with
'the circumference of the earth and of the sea'.[11]   Hecataeus, a
much-travelled man, is said to have corrected Anaximander's map,

[1] Diels, loc. cit., p. 233.   [2] Diog. L. ii. 1 (*Vors.* i², p. 12. 3).
[3] Herodotus, ii. 109.   [4] εἰσήγαγε, Suidas (*Vors.* i², p. 12. 18).
[5] Euseb. *Praep. Evang.* x. 14. 11 (*Vors.* i², p. 12. 24).
[6] Diog. L. ii. 1.   [7] Ibid. ii. 2.   [8] Cic. *De rep.* i. 14. 22.
[9] Agathemerus (from Eratosthenes), i. 1 (*Vors.* i², p. 12. 36).
[10] Gomperz, *Griechische Denker*, i³, pp. 41, 422.
[11] Diog. L. ii. 2 (*Vors.* i², p. 12. 5).

so that it became the object of general admiration. According to another account, Hecataeus left a written description of the world based on the map. In the preparation of the map Anaximander would of course take account of all the information which reached his Ionian home as the result of the many journeys by land and sea undertaken from that starting-point, journeys which extended to the limits of the then-known world ; the work involved of course an attempt to estimate the dimensions of the earth. We have, however, no information as to his results.[1]

Anaximander's remarkable theory of evolution does not concern us here.[2]

[1] On Anaximander's map see Berger, *Geschichte der wissenschaftlichen Erdkunde der Griechen*, 2 ed., 1903, pp. 35 sqq.

[2] See Plut. *Symp.* viii. 8. 4 (*Vors.* i², p. 17. 24) ; Aët. v. 19. 4 (*D. G.* p. 430 ; *Vors.* i², p. 17. 18) ; Ps. Plut. *Stromat.* 2 (*D. G.* p. 579) ; Hippol. *Refut.* i. 6. 6 (*D. G.* p. 560). According to Anaximander, animals first arose from slime evaporated by the sun ; they first lived in the sea and had prickly coverings ; men at first resembled fishes.

V

ANAXIMENES

FOR Anaximenes of Miletus (whose date Diels fixes at 585/4–528/4 B. C.) the earth is still flat, like a table,[1] but, instead of resting on nothing, as with Anaximander, it is supported by air, riding upon it, as it were.[2] Aristotle explains this assumption thus:[3]

'Anaximenes, Anaxagoras, and Democritus say that its flatness is what makes it remain at rest; for it does not cut the air below it but acts like a lid to it, and this appears to be characteristic of those bodies which possess breadth. Such bodies are, as we know, not easily displaced by winds, because of the resistance they offer. The philosophers in question assert that the earth resists the air below it, in the same way, by its breadth, and that the air, on the other hand, not having sufficient space to move from its position, remains in one mass with that which is below it, just as the water does in water-clocks.'

The sun, moon, and stars are evolved originally from earth; for it is from earth that moisture arises; then, when this is rarefied, fire is produced, and the stars are composed of fire which has risen aloft.[4] The sun, moon, and stars are all made of fire, and they ride on the air because of their breadth.[5] The sun is flat like a leaf;[6] it derives its very adequate heat from its rapid motion.[7] The stars, on the other hand, fail to warm because of their distance.[8]

The stars are fastened on a crystal sphere, like nails or studs.[9]

---

[1] Aët. iii. 10. 3 (*D. G.* p. 377; *Vors.* i², p. 20. 26).

[2] Ps. Plut. *Stromat.* 3 (*D. G.* p. 580; *Vors.* i², p. 18. 27); Hippol. *Refut.* i. 7. 4 (*D. G.* p. 560; *Vors.* i², p. 18. 40); Aët. iii. 15. 8 (*D. G.* p. 380; *Vors.* i², p. 20. 34).

[3] *De caelo* ii. 13, 294 b 13 (*Vors.* i², p. 20. 27).

[4] Ps. Plut. *Stromat.* 3 (*D. G.* p. 580; *Vors.* i², p. 18. 27); Hippol. *Refut.* i. 7. 5 (*D. G.* p. 561; *Vors.* i², p. 18. 42).

[5] Hippol., loc. cit. (*Vors.* i², p. 18. 41).

[6] Aët. ii. 22. 1 (*D. G.* p. 352; *Vors.* i², p. 20. 5).

[7] Ps. Plut. *Stromat.* 3 (*D. G.* p. 580; *Vors.* i², p. 18. 28).

[8] Hippol., loc. cit. (*Vors.* i², p. 19. 1).

[9] Aët. ii. 14. 3 (*D. G.* p. 344; *Vors.* i², p. 19. 38).

The stars do not move or revolve *under* the earth as some suppose, but round the earth, just as a cap can be turned round the head. The sun is hidden from sight, not because it is under the earth, but because it is covered by the higher parts of the earth and because its distance from us is greater.[1] With this statement may be compared the remark of Aristotle that

' Many of the ancient meteorologists were persuaded that the sun is not carried under the earth, but round the earth, and in particular our northern portion of it, and that it disappears and produces night because the earth is lofty towards the north.'[2]

The allusion is also to Anaximenes when we are told that some (i. e. Anaximenes) make the universe revolve like a millstone ($\mu\nu\lambda o\epsilon\iota\delta\hat{\omega}s$), others (i.e. Anaximander) like a wheel.[3]

Now it is difficult to understand how the stars which, being fixed on a crystal sphere, move bodily with it round a diameter of the sphere, and which are seen to describe circles cutting the plane of the horizon at an angle, can do otherwise than describe the portion of their paths between their setting and rising again by passing under the earth ; and all sorts of attempts have been made to explain the contradiction. Schaubach pointed out that the circles described by the stars could not all converge and meet, say, on the horizon to the north; for then they could not be parallel.[4] Ottinger[5] supposed that the attachment of the stars to the crystal sphere only held good while they were above the horizon; then, when they reached the horizon, they became detached and passed round in the plane of the horizon till they reached the east again ! Zeller, Martin, and Teichmüller all have explanations which are more or less violent attempts to make ' under ' mean not exactly 'under', but something else. Teichmüller,[6] to explain the simile of the cap, observes that the ancients wore their caps, not as we wear our hats, but tilted back on the neck. The simile of the cap worn

---

[1] Hippol., loc. cit. (*Vors.* i², pp. 18. 45–19. 1) ; cf. Aët. ii. 16. 6 (*D. G.* p. 346; *Vors.* i², p. 19. 39).

[2] Aristotle, *Meteorologica* ii. 1, 354 a 28.

[3] Aët. ii. 2. 4 (*D. G.* p. 329 b, note ; *Vors.* i², p. 19. 32).

[4] Schaubach, *Geschichte der griechischen Astronomie bis auf Eratosthenes*, p. 136.

[5] Quoted by Sartorius, op. cit., p. 33.

[6] Teichmüller, *Studien zur Geschichte der Begriffe*, 1874, p. 100.

in this way would no doubt be appropriate if Anaximenes had confined his comparison to some stars only, namely those in the north which are always above the horizon and never set; but he does not make this limitation; and this view of the cap does not correspond very well to the revolution 'like a millstone'.

More important is the distinction between the motion of the fixed stars, which are fastened like nails on the sphere, and the motion of the sun and moon. Anaximenes says that

'The sun and the moon and the other stars float on the air on account of their breadth.'[1]

This is intelligible as regards the sun, because it is like a leaf; but, as regards 'the other stars' it seems clear that floating on the air is inconsistent with their being fastened to the heavenly sphere; it is almost necessary therefore to suppose that 'the other stars' are here, not the fixed stars, but the *planets*, and that this 'floating on the air' is a hypothesis to explain the disagreement between the observed motions of the sun, moon, and planets on the one hand, and the simple rotation of the stars in circles on the other. We are told in another place that, while Anaximenes said that the stars are fastened like nails on the crystal sphere, 'some' say that they are 'leaves of fire, like pictures';[2] it is tempting, therefore, to read, instead of ἔνιοι in the nominative, the accusative ἐνίους (ἀστέρας), when the meaning would be 'but that *some of the stars* are leaves of fire', &c. The idea that the planets are meant in the above passage is further supported by another statement that

'The stars execute their turnings (τὰς τροπὰς ποιεῖσθαι) in consequence of their being driven out of their course by condensed air which resists their free motion.'[3]

It seems clear that the 'turnings' here referred to are not the 'solstices', but simply the turnings of the stars in the sense of their revolution in their respective orbits, *so far as they are not fixed on the crystal sphere*;[4] that is to say, the statement refers to the planets only.

---

[1] Hippol. *Refut.* i. 7. 4 (*D. G.* p. 561; *Vors.* i², p. 18. 41).
[2] Aët. ii. 14. 4 (*D. G.* p. 344; *Vors.* i², p. 19. 38).
[3] Aët. ii. 23. 1 (*D. G.* p. 352; *Vors.* i², p. 20. 5).
[4] Zeller, i⁵, p. 250.

It would seem certain therefore that Anaximenes was the first to distinguish the planets from the fixed stars in respect of their irregular movements, which he accounted for in the same way as the motions of the sun and moon. This being so, it seems not impossible that the passages about the sun and the stars not moving *under*, but laterally *round*, the earth refer exclusively to the sun, moon, and planets;[1] the fact of their floating on the air might be supposed to be a reason why they should not ever fall below the earth, which itself rests on the air, and in this way the difficulty with regard to the motion of the fixed stars would disappear.

Another improvement on the system of Anaximander is the relegation of the stars to a more distant region than that in which the sun moves. Anaximander had made the sun's wheel the most remote, the moon's next to it, and those of the stars nearer still to the earth ; Anaximenes, however, explains that the stars do not give warmth because they are too far off, and with this may be compared his statement that

'The rotation which is the furthest away from the earth is (that of) the heaven,'[2]

which view is attributed to him in common with Parmenides.

Anaximenes made yet another innovation of some significance. He said that

'There are also, in the region occupied by the stars, bodies of an earthy nature which are carried round along with them,'[3]

and that,

'While the stars are of a fiery nature, they also include (or contain) certain earthy bodies which are carried round along with them but are not visible.'[4]

Zeller[5] interprets these passages as ascribing an earthy nucleus to the stars; and this is not unnaturally suggested by the second of the two passages. But the first passage suggests another possible

[1] This was the suggestion of Heeren (Stobaeus, i, p. 511).
[2] Aët. ii. 11. 1 (*D. G.* p. 339; *Vors.* i², p. 19. 34).
[3] Hippol. *Refut.* i. 7. 5 (*D. G.* p. 561; *Vors.* i², p. 18. 44).
[4] Aët. ii. 13. 10 (*D. G.* p. 342; *Vors.* i², p. 19. 36).
[5] Zeller, i⁵, pp. 247, 248.

interpretation ; bodies of an earthy nature *in the region* occupied by the stars (ἐν τῷ τόπῳ τῶν ἀστέρων) might be separate from them and not 'contained in them', although carried round with them. 'The stars' in the two passages no doubt include the sun and moon ; but the sun is flat like a leaf ; why then should Anaximenes attach to it an earthy substance as well ? The object of the invisible bodies of an earthy nature carried round along with 'the stars' is clearly to explain eclipses and the phases of the moon. If, then, Anaximenes supposed that one side in both the sun and the moon was bright and the other dark, his idea would doubtless be that they might sometimes turn their dark side to us in such a way as to hide from us more or less the bright side. (This was the idea of Heraclitus, though with him the heavenly bodies had not a flat surface but were hollowed out like a basin or bowl.) But the phenomena of eclipses are more simply accounted for if we suppose the earthy bodies of Anaximenes to be separate from the sun and moon, and to get in front of them ; we need not therefore hesitate to attribute to him this fruitful idea which ultimately led to the true explanation. Anaxagoras said that the moon is eclipsed because the earth is interposed, but, not being able to account for all the phenomena in this way, he conceived that eclipses were also sometimes due to obstruction by bodies 'below the moon', which he describes in almost the same words as Anaximenes, namely as 'certain bodies (in the region) below the stars which are carried round with the sun and moon and are invisible to us'. Clearly therefore Anaxagoras was indebted to Anaximenes for this conception ; and again the rôle of the counter-earth in the Pythagorean system is much the same as that of the 'earthy bodies' now in question.

Tannery[1] goes further and maintains that Anaximenes' hypothesis was bound to lead to the true explanation of eclipses. 'For, if any one asked himself why these dark bodies were not seen at all, the question of their being illuminated by the sun would present itself, and it was easy to recognize that, under the most general conditions, the phenomena which such a dark body would necessarily present were really similar to the phases of the moon. From this to the

---

[1] Tannery, *Pour l'histoire de la science hellène*, pp. 153, 154.

recognition of the fact that the moon itself is opaque there was only one step more. The rôle of the moon in regard to the eclipses of the sun was easy to deduce, while the question of the lighting up of the moon by the sun at night naturally brought into play the shadow of the earth and, through that, led to the discovery of the cause of eclipses of the moon. The hypothesis then of Anaximenes has a true scientific character, and constitutes for him a title to fame, the more rare because the conception appears to have been absolutely original, while his other ideas are not in general of the same stamp.' While the successive steps towards the discovery of the truth may no doubt have been taken in the order suggested, it must, I think, be admitted that, at the point where the question of the illumination of the opaque bodies by the sun would present itself ('se posait'), a very active imagination would be required to suggest the transition to this question ; and, even after the transition was made, it would be necessary to assume further that the opaque bodies are spherical in form, an assumption nowhere suggested by Anaximenes.

Tannery[1] adds that the only feature of Anaximenes' system that was destined to an enduring triumph is the conception of the stars being fixed on a crystal sphere as in a rigid frame. Although attempts were made later to arrive at a more immaterial and less gross conception of the substance rigidly connecting the fixed stars, the character of this connexion was not modified, and the rigidity of the sphere really remained the fundamental postulate of all astronomy up to Copernicus. The exceptions to the general adoption of this view were, curiously enough, the Ionian physicists of the century immediately following Anaximenes.

It would appear that Anaximenes anticipated the Pythagorean notion that the world breathes, for he says :

' Just as our soul, being air, holds us together, so does breath and air encompass the whole world.' [2]

---

[1] Tannery, op. cit., p. 154.
[2] Fragment in Aët. i. 3. 4 (*D. G.* p. 278; *Vors.* i², p. 21. 17).

VI

PYTHAGORAS

PYTHAGORAS, undoubtedly one of the greatest names in the history of science, was an Ionian, born at Samos about 572 B.C., the son of Mnesarchus. He spent his early manhood in Samos, removed in about 532 B.C. to Croton, where he founded his school, and died at Metapontium at a great age (75 years according to one authority, 80 or more according to others). His interests were as various as those of Thales, but with the difference that, whereas Thales' knowledge was mostly of practical application, with Pythagoras the subjects of which he treats become sciences for the first time. Mathematicians know him of course, mostly or exclusively, as the reputed discoverer of the theorem of Euclid I. 47; but, while his share in the discovery of this proposition is much disputed, there is no doubt that he was the first to make theoretical geometry a subject forming part of a liberal education, and to investigate its first principles.[1] With him, too, began the Theory of Numbers. A mathematician then of brilliant achievements, he was also the inventor of the science of acoustics, an astronomer of great originality, a theologian and moral reformer, founder of a brotherhood 'which admits comparison with the orders of mediaeval chivalry.'[2]

The epoch-making discovery that musical tones depend on numerical proportions, the octave representing the proportion of $2:1$, the fifth $3:2$, and the fourth $4:3$, may with sufficient certainty be attributed to Pythagoras himself,[3] as may the first exposition of the theory of *means*, and of proportion in general applied to commensurable quantities, i.e. quantities the ratio between which can be expressed as a ratio between whole numbers. The all-

---

[1] Proclus, *Comm. on Eucl. I*, p. 65. 15–19.
[2] Gomperz, *Griechische Denker*, i³, pp. 80, 81.
[3] Burnet, *Early Greek Philosophy*, p. 118.

pervading character of number being thus shown, what wonder that the Pythagoreans came to declare that number is the essence of all things? The connexion so discovered between number and music would also lead not unnaturally to the idea of the 'harmony of the heavenly bodies'.

Pythagoras left no written exposition of his doctrines, nor did any of his immediate successors in the school; this statement is true even of Hippasus, about whom the different stories arose (1) that he was expelled from the school because he published doctrines of Pythagoras,[1] (2) that he was drowned at sea for revealing the construction of the dodecahedron in a sphere and claiming it as his own,[2] or (as others have it) for making known the discovery of the irrational or incommensurable.[3] Nor is the absence of any written record of early Pythagorean doctrine to be put down to any pledge of secrecy binding the school; there does not seem to have been any secrecy observed at all unless perhaps in matters of religion or ritual; the supposed secrecy seems to have been invented to explain the absence of any trace of documents before Philolaus. The fact appears to be merely that oral communication was the tradition of the school, and the closeness of their association enabled it to be followed without inconvenience, while of course their doctrine would be mainly too abstruse to be understood by the generality of people outside.

Philolaus was the first Pythagorean to write an exposition of the Pythagorean system. He was a contemporary of Socrates and Democritus, probably older than either, and we know that he lived in Thebes in the last decades of the fifth century.[4]

It is difficult in these circumstances to disentangle the portions of the Pythagorean philosophy which may safely be attributed to the founder of the school. Aristotle evidently felt this difficulty; he clearly knew nothing for certain of any ethical or physical doctrines going back to Pythagoras himself; and, when he speaks of the Pythagorean system, he always refers it to ' the Pythagoreans ', sometimes even to 'the so-called Pythagoreans'.[5] The account

---

[1] Clem. *Stromat.* v. 58 (*Vors.* i², p. 30. 18); Iamblichus, *Vit. Pyth.* 246, 247 (*Vors.* i², p. 30. 10, 14).
[2] Iamblichus, *Vit. Pyth.* 88 (*Vors.* i², p. 30. 2).
[3] Ibid. 247 (*Vors.* i², p. 30. 17).
[4] Zeller, i⁵, pp. 337, 338. [5] Burnet, *Early Greek Philosophy*, p. 100.

which he gives of the Pythagorean planetary system corresponds to the system of Philolaus as we know it from the *Doxographi*.

For Pythagoras's own system, therefore, that of Philolaus affords no guide; we have to seek for traces, in the other writers of the end of the sixth and the beginning of the fifth centuries, of opinions borrowed from him or of polemics directed against him.[1] On these principles we have seen reason to believe that he was the first to maintain that the earth is spherical and, on the basis of this assumption, to distinguish the five zones.

How Pythagoras came to conclude that the earth is spherical in shape is uncertain. There is at all events no evidence that he borrowed the theory from any non-Greek source.[2] On the assumption, then, that it was his own discovery, different suggestions [3] have been put forward as to the considerations by which Pythagoras convinced himself of its truth. One suggestion is that he may have based his opinion upon the correct interpretation of phenomena, and above all, on the round shadow cast by the earth in the eclipses of the moon. But it is certain that Anaxagoras was the first to suggest this, the true explanation of eclipses. The second possibility is that Pythagoras may have extended his assumption of a spherical sky to the separate luminaries of heaven; the third is that his ground was purely mathematical, or mathematico-aesthetical, and that he attributed spherical shape to the earth for the simple reason that 'the sphere is the most beautiful of solid figures'.[4] I prefer the third of these hypotheses, though the second and third have the point of contact that the beauty of the spherical shape may have

---

[1] Tannery, op. cit., p. 203.

[2] The question is discussed by Berger (*Geschichte der wissenschaftlichen Erdkunde der Griechen*, pp. 171-7) who is inclined to think that, along with the facts about the planets and their periods discovered, as the result of observations continued through long ages, by the Egyptians and Babylonians, the doctrine of a suspended spherical earth also reached the Greeks from Lydia, Egypt, or Cyprus. Berger admits, however, that Diodorus (ii. 31) denies to the Babylonians any knowledge of the earth's sphericity. Martin, it is true, in a paper quoted by Berger (p. 177, note), assumed that the Egyptians had grasped the idea of a spherical earth, but, as Gomperz observes (*Griechische Denker*, i³, p. 430), this assumption is inconsistent with the Egyptian representation of the earth's shape as explained by one of the highest authorities on the subject, Maspero, in his *Hist. ancienne des peuples de l'Orient classique, Les origines*, pp. 16, 17.

[3] Gomperz, *Griechische Denker*, i³, p. 90.

[4] Diog. L. viii. 35 (*Vors.* i², p. 280. 1) attributes this statement to the Pythagoreans.

dictated its application *both* to the universe and to the earth.   But, whatever may have been the ground, the declaration that the earth is spherical was a great step towards the true, the Copernican view of the universe.[1]   It may well be (though we are not told) that Pythagoras, for the same reason, gave the same spherical shape to the sun and moon and even to the stars, in which case the way lay open for the discovery of the true cause of eclipses and of the phases of the moon.

There is no doubt that Pythagoras's own system was *geocentric*. The very fact that he is credited with distinguishing the zones is an indication of this; the theory of the zones is incompatible with the notion of the earth moving in space as it does about the central fire of Philolaus.   But we are also directly told that he regarded the universe as living, intelligent, spherical, enclosing the earth *in the middle*, the earth, too, being spherical in shape.[2]   Further, it seems clear that he held that the universe rotated about an axis passing through the centre of the earth.   Thus we are told by Aristotle that

'Some (of the Pythagoreans) say that *time* is the *motion of the whole* (universe), others that it is the sphere itself'; [3]

and by Aëtius that

'Pythagoras held time to be the sphere of the enveloping (heaven).' [4]

Alcmaeon, a doctor of Croton, although expressly distinguished from the Pythagoreans by Aristotle,[5] is said to have been a pupil of Pythagoras; [6] even Aristotle says that, in the matter of the Pythagorean pairs of opposites, Alcmaeon, who was a young man when Pythagoras was old, expressed views similar to those of the Pythagoreans, 'whether he got them from the Pythagoreans or they from him'.[7]   Hence he was clearly influenced by Pythagorean

---

[1] Gomperz, *Griechische Denker*, i³, p. 90.
[2] Alexander Polyhistor in Diog. L. viii.
[3] Aristotle, *Phys.* iv. 10, 218 a 33.
[4] Aët. i. 21. 1 (*D. G.* p. 318; *Vors.* i², p. 277. 19).
[5] Aristotle, *Metaph.* A. 5, 986 a 27–31.
[6] Diog. L. viii. 83 (*Vors.* i², p. 100. 19); Iamblichus, *Vit. Pyth.* 104.
[7] Aristotle, *Metaph.* i. 5, 986 a 28.

doctrines. Now the doxographers' account of his astronomy includes one important statement, namely that

'Alcmaeon and the mathematicians hold that the planets have a motion from west to east, in a direction opposite to that of the fixed stars.'[1]

Incidentally, the assumption of the motion of the fixed stars suggests the immobility of the earth. But this passage is also the first we hear of the important distinction between the diurnal revolution of the fixed stars from east to west and the independent movement of the planets *in the opposite direction*; the Ionians say nothing of it (though perhaps Anaximenes distinguished the planets as having a different movement from that of the fixed stars); Anaxagoras and Democritus did not admit it; the discovery, therefore, appears to belong to the Pythagorean school and, in view of its character, it is much more likely to have been made by the Master himself than by the physician of Croton.[2] For the rest of Alcmaeon's astronomy is on a much lower level; he thought the sun was flat,[3] and, like Heraclitus, he explained eclipses and the phases of the moon as being due to the turning of the moon's bowl-shaped envelope.[4] It is right to add that Burnet[5] thinks that the fact of the discovery in question being attributed to Alcmaeon implies that it was *not* due to Pythagoras. Presumably this is inferred from the words of Aristotle distinguishing Alcmaeon from the Pythagoreans; but either inference is possible, and I prefer Tannery's. It is difficult to account for Alcmaeon being credited with the discovery if, as Burnet thinks, it was really Plato's.

But we have also the evidence of Theon of Smyrna, who states categorically that Pythagoras was the first to notice that the planets move in independent circles:

'The impression of variation in the movement of the planets is produced by the fact that they appear to us to be carried through the signs of the zodiac in certain circles of their own, being fastened in spheres of their own and moved by their motion, *as Pythagoras*

---

[1] Aët. ii. 16. 2–3 (*D. G.* p. 345 ; *Vors.* i², p. 101. 8).
[2] Tannery, op. cit., p. 208.
[3] Aët. ii. 22. 4 (*D. G.* p. 352 ; *Vors.* i², p. 101. 10).
[4] Aët. ii. 29. 3 (*D. G.* p. 359 ; *Vors.* i², p. 101. 10-12).
[5] Burnet, *Early Greek Philosophy*, p. 123, note.

was the first to observe, a certain varied and irregular motion being thus grafted, as a qualification, upon their simply and uniformly ordered motion in one and the same sense ' [i. e. that of the daily rotation from east to west].[1]

It appears probable, therefore, that the theory of Pythagoras himself was that the universe, the earth, and the other heavenly bodies are spherical in shape, that the earth is at rest in the centre, that the sphere of the fixed stars has a daily rotation from east to west about an axis passing through the centre of the earth, and that the planets have an independent movement of their own in a sense opposite to that of the daily rotation, i.e. from west to east.

[1] Theon of Smyrna, p. 150. 12-18.

VII

XENOPHANES

XENOPHANES of Colophon was probably born about 570 and died after 478 B.C. What we know for certain is that he spoke of Pythagoras in the past tense,[1] that Heraclitus mentions him along with Pythagoras,[2] and that he says of himself that, from the time when he was 25 years of age, three-score years and seven had 'tossed his care-worn soul up and down the land of Hellas.'[3] He may have left his home at the time when Ionia became a Persian province (545 B.C.) and gone with the Phocaeans to Elea,[4] founded by them in 540/39 B.C., six years after they left Phocaea.[5] As he was writing poetry at 92 and is said to have been over 100 when he died,[6] the above dates are consistent with the statement that he was a contemporary of Hieron, who reigned from 478 to 467 B.C.[7] According to Theophrastus, he had 'heard' Anaximander.[8]

Xenophanes was more a poet and satirist than a natural philosopher, but Heraclitus credited him with wide learning,[9] and he is said to have opposed certain doctrines of Pythagoras and Thales.[10] We are told that he wrote epics as well as elegies and iambics attacking Homer and Hesiod. In particular, 2,000 verses on the foundation of Colophon and the settlement at Elea are attributed to him.[11] He is supposed to have written a philosophical poem; Diels refers about sixteen fragments to such a poem, to which the

---

[1] Fr. 7 (*Vors.* i², p. 47. 20-23). [2] Heraclitus, Fr. 40 (*Vors.* i², p. 68. 10).
[3] Fr. 8 (*Vors.* i², p. 48. 3-6).
[4] Gomperz, *Griechische Denker*, i³, pp. 127, 436.
[5] Herodotus, i. 164-7.
[6] Censorinus, *De die natali* c. 15. 3, p. 28. 21, ed. Hultsch.
[7] Timaeus in Clem. *Stromat.* i. 14, p. 353 (*Vors.* i², p. 35. 2).
[8] Diog. L. ix. 21 (*Vors.* i², p. 34. 35).
[9] Heraclitus, loc. cit.: 'Wide learning does not teach one to have understanding; if it did, it would have taught Hesiod and Pythagoras, and again Xenophanes and Hecataeus.'
[10] Diog. L. ix. 18 (*Vors.* i², p. 34. 12). [11] Ibid. ix. 20 (*Vors.* i², p. 34. 26).

name *On Nature* (Περὶ φύσεως) was given; but such titles are of later date than Xenophanes, and Burnet[1] holds that all the fragments might have come into the poems directed against Homer and Hesiod, the fact that a considerable number of them come from commentaries on Homer being significant in this connexion.

Xenophanes attacked the popular mythology, proving that God must be one, not many (for God is supreme and there can only be one supreme power),[2] eternal and not born (for it is as impious to say that the gods are born as it would be to say that they die; in either case there would be a time when the gods *would not be*);[3] he reprobated the scandalous stories about the gods in Homer and Hesiod[4] and ridiculed the anthropomorphic view which gives the gods bodies, voices, and dress like ours, observing that the Thracians made them blue-eyed and red-haired, the Aethiopians snub-nosed and black,[5] while, if oxen or horses or lions had hands and could draw, they would draw them as oxen, horses, and lions respectively.[6] God is the One and the All, the universe;[7] God remains unmoved in one and the same place;[8] God is eternal, one, alike every way, finite, spherical and sensitive in all parts,[9] but does not breathe.[10] It is difficult to reconcile the finite and spherical God with Xenophanes' description of the world, which may be summarized as follows.

The world was evolved from a mixture of earth and water,[11] and the earth will gradually be dissolved again by moisture; this he infers from the fact that shells are found far inland and on mountains, and in the quarries of Syracuse there have been found imprints (fossils) of a fish and of seaweed,[12] and so on, these imprints showing that everything was covered in mud long ago,

---

[1] Burnet, *Early Greek Philosophy*, p. 128.
[2] Simpl. *in Phys.* p. 22. 31 (*Vors.* i², p. 40. 30).
[3] Aristotle, *Rhetoric* ii. 23, 1399 b 6.
[4] Fr. 11 (*Vors.* i², p. 48. 13).   [5] Fr. 14, 16 (*Vors.* i², p. 49. 2, 11).
[6] Fr. 15 (*Vors.* i², p. 49. 5).
[7] Aristotle, *Metaph.* A. 5, 986 b 21 (*Vors.* i², p. 40. 15); Simpl., loc. cit. (*Vors.* i², p. 40. 29); cf. Cicero, *De nat. deor.* i. 11. 28 (*Vors.* i², p. 41. 44); *Acad. pr.* ii. 37. 118 (*Vors.* i², p. 41. 42).
[8] Fr. 26 (*Vors.* i², p. 50. 22).
[9] Hippol. *Refut.* i. 14. 2 (*D. G.* p. 565; *Vors.* i², p. 41. 26).
[10] Diog. L. ix. 19 (*Vors.* i², p. 34. 18).
[11] Fr. 29. 33 (*Vors.* i², p. 51. 5, 20).
[12] I read, with Burnet, after Gomperz φυκῶν (seaweed) instead of φωκῶν.

and that the imprints dried on the mud. All men will disappear
when the earth is absorbed into the sea and becomes mud, after
which the process of coming into being starts again; all the worlds
(alike) suffer this change.[1] This is, of course, the theory of
Anaximander.

As regards the earth we are told that

'This upper side of the earth is seen, at our feet, to touch the air,
but the lower side reaches to infinity.'[2]

'This is why some say that the lower portion of the earth is
infinite, asserting, as Xenophanes of Colophon does, that its roots
extend without limit, in order that they may not have the trouble
of investigating the cause (of its being at rest). Hence Empedocles'
rebuke in the words "if the depths of the earth are without limit
and the vast aether (above it) is so also, as has been said by the
tongues of many and vainly spouted forth from the mouths of men
who have seen little of the whole".'[3]

'Xenophanes said that on its lower side the earth has roots
extending without limit.'[4]

'The earth is infinite, and is neither surrounded by air nor by the
heaven.'[5]

Simplicius[6] (on the second of the above passages) observes that,
not having seen Xenophanes' own verses on the subject, he cannot
say whether Xenophanes meant that the under side of the earth
extends without limit, and that this is the reason why it is at rest, or
meant to assert that the space below the earth, and the aether, is
infinite, and consequently the earth, though it is in fact being carried
downwards without limit, appears to be at rest; for neither Aristotle
nor Empedocles made this clear. Presumably, however, as
Simplicius had not seen Xenophanes' original poem, he had not
seen Fr. 28, the first of the above passages; for this passage seems
to be decisive; there is nothing in it to suggest *motion* downwards,
and, if it meant that there was infinite air below the earth as there
is above, there would be no contrast between the upper and the
under side such as it is the obvious intention of the author to draw.[7]

[1] Hippol. *Refut.* i. 14. 5-6 (*D. G.* p. 566; *Vors.* i², p. 41. 33-41).
[2] Fr. 28 (*Vors.* i², p. 51. 2).
[3] Aristotle, *De caelo* ii. 13, 294 a 21-28.
[4] Aët. iii. 9. 4; 11. 1, 2 (*D. G.* pp. 376, 377; *Vors.* i², p. 43. 33, 35).
[5] Hippol. *Refut.* i. 14. 3 (*D. G.* p. 565; *Vors.* i², p. 41. 29).
[6] Simplicius on *De caelo*, p. 522. 7, ed. Heib. (*Vors.* i², p. 43. 28).
[7] As witness the μέν and the δέ and the clear opposition of 'touching the air'

According to Xenophanes the stars, including comets and
meteors, are made of clouds set on fire; they are extinguished
each day and are kindled at night like coals, and these happenings
constitute their setting and rising respectively.[1] The so-called
Dioscuri are small clouds which emit light in virtue of the motion,
whatever it is, that they have.[2]

Similarly the sun is made of clouds set on fire; clouds formed
from moist exhalation take fire, and the sun is formed from the
resulting fiery particles collected together.[3] The moon is likewise
so formed, the cloud being here described as 'compressed'
($\pi\epsilon\pi\iota\lambda\eta\mu\acute{\epsilon}\nu o\nu$),[4] following an expression of Anaximander's for
compressed portions of air; the moon's light is its own.[5]

When the sun sets, it is extinguished, and when it next rises, it is
a fresh one; it is likewise extinguished when there is an eclipse.[6]

($\mathring{\eta}\acute{\epsilon}\rho\iota$ $\pi\rho o\sigma\pi\lambda\acute{a}\zeta o\nu$) and reaching to infinity ($\acute{\epsilon}s$ $\mathring{a}\pi\epsilon\iota\rho o\nu$ $\mathring{\iota}\kappa\nu\epsilon\hat{\iota}\tau a\iota$). $\mathring{\iota}\kappa\nu\epsilon\hat{\iota}\tau a\iota$ implies,
not *motion* towards, but *arrival at*, or *reaching*, a destination. Berger, it is true,
rejects as a misapprehension the whole of the traditional view of Xenophanes'
system (*Gesch. der wissenschaftlichen Erdkunde der Griechen*, pp. 191 sqq.). We
shall have to consider his argument later; but it necessitates getting a sense out
of the fragment and the passage of Aristotle other than the literal interpretation.
The significant words in the passage of Aristotle are 'saying that it (the earth)
is *rooted ad infinitum* ($\acute{\epsilon}\pi$' $\mathring{a}\pi\epsilon\iota\rho o\nu$ $\acute{\epsilon}\rho\rho\iota\zeta\hat{\omega}\sigma\theta a\iota$)'. Berger (p.194, note) holds that the
expression is not used in the literal sense of having *roots* extending *ad infinitum*,
but that 'we use the word $\acute{\epsilon}\rho\rho\iota\zeta\hat{\omega}\sigma\theta a\iota$ only as an expression for a supporting force
not capable of closer definition'; he can only quote in favour of this certain
metaphorical uses of $\acute{\rho}\acute{\iota}\zeta a$ 'root' and other words connected with it, $\acute{\rho}\iota\zeta\acute{\omega}\mu a\tau a$ and
$\acute{\rho}\iota\zeta\acute{\omega}\delta\epsilon s$, which of course do not in the least prove that $\acute{\epsilon}\rho\rho\iota\zeta\hat{\omega}\sigma\theta a\iota$ is used in
a metaphorical sense in our passage; indeed, if it is used in so vague a sense, it
is difficult to see how Xenophanes thereby absolved himself from giving a further
explanation of the cause of the earth's remaining at rest, which, according to
Aristotle, was his object. As regards the fragment from Xenophanes' own
poem, Berger says that he prefers to regard it as an attempt to give in few
words an idea of the *horizon* which divides earth and heaven into an upper,
visible, half, and an invisible lower half. This again leaves no *contrast* between
the upper and lower sides of the earth such as the fragment is obviously intended
to draw. On both points Berger's arguments are of the nature of special
pleading, which can hardly carry conviction.

[1] Aët. ii. 13. 14, iii. 2. 11 (*D. G.* pp. 343, 367; *Vors.* i², pp. 42. 39, 43. 15).
[2] Aët. ii. 18. 1 (*D. G.* p. 347; *Vors.* i², p. 42. 42).
[3] Aët. ii. 20. 3 (*D. G.* p. 348; *Vors.* i², p. 42. 45); Hippol. *Refut.* i. 14. 3 (*D. G.*
p. 565).
[4] Aët. ii. 25. 4 (*D. G.* p. 356; *Vors.* i², p. 43. 12).
[5] Aët. ii. 28. 1 (*D. G.* p. 358; *Vors.* i², p. 43. 13).
[6] Aët. ii. 24. 4 (*D. G.* p. 354; *Vors.* i², p. 43. 1). The passage, which is under
the heading 'On eclipse of the sun', implies that it is an eclipse which comes
about by way of extinguishment ($\kappa a\tau\grave{a}$ $\sigma\beta\acute{\epsilon}\sigma\iota\nu$), but the next words to the effect
that the sun is a new one on rising again suggest that it is 'setting' rather
than 'eclipse', which should be understood.

The phases of the moon are similarly caused by (partial) extinction.[1]

According to Xenophanes, the sun is useful with reference to the coming into being and the ordering of the earth and of living things in it; the moon is, in this respect, otiose.[2]

More remarkable are Xenophanes' theory of a multiplicity of suns and moons, and his view of the nature of the sun's motion; and here it is necessary to quote the actual words of Aëtius:

'Xenophanes says that there are many suns and moons according to the regions (κλίματα), divisions (ἀποτομαί) and zones of the earth; and at certain times the disc lights upon some division of the earth not inhabited by us and so, as it were, stepping on emptiness, suffers eclipse.

'The same philosopher maintains that the sun goes forward *ad infinitum*, and that it only appears to revolve in a circle owing to its distance (away from us).'[3]

The idea that the sun, on arriving at an uninhabited part of the earth, straightway goes out, as it were, is a curious illustration of the final cause.[4] For the rest, the passage, according to the most natural interpretation of it, implies that the sun does not revolve about the earth in a circle, but moves in a straight line *ad infinitum*, that the earth is flat, and that its surface extends without limit. On this interpretation we are presumably to suppose that the sun of any one day passes out of our sight and is seen successively in regions further and further distant towards the west until it is finally extinguished, while in the meantime the new sun of the next day follows the first, at an interval of 24 hours, over our part of the earth, and so on, with the result that at any given time there are many suns all travelling in the same straight direction *ad infinitum*. If this is the correct interpretation of Xenophanes' theory (and this is the way in which it is generally understood), it shows no advance upon, but a distinct falling off from, the systems of Anaximander and Anaximenes. Berger,[5] deeming it incredible that Xenophanes could have put forward views so crude, not to say childish, at a time when the notion of the sphericity of the earth discovered by

[1] Aët. ii. 29. 5 (*D. G.* p. 360; *Vors.* i², p. 43. 14).
[2] Aët. ii. 30. 8 (*D. G.* p. 362; *Vors.* i², p. 43. 9).
[3] Aët. ii. 24. 9 (*D. G.* p. 355; *Vors.* i², p. 43. 3-8).
[4] Tannery, op. cit., p. 133.   [5] Berger, op. cit., pp. 190 sqq.

the earliest Pythagoreans and by Parmenides must already have spread far and wide, seeks to place a new interpretation upon the passages in question.

For the Ionians, with their flat earth, there was necessarily one horizon, so that the solar illumination and the length of the day were the same for all parts of the inhabited earth. As soon, however, as the spherical shape of the earth was realized, it would necessarily appear that there were different horizons according to the particular spot occupied by an observer on the earth's surface. It was then, argues Berger, the *different horizons* which Xenophanes had in view when he spoke of many suns and moons according to the different regions or climates, divisions and zones of the earth ; he realized the difference in the appearances and the effects of the same phenomena at different places on the earth's surface, and he may have been the first to introduce, in this way, the mode of expression by which we commonly speak of different suns, the tropical sun, the Indian sun, the midnight sun, and the like.   This is ingenious, but surely not reconcilable with other elementary opinions stated by Xenophanes, such as that there is a new sun every day. Then again, Berger has to explain the sun's 'going-forward *ad infinitum*' as contrasted with circular motion ; as, on his theory, it cannot be motion *in a straight line* without limit, he takes it to be the motion in a *spiral* which the sun actually exhibits owing to the combination of its two motions, that of the daily rotation, and its yearly motion in the ecliptic, which causes a slight change in its latitude day by day. But in the first place this motion in a spiral is not motion forward *ad infinitum*, for the spiral returns on itself in a year just as a simple circular motion would in 24 hours.   Indeed, Berger's interpretation would make Xenophanes' system purely Pythagorean, and advanced at that, for we do not hear of the spiral till we find it in Plato.[1]   And, if Heraclitus's system also represents (as we shall find it does) a setback in astronomical theory, why should not Xenophanes' ideas have been equally retrograde?

There remains the story that Xenophanes told of an eclipse of the sun which lasted a whole month.[2]   Could he have intended, by

---

[1] Plato, *Timaeus* 39 A.
[2] Aët. ii. 24. 4 (*D. G.* p. 354 ; *Vors.* i², p. 43. 2–3).

this statement, to poke fun at Thales?[1] Berger, full of his theory
that Xenophanes' ideas were based on the sphericity of the earth,
thinks that he must have inferred that the length of the day would
vary in different latitudes and according to the position of the sun
in the ecliptic, and must have seen that, at the winter solstice for
example, there would be a point on the earth's surface at which the
longest night would last 24 hours, another point nearer the north
pole where there would be a night lasting a month, and so on, and
finally that at the north pole itself there would be a night six
months long as soon as the sun passes to the south of the equator ;
Xenophanes therefore, according to Berger, must simply have been
alluding to the existence of a place where a night may last a month.
If, as seems certain, Xenophanes' earth was flat, this explanation
too must fall to the ground.

[1] Tannery, op. cit., p. 132.

VIII

HERACLITUS

If the astronomy of Xenophanes represents a decided set-back in comparison with the speculations of Anaximander and Anaximenes, this is still more the case with Heraclitus of Ephesus (fl. 504/0, and therefore born about 544/0 B.C.); he was indeed no astronomer, and he scarcely needs mention in a history of astronomy except as an illustration of the vicissitudes, the ups and downs, through which a science in its beginnings may have to pass. Heraclitus's astronomy, if it can be called such, is of the crudest description. He does not recognize daily rotation; he leaves all the apparent motions of the heavenly bodies to be explained by a continued interchange of matter between the earth and the heaven.[1] His original element, fire, condenses into water, and water into earth; this is the downward course. The earth, on the other hand, may partly melt; this produces water, and water again vaporizes into air and fire; this is the upward course. There are two kinds of exhalations which arise from the earth and from the sea; the one kind is bright and pure, the other dark; night and day, the months, the seasons of the year, the years, the rains and the winds, &c., are all produced by the variations in the proportion between the two exhalations. In the heavens are certain basins or bowls (σκάφαι) turned with their concave sides towards us, which collect the bright exhalations or vaporizations, producing flames; these are the stars.[2] The sun and the moon are bowl-shaped, like the stars, and they are similarly lit up.[3] The flame of the sun is brightest and hottest; the other stars are further away from the earth and

---

[1] Tannery, op. cit., pp. 168, 169.

[2] Diog. L. ix. 9–10 (*Vors.* i², pp. 55. 25 sqq.); cf. Aët. ii. 28. 6 (*D. G.* p. 359; *Vors.* i², p. 59. 8).

[3] Aet. ii. 22. 2; 27. 2; 28. 6 (*D. G.* pp. 352, 358, 359; *Vors.* i², p. 59. 4, 6, 7–10).

consequently they give out less light and warmth. The moon, although nearer the earth, moves in less pure air and is consequently dimmer than the sun; the sun itself moves in pure and transparent air and is at a moderate distance from us, so that it warms and illuminates more.[1] 'If there were no sun, it would be night for anything the other stars could do.'[2] Both the sun and the moon are eclipsed when the bowls are turned upwards (i.e. so that the concave side faces upwards and the convex side faces in our direction); the changes in the form of the moon during the months are caused by gradual turning of the bowl.[3]

According to Heraclitus there is a new sun every day,[4] by which is apparently meant that, on setting in the west, it is extinguished or spent,[5] and then, on the morrow, it is produced afresh in the east by exhalation from the sea.[6]

The question arises, what happens to the bowl or basin supposed to contain the sun if the sun has to be re-created in this way each morning? Either a fresh envelope must be produced every day for the rising of the sun in the east or, if the envelope is supposed to be the same day after day, it must travel round from the west to the east, presumably in the encircling water, laterally.[7] Diogenes Laertius (i. e. in this case Theophrastus) complains that Heraclitus

---

[1] Diog. L., loc. cit.; Aët. ii. 28. 6 (*D. G.* p. 358; *Vors.* i², p. 59. 10).

[2] Plutarch, *De fort.* 3, p. 98 C (*Vors.* i², p. 76. 8).

[3] Diog. L., loc. cit.; Aët. ii. 24. 3 (*D. G.* p. 354; *Vors.* i², p. 59. 5). The explanation that the hollow side of the basins is turned towards us itself shows how crude were the ideas of Heraclitus. For it is clear that to account for the actual variations which we see in the shape of the moon, it is the *outer* side of a hemispherical bowl which should be supposed bright and turned towards us when the moon is full.

[4] Aristotle, *Meteor.* ii. 2, 355 a 14.

[5] Plato, *Rep.* vi. 498 A.

[6] Aristotelian *Problems*, xxiii. 30, 934 b 35. It is true that a certain passage of Aristotle may be held to imply that Heraclitus did not maintain that the moon and the stars, as well as the sun, are fed and renewed by exhalations. Aristotle (*Meteor.* ii. 2, 354 b 33 sqq.) is speaking of those who maintain that the sun is fed by moisture. He first argues that, although fire may be said to be nourished by water (the flame arising through continuous alternation between the moist and the dry), this cannot take place with the sun ; 'and if the sun were fed in this same way, then it is clear that not only is the sun new every day, as Heraclitus says, but it is continuously becoming new (every moment)' (355 a 11–15). 'And,' he adds (355 a 18–21), 'it is absurd that these thinkers should only concern themselves with the sun, and neglect the conservation of the other stars, seeing that their number and their size is so great.'

[7] Zeller, i⁵, p. 684.

gave no information as to the nature of these cups or basins. The idea, however, of the sun and moon being carried round in these σκάφαι reminds us forcibly of the Egyptian notion of the sun in his barque floating over the waters above, accompanied by a host of secondary gods, the planets and the fixed stars.[1]

Heraclitus held (as Epicurus did long afterwards) that the diameter of the sun is one foot,[2] and that its actual size is the same as its apparent size.[3] This in itself shows that Heraclitus was no mathematician; as Aristotle says, 'it is too childish to suppose that each of the moving heavenly bodies is small in size because it appears so to us observing it from where we stand.'[4]

He called the arctic circle by the more poetical name of 'the Bear', saying that 'the Bear represents the limits of morning and evening' . . . whereas of course it is the arctic circle, not the Bear itself, which is the confine of setting and rising[5] (i.e. the stars within the arctic circle never set).

According to Diogenes Laertius, Heraclitus said absolutely nothing about the nature of the earth;[6] but we may judge that in his conception of the universe he was closer to Thales than to Anaximander; that is, he would regard the universe as a hemisphere rather than a sphere, and the base of the hemisphere as a plane containing the surface of the earth surrounded by the sea; if he recognized a subterranean region, under the name of Hades, he does not seem to have formed any idea with regard to it beyond what was contained in the current mythology.[7]

When he gave 10,800 solar years as the length of a Great Year,[8] he meant no astronomical Great Year, but the period of duration of the world from its birth to its resolution again into fire and *vice versa*. He arrived at it, apparently, by taking a generation of 30 years as a day and multiplying it by 360 as the number of days in a year.[9]

---

[1] See pp. 19, 20 above.   [2] Aët. ii. 21. 4 (*D. G.* p. 351; *Vors.* i², p. 62. 7).
[3] Diog. L. ix. 7 (*Vors.* i², p. 55. 12).
[4] Aristotle, *Meteor.* i. 3, 339 b 34.
[5] Strabo, i. 1. 6, p. 3 (*Vors.* i², p. 78. 15).
[6] Diog. L. ix. 11 (*Vors.* i², p. 55. 46).
[7] Tannery, op. cit., p. 169.
[8] Aët. ii. 32. 3 (*D. G.* p. 364; *Vors.* i², p. 59. 13); Censorinus, *De die natali* 18. 11 (*Vors.* i², p. 59. 16).
[9] Tannery, op. cit., p. 168.

IX

PARMENIDES

WITH regard to the date of Parmenides there is a conflict of authority. On the one hand Plato says that Parmenides and Zeno paid a visit to Athens, Parmenides being then about 65 and Zeno nearly 40 years of age, and that Socrates, who was then very young (σφόδρα νέος), conversed with them on this occasion.[1] Now if we assume that Socrates was about 18 or 20 years of age at this time, the date of the meeting would be about 451 or 449 B.C., and this would give 516 or 514 as the date of Parmenides' birth. On the other hand, Diogenes Laertius[2] says (doubtless on the authority of Apollodorus) that Parmenides flourished in Ol. 69 (504/0 B.C.), in which case he must have been born about 540 B.C. In view of the number of cases in which, for artistic reasons, Plato indulged in anachronisms, it is not unnatural to feel doubt as to whether the meeting of Socrates with Parmenides was a historical fact. Zeller[3] firmly maintained that it was a poetic fiction on the part of Plato; but Burnet, on grounds which seem to be convincing, accepts it as a fact, exposing at the same time the rough and ready methods on which Apollodorus proceeded in fixing his dates.[4]

---

[1] Plato, *Parmenides* 127 A–C.   [2] Diog. L. ix. 23 (*Vors.* i², p. 106. 10).
[3] Zeller, i⁵, pp. 555, 556.
[4] Burnet, *Early Greek Philosophy*, pp. 192, 193. The story was early questioned. Athenaeus (xi. 15, p. 505 F; *Vors.* i², p. 106. 47) doubted whether the age of Socrates would make it possible for him to have conversed with Parmenides or at any rate to have held or listened to such a discourse. But Plato refers to the meeting in two other places (*Theaet.* 183 E, *Sophist* 217 C), and (as Brandis and Karsten also pointed out) we should have to assume a deliberate falsification of facts on the part of Plato if he had inserted these two allusions solely for the purpose of inducing people to believe a fiction contained in another dialogue. We have, too, independent evidence of the visit of Zeno to Athens. Plutarch (*Pericles* 4. 3) says that Pericles 'heard' Zeno. The date given by Apollodorus, on the other hand, seems to be based solely on that of the foundation of Elea. As he adopts that date as the *floruit* of Xenophanes, so he makes it the date of Parmenides' birth. In like manner he makes Zeno's birth contemporaneous

Parmenides is said to have been a disciple of Xenophanes;[1] he was also closely connected with the Pythagorean school, being specially associated with a Pythagorean, Ameinias Diochaites, for whom he conceived such an affection that he erected a ἡρῷον to him after his death;[2] Proclus quotes Nicomachus as authority for the statement that he actually belonged to the school,[3] and Strabo has a notice to the same effect.[4] It is not therefore unnatural that Parmenides' philosophical system had points in common with that of Xenophanes, while his cosmogony was on Pythagorean lines, with of course some differences. Thus his Being corresponds to the One of Xenophanes and, like it, is a well-rounded sphere always at rest; he excluded, however, any idea of its infinite extension; according to Parmenides it is definitely limited, rounded off on all sides, extending equally in all directions from the centre.[5] Parmenides differs from Xenophanes in denying genesis and destruction altogether; these phenomena, he holds, are only apparent.[6] Being is identified with Truth; anything else is Not-Being, the subject of opinion. Physics belongs to the latter deceptive domain.[7]

The main difference between the cosmologies of Parmenides and the Pythagoreans appears to be this. It seems almost certain that Pythagoras himself conceived the universe to be a sphere, and attributed to it daily rotation round an axis[8] (though this was denied by Philolaus afterwards); this involved the assumption that it is itself finite but that something exists round it; the Pythagoreans, therefore, were bound to hold that, beyond the finite rotating sphere, there was limitless void or empty space;

with Parmenides' *floruit*, thereby making Zeno forty years younger than Parmenides, whereas Plato makes him about twenty-five years younger. Burnet quotes E. Meyer (*Gesch. des Alterth.* iv. § 509, note) in support of his view.

[1] Aristotle, *Metaph.* A. 5, 986 b 22; Simplicius, *In phys.* p. 22. 27 (*Vors.* i², p. 107. 16). Diog. L. (ix. 21; *Vors.* i², p. 105. 26) says that Parmenides 'heard' Xenophanes but did not follow him.

[2] Diog. L. ix. 21 (*Vors.* i², p. 105. 29).

[3] Proclus, *In Parm.* i, ad init. (*Vors.* i², p. 106. 30).

[4] Strabo, vi. 1. 1, p. 252 (*Vors.* i², p. 107. 39).

[5] Aristotle, *Phys.* iii. 6, 207 a 16; Fr. 8, line 42 (*Vors.* i², p. 121. 3).

[6] Aristotle, *De caelo* iii. 1, 298 b 14; Aët. i. 24. 1 (*D. G.* p. 320; *Vors.* i², p. 110. 18).

[7] Fr. 8. 50–53 (*Vors.* i², p. 121. 11–13).

[8] Tannery, op. cit., p. 123.

this agrees with their notion that the universe *breathes*,[1] a supposition
which Tannery attributes to the Master himself because Xenophanes
is said to have denied it.[2] Parmenides, on the other hand, denied
the existence of the infinite void, and was therefore obliged to
make his finite sphere motionless, and to hold that its apparent
rotation is only an illusion.[3]

As in other respects the cosmology of Parmenides follows so
closely that of the Pythagoreans, it is not surprising that certain
astronomical innovations are alternatively attributed to Parmenides
and to Pythagoras. Parmenides is said to have been the first to
assert that the earth is spherical in shape and lies in the centre ;[4]
this statement has the great authority of Theophrastus in its favour ;
there was, however, an alternative tradition stating that it was
Pythagoras who first called the heaven κόσμος, and held the earth
to be round (στρογγύλην).[5] As the idea that the earth is spherical
was probably suggested by mathematical considerations, Pythagoras
is the more likely to have conceived it, though Parmenides may
have been the first to state it publicly (the Pythagorean secrecy,
such as it was, seems to have applied only to their ritual, not to their
mathematics or physics). Parmenides is associated with Democritus
as having argued that the earth remains in the centre because,
being equidistant from all points (on the sphere of the universe),
it is in equilibrium, and there is no more reason why it should
tend to move in one direction than in another.[6] Parmenides
therefore here practically repeats the similar argument used by
Anaximander (see above, p. 24), and we shall find that in other
physical portions of his system he follows Anaximander and other
Ionians pretty closely.

---

[1] Aristotle, *Phys.* iv. 6, 213 b 24.

[2] Tannery, op. cit., p. 121. Zeller (i⁵, p. 525), however, does not believe that
the remark μὴ μέντοι ἀναπνεῖν, if Xenophanes really made it, is directed against
the Pythagorean view. He points out, too, that the statement in Diog. L. ix. 19
(*Vors.* i², p. 34. 18), so far as these words ('but that it does not breathe') are
concerned, may only represent an inference from the fact that Fr. 24 only
mentions seeing, hearing, and thinking. This, however, assumes greater intelligence on the part of Diogenes than we are justified in attributing to him.

[3] Tannery, op. cit., p. 125.

[4] Diog. L. ix. 21 (*Vors.* i², p. 105. 32).

[5] Diog. L. viii. 48 (*Vors.* i², p. 111. 38).

[6] Aët. iii. 15. 7 (*D. G.* p. 380 ; *Vors.* i², p. 111. 40) ; cf. Aristotle, *De caelo*, ii.
13, 295 b 10, and the similar views in Plato, *Phaedo* 108 E–109 A.

Secondly, Parmenides is said to have been the first to 'define the habitable regions of the earth under the two tropic zones';[1] on the other hand we are told that Pythagoras and his school declared that the sphere of the whole heaven was divided into five circles which they called 'zones'.[2]   Hultsch[3] bids us reject the attribution to Pythagoras on the ground that these zones would only be possible on a system in which the axis of the universe about which it revolves passes through the centre of the earth; the zones are therefore incompatible with the Pythagorean system, according to which the earth moves round the central fire. Hultsch admits, however, that this argument does not hold if the hypothesis of the central fire was not thought of by any one before Philolaus; and there is no evidence that it was.   As soon as Pythagoras had satisfied himself that the universe and the earth were concentric spheres, the centre of both being the centre of the earth, the definite portion of the heaven marked out by the extreme deviations of the sun in latitude (north and south) might easily present itself to him as a *zone* on the heavenly sphere.   The Arctic Circle, already known in the sense of the circle including within it the stars which never set, would make another division, while a corresponding Antarctic Circle would naturally be postulated by one who had realized the existence of antipodes.[4]   With the intervening two zones, five divisions of the heaven were ready to hand.   It would next be seen that straight lines drawn from the centre of the earth to all points on all the dividing circles in the heaven would cut the surface of the earth in points lying on exactly corresponding circles, and the zone-theory would thus be transferred to the earth.[5]   We are told, however, that Parmenides' division of the earth into zones was different from the division which would be arrived at in this way, in that he made his torrid zone about

<hr/>

[1] Aët. iii. 11. 4 (*D. G.* p. 377).

[2] Aët. ii. 12. 1 (*D. G.* p. 340).

[3] Hultsch, art. 'Astronomie' in Pauly-Wissowa's *Real-Encyclopädie der classischen Altertumswissenschaft*, ii. 2, 1896, p. 1834.

[4] Alexander Polyhistor in Diog. L. viii. 1. 26.

[5] Aët. iii. 13. 1 (*D. G.* p. 378), 'Pythagoras said that the earth was divided, correspondingly to the sphere of the universe, into five zones, the arctic, antarctic, summer and winter zones, and the equatorial zone; the middle of these defines the middle portion of the earth, and is for this reason called the torrid zone; then comes the habitable zone which is temperate.'

twice as broad as the zone intercepted between the tropic circles, so that it spread over each of those circles into the temperate zones.[1] This seems to be the first appearance of zones viewed from the standpoint of physical geography.

Thirdly, Diogenes Laertius says, on the authority of Favorinus, that Parmenides is thought to have been the first to recognize that the Evening and the Morning Stars are one and the same, while others say that it was Pythagoras.[2] In this case, although Parmenides may have learnt the fact from the Pythagoreans, it is probable that Pythagoras did not know it as the result of observations of his own, but acquired the information from Egypt or Chaldaea along with other facts about the planets.[3]

On the purely physical side Parmenides in the main followed one or other of the Ionian philosophers. The earth, he said, was formed from a precipitate of condensed air.[4] He agreed with Heraclitus in regarding the stars as 'compressed' fire (literally close-pressed packs of fire, πιλήματα πυρός).[5]

Parmenides' theory of 'wreaths' (στεφάναι) seems to be directly adapted from Anaximander's theory of hoops or wheels. Anaximander had distinguished hoops belonging to the sun, the moon, and the stars respectively, which were probably concentric with the earth; the hoops were of different sizes, the sun's being the largest, the moon's next, and those of the stars smaller still. These hoops were rings of compressed air filled with fire which burst out in flame at outlets, thereby producing what we see as the sun, moon, and stars. The corresponding views of Parmenides are not easy to understand; I will therefore begin by attempting a translation of the passage of Aëtius in which they are set out.[6]

'There are certain wreaths twined round, one above the other [relatively to the earth as common centre]; one sort is made of the rarefied (element), another of the condensed; and between these are others consisting of light and darkness in combination. That

---

[1] Posidonius in Strabo, ii. 2. 2, p. 94.
[2] Diog. L. ix. 23 (*Vors.* i², p. 106. 11).
[3] Tannery, op. cit., p. 229.
[4] Λέγει δὲ τὴν γῆν πυκνοῦ καταρρυέντος ἀέρος γεγονέναι, Ps. Plut. *Stromat.* 5 (*D. G.* p. 581. 4; *Vors.* i², p. 109. 1).
[5] Aët. ii. 13. 8 (*D. G.* p. 342; *Vors.* i², p. 111. 25). Cf. Anaximander's πιλήματα ἀέρος.
[6] Aët. ii. 7. 1 (*D. G.* p. 335; *Vors.* i², p. 111. 5–16).

which encloses them all is solid like a wall, below which is a wreath
of fire; that which is in the very middle of all the wreaths is solid,
about which (περὶ ὅ) [under which (ὑφ' ᾧ, Diels)] again is a wreath
of fire.　And of the mixed wreaths the midmost is to all of them
the beginning and cause of motion and becoming,[1] and this he calls
the Deity which directs their course and holds sway (κληροῦχον) [2]
[holds the keys (κληδοῦχον, Fülleborn)], namely Justice and Necessity.
Moreover, the air is thrown off the earth in the form of vapour
owing to the violent pressure of its condensation; the sun and the
Milky Way are an exspiration [3] of the fire; the moon is a mixture
of both elements, air and fire.　And, while the encircling aether
is uppermost of all, below it is ranged that fiery (thing) which we
call heaven, under which again are the regions round the earth.'

But in addition we are told that

'It is the mixture of the dense and the rarefied which produces
the colour of the Milky Way.' [4]
'The sun and the moon were separated off from the Milky Way,
the sun arising from the more rarefied mixture which is hot, and
the moon from the denser which is cold.' [5]

The fragments of Parmenides do not add much to this.　The
relevant lines are as follows:

'The All is full of light and, at the same time, of invisible
darkness, which balance each other; for neither of them has any
share in the other.' [6]
'Thou shalt learn the nature of the aether and all the signs in
the aether, the scorching function of the pure clear sun, and whence
they came; thou shalt hear the wandering function and the nature
of the round-eyed moon, and thou shalt learn of the surrounding
heaven, whence it arose, and how Necessity, guiding it, compelled
it to hold fast the bounds of the stars.' [7]
'⟨I will begin by telling⟩ how the earth, the sun and the moon,
the common aether, the milk of the heaven, furthest Olympus, and
the hot force of the stars strove to come to birth.' [8]

---

[1] I follow the reading adopted by Diels in the *Vorsokratiker*, ἁπάσας ⟨ἀρχήν⟩
τε καὶ ⟨αἰτίαν⟩ κινήσεως καὶ γενέσεως ὑπάρχειν.
[2] Burnet (*Early Greek Philosophy*, p. 219) observes that κλῆρος in the Myth
of Er suggests κληροῦχον as the right reading.　Fülleborn suggested κληδοῦχον
in view of the use of κληῖδας (keys) in Fr. 1. 14.
[3] The word ἀναπνοή is of course ambiguous; I follow Diels' interpretation,
'Ausdünstung', 'evaporation' or 'exhalation'.　Diels (*Parmenides Lehrgedicht*,
1897, p. 105) compares ἀναπνοὰς ἴσχον in the *Timaeus* 85 A.
[4] Aët. iii. 1. 4 (*D. G.* p. 365).
[5] Aët. ii. 20. 8 a (*D. G.* p. 349; *Vors.* i², p. 111. 35).
[6] Fr. 9 (*Vors.* i², p. 122. 11–12).
[7] Fr. 10 (*Vors.* i², pp. 122. 21–123. 2).
[8] Fr. 11 (*Vors.* i², p. 123. 5–7).

Of the wreaths he says that

'The narrower (wreaths) were filled with unmixed[1] fire; those next in order to them (were filled) with night, and along with them the share of flame spreads itself. In the middle of these is the Deity which controls all.'[2]

It is not surprising that there have been a number of interpretations of these passages taken in combination.[3] To begin with the outside, there is a doubt as to the relative positions of the 'heaven' and the aether. According to Aëtius 'the encircling aether is uppermost of all, and below it is ranged that fiery thing which we call heaven', whereas the fragments suggest that the 'common aether' is within the 'encircling heaven' or 'furthest Olympus', which latter clearly seems to be the solid envelope compared to a wall. The fragments presumably better represent Parmenides' own statement, and possibly Aëtius's version (which seems practically to interchange the 'heaven' and the 'aether') is due to some confusion.

The next question is, what was the shape of the 'wreaths' or bands?[4] Zeller, in view of the spherical form of the envelope, does not see how they can be anything but hollow globes.[5] But surely 'wreaths' or 'garlands', i.e. bands, would not in that case be a proper description. Tannery[6] takes them to be cylindrical bands fixed one inside the other, comparing with our passage the description in Plato's Myth of Er,[7] where 'the distaff of Necessity by means of which all the revolutions of the universe are kept up' distinctly suggests that Plato had Parmenides' system in mind; Plato there speaks of eight *whorls* (σφόνδυλοι), one inside the other, 'like those boxes which fit into one another,' and of the *lips* of

---

[1] Reading ἀκρήτοιο. The reading ἀκρίτοιο (literally 'confused' or 'undistinguishable', that is to say, *diluted* fire) is impossible, because (1) it does not give the required sense, and (2) it offends against prosody, since ι in ἀκριτος is short (Diels, *Parmenides Lehrgedicht*, p. 104).

[2] Fr. 12 (*Vors.* i², p. 123. 18–20).

[3] Zeller (i⁵, p. 573) gives references to the explanations suggested by Brandis, Karsten, and Krische. More recent views (those of Tannery, Diels, Berger, and Otto Gilbert) are referred to in the text above.

[4] στεφάνη is sometimes translated as 'crown'; but this rendering is open to the objection of suggesting a definite shape. Moreover, it is inapplicable to a series of wreaths or bands entwined the one within the other.

[5] Zeller, i⁵, p. 572.　　　　　　　　[6] Tannery, op. cit., p. 230.

[7] Plato, *Republic* x. 616 D.

the whorls. In the *Timaeus* too there are no spheres, but bands
or strips crossing one another at an angle.[1] We may perhaps take
the bands to be, not cylinders, but zones of a sphere bisected by
a great circle parallel to the bounding circles. Burnet[2] thinks that
the solid circle which surrounds all the bands cannot be a sphere
either, because in that case 'like a wall' would be inappropriate.
I do not, however, see any real difficulty in such a use of 'like
a wall', and certainly Parmenides' All was spherical.[3]

We now come to the main question of the nature of the bands,
their arrangement relatively to one another, and the meaning to
be attached to them severally. What we learn about them from
Aëtius and the fragments taken together amounts to this. First,
the material of which they are composed is of two kinds; one is
alternatively described as the 'rarefied' (ἀραιόν), light, flame (φλόξ)
or fire; the other as the 'condensed' (πυκνόν), darkness, or night.
The bands are of three kinds, the first composed entirely of the
'rarefied' element or fire, the second of the 'condensed' or darkness,
and the third of a mixture of the two. Secondly, as regards their
arrangement, we are told that there is a solid envelope, a spherical
shell, enclosing them all; two bands of unmixed fire are mentioned,
of which one is immediately under the envelope, the other is *about*
(reading περί with the MSS.) or *under* (reading ὑπό with Diels)
'that which is in the very midst of all the bands' and which is
'solid'; these two bands are also 'narrower' (than something),
where 'narrower' means that their radii are smaller, that is to say,
their inner surfaces are nearer (than something) to the centre of
the earth, which is the common centre of all the bands. The mixed
bands, according to Aëtius, are 'between' the bands of fire and the
bands of darkness; the fragment (12) makes them come next to
both the 'narrower' bands, the bands of fire.

There seems to be general agreement that the 'mixed' bands
include the sun, the moon, and the planets; it is with regard to
the meaning and position of the bands of fire, and to the place
occupied by the Deity called by the names of Justice and Necessity,
that there has been the greatest difference of opinion. Tannery's

---

[1] Plato, *Timaeus* 36 B.   [2] Burnet, *Early Greek Philosophy*, p. 216.
[3] 'It is complete on every side, like the mass of a well-rounded sphere poised
from the centre in every direction' (Fr. 8. 42-4; *Vors.* i², p. 121. 3-5).

view is that the outermost band of fire under the solid envelope (which envelope may be regarded as one of the bands made of the 'condensed' element) is the Milky Way. In that case, however, the fire is not pure; for 'it is the mixture of the dense and the rarefied which produces the colour of the Milky Way'. Tannery would get over this difficulty by supposing the band to be only *full* of fire, like the hoops of Anaximander, the almost continuous brightness being due to *exspiration* through the covering. But Aëtius says that both the Milky Way and the sun are an exspiration of fire, and the sun is certainly represented by one of the *mixed* bands, so that the Milky Way should also be one of the mixed bands. The band of fire which (with the reading περί) is about the solid in the very centre of all the bands (i. e. the earth) Tannery takes to be our atmosphere. This seems possible, for Parmenides may have regarded air *lit up* as being fire. In Diels' interpretation a similar view seems to be taken of the outermost band of fire which he calls 'aether-fire'; and the assumption that the aether is fire is perhaps justified by the fact, if true, that Parmenides declared the heaven to be of fire.[1] The intermediate bands consisting of the two elements, light and dark, in combination correspond in Tannery's view to the orbits of the moon, the sun, and the planets respectively, which (starting from the earth) come in that order; possibly among these mixed bands there may be bands entirely dark as well (cf. Fr. 12).

Diels[2] takes the bands which consist exclusively of the 'condensed' element to be made of earth simply. There are two of these; one is the solid envelope, the solid firmament, 'Outer Olympus'; the other is the *crust* of the earth. Just beneath the solid envelope comes the outer band of fire, which is the aether-fire. Next within this come the mixed class of bands which are the bands of stars containing both elements, earth and fire, not separate from one another but mixed together. Such dark rings, out of which the fire flashes out here and there, are the Milky Way, the sun, the moon, and the planets. After the mixed bands comes the solid earth-*crust*, *below* which again (reading ὑφ' ᾧ, which Diels substitutes

---

[1] Aët. ii. 11. 4 (*D. G.* p. 340; *Vors.* i², p. 111. 23).
[2] Diels, *Vors.* ii², i, p. 675; cf. *Parmenides Lehrgedicht*, 1897, pp. 104 sqq.

for περὶ ὅ) comes the inner band of fire, which therefore is *inside* the earth and forms a *kernel* of fire.

It will be seen that the idea of Anaximander that stars are dark rings with fire shining out at certain points is supposed, both by Tannery and Diels, to be more or less present in Parmenides' conception, though Tannery only assumes it as applying to the Milky Way, which he wrongly identifies with the outer band of undiluted fire. Diels, more correctly, implies that it is the mixed rings made up of light and darkness in combination which exhibit the phenomenon of 'fire shining out here and there', these mixed rings including the Milky Way as well as the sun, moon, and planets. It is possible that Aëtius's 'mixed rings' may be no more than his interpretation of the line in Fr. 12 which says that after the 'narrower' bands 'filled with unmixed fire' there come 'bands filled with night and *with* them (μετά, which Diels translates by 'between') is spread (or is set in motion, ἵεται) a share of fire'. And this line itself may mean either that the bands of night have a portion of fire mixed in them, or that each of the bands of night has a stream of fire (its 'share of fire') coursing through it. If the fire were enclosed in the darkness as under the second alternative, we should have a fairly exact reproduction of Anaximander's tubes containing fire; but there is nothing in the fragment to suggest that fire shines out of *vents* in the dark covering; hence the mixture of light and dark, with light shining out at certain points (without enclosure in tubes), as assumed by Diels, seems to be the safer interpretation.

Tannery and Diels differ fundamentally about the inner band of fire. According to the former, it is the atmosphere round the earth, and, if the 'atmosphere' be taken to include the empty space outside the actual atmosphere as far as the nearest of the mixed bands, this seems quite possible. Diels, however, (reading ὑφ᾽ ᾧ, 'under which', instead of περὶ ὅ, 'round which'), makes it a kernel of fire *inside* the earth and concludes that 'Parmenides is for us the first who stated the truth not only as regards the form of the earth but also as regards its constitution, whether he guessed the latter or inferred it correctly from indications such as volcanoes and hot springs'.[1] But it seems to me that there are great difficulties in

---

[1] Diels, *Parmenides Lehrgedicht*, pp. 105, 106.

the way of Diels' interpretation. First, it is difficult to regard a *kernel* of fire, which would presumably be a solid mass of fire, spherical in shape, as satisfying the description of a wreath or band. Secondly, whereas Fr. 12 speaks of the narrower bands as filled with unmixed fire and then of the mixed bands being 'next to *these*' (αἱ δ' ἐπὶ ταῖς νυκτός . . .), the mixed bands would, on Diels' interpretation, be next to only one of the bands of fire (the outer one) and would not be next to the inner one but would be separated from it by the earth's crust. Diels seems to have anticipated this objection, for he explains that it is *both* the unmixed kinds of bands (i.e. those made of unmixed fire and those of unmixed earth, and not only the former, the 'narrower' bands) on which the mixed bands follow, in the inward direction starting from the outside envelope and in the outward direction starting from the centre;[1] but ταῖς would much more naturally mean the narrower bands only. Thirdly, it seems to me to be difficult to assume that there is no band intervening between the surface of the earth and the nearest of the mixed bands; if there were no intervening band, the nearest mixed band, say that of the moon, would have to be in contact with the earth, and therefore the moon also, shining out of it, must practically touch the earth. Therefore there must be some intervening band. But, if there is an intervening band, it must be one of three kinds, dense, mixed, or fiery. It cannot be a dense band, for, if it were, the sun, moon and stars would never be visible; if it were a mixed band, there would again be some heavenly body or bodies in the same position of virtual contact with the earth; therefore the intervening band can only be a band of fire. I am disposed, therefore, to accept Tannery's view that the inner band of fire is our atmosphere with the empty space beyond it reaching to the mixed bands.

If the above arguments are right, the order would be, starting from the outside: (1) the solid envelope like a wall; (2) a band of fire = the aether-fire; (3) mixed bands, in which are included the Milky Way, the planets, the sun, and the moon; (4) a band of fire, the inner side of which is our atmosphere, touching the earth; (5) the earth itself; which is Diels' solution except as regards (4).

[1] *Parmenides Lehrgedicht*, p. 106.

Berger[1] has an ingenious theory as regards the inner band of fire round the earth. If I understand him rightly, he argues that the bands in the heaven containing the stars were described in one part of Parmenides' poem, and the zones of the earth in another, and that Fr. 12 refers to the zones; that the two descriptions then got confused in the *Doxographi*, and that the inner band of fire is really nothing but the *torrid zone*, which has no business in the description at all. Diels has shown that this cannot be correct.[2] Gilbert[3] disagrees with Diels' view of the inner band of fire as a kernel of fire inside the earth; he himself thinks that there was not a *band* of fire about the earth, but that πυρώδης (with στεφάνη understood), 'a band of fire', is a mistake for πῦρ, 'fire', or πυρῶδες in the neuter, and that the meaning is a fire or a fiery space *connected with* the earth (περί in that sense being possible) 'downwards', which fire or fiery space he says we must suppose to embrace the under surface of the earth's sphere.

Lastly, there is a difficulty as to the position occupied by the 'goddess who steers all things', Justice or Necessity. This mythological personification of Necessity and Justice is, of course, after the Pythagorean manner,[4] and reminds us of the similar introduction of Necessity in Plato's Myth of Er, which has so many other points of resemblance to Parmenides' theory. Fragment 12 says that this Deity is 'in the middle of these', i.e. presumably 'these *bands*', and Aëtius, that is to say Theophrastus, took this to mean in the midst of the 'bands filled with night but with a share of fire in them'. Simplicius, on the other hand, takes it to mean 'in the middle of the whole system (ἐν μέσῳ πάντων)',[5] i.e. in the middle of the whole world, clearly identifying the goddess with the central fire or hearth of the Pythagoreans. Diels seems to favour Simplicius's view, taking the centre of the universe to be the centre of the earth,[6] without, how-

---

[1] Berger, *Geschichte der wissenschaftlichen Erdkunde der Griechen*, p. 204 sq.

[2] *Parmenides Lehrgedicht*, p. 104. Since the torrid zone, as viewed by Parmenides, is twice the size of the zone between the tropics, the 'narrower' zones must be the temperate zones, which requires the impossible reading ἀκρίτοιο; with the true reading ἀκρήτοιο, the torrid zone would be 'broader', not 'narrower'. Besides, Aëtius's paraphrase agrees so closely with the fragment, especially in the striking introduction of the Deity, that it cannot be regarded as being anything else than Theophrastus's paraphrase of the verses.

[3] Gilbert, 'Die δαίμων des Parmenides', in *Archiv für Gesch. der Philosophie*, xx, 1906, pp. 25–45.　　　　[4] Tannery, loc. cit.

[5] Simpl. *in Phys.* p. 34. 15 (*Vors.* i², p. 123. 16).

[6] Diels, *Parmenides Lehrgedicht*, pp. 107–8.

ever, attempting to reconcile this with Aëtius's statement that she is placed in the middle of the mixed bands. It is in any case difficult to suppose that Parmenides treated his goddess who 'guides the encircling heaven and compels it to hold fast the bounds of the stars' as shut up within a solid spherical earth with no outlet; the difficulty is even greater than in the Myth of Er, where at all events there is 'a straight light like a pillar which extends from above through all the heaven and earth', and which accordingly passes through the place where Necessity is assumed to be seated. The statement of Aëtius that she is placed in the middle of the mixed bands suggested to Berger [1] the possibility that her place was in the sun, in view of the pre-eminent position commonly assigned to the sun in the celestial system.[2] Gilbert holds that the goddess had her abode in the fiery space under the earth above mentioned; he quotes from other poets, Hesiod, Heraclitus, Aeschylus and Sophocles, references to Dikê as connected with the gods of the lower world, his object being to show that, in connecting Justice or Necessity with the earth, night, and the under-world, Parmenides was only adopting notions generally current.[3] Gilbert (like Diels) is confronted with the difficulty of Aëtius's location of the goddess 'in the middle of *the mixed bands*,' and he disposes of this objection by assuming that the words were interpolated by some one who wished to find her in the sun.[4] This, however, seems too violent.

Both Tannery and Diels specially mention the planets, and Tannery makes Parmenides arrange the heavenly bodies in the following order, starting from the earth: moon, sun, planets, fixed stars. There is, however, nothing in the texts about the bands which distinguishes the planets from the fixed stars or indicates their relative distances.

---

[1] Berger, op. cit., pp. 204, 205.
[2] e. g. Cleanthes (Aët. ii. 4. 16) saw in the sun the seat of authority in the universe (τὸ ἡγεμονικὸν τοῦ κόσμου): cf. also such passages as Theon of Smyrna, pp. 138. 16, 140. 7, 187. 16; Plut. *De fac. in orbe lunae* 30, 945 C; Proclus, *in Timaeum* 258 A, 'The sun, where the justice ordering the world is placed.'
[3] Gilbert, loc. cit., p. 36.
[4] The text in Diels' *Doxographi* (p. 335. 10 sq.) being καὶ τὸ μεσαίτατον πασῶν περὶ ὃ πάλιν πυρῶδης· τῶν δὲ συμμιγῶν τὴν μεσαιτάτην ἁπάσαις τοκέα πάσης κινήσεως καὶ γενέσεως ὑπάρχειν, ἥντινα καὶ δαίμονα κ.τ.έ., Gilbert would reject τῶν δὲ συμμιγῶν τὴν μεσαιτάτην as an interpolation, leaving καὶ τὸ μεσαίτατον πασῶν, περὶ ὃ πάλιν πυρώδης (? στεφάνη), ἁπάσαις τοκέα πάσης κινήσεως καὶ γενέσεως ὑπάρχειν κ.τ.έ.

The only passage in the *Doxographi* throwing light on the matter is a statement that

'Parmenides places the Morning Star, which he thinks the same as the Evening Star, first in the aether; then, after it, the sun, and under it again the stars in the fiery (thing) which he calls heaven.' [1]

Tannery thinks that, if Parmenides distinguished Venus, and if it was from the first Pythagoreans that he learnt to do so, the other planets must equally have been known to the Pythagoreans and therefore to Parmenides. Tannery's view, however, of Parmenides' arrangement of the stars can hardly be reconciled with the distinct statement of Aëtius that, while Venus is outside the sun, the other stars are below it; this, except as regards Venus, agrees with Anaximander's order, according to which both the planets and the other stars are all placed below the sun and moon. Tannery is therefore obliged to assume that Aëtius's remark is an error based on a too rigorous interpretation of the terms aether and heaven; this, however, seems somewhat arbitrary.

It remains to deal with the statement of the *Doxographi* that Parmenides held the moon to be illuminated by the sun:

'The moon Parmenides declared to be equal to the sun; for indeed it is illuminated by it.' [2]

This is the more suspicious because in another place Aëtius attributes the first discovery of this fact to Thales, and adds that Pythagoras, Parmenides, and Empedocles, as well as Anaxagoras and Metrodorus, held the same view. [3] Parmenides was doubtless credited with the discovery on the ground of two lines from his poem. [4] The first is quoted by Plutarch: [5]

'For even if a man says that red-hot iron is not fire, or that the moon is not a sun because, as Parmenides has it, the moon is

"a night-shining foreign light wandering round the earth",

he does not get rid of the use of iron or of the existence of the moon.'

---

[1] Aët. ii. 15. 7 (*D. G.* p. 345).
[2] Aet. ii. 26. 2 (*D. G.* p. 357; *Vors.* i², p. 111. 32).
[3] Aët. ii. 28. 5 (*D. G.* p. 358; *Vors.* i², p. 111. 33).
[4] Fr. 14 and 15 (*Vors.* i², p. 124. 6, 10).
[5] Plutarch, *Adv. Colot.* 15, p. 1116 A (*Vors.* i², p. 124, 4-7).

But, even if the verse is genuine, 'foreign' (ἀλλότριον) need not have meant 'borrowed'; the expression ἀλλότριον φῶς is, as Diels says,[1] a witty adaptation of Homer's ἀλλότριος φῶς used of persons, 'a stranger'.[2] Tannery thinks that the line is adapted from one of Empedocles', and was probably interpolated in Parmenides' poem by some Neo-Pythagorean who was anxious to refer back to the Master the discovery which gives Anaxagoras his greatest title to fame.[3]

Boll,[4] on the other hand, considers it absolutely certain that Parmenides knew of the illumination of the moon by the sun. He admits, however, that we cannot suppose Parmenides to have discovered the fact for himself, and that we cannot be certain whether he got it from Anaximenes or the Pythagoreans. We have seen (p. 19) good reason for thinking that it was not Anaximenes who made the discovery; and the only support that Boll can find for the alternative hypothesis is the statement of Aëtius that Pythagoras considered the moon to be a 'mirror-like body' (κατοπτροειδὲς σῶμα).[5] But this is an uncertain phrase to build upon, especially when account is taken of the tendency to attribute to Pythagoras himself the views of later Pythagoreans; and indeed the evidence attributing the discovery to Anaxagoras is so strong that it really excludes all other hypotheses.

The other line speaks of the moon as 'always fixing its gaze on the beams of the sun'. This remark is certainly important, but is far from explaining the cause of the observed fact. But we have positive evidence against the attribution of the discovery of the opacity of the moon to Parmenides or even to Pythagoras. It is part of the connected prose description of Parmenides' system[6] that the moon is a mixture of air and fire;[7] in other passages we are told that Parmenides held the moon to be of fire[8]

---

[1] Diels, Vors. ii². 1, p. 675 ; Parmenides Lehrgedicht, p. 110.

[2] Homer, Iliad v. 214 ; Od. xviii. 219, &c.

[3] Tannery, op. cit., p. 210. The lines are respectively—

Νυκτιφαὲς περὶ γαῖαν ἀλώμενον ἀλλότριον φῶς (Parm.).

Κυκλοτερὲς περὶ γαῖαν ἑλίσσεται ἀλλότριον φῶς (Emped.).

[4] Boll, art. 'Finsternisse' in Pauly-Wissowa's Real-Encyclopädie der classischen Altertumswissenschaft, vi. 2, 1909, p. 2342.

[5] Aët. ii. 25. 14 (D. G. p. 357).

[6] Aët. ii. 7. 1 (D. G. p. 335 ; Vors. i², p. 111. 5 sqq.).

[7] Ibid. (D. G. p. 335 ; Vors. i², p. 111. 13).

[8] Aët. ii. 25. 3 (D. G. p. 356 ; Vors. i², p. 111. 31).

and to be an excretion from the denser part of the mixture in the
Milky Way,[1] which itself (like the sun) is an exspiration of fire.[2]
More important still is the evidence of Plato, who speaks of 'the
fact which Anaxagoras lately asserted, that the moon has its light
from the sun'.[3] It seems impossible that Plato should have spoken
in such terms if the fact had been stated for the first time by
Parmenides or the Pythagoreans.

[1] Aët. ii. 20. 8 a (*D. G.* p. 349 ; *Vors.* i², p. 111. 35).
[2] Aët. ii. 7. 1 (*D. G.* p. 335 ; *Vors.* i², p. 111. 13).
[3] Plato, *Cratylus* 409 A.

X

ANAXAGORAS

ANAXAGORAS was born at Clazomenae in the neighbourhood of Smyrna about 500 B.C. He neglected his possessions, which were considerable, in order to devote himself to science.[1] Some one once asked him what was the object of being born, to which he replied, 'The investigation of sun, moon, and heaven.'[2] He seems to have been the first philosopher to take up his abode at Athens, where he enjoyed the friendship of Pericles, who had probably induced him to come thither. When Pericles became unpopular shortly before the outbreak of the Peloponnesian war, he was attacked through his friends, and Anaxagoras was accused of impiety for holding that the sun was a red-hot stone and the moon earth.[3] According to one account he was fined five talents and banished;[4] another account says that he was put in prison and it was intended to put him to death, but Pericles got him set at liberty;[5] there are other variations of the story. He went and lived at Lampsacus, where he died at the age of 72.

A great man of science, Anaxagoras enriched astronomy by one epoch-making discovery. This was nothing less than the discovery of the fact that the moon does not shine by its own light but receives its light from the sun. As a result, he was able to give (though not without an admixture of error) the true explanation of eclipses. I quote the evidence, which is quite conclusive :

'. . . the fact which he (Anaxagoras) recently asserted, namely that the moon has its light from the sun.'[6]

'Now when our comrade, in his discourse, had expounded that proposition of Anaxagoras, that "the sun places the brightness in the moon", he was greatly applauded.'[7]

---

[1] Plato, *Hippias Major* 283 A. [2] Diog. L. ii. 10 (*Vors.* i², p. 294. 17).
[3] Plato, *Apology* 26 D. [4] Diog. L. ii. 12 (*Vors.* i², p. 294. 32).
[5] Ibid. ii. 13 (*Vors.* i², p. 294. 42). [6] Plato, *Cratylus*, p. 409 A.
[7] Plutarch, *De facie in orbe lunae* 16, p. 929 B (*Vors.* i², p. 321. 5–7).

'The moon has a light which is not its own, but comes from the sun.'[1]

'The moon is eclipsed through the interposition of the earth, sometimes also of the bodies below the moon'[2] [i.e. the 'bodies below the stars which are carried round along with the sun and the moon but are invisible to us'.[3]]

'The sun is eclipsed at the new moon through the interposition of the moon.'[4] 'He was the first to set out distinctly the facts about eclipses and illuminations.'[5]

'For Anaxagoras, who was the first to put in writing, most clearly and most courageously of all men, the explanation of the moon's illumination and darkness, did not belong to ancient times, and even his account was not common property but was still a secret, current only among a few and received by them with caution or simply on trust. For in those days they refused to tolerate the physicists and star-gazers as they were called, who presumed to fritter away the deity into unreasoning causes, blind forces, and necessary properties. Thus Protagoras was exiled, and Anaxagoras was imprisoned and with difficulty saved by Pericles.'[6]

'Anaxagoras, in agreement with the mathematicians, held that the moon's obscurations month by month were due to its following the course of the sun by which it is illuminated, and that the eclipses of the moon were caused by its falling within the shadow of the earth, which then comes between the sun and the moon, while the eclipses of the sun were due to the interposition of the moon.'[7]

'Anaxagoras, as Theophrastus says, held that the moon was also sometimes eclipsed by the interposition of the (other) bodies below the moon.'[8]

Here, then, we have the true explanation of lunar and other eclipses, though with the unnecessary addition that, besides the earth, there are other dark bodies invisible to us which sometimes

---

[1] Hippolytus, *Refut.* i. 8. 8 (from Theophrastus: see *D. G.* p. 562; *Vors.* i², p. 301. 46).

[2] Ibid. i. 8. 9. (*D. G.* p. 562; *Vors.* i², p. 301. 47).

[3] Ibid. i. 8. 6 (*D. G.* p. 562; *Vors.* i², p. 301. 41).

[4] Ibid. i. 8. 9 (*D. G.* p. 562; *Vors.* i², p. 301. 48).

[5] Ibid. i. 8. 10 (*D. G.* p. 562; *Vors.* i², p. 302. 3).

[6] Plutarch, *Nic.* 23 (*Vors.* i², p. 297. 40–6).

[7] Aët. ii. 29. 6 (*D. G.* p. 360; *Vors.* i², p. 308. 17). I have in the last phrase translated Diels' conjecturally emended reading ἥλιον δὲ τῆς σελήνης instead of μᾶλλον δὲ τῆς σελήνης ἀντιφραττομένης (*D. G.* pp. 53–4). The difficulty, however, is that, according to the heading, the passage deals with the eclipses of the moon *only*.

[8] Aët. ii. 29. 7 (*D. G.* p. 360; *Vors.* i², p. 308. 20).

obscure the moon and cause eclipses. In this latter hypothesis, as
in much else, Anaxagoras followed Anaximenes.[1]

Whether Anaxagoras reached the true explanation of the *phases*
of the moon is much more doubtful. It is true that Parmenides
had observed that the moon has its bright portion always turned in
the direction of the sun ; when to this was added Anaxagoras's
discovery that the moon derived its light from the sun, the explanation of the phases was ready to hand. But it required that the
moon should be spherical in shape ; Anaxagoras, however, held
that the earth, and doubtless the other heavenly bodies also, were

---

[1] The same idea is attributed by Aristotle (*De caelo* ii. 13, 293 b 21–25) to
certain persons whom he does not name : ' Some think it is possible that more
bodies of the kind [i.e. such as the Pythagorean counter-earth] may move about
the centre but may be invisible to us owing to the interposition of the earth.
This, they say, is the reason why more eclipses of the moon occur than of the
sun, for each of the bodies in question obscures the moon, and it is not only the
earth which does so.' An interesting suggestion has been made (by Boll in art.
'Finsternisse' in Pauly-Wissowa's *Real-Encyclopädie d. class. Altertumsw.* vi. 2,
p. 2351), which furnishes a conceivable explanation of the persistence of the
idea that lunar eclipses are sometimes caused by the interposition of dark bodies
other than the earth.   Cleomedes (*De motu circulari* ii. 6, p. 218. 8. sqq.)
mentions that there were stories of extraordinary eclipses which 'the more
ancient of the mathematicians' had vainly tried to explain; the supposed
'paradoxical' case was that in which, while the sun seems to be still above the
horizon, the *eclipsed* moon rises in the east.   The phenomenon appeared to be
inconsistent with the explanation of lunar eclipses by the entrance of the moon
into the earth's shadow ; how could this be if both bodies were above the
horizon at the same time ? The 'more ancient' mathematicians tried to argue
that it was possible that a spectator standing on an *eminence* of the spherical
earth might see along the generators of a *cone*, i.e. a little downwards on all
sides, instead of merely in the *plane* of the horizon, and so might see both the
sun and the moon even when the latter was in the earth's shadow.   Cleomedes
denies this and prefers to regard the whole story of such cases as a fiction
designed merely for the purpose of plaguing astronomers and philosophers ; no
Chaldean, he says, no Egyptian, and no mathematician or philosopher has
recorded such a case. But we do not need the evidence of Pliny (*N.H.* ii, c. 57,
§ 148) to show that the phenomenon is possible ; and Cleomedes himself really
gives the explanation (pp. 222. 28–226. 3), namely, that it is due to atmospheric
refraction.   Observing that such cases of atmospheric refraction were especially
noticeable in the neighbourhood of the Black Sea, he goes on to say that it is
possible that the visual rays going out from our eyes are refracted through falling
on wet and damp air, and so reach the sun though it is already below the
horizon ; and he compares the well-known experiment of the ring at the bottom
of a jug, where the ring, just out of sight when the jug is empty, is brought into
view when water is poured in.   Unfortunately there is nothing to indicate the
date of the 'more ancient mathematicians' who gave the somewhat primitive
explanation which Cleomedes refutes ; but was it the observation of the phenomenon, and their inability to explain it otherwise, which made Anaxagoras
and others adhere to the theory that there are other bodies besides the earth
which sometimes, by their interposition, cause lunar eclipses ?

flat, and accordingly his explanation of the phases could hardly have been correct.[1]

Anaxagoras's cosmology contained other fruitful ideas. According to him the formation of the world began with a vortex set up, in a portion of the mixed mass in which 'all things were together', by his *deus ex machina*, Nous.[2] This rotatory movement began at one point and then gradually spread, taking in wider and wider circles. The first effect was to separate two great masses, one consisting of the rare, hot, light, dry, called the 'aether', and the other of the opposite categories and called 'air'. The aether or fire took the outer position, the air the inner.[3] The next step is the successive separation, out of the air, of clouds, water, earth, and stones.[4] The dense, the moist, the dark and cold, and all the heaviest things collect in the centre as the result of the circular motion; and it is from these elements when consolidated that the earth is formed.[5] But, after this, 'in consequence of the violence of the whirling motion, the surrounding fiery aether tore stones away from the earth and kindled them into stars.'[6] Reading this with the remark that stones 'rush outwards more than water',[7] we see that Anaxagoras conceived the idea of a *centrifugal* force as distinct from that of concentration brought about by the motion of the vortex, and further that he assumed a series of projections or 'hurlings-off' of precisely the same kind as the theory of Kant and Laplace assumes for the formation of the solar system.[8]

Apart from the above remarkable innovations, Anaxagoras did not make much advance upon the crude Ionian theories; indeed he showed himself in the main a follower of Anaximenes.

According to Anaxagoras

'The earth is flat in form and remains suspended because of its size, because there is no void, and because the air is very strong and supports the earth which rides upon it.'[9]

'The sun, the moon, and all the stars are stones on fire, which are carried round by the revolution of the aether.'[10]

---

[1] Tannery, op. cit., p. 278.   [2] Fragment 13 (*Vors.* i², p. 319. 20).

[3] Fr. 15 (*Vors.* i², p. 320. 11).   [4] Fr. 16 (*Vors.* i², p. 320. 20).

[5] Hippol. *Refut.* i. 8. 2 (from Theophrastus); *D. G.* p. 562; *Vors.* i², p. 301. 28–30.   [6] Aët. ii. 13. 3 (*D. G.* p. 341 ; *Vors.* i², p. 307. 16).

[7] Fr. 16 (*Vors.* i², p. 320. 22–3).

[8] Gomperz, *Griechische Denker*, i³, p. 176.

[9] Hippol. *Refut.* i. 8. 3 (*D. G.* p. 562; *Vors.* i², p. 301. 31).

[10] Ibid. i. 8. 6 (*Vors.* i², p. 301. 39).

' The sun is a red-hot mass or a stone on fire.' [1]

' It is larger' (or ' many times larger'[2]) than the Peloponnese.[3]

' The moon is of earthy nature and has in it plains and ravines.' [4]

'The moon is an incandescent solid, having in it plains, mountains, and ravines.' [5]

' It is an irregular compound because it has an admixture of cold and of earth. It has a surface in some places lofty, in others low, in others hollow. And the dark is mixed along with the fiery, the joint effect being an impression of the shadowy ; hence it is that the moon is said to shine with a false light.' [6]

Anaxagoras explained the 'turning' of the sun at the solstice thus :

' The turning is caused by the resistance of the air in the north which the sun itself compresses and renders strong through its condensation.' [7]

' The turnings both of the sun and of the moon are due to their being thrust back by the air. The moon's turnings are frequent because it cannot get the better of the cold.' [8]

Again :

' We do not feel the warmth of the stars because they are at a great distance from the earth ; besides which they are not as hot as the sun because they occupy a colder region. The moon is below the sun and nearer to us.' [9]

' The stars were originally carried round (laterally) like a dome, the pole which is always visible being vertically above the earth, and it was only afterwards that their course became inclined.' [10]

'After the world was formed and the animals were produced from the earth, the world received as it were an automatic tilt towards its southern part, perhaps by design, in order that some

[1] Aët. ii. 20. 6 (*D. G.* p. 349; *Vors.* i², p. 307. 19).
[2] Aët. ii. 21. 3 (*D. G.* p. 351 ; *Vors.* i², p. 307. 20).
[3] Diog. L. ii. 8 (*Vors.* i², p. 293. 38).
[4] Hippol. *Refut.* i. 8. 10 (*D. G.* p. 562; *Vors.* i², p. 302. 4).
[5] Aët. ii. 25. 9 (*D. G.* p. 356 ; *Vors.* i², p. 308. 10).
[6] Aët. ii. 30. 2 (*D. G.* p. 361; *Vors.* i², p. 308. 12). As Dreyer observes (*Planetary Systems*, p. 32, note), the moon has some light of its own which we see during lunar eclipses ; cf. Olympiodorus on Arist. *Meteor.* (p. 67. 36, ed. Stüve; *Meteor.*, ed. Ideler, vol. i, p. 200), 'The moon's own light is of one kind, the sun's of another ; for the moon's own light is like charcoal (ἀνθρακῶδες), as we can plainly see during an eclipse.'
[7] Aët. ii. 23. 2 (*D. G.* p. 352; *Vors.* i², p. 307. 20).
[8] Hippol. *Refut.* i. 8. 9 (*D. G.* p. 562 ; *Vors.* i², p. 302. 1).
[9] Ibid. i. 8. 7 (*D. G.* p. 562 ; *Vors.* i², p. 301. 42).
[10] Diog. L. ii. 9 (*Vors.* i², p. 294. 3).

parts of the world might become uninhabitable and others inhabit-
able, according as they are subject to extreme cold, torrid heat,
or moderate temperature.'[1]

' The revolution of the stars takes them round under the earth.'[2]

Gomperz[3] finds a difficulty in reconciling the last of these
passages with the other statement that the earth is flat and rests on
air, in which Anaxagoras had followed Anaximenes. Anaximenes
seems to have regarded the basis of air on which the flat earth
rested in the same way as Thales the water on which his earth
floated ; and Anaximenes said that the stars did not pass under the
earth but laterally round it. I do not, however, feel sure that
Anaxagoras could not have supposed the stars to pass in their
revolution through the basis of *air* under the earth, although no
doubt Thales was almost precluded from supposing them to pass
through his basis of *water*. If, as Gomperz says, Simplicius[4] is alone
in attributing to Anaxagoras's earth the shape of a drum or cylinder,
Aristotle as well as Simplicius seems to imply that at all events
the earth occupied the *centre* of the universe.[5]

Anaxagoras put forward a remarkable and original hypothesis to
explain the Milky Way. As we have seen, he thought the sun to be
smaller than the earth. Consequently, when the sun in its revolution passes below the earth, the shadow cast by the earth extends
without limit. The trace of this shadow on the heavens is the
Milky Way. The stars within this shadow are not interfered with
by the light of the sun, and we therefore see them shining ; those
stars, on the other hand, which are outside the shadow are overpowered by the light of the sun, which shines on them even during
the night, so that we cannot see them. Such appears to be the
meaning of the passages in which Anaxagoras's hypothesis is
explained. According to Aristotle, Anaxagoras and Democritus
both held that

' The Milky Way is the light of certain stars. For when the sun
is passing below the earth some of the stars are not within its
vision. Such stars then as are embraced in its view are not seen to

---

[1] Aët. ii. 8. 1 (*D. G.* p. 337 ; *Vors.* i², p. 306. 12).
[2] Hippol. *Refut.* i. 8.8 (*D. G.* p. 562 ; *Vors.* i², p. 301. 47).
[3] Gomperz, *Griechische Denker,* i³, pp. 178, 442.
[4] Simplicius on *De caelo,* p. 520. 30.
[5] Arist. *De caelo* ii. 13, 295 a 13.

give light, for they are overpowered by the rays of the sun ; such of the stars, however, as are hidden by the earth, so that they are not seen by the sun, form by their own proper light the Milky Way.'[1]

'Anaxagoras held that the shadow of the earth falls in this part of the heaven (the Milky Way) when the sun is below the earth and does not cast its light about all the stars.'[2]

'The Milky Way is the reflection (ἀνάκλασις) of the light of the stars which are not shone upon by the sun.'[3]

As Tannery[4] and Gomperz[5] point out, this conjecture, however ingenious, could easily have been disproved by simple observation. For Anaxagoras might have observed the obvious fact, noted as an objection by Aristotle,[6] that the Milky Way always retains the same position relatively to the fixed stars, whereas the hypothesis would require the trace of it to change its position along with the sun ; indeed the Milky Way should have coincided with the ecliptic, whereas it is actually inclined to it. Again, if the theory were true, an eclipse of the moon would have been bound to occur whenever the moon passed over the Milky Way, and it would have been easy to verify that this is not so. As the Milky Way is much longer than it is broad, it would seem that Anaxagoras thought that the flat earth was not round but 'elongated' (προμήκης), as Democritus afterwards conceived it to be,[7] though Democritus only made its its length half as much again as its breadth.[8]

Aristotle[9] adds an interesting criticism of this theory : ' Besides, if what is proved in the theorems on astronomy is correct, and the size of the sun is greater than that of the earth, and the distance of the stars from the earth is many times greater than the distance of the sun, just as the distance of the sun is many times greater than the distance of the moon, the cone emanating from the sun and marking the convergence of the rays would have its vertex not very far from the earth, and consequently the shadow of the earth,

[1] Arist. *Meteorologica* i. 8, 345 a 25–31 (*Vors.* i², p. 308. 26–31).
[2] Aët. iii. 1. 5 (*D. G.* p. 365 ; *Vors.* i², p. 308. 31).
[3] Hippol. *Refut.* i. 8. 10 (*D. G.* p. 561 ; *Vors.* i², p. 302. 5) ; Diog. L. ii. 9 (*Vors.* i², p. 294. 5).
[4] Tannery, op. cit., p. 279.
[5] Gomperz, *Griechische Denker*, i³, p. 179.
[6] Aristotle, *Meteorologica* i. 8, 345 a 32.
[7] Eustathius *in Homer. Il.* vii. 446, p. 690 (*Vors.* i², p. 367. 42).
[8] Agathemerus, i. 2 (*Vors.* i², p. 393. 10).
[9] Aristotle, *Meteorologica* i. 8, 345 b 1–9.

which we call night, would not reach the stars at all.   In fact the sun must embrace in his view *all* the stars and the earth cannot hide any one of them from him.'

According to Proclus,[1] who quotes the authority of Eudemus, Anaxagoras anticipated Plato in holding that in the order of the revolution of the sun, moon, and planets round the earth the sun came next to the moon, whereas Ptolemy[2] says that according to 'the more ancient' astronomers (by which phrase he appears to mean the Chaldaeans[3]) the order (starting from the earth) was Moon, Mercury, Venus, Sun, Mars, Jupiter, Saturn.

It seems clear that Anaxagoras held that there were other worlds than ours.   Aëtius,[4] it is true, includes Anaxagoras among those who said that there was only one world; but the fragments must be held to be more authoritative, and one of these leaves no room for doubt on the subject.[5]   According to this fragment

'Men were formed and the other animals which have life; the men too have inhabited cities and cultivated fields as with us; they have also a sun and moon and the rest as with us, and their earth produces for them many things of various kinds, the best of which they gather together into their dwellings and live upon.'

Thus much have I said about separating off, to show that it will not be only with us that things are separated off, but elsewhere as well.' [6]

[1] Proclus *in Timaeum*, p. 258 C (on Timaeus 38 D) ; *Vors.* i², p. 308. 1–4.
[2] Ptolemy, *Syntaxis* ix. 1, vol. ii, p. 207, ed. Heiberg.
[3] Tannery, op. cit., p. 261.
[4] Aët. ii. 1. 2 (*D. G.* p. 327 ; *Vors.* i², p. 305. 44).
[5] Burnet, *Early Greek Philosophy*, pp. 312, 313.
[6] Fr. 4 (*Vors.* i², p. 315. 8–16).

XI

EMPEDOCLES

THE facts enabling the date of Empedocles of Agrigentum to be approximately determined are mainly given by Diogenes Laertius.[1] His grandfather, also called Empedocles, won a victory in the horse-race at Olympia in 496/5 B.C.; and Apollodorus said that his father was Meton, and that Empedocles himself went to Thurii shortly after its foundation. Thurii was founded in 445 B.C. and, when Diogenes Laertius says that Empedocles flourished in Ol. 84 (444/1), it is clear that the visit to Thurii was the basis for this assumption. According to Aristotle[2] he died at the age of sixty; hence, assuming him to be forty in 444 B.C., we should have 484–424 B.C. as the date. But there is no reason why he should be assumed to have been just forty at the date of his visit to Thurii; and other facts suggest that the date so arrived at is about ten years too late. Theophrastus said that Empedocles was born ' not long after Anaxagoras';[3] according to Alcidamas he and Zeno were pupils of Parmenides at the same time;[4] and Satyrus said that Gorgias was a disciple of Empedocles.[5] Now Gorgias was a little older than Antiphon (of Rhamnus), who was born in 480 B.C.[6] It follows that we must go back *at least* to 490 B.C. for the birth of Empedocles; most probably he lived from about 494 to 434 B.C.[7]

Empedocles is said to have been the inventor of rhetoric;[8] as an active politician of democratic views he seems to have played

---

[1] Diog. L. viii. 51-74 (*Vors.* i², pp. 149-53).
[2] In Diog. L. viii. 52 (*Vors.* i², p. 150. 15).
[3] Theophrastus in Simpl. *Phys.* p. 25. 19 (*D. G.* p. 477; *Vors.* i², p. 154. 33).
[4] Diog. L. viii. 56 (*Vors.* i², p. 150. 41).
[5] Diog. L. viii. 58 (*Vors.* i², p. 151. 10).
[6] [Plutarch] *Vit. X orat.* i. 1. 9, p. 832 F (*Vors.* ii². 1, p. 546. 25).
[7] Cf. Diels' ' Empedokles und Gorgias', 2 (*Berl. Sitzungsb.*, 1884); Burnet, *Early Greek Philosophy*, pp. 228-9.
[8] Aristotle in Diog. L. viii. 57 (*Vors.* i², p. 150. 46).

a prominent part in many a stirring incident; he was a religious teacher, a physiologist and, according to Galen,[1] the founder of an Italian school of Medicine, which vied with those of Cos and Cnidus. That he was no mean poet is sufficiently attested by the fragments which survive, amounting to 350 (or so) lines or parts of lines in the case of the poem *On Nature* and over 100 in the case of the *Purifications*.

Empedocles followed Anaximenes in holding that the heaven is a crystal sphere and that the fixed stars are attached to it.[2] The sphere, which is 'solid and made of air condensed or congealed by the action of fire, like crystal',[3] is, however, not quite spherical, the height from the earth to the heaven being less than its distance from it laterally, and the universe being thus shaped like an egg.[4] While the fixed stars are attached to the crystal sphere, the planets are free.[5]

The sun's course is round the extreme circumference of the world (literally 'is the circuit of the limit of the world');[6] in this particular Empedocles follows Anaximander. The circuit must be just inside the circumference because, under the heading 'tropics' or 'turnings' of the sun, Aëtius says that, according to Empedocles, the sun is prevented from moving always in a straight line by the resistance of the enveloping sphere and by the tropic circles.[7]

A special feature of Empedocles' system is his explanation (1) of day and night, (2) of the nature of the sun.

(1) Within the crystal sphere, and filling it, is a sphere consisting of two hemispheres, one of which is wholly of fire and therefore light, while the other is a mixture of air with a little fire, which mixture is darkness or night. The revolution of these two hemi-

---

[1] Galen, *Meth. Med.* i. 1 (*Vors.* i², p. 154. 19-23).

[2] Aët. ii. 13. 11 (*D. G.* p. 342; *Vors.* i², p. 162. 12).

[3] Aët. ii. 11. 2 (*D. G.* p. 339; *Vors.* i², p. 161. 40).

[4] Aët. ii. 31. 4 (*D. G.* p. 363; *Vors.* i², p. 161. 34). The statement as to height and breadth is mathematically inconsistent with the comparison of the figure to an egg, unless we suppose that Empedocles regarded the section of it by the plane containing the surface of the earth as an oval and not a circle, which does not seem likely. If the said section is a circle, the figure would be what we call an *oblate spheroid* (the solid described by the revolution of an ellipse about its *minor* axis) rather than egg-shaped.

[5] Aët. ii. 13. 11 (see above).

[6] Aët. ii. 1. 4 (*D. G.* p. 328; *Vors.* i², p. 161. 37) τὸν τοῦ ἡλίου περίδρομον εἶναι περιγραφὴν τοῦ πέρατος τοῦ κόσμου.

[7] Aët. ii. 23. 3 (*D. G.* p. 353; *Vors.* i², p. 162. 37).

spheres round the earth produces at each point on its surface the succession of day and night.[1] The beginning of this motion was due to the collection of the mass of fire in one of the hemispheres, the result being that the pressure of the fire upset the equilibrium of the heaven and caused it to revolve.[2] Apparently connected with this theory of the two hemispheres is Empedocles' explanation of the difference between winter and summer. It is winter when the air (forming one hemisphere) gets the upper hand through condensation and is forced upwards (into the fiery hemisphere), and summer when the fire gets the upper hand and is forced downwards (into the dark hemisphere) ;[3] that is, in the winter the fire occupies less than half of the whole sphere of heaven, while in the summer it occupies more than half. The idea seems to be that the greater half of the sphere takes longer to revolve about a particular point on the earth's surface than the smaller half, and that this explains why the days are longer in the summer than in the winter. We are not told what was the axis about which the two hemispheres were supposed to revolve, but it seems hardly likely that Empedocles could have assumed a definite axis different from that of the daily rotation of the heavenly sphere.

According to Empedocles it was the swiftness of the revolution of the heaven which kept the earth in its place, just as we may swing a cup with water in it round and round so that in some positions the top of the cup may actually be turned downwards without the water escaping.[4] The analogy is, of course, not a good one, because the water in that case is kept in its place by centrifugal force which throws it, as it were, against the side of the vessel, whereas the earth is presumably at rest in the centre during the revolution of the heaven, and is not acted on by such a force.

Empedocles further held that the revolution of the heaven, which now takes 24 hours to complete, was formerly much slower. At one time a single revolution was only accomplished in a period equal to ten of our months ; later it required a period equal to seven

---

[1] Ps. Plut. *Stromat.* apud Euseb. *Praep. Evang.* i. 8. 10 (from Theophrastus); *D. G.* p. 582 ; *Vors.* i², p. 158. 19–23.
[2] Ps. Plut. *Stromat.*, loc. cit. (*Vors.* i², p. 158. 33–4).
[3] Aët. iii. 8. 1 (*D. G.* p. 375 ; *Vors.* i², p. 163. 16).
[4] Aristotle, *De caelo* ii. 13, 295 a 17 (*Vors.* i², p. 163. 39).

of our months.[1]   These views have, however, no astronomical basis ;
they were put forward solely in order to explain the exceptions
to the usual period of gestation afforded by ten-months' and seven-
months' children, the period being in each case taken as one day !

Coming now to Empedocles's conception of the nature of the sun,
we find the following opinions attributed to him :

'The sun is, in its nature, not fire, but a reflection of fire similar
to that which takes place from (the surface of) water.'[2]

'There are two suns; one is the original sun which is the fire
in one hemisphere of the world, filling the whole hemisphere and
always placed directly opposite the reflection of itself; the other
is the apparent sun which is a reflection in the other hemisphere
filled with air and an admixture of fire, and in this reflection what
happens is that the light is bent back from the earth, which is
circular, and is concentrated into the crystalline sun where it is
carried round by the motion of the fiery (hemisphere).   Or, to
state the fact shortly, the sun is a reflection of the fire about the
earth.'[3]

'The sun which consists of the reflection is equal in size to
the earth.'[4]

'You laugh at Empedocles for saying that the sun is produced
about the earth by a reflection of the light in the heaven and " once
more flashes back to Olympus with fearless countenance ".'[5]

The second of the above passages is scarcely intelligible at the
point where the reflection is called 'a reflection *in the other
hemisphere*'; it can hardly be in the other hemisphere because
that hemisphere is night. Accordingly Tannery conjectures that the
reading should be 'a reflection (*invisible*) in the other hemisphere'.[6]
The meaning must apparently be that the fire in the fiery hemisphere is reflected from the earth upon the crystal vault, the
reflected rays being concentrated in what we see as the sun. The
equality of the size of the sun and the earth may have been a hasty
inference founded upon the supposition of an analogy with the
recently discovered fact that the moon shines with light borrowed

---

[1] Aët. v. 18. 1 (*D. G.* p. 427 ; *Vors.* I², p. 165. 31).
[2] Ps. Plut. *Stromat.*, loc. cit. (*D. G.* p. 582 ; *Vors.* i², p. 158. 35).
[3] Aët. ii. 20. 13 (*D. G.* p. 350; *Vors.* i², p. 162. 18-24).
[4] Aët. ii. 21. 2 (*D. G.* p. 351 ; *Vors.* i², p. 162. 25).
[5] Plutarch, *De Pyth. or.* 12, p. 400 B (*Vors.* i², p. 188. 8-11).
[6] Tannery, op. cit., p. 323.

from the sun.[1] The theory that the sun which we see is a concentration of rays reflected from the earth upon the crystal sphere
agrees exactly with the statement already quoted that the sun's
course is confined just within the inner surface of the spherical
envelope. Why it is just confined within the tropical circles and
prevented from deviating further in latitude is not so clear. If, as
Dreyer supposes,[2] the airy and the fiery hemispheres, which in turn
occupy more than half of the heavenly sphere, ' thereby make
the sun, the image of the fiery hemisphere, move south or north
according to the seasons ', it would seem necessary to suppose that
the advance of the hemisphere of fire in the summer (and its retreat
in the winter) does not take place uniformly over the whole of its
circular base (which is the division between the two hemispheres),
i. e. in such a way that the base of the new hemisphere is parallel
to the base of the old, but that the advance (or retreat) takes place
obliquely with reference to the circular base, being greatest at a
certain point on the rim of that base and least at the opposite
point, so that the plane base of the new hemisphere is obliquely
inclined to that of the old; in other words, that the *axis* of the
fiery hemisphere changes its position as the advance (or retreat)
proceeds, and in fact swings gradually (completing an oscillation
in a year) between two extreme positions inclined to the mean
position at an angle equal to the obliquity of the ecliptic. But it is
very unlikely that Empedocles, with his elementary notions of
astronomy, worked out his theory in this way.

It would appear that Empedocles' theory of the sun gave a lead
to the later Pythagoreans, for we shall find Philolaus saying that
' there are in a manner two suns . . . unless [in Aëtius's words]

[1] Cf. Plutarch, *De fac. in orbe lunae* 16, p. 929 E (*Vors.* i², p. 187. 21-6):
' There remains then the view of Empedocles that the illumination which we
get here from the moon is produced by a sort of reflection of the sun at the
moon [the same word ἀνάκλασιν being used in this case]. Hence we get neither
heat nor brightness from it, whereas we should expect both if there had been
a kindling and mixing of ⟨the⟩ lights, and, just as when sounds are reflected
the echo is less distinct than the original sound, ... "even so the ray which
struck the moon's wide orb" passes on to us a reflux which is weak and indistinct,
owing to the loss of power due to the reflection.' But, if Empedocles spoke in
this way of the moon's light, he could hardly have conceived the light of the
sun, which is bright and hot, to be a reflection of light in the same sense as the
light of the moon is; the 'reflection of light' which constitutes the sun is more
like the effect of a burning-glass than ordinary reflection.

[2] Dreyer, *Planetary Systems*, p. 25.

we prefer to say that there are three, the third consisting of the rays which are reflected again from the mirror or lens [the second sun] and spread in our direction'.[1]

Empedocles does not seem to have mentioned the annual motion of the sun relatively to the fixed stars, although, as we have seen, he speaks of the tropic circles as limiting its motion (i. e. motion in latitude).

Empedocles, like Anaxagoras, held that the moon shone with light borrowed from the sun.[2] The moon itself he regarded as 'a mass of frozen air, like hail, surrounded by the sphere of fire',[3] or as 'condensed air, cloudlike, solidified (or congealed) by fire, so that it is of mixed composition'.[4] This idea may have been put forward to account for the apparent change of shape in the phases; for we find Plutarch saying that 'the apparent form of the moon, when the month is half past, is not spherical, but lentil-shaped and like a disc, and, in the opinion of Empedocles, its actual substance is so too'.[5]

The stars he thought to be 'of fire (arising) out of the fiery (element) which the air contained in itself but squeezed out upwards in the original separation'.[6]

We are not definitely told whether Empedocles held the earth to be spherical or flat. He might, it is true, have adopted the view of the Pythagorean school and Parmenides that it was spherical, but it is more probable that he considered it to be flat. For we are told that he regarded the moon as 'like a disc'[7]; in this he probably followed Anaxagoras, who undoubtedly thought the earth flat, and therefore most probably the moon also.

He also shared the view of Anaxagoras that the axis of the world was originally perpendicular to the surface of the earth, the north pole being in the zenith, and that it was displaced afterwards. This view Anaxagoras combined with the hypothesis of a flat

---

[1] Aët. ii. 20. 12 (*D. G.* p. 349 ; *Vors.* i², p. 237. 39).
[2] Fr. 43, quoted in note on preceding page ; Aët. ii. 28. 5 (*D. G.* p. 358 ; *Vors.* i², p. 162. 48).
[3] Plutarch, *De fac. in orbe lunae* 5, p. 922 C (*Vors.* i², p. 162. 43).
[4] Aët. ii. 25. 15 (*D. G.* p. 357; *Vors.* i², p. 162. 41).
[5] Plutarch, *Quaest. Rom.* 101, p. 288 B (*Vors.* i², p. 162. 45).
[6] Aët. ii. 13. 2 (*D. G.* p. 341 ; *Vors.* i², p. 162. 10).
[7] Diog. L. viii. 77 (*Vors.* i², p. 153. 37) ; Aët. ii. 27. 3 (*D.G.* p. 358; *Vors.* i², p. 162. 44).

earth; indeed, a flat earth is almost necessary if the axis of the universe was originally perpendicular to its surface. Empedocles, however, differed from Anaxagoras in his explanation of the cause of the subsequent displacement; whereas Anaxagoras could only account for it tentatively by assuming 'design', Empedocles gave a mechanical explanation:

'The air having yielded to the force of the sun, the north pole became inclined, the northern parts were heightened, and the southern lowered, and the whole universe was thereby affected.' [1]

'There are many fires burning beneath the earth',[2] said Empedocles. He seems to have inferred this truth from the existence of hot springs, the water of which he supposed to be heated, like the water in baths, by running a long course, as it were in tubes, through fire.[3]

According to Empedocles the sun is a great collection of fire and greater than the moon,[4] and the sun is twice as distant from the earth as the moon is.[5]

He was aware of the true explanation of eclipses of the sun, for he says that

'The moon shuts off the beams of the sun as it passes across it, and darkens so much of the earth as the breadth of the blue-eyed moon amounts to.' [6]

With this may be compared his description of night as caused by the shadow of the earth which obstructs the rays of the sun as the sun passes under the earth.[7]

Empedocles' one important scientific achievement, so far as we know, was his theory that light travels and takes time to pass from one point to another. The theory is alluded to by Aristotle in the following passages:

[1] Aët. ii. 8. 2 (*D. G.* p. 338; *Vors.* i², p. 162. 35).
[2] Fr. 52 (*Vors.* i², p. 189. 14).
[3] Seneca, *Nat. Quaest.* iii. 24, quoted by Burnet, *Early Greek Philosophy*, p. 277, note.
[4] Diog. L. viii. 77 (*Vors.* i², p. 153. 36).
[5] Aët. ii. 31. 1 (*D. G.* p. 362; *Vors.* i², p. 163. 1–3). I follow the text as corrected by Diels after Karsten. The reading of Stobaeus is corrupt. That of the *Placita* says that the moon is twice as far from the sun as it is from the earth.
[6] Fr. 42 (*Vors.* i², p. 187. 28): cf. Aët. ii. 24. 7 (*D. G.* p. 354; *Vors.* i², p. 162. 40).
[7] Fr. 48 (*Vors.* i², p. 188. 31).

'Empedocles, for instance, says that the light from the sun reaches the intervening space before it reaches the eye or the earth. And this might well seem to be the fact. For, when a thing is moved, it is moved from one place to another, and hence a certain time must elapse during which it is being moved from the one place to the other. But every period is divisible. Therefore there was a time when the ray was not yet seen, but was being transmitted through the medium.'[1]

'Empedocles represented light as moving in space and arriving at a given point of time between the earth and that which surrounds it, without our perceiving its motion.'[2]

Aristotle of course rejected this theory because he himself held a different view, namely, that light was not a movement in space but was a qualitative change of the transparent medium which, he considered, could be changed all at once and not only (say) half at a time, just as a mass of water is all simultaneously congealed.[3] But he had no better argument to oppose to Empedocles than that 'though a movement of light might elude our observation within a short distance, that it should do so all the way from east to west is too much to assume'.[4]

[1] Aristotle, *De sensu* 6, 446 a 25–b 2.
[2] Aristotle, *De anima* ii. 7. 418 b 21.
[3] Aristotle, *De sensu* 6, 447 a 1–3.
[4] Aristotle, *De anima* ii. 7, 418 b 24.

XII

THE PYTHAGOREANS

IN a former chapter we tried to differentiate from the astronomical system of 'the Pythagoreans' the views put forward by the Master himself, and we saw reason for believing that he was the first to give spherical shape to the earth and the heavenly bodies generally, and to assign to the planets a revolution of their own in a sense opposite to that of the daily rotation of the sphere of the fixed stars about the earth as centre.

But a much more remarkable development was to follow in the Pythagorean school. This was nothing less than the abandonment of the geocentric hypothesis, and the reduction of the earth to the status of a planet like the others. Aëtius (probably on the authority of Theophrastus) attributes the resulting system to Philolaus, Aristotle to 'the Pythagoreans'.

Schiaparelli[1] sets out the considerations which may have suggested to the Pythagoreans the necessity of setting the earth itself in motion. If the proper movement of the sun, moon, and planets along the zodiac had been a rotation about the same axis as that of the daily rotation of the fixed stars, it would have been easy to account for the special movements of the former heavenly bodies by assuming for each of them a daily rotation somewhat slower than that of the fixed stars; if the movement of each of them had been thus simple, a moving force at the centre operating with various degrees of intensity (depending on distance and the numerical laws of harmony) would have served to explain everything. But, since the daily rotation follows the plane of the equator, and while special movement of the planets follows the plane of the ecliptic, it is clear that, with one single moving force

---

[1] Schiaparelli, *I precursori di Còpernico nell' antichità* (Milano, Hoepli, 1873), p. 4.

situated at the centre, it was not possible to account for both movements. Hence the necessity of attributing the daily rotation, which is apparently common to the fixed stars and the planets, to a motion of the earth itself. But another reason too would compel the Pythagoreans to avoid attributing to the sun, moon, and planets the movement compounded of the daily rotation and the special movement along the zodiac. For such a composite movement would take place in a direction and with a velocity continually altering and it would follow that, if at a given instant the harmonical proportions of the velocities and the distances held good, these proportions would not hold good for the next instant. Accordingly it was necessary to assign to each heavenly body one single simple and uniform movement, and this could not be realized except by attributing to the earth that one of the component movements which observation showed to be common to all the stars.

Whether the system attributed to Philolaus was really founded on arguments so scientific, combining the data furnished by observations with an antecedent principle based on the nature of things and on a living spirit animating the world, must be left an open question.

It is time to attempt a description of the system itself, and I think that this can best be done in the words of our authorities.

Motion round the central fire.

'While most philosophers say that the earth lies in the centre ... the philosophers of Italy, the so-called Pythagoreans, assert the contrary. They say that there is fire in the middle, and the earth, being one of the stars, is carried round the centre, and so produces night and day. They also assume another earth opposite to ours, which they call counter-earth, and in this they are not seeking explanations and causes to fit the observed phenomena, but they are rather trying to force the phenomena into agreement with explanations and views of their own and so adjust things. Many others might agree with them that the place in the centre should not be assigned to the earth, if they looked for the truth not in the observed facts but in *a priori* arguments. For they consider that the worthiest place is appropriate to the worthiest occupant, and fire is worthier than earth, the limit worthier than the intervening parts, while the extremity and the centre are limits ; arguing from these considerations they think that it is not the earth which is in the centre of the (heavenly) sphere but rather the fire. Further, the Pythagoreans give the additional reason that it is most fitting that the most important part of the All—and the centre may be so described—should be safe-guarded; they accordingly give the name of "Zeus's watch-tower" to the fire which occupies this position, the term "centre" being here used absolutely and the implication being that the centre of the (thing as a) magnitude is also the centre of the thing in its nature . . . . Such are the opinions of certain philosophers about the position of the earth; and their opinions about its rest or motion correspond. For they do not all take the same view; those who say that the earth does not so much as occupy the centre make it revolve in a circle round that centre, and not only the earth but the counter-earth also, as we said before. Some again think that there may be even more bodies of the kind revolving round the centre; only they are invisible to us because of the interposition of the earth. This they give as the reason why there are more eclipses of the moon than of the sun; for the moon is obscured by each of the other revolving bodies as well, and not only by the earth. The fact that the earth is not the centre, but is at a distance represented by the whole (depth, i.e. radius) of half the sphere (in which it revolves) constitutes, in their opinion, no reason why the phenomena should not present the same appearance to us if we lived (on an earth) away from the centre as they would if our earth were at the centre; seeing that, as it is, we are at a distance (from the centre) represented by half the earth's diameter and yet this does not make any obvious difference.'[1]

'The Pythagoreans, on the other hand, say that the earth is not at the centre, but that in the centre of the universe is fire, while round the centre revolves the counter-earth, itself an earth, and called counter-earth because it is opposite to our earth, and next to the counter-earth comes our earth, which itself also revolves round the centre, and next to the earth the moon; this is stated by Aristotle in his work on the Pythagoreans. The earth then, being like one of the stars, moves round the centre and, according to its position with reference to the sun, makes night and day. The counter-earth, as it moves round the centre and accompanies our earth, is invisible to us because the body of the earth is continually interposed in our way. . . . The more genuine exponents of the doctrine describe as fire at the centre the creative force which from the centre imparts life to all the earth and warms afresh the part of it which has cooled. Hence some call this fire the Tower of Zeus, as Aristotle states in his Pythagorean Philosophy, others the

[1] Aristotle, *De caelo* ii. 13, 293 a 18-b 30 (partly quoted in *Vors.* i², p. 278. 4-20, 38-40).

Watch-tower of Zeus, as Aristotle calls it here [*De caelo* ii. 13],
and others again the Throne of Zeus, if we may credit different
authorities.   They called the earth a star as being itself too
an instrument of time ; for it is the cause of days and nights,
since it makes day when it is lit up in that part of it which
faces the sun, and it makes night throughout the cone formed by
its shadow.' [1]

' Philolaus calls the fire in the middle about the centre the Hearth
of the universe, the House of Zeus, the Mother of the Gods, the
Altar, Bond and Measure of Nature.   And again he assumes another
fire in the uppermost place, the fire which encloses (all).   Now the
middle is naturally first in order, and round it ten divine bodies
move as in a dance, [the heaven] and (after the sphere of the fixed
stars) [2] the five planets, after them the sun, under it the moon,
under the moon the earth, and under the earth the counter-earth ;
after all these comes the fire which is placed like a hearth round
the centre.   The uppermost part of the (fire) which encloses (all),
in which the elements exist in all their purity, he calls Olympus,
and the parts under the moving Olympus, where are ranged the
five planets with the moon and the sun, he calls the Universe, and
lastly the part below these, the part below the moon and round
the earth, where are the things which suffer change and becoming,
he calls the Heaven.' [3]

' Philolaus the Pythagorean places the fire in the middle (for this
is the Hearth of the All), second to it he puts the counter-earth,
and third the inhabited earth which is placed opposite to, and
revolves with, the counter-earth ; this is the reason why those who
live in the counter-earth are invisible to those who live in our
earth.' [4]

' The governing principle is placed in the fire at the very centre,
and the Creating God established it there as a sort of keel to the
⟨sphere⟩ of the All.' [5]

' Others maintain that the earth remains at rest.   But Philolaus
the Pythagorean held that it revolves round the fire in an oblique
circle in the same way as the sun and moon.' [6]

---

[1] Simplicius on *De caelo* ii. 13, 293 a 15, pp. 511. 25-34 and 512. 9-17 Heib.
(*Vors.* i², p. 278. 20-36).
[2] The words are supplied by Diels in view of similar words in a passage of
Alexander Aphrodisiensis quoted below (Alex. on *Metaph.* 985 b 26, p. 540 b 4-7
Brandis, p. 38. 22-39. 3 Hayduck).
[3] Aët. ii. 7. 7 (*D. G.* p. 336-7 ; *Vors.* i², p. 237. 13 sqq.).   This and the next
extract probably come from Theophrastus, through Posidonius.
[4] Aët. iii. 11. 3 (*D. G.* p. 377 ; *Vors.* i², p. 237. 27 sq.).
[5] Aët. ii. 4. 15 (*D. G.* p. 332 ; *Vors.* i², p. 237. 31).
[6] Aët. iii. 13. 1, 2 (*D. G.* p. 378 ; *Vors.* i², p. 237. 46).

As regards the assumption of *ten* bodies we have the following further explanations. In a passage of the *Metaphysics* Aristotle is describing how the Pythagoreans find the elements of all existing things in numbers; he then proceeds thus :

'They conceived that the whole heaven is harmony and number ; thus, whatever admitted facts they were in a position to prove in the domain of numbers and harmonies, they put these together and adapted them to the properties and parts of the heaven and its whole arrangement. And if there was anything wanting anywhere, they left no stone unturned to make their whole system coherent. For example, regarding as they do the number ten as perfect and as embracing the whole nature of numbers, they say that the bodies moving in the heaven are also ten in number, and, as those which we see are only nine, they make the counter-earth a tenth.'[1]

Alexander adds in his note on this passage :

'If any of the phenomena of the heaven showed any disagreement with the sequence in numbers, they made the necessary addition themselves, and tried to fill up any gap, in order to make their system as a whole agree with the numbers. Thus, considering the number ten to be a perfect number, and seeing the number of the moving spheres shown by observation to be nine only, those of the planets being seven, that of the fixed stars an eighth, and the earth a ninth (for they considered that the earth too moved in a circle about the Hearth which remains fixed and, in their view, is fire), they straightway added to them in their doctrine the counter-earth as well, which they supposed to move counter to the earth and so to be invisible to the inhabitants of the earth.'[2]

Speaking of the sun in an earlier passage, Alexander says :

'(The sun) they placed seventh in order among the ten bodies which move about the centre, the Hearth ; for the movement of the sun comes next after (that of) the sphere of the fixed stars and the five movements belonging to the planets, while after the sun the moon comes eighth, and the earth ninth, after which again comes the counter-earth.'[3]

The system may be described briefly thus. The universe is spherical in shape and finite in size. Outside it is infinite void

[1] Aristotle, *Metaph.* A. 5, 986 a 2–12 (*Vors.* i³, p. 270. 40–47).
[2] Alexander on *Metaph.* 986 a 3 (p. 542 a 35–b 5 Brandis, p. 40, 24–41. 1 Hayduck).
[3] Ibid. 985 b 26 (p. 540 b 4–7 Brandis, p. 38. 22–39. 3 Hayduck).

which enables the universe to breathe, as it were.   At the centre is
the central fire, the Hearth of the universe, called by the various
names, the Tower or Watch-tower of Zeus, the Throne of Zeus,
the House of Zeus, the Mother of the Gods, the Altar, Bond and
Measure of Nature.   In this central fire is located the governing
principle, the force which directs the movement and activity of
the universe.   The outside boundary of the sphere is an envelope
of fire; this is called Olympus, and in this region the elements
are found in all their purity; below this is the Universe.   In the
universe there revolve in circles round the central fire the following
bodies.   Nearest to the central fire revolves the counter-earth,
which always accompanies the earth, the orbit of the earth coming
next to that of the counter-earth ; next to the earth, reckoning
in order from the centre outwards, comes the moon, next to the
moon the sun, next to the sun the five planets, and last of all,
outside the orbits of the planets, the sphere of the fixed stars.

The counter-earth, which accompanies the earth and revolves
in a smaller orbit, is not seen by us because the hemisphere of the
earth on which we live is turned away from the counter-earth.
It follows that our hemisphere is always turned away from the
central fire, that is, it faces outwards from the orbit towards
Olympus (the analogy of the moon which always turns one side
towards us may have suggested this); this involves a rotation of
the earth about its axis completed in the same time as it takes the
earth to complete a revolution about the central fire.

What was the object of introducing the counter-earth which
we never see?   Aristotle says in one place that it was to bring
up the number of the moving bodies to ten, the perfect number
according to the Pythagoreans.   But clearly Aristotle knew better ;
indeed he himself indicates the true reason in another passage
where he says that eclipses of the moon were considered to be
due sometimes to the interposition of the earth, sometimes to the
interposition of the counter-earth (to say nothing of other bodies
of the same sort assumed by 'some' in order to explain why there
appear to be more lunar eclipses than solar).[1]   The counter-earth,

[1] *De caelo* ii. 13, 293 b 21.   Cf. Aët. ii. 29. 4 (*D. G.* p. 360; *Vors.* i², p. 277. 46) :
'Some of the Pythagoreans, according to the account of Aristotle and the
statement of Philippus of Opus, say that the moon is eclipsed through reflection
and the interposition sometimes of the earth, sometimes of the counter-earth.'

therefore, we may take to have been invented for the purpose of explaining eclipses of the moon, and particularly the frequency with which they occur.

The earth revolves round the central fire in the same sense as the sun and moon (that is, from west to east), but its orbit is obliquely inclined; that is to say, the earth moves in the plane of the *equator*, the sun and the moon in the plane of the zodiac circle. It would no doubt be in this way that Philolaus would explain the seasons.

Next we are told that the revolution of the earth produces day and night, which depend on its position relatively to the sun; it is day in that part which is lit up by the sun and night in the cone formed by the earth's shadow. As the same hemisphere is always turned outwards, it seems to follow from the natural meaning of these expressions that the earth completes one revolution round the central fire in a day and a night, or in 24 hours.[1] This would, of course, account for the apparent diurnal rotation of the heavens from east to west; from this point of view it is equivalent to the rotation of the earth on its own axis in 24 hours But there is a considerable difficulty here, of which, if we may trust Aristotle, the Pythagoreans made light. According to him the Pythagoreans said that whether (1) the earth revolves in a circle round the centre of the universe or (2) the earth is itself stationary at that centre could make no difference in the appearance of the phenomena as observed by us. They argued that, even if we assume the earth to be at the centre, there is a distance between the centre and an observer on the earth's surface equal to the radius of the earth. On their assumption that the earth revolves round the centre of the universe, the distance of an observer from that centre would be greater than the radius of the earth's *orbit*; therefore to assert that the phenomena under the two assumptions would be exactly the same was to argue in effect that parallax is as negligible in one case as in the other. This is a somewhat extreme case of making the phenomena fit a preconceived hypothesis; but we may no doubt infer that the difficulty would lead the Pythagoreans to maintain that the distance of the earth from the centre of the universe was very small relatively to the distance

---

[1] Burnet apparently disputes this inference (*Early Greek Philosophy*, p. 352, note). We shall return to the point later.

of the other heavenly bodies from that centre, and that the radius of the earth's orbit was not in fact many times greater than the radius of the earth itself.[1]

But a still greater difficulty remains. On the assumption that the earth revolves round the central fire in a day and a night, and that the sun, the moon, and the five planets complete one revolution in their own several periods respectively, the observed movements of these heavenly bodies are accounted for. But, since the apparent daily rotation of the heavens is due to the revolution of the earth about the central fire in a day and a night, it would follow that the sphere of the fixed stars does not move at all, and therefore it could not be said that ' *ten* bodies' (of which that sphere is one) revolve about the central fire.

Boeckh suggested in his *Philolaus* that the motion of the sphere of the fixed stars could only be the precession of the equinoxes. This he thought might have been discovered by the Egyptians,[2] and Lepsius, later, took the same view, even suggesting that the Egyptians might have communicated the discovery to Eudoxus.[3] Boeckh afterwards, as a result of a study of Egyptian monuments, withdrew his suggestion;[4] but, later still, he seems to have taken it up again as preferable to the supposition of a very slow movement serving no purpose and frankly faked. But, so far as we know, Hipparchus was the first to discover precession. Martin passed through two stages corresponding to Boeckh's first and second. In his commentary on the *Timaeus* of Plato, Martin observed that precession only ' required long and steady observations, without any mathematical theory, in order to be recognized';[5] but Martin, too, changed his opinion later and satisfied himself that precession was not known to any of Hipparchus's predecessors.[6]

Schiaparelli thought it probable that Philolaus attributed *no*

---

[1] Schiaparelli, *I precursori*, p. 6.
[2] Boeckh, *Philolaos des Pythagoreers Lehren*, 1819, pp. 118, 119.
[3] Lepsius, *Chronologie der alten Aegypter*, p. 207.
[4] Boeckh, *Manetho und die Hundsternperiode*, 1845, p. 54.
[5] Martin, *Études sur le Timée de Platon*, ii, p. 98.
[6] Martin, ' La précession des équinoxes a-t-elle été connue des Égyptiens ou de quelque autre peuple avant Hipparque?' in vol. viii, pt. 1, of *Mémoires de l'Académie des Inscriptions et Belles-lettres, Savants Étrangers*, Paris, 1869; see also *Hypothèse astronomique de Philolaüs*, by the same author, Rome, 1872, p. 14.

movement to the sphere of the fixed stars,[1] his ground being the following. Censorinus attributes to Philolaus the statements that a 'Great Year' consists of 59 years, and that the solar year has $364\frac{1}{2}$ days. This gives a Great Year consisting of $21,505\frac{1}{2}$ days, which period contains very approximately 2 revolutions of Saturn, 5 of Jupiter, 31 of Mars, 59 of the sun, Mercury, and Venus, and 729 of the moon.[2] If, then, says Schiaparelli, Philolaus had attributed any movement to the stars, he would probably have included its period in his Great Year; which apparently he did not. Tannery, however, has given reason for thinking that the 729 lunations, and consequently the $364\frac{1}{2}$ days, were not the result of any independent calculation made by Philolaus, but were an arbitrary variation from the figures of Oenopides of Chios, of whom we are told by Censorinus that he made the year to be $365\frac{22}{59}$ days, so that 59 years would give 21,557 days or 730 lunations, not 729. Philolaus said, as Plato said after him, that the cube of 9 represents the number of months in a Great Year, and so it does *less* 1; the arbitrary variation is characteristic of the Pythagorean fanciful speculations with regard to numbers.[3]

---

[1] Schiaparelli, *I precursori*, p. 7.

[2] Schiaparelli (*I precursori*, p. 8, note) compares the periods of revolution based on the figures attributed to Philolaus with the true periods, thus:

Period of revolution.

Planet.	Philolaus.	Modern view.
Saturn	10752·75 days	10759·22 days
Jupiter	4301·10 ,,	4332·58 ,,
Mars	693·71 ,,	686.98 ,,
Venus, Mercury, Sun	364·50 ,,	365·26 ,,
Moon	29·50 ,,	29·53 ,,

Schiaparelli admits that the number of days for Mars (693·71) is uncertain, as it is not clear that Philolaus assumed 31 revolutions of Mars in his Great Year. But neither does there appear to be any evidence that he definitely fixed the number of revolutions made by the other planets in the Great Year.

[3] Tannery, 'La grande année d'Aristarque', in *Mémoires de la Société des sciences physiques et naturelles de Bordeaux*, 3e sér. iv, 1888, p. 90.

Tannery holds that Philolaus simply took his Great Year, equal to 59 solar years, from Oenopides, while Oenopides arrived at it in a very simple way, namely, by taking the number of days in the year as 365, and the period of the moon as $29\frac{1}{2}$ days, and observing the natural inference that, in whole numbers, 59 years are equal to 730 lunar months, after which he had only to determine the number of days in 730 lunar months.

But indeed, as Burnet points out,[1] it is incredible that the Pythagoreans should have put forward the theory that the sphere of the fixed stars is absolutely stationary. Such a suggestion would have seemed such a startling paradox that it is inconceivable that Aristotle should have said nothing about it, especially as he made the circular motion of the heavens the keystone of his own system. As it is, he does not attribute to any one the view that the heavens are stationary; and, in writing of the Pythagorean system, he makes it perfectly clear that the bodies *moving* in the heaven are ten in number,[2] from which it follows that the sphere of the fixed stars (which is one of the ten) must move. It may be observed, too, that Alcmaeon, whom Aristotle mentions as having held views similar to the Pythagoreans, distinctly said that 'all the divine bodies, the moon, the sun, the stars, *and the whole heaven*, move continually'.[3]

Now, if the Pythagoreans gave a movement of rotation to the sphere of the fixed stars, there are three possibilities. The first is that they may have assumed the universe *as a whole* to share in the rotation of the sphere of the fixed stars, while the independent revolutions of the earth, sun, moon, and planets were all *in addition to* their rotation as part of the universe. If this were the assumption, the rotation of the *whole universe* might be at any speed whatever without altering the phenomena as observed by us; the phenomena would present exactly the same appearance to us as they would on the assumption that the sphere of the fixed stars is stationary, and the planets, sun, moon, earth, and counter-earth have only their own proper revolutions round the central fire; only to a person situated at the central fire, supposed exempt from the general movement, would the general movement of the universe be perceptible. Thus the assumption of such a general movement would serve no purpose (apart from the objection that it would leave the speed of the rotation of the whole universe quite indeterminate); indeed, it would defeat what seems to have been

---

[1] Burnet, *Early Greek Philosophy*, p. 347.

[2] Aristotle, *Metaph.* A. 5, 986 a 10 τὰ φερόμενα κατὰ τὸν οὐρανὸν δέκα μὲν εἶναί φασιν. Cf. the passages of Alexander, quoted above (p. 98); also Simplicius on *De caelo* 293 a 15 (p. 512. 5), 'They wished to bring up to ten the number of the bodies which have a circular motion (κυκλοφορητικῶν).'

[3] Aristotle, *De anima* i. 2, 405 a 33.

the whole object of Philolaus's scheme, namely, to separate the daily rotation from the periodical revolutions of the sun, moon, earth, and planets, and to account for all the phenomena by simple motions instead of a combination of two in each case.

The second possibility is only slightly different. The sphere of the fixed stars might have a movement of rotation and carry with it all the heavenly bodies *except the earth* (and of course its inseparable companion, the counter-earth). The effect would be that the earth (with the counter-earth) would complete an actual revolution round the central fire in a period greater or less than 24 hours according to the speed and the direction of the rotation of the rest of the heavenly bodies;[1] the period would be less than 24 hours if the latter rotation were in the same sense as that of the earth's revolution from west to east, and greater if it were in the opposite sense, from east to west. This alternative is more complicated than the first, and is open to the same or stronger objections.

The third possibility is that the sun, moon, planets, earth, and counter-earth have their own special movements only, and that the sphere of the fixed stars moves *very slowly*, so slowly that its movement is imperceptible. This is the view of Martin[2] and of Apelt,[3] and it amounts to assuming that Philolaus gave a movement to the sphere of the fixed stars which, though it is not the precession of the equinoxes, is something very like it. If this is right, we must suppose that Philolaus gave the sphere of the fixed stars a merely nominal rotation for the sake of uniformity and nothing else; and perhaps, as Martin says, to assume an imperceptible motion would not be a greater difficulty for Philolaus than it was to postulate an invisible planet or to maintain that the enormous parallaxes which would be produced by the daily revolution of the earth about the central fire are negligible.

It is to be feared that a convincing solution of the puzzle will

---

[1] Martin (*Hypothèse astronomique de Philolaüs*, Rome, 1872, p. 16) compares an allusion in Ptolemy's *Syntaxis* (i. 7, p. 24. 11–13 Heib.) to the possibility of assuming (as an alternative to a scheme in which the fixed stars are stationary and the earth rotates on its own axis once in twenty-four hours) that *both* the earth and the sphere of the fixed stars rotate, at different speeds, about one and the same axis, the axis of the earth.

[2] Martin, *Hypothèse astronomique de Philolaüs*, pp. 14–16.

[3] Apelt, Untersuchungen über die Philosophie und Physik der Alten (*Abh. der Fries'schen Schule*, Heft 1, p. 68).

never be found.   After all that has been written on the subject,
Gomperz[1] still seems to prefer Boeckh's original suggestion that the
movement attributed by Philolaus to the fixed stars was actually
the precession of the equinoxes, but the new matter contained in
his note on the subject does not help his case.   He relies partly
on the *a priori* arguments originally put forward by Martin; 'it
is', he suggests, 'in itself hardly credible that a deviation in the
position of the luminaries which in the course of a single year
amounts to more than 50 seconds of an arc could remain unnoticed
for long'; he is aware, however, that Martin himself, as the result
of further investigation, could find no confirmation of his earlier
view.   He admits, too, that the Babylonians were still unacquainted
with precession in the third century B.C.[2]   The other main argument
used by Gomperz is that the estimates of the angular velocities
of the planetary movements which go back to Philolaus or other
early Pythagoreans are approximately correct, while only prolonged
observations of the stars could have made them so.   But, so far as
Philolaus is concerned, the data are apparently the same as those
from which Schiaparelli drew the opposite inference, namely, that
Philolaus was not aware of precession and considered the sphere of
the fixed stars to be stationary!

Harmony and distances.

'Philolaus holds that all things take place by necessity and by
harmony.'[3]

'It is clear too from this that, when it is asserted that the movement of the stars produces harmony, the sounds which they make
being in accord, the statement, although it is a brilliant and remarkable suggestion on the part of its authors, does not represent the
truth.   I refer to the view of those who think it inevitable that,
when bodies of such size move, they must produce a sound;
this, they argue, is observed even of bodies within our experience
which neither possess equal mass nor move with the same speed;
hence, when the sun and moon, and the stars which are so many
and of such size move with such a velocity, it is impossible that they

---

[1] Gomperz, *Griechische Denker*, i³, p. 93, and note on pp. 430, 431.

[2] Gomperz (p. 431) gives this as the opinion of the highest authority on the
subject, Pater Kugler, who is to argue the point anew in a forthcoming tract,
'Im Bannkreis Babels'.   This must be set against the opposite inference drawn
by Burnet (*Early Greek Philosophy*, p. 25, note) from another work of Kugler's,
and apparently confirmed by Hilprecht (*The Babylonian Expedition of the
University of Pennsylvania*, Philadelphia, 1906).

[3] Diog. L. viii. 84 (*Vors.* i³, p. 233. 33).

should not produce a sound of intolerable loudness. Supposing then that this is the case, and that the velocities depending on their distances correspond to the ratios representing chords, they say that the tones produced by the stars moving in a circle are in harmony. But, as it must seem absurd that we should not all hear these tones, they say the reason of this is that the sound is already going on at the moment we are born, so that it is not distinguishable by contrast with its opposite, silence ; for the distinction between vocal sound and silence involves comparison between them ; thus a coppersmith is apparently indifferent to noise through being accustomed to it, and so it must be with men in general.'[1]

' For (they said that) the bodies which revolve round the centre have their distances in proportion, and some revolve more quickly, others more slowly, the sound which they make during this motion being deep in the case of the slower and high in the case of the quicker; these sounds, then, depending on the ratio of their distances, are such that their combined effect is harmonious. . . . They said that those bodies move most quickly which move at the greatest distance, that those bodies move most slowly which are at the least distance, and that the bodies at intermediate distances move at speeds corresponding to the sizes of their orbits.'[2]

We have no information as to the actual ratios which the Pythagoreans assumed to exist between the respective distances of the earth, moon, sun, and planets from the centre of the universe. When Plutarch says that the distances of the ten heavenly bodies formed, according to Philolaus, a geometrical progression with 3 as the common ratio,[3] he can only be referring to some much later Pythagoreans. For if, on the basis of this progression, the distance of the counter-earth is represented by 3, that of the earth by 9, and that of the moon by 27, it is obvious that the enormous parallaxes due to the revolution of the earth round the centre would

---

[1] Arist. *De caelo* ii. 9, 290 b 12–29 (*Vors.* i², p. 277. 28–42). Yet when Aristotle is trying to prove his own contention that the stars do not move of themselves but are carried by spheres which revolve, he does not hesitate to use the argument that, if the planets moved freely through a mass of air or fire spread through the universe, 'as is universally alleged', they would, in consequence of their size, inevitably produce a sound so overpowering that it would not only be transmitted to us but would actually shiver things. He maintains, however, that, if a body is carried by something else which moves continuously and does not cause actual concussion, it does not produce sound ; hence, in his view, the fact that we do not hear sounds from the motion of the planets implies that they have no motion of their own but are carried by something (*De caelo* ii. 9, 291 a 16–28).

[2] Alexander on *Metaph.* A. 5, p. 542 a 5–10, 16–18 Brandis, pp. 39. 24–40. I, 40. 7–9 Hayduck.　　　[3] Plutarch, *De animae procreatione*, c. 31, p. 1028 B.

be quite inconsistent with 'saving the phenomena'.[1] Moreover, the order of the heavenly bodies given in this passage, counter-earth, earth, moon, Mercury, Venus, Sun, is not the order in which they were placed by Philolaus (and by Plato later) but the Chaldaean order, which does not seem to have been adopted by any Greek before the Stoic Diogenes of Babylon (second century B.C.).

Of the 'harmony of the spheres' there are many divergent accounts,[2] and it would appear that the places and the number of the heavenly bodies supposed to take part in it varied at different periods. Burnet[3] suggests that we cannot attribute to Pythagoras himself more than an identification of his newly-discovered musical intervals, the fourth, fifth, and octave, with the *three* rings which we find in Anaximander, that of the stars (nearest to the earth), that of the moon (next) and that of the sun (which is the furthest from the earth), and that this would be the most natural beginning for the later doctrine of the 'harmony of the spheres'. This is an attractive supposition, but it depends on the assumption that Pythagoras attributed to the planets and the fixed stars the same revolution from east to west ; whereas he certainly distinguished the planets from the fixed stars, and he must have known that their movement was not the same as that of the fixed stars (this is clear from his identification of the Morning and Evening Stars), even if he did not assign to the planets the independent movement, in the opposite sense to the daily rotation, which Alcmaeon is said to have observed. The original form of the theory of the 'harmony of the spheres' no doubt had reference to the seven planets only (including in that term the sun and moon), the seven planets being supposed, by reason of their several motions, to give out notes corresponding to the notes of the Heptachord ;[4]

---

[1] Schiaparelli, *I precursori*, pp. 6, 44.

[2] I must refer for full details to Boeckh, *Studien* iii, pp. 87 sqq. (*Kleine Schriften*, iii, pp. 169 sq.), Carl v. Jan, *Philol.* 1893, pp. 13 sqq., and for a summary to Zeller, i[5], pp. 431-4.

[3] Burnet, *Early Greek Philosophy*, p. 122.

[4] Cf. Hippol. *Refut.* i. 2. 2, (*D. G.* p. 555), 'Pythagoras maintained that the universe *sings* and is constructed in accordance with a harmony ; and he was the first to reduce the motion of the *seven* heavenly bodies to rhythm and song'; Censorinus, *De die natali* 13. 5, 'Pythagoras showed that the whole of our world constitutes a harmony. Accordingly, Dorylaus wrote that the world is an instrument of God ; others added that it is a heptachord, because there are seven planets which have the most motion.'

it could not have related to the *ten* heavenly bodies of the Pythagorean system, for this would have required ten notes, whereas the
Pythagorean theory of tones only recognized the seven notes of
the Heptachord.   This may, as Zeller says,[1] be the reason why
Philolaus himself, so far as we can judge from the fragments, said
nothing about the harmony of the spheres.   Aristotle, however,
clearly implies that in the harmony of the Pythagoreans whom he
knew the sphere of the fixed stars took part ; for he speaks of the
intolerable noise which, on the assumption that the motion of the
heavenly bodies produced sound, would be caused by 'the stars
which are so many in number and so great.'[2]   Consequently eight
notes are implied : and accordingly we find Plato (in *Republic* x)
including in his harmony eight notes produced by the sphere
of the fixed stars and by the seven planets respectively, and
corresponding to the Octachord, the eight-stringed lyre which had
been invented in the meantime.   The old theory being that all the
heavenly bodies revolved in the same direction from east to west,
only the planets revolved more slowly, their speeds diminishing in
the order of their distances from the sphere of the fixed stars,
which rotates once in about 24 hours, it would follow that Saturn,
being the nearest to the said sphere, would be supposed to move the
most quickly ; Jupiter, being next, would be the next quickest ;
Mars would come next, and so on ; while the moon, being the
innermost, would be the slowest ; on this view, therefore, the note
of Saturn would be the highest (νήτη), that of Jupiter next, and so
on, that of the moon being the lowest (ὑπάτη) ; and the speeds
determining this order are *absolute* speeds in space.   Nicomachus,[3]
though he mentions that his predecessors assigned notes to the
seven planets in this order, himself took the opposite view,
placing the moon's tone as the highest and Saturn's as the lowest
(incidentally he places the sun in the middle of the seven instead
of next to the moon as the older system did).   Nicomachus's order
is explicable if we assume that the independent revolutions of the
planets (in their orbits) was the criterion for the assignment of the
notes ; for the moon describes its orbit the quickest (in about
a lunar month), the sun the next quickest (in a year), and so on,
Saturn being the slowest in describing its orbit ; these speeds are

---

[1] Zeller, i⁵. p. 432, note 2.   [2] Aristotle, *De caelo* ii. 9, 290 b 18 (*Vors.* i², p. 277. 33).
[3] Nicomachus, *Harm.* 6. 33 sq. ; cf. Boethius, *Inst. Mus.* i. 27.

relative speeds, i.e. relative to the sphere of the fixed stars regarded as stationary. The *absolute* and *relative* angular speeds of the planets are of course connected in the following way: for any one planet its *absolute* speed is the speed of the sphere of the fixed stars *minus* the *relative* speed of the planet ; hence their order in respect of *absolute* speed is the reverse of their order in respect of *relative* speed and, so long as only the seven planets (including the sun and moon) come into the scale of notes, it is possible to assign notes to them in either order. But this is no longer the case when the sphere of the fixed stars is brought in as having a note of its own, making altogether eight notes corresponding to the Octachord. The speed of the fixed stars is of course an *absolute* speed, and it is faster than either the *absolute* or *relative* speed of any of the planets; it must, therefore, give out the highest note (νήτη). Now, in assigning the rest of the notes, we cannot take the *relative* speeds of the planets for the purpose of comparison with the *absolute* speed of the sphere of the fixed stars ; we must compare like with like; and indeed, on the hypothesis that the body which moves more swiftly gives out a higher note than the body which moves more slowly, it is only the *absolute* speed of the heavenly bodies *in space*, and nothing else, which can properly be taken as determining the order of their notes. Now Plato says [1] in the Myth of Er that eight different notes forming a harmony are given out by the Sirens seated on the eight whorls of the Spindle, which represent the sphere of the fixed stars and the seven planets, and that, while all the seven inner whorls (representing the planets) are carried round bodily in the revolution of the outermost whorl (representing the sphere or circle of the fixed stars), each of the seven inner whorls has a slow independent movement of its own in a sense opposite to that of the movement of the whole, the second whorl starting from the outside (the first of the seven inner ones) which represents Saturn having the slowest movement, the third representing Jupiter the next faster, the fourth representing Mars the next faster, the fifth, sixth, and seventh, which represent Mercury, Venus, and the Sun respectively and which go 'together' (i.e. have the same angular speed) the fastest but one, and the eighth representing the moon the fastest of all. Plato, therefore, while speaking

[1] Plato, *Republic* x. 617 A–B.

of *absolute* angular speed in the case of the circle of the fixed stars, refers to the *relative* speed in the case of the seven planets. To get the order of his tones therefore we must turn the relative speeds of the planets into absolute speeds by subtracting them respectively from the speed of the circle of the fixed stars, and the order of their respective notes is then as follows:

Circle of fixed stars . . . highest note (νήτη)
    Saturn
    Jupiter
    Mars
    Mercury⎫
    Venus ⎬
    Sun   ⎭
    Moon . . . . . . lowest note (ὑπάτη).[1]

[1] Dr. Adam, in his edition of the *Republic* (vol. ii, p. 452), supposes that, after the circle of the fixed stars giving the highest note, the seven planets would come in the order of their *relative* velocities, thus—

Circle of the fixed stars . . . highest note (νήτη)
    ,,   Moon
    ,,   Sun   ⎫
    ,,   Venus ⎬ . . . μέση
    ,,   Mercury⎭
    ,,   Mars
    ,,   Jupiter
    ,,   Saturn . . . . lowest note (ὑπάτη)

For the reason given above, I do not think it possible that Plato, who was a mathematician, would have assigned the notes to the eight circles in this order, though it is likely enough that, when writing the passage, he had not in his mind any definite allocation of notes at all. A further difficulty in the way of Adam's order is the following. He observes that, if we understand 'together' (ἅμα ἀλλήλοις), used of the motion of the sun, Venus, and Mercury, in a strict sense, there will only be six notes, as the three bodies will have the same note. He gets over this difficulty quite properly by supposing that Plato really had in his mind the period taken by the three bodies in describing their orbits, in other words, their *angular* velocity, rather than their linear velocity. ' In that case the octave will be complete, because, in order to complete their orbits in the same time, the sun, Venus, and Mercury will have to travel at different rates of speed.' True ; but, as the planet with the longer orbit must have a *linear* velocity greater than the planet with the shorter orbit, it follows that the linear velocity of Venus in the above scheme will be greater than that of the sun, and the linear velocity of Mercury greater than that of Venus. Thus the supposed linear velocities, instead of diminishing all the way from the circle of the fixed stars down to Saturn in the above table, will diminish from the circle of the fixed stars down to the sun, but will *increase* after that down to Mercury, before they diminish again with Mars and the rest; and this upsets the proper order of the notes altogether. On the other hand, with the arrangement according to absolute speeds, as in the text above, the linear velocities of Mercury, Venus, and the sun come in the correct diminishing order.

This order agrees with Cicero's arrangement, in which the highest circle, that of the fixed stars, has the highest note and the moon the lowest.[1]

Although Alexander clearly says that, in the Pythagorean theory of the harmony of the spheres, the different notes correspond to the ratios of the distances of the heavenly bodies, we have little or no authentic information as to how the early Pythagoreans translated the theory into an actual estimate of the relative distances.[2] It is true that some later writers such as Censorinus and Pliny give some definite ratios of distances and, as usual, refer them back to Pythagoras himself; but their statements contain such an admixture of elements foreign to the early Pythagorean theory that no certain conclusion can be drawn.

Plato implies, in his Myth of Er, that the breadths of the whorls of the spindle represent the distances separating successive planets; but he does not do more than state the order of magnitude in which the successive distances come; he makes no attempt to give absolute ratios between them.

Tannery[3] ingeniously conjectures that Eudoxus's view of the ratio of the distances of the sun and moon from the earth, which he put at 9:1, may have been suggested or confirmed by the theory of the harmony. The original discovery of the octave, the fourth and the fifth, stated in one of its forms,[4] showed that they represented ratios of lengths of string assumed to be under equal tension as follows, namely 1:2, 3:4, and 2:3 respectively. Bringing these ratios to their least common denominator, we see that strings at equal tension and of lengths 6, 8, 9, 12 respectively give the three intervals. The interval between the first and second strings being a fourth, and that between the first and third a fifth, the interval between the second and third is a tone, which may therefore be regarded as represented by the difference between

[1] Cicero, *Somn. Scip.* c. 5.

[2] Alexander's own figures (Alex. on *Metaph.* 986 a 2, p. 542 a 12–15 Brandis, p. 40. 3–6 Hayduck) seem to be illustrations only: 'The distance of the sun from the earth being, say (φέρε εἰπεῖν), double the distance of the moon, that of Aphrodite triple, and that of Hermes quadruple, they considered that there was some arithmetical ratio in the case of each of the other planets as well.' The ratios of 1, 2, 3, 4 for the distances of the moon, the sun, Venus, and Mercury are the same as those indicated by Plato in the *Timaeus* 36 D.

[3] Tannery, *Recherches sur l'histoire de l'astronomie ancienne*, pp. 293, 328.

[4] Cf. Theon of Smyrna, pp. 59. 21–60. 6, ed. Hiller; Boethius, *Inst. Mus.* i. 10.

9 and 8, or 1. Now the *Didascalia caelestis* of Leptines, known as
Ars Eudoxi, which was written in Egypt between 193 and 165 B.C.,
contains a number of things derived from Eudoxus, and the ratio
of the distance of the sun from the earth to the distance of the moon
from the earth is there said to correspond to the relation of the fifth
to the tone.[1] If we take the respective notes as represented by the
above numbers, the ratio of the fifth to the tone is 9 : (9 − 8), or 9 : 1.

It would appear from passages in Theon of Smyrna[2] and
Achilles,[3] doubtless taken in substance from Adrastus or Thrasyllus,
that the harmony was next spoken of in poems by Aratus and
Eratosthenes (third century B.C.); but there is no indication that
they did more than point out the correspondence between the
planets, in their order from the moon to Saturn or to the sphere
of the fixed stars, and the notes of the heptachord or octachord
from the ὑπάτη, the lowest, to the νήτη, the highest (Eratosthenes
certainly took the octachord for this purpose).[4]

Achilles tells us that, after Aratus and Eratosthenes, and before
Adrastus and Thrasyllus, Hypsicles the mathematician (the author
of the so-called Book XIV of Euclid) treated of the question of
the harmony of the spheres; and he proceeds to give, as generally
accepted by musicians, a remarkable musical scale in which an
octave is divided into *eight intervals* and *nine notes* (including the
two extreme notes of the octave), the nine notes corresponding
to the sphere of the fixed stars, Saturn, Jupiter, Mars, Mercury,
Venus, Sun, Moon, and Earth respectively, in that order. This
scale is the same as that described in verses quoted by Theon
of Smyrna from one Alexander (who was not Alexander of
Aetolia, as Theon wrongly calls him, but Alexander of Ephesus,
a contemporary of Cicero, or possibly, as Chalcidius calls him,
Alexander of Miletus, Alexander Polyhistor). The only difference

---

[1] The text, indeed, of Leptines has to be filled out in order to get this, and it
is the sizes of the sun and moon, not their distances respectively from the earth,
that are mentioned (though the effect is the same on the assumption that their
apparent angular diameters are equal). The sentence as corrected by Tannery
is ' Thus the sun is greater than the moon, and the moon greater than ⟨the
part of⟩ the earth ⟨which sees the eclipse⟩; the ratio is that of the fifth to ⟨the
difference between the fifth and⟩ the fourth.'

[2] Theon of Smyrna, pp. 105. 13 – 106. 2 ; pp. 142. 7 sqq.

[3] Petav. *Uranolog.* p. 136; see Tannery, *Recherches sur l'histoire de l'astronomie ancienne*, p. 330.

[4] Theon of Smyrna, loc. cit.

is that Alexander has the later order for the planets, his order
being: sphere of fixed stars, Saturn, Jupiter, Mars, Sun, Venus,
Mercury, Moon, Earth.[1]   Tannery infers that this peculiar division
of the octave, with the order of the planets as given by Achilles,
is due to Hypsicles.[2]

Theon of Smyrna criticizes this peculiar scale of nine notes as
described by Alexander.   First, he observes that in the last of
the verses Alexander says the heptachord is the image of the
world, whereas he has made an octave, consisting of six tones, out
of *nine* strings; his notes therefore do not correspond to the
diatonic scale.   Again, the lowest note is given to the earth,
whereas, being at rest, it gives out no sound.   The sun, too, is
given the 'middle' note ($\mu\acute\epsilon\sigma\eta$), whereas the interval from the
lowest ($\acute\upsilon\pi\acute\alpha\tau\eta$) to the 'middle' is not a fifth but a fourth; and
so on.

The scale, however, of nine notes with the sun in the middle,
as Alexander has it, is apparently the common foundation of three
scales of eight intervals given by Censorinus,[3] Pliny,[4] and Martianus
Capella[5] respectively, who apparently got them from a work of
the encyclopaedic writer Varro (116–27 B.C.).   The three scales
given by these three authors differ slightly in that Censorinus's
eight intervals add up to 6 tones (the proper amount), Pliny's to
7 tones, and Martianus Capella's to $6\frac{1}{2}$ tones; the differences may,
Tannery thinks, be due to errors in the MSS. of Varro, whence
the one scale which is the foundation of all three was taken.   We
need only set down Censorinus's version, which is:

From Earth to Moon	1	tone	
„ Moon to Mercury	$\frac{1}{2}$	„	$3\frac{1}{2}$ tones (a fifth)
„ Mercury to Venus	$\frac{1}{2}$	„	
„ Venus to Sun	$1\frac{1}{2}$	„	
„ Sun to Mars	1	„	
„ Mars to Jupiter	$\frac{1}{2}$	„	$2\frac{1}{2}$ tones (a fourth)
„ Jupiter to Saturn	$\frac{1}{2}$	„	
„ Saturn to fixed stars	$\frac{1}{2}$	„	

6 tones

[1] Theon of Smyrna, pp. 140. 5–141. 4.   [2] Tannery, loc. cit.
[3] Censorinus, *De die natali* 13. 3–5.   [4] Pliny, *N. H.* ii, c. 22, § 84.
[5] Mart. Capella, *De nuptiis philologiae et Mercurii*, ii. 169–98.

The difference between this and Pliny's scale is that Pliny takes the distance from Saturn to the sphere of the fixed stars to be $1\frac{1}{2}$ tones instead of half a tone, so that with him the distance between the sun and the fixed stars is $3\frac{1}{2}$ tones, or a fifth instead of a fourth. Both Censorinus and Pliny make the interval from the earth to the sun to be a fifth, and from the earth to the moon one tone, wherein they agree with the view attributed by Tannery to Eudoxus.

Both Pliny and Censorinus add a further detail which apparently must have come from some source other than the poem of Alexander; this is that Pythagoras made the actual distance between the moon and the earth, which he called one tone, to be 126,000 stades. This would of course enable the other distances between the heavenly bodies to be calculated on the basis of the scale; e.g. the distance from the earth to the sun would be $3\frac{1}{2}$ times 126,000 stades, and so on. But this evaluation of the distance from the earth to the moon, 126,000 stades, is exactly half of 252,000 stades, which is the estimate of the circumference of the earth made by Eratosthenes and Hipparchus. This exact coincidence is enough to make it plain that the 126,000 stades does not go back to Pythagoras, and can hardly have been suggested before the second century B.C.

Pliny, however, in a passage immediately preceding that in which he describes his scale, says that Pythagoras made the distance from the earth to the moon 126,000 stades, the distance from the moon to the sun twice that distance, and the distance from the sun to the sphere of the fixed stars thrice the same distance.[1] Pliny is here evidently quoting from a quite different authority; as he says that Sulpicius Gallus was of the same opinion, he would appear to be citing some book by Sulpicius Gallus, who may have got it from some tradition which cannot now be traced.

It is no doubt possible that, if Pythagoras did not estimate the distance of the moon from the earth in stades, he may have expressed it in terms of the circumference of the earth. But, seeing that Anaximander had already estimated the radius of the orbit of the moon at 18 times the radius of the earth, how could Pythagoras have put the distance of the moon so low as half the circumference of the earth, or about 3 times the earth's radius? Tannery

[1] Pliny, *N. H.* ii, c. 21, § 83.

conjectures that in the number of stades (126,000) given by Varro there is a mistake, *milia* having been written instead of myriads ($\mu\nu\rho\iota\acute{\alpha}\delta\epsilon\varsigma$); in that case the source from which Varro drew might have given the distance of the moon as 10 times the half-circumference of the earth. Hultsch,[1] however, thinks it incredible that *milia* could have been written in error for $\mu\nu\rho\iota\acute{\alpha}\delta\epsilon\varsigma$; and even if it had been, and the moon's distance were thus made up to about 30 times the earth's radius, the absurdity would still be left that the sun's distance is only $3\frac{1}{2}$ times as great.

It is true, as Martin observes,[2] that the sounding by the planets of all the notes of an octave at once would produce no 'harmony' in our sense of the word; but the Pythagoreans would not have been deterred by this consideration from putting forward their fanciful view.[3] We have, it is true, allusions to other arrangements of the notes which would make them cover more than an octave, but these must have been later than Plato's time. Thus Plutarch speaks of one view which made the seven planets correspond to the seven invariable strings of the fifteen-stringed lyre, and of another which made their distances correspond to the five tetrachords of the complete system.[4] Anatolius[5] has a peculiar distribution of tones between the heavenly bodies which gives altogether two octaves and a tone. Macrobius[6] bases his view on the successive numbers 1, 2, 3, 4, 8, 9, 27 applied to the planets in the *Timaeus* and supposed to represent their relative distances from the earth; Macrobius makes the first four (from 1 to 4) cover two octaves, and he seems to make the seven notes cover, in all, four octaves, a fifth, and one tone.[7]

The Sun.

'The Pythagoreans declared the sun to be spherical.'[8]

'Philolaus the Pythagorean holds that the sun is transparent like glass, and that it receives the reflection of the fire in the universe

---

[1] Hultsch, *Poseidonios über die Grösse und Entfernung der Sonne*, Berlin, 1897, p. 11, note 1.

[2] Martin, *Études sur le Timée*, ii, p. 37.　　　[3] Zeller, i[5], p. 432, note.

[4] Plutarch, *De animae procr.* c. 32, p. 1029 A, B. The five distances are (1) Moon to Sun with its concomitants Mercury and Venus, (2) Sun, &c. to Mars, (3) Mars to Jupiter, (4) Jupiter to Saturn, (5) Saturn to sphere of fixed stars.

[5] Anatolius in Iambl. *Theol. Ar.* p. 56; cf. Zeller, loc. cit.

[6] Macrobius, *In Somn. Scip.* ii, cc. 1, 2.

[7] Zeller, ii[4], pp. 777 sqq.　　　[8] Aët. ii. 22. 5 (*D. G.* p. 352).

and transmits to us both light and warmth, so that there are in some sort two suns, the fiery (substance) in the heaven and the fiery (emanation) from it which is mirrored, as it were, not to speak of a third also, namely the beams which are scattered in our direction from the mirror by way of reflection (or refraction); for we give this third also the name of sun, which is thus, as it were, an image of an image.' [1]

' Philolaus says that the sun receives its fiery and radiant nature from above, from the aethereal fire, and transmits the beams to us through certain pores, so that according to him the sun is triple, one sun being the aethereal fire, the second that which is transmitted from it to the glassy thing under it which is called sun, and the third that which is transmitted from the sun in this sense to us.' [2]

Thus, according to Philolaus, the sun was not a body with light of its own, but it was of a substance comparable to glass, and it concentrated rays of fire from elsewhere, and transmitted them to us. This idea was no doubt suggested in order to give a uniform nature to all the moving heavenly bodies. But there are difficulties in the descriptions above given of the sources of the beams of fire. The natural supposition would be that they would come from the central fire ; in that case the sun would act like a mirror simply; and the phenomena would be accounted for because the beams of the fire would always reach the sun except when obstructed by the moon, earth, or counter-earth, and, as the earth and counter-earth move in a different plane from the sun and moon, eclipses would occur at the proper times. But the first of the above passages says that the beams come from the fire in the *universe*, and that one of the suns is the fiery substance in the *heaven*, while the second passage says that the beams come from *above*, from the fire of the aether. Burnet takes ' heaven' in the narrow sense of the ' portion of the universe below the moon and round about the earth' which, according to the *Doxographi*, was called 'heaven',[3] and he thinks that 'the fire in the heaven' is therefore exclusively the central fire.[4] But this leaves out of account the alternative term ' the fire in the universe' and also Achilles' ' fire from *above*'; and,

---

[1] Aët. ii. 20. 12 (*D. G.* p. 349, 350; *Vors.* i², p. 237. 36).
[2] Achilles, *Isagoge in phaenomena* (Petav. *Uranolog.*, p. 138; *D. G.* pp. 349, 350).
[3] See above, p. 97 (Aët. ii. 7. 7 ; *D. G.* p. 337 ; *Vors.* i², p. 237. 22).
[4] Burnet, *Early Greek Philosophy*, p. 348.

as the central fire seems in other passages always to be called 'the fire in the middle', Burnet's interpretation seems scarcely possible. Boeckh originally took the same view that the beams could only be those from the central fire, holding to the strict interpretation of *universe* as being below the outer *Olympus*;[1] but he afterwards admitted,[2] with Martin, that the beams might come from the *outer* fire, the fire of Olympus, as well. Accordingly the beams coming from outside would be *refracted* by the sun, which would act as a sort of lens.[3] Tannery[4] takes a similar view, from which he develops another interesting hypothesis. We are to suppose two cones opposite to one another and each truncated at the sun, where they meet in a common section; these two cones form a luminous column (that of the Myth of Er) by which a stream of light flows from the fire of Olympus (supposed to be the Milky Way) in the direction of the earth. But there remains a difficulty as regards the central fire. What is the relation between the central fire and the fire of the sun, and why does not the central fire always light up the moon sufficiently for us to see it full? The beams of the central fire must, Tannery conceives, be relatively feeble in comparison with those from the Milky Way, and though they may suitably light up and warm the side of the counter-earth turned towards the central fire, they have no appreciable power at the distance of the moon, still less at the distance of the sun. The outer cone and the inner cone meeting at the sun are supposed by Tannery to have a small angular aperture. The base of the outer cone is therefore presumably a *part* of the *Milky Way*,[5] which part is accordingly the first sun of the texts, and Tannery suggests that we have in this portion of the Milky Way the *tenth* of the heavenly bodies which revolve round the central fire, leaving the sphere of the fixed stars motionless, as the complete system of Philolaus requires it to be. This suggestion is brilliant but scarcely, I think, consistent with what we are told of the tenth body; for

[1] Boeckh, *Philolaus*, pp. 123-30.
[2] Boeckh, *Das kosmische System des Platon*, p. 94.
[3] Martin, *L'hypothèse astronomique de Philolaüs*, pp. 9, 10.
[4] Tannery, *Pour l'histoire de la science hellène*, pp. 237, 238.
[5] Cf. Aët. i. 14. 2 (*D. G.* p. 312), where it is stated that only the fire in the very uppermost place is conical. The passage occurs in a section dealing mainly with the shapes of the *elements*, but it may perhaps have strayed into the wrong context.

on this assumption it would presumably be, from time to time, a different portion of the Milky Way varying as the sun revolves.

With Tannery's idea of the connexion between the sun and the Milky Way, the following passages should be compared :

' Of the so-called Pythagoreans some say that this [the Milky Way] is the path of one of the stars which fell out of their places in the destruction said to have taken place in Phaethon's time ; others say that the sun formerly revolved in this circle, and accordingly this region was, so to say, burnt up, or suffered some such change, through the revolution of the sun. [1]

' Of the Pythagoreans some explain the Milky Way as due to the burning-up of a star which fell out of its proper place and set on fire the region through which it circulated during the conflagration caused by Phaethon ; others say that the sun's course originally lay along the Milky Way. Some, again, say that it is the mirrored image of the sun as it reflects its rays at the heaven, the process being the same as with the rainbow on the clouds.' [2]

The Moon.

A fanciful view of the moon is quoted by the *Doxographi* as held by some of the Pythagoreans, including Philolaus.

' Some of the Pythagoreans, among whom is Philolaus, say that the moon has an earthy appearance because, like our earth, it is inhabited throughout by animals and plants, only larger and more beautiful (than ours): for the animals on it are fifteen times stronger than those on the earth . . . and the day in the moon is correspondingly longer.' [3]

No doubt the fact that the animals on the moon are superior to those on the earth ' in force ($\tau\hat{\eta}$ $\delta\upsilon\upsilon\acute{a}\mu\epsilon\iota$)' to the extent of fifteen times is an inference from the fact that the day is fifteen times longer than ours. Boeckh points out, as regards the day, that the length of it is clearly meant to be half the time occupied by one revolution of the moon (in $29\frac{1}{2}$ days) round the central fire. Assuming that, as with the earth, the same hemisphere is always turned outwards (which involves one rotation of the moon round its axis in

---

[1] Aristotle, *Meteorologica* i. 8, 345 a 13–18 (*Vors.* i², p. 230. 37–41). In the last words of this passage Diels (loc. cit.) reads $\phi\theta o\rho\hat{a}s$, ' destruction ' or ' wasting ', instead of $\phi o\rho\hat{a}s$, ' revolution '.

[2] Aët. iii. 1. 2 (*D. G.* p. 364 ; *Vors.* i², p. 278. 42).

[3] Aët. ii. 30. 1 (*D. G.* p. 361 ; *Vors.* i², p. 237. 42).

the same time as it takes the moon to revolve round the central fire),
an inhabitant of that hemisphere would see the sun, that is, it would
be day for him, for roughly half the period of the moon's revolution; during the same half of the period an inhabitant of the
hemisphere turned towards the earth would not see the sun, and it
would be night for him; and *vice versa*. Therefore the 'day' for
an inhabitant of the moon, which receives its light from the sun,
would be equal to fifteen of our days *and nights* added together.
According to the actual wording of the text it should be fifteen
times our day only; this would require that the moon should
revolve on its axis *twice* (instead of the once which is automatic,
as it were) during a lunation.   Martin[1] develops this supposition,
but it seems clear that the 'day' of the inhabitants of the moon
was meant to be equal to fifteen of our days *and nights* together,
and that the form of the statement in the text is due to
inadvertence.

According to 'other Pythagoreans' what we see on the moon
is a reflection of the sea which is beyond the torrid circle or zone in
our earth.[2]

Eclipses.

We have seen that the counter-earth was probably invented in
order to explain the frequency of eclipses of the moon, and that
there were some who thought there might be more bodies of the
kind which by their interposition caused eclipses of the moon. The
latter bodies would of course, like the counter-earth, be invisible to
the inhabitants of our hemisphere, from which it follows that they
would also, like the counter-earth, revolve along with the earth round
the central fire and always have the same right ascension with
the earth.

Eclipses of the moon are then caused by the interposition either
of the earth or of the counter-earth (or other similar body) between
the sun and the moon.[3]

Eclipses of the sun on the other hand are, and can only be, caused
by the moon 'getting under the sun',[4] i.e. by the interposition of
the moon between the sun and the earth.

---

[1] Martin, *Hypothèse astronomique de Philolaüs*, p. 22.
[2] Aët. ii. 30. 1 (*D. G.* p. 361 b 10–13).
[3] Aët. ii. 29. 4 (*D. G.* p. 360; *Vors.* i², p. 277. 46).
[4] σελήνης αὐτὸν ὑπερχομένης, Aët. ii. 24. 6 (*D. G.* p. 354).

The Phases of the Moon.

In the same passage (under the heading 'On the Eclipse of the Moon') in which Aëtius says that 'some of the Pythagoreans' give the explanation of lunar eclipses just referred to, a curious view is mentioned as having been held by 'some of the later (Pythagoreans)'. The words must apparently (notwithstanding their context) refer to the *phases*, and not to eclipses, of the moon ; the change is said to come about 'by way of spreading of flame, which is kindled by degrees and in a regular manner until it produces the perfect full moon, after which again the flame is curtailed by corresponding degrees until the conjunction, when it is completely extinguished'. It would seem that these 'later' Pythagoreans had forgotten the fact that the moon gets its light from the sun, or at least had no clear understanding of the way in which the variations in the positions of the sun and moon relatively to the earth produce the variations in the shape of the portion of the illuminated half which is visible to us from time to time.

XIII

THE ATOMISTS, LEUCIPPUS AND DEMOCRITUS

LEUCIPPUS of Elea or Miletus (it is uncertain which[1]) was a contemporary of Anaxagoras and Empedocles; and Democritus of Abdera was also a contemporary of Anaxagoras, though younger, for he was, according to his own account,[2] 'young when Anaxagoras was old', from which it is inferred that he was born about 460 B.C. The place of the two Atomist philosophers in the history of astronomy is not a large one, for they made scarcely any advance upon their predecessors; most of the views of Democritus are a restatement of those of Anaxagoras, even down to the crudest parts of his doctrine. As Burnet[3] says, the primitive character of the astronomy taught by Democritus as compared with that of Plato is the best evidence of the value of the Pythagorean researches. The weakness of Democritus's astronomy is the more remarkable because we have conclusive evidence that he was a really able mathematician. Archimedes[4] says that Democritus was the first to state that the volumes of a cone and a pyramid are one-third of the volumes of the cylinder and prism respectively which have the same base and height, though he was not able to prove these facts in the rigorous manner which alone came up to Archimedes' standard of what a scientific proof should be (the discovery of the proofs of the propositions by the powerful 'method of exhaustion' was

[1] Simplicius *in Phys.* p. 28. 4 (from Theophrastus); see *D. G.* p. 483; *Vors.* i², p. 344. 46.
[2] Diog. L. ix. 41 (*Vors.* i², p. 387. 12).
[3] Burnet, *Early Greek Philosophy*, p. 345.
[4] Heiberg, 'Eine neue Archimedes-Handschrift' in *Hermes*, xlii, 1907, pp. 245, 246; cf. the translation and commentary by Heiberg and Zeuthen in *Bibliotheca Mathematica*, vii₃, 1906–7, p. 323; *The Thirteen Books of Euclid's Elements*, 1908, vol. iii, pp. 366, 368.

reserved for Eudoxus). There is evidence, too, that Democritus investigated (1) the relation in size between two sections of a cone parallel to the base and very close to each other, and (2) the nature of the contact of a circle or sphere with a tangent. These facts taken together suggest that he was on the track of infinitesimals and of the Integral Calculus.

The *Great Diakosmos*, attributed by Theophrastus to Leucippus, is also given in the lists of Democritus's works;[1] indeed no one later than Theophrastus seems to have been able to distinguish between the work of Leucippus and Democritus, all the writings of the school of Abdera being apparently regarded by later authors as due to Democritus. However, the information which we possess about the cosmology of the two philosophers goes back to Theophrastus, so that we are not without some guidance as to details in which they differed. Diogenes Laertius,[2] in a passage drawn from an epitome of Theophrastus, attributes the following views to Leucippus. The worlds, unlimited in number, arise through 'bodies', i.e. atoms, falling into the void and meeting one another. By abscission from the infinite many 'bodies' of all sorts of shapes are borne into a great void, and their coming together sets up a vortex. By the usual process, in the case of our world, the earth collects at the centre. The earth is like a tambourine in shape and rides or floats by virtue of its being whirled round in the centre.

The sun revolves in a circle, as does the moon; the circle of the sun is the outermost, that of the moon the nearest to the earth, and the circles of the stars are between. All the stars are set on fire because of the swiftness of their motion; the sun is also ignited by the stars; the moon has only a little fire in its composition.

The 'inclination of the earth',[3] i.e. the angle between the zenith

---

[1] *Vors.* i², p. 357. 21, p. 387. 4; cf. Achilles, *Isagoge* i. 13 (*Vors.* i², p. 349. 29).

[2] Diog. L. ix. 30–33 (*Vors.* i², pp. 342. 35 – 343. 27).

[3] The words 'inclination of the earth' are missing in the text of Diogenes. Diels (*Vors.* i², p. 343. 22) supplies words thus: ⟨τὴν δὲ λόξωσιν τοῦ ζῳδιακοῦ γενέσθαι⟩ τῷ κεκλίσθαι τὴν γῆν πρὸς μεσημβρίαν, '⟨the obliquity of the zodiac circle is due⟩ to the tilt of the earth towards the south.' But this can hardly be right; the reference must be to the same 'inclination of the earth' (ἔγκλισις γῆς), i.e. the angle between the zenith and the pole or between the earth's (flat) surface and the plane of the apparent circular revolution of a star, which is spoken of in Aët. iii. 12. 1–2 (*D. G.* p. 377; *Vors.* i², pp. 348. 15, 367. 47). The words which have fallen out may perhaps have been 'the obliquity of the circles

and the visible (north) pole, or the angle between the (flat) surface of the earth and the plane of the apparent circular movement of a star in the daily rotation, is due to the tilt of the earth towards the south, the explanation of this tilt being on lines which recall Empedocles rather than Anaxagoras;[1] the northern parts have perpetual snow and are cold and frozen.

The sun rarely suffers eclipse, while the moon is continually darkened, because their circles are unequal.

We have here reminiscences of Anaximander in the description of the shape of the earth and partly also in the statement about the relative distances of the sun, moon, and stars from the earth, while the idea of the earth riding on the air recalls Anaximenes, with a difference. There are traces of Anaxagoras's views in the vortex causing the earth to take the central position, and in the kindling of the stars due to their rapid motion; but there is the difference that the atoms take the place of the mixture in which 'all things are together', and no force such as Anaxagoras's *Nous* is considered to be required in order to start the motion of the vortex, the atoms being held to have been in motion always.

Democritus's views are much more uniformly those of Anaxagoras. Thus with him the stars are stones,[2] the sun is a red-hot mass or a stone on fire;[3] the sun is of considerable size.[4] The moon has in it plains, mountains (or, according to one passage, lofty elevations casting shadows[5]), and ravines,[6] or valleys.[5] Democritus said that the moon is 'plumb opposite' to the sun at the conjunctions, and

---

of the stars ', or they may have referred to differences of climate in different parts of the earth.

[1] Leucippus's explanation of the tilt (Aët., loc. cit.) is that ' the earth turned sideways towards the southern regions because of the rarefaction (ἀραιότητα) in those parts, due to the fact that the northern regions became frozen through excessive cold while the southern parts were set on fire'.

Democritus's explanation is slightly different : ' The earth as it grew became inclined southwards because the southern portion of the enveloping (substance) is weaker (i. e. presumably weaker in resisting power) ; for the northern regions are intemperate (ἄκρατα), i.e. frigid, the southern temperate (κέκραται) ; hence it is in the south that the earth *sags* (βεβάρηται), namely, where fruits and all growth are in excess.'

[2] Aët. ii. 13. 4 (*D. G.* p. 341 ; *Vors.* i², p. 366. 31).
[3] Aët. ii. 20. 7 (*D. G.* p. 349 ; *Vors.* i², p. 366. 35).
[4] Cicero, *De fin.* i. 6. 20 (*Vors.* i², p. 366. 36).
[5] Aët. ii. 30. 3 (*D. G.* p. 361 ; *Vors.* i², p. 367. 13).
[6] Aët. ii. 25. 9 (*D. G.* p. 356; *Vors.* i², p. 308. 11).

it is evident that he fully accepted the doctrine that the moon receives its light from the sun.[1]

As regards the earth, Democritus differed from Anaxagoras in that, while Anaxagoras said it was flat, Democritus regarded it as 'disc-like but hollowed out in the middle'[2] (i.e. depressed in the middle and raised at the edges); but this latter view was also held by Archelaus, a disciple of Anaxagoras, and may therefore have been that of Anaxagoras himself; the proof of the hollowness, Archelaus thought, was furnished by the fact that the sun does not rise and set everywhere on the earth's surface at the same time, as it would have been bound to do if the surface had been level.[3] How, asks Tannery,[4] did Anaxagoras or Archelaus come to draw from the observed facts with regard to the rising and setting of the sun a conclusion the very opposite of the truth?

Again, while Anaxagoras, like Anaximenes, supposed the flat earth to ride on the air, being supported by it,[5] Democritus is associated with Parmenides' view that the earth remains where it is because it is in equilibrium and there is no reason why it should move one way rather than another.[6]

We are told that the ancients represented the inhabited earth as circular, and regarded Greece as lying in the middle of it and Delphi as being in the centre of Greece, but that Democritus was the first to recognize that the earth is elongated, its length being $1\frac{1}{2}$ times its breadth.[7] Democritus is also, along with Eudoxus, credited with having compiled a geographical and nautical survey of the earth as, after Anaximander, Hecataeus of Miletus and Damastes of Sigeum had done.[8]

Democritus agreed with Anaxagoras's remarkable view of the Milky Way as consisting of the stars which the sun 'does not see'

[1] Plutarch, *De facie in orbe lunae* 16, p. 929 C (*Vors.* i², p. 367. 9–11). Plutarch is arguing that the moon is made of an opaque substance, like earth. Were it otherwise, he says, the moon would not be invisible at the conjunctions when 'plumb opposite' the sun; if, e.g., the moon were made of a transparent material like glass or crystal, then, at the conjunctions, it should not only be visible itself, but it should allow the sun's light to shine through it, whereas it is in fact invisible at those times and often actually hides the sun from our sight.

[2] Aët. iii. 10. 5 (*D. G.* p. 377; *Vors.* i², p. 367. 41).

[3] Hippolytus, *Refut.* i. 9. 4 (*D. G.* pp. 563–4; *Vors.* i², p. 324. 16).

[4] Tannery, *Pour l'histoire de la science hellène*, p. 279.

[5] Hippol. *Refut.* i. 8. 3 (*D. G.* p. 562. 5–7; *Vors.* i², p. 301. 32).

[6] Aët. iii. 15. 7 (*D. G.* p. 380; *Vors.* i², p. 111. 40).

[7] Agathemerus, i. 1. 2 (*Vors.* i², p. 393. 10).

[8] Ibid.

when it is passing under the earth during the night;[1] but, at the same time, he seems to have been the first to appreciate its true character as a multitude of small stars so close together that the narrow spaces between them seem even to be covered by the diffusion of their light in all directions, so that it has the appearance, almost, of a continuous body of light.[2]

With Anaxagoras he thought that comets were 'a conjunction of planets when they come near and appear to touch one another',[3] or a 'coalescence of two or more stars so that their rays unite'.[4]

In his remark, too, about the infinite number of worlds he seems to have done little more than expand what Anaxagoras had said about the men in other worlds than ours who have inhabited cities and cultivated fields, a sun and moon of their own, and so on.[5] It is worth while to quote Democritus's actual words in full, in order to see how slight is the foundation for the rhapsodical estimate which Gomperz gives of his significance as a forerunner of Copernicus. Hippolytus relates of Democritus that

'He said that there are worlds infinite in number and differing in size. In some there is neither sun nor moon, in others the sun and moon are greater than with us, in others there are more than one sun and moon. The distances between the worlds are unequal, in some directions there are more of them, in some fewer, some are growing, others are at their prime, and others again declining, in one direction they are coming into being, in another they are waning. Their destruction comes about through collision with one another. Some worlds are destitute of animal and plant life and of all moisture. . . . A world is at its prime so long as it is no longer capable of taking in anything from without.'[6]

Let us now hear Gomperz.[7] 'Democritus's doctrine was far from admitting the plausible division of the universe into essentially different regions. It recognized no contrast between the sublunary world of change and the changeless steadiness of the divine stars, important and fatal though that difference became in the Aristotelian

[1] Aristotle, *Meteorologica* i. 8, 345 a 25 (*Vors.* i², p. 308. 26).
[2] Macrobius, *In Somn. Scip.* i. 15. 6; Aët. iii. 1. 6 (*D. G.* p. 365; *Vors.* i², p. 367. 21).
[3] Aristotle, *Meteorologica* i. 6, 342 b 27 (*Vors.* i², p. 308. 34).
[4] Aët. iii. 2. 2 (*D. G.* p. 366; *Vors.* i², p. 308. 37).
[5] Anaxagoras, Fr. 4 (*Vors.* i², p. 315. 8–16).
[6] Hippolytus, *Refut.* i. 13. 2–4 (*D. G.* p. 565; *Vors.* i², p. 360. 10–19).
[7] Gomperz, *Griechische Denker*, i³, pp. 295, 296.

system. At this point Democritus was once more fully in agreement not merely with the opinions of great men like Galilei, who released modern science from the fetters of Aristotelianism, but even with the actual results of the investigation of the last three centuries. It is almost miraculous to observe how the mere dropping of the scales from his eyes gave Democritus a glimpse of the revelations which we owe to the telescope and to spectrum analysis. In listening to Democritus, with his accounts of an infinitely large number of worlds, different in size, some of them attended by a quantity of moons [why not suns too, as in the fragment?], others without sun or moon, some of them waxing and others waning after a collision, others again devoid of every trace of fluid, we seem to hear the voice of a modern astronomer who has seen the moons of Jupiter, has recognized the lack of moisture in the neighbourhood of the moon, and has observed the nebulae and obscured stars which the wonderful instruments that have now been invented have made visible to his eyes. Yet this consentaneity rested on scarcely anything else than the absence of a powerful prejudice concealing the real state of things, and on a bold, but not an over-bold, assumption that in the infinitude of time and space the most diverse possibilities have been realized and fulfilled. So far as the endless multiformity of the atoms is concerned, that assumption has not won the favour of modern science, but it has been completely vindicated in respect to cosmic processes and transformations. It may legitimately be said that the Democritean theory of the universe deposed in principle the geocentric point of view. Nor would it be unfair to suppose that Democritus smoothed the way for its actual deposition at the hands of Aristarchus of Samos.' . . . ' Democritus contended that some worlds were without animals and plants because the requisite fluid was lacking which should supply them with nourishment. And this dictum of the sage is especially remarkable inasmuch as it was obviously based on the assumption of the uniformity of the universe in the substances composing it and in the laws controlling it, which the sidereal physics of our own day has proved beyond dispute. He evinced the same spirit which animated Metrodorus of Chios, himself a Democritean, in his brilliant parable: "a single ear of corn on a wide-spreading champaign would not be more wonderful than

a single cosmos in the infinitude of space." The genius of Democritus
did not stop at anticipating modern cosmology.' . . .

This is a fascinating picture, but surely it is, in any case, much
overdrawn. And, even if it were true, we cannot but ask, why is
Anaxagoras, who, before Democritus, spoke of other worlds than
ours, with their suns and moons, their earths inhabited by men and
animals, where there are cities and cultivated fields, 'as with us',
given none of the credit for a theory which 'deposed in principle the
geocentric hypothesis'? Anaxagoras clearly set no limit to the
number of such worlds, and Democritus added little to his statement
except the details that at any given time some of the infinite number
of worlds are coming into being, others waxing, others waning, others
being destroyed, and that they represent all possible varieties of
composition (some with suns and moons, some without, &c.), instead
of being more or less on the same plan with ours, as Anaxagoras
perhaps implied. Again, the abandonment of the geocentric hypothesis does not carry us a step towards the Copernican theory
unless some other and truer centre is substituted for the earth.
But Democritus's theory of the infinity of worlds does not suggest
any such centre, nay, it destroys the possibility of there being such
a centre at all.[1]

With regard, however, to our sun and moon, Democritus puts
forward a rather remarkable hypothesis connected with the infinite
multiplication of his worlds. With Anaxagoras the stars, and
presumably the sun and moon also, were stones torn from the
earth by the whirling motion of the universe, and afterwards
kindled into fire by the rapidity of that motion. But according to
Democritus the sun and moon, which at the time of their coming
into being 'had not yet completely acquired the heat characteristic
of them, still less their great brilliance, but on the contrary were
assimilated to the nature subsisting in the earth' were then 'moving
in independent courses of their own ($\kappa\alpha\tau'$ $\iota\delta\iota\alpha\nu$)' ; 'for each of the
two bodies, when it first came into being, was still in the nature of
a separate foundation or nucleus for a world, but afterwards, as the
circle about the sun became larger, the fire was caught up in it '.[2]

---

[1] Cf. Aristotle's argument (*De caelo* i. 6, 275 b 13) that the universe cannot
be infinite because the infinite cannot have a centre.
[2] Ps. Plut. *Stromat.* (apud Euseb. *Pr. Ev.* i. 8. 7); *D. G.* p. 581; *Vors.* i²,
p. 359. 47.

The last words appear to relate only to the addition of fire to the earthy nucleus of the sun, which may be connected with the idea of Leucippus that 'the sun was kindled by the stars': but it seems to be implied by the whole passage that the sun and the moon, after beginning to come into being as the nucleus of separate worlds, were caught up by the masses moving round the earth and then carried round the earth with them so as to form part of our universe.

As regards the planets, we have seen that Anaxagoras, like Plato, placed the moon nearest to the earth, the sun further from it, and the planets further still; Democritus made the order, reckoning from the earth, to be Moon, Venus, Sun, the other planets, the fixed stars.[1] 'Even the planets have not all the same height' (i.e. are not at the same distance from us).[2] Seneca observes that 'Democritus, the cleverest of all the ancients, says he suspects that there are several stars which have a motion of their own, but he has neither stated their number nor their names, the courses of the five planets not having been at that time understood'.[3] This seems to imply that Democritus did not even venture to say how many planets there were; Zeller, however, holds that he could not but have known of the five planets, especially as he wrote a book 'about the planets';[4] it may be that he said in this work that there might perhaps be more planets than the five generally known, and Seneca, who had this at third hand, may have misunderstood the observation.[5]

An interesting remark about Democritus's views on the motion of the sun and moon is contained in a passage of Lucretius,[6] where the question is raised, why the sun takes a year to describe the full circle of the zodiac while the moon completes its course in a month; perhaps, says Lucretius, Democritus may be right when he says that the nearer any body is to the earth, the less swiftly can it be carried round by the revolution of the heaven; now the moon is nearer than the sun, and the sun than the signs of the zodiac; therefore the moon seems to get round faster than the sun because, while the sun, being lower and therefore slower than the signs, is left behind

---

[1] Aët. ii. 15. 3 (*D. G.* p. 344; *Vors.* i², p. 366. 32).
[2] Hippol. *Refut.* i. 13. 4 (*D. G.* p. 565; *Vors.* i², p. 360. 17).
[3] Seneca, *Nat. Quaest.* vii. 3. 2 (*Vors.* i², p. 367. 29).
[4] Thrasyllus ap. Diog. L. ix. 46 (*Vors.* i², p. 357. 22).
[5] Zeller, i⁵, p. 896 note.   [6] Lucretius, v. 621 sqq.

by them, the moon, being still lower and therefore slower still, is still more left behind. Therefore it is the moon which appears to come back to every sign more quickly than the sun does, because the signs go more quickly back to her. The view that the bodies which move round at the greatest distance move the most quickly and *vice versa* is the same as we find attributed by Alexander Aphrodisiensis to the Pythagoreans.[1]

Lastly, we are told by Censorinus[2] that Democritus put the Great Year at ' 82 years with the same number, 28, of intercalary months ', where the 'same number' is the number of intercalary months assumed by Callippus in his cycle of 76 years. Tannery[3] conjectures that the reading should be 77 years (LXXVII) instead of 82 years (LXXXII), which seems probable enough ; but, as he says, it is impossible to draw any certain conclusion from the passage.

[1] Alexander, *In metaphysica* A. 5, p. 542 a 16–18 Brandis, p. 40. 7–9 Hayduck.
[2] Censorinus, *De die natali* 18. 8 (*Vors.* i², p. 390. 19).
[3] Tannery in *Mém. de la Société des sciences phys. et nat. de Bordeaux*, 3ᵉ sér. iv, 1888, p. 92.

XIV

OENOPIDES

THE date of Oenopides of Chios is fairly determined by the statement of Proclus that he was a little younger than Anaxagoras.[1] He was a geometer of some note; Eudemus credited him with having been the first to investigate the problem of Eucl. I. 12 (the drawing of a perpendicular to a given straight line from a given point outside it), which he 'thought useful for astronomy', and to discover the problem solved in Eucl. I. 23 (the construction on a given straight line and at a point on it of an angle equal to a given rectilineal angle). No doubt perpendiculars had previously been drawn by means of some mechanical device such as a set square, and Oenopides was the first to give the theoretical construction as we find it in Euclid; and in like manner he probably discovered, not the problem of Eucl. I. 23 itself, but the particular solution of it given by Euclid.

In astronomy he is said to have made two discoveries of importance. The first is that of the obliquity of the ecliptic. It is true that Aëtius says that both Thales and Pythagoras, as well as the successors of the latter, distinguished the oblique circle of the zodiac as touching or meeting three of the 'five circles which are called zones';[2] Aëtius further states that 'Pythagoras is said to have been the first to observe the obliquity of the zodiac circle, a fact which Oenopides put forward as his own discovery'.[3] Now Thales could not possibly have known anything of the zones, and no doubt ' Pythagoras and his successors' may have been substituted for 'the Pythagoreans' in accordance with the usual tendency to attribute everything to the Master himself; in like manner the second

---

[1] Proclus, *Comm. on Eucl. I*, p. 66. 2 (*Vors.* i², p. 229. 36).
[2] Aët. ii. 12. 1 (*D. G.* p. 340).
[3] Aët. ii. 12, 2 (*D. G.* p. 340–1 ; *Vors.* i², p. 230. 14).

passage is probably the result of the same jealousy for the reputation of Pythagoras. And for the attribution of this particular discovery to Oenopides we have the better authority of Eudemus in a passage taken from Dercyllides by Theon of Smyrna.[1] Macrobius observes that Apollo (meaning the sun) is called Loxias, as Oenopides says, because he traverses the oblique circle (λοξὸν κύκλον), moving from west to east.[2] The Egyptian priests, we are told, claimed that it was from them that Oenopides learned that the sun moves in an inclined orbit and in a sense opposite to that of the motion of the other stars.[3] It does not appear that Oenopides made any measurement of the obliquity; at all events he cannot be credited with the estimate of 24°, which held its own till the time of Eratosthenes (*circa* 275–194 B. C.).[4]

[1] Theon of Smyrna, p. 198. 14, Hiller (*Vors.* i², p. 230. 11).
[2] Macrobius, *Sat.* i. 17. 31 (*Vors.* i², p. 230. 22).
[3] Diodorus Siculus, i. 98. 2 (*Vors.* i², p. 230. 19).
[4] Dercyllides' quotation from Eudemus (Theon of Smyrna, pp. 198, 199), which states that Oenopides was the first to discover the obliquity of the zodiac circle, also mentions that it was other astronomers not named in the particular passage who added (among other things) the discovery that the measure of the obliquity was the angle subtended at the centre of a circle by the side of a regular fifteen-angled figure inscribed in the circle, that is to say, 24°. But this value was discovered before Euclid's time, for Proclus, quite credibly, mentions (*Comm. on Eucl. I*, p. 269. 11–21) that the proposition Eucl. IV. 16, showing how to describe a regular fifteen-angled figure in a circle, was inserted in view of its use in astronomy. The value was doubtless known to Eudoxus also, if it does not even go back to the Pythagoreans. The angle might no doubt have been calculated by means of Pytheas's measurement of the midday height of the sun at Marseilles at the summer solstice. According to Strabo (ii. 5. 8, p. 115, and ii. 5. 41, p. 134, Cas.), Pytheas found that the ratio of the gnomon to its midday shadow at the summer solstice at Marseilles was 120 : 41⅘ (Ptolemy made it 60 : 20⅗, or 120 : 41⅔, *Syntaxis*, ii. 6, p. 110. 5). But we are not told of any value that Pytheas gave for the latitude of Massalia. According to Strabo, Hipparchus said that the same ratio of the gnomon to the shadow as Pytheas found at Massalia held good at Byzantium also, whence, relying on Pytheas's accuracy, he inferred that the two places were on the same parallel of latitude. As, however, Marseilles is 2° further north than Byzantium, it is clear that there must have been an appreciable error of calculation somewhere. Theon of Alexandria (*On Ptolemy's Syntaxis*, p. 60) states that Eratosthenes discovered the distance between the tropic circles to be 11/83rds of the whole meridian circle = 47° 42′ 40″, which gives 23° 51′ 20″ for the obliquity of the ecliptic. Berger, however (*Die geographischen Fragmente des Eratosthenes*, 1880, p. 131), is inclined to infer from Ptolemy's language that it was Ptolemy himself who invented the ratio 11 : 83, and that Eratosthenes still adhered to the value 24°. For Ptolemy (*Syntaxis* i. 12, p. 67. 22 – 68. 6) says that he himself found the distance between the tropic circles to lie always between 47° 40′ and 47° 45′, 'from which we obtain *about* (σχεδόν) the same ratio as that of Eratosthenes, which Hipparchus also used. For the distance between the tropics *becomes* (or *is found to be*, γίνεται) very nearly 11 parts out of 83 contained in the whole

The second discovery attributed to Oenopides is that of a 'Great Year, the duration of which he put at 59 years.[1] In addition, we are told by Censorinus that Oenopides made the length of the year to be $365\frac{22}{59}$ days.[2] Tannery[3] suggests the following as the method by which he arrived at these figures. Starting first of all with 365 days as the length of a year, and $29\frac{1}{2}$ days as the length of the lunar month, approximate values known before his time, Oenopides had to find the least integral number of complete years which would contain an exact number of lunar months; this is clearly 59 years, which contains a number of lunar months represented by twice 365, or 730. He had then to determine how many days there were in 730 months. This his knowledge of the calendar would doubtless enable him to do, and he would appear to have arrived at 21,557 days as the result,[4] since this, when divided by 59, gives $365\frac{22}{59}$ days as the length of the year.[5] Tannery gives good

meridian circle.' The mean between 47° 40′ and 47° 45′ is of course 47° 42′ 30″, or only 10″ different from 47° 42′ 40″; but the wording is somewhat curious if Ptolemy meant to imply that the actual ratio 11 : 83 represented Eratosthenes' estimate. For 'the same ratio' would then be 11/83 and σχεδόν and ἔγγιστα would have to mean exactly the same thing. Moreover, in that case, to make a separate sentence of the comparison with the fraction 11/83 was quite unnecessary ; all that was necessary was to add to the preceding sentence some words such as ' namely 11/83rds of the meridian circle' in explanation of 'the same ratio'. On the other hand, if the intention was to compare the mean value 47° 42′ 30″ with a value 48°, or 2/15ths of a great circle, used by Eratosthenes and Hipparchus, there was a sort of excuse for a separate sentence converting 47° 42′ 30″ into a fraction of a great circle as nearly as possible equivalent, namely 11/83rds, for the purpose of comparison with 2/15ths, the difference between the fractions being 1/1245. Hipparchus, in his Commentary on the Phaenomena of Aratus and Eudoxus (p. 96. 20-21, Manitius) said that the summer tropical circle is ' very nearly 24° north of the equator'. Another value for the obliquity of the ecliptic is derivable from an *obiter dictum* of Pappus (vi. 35, p. 546. 22-7, ed. Hultsch). Pappus, without any indication of his source, there says that the value of the ratio which we should call the tangent of the angle is 10/23. We should scarcely have expected a ratio between such small numbers to give a very accurate value, but 10/23 = 0·4347826, which is the tangent of an angle of 23° 29′ 55″ nearly.

[1] Theon of Smyrna, p. 198. 15 (*Vors.* i², p. 230. 13) : Aelian, *V. H.* x. 7 (*Vors.* i², p. 230. 27) ; Aët. ii. 32. 2 (*D. G.* p. 363 ; *Vors.* i², p. 230. 34).

[2] Censorinus, *De die natali* 19. 2.

[3] Tannery in *Mém. de la Société des sciences phys. et nat. de Bordeaux*, 3ᵉ sér. iv. 1888, pp. 90, 91.

[4] The true synodic month being 29·53059 days, 730 times this gives, as a matter of fact, $21557\frac{1}{3}$ days nearly.

[5] This year of a little less than 365 days 9 hours is slightly more correct than the average year of the *octaëteris* of $2923\frac{1}{2}$ days, which works out to 365 days $10\frac{1}{2}$ hours (Ginzel, *Handbuch der mathematischen und technischen Chronologie*, vol. ii, 1911, p. 387).

ground for thinking that Oenopides cannot have taken account of
the motion of all the planets as well as of the sun and moon for
the purpose of calculating the Great Year. He would, no doubt,
know the approximate periods of revolution of Saturn, Jupiter,
and Mars, namely 30 years for Saturn, 12 years for Jupiter, and
2 years for Mars, which figures would give roughly, in his great
year of 59 years, 2 revolutions of Saturn, 5 of Jupiter, and 30 or
31 for Mars. Admitting the last number as the more exact, and
dividing 21,557 days by these numbers respectively, we obtain
periods for the revolution of the several planets which, like the
figures worked out by Schiaparelli for Philolaus, would show errors
not exceeding 1 per cent. of the true values. But Tannery considers
that this is not the proper way to judge of the error ; he would
rather judge the degree of inaccuracy by the error in the mean
position of the planet at the end of the period. He finds that,
calculated on this basis, the error would not reach as much as
2° in the case of Saturn, and 9° in the case of the sun ; but for
Mars the error would exceed 107°, which is quite inadmissible.
If Oenopides had ventured to indicate the sign of the zodiac in
which each planet would be found at the end of his period, the
error in the case of Mars would have been discovered when the
time came.

Aristotle [1] says that some of the so-called Pythagoreans held
that the sun at one time moved in the Milky Way. This same
view is attributed to Oenopides ; for Achilles says [2] that ' According
to others, among whom is Oenopides of Chios, the sun formerly
moved through this region [the Milky Way], but because of the
Thyestes-feast he was diverted and has (since) revolved in a path
directed the opposite way to the other, that namely which is
defined by the zodiac circle '.

---

[1] Aristotle, *Meteorologica* i. 8, 345 a 16 (*Vors.* i², p. 230. 39).
[2] Achilles, *Isagoge ad Arat.* 24, p. 55. 18, Maass (*Vors.* i², p. 230. 42).

XV

PLATO

In order to obtain an accurate view of Plato's astronomical system
as a whole, and to judge of the value of his contributions to the
advance of scientific astronomy, it is necessary, first, to collect and
compare the various passages in his dialogues in which astronomical
facts or theories are stated or indirectly alluded to ; then, secondly,
allowance has to be made for the elements of myth, romance, and
idealism which are, in a greater or less degree depending on the
character of the particular dialogue, invariably found as a setting
and embellishment of actual facts and theories. When these elements are as far as possible eliminated, we find a tolerably complete and coherent system which, in spite of slight differences of
detail and a certain development and even change of view between
the earlier and the later dialogues, remains essentially the same.

In considering this system we have further to take into account
Plato's own view of astronomy as a science. This is clearly stated
in Book VII of the *Republic*, where he is describing the curriculum
which he deems necessary for training the philosophers who are to
rule his State. The studies required are such as will lift up the
soul from Becoming to Being ; they should therefore have nothing
to do with the objects of sensation, the changeable, the perishable,
which are the domain of opinion only and not of knowledge. It is
true that sensible objects are useful in so far as they give the
stimulus to the purely intellectual discipline required, in so far, in
fact, as they suffice to show that sensations are untrustworthy or
even self-contradictory. Some objects of perception are adequately
appreciated by the perception ; these are non-stimulants ; others
arouse the intellect by showing that the mere perception produces
an unsound result. Thus the perception which reports that a thing
is hard frequently reports that it is also soft, and similarly with

thickness and thinness, greatness and smallness, and the like. In such cases the soul is perplexed and appeals to the intellect for help ; the intellect responds and looks at 'great' and 'small' (e.g.) as distinct and not confounded ; we are thus led to the question what *is* the 'great' and what *is* the 'small'. Science then is only concerned with realities independent of sense-perception ; sensation, observation, and experiment are entirely excluded from it. At the beginning of the formulation of the curriculum for philosophers gymnastic and music are first mentioned, only to be rejected at once ; gymnastic has to do with the growth and waste of bodies, that is, with the changeable and perishing ; music is only the counterpart, as it were, of gymnastic. Next, all the useful arts are tabooed as degrading. The first subject of the curriculum is then taken, namely the science of Number, in its two branches of ἀριθμη-τική, dealing with the Theory of Numbers, as we say, and of λογιστική, calculation, with the proviso that it is to be pursued for the sake of knowledge and not for purposes of trade. Next comes geometry, and here Plato, carrying his argument to its logical con-clusion, points out that the true science of geometry is, in its nature, directly opposed to the language which, for want of better terms, geometers are obliged to use ; thus they speak of 'squaring', 'applying' (a rectangle), 'adding', &c., as if the object were to *do* something, whereas the true purpose of geometry is knowledge. Geometrical knowledge is knowledge of that which *is*, not of that which becomes something at one moment and then perishes ; and, as such, geometry draws the soul towards truth and creates the philosophic spirit which helps to raise up what we wrongly keep down. Astronomy is next mentioned, but Socrates corrects him-self and gives the third place in the curriculum to stereometry, or solid geometry as we say, which, adding a third dimension, naturally follows plane geometry. And fourth in the natural order is astronomy, since it deals with the 'motion of body' (φορὰ βάθους, literally 'motion of depth' or of the third dimension).

When astronomy was first mentioned, Socrates' interlocutor hastened to express approval of its inclusion, because it is proper, not only for the agriculturist and the sailor, but also for the general, to have an adequate knowledge of seasons, months, and years ; whereupon Socrates rallies him upon his obvious anxiety lest the

philosopher should be thought to be pursuing useless studies.
When the speakers return to astronomy after the digression on
solid geometry, Glaucon tries a different tack : at all events, he says,
astronomy compels the soul to look upward and away from the
things of the earth.   But no! he is using the term 'upward' in the
sense of towards the material heaven, not, as Socrates had meant
it, towards the realm of ideas or truth; and Socrates at once takes
him up.   On the contrary, he says, as it is now taught by those
who would lead us upward to philosophy, it is calculated to turn
the soul's eye down.

'You seem with sublime self-confidence to have formed your
own conception of the nature of the learning which deals with the
things above.   At that rate, if a person were to throw his head
back and learn something by contemplating a carved ceiling, you
would probably suppose him to be investigating it, not with his
eyes, but with his mind.   You may be right, and I may be wrong.
But I, for my part, cannot think any other study to be one that
makes the soul look upwards except that which is concerned with
the real and the invisible, and, if any one attempts to learn anything
that is *perceivable*, I do not care whether he looks upwards with
mouth gaping or downwards with mouth closed: he will never, as
I hold, learn—because no object of sense admits of knowledge—
and I maintain that in that case his soul is not looking upwards but
downwards, even though the learner float face upwards on land or
in the sea.'   'I stand corrected,' said he; 'your rebuke was just.
But what is the way, different from the present method, in which
astronomy should be studied for the purposes we have in view?'
'This', said I, 'is what I mean.   Yonder broideries in the
heavens, forasmuch as they are broidered on a visible ground, are
properly considered to be more beautiful and perfect than anything
else that is visible; yet they are far inferior to those which are true,
far inferior to the movements wherewith essential speed and essential slowness, in true number and in all true forms, move in relation
to one another and cause that which is essentially in them to move:
the true objects which are apprehended by reason and intelligence,
not by sight.   Or do you think otherwise?'   'Not at all,' said he.
'Then', said I, 'we should use the broidery in the heaven as illustrations to facilitate the study which aims at those higher objects,
just as we might employ, if we fell in with them, diagrams drawn
and elaborated with exceptional skill by Daedalus or any other
artist or draughtsman; for I take it that any one acquainted with
geometry who saw such diagrams would indeed think them most

beautifully finished but would regard it as ridiculous to study them seriously in the hope of gathering from them true relations of equality, doubleness, or any other ratio.' 'Yes, of course it would be ridiculous,' he said. 'Then', said I, ' do you not suppose that one who is a true astronomer will have the same feeling when he looks at the movements of the stars? That is, will he not regard the maker of the heavens as having constructed them and all that is in them with the utmost beauty of which such works admit ; yet, in the matter of the proportion which the night bears to the day, both these to the month, the month to the year, and the other stars to the sun and moon and to one another, will he not, think you, regard as absurd the man who supposes these things, which are corporeal and visible, to be changeless and subject to no aberrations of any kind ; and will he not hold it absurd to exhaust every possible effort to apprehend their true condition ?' 'Yes, I for one certainly think so, now that I hear you state it.' 'Hence', said I, 'we shall pursue astronomy, as we do geometry, by means of problems, and we shall dispense with the starry heavens, if we propose to obtain a real knowledge of astronomy, and by that means to convert the natural intelligence of the soul from a useless to a useful possession.' 'The plan which you prescribe is certainly far more laborious than the present mode of studying astronomy.'[1]

We have here, expressed in his own words, Plato's point of view, and it is sufficiently remarkable, not to say startling. We follow him easily in his account of arithmetic and geometry as abstract sciences concerned, not with material things, but with mathematical numbers, mathematical points, lines, triangles, squares, &c., as objects of pure thought. If we use diagrams in geometry, it is only as illustrations ; the triangle which we draw is an imperfect representation of the real triangle of which we *think*. And in the passage about the inconsistency between theoretic geometry and the *processes* of squaring, adding, &c., we seem to hear an echo of the general objection which Plato is said to have taken to the mechanical constructions used by Archytas, Eudoxus, and others for the duplication of the cube, on the ground that ' the good of geometry is thereby lost and destroyed, as it is brought back to things of sense instead of being directed upward and grasping at eternal and incorporeal images '.[2] But surely, one would say, the case would be different with astronomy, a science dealing with

[1] *Republic* vii. 529 A–530 B.
[2] Plutarch, *Quaest. Conviv.* viii. 2. 1, p. 718 F (*Vors.* i², p. 255. 3–5).

the movements of the heavenly bodies which we see. Not at all, says Plato with a fine audacity, we do not attain to the real science of astronomy until we have 'dispensed with the starry heavens', i.e. eliminated the visible appearances altogether. The passage above translated is admirably elucidated by Dr. Adam in his edition of the *Republic*.[1] There is no doubt that Plato distinguishes two astronomies, the apparent and the real, the apparent being related to the real in exactly the same way as practical (apparent) geometry which works with diagrams is related to the real geometry. On the one side there are the visible broideries or spangles in the visible heavens, their visible movements and speeds, the orbits which they are seen to describe, and the number of hours, days, or months which they take to describe them. But these are only illustrations (παραδείγματα) of real heavens, real spangles, real or essential speed or slowness, real or true orbits, and periods which are not days, months, or years, but absolute numbers. The broideries or spangles in both the astronomies are stars, but stars regarded as moving bodies. Essential speed and essential slowness seem to be, as Adam says, simply mathematical counterparts of visible stars, because they are said to be *carried* in the true motions of real astronomy, and therefore cannot be the speed and slowness of the mathematical bodies of which the visible stars are illustrations, but must be those mathematical bodies themselves. The true figures in which they move are their mathematical orbits, which we might now say are the perfect ellipses of which the orbits of the visible material planets are imperfect copies. And lastly, as a visible planet carries with it all the sensible properties and phenomena which it exhibits, so does its mathematical counterpart carry with it the mathematical realities which are in it. In short, Plato conceives the subject-matter of astronomy to be a mathematical heaven of which the visible heaven is a blurred and imperfect expression in time and space; and the science is a kind of ideal kinematics, a study in which the visible movements of the heavenly bodies are only useful as illustrations.

But, we may ask, what form would astronomical investigations on Plato's lines have taken in actual operation? Upon this there is naturally some difference of opinion. One view is that of

---

[1] See, especially, vol. ii, pp. 128-31, notes, and Appendices II and X to Book VII, pp. 166-8, 186-7.

Bosanquet,[1] who relies upon the phrase 'we shall pursue astronomy as we do geometry by means of *problems*', and suggests that the discovery of Neptune, picturesquely described by De Morgan as 'Leverrier and Adams calculating an unknown planet into visible existence by enormous heaps of algebra',[2] is the kind of investigation which 'seems just to fulfil Plato's anticipations'. Plato was a master of method, and it is an attractive hypothesis to picture him as having at all events foreshadowed the methods of modern astronomy; but Adam seems to be clearly right in holding that the illustration does not fit the language of the passage in the *Republic* which we are discussing. For Plato says that the person who thought that the heavenly bodies should always move precisely in the same way and show no aberrations whatever would properly be thought 'absurd', and that it would be absurd to exhaust oneself in efforts to make out the truth about them ; hence, on this showing, the visible perturbations of Uranus would scarcely have seemed to Plato very extraordinary or worth any very deep investigation by 'heaps of algebra' or otherwise. Besides, the discovery of Uranus's perturbations could hardly have been made without observation, and observation is excluded by the words 'we shall let the heavens alone'. The fact is that, at the time when our passage was written, Plato's 'problems' were *a priori* problems which, when solved, would explain visible phenomena ; Adams began at the other end, with observations of the phenomena, and then, when these were ascertained, sought for their explanation.

It may be that, when Plato is banning sense-perception from the science of astronomy in this uncompromising manner, he is consciously exaggerating ; it would not be surprising if his enthusiasm and the strength of his imagination led him to press his point unduly. In any case, his attitude seems to have changed considerably by the time when he wrote the *Timaeus* and the *Laws*, both as regards the use made of sense-perception and the relation of astronomy to the visible heaven. In the *Republic* sense-perception is only regarded as useful up to the point at which, owing to its presentations contradicting one another, it stimulates the intellect. In the *Timaeus* the senses, e.g. sight, fulfil a much more important

[1] Bosanquet, *Companion to Plato's Republic*, 1895, pp. 292-3.
[2] De Morgan, *Budget of Paradoxes*, p. 53.

rôle. 'Sight, according to my judgement, has been the cause of the greatest blessing to us, inasmuch as of our present discourse concerning the universe not one word would have been uttered had we never seen the stars and the sun and the heavens. But now day and night, being seen of us, and months and revolutions of years have made number, and they gave us the notion of time and the power of searching into the nature of the All; whence we have derived philosophy, than which no greater good has come nor shall come hereafter as the gift of the gods to mortal man. This I declare to be the chiefest blessing due to the eyes.'[1] In the *Laws* Plato makes the Athenian stranger say that it is impious to use the term 'planets' of the gods in heaven as if they and the sun and moon never kept to one uniform course, but wandered hither and thither; the case is absolutely the reverse of this, 'for each of these bodies follows one and the same path, not many paths but one only, which is a circle, although it appears to be borne in many paths.'[2] Here then we no longer have the view that the visible heavenly bodies should be neglected as being subject to perturbations which it would be useless to attempt to fathom, and that true astronomy is only concerned with the true heavenly bodies of which they are imperfect copies; but we are told that the paths of the visible sun, moon, and planets are perfectly uniform, the only difficulty being to grasp the fact. Bosanquet observes, on the passage in the *Republic* contrasting the visible and the true heavens, that 'Plato's point is that there are no doubt true laws by which the periods, orbits, accelerations and retardations of the solids in motion can be explained, and that it is the function of astronomy to ascertain them'.[3] On the later view stated in the *Laws* this would be true with 'the visible heavenly bodies' substituted for 'solids in motion'.

We are told on the authority of Sosigenes,[4] who had it from Eudemus, that Plato set it as a problem to all earnest students to find 'what are the uniform and ordered movements by the assumption of which the apparent movements of the planets can be accounted for'. The same passage says that Eudoxus was the

---

[1] *Timaeus* 47 A, B.   [2] *Laws* vii. 822 A.
[3] Bosanquet, *Companion*, p. 291.
[4] Simplicius on *De caelo* ii. 12 (292 b 10), p. 488. 20-4, Heib.

first to formulate hypotheses with this object; Heraclides of Pontus followed with an entirely new hypothesis. Both were pupils of Plato, and it is a fair inference that the stimulus of the Master's teaching was a factor contributing to these great advances, although it is probable that Eudoxus attacked the problem on his own initiative.

When we come to extract from the different dialogues the details of Plato's astronomical system, we find, as already indicated, that, if allowance is made for the differences in the literary form in which they are presented, and for the greater or less admixture of myth, romance, and poetry, the successive presentations of the system at different periods of Plato's life merely show different stages of development; the system remains throughout fundamentally the same. Some of the passages have nothing mythical about them at all; e.g. the passage in the *Laws*, which is intended to combat prevailing errors, gives a plain statement of the view which Plato thought the most correct. In the passages in which myth has a greater or less share, that which constitutes the most serious part is precisely that which relates to astronomy; and that which proves that the astronomical part is serious is the fact that, in different forms, and with more or fewer details in different passages, we have only one and the same main hypothesis; the variations are on points which are merely accessory.[1] Nor was the system revolutionary as compared with previous theories; on the contrary, Plato evidently selected what appeared to him to be the best of the astronomical theories current in his time, and only made corrections which his inexorable logic and his scientific habit of mind could not but show to be necessary; and the theory which commended itself to him the most was that of Pythagoras and the early Pythagoreans —the system in which the earth was at rest in the centre of the universe—as distinct from that of the later Pythagorean school, with whom the earth became a planet revolving like the others about the central fire.

Plato's system is set out in its most complete form in the *Timaeus*, and on this ground Martin, in his last published memoir on the subject, began with the exposition in the *Timaeus* and then

---

[1] Cf. Martin in *Mémoires de l'Acad. des Inscriptions et Belles-Lettres*, xxx, 1881, pp. 6–13.

added, for the purpose of comparison, the substance of the astronomical passages in the other dialogues. This plan would perhaps
enable a certain amount of repetition to be avoided; but I think
that the development of the system is followed better if the usual
plan is adopted and the dialogues taken in chronological order.

We begin therefore with the *Phaedrus*, perhaps the earliest of all
the dialogues. The astronomy in the *Phaedrus* consists only in the
astronomical setting of the myth about souls soaring in the heaven
and then again falling to earth. Soaring in the heaven, they with
difficulty keep up for a time with the chariots of the gods in their
course round the heavens.

'Zeus, the great captain in heaven, mounted on his winged
chariot, goes first and disposes and oversees all things. Him follows
the army of Gods and Daemons ordered in eleven divisions; for
Hestia alone abides in the House of God, while, among the other
gods, those who are of the number of the twelve and are appointed
to command lead the divisions to which they were severally
appointed.

Many glorious sights are there of the courses in the heaven
traversed by the race of blessed gods, as each goes about his own
business; and whosoever wills, and is able, follows, for envy has no
place among the Heavenly Choir . . .

The chariots of the gods move evenly and, being always obedient
to the hand of the charioteer, travel easily; the others travel with
great difficulty . . .

The Souls which are called immortal, when they are come to the
summit of the Heaven, go outside and stand on the roof and, as
they stand, they are carried round by its revolution and behold
the things which are outside the Heaven.'[1]

Here, then, the army of Heaven is divided into twelve divisions.
One is commanded by Zeus, the supreme God, who also commands-
in-chief all the other divisions as well; subject to this, each division
has its own commander. Zeus is here the sphere of the fixed stars,
which revolves daily from east to west and carries round with it
the other divisions except one, Hestia, which abides unmoved in the
middle. Hestia, the Hearth in God's House, stays at home to
keep house; the other divisions follow the march of Zeus but
perform separate evolutions under the command of their several
leaders. Hestia is here undoubtedly the earth, unmoved in the

---

[1] Plato, *Phaedrus* 246 E–247 C.

centre of the world,[1] and is not the central fire of the Pythagoreans. The gods in command of the ten other divisions are, in the first place, the seven planets, i. e. the sun and moon and the five planets, and then between them and the earth come the three others which are the aether, the air, and the moist or water.[2] The sun, moon, and planets are all carried round in the general revolution of the whole heaven from east to west, but have independent duties and commands of their own, i. e. separate movements which (as later dialogues will tell us) are movements in the opposite sense, i. e. from west to east.

In the *Phaedo* Plato puts into the mouth of Socrates his views as to the shape of the earth, its position and its equilibrium in the middle of the universe. The first passage on the subject is that in which he complains of the inadequate use by Anaxagoras of his *Nous* in explaining phenomena.

'When once I heard some one reading from a book, as he said, of Anaxagoras, in which the author asserts that it is Mind which disposes and causes all things, I was pleased with this cause, as it seemed to me right in a certain way that Mind should be the cause of all things, and I thought that, if this is so, and Mind disposes everything, it must place each thing as is best. . . . With these considerations in view I was glad to think that I had found a guide entirely to my mind in this matter of the cause of existing things, I mean Anaxagoras, and that he would first tell me whether the earth is flat or round, and, when he had told me this, would add to it an explanation of the cause and the necessity for it, which would be the Better, that is to say, that it is better that the earth should be as it is; and further, if he should assert that it is in the centre, that he would add, as an explanation, that it is better that it should be in the centre. . . . Similarly I was prepared to be told in like manner, with regard to the sun, the moon, and the other stars, their relative speeds, their turnings or changes, and their other conditions, in what way it is best for each of them to exist, to act, and to be acted upon so far as they are acted upon. For I should never have supposed that, when once he had said that these things were ordered by Mind, he would have assigned to them in addition any cause except the fact that it is best that they should be as they are. . . . From what

---

[1] Cf. Theon of Smyrna, p. 200. 7; Plutarch, *De primo frigido*, c. 21, p. 954 F; Proclus, *In Timaeum*, p. 281 E; Chalcidius, *Timaeus*, c. 122, p. 187, and c. 178, pp. 227-8.

[2] Chalcidius, loc. cit.; cf. Proclus, *In remp.* vol. ii, p. 130, 6-9, Kroll.

a height of hope then was I hurled down when I went on with my reading and saw a man that made no use of Mind for ordering things, but assigned as their cause airs, aethers, waters, and any number of other absurdities.' [Then follows the sentence stating that it is as if one were to say that Socrates did everything he did by Mind and then gave as the cause of his sitting there the fact that his body was composed of bones and sinews, the former having joints, and the sinews serving to bend and stretch out the limbs consisting of the bones with their covering sinews and flesh and skin, and so on. This inability to distinguish between what is the cause of that which is and the indispensable conditions without which the cause cannot be a cause suggests that most people are fumbling in the dark.] 'Thus it is that one makes the earth remain stationary under the heaven by making it the middle of a vortex, another sets the air as a support to the earth, which is like a flat kneading-trough.' [1]

The last sentence alludes to some of the familiar early views as to the form of the earth. Only Parmenides and the Pythagoreans thought it to be spherical, the Ionians and others supposed it to be flat, though differing as to details ; the theory that it is the motion of a vortex with the earth in the middle that keeps it stationary is that of Empedocles, while the idea that it is a disc, or like a flat kneading-trough, supported by air, is of course that which Aristotle attributes to Anaximenes, Anaxagoras, and Democritus. [2]

Plato's own view is stated later in the dialogue.

'There are many and wondrous regions in the earth, and it is neither in its nature nor in its size what it is supposed to be by those whom we commonly hear speak about it ; of this I have been convinced, I will not say by whom. . . . My persuasion as to the form of the earth and the regions within it I need not hesitate to tell you . . . I am convinced then, said he, that, in the first place, if the earth, being a sphere, is in the middle of the heaven, it has no need either of air or of any other such force to keep it from falling, but that the uniformity of the substance of the heaven in all its parts and the equilibrium of the earth itself suffice to hold it ; for a thing in equilibrium in the middle of any uniform substance will not have cause to incline more or less in any direction, but will remain as it is, without such inclination. In the first place I am persuaded of this.' [3]

---

[1] *Phaedo* 97 B–99 B.   [2] Aristotle, *De caelo* ii. 13, 294 b 13.
[3] *Phaedo* 108 C–109 A.

When Socrates says he has been convinced by some one of the fact that the earth is different from what it was usually supposed to be, he is considered by some to be referring to Anaximander who drew the first map of the inhabited earth. But surely Anaximander's views, no doubt with improvements, would be represented in those of his successors, the geographers of the time, whom Socrates considers to be wrong (we are told, for instance, that Democritus, who, like Anaximander, thought the earth flat, compiled a geographical and nautical survey of the earth[1]). 'Some one' may possibly be no one in particular, in accordance with Plato's habit of 'giving an air of antiquity to his fables by referring them to some supposititious author'.[2] On the other hand, the explanation of the reason why the spherical earth remains in equilibrium in the centre of the universe, namely that there is nothing to make it move one way rather than another, is sufficiently like Anaximander's explanation of the same thing.[3]

Socrates proceeds:

'Moreover, I am convinced that the earth is very great, and that we who live from the river Phasis as far as the Pillars of Heracles inhabit a small part of it; like to ants or frogs round a pool, so we dwell round the sea; while there are many other men dwelling elsewhere in many regions of the same kind. For everywhere on the earth's surface there are many hollows of all kinds both as regards shapes and sizes, into which water, clouds, and air flow and are gathered together; but the earth itself abides pure in the purity of the heaven, in which are the stars, the heaven which the most part of those who use to speak of these things call aether, and it is the sediment of the aether which, in the forms we mentioned, is always flowing and being gathered together in the hollow places of the earth. We then, dwelling in the hollow parts of it, are not aware of the fact but imagine that we dwell above on its surface; this is just as if any one dwelling down at the bottom of the sea were to imagine that he dwelt on its surface and, beholding the sun and the other heavenly bodies through the water, were to suppose the sea to be the heaven, for the reason that, through being sluggish and weak, he had never yet risen to the top of the sea nor been able, by putting forth his head and coming up out of the sea into the place where we live, to see how much purer and more beautiful it is

---

[1] Agathemerus, i. 1 (*Vors.* i², p. 393. 6, 7).
[2] Archer-Hind, *The Phaedo of Plato*, p. 161 note.
[3] See pp. 24, 25, above: cf. Aristotle, *De caelo* ii. 13, 295 b 11.

than his abode, neither had heard this from another who had seen it. We are in the same case; for, though dwelling in a hollow of the earth, we think we dwell upon its surface, and we call the air heaven as though this were the heaven and through this the stars moved, whereas in fact we are through weakness and sluggishness unable to pass through and reach the limit of the air: for, if any one could reach the top of it or could get wings and fly up, then, just as fishes here, when they come up out of the sea, espy the things here, so he, having come up, would likewise descry the things there, and if his strength could endure the sight would know that there is the true heaven, the true light, and the true earth. For here the earth, with its stones and the whole place where we are, is corrupted and eaten away, as things in the sea are eaten away by the salt, insomuch that there grows in the sea nothing of moment nor anything perfect, so to speak, but there are hollow rocks, sand, clay without end, and sloughs of mire wherever there is also earth, things not worthy at all to be compared to the beautiful objects within our view ; but the things beyond would appear to surpass even more the things here.'[1] . . .

Then begins the myth of the things which are upon the real earth and under the heaven,

'First it is said that, if one saw it from above, the earth is like unto a ball made with twelve stripes of different colours, each stripe having its own colour. . . .'

We need not pursue the picture of the idealized earth with its varied hues, its precious stones, its race of men excelling us in sight, hearing, and intelligence in the same proportion as air excels water, and aether excels air, in purity, and so on.

Reading the story of the hollows in the earth, we recall the idea of Archelaus, which he perhaps learnt from Anaxagoras, that the earth was hollowed out in the middle but higher at the edges. This shape would correspond to the flat kneading-trough mentioned by Plato as the form given by some to the earth.[2] Plato, realizing that certain inhabited regions such as that from the river Phasis (descending from the Caucasus into the Black Sea) to the Pillars of Hercules, being partly bounded by mountains, did appear to be hollows, had to reconcile this fact with his earnest conviction of the earth's sphericity. Archelaus regarded the whole earth as one such

---

[1] *Phaedo* 109 A–110 A.   [2] Ibid. 99 B.

hollow; to which Plato replies that the inhabited earth may be a hollow, but it is not the whole earth. The earth itself is very large indeed, so that the apparent hollow formed by the portion in which we live is quite a small portion of the whole. There are any number of other hollows of all sorts and sizes; these hollows are separated by the ridges between them, and it is only the tops of these ridges that are on the real surface of the spherical earth. Consequently there is nothing in the existence of the hollows that is inconsistent with the earth being spherical; they are mere indentations. The impossibility of our climbing up the sides to the top of the bounding ridges, or taking wings and flying out of the hollows, and so reaching the real surface of the earth and obtaining a view of the real heavens, is of course poetic fancy and has nothing to do with astronomy.

The extreme estimate of the size of the earth made by Plato in the *Phaedo* seems to be peculiar to him. For the sake of contrast, Aristotle's remarks on the same subject may be referred to.[1] Aristotle says that observations of the stars show not only that the earth is spherical, but that it is 'not great'. For quite a small change of position from north to south or *vice versa* involves a change of the circle of the horizon. Thus some stars are seen in Egypt and Cyprus which are not seen in the northern regions, and some stars which in the northern regions are always above the horizon are, in Egypt, seen to rise and set. Such differences for so small a change in the position of an observer would not be possible unless the earth's sphere were of quite moderate size. Aristotle adds that the mathematicians of his day who tried to calculate the circumference of the earth made it approach 400,000 stades. This estimate had, according to Archimedes,[2] been reduced in his time to 300,000 stades, and Eratosthenes made the circumference to be 252,000 stades on the basis of a definite measurement of the arc separating Syene and Alexandria on the same meridian, compared with the known distance between those places.

On the negligibility of the height of the highest mountain in comparison with the diameter of the earth, Theon of Smyrna[3] has

---

[1] Aristotle, *De caelo* ii. 14, 297 b 30–298 a 20.
[2] Archimedes, *Sand-reckoner* (vol. ii, ed. Heib., p. 246. 15; ed. Heath, p. 222).
[3] Theon of Smyrna, pp. 124-6, Hiller.

some remarks based on the estimates of 252,000 stades for the circumference and of 10 stades (a low estimate, it is true) for the height of the highest mountain above the general level of the plains.

Coming now to the *Republic*, Book X, we get a glimpse of a more complete system, though again the astronomy is blended with myth. The story is that of Er, the son of Armenius, who, after being killed in battle, came to life twelve days afterwards and recounted what he had seen. He first came with other souls to a mysterious place where there were two pairs of mouths, one pair leading up into heaven, the other two down into the earth; between them sat judges who directed the righteous to take the road to the right hand leading up into the heaven and sent those who had wrought evil down the left-hand road into the earth; at the same time other souls were returning by the other road out of the earth, and others again by the other road coming down from the heaven: the two returning streams met, the former travel-stained after a thousand years' journeying under the earth, the latter returning pure from heaven, and they foregathered in the meadow where they related their several experiences.

'Now when seven days had passed since the spirits arrived in the meadow, they were compelled to arise on the eighth day and journey thence; and on the fourth day they arrived at a point from which they saw extended from above through the whole heaven and earth a straight light, like a pillar, most like to the rainbow, but brighter and purer. This light they reached when they had gone forward a day's journey, and there, at the middle of the light, they saw, extended from heaven, the extremities of the chains thereof; for this light it is which binds the heaven together, holding together the whole revolving firmament as the undergirths hold together triremes; and from the extremities they saw extended the Spindle of Necessity by which all the revolutions are kept up. The shaft and hook thereof are made of adamant, and the whorl is partly of adamant and partly of other substances.

Now the whorl is after this fashion. Its shape is like that we use; but from what he said we must conceive of it as if we had one great whorl, hollow and scooped out through and through, into which was inserted another whorl of the same kind but smaller, nicely fitting it, like those boxes which fit into one another; and into this again we must suppose a third whorl fitted, into this a fourth, and after that four more. For the whorls are altogether eight in number, set

one within another, showing their rims above as circles and forming
about the shaft a continuous surface as of one whorl; while the
shaft is driven right through the middle of the eighth whorl.

The first and outermost whorl has the circle of its rim the
broadest, that of the sixth is second in breadth, that of the fourth
is third, that of the eighth is fourth, that of the seventh is fifth,
that of the fifth is sixth, that of the third is seventh, and that of the
second is eighth.   And the circle of the greatest is of many colours,
that of the seventh is brightest, that of the eighth has its colour
from the seventh which shines upon it, that of the second and fifth
are like each other and yellower than those aforesaid, the third
is the whitest in colour, the fourth is pale red, and the sixth is the
second in whiteness.

The Spindle turns round as a whole with one motion, and within
the whole as it revolves the seven inner circles revolve slowly in the
opposite sense to the whole, and of these the eighth goes the most
swiftly, second in speed and all together go the seventh and sixth
and fifth, third in the speed of its counter-revolution the fourth
appears to move, fourth in speed comes the third, and fifth the
second.   And the whole Spindle turns in the lap of Necessity.

Upon each of its circles above stands a Siren, carried round with
it and uttering one single sound, one single note, and out of all the
notes, eight in number, is formed one harmony.

And again, round about, sit three others at equal distances apart,
each on a throne, the daughters of Necessity, the Fates, clothed
in white raiment and with garlands on their heads, Lachesis,
Clotho, and Atropos, and they chant to the harmony of the Sirens,
Lachesis the things that have been, Clotho the things that are, and
Atropos the things that shall be.

And Clotho at intervals with her right hand takes hold of the
outer revolving whorl of the Spindle and helps to turn it; Atropos
with her left hand does the same to the inner whorls; Lachesis
with both hands takes hold of the outer and inner alternately
(i.e. of the outer with her right hand and of the inner with
her left).'[1]

On the precise interpretation of the details of this description
there has been a great deal of discussion and difference of opinion.[2]
Some of the details are hardly astronomical, and this is not the
place for more than a short statement of the principal points at
issue.

[1] *Republic* x. 616 B–617 D.
[2] Very full information will be found in Adam's edition of the *Republic*; see
especially the notes in vol. ii, pp. 441–53, and Appendix VI to Book X,
pp. 470–9.

First, what is the form and position of the 'straight light, like a pillar', and at what point is 'the middle' of the light where the souls saw 'the extremities of the chains' binding the heavens together?   As early as Proclus's time one supposition was that the light was the Milky Way.[1] Proclus rejected this view, which in modern times is represented by Boeckh[2] and Martin.[3] Boeckh supposes the souls to be beyond the north pole, outside the circle of the Milky Way which, if seen from the outside *edgeways*, would look straight; the middle of the light is for him the north pole, from which stretch the chains of heaven, *one* of which is the light.   Martin makes the souls see the Milky Way as a straight column of light from *below*; thence they go quickly up in the day's journey to the middle of the light (Martin compares the souls in *Phaedrus* 247 B–248 B, which get to the outside of the sphere of the fixed stars); they there see both poles of the sphere, and the curved column is, for them, like a band forming a complete ring round the sphere and holding it together; this curved column can only be the Milky Way.   Martin supports his view by pressing the comparison of the column to a rainbow, which, he says, must refer to its form and not to its colours; and for the illusion of supposing the curved column to be straight he cites the parallel of Xenophanes, who thought the stars moved in straight lines which only *appeared* to be circles.   I agree with Adam's opinion that to suppose the column to be curved and only to appear straight does violence to the language of Plato.   Then again, it would be strange that the souls, one class of which has come back from a thousand years' journey in the heaven, and the other from the same length of journey under the earth, should next be taken up, all of them, to the top of the heavenly sphere; there is nothing to suggest that, either in the four days elapsing between the time when they leave the meadow and the time when they first see the straight column of light, or in the one day following which brings them to the middle of the light, they leave the earth at all.   The other alternative is to take the 'straight light' to be, in accordance with the natural meaning of the words, a straight line or straight

[1] Proclus, *In remp.* vol. ii, p. 194. 19, Kroll.
[2] Boeckh, *Kleine Schriften*, iii, pp. 266–320.
[3] Martin in *Mém. de l'Acad. des Inscriptions et Belles-Lettres*, xxx, 1881, pp. 94–7.

cylindrical column of light passing from pole to pole right through
the centre of the universe and of the earth (occupying the centre
of the universe), which column of light symbolizes the axis on
which the sphere of the heaven revolves.   Where then is 'the
middle' of this column of light which the souls are supposed to
reach one day after they first see the column?   Adam thinks
it can only be at the centre of the earth, and he seems to base
this view mainly on the fact that, later on, the souls, after passing
under the throne of Necessity and encamping by the river of
Unmindfulness in the plain of Lethe, are said (621 B) to go *up*,
'shooting like stars,' to be born again.   Here also I cannot but
think it strange that all the souls should be brought down to the
centre of the earth, seeing that one class of them had just returned
from a thousand years' wandering in the interior of the earth, to
say nothing of the shortness of the time allowed for reaching the
centre of the earth, namely, one day from the time when they first
saw the column of light, while there is nothing in the language
describing the five days' journey to suggest that they did anything
but walk (πορεύεσθαι).   Now the place of the judgement-seat which
was between the mouths of the earth and the heaven, and to
which the souls returned after their thousand years in the earth and
heaven respectively, was on the surface of the earth; presumably
therefore the meadow to which they turned aside from that place
was also on the surface of the earth (and not even on the surface
of the 'True Earth' of the *Phaedo*, as Adam supposes); and
Mr. J. A. Stewart[1] has pointed out that the popular belief as to
the river Lethe made it a river entirely above ground and not one
of the rivers of Tartarus.   Hence I am disposed to agree with
Mr. Stewart that the whole journey from the meadow by the
throne of Necessity to the plain of the river Lethe was along the
surface of the earth.   Although Adam rightly rejects Boeckh's
identification of the 'straight light' with the Milky Way, he is
induced by the parallel of the 'undergirths' (ὑποζώματα) of
triremes to assume, in addition to the straight light forming the
axis of the universe, a circular ring of light passing round it from
pole to pole and joining the straight portion at the poles;[2] this

---

[1] J. A. Stewart, *The Myths of Plato*, pp. 154 sqq.
[2] Adam, *The Republic of Plato*, vol. ii, pp. 445-7, notes.

he does because the more proper meaning of 'undergirths' appears
to be ropes passed round the vessel outside it and horizontally,
rather than planks passing longitudinally from stem to stern as
Proclus and others supposed.[1]   But there is nothing in the Greek
to suggest the addition of this circle to the straight light; and
the assumption seems, as Mr. Stewart says,[2] to make too much
of the man-of-war or trireme.   Moreover, the ground for assuming
a ring, as well as a straight line, of light vanishes altogether if
the ὑποζώματα are, after all, cables stretched tight, i.e. in straight
lines, inside the ship from stem to stern, as Tannery holds.[3]   It
seems to be enough to regard Plato as saying that the pillar (which
alone is mentioned) holds the universe together in its particular
way as the undergirths do the trireme in their way.   I prefer then
to believe that the light is simply a straight column or cylinder
of light, and that the 'middle of the light' is the point on the
surface of the earth which is in the centre of the column of light,
i.e. the centre of the circular projection of the cylinder of light on
the earth's surface.   I do not see why the souls, looking from that
point along the cylinder of light in both directions, should not in
this way be supposed to see (illuminated by the column as by a
searchlight) the poles of the universe, nor why these should not
be called the extremities of the chains holding the heaven together,
the pillar of light having by a sudden change of imagery become
those chains themselves.

The Spindle of Necessity.

By another sudden change of imagery the chains following the
course of the pillar of light become a spindle which is similarly
extended from the same 'extremities' or poles, and the spindle
with its whorls representing the movements of the universe is seen
to turn in the lap of Necessity.   The throne of Necessity must on

[1] Proclus, *In remp.* vol. ii, p. 200. 25, and scholium, ibid. p. 381. 10.
[2] Stewart, op. cit., p. 169.
[3] Tannery in *Revue de Philologie*, xix, 1895, p. 117 : 'Le *Thesaurus* constate,
d'ailleurs, que Boeckh a démontré que les ὑποζώματα νεῶν, dont il est assez
souvent fait mention dans les inscriptions, sont des câbles, ainsi que du reste
Hesychius [s.v. ζωμεύματα] explique ce mot : σχοινία κατὰ μέσον τὴν ναῦν δεσμευό-
μενα.   Ces câbles étaient tendus, d'après les *Origines* d'Isidore, entre l'étrave et
l'étambot, en tout cas, on ne peut se les figurer tendus autrement que suivant
une ligne droite.'

the above view be at the point on the surface of the earth which
is in the middle of the column of light; and on this hypothesis, as
on others, the attempt to translate the details of the poetic imagery
into a self-consistent picture of physical facts is hopeless, for the
simple reason that one thing cannot both be entirely outside
another thing and entirely within it at the same time. Let us
assume with Boeckh that the souls are outside the universe when
they see the *apparently* straight light; Necessity will then presumably be outside the universe which in the form of the spindle
and whorls she holds in her lap. It is on this assumption impossible to give an intelligible meaning to 'under the throne of
Necessity' as an intermediate point on the journey of the souls
from the meadow to the plain of Lethe. The same difficulty
arises if, with Zeller, we suppose Plato to be availing himself of
the external Necessity which, according to Aëtius, Pythagoras
regarded as 'surrounding the world'.[1] Plato's Necessity is certainly not outside but in the middle. If, however, Necessity
sits either at the centre of the earth as supposed by Adam, or at
a point on the surface of the earth as supposed by Mr. Stewart,
how can she, being inside the universe, hold the spindle and whorls
forming the universe in her lap? This is no doubt the difficulty
which makes Mr. Stewart infer that Necessity does not hold the
universe itself in her lap, but a model of the universe.[2]

The whorls.

The real astronomy of the *Republic* is contained in the description
of the whorls and their movements. The first question arising is,
what was the shape of the whorls? They are not spheres because
they have rims ('lips', $\chi\epsilon\hat{\iota}\lambda\eta$) one inside the other, which are all
visible and form one continuous flat surface as of one whorl. We
might, on the analogy of Parmenides' bands, suppose that they
are *zones* of hollow spheres symmetrical about a great circle, i.e. so
placed that the plane of the great circle is parallel to, and equidistant from, the outer circles bounding the zones. Adam supposes
them to be *hemispheres*, which Plato possibly obtained by cutting

---

[1] Aët. i. 25. 2 (*D. G.* p. 321).
[2] Stewart, op. cit., pp. 152-3, 165.

in half the Pythagorean spheres mentioned by Theon of Smyrna.[1]
It is true that there is nothing in the text of Plato requiring them
to be hemispheres, although Proclus regards them as segments of
spheres[2]; but the supposition that they are hemispheres has the
great advantage that it eliminates all question of the *depth* of
the whorls measured perpendicularly (downwards, let us say) from
the visible flat surface formed by their rims.　Plato says nothing
of the *depth* of the whorls, but merely gives the rims different
breadths.　The moment we suppose the whorls to be zones or rings
we have to consider what depth or thickness (i. e. perpendicular
distance between the two bounding surfaces) must be assigned to
them.　The thickness of the rings would presumably be great
enough to hold symmetrically the largest of the heavenly bodies
which the rings carry round with them.[3]　Martin[4] takes the
thickness of the rings to be greater than this; he supposes that
the outer whorl is an equatorial zone of the celestial sphere
included between two equal circular sections 'which are doubtless
the tropics'.　But Martin admits that there is, in the whole passage,
no reference to any obliquity of movements relatively to the
equator, and he can only suppose such obliquity to be *tacitly* implied
by the thickness of each whorl.　I think that this supposition is
unsafe, and that it is better to assume that, at this stage in the
development of his astronomy, or perhaps merely for the purpose
of the imagery of this particular myth, Plato did not recognize
any obliquity, still less any variations of obliquity in the movements
of the planets.[5]　I prefer therefore to suppose the whorls to be

[1] Theon of Smyrna, p. 150. 14.
[2] Proclus, *In remp.* vol. ii, p. 213. 19-22.
[3] The revolving whorls περιάγουσι τοὺς ἀστέρας (Proclus, *In remp.* vol. ii, p. 226, 12).
[4] Martin in *Mém. de l'Académie des Inscriptions et Belles-Lettres*, xxx, 1881, pp. 100-1.
[5] Yet Berger (*Geschichte der wissenschaftlichen Erdkunde der Griechen*, 1903, pp. 199-201) still insists on regarding Plato's 'breadths' as what I have called *depths*. According to him a 'lip' (χεῖλος) must *project* (cf. Plato, *Critias* 115 E); hence he thinks they must project and recede in comparison with one another. It is difficult, as he sees, to reconcile this with νῶτον συνεχές, 'a continuous *back*' as seen from above, say the pole; he is therefore driven to the supposition that the words may describe the appearance of the *outermost* whorl as seen from a position where it hides all the others, i.e. from a point between the planes of its bounding circles; but this clearly will not do. The object of Berger is to make out that Plato wished to distinguish by the 'breadths' of his rings the inclinations of the movements of the several planets. As I have said

hemispheres, or similar segments of spheres fitting one inside the other, and having their bases in one plane. The planets, sun, and moon would perhaps be regarded as fixed in such a position that their centres would be on the plane surface which is the common boundary of all the whorls, so that half of each planet would project above that surface and half of it would be below.

It is not difficult to see what is the astronomical equivalent of each of the concentric whorls. The outermost (the first) represents the sphere of the fixed stars ; and here we have somewhat the same difficulty as we saw in the case of Parmenides' wreaths or bands. The fixed stars being spread over the whole sphere, how can that sphere be represented by a hemisphere, or a segment of a sphere, or a ring or zone ? The answer is presumably that the whorls are pure mechanism, designed with reference to the necessity of making the movements of the inner whorls give plane circular orbits to the seven single heavenly bodies, the sun, the moon, and the five planets. Mr. Stewart, in accordance with his idea that it is a *model* which Necessity holds in her lap, suggests that the model might be an old-fashioned one with rings instead of spheres, or that, if it were an up-to-date model, with spheres, it might be one in which only the half of each sphere was represented so that the internal 'works' might be seen ; he compares the passage in the *Timaeus*[1] where the speaker says that, without the aid of a model of the heavens, it would be useless to attempt to describe certain motions.

above, there is nothing in the text to suggest any obliquity in the movements ; and, if the ' breadths ' are *depths*, the sizes of the rings as measured by their inner and outer radii become entirely indeterminate, so that the relative orbital distances are undistinguished. It is quite incredible that Plato should say nothing about the relative sizes of the orbits while carefully distinguishing their obliquities relatively to the equator. It is true that Aristotle, *Metaph.* Λ. 8, 1073 b 17 sq.) and Theon of Smyrna (p. 174. 1–3) admit different obliquities exhibited by the planetary motions ; and Cleomedes (*De motu circulari* ii. 7, p. 226. 9–14) gives some estimates of them. These are, however, all obliquities with reference to the ecliptic, not the equator. Moreover, Cleomedes' figures are quite irreconcilable with Plato's corresponding ' breadths'. Cleomedes says that the obliquity is the greatest in the case of the moon ; next comes Venus which diverges 5° on each side of the zodiac ; next Mercury, 4° ; next Mars and Jupiter, 2½° each ; and last of all Saturn, 1°. Plato places them in descending order of ' breadth' thus : Venus, Mars, Moon, Mercury, Jupiter, Saturn.

[1] *Timaeus* 40 D. Cf. Theon of Smyrna, p. 146. 4, where Theon alludes to the same passage of the *Timaeus*, and says that he himself made a model to represent the system described in the present passage of the *Republic*.

The second whorl (reckoning from the outside) carries the planet Saturn, the third Jupiter, the fourth Mars, the fifth Mercury, the sixth Venus, the seventh the sun, and the eighth the moon. The earth, as always in Plato, is at rest in the centre of the system. The outer rim of each whorl clearly represents the path of the heavenly body which that whorl carries. The breadth of each whorl, that is, the difference between the radii of its outer and inner rims respectively (the inner radius of the particular whorl being of course the outer radius of the next smaller whorl), is the difference between the distances from the earth of the planet carried by the particular whorl and of the planet carried by the next smaller whorl. The rim of the innermost whorl (the eighth) is the orbit of the moon, the outer rim of the next whorl (the seventh) is the orbit of the sun, and so on. Proclus [1] says that there was an earlier reading of the passage about the breadths of the rims of the successive whorls which made them dependent on, i.e. presumably proportional to, the sizes of the successive planets. Professor Cook Wilson observes that ' this principle would be a sort of equable distribution of planetary mass, allowing the greater body more space. It would come to allowing the same average of linear dimension of planetary mass to each unit of distance between orbits throughout the system.' [2] Adam, however, for reasons which he gives, decides in favour of our reading of the passage as against the ' earlier' reading of Proclus.

As regards the speeds we are told that, while the outermost whorl (the sphere of the fixed stars) and the whole universe (including the inner whorls) along with it are carried round in one motion of rotation in one direction (i.e. from east to west), the seven inner whorls have slow rotations of their own in addition, the seven rotations being at different speeds but all in the opposite sense to the rotation of the whole universe. Hence the quickest rotation is that of the fixed stars and the whole universe, which takes place once in about 24 hours ; the slower speeds of the rest are speeds which are not absolute but relative to the sphere of the fixed stars regarded as stationary, and of these *relative* speeds the quickest is that of the moon, the next quickest that of. the sun, Venus, and

---

[1] Proclus, *In remp.* vol. ii, p. 218, 1 sq. Cf. Theon of Smyrna, p. 143. 14–16.
[2] See Adam, Plato's *Republic*, vol. ii, pp. 475–9.

Mercury, which travel in company with one another, i.e. have the same angular velocity and take about a year to describe their orbits respectively ; the next is that of Mars, the next that of Jupiter, and the last and slowest relative motion is that of Saturn. The speeds here are all angular speeds because, if the sun, Venus, and Mercury describe their several orbits in the same time, the sun must have the least linear velocity of the three, Venus the next greater, and Mercury the greatest, since the actual length of the orbit of the sun is less than that of the orbit of Venus, and the length of the orbit of Venus is again less than that of the orbit of Mercury. To obtain the *absolute* angular speeds in the direction of the daily rotation, i. e. from east to west, we have to deduct from the speed of the daily rotation the slower *relative* speeds of the respective planets in the opposite sense ; the absolute angular speeds are therefore, in descending order, as follows :

Sphere of fixed stars, Saturn, Jupiter, Mars, $\begin{cases} \text{Mercury} \\ \text{Venus} \\ \text{Sun} \end{cases}$, Moon.

The following table gives the order of orbital distances, or breadths of rims of whorls, as compared with the order of the whorls themselves, the order of *relative* speeds, and the relation of the colours of the planets respectively :

Whorl.	Planet.	Order in breadth of rim according to our reading.	Order in breadth of rim according to Proclus's 'old' reading.	Order of relative speeds.	Relation of colours.
1 =	Sphere of fixed stars	1	1	—	Spangled.
2 =	Saturn	8	7	5	Yellower than sun and moon.
3 =	Jupiter	7	6	4	Whitest.
4 =	Mars	3	5	3	Rather red.
5 =	Mercury	6	8	⎧ 2	Like Saturn in colour.
6 =	Venus	2	4	⎨ 2	Second in whiteness.
7 =	Sun	5	2	⎩ 2	Brightest.
8 =	Moon	4	3	1	Light borrowed from sun.

As, according to either reading, Plato only gives the order of the successive rims as regards breadth, not the ratios of their breadths, we cannot gather from this passage what was his view as to the ratios of the distances of the respective heavenly bodies from the earth. Nor can his estimate of the ratios be deduced from the mere allusion to the harmony produced by the eight notes chanted by the Sirens perched upon the respective whorls; as to this harmony see pp. 105-15 above.

As regards the Sirens, Theon of Smyrna tells us that some supposed them to be the planets themselves; some, however, regarded them as representing the several notes which were produced by the motion of the several stars at their different speeds.[1] It is clear that the latter is the right view; the Sirens are a poetical expression of the notes.

It will be noticed that Plato has the correct theory with regard to the moon's light being derived from the sun, a fact which, as before stated, he evidently learned from Anaxagoras.

The *Timaeus* is one of the latest of Plato's dialogues and is the most important of all for our purpose because in it Plato's astronomical system is most fully developed and given with the fewest lacunae. I shall continue to follow the plan of quoting passages in Plato's own words and adding the explanations which appear necessary. First, we are told that the universe is one only, eternal, alive, perfect in all its parts, and in shape a perfect sphere,[2] that being the most perfect of all figures.

' He (the Creator) assigned it that motion which was proper to its bodily form, that motion of all the seven which most belongs to reason and intelligence. Wherefore turning it about uniformly, in the same place, and in itself, he made it to revolve round and round; but all the other six motions he took away from it and stablished it without part in their wanderings.'[3]

'And in the midst of it he put soul and spread it throughout the whole, and also wrapped the body with the same soul round about on the outside; and he made it a revolving sphere, a universe one and alone.'[4]

Here then we have all plurality of worlds denied and the one universe made to revolve uniformly, carrying with it in its revolution all that is within it, as in the *Republic*; the uniform revolution is of course the daily rotation. Turning 'in itself' means about its own axis and therefore, so to speak, coincidently with itself, so that one

---

[1] Theon of Smyrna, pp. 146. 8-147. 6.
[2] *Timaeus* 32 C-33 B.
[3] Ibid. 34 A.
[4] *Timaeus* 34 B.

position does not overlap another, but in all positions the sphere occupies exactly the same space and place. The other ' six motions' from which it is entirely free are the three pairs of translatory motions, forward and backward, right and left, up and down.

Next Plato explains how the Creator made the Soul by first combining in one mixture Same, Other, and Essence, and then ordering the mixture according to the intervals of a musical scale, so that its harmony pervaded the whole substance. This substance, considered as having taken the form of a bar or band, a soul-strip as it were, he proceeds to divide.

' Next he cleft the structure so formed lengthwise into two halves and, laying them across one another, middle upon middle in the shape of the letter X, he bent them in a circle and joined them, making them meet themselves and each other at a point opposite to that of their original contact; and he comprehended them in that motion which revolves uniformly and in the same place, and one of the circles he made exterior and one interior. The exterior movement he named the movement of the Same, the interior the movement of the Other. The revolution of the circle of the Same he made to follow the side (of a rectangle) towards the right hand, that of the circle of the Other he made to follow the diagonal and towards the left hand, and he gave the mastery to the revolution of the Same and uniform, for he left that single and undivided; but the inner circle he cleft, by six divisions, into seven unequal circles in the proportion severally of the double and triple intervals, each being three in number; and he appointed that the circles should move in opposite senses, three at the same speed, and the other four differing in speed from the three and among themselves, yet moving in a due ratio.'[1]

The two circles in two planes forming an angle and bisecting one another at the extremities of a diameter common to both circles are of course the equator and the zodiac or ecliptic. The equator is the circle of the Same, the ecliptic that of the Other. In the accompanying figure, *AEBF* is the circle of the Same (the equator), *CFDE* the circle of the Other (the ecliptic), and they intersect at the ends of their common diameter *EF*. *GH* is the axis of the universe which is at right angles to the plane of the circle *AEBF*. If we draw chords *DK*, *CL* parallel to the diameter *AB* common to the circles *AEBF*, *AGBH*, and join *CK*, *DL*, we have a rectangle

---

[1] *Timaeus* 36 B–D.

of which *KD* is a side and *CD* is a diagonal. As the universe
revolves round *GH*, each point on the circumference of the circle
AGBH describes a circle parallel to the circle *AEBF*, i.e. a

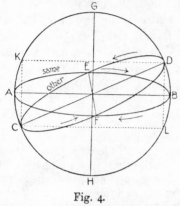

Fig. 4.

circle about a diameter parallel
to *AB* or *KD*; that is, the revolution 'follows the side' *KD* of
the rectangle. Similarly the
revolution of the circle of the
Other about an axis perpendicular to the plane of the circle
CFDE 'follows the diagonal'
CD of the rectangle.

The circle of the Same or the
equator is the outer, and the circle
of the Other, the ecliptic, is the
inner. When Plato says that the
Creator 'comprehended them' (i.e. both circles) in the motion of
the Same, and then again later that he gave the supremacy to that
circle, he means that the movement of that circle is common to the
whole heaven and carries with it in its motion the smaller circles,
the subdivisions of the circle of the Other, and everything in the
universe; this he makes still clearer in a later passage where he
speaks of the motion of the planets in the circle of the Other being
'controlled' by the motion of the Same, and the motion of the
Same twisting all their circles into spirals.[1] The subjection of all
that is in the universe, including all the independent motions of the
planets, to the one general movement of daily rotation is of course
the same as we saw in the *Republic*; but there all the circles were
in one plane, whereas the bodies moving in the opposite sense to
the daily rotation here move in a different plane, that of the ecliptic,
instead of that of the equator.

I have represented the directions of the motions in the two circles
by arrows in the figure. The motion in the circle *AEBF* is in the
direction represented by the order of the letters.

The statement of Plato that the Creator made the circle of the
Same (i.e. the circle of the fixed stars) revolve *towards the right
hand* and the circle of the Other (comprising the circles of the

[1] *Timaeus* 39 A.

planets) *towards the left hand* has given the commentators, from
Proclus downwards, much trouble to explain. It is also in contradiction to the observation in the *Laws* that motion to the *right*
is motion towards the *east*,[1] while the writer of the *Epinomis* again
represents the independent movement of the sun, moon, and planets
as being to the *right* and not to the left.[2]   There is of course no
difficulty in the circumstance that Plato has previously said that
the Creator took away from the world-sphere the six motions, up
and down, *right* and *left*, forwards and backwards ; for this refers
to movements of translation such as take place *inside* the sphere, not
to the revolution of the sphere itself.   The axis of such revolution
being once fixed, the revolution may be in one of two (and only
two) directions;[3] consequently there is nothing to prevent one of
the two directions being described as *to the right* and the other
as *to the left*.   But why did Plato speak of the revolution from
east to *west* as being motion to the *right*?   Boeckh has discussed
the question at great length, giving a full account of earlier views
before stating his own.[4]   Martin's explanation is that Plato is
speaking from the point of view of a spectator looking south, as
he would have to do in northern latitudes in order to see the
apparent revolution of the sun from east to west; that is, the
movement is from *left* to right.   Boeckh, however, points out that
the Greeks were accustomed, from the earliest times when diviners
foretold events by watching the flight of birds, to turn their faces
to the north; the east would therefore be on the right hand and
would naturally be regarded as the most auspicious, and therefore
as ' right '.   It is also true that the common view among the Greeks
(we find it later in Aristotle[5]) would make of the sphere of the
universe a sort of world-animal, which would have a right and left
of its own, as it might be a man masked in a sphere put over him ;
and no doubt, on such a view, the east would be sure to be
regarded as ' right' and the west as ' left '.   Boeckh therefore finds
it difficult to believe that Plato could have represented the east
as *left*.   Assuming then that Plato regarded the east as *right*,

[1] *Laws* vi. 8, 760 D.
[2] *Epinomis* 987 B.
[3] The sphere has, in mathematical language, only ' one degree of freedom '.
[4] Boeckh, *Das kosmische System des Platon*, pp. 28–32.
[5] Aristotle, *De caelo* ii. 2, 285 b 2–3.

Boeckh thinks Martin's view untenable, and concludes that the only possible alternative is to suppose that Plato must have thought, in the *Timaeus*, of a movement *from* the right *to* the right again, i.e. of the *whole* revolution from *east* to *east* instead of the portion from the east to the west.   But the movement, on the assumptions made, is undoubtedly *left-wise*, and it seems to me that Boeckh's explanation is almost as violent as the desperate method of interpretation suggested by Proclus.[1]   Where Boeckh is in error is, I think, in supposing that Plato would identify the east in his world-sphere with the right hand at all; it seems to me that he could not possibly have done so consistently with the scientific attitude he adopted in denying the existence of any absolute up and down, right and left, forward and backward in the spherical universe.   He explains, for example, that 'up' and 'down' have only a relative meaning as applied to different parts of the sphere,[2] and it is clear that, in the same connexion, he would say the same of right and left.   Now suppose that a particular point on the equator of the universe is *east* at a given moment; after about six hours the same point will be *south*, after six more *west*, and so on.   The case then is similar to that put by Plato when he says that a man going round the circumference of a solid body placed at the centre of the universe would at some time arrive at the antipodes of an earlier position and would therefore, on the usual view of 'up' and down, have to call 'down' what he had before described as 'up', and *vice versa*.[3]   Plato would never, surely, have made the same mistake in speaking of the universe.   On the contrary, when he spoke of the daily rotation, he properly ignored all question of a starting-point, whether east or west, right or left, or of the position of a *person* setting the sphere in motion, and confined himself to distinguishing by different names the two possible directions of motion in order to make it clear that the circles of the Same and of the Other moved in opposite directions. The expressions *to the right* and *to the left* were obviously well

[1] Proclus (*In Timaeum* 220 E) will have it that ἐπὶ δεξιά does not mean the same thing as εἰς τὸ δεξιόν, but that, while εἰς τὸ δεξιόν refers to motion *in a straight line*, ἐπὶ δεξιά only refers to motion *in a circle* and means ' the place to which the right moves (anything),' ἐφ' ᾧ τὸ δεξιὸν κινεῖ.

[2] Plato, *Timaeus* 62 D–63 E.

[3] *Timaeus* 62 E–63 A.

adapted to express the distinction, and it seems to me that the reason of Plato's particular application of them is simply this. He considered that the circle of the Same must have the superior motion; but *right* is superior to *left*; he therefore described the revolution of the circle of the Same as being *to the right*, and the revolution of the circle of the Other as being *to the left*, for this sole reason, without regard to any other considerations, just as in the *Republic* he confines himself to saying that Clotho at intervals, with her *right hand*, helps to turn the *outer* whorl of the spindle, and so on,[1] without saying anything about the actual directions in which the respective whorls revolve. On the other hand, when he says in the *Laws* that revolution from west to east is to the right and revolution from east to west is to the left, he is, as Boeckh properly observes, merely using popular language.

The cutting of the circle of the Other into seven concentric circles (including the original circumference as one of the seven) produces seven orbits in exactly the same way as the eight whorls in the Myth of Er give eight orbits, the difference being that the outermost circle of the *Republic*, the circle about which the sphere of the fixed stars moves, is not now in the same plane with the other seven, but is the circle of the Same in a different plane. Plato here says that the seven circles move in opposite directions, literally 'in opposite senses to one another', which, as there are only two directions, can only mean that a certain number of the seven revolve in one direction, and the rest in the other; we shall return later to this point, which presents great difficulty. The three which move at the same speed are of course the circles of the sun, Venus, and Mercury, as in the *Republic*, the same speed meaning, as there, not the same linear speed (as they are at different distances from the earth), but the same *angular* speed.

The seven circles are said to be 'in the proportion of the double and triple intervals, three of each'. The allusion is to the Pythagorean τετρακτύς represented in the annexed figure, the numbers on the one side after 1 being successive powers of 2 and those on the other side successive powers of 3. When the concentric circles into which the circle of the Other is divided are said to correspond to these numbers, it is clear that it must be

[1] *Republic* x. 617 C, D.

the circumferences (or, what is the same thing in other words, the radii), not the areas, which so correspond ; for, if it were the areas, the radii would not be commensurable with one another. The dictum is generally [1] taken to mean that the radii of the successive orbits, i.e. the distances between the successive planets and the earth, are in the ratio of the numbers 1, 2, 3, 4, 8, 9, 27. But Chalcidius [2] apparently takes the several numbers to indicate the successive differences between radii, for he says that, while the first distance (1) is that between the earth and the moon, the second (2) is the distance between the *moon* (not the earth) and the sun ;

Fig. 5.

on this view, the successive radii are 1, 1 + 2 = 3, 1 + 2 + 3 = 6, &c. Macrobius [3] says that the Platonists made the distances cumulative by way of multiplication, the distance of the sun from the earth being thus (in terms of the distance of the moon from the earth) 1 × 2 or 2, that of Venus 1 × 2 × 3 = 6, that of Mercury 6 × 4 = 24, that of Mars 24 × 9 = 216, that of Jupiter 216 × 8 = 1,728, and that of Saturn 1,728 × 27 = 46,656. (It will be observed that in this arrangement 9 comes before 8, Macrobius having previously explained this order by saying that, after 1, we first take the first even number, 2, then the first odd number, 3, then the second even number, 4, then the second odd number, 9, then the third even number, 8, and last of all the third odd number, 27.) But, whatever the exact meaning, it is obvious that we have here no serious estimate of the relative distances of the sun, moon, and planets based on empirical data or observations ; the statement is a piece of Plato's ideal *a priori* astronomy, in accordance with his statement in the *Republic*, Book VII, that the true astronomer should 'dispense with the starry heavens'.

Plato goes on to the question of Time and its measurement. As the ideal after which the world was created is eternal, but no created thing can be eternal, God devised for the world an image of abiding eternity 'moving according to number, even that which we have named time'.

[1] Cf. Zeller, ii⁴, p. 779 note.
[2] Chalcidius, *Timaeus*, c. 96, p. 167, ed. Wrobel.
[3] Macrobius, *In somn. Scip.* ii. 3. 14.

'For, whereas days and nights and months and years were not before the heaven was created, he then devised their birth along with the construction of the heaven. Now these are all portions of time...'[1]

'So, then, this was the plan and intent of God for the birth of time; the sun, the moon, and the five other stars which are called planets have been created for defining and preserving the numbers of time.

'And when God had made their several bodies, he set them in the orbits in which the revolution of the Other was moving, in seven orbits seven stars. The moon he placed in that nearest the earth, in the second above the earth he placed the sun; next, the Morning Star and that which is held sacred to Hermes he placed in those orbits which move in a circle having equal speed with the sun, but have the contrary tendency to it; hence it is that the sun and the star of Hermes and the Morning Star overtake, and are in like manner overtaken by, one another. And as to the rest, if we were to set forth the orbits in which he placed them, and the causes for which he did so, the account, though only by the way, would lay on us a heavier task than that which is our chief object in giving it. These things, perhaps, may hereafter, when we have leisure, find a fitting exposition.'[2]

The crux of this passage is the statement that, while Venus and Mercury have the same speed as the sun, i.e. have the same *angular* speed, describing their orbits in about the same time, 'they have the contrary tendency to the sun'; the words are ἐναντίαν δύναμιν, 'contrary tendency' or 'force'. In an earlier passage, as we have seen, Plato spoke of some of the seven planets moving on the concentric circles forming part of the circle of the Other as going 'the opposite way' (κατὰ τἀναντία)[3] to the others. Now, although δύναμις need not perhaps here be a 'principle of movement' as Aristotle defines it,[4] yet if we read the two passages together and give the most natural sense to the words in both cases, the meaning certainly seems to be that some of the planets describe their orbits in the contrary direction to the others, and that those which move, in the zodiac, the opposite way to the others are Venus and Mercury; that is to say, the sun, the moon, Mars, Jupiter, and Saturn all move in the direction of the motion of the circle of the Other, i.e. from west to east, while Venus and Mercury move in the same plane of the zodiac but in the opposite direction, i.e. from

---

[1] *Timaeus* 37 D, E.   [2] *Timaeus* 38 C–E.
[3] *Timaeus* 36 D, p. 159 above.   [4] Aristotle, *Metaph.* Δ. 12, 1019 a 15.

east to west. At the same time we are told that the periods in which the sun, Venus, and Mercury describe their orbits are the same. Thus if, say, Venus and the sun are close together at a particular time, they would according to this theory be nearly together again at the end of a year; but in the meantime Venus, moving in a sense contrary to the sun's motion, i.e. in the direction of the daily rotation from east to west, would pass through all possible angles of divergence from the sun and, after gaining a day, would appear with it again. But, as it is, Venus is never far away from the sun; and consequently Plato's statements, thus interpreted, are in evident contradiction to the facts, as easily verified by observation. It is not surprising that commentators have exhausted their ingenuity to find an interpretation less compromising to Plato's reputation as an astronomer. It is true that in the *Republic* all the seven planets revolve in one direction; but Plato is here referring to a phenomenon which is not mentioned in the *Republic*, namely, the fact that Venus and Mercury respectively on the one hand, and the sun on the other, 'overtake and are overtaken by one another', and the idea of the two planets having the 'contrary tendency to the sun' is clearly put forward for the precise purpose of explaining this phenomenon. It is accordingly with reference to the standings-still and the retrogradations of Venus and Mercury that the commentators try to interpret Plato's words. On the first passage (36 D) Proclus gives a number of alternatives, differing very slightly in substance, some importing the machinery of epicycles (which, as Proclus says, are foreign to Plato) and others not, but all designed to make Plato refer to nothing more than the stationary points and retrogradations; Proclus[1] on this occasion rejects them all, observing that the truest explanation is to suppose that Plato did not mean that there was any opposition of direction among the seven bodies at all, but only that all the seven, moving one way, moved in the opposite sense to the general movement of the daily rotation. This is cutting the knot with a vengeance. On the second passage (38 D) Proclus has the same kind of discussion, giving, as an alternative to the importation of epicycles, &c., the hypothesis that the 'overtakings' may be accounted for by the speeds of the sun, Venus, and Mercury varying relatively to one

---

[1] Proclus, *In Timaeum* 221 D sqq.

another at different points of their respective orbits.[1] Chalcidius[2] has much the same account of the different interpretations, but fortunately coupled with a precious passage about the view taken by Heraclides of Pontus of the movements of Venus and Mercury in relation to the sun: an account which, although it again wrongly imports epicycles into Heraclides' theory, as Theon of Smyrna and others erroneously import them into Plato's,[3] enables the true theory of Heraclides to be disentangled.[4]

Of modern editors Martin[5] refuses to accept any of these explanations which give a meaning to the passages other than that which the words naturally convey, and stoutly maintains that Plato did actually say that Venus and Mercury describe their orbits the contrary way to the motion of the sun, and meant what he said, incomprehensible as this may appear. He quotes in support of his view the evidence of Cicero in the fragments of his translation of the *Timaeus*. It is true that Cicero fences with the expression 'the contrary tendency', translating it as 'vim quandam contrariam', where 'quandam' has nothing corresponding to it in the Greek, but merely indicates a certain timidity or hesitation which Cicero felt in translating δύναμις by *vis*; Cicero, perhaps, may have had some idea, such as Proclus had, of a capricious force of some kind causing the two planets respectively to go faster at one time and slower at another. But by his translation of the other passage about the seven smaller circles making up the circle of the Other he shows that he interpreted Plato as meaning that some of the planets describing these circles move in the opposite direction to the others: his words are 'contrariis inter se cursibus'.

Archer-Hind[6] maintains that the phrase 'having the contrary tendency to it' does not mean that Venus and Mercury revolve in a direction contrary to the sun. He believes that 'Plato meant the Sun to share the contrary motion of Venus and Mercury in relation to the other planets'. 'It is quite natural,' he says, 'seeing that the sun and the orbits of Venus and Mercury are encircled by the

[1] Proclus, *In Timaeum* 259 A–C.
[2] Chalcidius, *Timaeus* c. 97, pp. 167–8; c. 109, p. 176, Wrobel.
[3] Theon of Smyrna, p. 186. 12–24.
[4] Hultsch, 'Das astronomische System des Herakleides von Pontos', in *Jahrbuch der classischen Philologie*, 1896, pp. 305–16.
[5] Martin, *Études sur le Timée*, ii, pp. 66–75.
[6] Archer-Hind, *Timaeus*, pp. 124–5 n.

orbit of the earth, while Plato supposed them all to revolve about
the earth, that he should class them together apart from the four
whose orbits really do encircle that of the earth: his observations
would very readily lead him to attributing to these three a motion
contrary to the rest.' This seems to be a very large assumption;
and indeed there is no evidence that Plato made any distinction
between the groups of planets which we now call inferior and
superior; in his system Venus and Mercury were not even inferior
to the sun, but above it. Besides, although Archer-Hind's view
would satisfy the first passage about some of the seven moving in
the contrary direction to the others, it still does not explain the
second statement that Venus and Mercury have 'the contrary tendency to *it*' (the sun). Accordingly he essays a new explanation.
'What I believe it' [the contrary tendency] 'to be may be understood from the accompanying figure which is copied from part of
a diagram in Arago's *Popular Astronomy.*' It represents the
motion of Venus relatively to the earth during one year as observed
in 1713, and is a sort of epicycloid with a loop. The 'tendency',
then, is the 'tendency on the part of Venus, as seen from the earth,
periodically to retrace her steps'. That is, Archer-Hind's explanation is really an explanation of retrogradations by the equivalent of
epicycles, and is therefore no better than the anachronistic explanations by Proclus and others to the same effect.

I do not think that Schiaparelli [1] is any more successful in his
explanations. He suggests that the first passage 'seems to allude
to the retrogradations, or perhaps to the opposite positions (with
reference to the sun) in which Mars, Jupiter, and Saturn on the one
hand, and Mercury and Venus on the other, carry out their standings-still and their retrogradations'. In the second passage he
translates the words about the 'contrary tendency' by '*receiving*
a force contrary to it' [2] (the sun), and he implies that this force is
really in the sun: 'it might be interpreted simply as a power, which
the sun seems to have, of making these planets go backward, as if it
attracted them to itself'. [3] This is not less vague than the explanations of Proclus and others; it has the disadvantage also that it is

[1] Schiaparelli, *I precursori*, p. 16 note.
[2] 'Ricevendo una forza contraria a lui.'
[3] 'Questo tuttavia si potrebbe interpretare semplicemente di una forza che sem-
bra avere il Sole, di far retrocedere questi pianeti, quasi li attirasse verso di sè.'

based on a mistranslation of the Greek.   The words mean 'having' or 'possessed of (εἰληχότας) the contrary tendency to the sun', which clearly shows that the tendency such as it is resides in the planets themselves.

We pass on to the next passage which is relevant to our subject.

'But when each of the beings [the planets] which were to join in creating time had arrived in its proper orbit, and they had been as animate bodies secured with living bonds and had learnt their appointed task, then in the motion of the Other, which was oblique and crossed the motion of the Same and was controlled by it, one planet described a larger, and another a smaller circle, and those which described the smaller circle went round it more swiftly and those which described the larger more slowly; but because of the motion of the Same those which went round most swiftly appeared to be overtaken by those which went round more slowly, though in reality they overtook them.   For the motion of the Same, which twists all their circles into spirals because they have two separate and simultaneous motions in opposite senses, is the swiftest of all, and displays closest to itself that which departs most slowly from it.'[1]

The spirals are easily understood by reference to the figure on p. 160.   Suppose a planet to be at a certain moment at the point F.   It is carried by the motion of the Same about the axis GH, round the circle $FAEB$.   At the same time it has its own motion along the circle $FDEC$.   After 24 hours accordingly it is not at the point F on the latter circle, but at a point some way from F on the arc FD.   Similarly after the next 24 hours, it is at a point on FD further from F; and so on.   Hence its complete motion is not in a circle on the sphere about GH as diameter but in a spiral described on it.   After the planet has reached the point on the zodiac (as D) furthest from the equator it begins to approach the equator again, then crosses it, and then gets further away from it on the other side, until it reaches the point on the zodiac furthest from the equator on that side (as C).   Consequently the spiral is included between the two small circles of the sphere which have KD, CL as diameters.

The remark about the overtakings of one planet by another is also easily explained.   Let us consider the matter with reference to two of the seven planets in the wider sense, namely the sun and the moon.   Plato says that the moon, which has the smaller orbit,

[1] *Timaeus* 38 E–39 B.

moves the faster, that is, the independent movement of the moon
in its orbit is faster than the independent movement of the sun in
its orbit, by which he means that the moon describes its orbit in
the shorter period. Thus the sun describes its orbit in about $365\frac{1}{4}$
days; the moon returns to the same position relatively to the fixed
stars in $27\frac{1}{3}$ days, a sidereal month, and relatively to the sun in $29\frac{1}{2}$
days, a synodic month. Now, if we consider the *whole apparent*
motion of the sun and moon, i.e. including the daily rotation as
well as the independent motion, the moon *appears* to go round the
earth *more slowly* than the sun. For at new moon it sets soon after
the sun. The next day it sets later, the day after later still, and so
on; it *appears* therefore to be gradually left behind by the sun, or
the sun appears to gain on it daily, that is, the moon 'appears to be
overtaken' by the sun. On the other hand, if we consider only the
relative motion of the sun and moon, i.e. if we leave out of account
the daily rotation as common to both, the moon, describing its
orbit more quickly than the sun describes its orbit, gains on the
sun, that is, 'in reality it overtakes' the sun, as Plato says.

'And that there might be some clear measure of the relative
slowness and swiftness with which they moved in their eight revolutions, God kindled a light in the second orbit from the earth,
which we now have named the Sun, in order that it might shine
most brightly through all the heaven, and that living things, so
many as was meet, should possess number, learning it from the
revolution of the Same and uniform. Night then and day have
been created in this manner and for these reasons, making the
period of the one and most intelligent revolution; a month has
passed when the moon, after completing her own orbit, overtakes
the sun, and a year when the sun has completed its own circle.

'But the courses of the others men have not grasped, save a few
out of many; and they neither give them names nor investigate the
measurement of them one against another by means of numbers, in
fact they can scarcely be said to know that time is represented by
the wanderings of these, which are incalculable in multitude and
marvellously intricate.

'None the less, however, can we observe that the perfect number
of time fulfils the perfect year at the moment when the relative
speeds of all the eight revolutions accomplish their course together
and reach their starting-point, being measured by the circle of the
Same and uniformly moving.'[1]

[1] *Timaeus* 39 B–D.

The 'month' in the above passage is the *synodic* month, the period in which the moon returns to the same position relatively to the sun. 'The courses of the others' are the periods of the planets, which are not called by separate names like 'year' and 'month', and which, Plato says, only a very few astronomers had attempted to measure one against another. The description of the 'wanderings' of the planets as 'incalculable in multitude and marvellously intricate' is an admission in sharp contrast to the assumption of the spirals regularly described on spheres of which the independent orbits are great circles, and still more so to the assertion in the *Laws* that it is wrong and even impious to speak of the planets as 'wandering' at all, since 'each of them traverses the same path, not many paths, but always one circular path'.[1] For the moment Plato condescends to use the language of *apparent* astronomy, the astronomy of observation; and this may remind us that Plato's astronomy, even in its latest form as expounded in the *Timaeus* and the *Laws*, is consciously and intentionally ideal, in accordance with his conception of the true astronomy which 'lets the heavens alone'.

What was the length of Plato's Great Year? Adam,[2] in his edition of the *Republic*, makes it to be 36,000 years, a figure which he bases on his interpretation of the famous passage in the *Republic*, Book VIII, about the Platonic 'perfect number', which is there called the 'period for a divine creature', just as, in the passage of the *Timaeus*, 'the perfect number of time fulfils the perfect year'. The perfect number of the *Republic* being, according to both Adam and Hultsch, the square of 3,600, or 12,960,000, Adam connects the perfect year with the two periods of the myth in the *Politicus*,[3] during the first of which God accompanies and helps to wheel the revolving world, while during the second he lets it go. Each of these periods contains 'many myriads of revolutions', the word for revolutions being περιόδων, the same word as is used in the *Republic* for the 'period for a divine creature'. Now in the *Politicus* περίοδοι, 'periods' or 'revolutions', refers to the revolutions of the world on its own axis. Hence Adam infers that the perfect or great year consists of 12,960,000 daily rotations or 12,960,000 days. Next, he cites the *Laws*, in which Plato divides the year into 360 days (which

---

[1] *Laws* vii. 22, 821 B–D, 822 A.
[2] Adam's *Republic*, vol. ii, pp. 204 sqq. notes, 295–305.   [3] *Politicus* 270 A.

is, it is true, an ideal division).[1] Dividing then 12,960,000 by 360, we obtain 36,000 years. Adam seeks confirmation of this in the fact that we find the period of 36,000 years sometimes actually called the 'great Platonic year' in early astronomical treatises. Thus Sacro-Bosco in his *Sphaera* says that 'the ninth circle in a hundred and a few years, according to Ptolemy, completes one degree of its own motion and makes a complete revolution in 36,000 years (which time is commonly called a great year or Platonic year)'. Since a text-book of Ptolemaic astronomy makes this statement, Adam infers that Ptolemy or some of his predecessors had understood the Platonic Number, and that we can perhaps trace the knowledge of the Number as far back as Hipparchus. For Hipparchus discovered the precession of the equinoxes and is supposed to have given 36,000 years as the time in which the equinoctial points make a complete revolution ; and Adam finds it difficult to believe that Hipparchus was uninfluenced by Plato's Number. There is, however, the strongest reason for doubting this, because Hipparchus's discovery of precession was based on something much more scientific than a recollection of the Platonic Number, namely actual recorded observations. It is true that Ptolemy estimated the movement of precession at $2\frac{2}{3}°$ in 265 years, i.e. about $1°$ in 100 years, or $36''$ a year,[2] and it is commonly supposed that this is precisely Hipparchus's estimate[3]. But it is probable that Hipparchus's estimate was much more correct. The evidence of Ptolemy[4] shows that Hipparchus found the bright star Spica to be, at the time of his observation of it, $6°$ distant from the autumnal equinoctial point, whereas he deduced from the observations recorded by Timocharis that Timocharis had made the distance $8°$. Consequently the motion had amounted to $2°$ in the period between 283 (or 295) and 129 B.C., a period of 154 (or 166) years ; this gives about $46.8''$ (or $43.4''$) a year, which is much nearer than $36''$ to the true value of $50.3757''$. It is true that, in a quotation which Ptolemy

---

[1] *Laws* vi. 756 B–C, 758 B.

[2] Ptolemy, *Syntaxis* vii. 2, vol. ii, p. 15. 9–17 Heib. Yet Ptolemy, in another place (vii. 3, pp. 28–30), infers from two observations made by Timocharis in 295 and 283 B.C. respectively that the movement amounted to $10'$ in about 12 years, which gives $50''$ a year.

[3] See Tannery, *Recherches sur l'histoire de l'astronomie ancienne*, pp. 265 sqq.

[4] Ptolemy, vii. 2, vol. ii, pp. 12, 13, Heib.

makes from Hipparchus's treatise on the Length of the Year,[1] 1° in 100 years is the rate mentioned; but Tannery points out that this is not conclusive, because Hipparchus is in the particular passage only giving a lower limit, for he says '*at least* one-hundredth of a degree' and 'in 300 years the movement would have to amount to *at least* 3°'. It would appear therefore that, if the estimate of 1° in a hundred years was due to Platonic influence at all, it must have been Ptolemy who Platonized rather than Hipparchus. And it seems clear that the Great Year of 36,000 years, if we assume it to be deducible from the passage of Plato, is certainly not 'best explained with reference to precession' as Burnet supposes.[2] Indeed the passage in the *Timaeus* is hardly consistent with this, for the Great Year is there distinctly said to be the period after which all the *eight* revolutions', i.e. those of the seven 'planets' as well as that of the sphere of the fixed stars, come back to the same relative positions; and the only revolution of the sphere of the fixed stars that is mentioned is the daily rotation.

'The visible form of the deities he made mostly of fire, that it might be most bright and most fair to behold, and, likening it to the All, he fashioned it like a sphere and assigned it to the intelligence of the supreme to follow after it; and he disposed it round about throughout all the heaven, to be an adornment of it in very truth, broidered over the whole expanse. And he bestowed two movements on each, one in the same place and uniform, as remaining constant to the same thoughts about the same things, the other a movement forward controlled by the revolution of the Same and uniform; but for the other five movements he made it motionless and at rest, in order that each star might attain the highest order of perfection.
'From this cause then have been created all the stars that wander not but remain fixed for ever, living beings, divine, eternal, and revolving uniformly and in the same place; while those which have turnings and wander as aforesaid have come into being on the principles which we have declared in the foregoing.'[3]

The deities are of course the stars, and 'the intelligence of the supreme' which they follow is the revolution of the circle of the Same which holds the mastery over all. The two movements common to the fixed stars are (1) rotation about their own axes

[1] Ptolemy, l. c., vol. ii, pp. 15, 16, Heib.
[2] Burnet, *Early Greek Philosophy*, p. 26 note.   [3] *Timaeus* 40 A–B.

and (2) their motion as part of the whole heaven in its daily rotation, the first being a motion in one and the same place, the other a motion 'forward', or of translation, in circles parallel to the equator, from east to west. The idea that the fixed stars rotate about their own axes is attributed by Achilles to the Pythagoreans.[1] The 'other five movements' (in addition to movement forward) are movements backward, right, left, up and down.

Rotation about their own axes is only attributed in express terms to the fixed stars; but Proclus is doubtless right in holding that Plato intended to convey that the planets also rotate about their own axes, the result of which is that, while the fixed stars have two motions, the planets have three, rotation about their own axes, revolution about the axis of the universe due to their sharing in the motion of the Same, and lastly their independent movements in their orbits. The 'turnings' refer to the fact that, like the sun, the planets, moving in the circle of the zodiàc, go as far from the equator as the tropic of Cancer and then turn, first approaching the equator and then passing it, until they reach the tropic of Capricorn when they again turn back.

'But the earth our foster-mother, globed round the axis stretched from pole to pole through the universe, he made to be guardian and creator of night and day, the first and chiefest of the gods that have been created within the heaven.

'But the circlings of these same gods and their comings alongside one another, and the manner of the returnings of their orbits upon themselves and their approachings, which of the deities meet one another in their conjunctions and which are in opposition, in what order they pass before one another, and at what times they are hidden from us and again reappearing send, to them who cannot calculate their movements, terrors, and portents of things to come— to declare all this without visible imitations of these same movements were labour lost.'[2]

It is mainly upon this passage, combined with a passage of Aristotle alluding to it, that some writers have based the theory that Plato asserted the earth's rotation about its own axis. There is now, however, no possibility of doubt that this view is wrong, and that Plato made the earth entirely motionless in the centre of the universe. This was proved by Boeckh in his elaborate

---

[1] Achilles, *Isagoge in Arati phaenomena*, c. 18 (*Uranologium*, p. 138 C).
[2] *Timaeus* 40 B–D.

examination of the whole subject[1] made in reply to a tract by
Gruppe[2], and again in a later paper[3] where Boeckh successfully refuted objections taken by Grote to his arguments. The
cause of the whole trouble is the ambiguity in the meaning of
the Greek word which is used of the earth '*globed* round the axis'.
It now appears that ἰλλομένην is the correct reading, although there
is MS. authority for εἰλλομένην and εἱλλομένην; but all three words
seem to be no more than variant forms meaning the same thing
(literally 'rolled'). Boeckh indeed seems to have gone too far in
saying that εἰλλομένην *can* only mean 'globed round' in Plato,
because no actual use of εἴλλεσθαι or εἴλεσθαι in the sense of rotation
about an axis or revolution in an orbit round a point can be found
in the *Timaeus* or elsewhere in the dialogues; for, as Teichmüller[4]
points out, εἴλλω is related to ἕλιξ (a spiral) and ἑλίττω (Ionic εἱλίσσω),
to 'roll' or 'wind', which latter word is actually used along with the
word στρέφεσθαι ('to be turned') in the *Theaetetus*.[5] But, while ἰλλομένην does not exclude the idea of motion, it does not necessarily
include it;[6] and the real proof that it does not imply rotation here
(but only being 'rolled round' in the sense of massed or packed
round) is not the etymological consideration, but the fact that the idea
of the earth rotating at all on its axis is quite inconsistent with the
whole astronomical system described in the *Timaeus*. An essential
feature of that system, emphasized over and over again, is the
motion of the Circle of the Same which carries every other motion
and all else in the universe round with it; this is the daily rotation
which carries round the earth the sphere of the fixed stars, and it is
this rotation of the fixed stars once completed which makes a day
and a night; cf. the passage 'night and day have been created . . .
and these are the revolution of the one and most intelligent circuit'.[7]

[1] Boeckh, *Untersuchungen über das kosmische System des Platon*, 1852.
[2] Gruppe, *Die kosmischen Systeme der Griechen*, 1851.
[3] Boeckh, *Kleine Schriften*, iii, p. 294 sqq.
[4] Teichmüller, *Studien zur Geschichte der Begriffe*, 1874, pp. 240-2.
[5] *Theaetetus* 194 B.
[6] Thus in Sophocles, *Antigone* 340, ἰλλομένων, used of ploughs, means '*going to and fro*'; but four instances occurring in Apollonius Rhodius tell in favour of Boeckh's interpretation of our passage: i. 129 δεσμοῖς ἰλλόμενον, where (as in ii. 1249 also) ἰλλόμενος means '*fast bound*'; i. 329 ἰλλομένοις ἐπὶ λαίφεσι, 'with sails *furled*'; ii. 27 ἰλλόμενός περ ὁμίλῳ, '*hemmed in* by a crowd.' Simplicius (on *De caelo*, p. 517, 15) cites Ap. Rh. i. 129 and adds that, even if the word is spelt εἰλλόμενος, it still means εἰργόμενος ('shut in'), as it does once in a play of Aeschylus (now lost). [7] *Timaeus* 39 C.

If the earth rotated about its axis in either direction, it would not be the rotation of the sphere of the fixed stars alone which would make night and day, but the sum or difference of the two rotations according as the earth rotated in the same or the opposite sense to the sphere of the fixed stars; but there is not a word anywhere to suggest any cause but the one rotation of the fixed stars in 24 hours.

This being so, how did Aristotle come to write ' Some say that, although the earth lies at the centre, it is yet wound *and moves* about the axis stretched through the universe from pole to pole, as is stated in the *Timaeus*'[1]? For three MSS. out of Bekker's five add the words καὶ κινεῖσθαι, ' *and is moved* ', to ἴλλεσθαι, ' is wound ', whereas the actual passage in the *Timaeus* has ἰλλομένην and nothing more. Alexander[2] held that Aristotle must have been right in adding the gloss ' *and moves* ' because he could not have been unaware either of the meaning of ἰλλομένην or of Plato's intention. Simplicius[3] is not so sure, but makes the best excuse he can. As the word ἰλλομένην might be interpreted by the ordinary person as implying rotation, Aristotle would be anxious to take account of the full apparent signification as well as the true one, in accordance with his habit of minutely criticizing the language of his predecessors with all its possible implications; he might then be supposed to say in this passage (which immediately follows his reference to those who held that the earth is not in the centre but moves round the central fire): ' And, if any one were to suppose that Plato affirmed its *rotation* in the centre through taking ἰλλο-μένην (being wound) to mean κινουμένην (being moved), we should at once have another class of persons coming under the more general category of those who assert that the earth moves; for the hypotheses will be that the earth moves in one of two ways, either round the centre or in the centre; and the person who understands Plato's remark in the sense of the latter hypothesis will be proved to be in error.' But Simplicius evidently feels that this is not a very satisfactory explanation, for he goes on to suggest the alternative that the words καὶ κινεῖσθαι, 'and moves', are an interpola-

---

[1] Aristotle, *De caelo* ii. 13, 293 b 30.
[2] Simplicius on *De caelo*, p. 518. 1-8, 20-21, ed. Heib.
[3] Simplicius, loc. cit., pp. 518. 9-519. 8.

tion; the passage will then, he says, be easy to understand; the contrast will be a double one, between those who say that the earth (1) is
not in the centre but (2) moves about the centre, and those who say
that (1) it is in the centre and (2) is at rest there. It would not be
unnatural if an unwise annotator had interpolated the words from
the passage at the beginning of the next chapter (14), where the
same remark is made without any mention of the *Timaeus*: 'for, *as
we said before*, some make the earth one of the stars, while others
place it in the centre and say that it is wound and moves (ἴλλεσθαι
καὶ κινεῖσθαι, as before) about the axis through the centre joining the
poles.'[1] Archer-Hind[2] is disposed to accept the suggestion that the
words are interpolated from the later into the earlier passage; but the
suggestion only helps if Aristotle is referring in the later passage to
some one other than Plato. Archer-Hind, it is true, thinks that
the added words in the second passage distinguish the theory there
stated from Plato's; but I think this is not so. The theory
alluded to in both passages is, I think, identically the same, as
indeed we may infer from the words 'as we said before'. Another
attempted explanation should be mentioned; it is to the effect that
the words 'as is stated in the *Timaeus*' in the passage of Aristotle
refer only to the words 'about the axis stretched through the universe from pole to pole' and not to the whole phrase 'it is yet wound
and moves about the axis, &c.'. This explanation was given, as much
as 600 years ago, by Thomas Aquinas;[3] in recent years it has been
independently suggested by Martin[4] and Zeller,[5] and Boeckh has
an explanation which comes to the same thing.[6] What seems to
me to be fatal to it is the word ἴλλεσθαι, 'is wound', immediately
preceding; this corresponds to Plato's word ἰλλομένην, and it is
impossible, I think, to suppose that ἴλλεσθαι does not, as much as

---

[1] Aristotle, *De caelo* ii. 14, 296 a 25.　　[2] Archer-Hind, *Timaeus*, p. 133 note.
[3] Dreyer (*Planetary Systems*, p. 78) was apparently the first to point this out.
The explanation was put forward in Thomas Aquinas's *Comment. in libros
Aristotelis de caelo*, lib. ii, lect. xxi (in *S. Thomae Aquinatis Opera omnia*,
iii, p. 205, Rome, 1886): 'Quod autem addit, *quemadmodum in Timaeo
scriptum est*, referendum est non ad id quod dictum est, *revolvi et moveri*, sed
ad id quod sequitur, *quod sit super statutum polum*.'
[4] Martin in *Mém. de l'Acad. des Inscriptions et Belles-Lettres*, xxx, 1881,
pp. 77, 78.
[5] Zeller, 'Ueber die richtige Auffassung einiger aristotelischen Citate,' in
Sitzungsber. der k. Preuss. Akad. der Wissenschaften, 1888, p. 1339.
[6] Boeckh, *Das kosmische System des Platon*, pp. 81-3.

the words about the axis, refer to the *Timaeus*. The only possible conclusion left is the earlier one of Martin,[1] in which Teichmüller[2] agrees, namely that Aristotle deliberately misrepresented Plato for the purpose of scoring a point. There are many other instances in Aristotle of this ' eristic ' and ' sophistical' criticism, as Teichmüller calls it, of Plato's doctrines.

Other writers seem to have been misled from the first by Aristotle's erroneous description of the theory of the *Timaeus*. Cicero, in speaking of the rotation of the earth about its axis, says : ' And some think that Plato also affirmed it in the *Timaeus* but in somewhat obscure terms.' [3] Plutarch[4] discusses and rejects this interpretation. Proclus is also perfectly clear that Plato made the earth absolutely at rest : ' Let ', he says, ' Heraclides of Pontus, who was not a disciple of Plato, hold this opinion and make the earth rotate round its axis ; but Plato made it unmoved.' [5] Proclus goes on to support this by a good argument. If, he says, Plato had not denied motion to the earth, he would not have described his ' perfect year ' with reference to *eight* motions only ; he would have had to take account of the earth's motion also as a ninth.

The words 'guardian and creator (φύλακα καὶ δημιουργόν) of night and day' have been thought by some to constitute a difficulty on the assumption that the earth abides absolutely unmoved in the centre. How, it is asked, can a thing which is purely passive be said to 'create' anything? Martin[6] furnishes the answer to this. If the earth were purely passive, it would not be at rest ; it would rotate about its axis once in 24 hours, since it would be carried round in the daily revolution of the universe. In order to remain at rest, as Plato requires, it has to exert a force in the opposite direction equal to that exerted by the daily revolution ; it produces day and night therefore by the energy of its resistance which keeps it at rest, while it is the 'guardian' by virtue of its immobility. A guardian is, as Boeckh says,[7] one who remains on the spot to watch and ward ; this is the rôle of the earth ; if it deserted its post,

---

[1] Martin, *Études sur le Timée*, ii, p. 87.
[2] Teichmüller, *Studien zur Geschichte der Begriffe*, 1874, pp. 238–45.
[3] Cicero, *Acad. Pr.* ii. 39, 123.   [4] Plutarch, *Quaest. Plat.* viii. 1–3, p. 1006 C–F.
[5] Proclus *in Tim.* p. 281 E.
[6] Martin, *Études sur le Timée*, ii, pp. 88, 90.
[7] Boeckh, *Das kosmische System des Platon*, p. 69.

if it were not there, there would only be light, and not day and
night; hence it is called the guardian of night and day. Proclus
observes that the earth is of course the 'creator' of night because
night is the effect of the earth's shadow which is cast in the shape
of a cone, and the earth can be said to be the creator of day by
virtue of the day's connexion with night, although one would say
that the sun rather than the earth is the actual cause of day.[1]
It is, however, the earth which is the cause of the *distinction*
between night and day; consequently it may fairly be called the
'creator' of both. In the *Timaeus Locrus*[2] the earth is called
the ὅρος (boundary, limit, or determining principle) of night and day;
and Plutarch[3] aptly compares it to the upright needle of the sundial:
it is its fixedness, he says, which gives the stars a rising and a setting.

Some expressions in the second paragraph of the passage quoted
on p. 174 call for a word or two in explanation. The 'circlings',
&c., are of course those of the planets; the circlings are their revolutions round the earth as common centre, as it were in a round dance
(χορεία), 'their well-ordered and harmonious revolutions,' as Proclus says.[4] The 'comings alongside one another' (παραβολαί, the
same word as is used in geometry of the 'application' of an area to
a straight line) are explained by Proclus as 'their comings together
in respect of longitude, while their positions in respect of latitude
or of depth are different, in other words, their rising simultaneously
and their setting simultaneously'.[5] 'The returnings of their orbits
upon themselves and their approachings' (αἱ τῶν κύκλων πρὸς ἑαυ-
τοὺς ἐπανακυκλήσεις καὶ προσχωρήσεις) are somewhat differently
interpreted. Proclus understands them as meaning retrogradations
and advance movements respectively: 'for when they advance they
are *approaching* their ἀποκατάστασις (their return to the same place
in the heavens); and, when their movement is retrograde, they return
upon themselves.'[6] Boeckh agrees in taking προσχωρήσεις to mean
their return to the same position in the heavens (ἀποκατάστασις)
but takes ἐπανακυκλήσεις, their return upon one another, to be an
earlier stage of the same motion; they 'turn upon themselves' in

[1] Proclus *in Tim.* 282 B, C; cf. Archer-Hind, *Timaeus*, p. 134 note.
[2] *Timaeus Locrus* 97 D.
[3] Plutarch, *Quaest. Plat.* viii. 3, p. 1006 F; cf. *De fac. in orbe lunae*, c. 25, p. 938 E.
[4] Proclus *in Tim.* p. 284 B.
[5] Ibid., p. 284 C.   [6] Ibid.

respect of the circular motion tending to bring them round again to the same point, and the 'approaching' is the arrival at the same point.[1]

Some allusions to the sun, moon, and planets as the 'instruments of time' (ὄργανα χρόνου) bring us to the end of the astronomy of the *Timaeus*. After a passage about the created gods and other gods born of them, the Creator makes a second blending of Soul.

'And when he had compounded the whole, he portioned off souls equal in number to the stars and distributed a soul to each star and, setting them in the stars as in a chariot, he showed them the nature of the universe and declared to them its fated laws . . . . and how they must be sown into the instruments of time befitting them severally.'[2]

Archer-Hind explains that the 'souls' here distributed among the stars, one to each, are different from the souls of the stars themselves and are rather portions of the whole substance of soul ; this was so distributed in order that it might learn the laws of the universe; then finally, he thinks, it was redistributed among the planets for division into separate souls incorporated in bodies.[3] The instruments of time are mentioned again a little later on :

'And when he had ordained all these things for them . . . God sowed some in the earth, some in the moon, and some in the other instruments of time.'[4]

Gruppe seizes upon this passage to argue that the earth is included with the moon and the other planets among the 'instruments of time', and hence that, as a measurer of time, the earth cannot be at rest but must rotate round its axis. But Boeckh[5] points out that even in this passage the earth itself need not be an instrument of time, for 'the other instruments of time' may mean 'other *than the moon*' just as well as 'other than the earth and moon'; and it is clear from another passage that the earth is *not* one of the 'instruments of time'. For in a sentence already quoted we are told that 'the sun and the moon and five other stars which have the name of planets have been created for defining and preserving

---

[1] Boeckh, *Das kosmische System des Platon*, p. 60.
[2] *Timaeus* 41 D, E.   [3] Archer-Hind, *Timaeus*, p. 141-2 note.
[4] *Timaeus* 42 D.
[5] Boeckh, *Das kosmische System des Platon*, pp. 71-3.

the numbers of time',[1] i. e. as the instruments of time. It is true that the remaining 'instrument', which measures the day of about 24 hours, is not here mentioned; but, when it does come to be mentioned, this instrument is not the earth, but the motion of the circle of the Same, or the sphere of the fixed stars: 'Night and day ... are one revolution of the undivided and most intelligent circuit.'[2]

We have next to inquire whether still later dialogues contain or indicate any modification of the system of the *Timaeus*. We come then to the *Laws*.

In Book VII occurs the passage already alluded to above, which in the first place exposes what appeared to Plato to be errors in the common notions about the movements of the planets current in his time, and then states, in a matter of fact way, the view which seems to him the most correct. After arithmetic and the science of calculation, and geometry as the science of measurement, with the distinction between commensurables and incommensurables, astronomy is introduced as a subject for the instruction of the young, when the following conversation takes place between the Athenian stranger and Clinias.

'*Ath.* My good friends, I make bold to say that nowadays we Greeks all affirm what is false of the great gods, the sun and the moon.

Cl. What is the falsehood you mean?

Ath. We say that they never continue in the same path, and that along with them are certain other stars which are in the same case, and which we therefore call planets.

Cl. By Zeus, you are right, O stranger; for many times in my life I too have noticed that the Morning Star and the Evening Star never follow the same course but wander in every possible way, and of course the sun and the moon behave in the way which is familiar to everybody.

Ath. These are just the things, Megillus and Clinias, which I say citizens of a country like ours and the young should learn with regard to the gods in heaven; they should learn the facts about them all so far as to avoid blasphemy in this respect, and to honour them at all times, sacrificing to them and addressing to them pious prayers.

Cl. You are right, assuming that it is at all possible to learn that to which you refer; if there is anything in our present views about

---

[1] *Timaeus* 38 C.   [2] Ibid. 39 B, C.

the gods that is not correct, and instruction will correct it, I too agree that we ought to learn a thing of such magnitude and importance. Do you then try your best to explain how these things are as you say, and we will try to follow your instruction.

Ath. Well, it is not easy to grasp what I mean, nor yet is it very difficult or a very long business. And the proof of this is that, although it is not a thing I learnt when I was young or have known a long time, I shall not take long to explain it to you; whereas, if it had been difficult, I at my age should never have been able to explain it to you at yours.

Cl. I dare say. But what sort of doctrine is this you speak of, which you call surprising, and proper to be taught to the young, but which we do not know? Try to tell us this much about it as clearly as you can.

Ath. I will try. Well, my good friends, this view which is held about the moon, the sun, and the other stars, to the effect that they ever wander, is not correct, but the very contrary is the case. *For each of them traverses the same path, not many paths, but always one, in a circle, whereas it appears to move in many paths.* And again, the swiftest of them is incorrectly thought to be the slowest, and *vice versa.* Now, if the truth is one way and we think another way, it is as if we had the same idea with regard to horses or long-distance runners at Olympia and were to address the swiftest as the slowest, and the slowest as the swiftest, and to award the praise accordingly, notwithstanding that we knew that the so-called loser had really won. I imagine that in that case we should not be awarding the praise in the proper way or a way agreeable to the runners, who are only human. When then we make this very same mistake with regard to the gods, should we not expect that the same ridicule and conviction of error would attach to us here and in this question as we should have suffered on the racecourse?

Cl. Nay, it would be no laughing matter at all.

Ath. No, nor would it be consistent with respect for the gods, if we repeated a false report against them.' [1]

The sentence italicized above is cited by Gruppe as another argument in favour of his hypothesis that Plato attributed to the earth rotation about its axis. Plato says that the apparent multiplicity of the courses of each planet is an illusion, and that each has one path only. Now, says Gruppe, this is only true if we reject the motion of the sphere of the fixed stars as only apparent, and substitute for it the rotation of the earth round its axis; for only then can it be said, e.g., that the sun and moon have only *one* movement

---

[1] Plato, *Laws* vii. 821 B–822 C.

in a circle.   If we assume the actual motion of the sun along with
the sphere of the fixed stars, while the earth remains at rest, the
circle becomes a spiral as described in the *Timaeus*.   Schiaparelli,[1]
influenced also by the passage of Aristotle which he thinks represents what Aristotle must have known to be the final view of Plato
through hearing the matter discussed in his school, accepts Gruppe's
conclusion, not apparently having been aware, at the time that he
did so, of Boeckh's complete refutation of it.   Boeckh[2] answers in
the first place that the unity of the movement of the planets
in single circles is not supposed, here any more than in the *Timaeus*,
to be upset by the fact that the movement of the circle of the Same
turns them into spirals.   Thus in the *Timaeus*, in the very next
sentence but one to that about the spirals, Plato speaks of the moon
as describing 'its own *circle* ' in a month, and of the sun as describing
'its own *circle*' in a year.   Similarly, Dercyllides[3] says that the
orbits of the planets are primarily simple and uniform circles
round the earth ; the turning of these circles into spirals is merely
incidental.

Gruppe goes so far as to find the heliocentric system in the
passage before us, by means of a forced interpretation of the words
about the planets which are really the quickest being regarded as
the slowest and *vice versa*.   He relies in the first place on two
passages of Plutarch as follows : (1) ' Theophrastus also adds that
Plato in his old age regretted that he had given the earth the
middle place in the universe, which was not appropriate to it,'[4] and
(2) 'they say that Plato in his old age was moved by these considerations [the Pythagorean theory of the central fire] to regard
the earth as placed elsewhere than in the centre, and the middle
and chiefest place as belonging to some worthier body ';[5] he then
straightway proceeds to assume the worthier body to be the sun,
and the ambiguity as regards swiftness and slowness to refer to the
stationary points and the retrogradations of the planets.   Schiaparelli,[6] however, points out, as Boeckh[7] had done before him, that

---

[1] Schiaparelli, *I precursori*, p. 19 sq.
[2] Boeckh, *Das kosmische System des Platon*, pp. 52 sqq.
[3] Theon of Smyrna, p. 200. 23 sq.
[4] Plutarch, *Quaest. Plat.* viii. 1, p. 1006 C.
[5] Plutarch, *Numa*, c. 11.   [6] Schiaparelli, *I precursori*, p. 21.
[7] Boeckh, *Das kosmische System des Platon*, p. 57.

this cannot be correct, as it is indicated a little earlier in the same passage of the *Laws* that everybody sees the same phenomena illustrated in the case of the sun and moon : this clearly implies, first, that the sun moves and, secondly, that the irregularities cannot be retrogradations, seeing that they do not exist in the case of the sun and moon. The fact is that the ambiguity pointed out in the *Laws* with regard to the speed of the planets is exactly the same as that which we have read of in the *Timaeus*, and that the passage in the *Laws* changes nothing whatever in the system expounded in the earlier dialogue. The remarks quoted from Plutarch will be dealt with later.

But we have not even yet finished with the arguments as regards the supposed rotation of the earth in Plato's final system. Schiaparelli[2] finds another argument in its favour in the *Epinomis*, a continuation of the *Laws* attributed to Philippus of Opus, a disciple of Plato, who is also said to have revised and published the *Laws*, which had been left unfinished. The system described in the *Epinomis* is the same as the system of the *Timaeus*. There are eight revolutions. Two are those of the moon and the sun;[3] then come two others, those of Venus and Mercury, of which it is said that their periods are about the same as that of the sun,[4] so that no one of the three can be said to be slower or faster than the others;[5] after these are mentioned the three revolutions of the other planets, Mars, Jupiter, and Saturn, which are said to travel in the same direction as the sun and moon, i.e. from west to east. The eighth revolution is not that of the earth, so that here, as in the *Timaeus* and the *Laws*, no rotation is attributed to the earth. Of the eighth revolution we read :

'And one of the moving bodies, the eighth, is that which it is most usual to call the universe above [i.e. the sphere of the fixed stars], which travels in the opposite sense to all the others, while carrying the others with it, *as men with little knowledge of these things would suppose.* But whatever we adequately know we must affirm and we do affirm.'[6]

Upon this Schiaparelli remarks, adverting to the italicized words : 'Plato then declares, in the *Epinomis* also, that men who under-

---

[1] *Laws* 821 C.   [2] Schiaparelli, *I precursori*, pp. 20–21.
[3] *Epinomis* 986 A, B.   [4] Ibid. 986 E, 987 B.   [5] Ibid. 987 B.   [6] Ibid. 987 B.

stand little about astronomy believe in the daily revolution of the heaven. If he expresses himself according to this system, it is for the purpose of adapting himself to the intelligence of the ordinary person.   Here we have what Aristotle ˎdoubtless had in mind when he wrote his celebrated remark about the rotation of the earth.'[1] But if this is the meaning of the passage, why did the author, after saying (apparently by way of contrast) ' but what we adequately know we must affirm and do affirm ', stop there and say not a single word of any alternative to the general rotation of the ' heaven ' ? There is still not a word of the earth's rotation, and indeed it is excluded by the limitation of the revolutions to eight, as remarked above. We must therefore, I think, reject Schiaparelli's interpretation of the passage and seek another.   It occurs to me that the emphasis is on the word ' *men* ' (ἀνθρώποις without the article), and that the meaning is ' so far as mere human beings can judge, who can have little knowledge of these things '. The words immediately following are then readily intelligible ; they would mean ' but if we are reasonably satisfied of a thing we must have the courage to state our view '.[2]

One other passage of the *Epinomis* is quoted by Martin[3] as evidence that it only repeats the theory of the *Timaeus* without change. All the stars are divine beings with body and soul. A proof that stars have intelligence is furnished by the fact that ' they always do the same things, because they have long been doing things which had been deliberated upon for a prodigious length of time, and they do not change their plans up and down, do one thing at one time and another at another, or wander and change their orbits '.[4] Consequently, as the stars include the planets, the *Epinomis*, like the *Timaeus*,[5] seems to deny the distinction between perigee and apogee, all variations of angular speed, stationary positions and retrogradations, and all movement in celestial latitude.

We have, lastly, to consider the two passages of Plutarch quoted above (p. 183) to the effect that Plato is said to have repented in his

---

[1] Schiaparelli, *I precursori*, pp. 20–1.
[2] Cf. *Laws* 716 C, to the effect that God is the real measure of all things, much more so than any man.
[3] Martin in *Mém. de l'Acad. des Inscriptions et Belles-Lettres*, xxx, 1881, p. 90.
[4] *Epinomis* 982 C, D.
[5] *Timaeus* 40 B ; cf. 34 A, 43 B, &c.

old age of having put the earth in the centre instead of assigning the worthier place to a worthier occupant. These passages have been fully dealt with by Boeckh[1] and by Martin[2] after him, and it is difficult or impossible to dissent from their conclusion, which is that the tradition is due to a misunderstanding and is unworthy of credence. To begin with, although the *Laws* is later than the *Timaeus* and so late that Plato did not finish it, there is in it no sign of a change of view. Nor is there any sign of such in the *Epinomis* written by Plato's disciple, Philippus of Opus ; and it is incredible that, if the supposed change of view had come out in the last oral discussions with the Master, Philippus would not have known about it and mentioned it. Even assuming the tradition to be true, we can at all events reject without hesitation the inference of Gruppe that the sun was Plato's new centre of the universe. If the sun had been the centre, this would surely have been stated, and we should not have been put off with the vague phrase ' some worthier occupant'. As, in the *Numa* where this expression occurs, Plutarch has just been speaking of the central fire of the Pythagoreans, the natural inference is that Plato's new centre, if he came to assume one at all, would be either the Pythagorean central fire or some imaginary centre of the same sort. But from what source did Theophrastus get the story which he repeats? Obviously from hearsay, since there is not a particle of written evidence to confirm it. The true explanation seems to be that some of Plato's immediate followers in the Academy altered Plato's system in a Pythagorean sense, and that the views of these Pythagorizing Platonists were then put down to Plato himself. In confirmation of this Boeckh quotes the passage of Aristotle in which, after speaking of the central fire of the Pythagoreans and the way in which they invented the counter-earth in order to force the phenomena into agreement with their preconceived theory, he goes on to indicate that there was in his time a school of philosophers other than the Pythagoreans who held a similar view : ' And no doubt many others too would agree (with the Pythagoreans) that the place in the centre should not be assigned to the earth, if they looked for

[1] Boeckh, *Das kosmische System des Platon*, pp. 144–50.
[2] Martin in *Mém. de l'Acad. des Inscriptions et Belles-Lettres*, xxx, 1881, pp. 128–32.

the truth, not in the observed facts, but in *a priori* arguments. For *they hold* that it is appropriate to the worthiest object that it should be given the worthiest place. Now fire is worthier than earth, the limit worthier than the things which are between the limits, while both the extremity and the centre are limits: consequently, reasoning from these premises, they hold that it is not the earth which is placed at the centre of the sphere, but rather fire.'[1] Simplicius[2] observes upon this that Archedemus, who was younger than Aristotle, held this view, but that, as Alexander says, it is necessary to inquire historically who were the persons earlier than Aristotle who also held it. As Alexander could not find any such, he concluded that it was not necessary to suppose that there were any except the Pythagoreans. But the present indicative ' they hold ' makes it clear that Aristotle had certain other persons in mind who, however, were not philosophers of an earlier time but were contemporaries of his own. These may well have been members of, or an offshoot from, the Academy who expressed the views in question, not in written works, but in discussion ; and, if this were so, nothing would be more natural than that a tradition which referred to the views of these persons should be supposed to represent the views of Plato in his old age.

Tannery[3] has a different and very ingenious explanation of Theophrastus's dictum about Plato's supposed change of view. This explanation is connected with Tannery's explanation of another mystery, that of the attribution to one Hicetas of Syracuse of certain original discoveries in astronomy. Diogenes Laertius[4] says of Philolaus that ' he was the first to assert that the earth moves in a circle, though other authorities say that it was Hicetas the Syracusan '. Aëtius says[5] that ' Thales and those who followed him said that the earth was one; Hicetas the Pythagorean that there were two, our earth and the counter-earth '. From these two passages taken together we should naturally infer that Hicetas was by some considered to be the real author of the doctrine attributed

---

[1] Aristotle, *De caelo* ii. 13, 293 a 27–b 1.
[2] Simplicius on *De caelo*, p. 513, ed. Heib.
[3] Tannery, ' Pseudonymes antiques ' in *Revue des Études grecques*, x, 1897, pp. 127–37.
[4] Diog. L. viii. 85 (*Vors.* i², p. 233. 33).
[5] Aët. iii. 9. 1. 2 (*D. G.* p. 376; *Vors.* i², p. 265. 25).

to Philolaus, in which the earth and counter-earth, along with the sun, moon, and planets, revolve round the central fire. Cicero,[1] however, has a different story: 'Hicetas of Syracuse, as Theophrastus says, holds that the heaven, the sun, the moon, the stars, and in fact all things in the sky remain still, and nothing else in the universe moves except the earth ; but, as the earth turns and twists about its axis with extreme swiftness, all the same results follow as if the earth were still and the heaven moved.' This is of course not well expressed, because, on the assumption that the earth rotates about its axis once in every 24 hours, the sun, moon, and planets would not in fact remain at rest any more than on the assumption of a stationary earth, for they would still have their independent movements; but Cicero means no more than that the rotation of the earth is a complete substitute for the apparent daily rotation of the heaven as a whole. However, the passage clearly implies that Hicetas asserted the axial rotation of the earth, and not its revolution with the counter-earth, &c., round the central fire. The statements therefore of Cicero on the one side, and of Diogenes and Aëtius on the other, are inconsistent. Tannery agrees with Martin[2] that we must accept as the more correct the version of Diogenes and Aëtius identifying Hicetas with the theory commonly attributed to Philolaus. Now, says Tannery, Aristotle, when speaking of the doctrine of the central fire as that of 'the philosophers of Italy, the so-called Pythagoreans', clearly shows that he did not attribute the doctrine to the Pythagoreans in general or to Philolaus; if he had seen the book of Philolaus of which our fragments formed part, and if he had referred to that work in this passage, he would have spoken of Philolaus by name instead of using the circumlocution; hence Aristotle must have been quoting from a book by some contemporary purporting to give an account of Pythagorean doctrines or doctrines claiming to be such. Tannery supposes therefore that Aristotle was referring to Hicetas, and that Hicetas was one of the personages in a certain dialogue, in which Hicetas represented the system known by the name of Philolaus, while Plato was his interlocutor. This dialogue

---

[1] Cicero, *Acad. Pr.* ii. 39. 123 (*Vors.* i², p. 265. 20).
[2] Martin, *Études sur le Timée*, vol. ii, pp. 101, 125 sq.

would be one of those written by Heraclides of Pontus. One of Heraclides' dialogues was 'On the Pythagoreans', and an account of the system of the central fire might easily form part of one of the others, e.g. that 'On Nature' or 'On the things in heaven'. Now there was a historical personage of the name of Hicetas of Syracuse whom Plato might well have known. He was a friend of Dion and he appears in Plutarch's lives of Dion and Timoleon as a political personage of some importance. Faithful to Dion, and for a time to his family after Dion's assassination, he threw over that family and seized the tyranny at Leontini, remaining the principal adversary of Dionysius the Younger until the arrival of Timoleon, when he was conquered and killed by the latter. There is nothing to suggest that he was a physicist or a Pythagorean; but he might quite well be represented in the dialogue as one who knew by oral tradition the doctrines of the school, and was therefore a suitable interlocutor with Plato. Plato's remarks in the dialogue might no doubt easily indicate a change from the views which we find in his own dialogues, and this is a possible explanation of the misconception on the part of Theophrastus and the *Doxographi*. Tannery adds that, on his hypothesis, we can hardly any longer consider the so-called Philolaic system as anything else but a brilliant phantasy due to that clever raconteur Heraclides. I do not see the necessity for this, and it is extremely difficult to believe that Heraclides invented *both* the theory of Philolaus and his own theory of the rotation of the earth about its axis; I do not see why we should not suppose that the system known by the name of Philolaus actually belonged to him or to the Pythagoreans proper, and that Hicetas represented the Pythagorean view rather than a new discovery of Heraclides. Tannery's attractive hypothesis is accepted by Otto Voss.[1]

---

[1] Otto Voss, *De Heraclidis Pontici vita et scriptis*, Rostock, 1896, p. 64.

XVI

THE THEORY OF CONCENTRIC SPHERES.
EUDOXUS, CALLIPPUS, AND ARISTOTLE

DIOGENES LAERTIUS[1] tells us that Eudoxus of Cnidus was celebrated as geometer, astronomer, physician, and legislator. Philosopher and geographer in addition, he commanded and enriched almost the whole field of learning; no wonder that (though it was a poor play on his name) he was called ἔνδοξος ('celebrated') instead of Eudoxus. In geometry he was a pupil of Archytas of Tarentum, and it is clear that he could have had no better instructor, for Archytas was a geometer of remarkable ability, as is shown by his solution of the problem of the two mean proportionals handed down by Eutocius.[2] This solution furnishes striking evidence of the boldness and breadth of conception which already characterized Greek geometry, seeing that even in that early time it did not shrink from the use of complicated curves in space produced by the intersection of two or more solid figures. Archytas solved the problem of the two mean proportionals by finding a point in space as the intersection of three solid figures. The first was an anchor-ring or *tore* with centre C, say, inner radius equal to zero, and outward radius $2a$, say; the second was a right cylinder of radius a so placed that its surface passes through the centre C of the tore and its axis is parallel to the axis of the tore or perpendicular to the plane bisecting the tore in the same way as a split ring is split; the third surface was a certain right cone with C as vertex. The intersection of the first two surfaces gives of course a curve (or curves) of double curvature in space, and the third surface cuts it in points, one of which gives Archytas what he seeks. There is, as we shall see,

---

[1] Diog. L. viii. 86–91.
[2] See Heiberg's *Archimedes*, vol. iii, pp. 98–102; or my *Apollonius of Perga*, pp. xxii, xxiii.

a remarkable similarity between this construction and the way in
which Eudoxus's ' spherical lemniscate' (*hippopede*) is evolved as the
intersection between a sphere, a cylinder touching it internally, and
a certain cone, so that we may well believe that Eudoxus owed
much to Archytas. To Eudoxus himself geometry owes a debt
which is simply incalculable, and it is doubtful, I think, whether, for
originality and power, any of the ancient mathematicians except
Archimedes can be put on the same plane with him. Although no
geometrical work of Eudoxus is preserved, there is, in the first
place, a monument to him *aere perennius* in Book V of Euclid's
Elements; it was Eudoxus who invented and elaborated the great
theory of proportion there set out, the essence of which is its
applicability to incommensurable as well as commensurable quantities. The significance of this theory of proportion, discovered
when it was, cannot be over-rated, for it saved geometry from the
impasse into which it had got through the discovery of the irrational
at a time when the only theory of proportion available for geometrical demonstrations was the old Pythagorean numerical theory,
which only applied to commensurable magnitudes. Nor can any
one nowadays even attempt to belittle the conception of equal
ratios embodied in Euclid V, Def. 5, when it is remembered that
Weierstrass's definition of equal numbers is word for word the same,
and Dedekind's theory of irrational numbers corresponds exactly
to, nay, is almost coincident with, the same definition. Eudoxus's
second great discovery was that of the powerful *method of
exhaustion* which not only enabled the areas of circles and the
volumes of pyramids, cones, spheres, &c., to be obtained, but is at
the root of all Archimedes' further developments in the mensuration
of plane and solid figures. It is not then surprising that Eudoxus
should have invented a geometrical hypothesis for explaining the
movements of the planets which for ingenuity and elegance yields
to none.

Eudoxus flourished, according to Apollodorus, in Ol. 103 = 368–
365 B.C., from which we infer that he was born about 408 B.C., and
(since he lived 53 years) died about 355 B.C. In his 23rd year he
went to Athens with the physician Theomedon, and there for two
months he attended lectures on philosophy and oratory, and in
particular the lectures of Plato; so poor was he that he took up his

abode at the Piraeus and trudged to Athens and back on foot each day. It would appear that his journey to Italy and Sicily to study geometry with Archytas and medicine with Philistion must have been earlier than the first visit to Athens at 23, for from Athens he returned to Cnidus, after which he went to Egypt with a letter of introduction to the king Nectanebus, given him by Agesilaus; the date of this journey was probably 381–380, or a little later, and he stayed in Egypt sixteen months. After that he went to Cyzicus, where he collected round him a large school with whom he migrated to Athens in 368 B.C. or a little later. There is apparently no foundation for the story mentioned by Diogenes Laertius that he took up a hostile attitude to Plato, nor, on the other side, for the stories that he went with Plato to Egypt and spent thirteen years in the company of the Egyptian priests, or that he visited Plato when Plato was with Dionysius, i.e. the younger Dionysius, on his third visit to Sicily in 361 B.C. Returning later to his native place, Eudoxus was by a popular vote entrusted with legislative office.

When in Egypt Eudoxus assimilated the astronomical knowledge of the priests of Heliopolis and himself made observations. The observatory between Heliopolis and Cercesura used by him was still pointed out in Augustus's time;[1] he also had one built at Cnidus, from which he observed the star Canopus which was not then visible in higher latitudes.[2] He wrote two books entitled respectively the *Mirror* (ἔνοπτρον) and the *Phaenomena*: the poem of Aratus was, so far as verses 19–732 are concerned, drawn from the *Phaenomena* of Eudoxus. It is probable that he also wrote a book on *Sphaeric*, dealing with the same subjects as Autolycus's *On the moving sphere* and Theodosius's *Sphaerica*.

In order to fix approximately the positions of the stars, including in that term the fixed stars, the planets, the sun, and the moon, Eudoxus probably used a *dioptra* of some kind, though doubtless of more elementary construction than that used later by Hipparchus;

---

[1] Strabo, xvii. 1. 30, pp. 806–7 Cas.

[2] Strabo, ii. 5. 14, p. 119 Cas. Hipparchus (*In Arati et Eudoxi phaenomena Commentariorum libri tres*, p. 114, 20–28) observes that Eudoxus placed the star Canopus exactly on the 'always invisible circle', but that this is not correct, since at Rhodes the circumference of this circle is 36° and at Athens 37° from the South pole, while Canopus is about 38½° distant from that pole, so that Canopus is seen in Greece *north* of the said circle. But, at the time when this was written, Hipparchus had not yet discovered Precession.

and he is credited with the invention of the *arachne* (spider's web), which, however, is alternatively attributed to Apollonius,[1] and which seems to have been a sun-clock of some kind.[2]

But it was on the theoretic even more than the observational side of astronomy that Eudoxus distinguished himself, and his theory of concentric spheres, by the combined movements of which he explained the motions of the planets (thereby giving his solution of the problem of accounting for those motions by the simplest of regular movements), may be said to be the beginning of scientific astronomy.

Two pupils of Eudoxus achieved fame, one in geometry, Menaechmus, the reputed discoverer of the conic sections, and the other in astronomy, Helicon of Cyzicus, who was said to have successfully predicted a solar eclipse.

The ancient evidence of the details of Eudoxus's system of concentric spheres (which he set out in a book entitled *On speeds*, Περὶ ταχῶν, now lost) is contained in two passages. The first is in Aristotle's *Metaphysics*,[3] where a short notice is given of the numbers and relative positions of the spheres postulated by Eudoxus for the sun, moon, and planets respectively, the additions which Callippus thought it necessary to make to the numbers of the spheres assumed by Eudoxus, and lastly the modification of the system which Aristotle himself considers necessary ' if the phenomena are to be produced by all the spheres acting in combination'. A more elaborate and detailed account of the system is contained in Simplicius's commentary on Book II of the *De caelo* of Aristotle ;[4] Simplicius quotes largely from Sosigenes the Peripatetic (second century A.D., the teacher of Alexander Aphrodisiensis, not the astronomer who assisted Caesar in his reform of the calendar), observing that Sosigenes drew from Eudemus, who dealt with the subject in the second book of his *History of Astronomy*.[5] Ideler was the first to appreciate the elegance of the theory and to attempt

[1] Vitruvius, *De architect.* ix. 8 (9). 1.
[2] Bilfinger, *Die Zeitmesser der antiken Völker*, p. 22.
[3] Aristotle, *Metaph.* Λ. 8, 1073 b 17 - 1074 a 14.
[4] *Simplicii in Aristotelis de caelo commentaria*, p. 488. 18–24, pp. 493. 4 – 506. 18, Heiberg; p. 498 a 45–b 3, pp. 498 b 27 – 503 a 33, Brandis.
[5] Simpl. on *De caelo*, p. 486, 18–21, Heib. ; p. 498 a 46–8, Brandis.

to explain its working;[1] he managed by means of an ordinary globe to indicate roughly how Eudoxus explained the stationary points and retrogradations of the planets and their movement in latitude. E. F. Apelt[2] too gave a fairly full exposition of the theory in a paper of 1849. But it was reserved for Schiaparelli to work out a complete restoration of the theory and to investigate in detail the extent to which it could account for the phenomena ; this Schiaparelli did in a paper which has become classical,[3] and which will no doubt be accepted by all future historians (in the absence of the discovery of fresh original documents) as the authoritative and final exposition of the system.[4]

The passages of Aristotle and Simplicius are translated in full in Appendices I and II to Schiaparelli's paper. The former may properly be reproduced here.

'Eudoxus assumed that the sun and moon are moved by three spheres in each case ; the first of these is that of the fixed stars, the second moves about the circle which passes through the middle of the signs of the zodiac, while the third moves about a circle latitudinally inclined to the zodiac circle ; and, of the oblique circles, that in which the moon moves has a greater latitudinal inclination than that in which the sun moves. The planets are moved by four spheres in each case ; the first and second of these are the same as for the sun and moon (the first being the sphere of the fixed stars which carries all the spheres with it, and the second, next in order to it, being the sphere about the circle through the middle of the signs of the zodiac which is common to all the planets[5]) ; the third is in all cases a sphere with its poles on the circle through the middle of the signs ; the fourth moves about

---

[1] Ideler, ' Ueber Eudoxus ' in *Abh. der Berliner Akademie, hist.-phil. Classe*, 1828, pp. 189–212, and 1830, pp. 49–88.

[2] E. F. Apelt, 'Die Sphärentheorie des Eudoxus und Aristoteles ' in the *Abhandlungen der Fries'schen Schule*, Heft ii (Leipzig, 1849).

[3] Schiaparelli, ' Le sfere omocentriche di Eudosso, di Callippo e di Aristotele ', in *Pubblicazioni del R. Osservatorio di Brera in Milano*, No. ix, Milano, 1875 ; German translation by W. Horn, in *Abh. zur Gesch. der Math.*, 1. Heft, Leipzig, 1877, pp. 101–98.

[4] It is true that Martin (*Mém. de l'Acad. des Inscr.* xxx, 1881) took objection to Schiaparelli's interpretation of the theories of the sun and moon, but he was sufficiently answered by Tannery (' Seconde note sur le système astronomique d'Eudoxe ' in *Mém. de la Soc. des sci. phys. et nat. de Bordeaux*, 2ᵉ série, v, 1883, pp. 129 sqq., republished in *Paul Tannery, Mémoires scientifiques*, ed. Heiberg and Zeuthen, vol. i, 1912, pp. 317–38.

[5] ἁπασῶν, with which we must, strictly speaking, understand σφαιρῶν (spheres) or possibly φορῶν (motions).

a circle inclined to the middle circle (the equator) of the third sphere ; the poles of the third sphere are different for all the planets except Aphrodite and Hermes, but for these two the poles are the same.[1]

Fuller details are given by Simplicius, but, before we pass to the details, we may, following Schiaparelli, here as throughout, inter- pose a few general observations on the essential characteristics of the system.[2] Eudoxus adopted the view which prevailed from the earliest times to the time of Kepler, that circular motion was suffi- cient to account for the movements of all the heavenly bodies. With Eudoxus this circular motion took the form of the revolution of different spheres, each of which moves about a diameter as axis. All the spheres were concentric, the common centre being the centre of the earth ; hence the name of 'homocentric spheres' used in later times to describe the system. The spheres were of different sizes, one inside the other. Each planet was fixed at a point in the equator of the sphere which carried it, the sphere revolving at uniform speed about the diameter joining the corresponding poles ; that is, the planet revolved uniformly in a great circle of the sphere perpendicular to the axis of rotation. But one such circular motion was not enough ; in order to explain the changes in the speed of the planets' motion, their stations and retrogradations, as well as their deviations in latitude, Eudoxus had to assume a number of such circular motions working on each planet and producing by their combination that single apparently irregular motion which can be deduced from mere observation. He accordingly held that the poles of the sphere which carries the planet are not fixed, but themselves move on a greater sphere concentric with the carrying sphere and moving about two different poles with a speed of its own. As even this was not sufficient to explain the phenomena, Eudoxus placed the poles of the second sphere on a third, which again was concentric with and larger than the first and second and moved about separate poles of its own, and with a speed peculiar to itself. For the planets yet a fourth sphere was required

---

[1] Aristotle, *Metaph.* Λ. 8, 1073 b 17-32.

[2] A very useful summary of the results of Schiaparelli's paper is given in Dreyer's *History of the Planetary Systems from Thales to Kepler* (Camb. Univ. Press, 1906), pp. 90-103. My account must necessarily take the same line ; and my apology for inserting it instead of merely referring to Dreyer's chapter on the subject must be that a sketch of the history of Greek astronomy such as the present would be incomplete without it.

similarly related to the three others; for the sun and moon he found that, by a suitable choice of the positions of the poles and of speeds of rotation, he could make three spheres suffice. In the accounts of Aristotle and Simplicius the spheres are described in the reverse order, the sphere carrying the planet being the last. The spheres which move each planet Eudoxus made quite separate from those which move the others. One sphere sufficed of course to produce the daily rotation of the heavens. Thus, with three spheres for the sun, three for the moon, four for each of the planets and one for the daily rotation, there were 27 spheres in all. It does not appear that Eudoxus speculated upon the causes of these rotational motions or the way in which they were transmitted from one sphere to another; nor did he inquire about the material of which they were made, their sizes and mutual distances. In the matter of distances the only indication of his views is contained in Archimedes' remark that he supposed the diameter of the sun to be nine times that of the moon,[1] from which we may no doubt infer that he made their distances from the earth to be in the same ratio 9 : 1. It would appear that he did not give his spheres any substance or mechanical connexion; the whole system was a purely geometrical hypothesis, or a set of theoretical constructions calculated to represent the apparent paths of the planets and enable them to be computed. We pass to the details of the system.

The moon has a motion produced by three spheres; the first and outermost moves in the same sense as the fixed stars from east to west in twenty-four hours; the second moves about an axis perpendicular to the plane of the zodiac circle or the ecliptic, and in a sense opposite to that of the daily rotation, i. e. from west to east; the third moves about an axis inclined to the axis of the second, at an angle equal to the highest latitude attained by the moon, and in the sense of the daily rotation from east to west; the moon is fixed on the equator of this third sphere. Simplicius observes that the third sphere is necessary because it is found that the moon does not always reach its highest north and south latitude at the same points of the zodiac, but at points which travel round the zodiac in the inverse order of the signs.[2] He says at the same time that

---

[1] Archimedes, ed. Heib., vol. ii, p. 248. 4–8; *The Works of Archimedes*, p. 223.
[2] Simplicius on *De caelo*, p. 495. 10–13, Heib.

the motion of the third sphere is slow, the motion of the node being 'quite small during each month', while he implies that the monthly motion round the heavens is produced by the second sphere, the equator of which is in the plane of the zodiac or ecliptic. The object of the third sphere was then to account for the retrograde motion of the nodes in about 18½ years. But it is clear (as Ideler saw) that Simplicius's statement about the speeds of the third and second spheres is incorrect. If it had been the third sphere which moved very slowly, as he says, the moon would only have passed through each node once in the course of 223 lunations, and would have been found for nine years north, and then for nine years south, of the ecliptic. In order that the moon may pass through the nodes as often as it is observed to do, it is necessary to interchange the speeds of the second and third spheres as given by Simplicius; that is, we must assume that the third sphere produces the monthly revolution of the moon from west to east in 27 days 5h. 5m. 36sec. (the draconitic or nodal month) round a circle inclined to the ecliptic at an angle equal to the greatest latitude of the moon, and then that this oblique circle is carried round by the second sphere in a retrograde sense along the ecliptic in a period of 223 lunations; lastly, we must assume that both the inner spheres, the second and third, are bodily carried round by the first sphere in 24 hours in the sense of the daily rotation. There can be no doubt that this was Eudoxus's conception of the matter. The mistake made by Simplicius seems to go back as far as Aristotle himself, since, in the passage of the *Metaphysics* quoted above, Aristotle clearly implies that the second sphere corresponds to the movement in longitude for all the seven bodies including the sun and moon, whereas in fact it only does so in the case of the five planets ; and no doubt Sosigenes, Simplicius's authority, accepted the statement of Aristotle, without suspecting that the Master might be an unsafe guide on such a subject. From the theory of Eudoxus as thus restored we can judge how far by his time the Greeks had progressed in the study of the motions of the moon. Observations had gone far enough to enable the movement in latitude and the retrogression of the nodes of the moon's orbit to be recognized. Eudoxus knew nothing of the variation of the moon's speed in longitude, or at least took no account of it, whereas Callippus was aware of it about 325 B.C., that is, about twenty or thirty years after Eudoxus's time.

As regards the sun, we learn from Aristotle that Eudoxus again assumed three spheres to explain its motion. As in the case of the moon, the first or outermost sphere revolved like the sphere of the fixed stars, the second moved about an axis perpendicular to the plane of the zodiac, its equator revolving accordingly in the plane of the zodiac, while the third moved so that its equator described a plane slightly inclined to that of the zodiac, the inclination being less in the case of the sun than in the case of the moon. Simplicius adds that the third sphere (which is necessary because the sun does not at the summer and winter solstices always rise at the same point on the horizon) moves much more slowly than the second and (unlike the corresponding sphere in the case of the moon) in the direct order of the signs.[1] Simplicius makes the same mistake as regards the speeds of the second and third spheres as he made in the case of the moon. If it were the third sphere which moved very slowly, the sun would for ages remain in a north or a south latitude and in the course of a year would describe, not a great circle, but (almost) a small circle parallel to the ecliptic. The slow motion must therefore belong to the second sphere, the equator of which revolves in the ecliptic, while the revolution of the third sphere must take place in about a year (strictly speaking, a little more than a tropic year in consequence of the supposed slow motion of the second sphere in the same sense), the plane of its equator being inclined, at the small angle mentioned, to the plane of the ecliptic. The slightly inclined great circle of the third sphere which the sun appears to describe is then carried round bodily in the revolution of the second sphere about the axis of the ecliptic, the nodes on the ecliptic thus moving slowly forward, in the direct order of the signs; and lastly both the second and third spheres are carried round by the revolution of the first sphere following the daily rotation.

The strange thing in this description of the sun's motion is the imaginary idea that its path is not in the ecliptic but in a circle inclined at a small angle to the latter. Simplicius says that Eudoxus ' and those who preceded him ' (τοῖς πρὸ αὐτοῦ) thought the sun had the three motions described, and that this was inferred

---

[1] Simplicius on *De caelo*, pp. 493. 15–17, 494. 6–7, 9–11.

from the fact that the sun, in the summer and winter solstices, does not always rise at the same point of the horizon.[1] We gather from this that even before Eudoxus's time astronomers had suspected a certain deviation in latitude on the part of the sun. Schiaparelli suggests as an explanation that, the early astronomers having discovered, by comparison with the fixed stars, the deviation of the moon and the five planets in latitude, it was natural for them to suppose that the sun also must deviate from the circle of the ecliptic; indeed it would be difficult for them to believe that the sun alone was exempt from such deviation. However this may be, the notion of the nutation of the sun's path survived for centuries. Hipparchus[2] quotes a sentence from the lost *Enoptron* of Eudoxus to the effect that 'it appears that the sun too shows a difference in the places where it appears at the solstices, though the difference is much less noticeable and indeed is quite small'; Hipparchus goes on to deny this on the ground that, if it were so, the prophecies by astronomers of lunar eclipses, which they made on the assumption that there was no deviation of the sun from the ecliptic, would sometimes have proved appreciably wrong, whereas in fact the eclipses never showed a difference of more than two 'finger-breadths', and only very rarely that, in comparison with the most accurately calculated predictions. Notwithstanding Hipparchus's great authority, the idea persisted, and we find later authors giving a value to the supposed inclination to the ecliptic. We are not told what Eudoxus supposed the angle to be, nor what he assumed as the period of revolution of the nodes. Pliny[3] gives the inclination as $1°$ on each side of the ecliptic; perhaps he misunderstood his source and took a range of $1°$ to be an inclination of $1°$. For Theon of Smyrna,[4] on the authority of Adrastus, says that the inclination is $\frac{1}{2}°$; Theon also says that the sun returns to the same latitude after $365\frac{1}{8}$ days, whereas it takes $365\frac{1}{4}$ days to return to the same equinox or solstice and $365\frac{1}{2}$ days to return to the same distance from us.[5] This shows that the solar nodes were thought to have a retrograde motion (not a motion in the order of the signs,

[1] Simplicius, loc. cit., p. 493. 11–17.
[2] Hipparchus, *In Arati et Eudoxi phaenomena*, i. 9, pp. 88–92, ed. Manitius.
[3] Pliny, *N.H.* ii. c. 16, § 67.
[4] Theon of Smyrna, ed. Hiller, pp. 135. 12–14, 194. 4–8.
[5] Ibid., p. 172. 15 – 173. 16.

as assumed by Eudoxus) and a period of $365\frac{1}{4} \div \frac{1}{8}$ or 2922 years. It is not known who invented this theory in the first instance. Schiaparelli shows that it was not started for the purpose of explaining the motion of the equinoctial points, or the precession of the equinoxes, which was discovered by Hipparchus, but was unknown to Eudoxus, Pliny, and Theon.

Eudoxus supposed the annual motion of the sun to be perfectly uniform ; he must therefore have deliberately ignored the discovery, made by Meton and Euctemon 60 or 70 years before, that the sun does not take the same time to describe the four quadrants of its orbit between the equinoctial and solstitial points. Eudoxus, in fact, seems to have definitely regarded the length of the seasons as being as nearly as possible equal, since he made three of them 91 days in length, only giving 92 days to the autumn in order to make up 365 days in the year.[1]

In the case of each of the planets Eudoxus assumed four spheres. The first and outermost produced the daily rotation in 24 hours, as in the case of the fixed stars ; the second produced the motion along the zodiac ' in the respective periods in which the planets appear to describe the zodiac circle ',[2] which periods, in the case of the superior planets, are respectively equal to the sidereal periods of revolution, and in the case of Mercury and Venus (on a geocentric system) one year. As the revolution of the second sphere was taken to be uniform, we see that Eudoxus had no idea of the zodiacal anomaly of the planets, namely that which depends on the eccentricity of their paths, and which later astronomers sought to account for by the hypothesis of eccentric circles ; for Eudoxus the points on the ecliptic where successive oppositions or conjunctions took place were always at the same distances, and the arcs of retrogradation were constant for each planet and equal at all parts of the ecliptic. Nor with him were the orbits of the planets inclined at all to the ecliptic ;

---

[1] This appears from the papyrus known under the title of *Ars Eudoxi*, deciphered by Letronne and published by Brunet de Presle (*Notices et extraits des manuscrits*, xviii. 2, 1865, p. 25 sq.). The papyrus was edited by Blass (Kiel, 1887), and a translation will be found in Tannery's *Recherches sur l'histoire de l'astronomie ancienne*, pp. 283–94. Tannery prefers the title restored by Letronne, *Didascalie céleste de Leptine*. The document, written in Egypt between the years 193 and 165 B. C., seems to have been a student's note-book, written perhaps during or after a course of lectures.

[2] Simplicius, loc. cit., p. 495. 25.

their motion in latitude was believed by Eudoxus to depend exclusively on their elongation from the sun and not on their longitude.
The third sphere had its poles at two opposite points on the zodiac
circle, the poles being carried round in the motion of the second
sphere; the revolution of the third sphere about the poles was
again uniform and took place in a period equal to the synodic
period of the planet or the time which elapsed between two successive oppositions or conjunctions with the sun. The poles of the third
sphere were different for all the planets, except that they were the
same for Mercury and Venus. The third sphere rotated according
to Simplicius ' from south to north and from north to south '[1] (this
followed of course from the position of the poles on the ecliptic);
the actual sense of the rotation is not clear from this, but Schiaparelli's exposition shows that it is immaterial whether we take the
one or the other. On the surface of the third sphere the poles of
the fourth sphere were fixed, the axis of the latter being inclined to
that of the former at an angle which was constant for each planet
but different for the different planets. And the rotation of the
fourth sphere about its axis took place in the same time as the rotation of the third about its axis but in the opposite sense. On the
equator of the fourth sphere the planet was fixed, the planet having
thus four motions, the daily rotation, the circuit in the zodiac, and
two other rotations taking place in the synodic period.

Simplicius gives the following clear explanation with regard to
the combined effect of the rotations of the third and fourth spheres.

' The third sphere, which has its poles on the great circle of the
second sphere passing through the middle of the signs of the zodiac,
and which turns from south to north and from north to south, will
carry round with it the fourth sphere which also has the planet
attached to it, and will moreover be the cause of the planet's movement in latitude. But not the third sphere only; for, so far as it
was on the third sphere (by itself), the planet would actually have
arrived at the poles of the zodiac circle and would have come near
to the poles of the universe; but, as things are, the fourth sphere,
which turns about the poles of the inclined circle carrying the
planet and rotates in the opposite sense to the third, i.e. from east
to west, but in the same period, will prevent any considerable divergence (on the part of the planet) from the zodiac circle, and will

---

[1] Simplicius, loc. cit., p. 496. 23.

cause the planet to describe about this same zodiac circle the curve called by Eudoxus the *hippopede*, so that the breadth of this curve will be the (maximum) amount of the apparent deviation of the planet in latitude, a view for which Eudoxus has been attacked.' [1]

Following up the hint here given, Schiaparelli set himself to investigate the actual path of a planet subject to the rotations of the third and fourth spheres only, leaving out of account for the moment the motions of the first two spheres producing respectively the daily rotation and the motion along the zodiac. The problem is, as he says, in its simplest expression, the following. 'A sphere rotates uniformly about the fixed diameter AB. P, P' are two

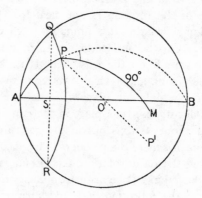

Fig. 6.

opposite poles on this sphere, and a second sphere concentric with the first rotates uniformly about PP' in the same time as the former sphere takes to turn about AB, but in the opposite direction. M is a point on the second sphere equidistant from the poles P, P' (in other words, a point on the equator of the second sphere). Required to find the path of the point M.' This is not difficult nowadays for any one familiar with spherical trigonometry and analytical geometry; but it was necessary for Schiaparelli to show that the solution was within the powers of Eudoxus. He accordingly develops a solution by means of a series of seven propositions or problems involving only elementary geometrical considerations, which would have

[1] Simplicius, loc. cit., pp. 496. 23 – 497. 5.

presented no difficulty to a geometer of the calibre of Eudoxus;
and he finds that, sure enough, the path of M in space is a figure
like a lemniscate but described on the surface of a sphere, that is, the
fixed sphere about AB as diameter. This 'spherical lemniscate',
as Schiaparelli calls it, is shown as well as I can show it in the
annexed figure (Fig. 7). Its double point is on the circumference of
the plane section of the sphere which is at right angles to AB, and
it is symmetrical about that plane as well as about the circumference of a circular section which has AB for diameter and is in what
Schiaparelli calls the 'fundamental plane', the plane of the great
circle with diameter AB on which the pole P and the planet M are

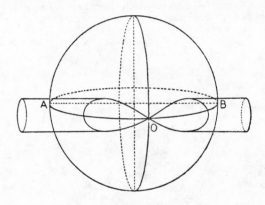

Fig. 7.

found at the same moment. The curve is actually the intersection
of the sphere with a certain cylinder touching it internally at the
double point, namely a cylinder with diameter equal to AS,
the *sagitta* (see Fig. 6) of the diameter of the small circle of
the sphere on which the pole P revolves. But the curve is also
the intersection of *either* the sphere *or* the cylinder with a certain
cone with vertex O, axis parallel to the axis of the cylinder
(i.e. touching the circle AOB at O) and vertical angle equal to
the 'inclination' (the angle $AO'P$ in Fig. 6).[1] For clearness' sake

---

[1] Schiaparelli's geometrical propositions are too long to be quoted here, but
the whole thing can be worked out analytically in a reasonable space. This is
done by Norbert Herz (*Geschichte der Bahnbestimmung von Planeten und*

I show in another figure (Fig. 9, p. 206) a right section of the cylinder by a plane passing through O and perpendicular to AB in the figure immediately preceding (Fig. 7).

The arc of the great circle AOB which bisects the 'spherical lemniscate' laterally is equal in length to the arc QAR of the great circle $AQBR$ (Figs. 6 and 8) and is of course divided at the double point O into equal halves of length equal to the arc AQ.

Kometen, Part I, Leipzig, 1887, pp. 20, 21), and I quote the solution exactly as he gives it :—

Let AB be the axis of the first sphere, and the circle AOB the circle in which P, P', the poles of the second sphere, and M the position of the planet, are found together at the same moment. Suppose that the motion of the two spheres is in the direction of the arrows and that, when the circle APB has moved through an angle θ, PM, the circle carrying the planet has also moved through the same angle, M being the position of the planet.

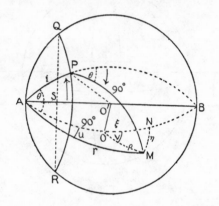

Fig. 8.

Let i be the *inclination* $AO'P$, r the arc of a great circle AM, u (measured positively downwards) the angle OAM.

Then in the triangle PAM we have, since $PM = 90°$,

$$\cos r = -\sin i \cos \theta,$$
$$\sin r \cos (\theta + u) = +\cos i \cos \theta,$$
$$\sin r \sin (\theta + u) = +\sin \theta.$$

Multiplying the second equation by $(-\sin \theta)$ and the third by $\cos \theta$, and adding, we have

$$\sin r \sin u = \sin \theta \cos \theta (1 - \cos i) = \sin^2 \tfrac{1}{2} i \sin 2\theta.$$

Multiplying the second equation by $\cos \theta$ and the third by $\sin \theta$, and adding, we have

$$\begin{aligned}
\sin r \cos u &= \sin^2 \theta + \cos i \cos^2 \theta \\
&= (\cos^2 \tfrac{1}{2} i + \sin^2 \tfrac{1}{2} i) \sin^2 \theta + (\cos^2 \tfrac{1}{2} i - \sin^2 \tfrac{1}{2} i) \cos^2 \theta \\
&= \cos^2 \tfrac{1}{2} i - \sin^2 \tfrac{1}{2} i \cos 2\theta \\
&= 1 - 2 \sin^2 \tfrac{1}{2} i \cos^2 \theta.
\end{aligned}$$

The breadth of the 'lemniscate', i.e. the *linear* distance between the two points on either loop of maximum latitude, north and south is equal to the diameter of the cylinder, i.e. to the sagitta AS. The angle at which the curve intersects itself at O is equal to the *inclination* $(PO'A)$ of the axes of rotation of the two spheres. The four points on the curve of greatest latitude, the double point and the two extreme points at which it intersects

Next, in the triangle AOM, if $OM = \rho$, and v is the exterior angle at O, we have, since $AO = 90°$,

$$\cos\rho = \sin r \cos u,$$
$$\sin\rho \sin v = \sin r \sin u,$$
$$\sin\rho \cos v = -\cos r;$$

therefore, if ξ, η be the 'spherical coordinates' of M with reference to origin O, we have, in the triangle OMN, and by using the results obtained above,

$$\sin\eta = \sin v \sin\rho = \sin^2 \tfrac{1}{2}i \sin 2\theta,$$
$$\cot\xi = \frac{\cot\rho}{\cos v} = -\tan r \cos u = \frac{1 - 2\sin^2\tfrac{1}{2}i\cos^2\theta}{\sin i \cos\theta}.$$

If now we use a system of rectangular coordinates x, y, z, with origin at O, z being measured along OO', and x, y being the projections of the arcs ξ, η on the plane AQB at right angles to OO' (y being positive in the upward direction, i. e. in the opposite direction to u, v), we have for the projections $O'N'$, $M'N'$, v', ρ' of ON, MN, v, ρ respectively

$$O'N' = x; \quad M'N' = -y,$$
$$v' = v,$$
$$\rho' = R\sin\rho,$$

where R is the radius of the sphere.

Consequently $x = \rho'\cos v' = R\sin\rho\cos v = -R\cos r,$
$$y = -\rho'\sin v' = -R\sin\rho\sin v = -R\sin r \sin u;$$

whence we have

$$x = R\sin i \cos\theta,$$
$$y = -R\sin^2\tfrac{1}{2}i\sin 2\theta.$$

This gives at once the projection of the *hippopede* on the plane AQB as constructed by Schiaparelli.

So far Norbert Herz. But we can also obtain the remainder of Schiaparelli's results, as follows.

We have for z, the third coordinate of M,

$$z = R(1 - \cos\rho) = R(1 - \sin r \cos u)$$
$$= 2R\sin^2\tfrac{1}{2}i\cos^2\theta = R\sin^2\tfrac{1}{2}i(1 + \cos 2\theta).$$

Eliminating θ from the equations for y and z, we obtain

$$(z - R\sin^2\tfrac{1}{2}i)^2 + y^2 = R^2\sin^4\tfrac{1}{2}i.$$

Therefore M lies on a cylinder which has its axis parallel to AB, touches the sphere internally at O, and has its radius equal to $R\sin^2\tfrac{1}{2}i$, i.e. its diameter equal to $R(1 - \cos i)$, which is the sagitta AS in Fig. 6 and Fig. 8. That is, the *hippopede* is the curve of intersection of this cylinder with the sphere.

The sphere being $x^2 + y^2 + z^2 = 2Rz$, and the cylinder $y^2 + z^2 = 2Rz\sin^2\tfrac{1}{2}i$, the cone is easily found to be

$$x^2 + y^2 + z^2 = x^2\sec^2\tfrac{1}{2}i.$$

the 'fundamental plane' through AB, divide the curve into eight arcs which are described by the planet in equal times. Schiaparelli shows how to construct the projection of the curve upon the plane through AB perpendicular to the plane which bisects the curve longitudinally. Describe, he says, a circle with radius equal to QS, the radius of the small circle described by P (Fig. 6). Then, with the same centre, draw a smaller circle with radius equal to half the sagitta AS. Divide the lesser circle into any number of equal parts, say 8, as at the points marked 0, 1, 2, 3 . . . 7 round the circle, and suppose the same points marked again with the numbers 8, 9, 10 . . . 15 respectively ; divide the greater circle into double the

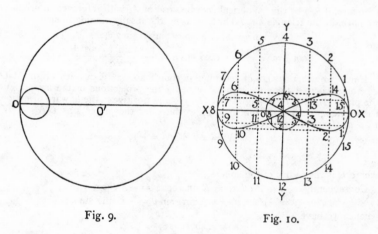

Fig. 9.   Fig. 10.

number of equal parts as at the points marked 0, 1, 2, 3, 4, 5 . . . 15 (arranging the points so that those marked 0 are opposite one another on a common diameter XX, while the numbers go round in the same sense). Draw YY through the centre perpendicular to XX, and through the points of division of the outer circle draw chords parallel to YY, and through the points of division of the inner circle straight lines parallel to XX. The points of intersection of the lines give a series of points on the projection of the 'spherical lemniscate'. These points are again marked in the figure by the numbers 0, 1, 2 . . . . 15. The projection of the position of the planet moves along this curve in the direction indicated by the successive numbers.

There is no doubt that Schiaparelli has restored, in his 'spherical lemniscate ', the *hippopede* of Eudoxus, the fact being confirmed by the application of the same term *hippopede* (horse-fetter) by Proclus[1] to a plane curve of similar shape formed by a plane section of an anchor-ring or *tore* touching the tore internally and parallel to its axis.

So far account has only been taken of the motion due to the combination of the rotations of the third and fourth spheres. But A, B, the poles of the third sphere (Figs. 6–8), are carried round the zodiac or ecliptic by the motion of the second sphere and in a time equal to the ' zodiacal' period of the planet. Now the longitudinal axis of the 'spherical lemniscate' (the arc of the great circle bisecting it longitudinally) always lies on the ecliptic. We may therefore substitute the 'lemniscate' moving bodily round the ecliptic for the third and fourth spheres, the planet meantime moving round the 'lemniscate' in the manner described above. The combination of the two motions (that of the ' lemniscate' and that of the planet on it) gives the motion of the planet through the constellations. The motion of the planet round the curve is an oscillatory motion, now forward in acceleration of the motion round the ecliptic due to the second sphere, now backward in retardation of the same motion ; the period of the oscillation is the period of the synodic revolution, and the acceleration and retardation occupy half the period respectively. When the retardation in the sense of longitude due to the backward oscillation is greater than the speed of the forward motion of the ' lemniscate' itself, the planet will for a time have a retrograde motion, at the beginning and end of which it will appear stationary for a little while, when the two opposite motions balance each other. The greatest acceleration of the planet in longitude, and the greatest retardation (or the quickest rate of retrograde motion), occur at the times when the planet passes through the double point of the curve. The movements must therefore be so combined that the planet is at the double point and moving in the forward direction at the time of superior conjunction with the sun, when the apparent speed of the planet in longitude is greatest, while it is again at the double point but moving in the backward direction when it is in opposition or inferior conjunction, at which times the apparent

[1] Proclus, *Comm. on Eucl. I*, ed. Friedlein, p. 112. 5.

retrograde motion of the planet is quickest. This combination of motions will be accompanied by motion in latitude within limits defined by the breadth of the lemniscate ; the planet will, during a synodic revolution, twice reach its greatest north and south latitude respectively and four times cross the ecliptic.

The actual shape of the *hippopede* and its dimensions relatively to the sphere on which it is drawn are fully determined when we know the inclination of the axis of the fourth sphere to that of the third, since they depend on this inclination exclusively. In order to test the working of the theory with regard to the several planets we need to know three things, (1) the inclination referred to, (2) the period of the 'zodiacal' or sidereal revolution, (3) the synodic period, in the case of each planet. We are not told what angles of inclination Eudoxus assumed, but the zodiacal and synodic periods which he ascribed to the five planets are given in round figures by Simplicius.[1] The following is a comparison of Eudoxus's figures with the modern values :

	Synodic period		Zodiacal period	
	Eudoxus	*Modern value*	*Eudoxus*	*Modern value*
Saturn	13 months	378 days	30 years	29 years 166 days
Jupiter	13 months	399 days	12 years	11 years 315 days
Mars	8 months 20 days	780 days	2 years	1 year 322 days
Mercury	110 days	116 days	1 year	1 year
Venus	19 months	584 days	1 year	1 year

Except in the case of Mars, these figures are tolerably accurate, while the papyrus purporting to contain the *Ars Eudoxi* gives for the synodic period of Mercury the exact modern figure of 116 days ; it is therefore clear that Eudoxus went on the basis of very careful observations, whether he obtained the results from Egypt or from Babylonian sources. As unfortunately the inclinations assumed by Eudoxus (the third factor required for the reconstruction of the system) are not recorded, Schiaparelli has to conjecture them for himself. Assuming that they would be such as to produce ' lemniscates ' which would give arcs of retrogradation corresponding to those actually observed, he takes the known retrograde arc of Saturn (6°) and observes that by the help of the zodiacal period of 30 years and the synodic period of 13 months, and by assuming

[1] Simplicius, loc. cit., pp. 495. 26-9, 496. 6-9.

6° as the 'inclination', a retrograde arc of about 6° is actually obtained; the length of the *hippopede* (the arc of the great circle of the sphere bisecting the curve longitudinally) is 12°, and the half of its breadth about 9′, a maximum deviation from the ecliptic which would of course be imperceptible to the observers of those days. In the case of Jupiter, assuming an inclination of 13°, and consequently a *hippopede* of 26° in length and twice 44′ in breadth, with a zodiacal period of 12 years and a synodic period of 13 months, he deduces a retrograde arc of about 8°; and again the divergence in latitude of 44′ would hardly be noticed. For these two planets, therefore, Eudoxus's method gave an excellent solution of Plato's problem of finding how the motion of the planets can be accounted for by a combination of uniform circular motions.

With Mars, however, the system fails. We have no means of knowing how Eudoxus came to put the synodic period at 8 months and 20 days, or 260 days, whereas it is really 780 days, or three times as long. But, whether we take 780 days or 260 days, the theory does not account for the facts. If the synodic period is 780 days, and we take for the length of the *hippopede* the greatest arc permissible according to Simplicius's account, namely an arc of 180°, corresponding to an 'inclination' of 90°, the breadth of the curve becomes 60°, so that Mars ought to diverge in latitude to the extent of 30°. Also, even under this extreme hypothesis, the retrograde motion of Mars on the *hippopede* cannot reach a speed equal to that of the direct motion of the *hippopede* itself along the ecliptic (the zodiacal period being 2 years); consequently Mars should not have any retrograde motion at all and should only move very slowly at opposition. To obtain a retrograde motion at all we should require an 'inclination' greater than 90°, and consequently the third and fourth spheres would rotate in the same instead of the opposite sense, which is contrary to Simplicius's statement; and, even if this were permissible, there is the objection that Mars's deviations in latitude would exceed 30°, and Eudoxus would never have assumed such an amount of deviation. On the other hand, to assume a synodic period of 260 days would produce a retrograde motion; by assuming an inclination of 34° we get 68° as the length of the *hippopede* and a maximum deviation in latitude of 4° 53′, which is not very far from the true deviation; the retrograde arc becomes about 16°, which is little greater than that disclosed by observation. This way of producing approximate agreement with observed facts may perhaps have been what led Eudoxus to assume a synodic period one third as long as the real period; but unfortunately the hypothesis gives two retrograde motions outside the oppositions with the sun, and six stationary points, four of which have no real existence.

As regards Mercury and Venus, inasmuch as their mean positions coincide with the mean position of the sun, Eudoxus must have assumed that the centre of the *hippopede* always coincides with the sun. This centre being on the ecliptic and at a distance of 90° from each of the poles of rotation of the third sphere, the poles of the third sphere of Mercury and the poles of the third sphere of Venus coincide, a fact for which we have the independent testimony of Aristotle in the passage quoted above. As the mean position of each of the two planets coincides with that of the sun, and the greatest elongation of each from the sun is half the length of the corresponding *hippopede*, Eudoxus doubtless determined the 'inclination' from the observed elongations. In the case of Mercury, with a maximum elongation of 23°, the length of the *hippopede* becomes 46°, and the half of its breadth or the greatest latitude is 2° 14', nearly as great as the observed deviation. The retrograde arc for Mercury would be about 6°, which is much smaller than the true length; but, as this mistake occurs in a part of the synodic circuit which cannot be observed, the theory cannot be blamed for this. In the visible portions of the circuit the longitudes are represented with fair accuracy, though the times of greatest elongation do not exactly agree with the facts. For Venus, taking the greatest elongation (and consequently the 'inclination') at 46°, we have a *hippopede* 92° in length, and a half-breadth or maximum latitude of 8° 54', which is roughly in agreement with the greatest latitude as observed. But, since the synodic period as given by Eudoxus, 570 days, is more than 1½ times the zodiacal period, Venus, like Mars, can never have a retrograde motion; and this error cannot be avoided whatever value we choose to substitute for 46° as the inclination. Another serious fault of the theory is that it requires Venus to take the same time to pass from the extreme eastern point to the extreme western point

of the *hippopcde* as it takes to return from the extreme
western to the extreme eastern point, whereas in fact Venus takes
441 days (out of the synodic period of 584 days) to pass from the
greatest eastern to the greatest western elongation and only 143
days to return from the greatest western to the greatest eastern
elongation. As regards latitude, too, the imperfection of the theory
is more marked in the case of Venus than in that of the other
planets; for the *hippopede* intersects the ecliptic four times, once
at each extremity, and twice at the double point; consequently
the planet ought to cross the ecliptic four times during each synodic
period, which is not the case, as the latitude of Venus is only *nil*
twice during each sidereal revolution.

   To sum up. For the sun and moon the hypothesis of Eudoxus
sufficed to explain adequately enough the principal phenomena,
except the irregularities due to the eccentricities, which were either
unknown to Eudoxus or neglected by him. For Jupiter and
Saturn, and to some extent for Mercury also, the system was
capable of giving on the whole a satisfactory explanation of their
motion in longitude, their stationary points and their retrograde
motions; for Venus it was unsatisfactory, and it failed altogether
in the case of Mars. The limits of motion in latitude represented
by the various *hippopedes* were in tolerable agreement with observed
facts, although the periods of the deviations and their places in
the cycle were quite wrong. But, notwithstanding the imper-
fections of the system of homocentric spheres, we cannot but
recognize in it a speculative achievement which was worthy of the
great reputation of Eudoxus and all the more deserving of admiration because it was the first attempt at a scientific explanation of
the apparent irregularities of the motions of the planets. And,
as Schiaparelli says, if any one, as the result of a superficial study
of the theory, finds it complicated, let him remember that in
none of his hypotheses does Eudoxus make use of more than three
constants or elements, namely the epoch of a superior conjunction,
the period of sidereal revolution (on which the synodic period is
dependent), and the inclination to one another of the axes of the
third and fourth spheres, which inclination determines completely
the dimensions of the *hippopede*; whereas in our time we require, for
the same purpose, six elements in the case of each planet.

212 THEORY OF CONCENTRIC SPHERES PART I

Eudoxus died in 355 B.C. at the age of 53. His doctrine of homocentric spheres was further studied in his school. Menaechmus, the reputed discoverer of the conic sections, and one of his pupils, is mentioned as a supporter of the theory.[1] Polemarchus of Cyzicus, a friend of Eudoxus, is also mentioned as having studied the subject, and, in particular, as having been aware of the objection raised to the system of homocentric spheres on the ground that the difference in the brightness of the planets, especially Venus and Mars, and in the apparent size of the moon, at different times, showed that they could not always be at the same distance from us; 'Polemarchus appears to have been aware of it' (the variation in the distances of each planet) 'but to have neglected it as not perceptible, because he preferred the assumption that the spheres themselves are about the centre of the universe'.[2] But it is Callippus to whom definite improvements in the system are attributed. Callippus of Cyzicus, the most famous and capable astronomer of his time, probably lived between 370 and 300 B.C.; he was therefore perhaps too young to be a pupil of Eudoxus himself; but he studied with Polemarchus and he followed [3] Polemarchus to Athens, where 'he stayed with Aristotle correcting and completing, with Aristotle's help, the discoveries of Eudoxus'.[4] This must have been during the reign of Alexander the Great (336–323 B.C.), at which time Aristotle was in Athens; it must also have been about the time when Callippus brought out his improvement of Meton's luni-solar cycle, since the beginning of Callippus's cycle was in 330 B.C. (28th or 29th June). Aristotle himself gives Callippus the sole credit for certain improvements on Eudoxus's system; immediately after the passage above quoted from the *Metaphysics* he says:

'Callippus agreed with Eudoxus in the position he assigned to the spheres, that is to say, in their arrangement in respect of distances, and he also assigned the same number of spheres as Eudoxus did to Zeus and Kronos respectively, but he thought it necessary to add two more spheres in each case to the sun and moon respectively, if one wishes to account for the phenomena, and one more to each of the other planets.'[5]

---

[1] Theon of Smyrna, ed. Hiller, pp. 201. 25 – 202. 1.

[2] Simplicius on *De caelo* ii. 12, p. 505. 21, Heib.

[3] μετ᾽ ἐκεῖνον εἰς Ἀθήνας ἐλθών. Schiaparelli translates μετ᾽ ἐκεῖνον as if it were μετ᾽ ἐκείνου, 'with him'.

[4] Simplicius, op. cit., p. 493. 5–8. [5] Aristotle, *Metaph.* Λ. 8, 1073 b 32–8.

Simplicius says that no book by Callippus on the subject was extant in his time, nor did Aristotle give any explanation of the reasons why Callippus added the extra spheres;

' but Eudemus shortly stated what were the phenomena in explanation of which Callippus thought it necessary to assume the additional spheres. According to Eudemus, Callippus asserted that, assuming the periods between the solstices and equinoxes to differ to the extent that Euctemon and Meton held that they did, the three spheres in each case (i. e. for the sun and moon) are not sufficient to save the phenomena, in view of the irregularity which is observed in their motions. But the reason why he added the one sphere which he added in the case of each of the three planets Ares, Aphrodite, and Hermes was shortly and clearly stated by Eudemus.' [1]

As regards the planets therefore, although we are informed that Eudemus gave the reason for the addition of a fifth sphere in each case, we are not told what the reason was, and we can only resort to conjecture. Schiaparelli observes that, since Callippus was content with Eudoxus's hypothesis about Jupiter and Saturn, we may conclude that their zodiacal inequality was still unknown to him, although it can reach the value of 6° in each case, and also that he regarded their deviations in latitude as non-existent or negligible. But the glaring deficiencies in the theory of Eudoxus when applied to Mars would suggest the urgent need for some improvement which should, in particular, produce the necessary retrograde motion in this case without the assumption of a synodic period different from the true one. It is sufficiently probable therefore that the fifth sphere was intended for the purpose of satisfying this latter condition. Schiaparelli observes that, on the assumption of a synodic period of 780 days, it is possible, by a combination of *three* spheres taking the place of Eudoxus's last two (the third and fourth), to obtain a retrograde motion agreeing sufficiently with observed facts, and this can be done in various ways without involving too considerable deviations in latitude; he gives, as the simplest arrangement leading to the desired result, the following.

Let AOB (Fig. 11) represent the ecliptic and A, B two opposite points on it which make the circuit of the zodiac in the zodiacal period of Mars. Let a sphere (the third of Eudoxus) revolve about

---

[1] Simplicius on *De caelo* ii. 12, p. 497. 17–24.

A, B as poles in the period of the synodic revolution. Take any point P_1 on the equator of this sphere as pole of another sphere (the fourth) rotating about its poles at twice the speed of the third sphere, in the opposite direction to the latter, and carrying with it P_2, distant from P_1 by an arc $P_1 P_2$ (which we will call the 'inclination'). About P_2 as pole, let a fifth sphere rotate at the same speed and

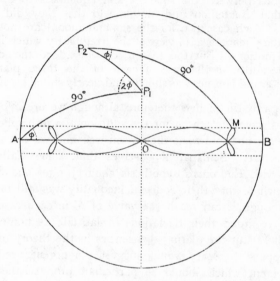

Fig. 11.

in the same direction as the third, carrying the planet fixed on its equator at the point M. It is easy to see that, if at the beginning of the motion the three points P_1, P_2, M lie on the ecliptic in the order $AP_2 P_1 MB$, then at any time afterwards the angle ϕ at A will be equal to the angle at P_2 between $P_2 P_1$ and $P_2 M$, while the angle $AP_1 P_2$ at P_1 will be twice as large. And, since $AP_1 = P_2 M = 90°$, the planet M will in the synodic period describe a curve adjacent to the ecliptic and symmetrical about it which will take a different form according to the value given to the 'inclination' $P_1 P_2$. This curve will for certain values of $P_1 P_2$ extend considerably in length but little in breadth and, as it has its centre at O midway between the poles A, B, it will, like the *hippopede*, produce a direct and retrograde motion alternately, but will have the advantage over the *hippopede* that it can give the planet in the neighbourhood of O a much greater direct and retrograde velocity with the same motion in latitude. Hence it is capable of giving the planet a retrograde motion where the *hippopede* fails to do so. If, for example, P_1P_2 is put equal to ⁻45°, the curve takes a form like that shown in the figure (in projection). The greatest deviation in latitude does not exceed 4° 11′, the curve has a length along the ecliptic of $95\frac{1}{3}°$, and has two triple points near the ends at a distance of 45° from the centre O. When the planet is passing O, its velocity is 1·2929 times the speed of the rotation of P_1 about AB. As the period of rotation of P_1 about AB is equal to the synodic period, 780 days, the daily motion of P_1 is 360°/780 or 0°·462, which multiplied by 1·2929 gives 0°·597 as the daily retrograde motion on the curve at O. And, as O has a direct motion on the ecliptic of 360°/686 = 0°·525, the resulting daily retrograde motion is 0°·072, which is a reasonable approximation to the fact.

Similarly an additional sphere might be made to remove the imperfection of the theory as applied to Venus. If the 'inclination' P_1P_2 is made 45°, the greatest elongation is $47\frac{2}{3}°$, which is very near the truth; and the different speed of the planet in the four parts of the synodic revolution is also better accounted for, since, in the curve above drawn, the passage from one triple point to the other takes one fourth of the time, the same passage back again another fourth, while the remaining two fourths are occupied by the very slow motion round the small loops at the ends. For Mercury the theory of Eudoxus gave a fairly correct result, and doubtless it would be possible by means of another sphere to attain a still greater degree of accuracy.

According to Eudemus, Callippus added two new spheres (making five) in the case of the sun, in order to account for the unequal motion in longitude which had been discovered a hundred years earlier by Meton and Euctemon. Euctemon had made the length of the seasons (beginning with the vernal equinox) 93, 90, 90, and 92 days respectively, showing errors ranging from 1·23 to 2·01 days; this was about 430 B.C. Callippus, about 330 B.C., made the corresponding lengths 94, 92, 89, 90 days respectively,[1] the errors

[1] *Ars Eudoxi*, § 55.

ranging from c·08 to 0·44 days only; this shows the great advance made in observations of the sun during the century between the two dates. Now Callippus had only to retain the three spheres assumed by Eudoxus for the sun and then to add two spheres, (1) a sphere with its poles on the third sphere of Eudoxus which described the orbit of the sun at uniform speed in the course of a year, and (2) a sphere carrying the sun on its equator and having its poles on the preceding sphere and its axis slightly inclined to the axis of the same sphere; the second of these spheres would rotate at the same speed as the first but in the opposite direction. If the inclination of the axes is equal to the greatest inequality (which was for Callippus, as it is for us, 2°), the two new spheres give for the sun a *hippopede*, the length of which along the ecliptic is 4° and the breadth nearly 1′ on each side of it; this representation of the motion of the sun is almost as accurate as that obtained later by means of the eccentric circle and the epicycle.

Simplicius's explanation of the reason why Callippus added two spheres in the case of the moon also is rather confused, because he tries to deal with the sun and moon in one sentence. But he presumably meant that the reason in the case of the moon was similar to the reason in the case of the sun; in other words, Callippus was aware of the inequality in the motion of the moon in longitude. This inequality, which often reaches as much as 8°, would necessarily reveal itself as soon as the intervals between a large number of successive lunar eclipses were noted and compared with the corresponding longitudes of the moon, which can in this case easily be deduced from those of the sun. The inclination between the axes of the two new spheres would in this case have to be taken equal to the mean inequality of 6°, and a *hippopede* of 12° would mean a maximum deviation from the moon's path of 9′, so that the moon's motion in latitude would not be sensibly affected.

Whether Callippus actually arranged his additional spheres in the way suggested by Schiaparelli or not, the improvements which he made were doubtless of the nature indicated above; and his motive was that of better 'saving the phenomena', his comparison of the theory of Eudoxus with the results of actual observation having revealed differences sufficiently pronounced to necessitate a remodelling of the theory.

We now come to the changes which Aristotle thought it necessary to make in the system of Eudoxus and Callippus. We have seen that that system was purely geometrical and theoretical; there was nothing mechanical about it. Aristotle's point of view was entirely different. Aristotle, as we shall see, transformed the purely abstract and geometrical theory into a mechanical system of spheres, i.e. spherical shells, in actual contact with one another; this made it almost necessary, instead of assuming separate sets of spheres, one set for each planet, to make all the sets part of one continuous system of spheres. For this purpose yet other spheres had to be added which Aristotle calls 'unrolling' or 'back-rolling' (ἀνελίττουσαι),[1] by which is meant 'reacting' in the sense of counteracting the motion of certain of Eudoxus's and Callippus's spheres which, for the sake of distinction, we may with Schiaparelli call 'deferent'. Aristotle's theory and its motive are given quite clearly in the chapter of the *Metaphysics* to which reference has already been made. The words come immediately after the description of Callippus's additions to the theory.

'But it is necessary, if the phenomena are to be produced by all the spheres acting in combination (συντεθεῖσαι), to assume in the case of each of the planets other spheres fewer by one [than the spheres assigned to it by Eudoxus and Callippus]; these latter spheres are those which unroll, or react on, the others in such a way as to replace the first sphere of the next lower planet in the same position [as if the spheres assigned to the respective planets above it did not exist], for only in this way is it possible for a combined system to produce the motion of the planets. Now the deferent spheres are, first, eight [for Saturn and Jupiter], then twenty-five more [for the sun, the moon, and the three other planets]; and of these only the last set [of five] which carry the planet placed lowest [the moon] do not require any reacting spheres. Thus the reacting spheres for the first two bodies will be six, and for the next four will be sixteen; and the total number of spheres, including the deferent spheres and those which react on them, will be fifty-five. If, however, we choose not to add to the sun and moon the [additional deferent] spheres we mentioned [i.e. the two added to each by Callippus], the total number of the spheres will be forty-seven. So much for the number of the spheres.'[2]

---

[1] Theophrastus, we are told (Simplicius, loc. cit., p. 504. 6), called them ἀνταναφέρουσαι.

[2] Aristotle, *Metaph.* Λ. 8, 1073 b 38 – 1074 a 15.

The way in which the system would work is explained very diffusely by Sosigenes in Simplicius;[1] Schiaparelli puts the matter quite clearly and shortly, thus. The different sets of spheres being merged into one, it is necessary to provide against the motion of the spheres assigned to a higher planet affecting the motion of the spheres assigned to a lower planet. For this purpose Aristotle interpolated between the last (the innermost) sphere of each planet and the first (or outermost) sphere of the planet next below it a certain number of spheres called 'reacting' spheres. Thus, suppose A, B, C, D to be the four spheres postulated for Saturn, A being the outermost and D the innermost on which the planet is fixed. If inside the sphere D we place a first reacting sphere D' which turns about the poles of D with equal speed, but in the opposite sense, to D, the rotations of D and D' will mutually cancel each other and any point of D' will move as though it was rigidly connected with the sphere C. Again, if we place inside the sphere D' a second reagent sphere C' rotating about the same poles with C and with equal speed, but in the opposite sense, the rotations of C and C' cancel each other, and any point of C' will move as if it were rigidly connected with the sphere B. Lastly, if inside C' a third reagent sphere B' is introduced which rotates about the same poles with B and at the same speed but in the opposite sense, the rotations of B and B' will cancel each other and any point of B' will move as if it were rigidly connected with the sphere A. But, as A is the outermost sphere for Saturn, A is the motion of the sphere of the fixed stars; hence B' will move in the same way as the sphere of the fixed stars ; and consequently Jupiter's spheres can move inside B' as if the spheres of Saturn did not exist and as if B' itself were the sphere of the fixed stars.

Hence it is clear that, if n is the number of the deferent spheres of a planet, the addition of $n-1$ reacting spheres inside them neutralizes the operation of $n-1$ of the original n spheres and prevents the inner set of spheres from being disturbed by the outer set. The innermost of the $n-1$ reacting spheres moves, as above shown, in the same way as the sphere of the fixed stars. But the first sphere of the next nearer planet (as of all the planets) is also a sphere with the same motion as that of the sphere of the fixed

[1] Simplicius on *De caelo* ii. 12, pp. 498. 1 - 503. 9.

stars, and consequently we have two spheres, one just inside the
other, with one and the same motion, that is, doing the work of one
sphere only. Aristotle could therefore have dispensed with the
second of these, namely the first of the spheres belonging to
the inner planet, without detriment to the working of his system ;
and, as the number of 'planets' inside the outermost, Saturn, is six,
he could have saved six spheres out of his total number.

Aristotle omits, as unnecessary, any reacting spheres for the
last and innermost planet, the moon. Yet, as Martin points out,[1]
Aristotle should have realized that, strictly speaking, the account
which he gives in the *Meteorologica* of shooting stars, comets, and
the Milky Way necessitates the introduction of four reacting
spheres below the moon. For, according to Aristotle, these
phenomena are the effects of exhalations rising to the top of the
sublunary sphere and there coming into contact with another
warm and dry substance which, being the last layer of the sublunary
sphere and in contact with the revolution of the outer heavenly
sphere, is carried round with it ; the rising exhalations are kindled
by meeting and being caught in the other substance and are carried
round with it. Hence there must be a sphere below the moon
which has the same revolution as that of the sphere of the fixed
stars, in order that comets, &c., may be produced and move as they
are said to do. The four inner spheres producing the moon's own
motion should therefore be neutralized as usual by the same
number of reacting spheres.

As it is, however, the hypotheses of Callippus, with the additions
of spheres actually made by Aristotle, work out thus :

	Deferent spheres	Reacting spheres
For Saturn	4	3
,, Jupiter	4	3
,, Mars	5	4
,, Mercury	5	4
,, Venus	5	4
,, Sun	5	4
,, Moon	5	0
Total	33	+ 22 = 55

In saying that, if Callippus's additional spheres for the sun and
moon are left out, the total number of spheres becomes 47, it would

[1] *Mémoires de l'Acad. des Inscr. et Belles-Lettres*, xxx. 1881, pp. 263-4.

seem that Aristotle made an arithmetical slip ;[1] for the omission would reduce the number 55 by 6 (4 deferent and 2 reacting), not by 8, and would leave 49, not 47. The remark would also seem to show that Aristotle did not feel quite certain that the two additional spheres assumed by Callippus for the sun and moon respectively were really necessary. We may compare the passage in the *De caelo* where he definitely regards the sun and moon as having fewer motions than some of the planets ; in that passage he endeavours to explain two 'difficulties' (ἀπορίαι), one of which is stated as follows :

'What can be the reason why the principle that the bodies which are at a greater distance from the first motion [the daily rotation of the sphere of the fixed stars] are moved by more movements does not apply throughout, but it is the middle bodies which have most movements? For it would appear reasonable that, as the first body [the sphere of the fixed stars] has one motion only, the nearest body to it should be moved by the next fewest movements, say two, the next to that by three, or in accordance with some other similar arrangement. But in practice the opposite is what happens ; for the sun and moon are moved by fewer movements than some of the planets, and yet the latter are further from the centre and nearer the first body [the sphere of the fixed stars] than the sun and moon are. In the case of some planets this is even observable by the eye ; for, at a time when the moon was halved, we have seen the star of Ares go behind it and become hidden by the dark portion of the moon and then come out at the bright side of it. And the Egyptians and Babylonians of old whose observations go back a great many years, and from whom we have a number of accepted facts relating to each of the stars, tell us of similar occultations of the other stars.'[2]

---

[1] There are other explanations, but they are all somewhat forced, and involve greater difficulties than they remove (see Simplicius on *De caelo*, pp. 503. 10–504. 3, and Martin, loc. cit., pp. 265–6). A further reduction of the number 49 to 47 which *might have been*, but obviously was not, made by Aristotle, is indicated by Martin (loc. cit., p. 268) and by Dreyer (*Planetary Systems*, p. 114 note). Aristotle might have abolished the '*third*' of the sun's spheres (as well as the fourth and fifth) ; this would have been a real improvement, since the 'third' sphere was meant to explain a movement which did not exist, namely, the supposed movement of the sun in latitude; the number of the spheres would thus have been reduced by two (one deferent and one reacting). But Aristotle had not the knowledge necessary to enable him to suggest this improvement.

[2] *De caelo* ii. 12, 291 b 29 – 292 a 9.

Aristotle's explanation is teleological, based on comparison with things which have life and are capable of action. We may perhaps say that that thing is in the best state which possesses the good without having to act at all, while those come nearest the best state which have to perform the fewest acts.[1] Now the earth is in the most happy state, being altogether without motion. The bodies nearest to it have few movements; they do not attain the ideal, but come as near as they can to 'the most divine principle'. The 'first heaven' [the sphere of the fixed stars] attains it at once by means of one movement only; the bodies between the first and the last [the last being the sun and the moon] attain it but only by means of a greater number of movements.[2]

The theory of concentric spheres was pursued for some time after Aristotle. Schiaparelli conjectures that even Archimedes still held to it. Autolycus, the author of the treatises *On the moving sphere* and *On risings and settings*, who lived till the end of the fourth or the beginning of the third century B.C., is said to have been the first to try, presumably by some modification of the theory, to meet the difficulties which had been seen from the first and were doubtless pointed out with greater insistence as time went on. What was ultimately fatal to it was of course the impossibility of reconciling the assumption of the invariability of the distance of each planet with the observed differences in the brightness, especially of Mars and Venus, at different times, and the apparent difference in the relative sizes of the sun and moon. The quotation by Simplicius from Sosigenes on this subject is worth giving in full.[4]

'Nevertheless the theories of Eudoxus and his followers fail to save the phenomena, and not only those which were first noticed at a later date, but even those which were before known and actually accepted by the authors themselves. What need is there for me to mention the generality of these, some of which, after Eudoxus had failed to account for them, Callippus tried to save,— if indeed we can regard him as so far successful? I confine myself to one fact which is actually evident to the eye; this fact no one before Autolycus of Pitane even tried to explain by means of hypotheses ($\delta\iota\grave{\alpha}$ $\tau\hat{\omega}\nu$ $\acute{\upsilon}\pi o\theta\acute{\epsilon}\sigma\epsilon\omega\nu$), and not even Autolycus was able to do so, as clearly appears from his controversy with

---

[1] *De caelo* ii. 12, 292 a 22-4.   [2] Ibid. 292 b 10-25.
[3] Simplicius on *De caelo*, pp. 504. 17 - 505. 11, 505. 19 - 506. 3.

Aristotherus[1]. I refer to the fact that the planets appear at times to be near to us and at times to have receded. This is indeed obvious to our eyes in the case of some of them; for the star called after Aphrodite and also the star of Ares seem, in the middle of their retrogradations, to be many times as large, so much so that the star of Aphrodite actually makes bodies cast shadows on moonless nights. The moon also, even in the perception of our eye, is clearly not always at the same distance from us, because it does not always seem to be the same size under the same conditions as to medium. The same fact is moreover confirmed if we observe the moon by means of an instrument; for it is at one time a disc of eleven fingerbreadths, and again at another time a disc of twelve fingerbreadths, which when placed at the same distance from the observer hides the moon (exactly) so that his eye does not see it. In addition to this, there is evidence for the truth of what I have stated in the observed facts with regard to total eclipses of the sun; for when the centre of the sun, the centre of the moon, and our eye happen to be in a straight line, what is seen is not always alike; but at one time the cone which comprehends the moon and has its vertex at our eye comprehends the sun itself at the same time, and the sun even remains invisible to us for a certain time, while again at another time this is so far from being the case that a rim of a certain breadth on the outside edge is left visible all round it at the middle of the duration of the eclipse. Hence we must conclude that the apparent difference in the sizes of the two bodies observed under the same atmospheric conditions is due to the inequality of their distances (at different times). . . . But indeed this inequality in the distances of each star at different times cannot even be said to have been unknown to the authors of the concentric theory themselves. For Polemarchus of Cyzicus appears to be aware of it, but to minimize it as being imperceptible, because he preferred the theory which placed the spheres themselves about the very centre in the universe. Aristotle too, shows that he is conscious of it when, in the Physical Problems, he discusses objections to the hypotheses of astronomers arising from the fact that even the sizes of the planets do not appear to be the same always. In this respect Aristotle was not altogether satisfied with the revolving spheres, although the supposition that, being concentric with the universe, they move about its centre attracted him. Again, it is clear from what he says in Book Λ of the Metaphysics that he thought that the facts about the movements of the planets had not been sufficiently explained by the

[1] Apparently a contemporary of Autolycus and, like him, a mathematician. The famous poet Aratus appears to have been a pupil of Aristotherus (Buhle's *Aratus*, Leipzig, 1793, vol. i, p. 4).

astronomers who came before him or were contemporary with him. At all events we find him using language of this sort: " (on the question how many in number these movements of the planets are), we must for the present content ourselves with repeating what some of the mathematicians say, in order that we may form a notion and our mind may have a certain definite number to apprehend ; but for the rest we must investigate some matters for ourselves and learn others from other investigators, and, if those who study these questions reach conclusions different from the views now put forward, we must, while respecting both, give our adherence to those which are the more correct " '.[1]

Schiaparelli observes that we must not be misled by these attempts to father on Aristotle doubts as to the truth of the theory of homocentric spheres; the object is to make an excuse for the line taken by the later Peripatetics in getting away from the revolving spheres of Aristotle and going over to the theory of eccentric circles and epicycles.

The allusion by Sosigenes to annular eclipses of the sun is particularly interesting, as it shows that he had much more correct notions on this subject than most astronomers up to Tycho Brahe. Even at the beginning of the seventeenth century, says Schiaparelli, some persons doubted the possibility of a total eclipse. Proclus points out that the views of Sosigenes are inconsistent with the opinion of Ptolemy that the apparent diameter of the sun is always the same, while that of the moon varies and is only at its apogee the same as that of the sun. 'If the latter contention is true,' says Proclus,[2] 'then that is not true which Sosigenes said in his work *On the revolving* (or *reacting*) *spheres*, namely, that in eclipses at perigee the sun is seen to be not wholly obscured, but to overlap with the edges of its circumference the circle of the moon, and to give light without hindrance. For if we accept this statement, then either the sun will show variation in its apparent diameter, or the moon will not, at its apogee, have its apparent diameter, as ascertained by observation, the same as that of the sun.' Cleomedes, too, alludes to the views of some of the more ancient astronomers who held that in total eclipses of the sun a bright rim

---

[1] Aristotle, *Metaph.* Λ. 8, 1073 b 10–17.
[2] Proclus, *Hypotyposis astronomicarum positionum*, c. 4, §§ 98, 99, p. 130, 16–26, ed. Manitius.

of the sun was visible all round (Cleomedes' words would imply that they asserted this to be true for *all* total eclipses, which is presumably a misapprehension), but adds that the statement has not been verified by observation.[1] Schiaparelli infers that Sosigenes was aware of the variations of the apparent diameter of the sun, as well as of the moon, and thinks that his object in alluding to annular eclipses in the above passage quoted from Simplicius, where the subject is again that of revolving spheres, was to use as an argument against that theory the fact that the distance of the sun from us is variable.

[1] Cleomedes, *De motu circulari* ii. 4, p. 190, 19–26, Ziegler.

XVII

ARISTOTLE (*continued*)

IT was convenient to give Aristotle's modified system of concentric spheres in close connexion with the systems of Eudoxus and Callippus, and to reserve the rest of his astronomy for separate treatment. While his modification of the beautiful theory of Eudoxus and Callippus was far from being an improvement, Aristotle rendered real services to astronomy in other respects. Those services consisted largely of thoughtful criticisms, generally destructive, of opinions held by earlier astronomers, but Aristotle also made positive contributions to the science which are of sufficient value to make it impossible to omit him from a history of Greek astronomy.

We have seen that he modified the purely geometrical hypotheses of Eudoxus and Callippus in a mechanical sense. A purely geometrical theory did not satisfy him; he must needs seek to assign causes for the motions of the several concentric spheres. We may therefore conveniently begin this chapter with an account of his views on Motion. Motion, according to Aristotle, is, like Form[1] and Matter,[2] eternal and indestructible, without beginning or end.[3] Motion presupposes a *primum movens* which is itself unmoved;[4] for that which is moved, being itself subject to change, cannot impart an unbroken and uniform movement;[5] the *primum movens*, then, must be one,[6] unchangeable, absolutely necessary;[7] there is nothing merely potential about it, no unrealized possibility;[8] it must therefore be incorporeal,[9] indivisible,[10] and unconditioned by space,[11] as

---

[1] *Metaph.* Z. 8, 1033 b 16, Z. 9, 1034 b 7, Λ. 3, 1069 b 35, &c.
[2] *Phys.* i. 9, 192 a 22-32.   [3] *Metaph.* Λ. 6, 1071 b 7.
[4] Ibid. 1071 b 4.   [5] *Phys.* viii. 6, 259 b 22; c. 10, 267 a 24.
[6] *Metaph.* Λ. 8, 1073 a 25, 1074 a 36, &c.   [7] Ibid. Λ. 7, 1072 b 7-11.
[8] Ibid. Λ. 6, 1071 b 12.   [9] Ibid. Λ. 6, 1071 b 20.
[10] Ibid. Λ. 9, 1075 a 7.
[11] *De caelo* i. 9, 279 a 18 sq.; *Phys.* viii. 10, 267 b 18.

well as motionless and passionless;[1] it is absolute Reality and pure
Energy,[2] that is, God.[3]   In another aspect the *primum movens* is the
Final Cause, pure Being, absolute Form, the object of thought and
desire ;[4] God is Thought,[5] self-sufficient,[6] contemplating unceasingly
nothing but itself,[7] the absolute activity of Thought, constituting
absolute reality and vitality and the source of all life.[8]   The *primum
movens* causes all the movements in the universe, not by any activity
of its own [9]—for that would be a movement and, as immaterial, it
can have no share in movement—but by reason of the fact that all
things strive after it and try to realize, so far as possible, its Form ;[10]
it operates like a beloved object, and that which is moved by it
communicates its motion to the rest.[11]

Motion takes place only by means of continuous contact between
the motive principle and the thing moved.   Aristotle insists upon
this even in a case where the contact might seem to be only
momentary, e.g. where a thing is *thrown*.   The motion in that case
seems to continue after contact with the thrower has ceased, but
Aristotle will not admit this; he assumes that the thrower moves
not only the thing thrown but also the medium through which the
thing is thrown, and makes the medium able to act as moved and
movent at the same time (i.e. to communicate the movement); and
further that the medium can continue to be movent even after it
has ceased to be moved.[12]   God then, as the first cause of motion,
must be in contact with the world,[13] though Aristotle endeavours to
exclude contiguity in space from the idea of 'contact', which he
often uses in the sense of immediate connexion, as of thought with
its object.[14]   The *primum movens* operates on the universe from the
circumference, because the quickest motion is that of the (outermost
limit of the) universe, and things move the quickest which are
nearest to that which moves them.[15]   Hence in a sense it could be

---

[1] *De anima* iii. 2, 426 a 10.   [2] *Metaph.* Λ. 7, 1072 a 25.   [3] *De caelo*, loc. cit.
[4] *Metaph.* Λ. 7, 1072 a 26; *De anima* iii. 10, 433 a 18.
[5] *Eth. N.* x. 8, 1178 b 21; *Metaph.* Λ. 9, 1074 b 25.
[6] *De caelo* ii. 12, 292 b 5; *Politics*, H. 1, 1323 b 23.
[7] *Metaph.* Λ. 9, 1075 a 10.   [8] *Metaph.* Λ. 7, 1072 b 28.
[9] *De caelo* ii. 12, 292 a 22; *Eth. N.* x. 8, 1178 b 20.
[10] *Metaph.* Λ. 7, 1072 a 26.   [11] Ibid. 1072 b 3.
[12] *Phys.* viii. 10, 266 b 27 - 267 a 18.   [13] *De gen. et corr.* i. 6, 323 a 31.
[14] *Metaph.* Θ. 10, 1051 b 24; Λ. 7, 1072 b 21.
[15] *Phys.* viii. 10, 267 b 7–9.

said that God is to Aristotle 'the extremity of the heaven';[1] but Aristotle is careful to deny that there can be any body or space or void outside the universe; what is outside is not in space at all; the 'end of the whole heaven' is life ($\alpha\iota\acute{\omega}\nu$), immortal and divine'.[2]

Motion in space is of three kinds, motion in a circle, motion in a straight line, and motion compounded of the two ('mixed').[3] Which of these can be endless and continuous? The 'mixed' would only be so if both the two components could; but movement in a straight line cannot have this character, since every finite rectilinear movement has terminal points at which it must turn back,[4] and an infinite rectilinear movement is impossible, both in itself,[5] and because the universe is finite; hence circular motion is the only motion which can be without beginning or end.[6] Simple bodies have simple motions; thus the four elements tend to move in straight lines; earth tends downwards, fire upwards; between the two are water, the relatively heavy, and air, the relatively light. Thus the order, beginning from the centre, in the sublunary sphere is earth, water, air, fire.[7] Now, says Aristotle, simple circular motion is more perfect than motion in a straight line. As, then, there are four elements to which rectilinear motion is natural and circular motion not natural, so there must be another element, different from the four, to which circular motion is natural.[8] This element is superior to the others in proportion to the greater perfection of circular motion and to its greater distance from us;[9] circular motion admits no such contraries as 'up' and 'down'; the superior element therefore can neither be heavy nor light;[10] the same absence of contrariety suggests that it is without beginning or end, imperishable, incapable of increase or change (because all becoming involves opposites and opposite motions).[11] This superior element which fills the uppermost space is called 'aether',[12] the 'first ele-

---

[1] Sextus Emp. *Adv. Math.* x. 33 ; *Hypotyp.* iii. 218.
[2] *De caelo* i. 9, 279 a 16–28.   [3] *Phys.* viii. 8, 261 b 29.
[4] *Phys.* viii. 8, 261 b 31–4.   [5] Ibid. iii. 5, 206 a 7 ; c. 6, 206 a 16.
[6] Ibid. viii. 8, 261 a 27 – 263 a 3, 264 a 7 sqq. ; c. 9, 265 a 13 sq.
[7] Aristotle is careful, however, to explain that the division between air and fire is not a strict one, as between two definite layers ; there is some intermixture (cf. *Meteor.* i. 3, 341 a 1–9). Further, the 'fire' is what from force of habit we *call* fire ; it is not really fire, for fire is an excess of heat, a sort of ebullition (ibid. 340 b 22, 23).   [8] *De caelo* i. 2, 268 b 26 – 269 b 17.   [9] Ibid.
[10] *De caelo* i. 3, 269 b 18–33.   [11] Ibid. 270 a 12–35.
[12] Ibid. 270 b 1–24.

ment ',[1] or 'a body other and more divine than the four so-called elements';[2] its changelessness is confirmed by long tradition, which contains no record of any alteration in the outer heaven itself or in any of its proper parts.[3] Of this element are formed the stars,[4] which are spherical,[5] eternal,[6] intelligent, divine.[7] It occupies the whole region from the outside limit of the universe down to the orbit of the moon, though it is not everywhere of uniform purity, showing the greatest difference where it touches the sublunary sphere.[8] Below the moon is the terrestrial region, the home of the four elements, which is subject to continual change through the strife of those elements and their incessant mutual transformations.[9]

There is, Aristotle maintains, only one universe or heaven, and that universe is complete, containing within it all the matter there is. For, he argues, all the simple bodies move to their proper places, earth to the centre, aether to the outermost region of the universe, and the other elements to the intervening spaces. There can be no simple body outside the universe, for that body has its own natural place inside, and, if it were kept outside by *force*, the place occupied by it would be the *natural* place for some other body; which is impossible, since *all* the simple bodies have their proper places inside. The same argument holds for mixed bodies; for, where mixed bodies are, there also are the simple bodies of which they are composed. Nor can there be any space or void outside the universe, for space or void is only that in which a body is or can be.[10] Another argument is that the *primum movens* is single and complete in itself; hence the world, which derives its eternal motion from the *primum movens*, must be so too.[11] If it be suggested that there may be many particular worlds as manifestations of one concept 'world', Aristotle replies that this cannot be; for the heaven is perceptible to our senses; hence it and other heavens

---

[1] *De caelo* iii. 1, 298 b 6 ; *Meteor.* i. 1, 338 b 21, &c.
[2] *De gen. an.* ii. 3, 736 b 29–31.   [3] *De caelo* i. 3, 270 b 11–16.
[4] *De gen. an.* ii. 3, 737 a 1.   [5] *De caelo* ii. 8, 290 a 7–b 11.
[6] *Metaph.* Λ. 8, 1073 a 34.
[7] Ibid. 1074 a 38–b 3 ; *Eth. N.* vi. 1143 b 1.   [8] *Meteor.* i. 3, 340 b 6–10.
[9] *Meteor.* ii. 3, 357 b 30.
[10] *De caelo* i. 9, 278 b 8 – 279 a 14.
[11] *Metaph.* Λ. 8, 1074 a 36–8.

(if any) must contain *matter* ; but our heaven contains all the matter there is, and therefore there cannot be any other.[1]

Next, the universe is *finite*. In the *Physics* Aristotle argues that an infinite body is inconceivable, thus. An infinite body must either be simple or composite. If composite, it is composed of elements ; these are limited in number ; hence an infinite body could only be made up of them if one or more were infinite in magnitude ; but this is impossible, because there would then be no room for the rest. Neither can it be simple ; for no perceptible simple body exists except the elements, and it has been shown that none of them can be infinite.[2] In the *De caelo* he approaches the subject from the point of view of motion. A body which has a circular motion, as the universe has, must be finite. For, if it is infinite, the straight line from the centre to a point on its circumference must be infinite ; now if, as being infinite, this distance can never be traversed, it cannot revolve in a circle, whereas we see that in fact the universe does so revolve.[3] Further, in an infinite body there can be no centre ; hence the universe which rotates about its centre cannot be infinite.[4]

Aristotle's arguments for the spherical shape of the universe are of the usual kind. As the circle, enclosed by one line, is the first of plane figures, so the sphere, bounded by one surface, is the first of solid figures ; hence the spherical shape is appropriate to the ' first body ', the subject of the ' outermost revolution '.[5] Next, as there is no space or void outside the universe, it must, as it revolves, continually occupy the same space ; therefore it must be a sphere ; for, if it had any other form, this condition would not be satisfied.[6] [Aristotle is not strictly correct here, since any solid of revolution revolving round its axis always occupies the same space, but it is true that only a sphere can remain in exactly the same position when revolving about any diameter whatever.] Further, we may infer the spherical form of the universe from the bodies in the centre. We have first the earth, then the water round the earth, air round the water, fire round the air, and similarly the bodies above the fire ;

[1] *De caelo* i. 9, 277 b 27 – 278 a 28.
[2] *Phys.* iii. 5, 204 b 3-35.
[3] *De caelo* i. 5, 271 b 28 – 272 a 7.
[4] *De caelo* i. 7, 275 b 12-15.
[5] Ibid. ii. 4, 286 b 10 – 287 a 5.
[6] Ibid. ii. 4, 287 a 11-22.

now the surface of the water is spherical; hence the surfaces of the layers following it, and finally the outermost surface, correspond.[1]

The fabric of the heavens is made up of spherical shells, as it were, one packed inside the other so closely that there is no void or empty space between them;[2] this applies not only to the astral spheres,[3] but right down to the earth in the middle;[4] it is necessary so far as the moving spheres are concerned because there must always be contact between the moving and the moved.[5]

We have above described the working of Aristotle's mechanical system of concentric spheres carrying the fixed stars and producing the motions of the planets respectively, and it only remains to add a word with reference to the motive power acting on the spheres other than that of the 'outermost revolution'. The outermost sphere, that of the fixed stars, is directly moved by the one single and eternal *primum movens*, Divine Thought or Spirit. Only one kind of motion is produced when one *movens* acts on one object;[6] how then do we get so many different movements in the spheres other than the outermost? Aristotle asks himself this question: Must we suppose that there is only one unmoved *movens* of the kind, or several, and, if several, how many are there? He is obliged to reply that, as eternal motion must be due to an eternal *movens*, and one such motion to one such *movens*, while we see that, in addition to the simple revolution of the whole universe caused by the unmoved *primum movens*, there exist other eternal movements, those of the planets, we must assume that each of the latter movements is due to a substance or essence unmoved in itself and eternal, without extension in space.[7] The number of them must be that of the separate spheres causing the motion of the separate planets.[8] The number of these spheres he had, as we have seen (p. 217), fixed provisionally, while recognizing that the progress of astronomy might make it necessary to alter the figures.[9] Of the several spheres which act on any one planet, the first or outermost alone is moved by its own motion exclusively; each of the inner spheres, besides having its own independent movement, is also

---

[1] *De caelo* ii. 4, 287 a 30–b 4.
[2] Cf. *Phys.* vii. 2, 243 a 5.
[3] *De caelo* i. 9, 278 b 16–18.
[4] *De caelo* ii. 4, 287 a 5–11.
[5] *Phys.* vii. 1, 242 b 24–6, vii. 2, 243 a 3–5.
[6] *Phys.* viii. 6, 259 a 18.
[7] *Metaph.* Λ. 8, 1073 a 14–b 10.
[8] *Metaph.* Λ. 8. 1074 a 13–16.
[9] Ibid. 1073 b 10–17.

carried round in the motion of the next sphere enveloping it, so that all the inner spheres, while themselves movent, are also moved by the eternal unmoved movent.[1]

In a chapter of the *De caelo*[2] Aristotle discusses the question which is the *right* side of the heaven and which the *left*. The disquisition is not important, but it is not unamusing.[3] He begins with a reference to the view of the Pythagoreans that there is a right and a left in the universe, and proceeds to investigate whether the particular distinction which they draw is correct or not, 'assuming that it is necessary to apply such principles as "right" and "left" to the body of the universe'.[4] There being three pairs of such opposites, up and down (or upper and lower), right and left, before and behind (or forward and backward), he begins with the distinctions (1) that 'up' is the principle of length, 'right' of breadth, and 'before' of depth, and (2) that 'up' is *the source of motion* ($\delta\theta\epsilon\nu$ $\dot{\eta}$ $\kappa\acute{\iota}\nu\eta\sigma\iota s$), 'right' the place *from which* it starts ($\dot{\alpha}\phi$' $o\hat{v}$), and '*to the front*' ($\epsilon\acute{\iota}s$ $\tau\grave{o}$ $\pi\rho\acute{o}\sigma\theta\epsilon\nu$) is the place *to which* it is directed ($\dot{\epsilon}\phi$' $\ddot{o}$). Now the fact that the shape of the universe is spherical, alike in all its parts, and continually in motion, is no obstacle to calling one part of it 'right' and the other 'left'. What we have to do is to think of something which has a right and left of its own (say a man) and then place a sphere round it.[5] Now, says Aristotle, I call the diameter through the two poles the *length* of the universe (because only the poles remain fixed), so that I must call one of the poles the *upper*, and the other the *lower*. He then proceeds to show that the proper relativities can only be preserved by calling the *south* (the invisible) pole the *upper* and the *north* (the visible) pole the *lower*, from which it follows that we live in the *lower* and *left* hemisphere, and the inhabitants of the regions towards the south pole live in the *upper* and *right* hemisphere; and this is precisely the opposite of what the Pythagoreans hold, namely that we live in the *upper* and *right* hemisphere, and the antipodes represent the *lower* and *left*. The argument amounts to this. 'Right' is the place from which motion in space starts; and the motion of

---

[1] *Phys.* viii. 6, 259 b 29–31. [2] *De caelo* ii. 2, 284 b 6 – 286 a 2.
[3] This matter also is fully discussed by Boeckh, *Das kosmische System des Platon*, pp. 112–19.
[4] *De caelo* ii. 2, 284 b 9–10. [5] Ibid. 285 b 1–3.

the heaven starts from the side where the stars rise, i.e. the east ;
therefore the east is 'right' and the west is 'left'.   If now (1) you
suppose yourself to be lying along the world's axis with your head
towards the *north* pole, your feet towards the *south* pole, and your
right hand towards the east, then clearly the apparent motion of the
stars from east to west is over your *back* from your right side towards
your left ; this motion, Aristotle maintains, cannot be called motion
'to the right', and therefore our hypothesis does not fit the assumption from which we start, namely that the daily rotation 'begins
from the right and is carried round towards the right (ἐπὶ τὰ δεξιά)'.[1]
We must therefore alter the hypothesis and suppose (2) that you
are lying with your head towards the *south* pole and your feet
towards the *north* pole.   If then your right hand is to the east, the
daily motion begins at your right hand and proceeds over the front
of your body from your right hand to your left.   We should nowadays regard this as giving precisely the wrong result, since motion
round us *in front* from right to left can hardly be described as ἐπὶ
τὰ δεξιά, 'to the right'; so that hypothesis (1) would, to us, seem
preferable to hypothesis (2).   But Aristotle's point of view is fairly
clear.   We are to suppose a man (say) standing upright and giving
a horizontal turn with his *right hand* to a circle about a vertical
diameter coincident with the longitudinal axis of his body.   Aristotle regards him as turning the circle towards the *right* when he
brings his right hand towards the *front* of his body, although we
should regard it as more natural to apply 'towards the right' to a
movement of his right hand *still more* to the right, i.e. round by
the right to the back.   The (to us) unnatural use of the terms
by Aristotle is attested by Simplicius who says that motion ἐπὶ
δεξιά *is in any case towards the front* (πάντως εἰς τὸ ἔμπροσθέν
ἐστι),[2] and it is doubtless due to what Aristotle would regard as the
necessity of making *front* (in the dichotomy front and back, or
before and behind) correspond to *right* (in the dichotomy right and
left), just as *up* (in the dichotomy up and down) must also correspond to *right*; this is indeed clear from his own statement quoted
above that, as 'the right' is the place *from which* motion starts, so
'to the front' is the place *towards which* it is directed.

   We come next to Aristotle's view as to the shape of the heavenly

[1] *De caelo* ii. 2, 285 b 20.   [2] Simplicius on *De caelo*, p. 392, 1, Heib.

bodies and the arguments by which he satisfied himself that they do not move of themselves but are carried by material spheres.

He held that the stars are spherical in form. One argument in support of this contention is curious. Nature, he says, does nothing without a purpose; Nature therefore gave the stars the shape most unfavourable for any movement on their own part; she denied to them all organs of locomotion, nay, made them as different as possible from the things which possess such organs. With this end in view, Nature properly made the stars spherical; for, while the spherical shape is the best adapted for motion in the same place (rotation), it is the most useless for progressive motion.[1] This is in curious contrast to the view of Plato who, with more reason, regarded the cube as being the shape least adapted for motion (ἀκινητότατον).[2] The second argument is from analogy. Since the moon is shown by the phases to be spherical, while we see similar curvature in the lines separating the bright part of the sun from the dark in non-total solar eclipses, we may conclude from this that the sun and, by analogy, the stars also are spherical in form.[3]

With regard to the spheres carrying the stars round with them, we note first that the 'heaven', in the sense of the 'outermost heaven' or 'the outermost revolution of the All' (ἡ ἐσχάτη περιφορὰ τοῦ παντός), which is the sphere of the fixed stars, was with Aristotle a material thing, a 'physical body' (σῶμα φυσικόν).[4] Now, says Aristotle,[5] seeing that both the stars and the whole heaven appear to change their positions, there are various *a priori* possibilities to be considered; (1) both the stars and the heaven may be at rest, (2) both the stars and the heaven may be in motion, or (3) the stars may move and the heaven be at rest, or *vice versa*. Hypothesis (1) is at once ruled out because, under it, the observed phenomena could not take place consistently with the earth being at rest also; and Aristotle assumes that the earth is at rest (τὴν δὲ γῆν ὑποκείσθω ἠρεμεῖν). Coming to hypothesis (2), we have to remember that the effect of a uniform rotation of the heaven about an axis passing through the poles is to make particular points on this spherical shell describe parallel circles about

[1] *De caelo* ii. 8, 290 a 31–b 5 ; c. 11, 291 b 11–17.
[2] Plato, *Timaeus* 55 D, E.   [3] *De caelo* ii. 11, 291 b 17–23.
[4] *De caelo* i. 9, 278 b 11–14.   [5] Ibid. ii. 8, 289 b 1 sqq.

the axis ; suppose then that the heaven rotates in this way, and that the stars also move. Now, says Aristotle, the stars and the circles cannot move independently ; if they did, it is inconceivable that the speeds of the stars would always be exactly the same as the speeds of the circles ; for, while the speeds of the circles must necessarily be in proportion to their sizes, i.e. to their radii, it is not reasonable to suppose that the stars, if they moved freely, would revolve at speeds proportional to the radii of the circles ; yet they would have to do so if the stars and the circles are always to return to the same places at the same times, as they appear to do. Nor can we, as in hypothesis (3), suppose the stars to move and the heaven to be at rest ; for, if the heaven were at rest, the stars would have to move of themselves at speeds proportional to the radii of the circles they describe, which has already been stated to be an unreasonable supposition. Consequently only one possibility remains, namely that the circles alone move, and the stars are fixed on them and carried round with them ;[1] that is, they are fixed on, and carried round with, the sphere of which the circles are parallel sections.

Again, says Aristotle, there are other considerations which suggest the same conclusion. If the stars have a motion of their own, they can, being spherical in shape, have only one of two movements, namely either (1) *whirling* (δίνησις) or (2) *rolling* (κύλισις). Now (1), if the stars merely whirled or rotated, they would always remain in the same place, and would not move from one position to another, as everybody admits that they do. Besides, if one heavenly body rotated, it would be reasonable to suppose that they all would. But, in fact, the only body which seems to rotate is the sun and that only at the times of its rising and setting ; this, however, is only an optical illusion due to the distance, 'for our sight, when at long range, wavers' (literally 'turns' or 'spins', ἐλίσσεται). This, Aristotle incidentally observes, may perhaps be the reason why the fixed stars, which are so distant, twinkle, while the planets, being nearer, do not. It is thus the tremor or wavering of our sight which makes the heavenly bodies seem to rotate.[2] In thus asserting that the stars do not *rotate*, Aristotle is of course opposed to Plato, who held that they do.[3]

---

[1] *De caelo* ii. 8, 289 b 32.   [2] Ibid. ii. 8, 290 a 9-23.   [3] Plato, *Timaeus* 40 A.

Again (2), if the stars *rolled* (along, like a wheel), they would necessarily turn round ; but that they do not turn round in this way is proved by the case of the moon, which always shows us one side, the so-called face.[1]

It is for a particular reason that I have reproduced so fully Aristotle's remarks about *rotation* and *rolling* as conceivable movements for stars as spherical bodies. It has been commonly remarked that Aristotle draws a curious inference from the fact that the moon has one side always turned to us, namely that the moon does not *rotate* about its own axis, whereas the inference should be the very opposite.[2] But this is, I think, a somewhat misleading statement of the case and less than just to Aristotle. What he says is that the moon does not turn round in the sense of *rolling along* ; and this is clear enough because, if it rolled along a certain path, it would roll once round while describing a length equal to 3·1416 times its diameter, but it manifestly does not do this. But Aristotle does not say that the moon does not *rotate* ; he does not, it is true, say that it does rotate either, but his hypothesis that it is fixed in a sphere concentric with the earth has the effect of keeping one side of the moon always turned towards us, and therefore *incidentally* giving it a rotation in the proper period, namely that of its revolution round the earth. I cannot but think that the fact of the moon always showing us one side was one of the considerations, if not the main consideration, which suggested to Aristotle that the stars were really fixed in material spheres concentric with the earth.

We pass to matters which are astronomically more important. And first as to the spherical shape of the earth. Aristotle begins by answering an objection raised by the partisans of a flat earth, namely that the line in which the horizon appears to cut the sun as it is rising or setting is straight and not curved.[3] His answer is confused ; he says that the objectors do not take account of the distance of the sun from the earth and of the size of its circumference,[4] the fact being that you can have an apparently straight line

---

[1] *De caelo* ii. 8, 290 a 26.
[2] Cf. Martin, 'Hypothèses astronomiques grecques' in *Mémoires de l'Acad. des Inscriptions et Belles-Lettres*, xxx. 1881, p. 287 ; Dreyer, *Planetary Systems*, p. 111, note.   [3] *De caelo* ii. 13, 294 a 1.
[4] τῆς περιφερείας seems clearly to be the circumference of the sun (not that of the horizon which cuts the solar disc).

as a section when you see it from afar in a circle which on account
of its distance appears small. He should no doubt have said, first,
that the sun, as we see it, looks like a flat disc of small size on
account of its distance, and then that the section of an object
apparently so small by the horizon is indistinguishable from a
section by a plane through our eye, so that the section of the disc
appears to be a straight line. He has, however, some positive
proofs based on observation. (1) In partial eclipses of the moon
the line separating the bright from the dark portion is always
convex (circular)—unlike the line of demarcation in the phases of
the moon, which may be straight or curved in either direction—
this proves that the earth, to the interposition of which lunar
eclipses are due, must be spherical.[1] He should no doubt have
said that a sphere is the *only* figure which can cast a shadow such
that a right section of it is *always* a circle; but his explanation
shows that he had sufficiently grasped this truth. (2) Certain stars
seen above the horizon in Egypt and in Cyprus are not visible
further north, and, on the other hand, certain stars set there which
in more northern latitudes remain always above the horizon. As
there is so perceptible a change of horizon between places so near
to each other, it follows not only that the earth is spherical, but
also that it is not a very large sphere. He adds that this makes it
not improbable that people are right when they say that the region
about the Pillars of Heracles is joined on to India, one sea connecting them. It is here, too, that he quotes the result arrived at
by mathematicians of his time, that the circumference of the earth
is 400,000 stades.[2] He is clear that the earth is much smaller
than some of the stars.[3] On the other hand, the moon is smaller
than the earth.[4] Naturally, Aristotle has *a priori* reasons for the
sphericity of the earth. Thus, using once more his theory of heavy
bodies tending to the centre, he assumes that, whether the heavy
particles forming the earth are supposed to come together from all
directions alike and collect in the centre or not, they will arrange
themselves uniformly all round, i.e. in the shape of a sphere, since, if
there is any greater mass at one part than at another, the greater

---

[1] *De caelo* ii. 14, 297 b 23-30.   [2] Ibid. 297 b 30 – 298 a 20.
[3] Ibid. 298 a 19; *Meteor.* i. 3, 339 b 7-9.
[4] Aëtius, ii. 26. 3 (*D. G.* p. 357 b 11).

mass will push the smaller until the even collection of matter all round the centre produces equilibrium.[1]

Aristotle's attempted proof that the earth is in the centre of the universe is of course a *petitio principii*. He begins by attempting to refute the Pythagorean theory that the earth, like the planets and the sun and moon, moves round the central fire. The Pythagoreans, he says, conceived the central fire to be the abode of sovereignty in the universe, the Watchtower of Zeus, while others might say that the centre, being the worthiest place, is appropriate for the worthiest occupant, and that fire is worthier than earth. To this he replies that the centre of a thing is not so worthy as the extremity, for it is the extremity which limits or defines a thing, while the centre is that which is limited and defined, and is more like a termination than a beginning or principle.[2] When Aristotle comes to state his own view, he rightly says that heavy bodies, e.g. parts of the earth itself, tend towards the centre of the earth; for bodies which fall towards the earth from different places do not fall in parallel lines but 'at equal angles', i.e. at right angles, to the (spherical) surface of the earth, and this proves that they fall in the direction of its centre. Similarly, if a weight is thrown upwards, however great the force exerted, it falls back again towards the centre of the earth.[3] But, he asks, do bodies tend towards the centre because it is the centre of the universe or because it is the centre of the earth, 'since both have the same centre'?[4] He replies that they must tend towards the centre of the universe because, in the reverse case of the light elements, e.g. fire, it is the extremities of the space which envelops the centre (i.e. the extremities of the *universe*) to which they naturally tend.[5] Even the show of argument in the last sentence does not prevent the whole of the reasoning from being a *petitio principii*. For it is exclusively based on the original assumption that, of the four elements, earth and, next to that, water tend to move in a straight line 'downwards', i.e., on Aristotle's view, towards the centre of the universe,[6] the effect of which is that not

---

[1] *De caelo* ii. 14, 297 a 8–b 18.
[2] Ibid. ii. 13, 293 a 17–b 15.   [3] Ibid. ii. 14, 296 b 18–25.
[4] Ibid. 296 b 9–12.   [5] Ibid. 296 b 12–15.
[6] *Phys.* iv. 4, 212 a 26; c. 8, 214 b 14; and especially *De caelo* iv. 1, 308 a 15–31. In the last-cited passage Aristotle, without mentioning Plato by name, attacks Plato's doctrine that, in a perfect sphere such as the universe is, you

only do the particles of the earth tend to the centre of the universe, but *a fortiori* the earth itself, which must therefore occupy the centre of the universe.[1]

Another argument is that, according to the astronomical views of the mathematicians, the phenomena which are observed as the heavenly bodies change their positions relatively to one another are just what they should be on the assumption that the earth is in the centre.[2] The answer to this is, as Martin says, 'How do you know? And how can you use the argument when you have quoted, without stating any objection to it, the argument of the Pythagoreans that their theory of the motion of the earth need cause no sensible difference of parallax in comparison with the theory that the earth is at the centre?'

The earth being in the centre of the universe, what keeps it there? Dealing with this question, Aristotle again begins by a consideration of the views of earlier philosophers. He rejects Thales' view that the earth floats on water as contrary to experience, since earth is heavier than water, and we see water resting or riding on earth, but not the reverse. He rejects, too, the view of Anaximenes, Anaxagoras, and Democritus that it rides on the air because it is flat and, acting like a lid to the air below it, is supported by it. Aristotle points out first that, if it should turn out that the earth is round and not flat, it cannot be the flatness which is the reason of the air supporting it; according to the argument it

cannot properly describe one part rather than another as 'up' or 'down'; on the contrary, says Aristotle, I call the centre, where heavy bodies collect, 'down', and the extremities of the sphere, whither light bodies tend to rise, 'up'. But, as usual, there is less difference between the two views than Aristotle would have us believe. Plato (*Timaeus* 62 D) said, it is true, that, as all points of the circumference are equidistant from the centre, it is incorrect to apply the terms 'up' and 'down' to different specific portions of that circumference, or to call any portion of the sphere 'up' or 'down' relatively to the centre, which is neither 'up' nor 'down', but simply the centre. But he goes on to say (63 B-E) that you can use the terms in a purely *relative* sense; any two localities may be 'up' and 'down' relatively to one another, and Plato proposes a criterion. If a body tends to move to a certain place by virtue of seeking for its like, this tendency is what constitutes its *heaviness*, and the place to which it tends is 'down'; and the opposite terms have the opposite meanings. The only difference made by Aristotle is in definitely allocating the *centre* of the universe as the place of the heaviest element, earth, and arranging the other elements in order of lightness in spherical layers round it, so that on his system the centre of the universe becomes 'down', and *any* direction outwards along a radius is 'up'.

[1] *De caelo* ii. 14, 296 b 6-9.   [2] Ibid. 297 a 2-6.

must rather be its size than its flatness, and, if it were large enough, it might even be a sphere. With this he passes on.[1] Nor does Empedocles' theory meet with more favour; if the earth is kept in its place in the same way as water in a cup which is whirled round, this means that the earth is kept in its place by *force*, and to this view Aristotle opposes his own theory that the earth must have some natural tendency, and a proper place, of its own. Even assuming that it came together by the whirling of a vortex, why do all heavy bodies now tend towards it ? The whirling is at all events too far away from us to cause this. And why does fire move upwards ? This cannot be through the whirling either ; and, if fire naturally tends to move to a certain region, surely the earth should too. But, indeed, the heavy and the light were prior to the whirling, and what determines their place is, not whirling, but the difference between 'up' and 'down'. Finally he deals with the view of Anaximander (followed by Plato) that the earth is in equilibrium through being equidistant from all points of the circumference, and therefore having no reason to move in one direction rather than another. Incidentally comparing the arguments (1) that, if you pull a hair with force and tension exactly equal throughout, it will not break, and (2) that a man would have to starve if he had victuals and drink equally disposed all round him, Aristotle again complains that the theory does not take account of the natural tendency of one thing to move to the centre, and of another to move to the circumference. It happens incidentally to be true that a body must remain at the centre if it is not more proper for it to move this way or that, but whether this is so or not depends on the body ; it is not the equidistance from the extremities which keeps it there, for the argument would require that, if fire were placed in the centre, it would remain there, whereas in fact it would not, since its tendency to fly upwards would carry it uniformly in all directions towards the extremities of the universe ; hence it is not the equidistance, but the natural tendency of the body, which determines the place where it will rest.[3]

In setting himself to prove that the earth has no motion whatever, Aristotle distinguishes clearly between the two views (1) of

[1] *De caelo* ii. 13, 294 a 28–b 30.   [2] Ibid. 295 a 16–b 9.
[3] Ibid. 295 b 10 – 296 a 21.

those who give it a motion of translation or 'make it one of the stars', and (2) of those who regard it as packed *and moving* about an axis through its centre.[1] Though he arbitrarily adds the words 'and moves' (καὶ κινεῖσθαι) to the phraseology of the *Timaeus*, thereby making it appear that Plato attributed to the earth a rotation about its axis, which, as we have seen, he could not have done, the second of the two views was actually held by Heraclides Ponticus, who was Aristotle's contemporary. It seems likely, as Dreyer suggests,[2] that, in speaking of a motion of the earth 'at the centre itself',[3] Aristotle is not thinking of a rotation of the earth *in twenty-four hours*, i.e. a rotation replacing the apparent revolution of the fixed stars, as Heraclides assumed that it did; for he does not mention the latter feature or give any arguments against it; on the contrary, he only deals with the general notion of a rotation of the earth, and moreover mixes up his arguments against this with his arguments against a translation of the earth in space. He uses against both hypotheses his fixed principle that parts of the earth, and therefore the earth itself, move naturally towards the centre.[4] Whether, he says, the earth moves away from the centre or *at* the centre, such movement could only be given to it by *force*; it could not be a natural movement on the part of the earth because, if it were, the same movement would also be natural to all its parts, whereas we see them all tend to move in straight lines towards the centre; the assumed movement, therefore, being due to force and against nature, could not be everlasting, as the structure of the universe requires.[5]

The second argument, too, though directed against both hypotheses, really only fits the first, that of motion in an orbit.

' Further, all things which move in a circle, except the first (outermost) sphere, appear to be left behind and to have more than one movement; hence the earth, too, whether it moves about the centre or in its position at the centre, must have two movements. Now, if this occurred, it would follow that the fixed stars would exhibit passings and turnings (παρόδους καὶ τροπάς). This, how-

---

[1] *De caelo* ii. 13, 293 a 20-3, b 18-20; c. 14, 296 a 25-7.
[2] Dreyer, *Planetary Systems*, pp. 116, 117.
[3] *De caelo* ii. 14, 296 a 29, b 2.　　　　　　[4] Ibid. 296 b 6-8.
[5] Ibid. 296 a 27-34.

ever, does not appear to be the case, but the same stars always rise
and set at the same places on the earth.'[1]

The bodies which appear to be 'left behind and to have more
movements than one' are of course the planets. The argument
that, if the earth has one movement, it must have two, is based upon
nothing more than analogy with the planets. Aristotle clearly
inferred as a corollary that, if the earth has two motions, one must
be oblique to the other, for it would be obliquity to the equator in
at least one of the motions which would produce what he regards
as the necessary consequence of his assumption, namely that the
fixed stars would not always rise and set at the same places. As
already stated, Aristotle can hardly have had clearly in his mind
the possibility of one single rotation about the axis *in twenty-four
hours* replacing exactly the apparent daily rotation ; for he would
have seen that this would satisfy his necessary condition that the
fixed stars shall always rise and set at the same places, and therefore that he would have to get some further support from elsewhere
to his assumption that the earth must have *two* motions. Still
less could he have dreamt of the possibility of Aristarchus's later
hypothesis that the earth has an annual revolution as well as a
daily rotation about its axis, which hypothesis satisfies, as a matter
of fact, both the condition as to two motions and the condition as
regards the fixed stars.

The *Meteorologica* deals with the sublunary portion of the
heavenly sphere, the home of the four elements and their combinations. Only a small portion of the work can be said to be astronomical, but some details bearing on our subject may be given. We
have seen the four elements distinguished according to their relative
heaviness or lightness, and the places which are proper to them
respectively ; in the *Meteorologica* they are further distinguished
according to the tangible qualities which are called their causes
(αἴτια). These tangible qualities are the two pairs of opposites,
hot—cold, and dry—moist ; and when we take the four combinations
of these in pairs which are possible we get the four elements ; hot
and dry = fire, hot and moist = air (air being a sort of vapour),
cold and moist = water, cold and dry = earth.[2] Of the four qualities

---

[1] *De caelo* ii. 14, 296 a 34–b 6.   [2] *De gen. et corr.* ii. 3, 330 a 30–b 7.

two, hot and cold, are regarded as active, and the other two, dry
and moist, as passive.[1] Since each element thus contains an active
as well as a passive quality, it follows that all act upon and are acted
upon by one another, and that they mingle and are transformed into
one another.[2] Every composite body contains all of them ;[3] they
are never, in our experience, found in perfect purity.[4] Elemental fire
is warm and dry evaporation,[5] not flame ; elemental fire is a sort of
' inflammable material ' which ' can often be kindled by even a little
motion, like smoke ';[6] but flame, or fire in the sense of flame, is
' an excess of heat or a sort of ebullition ',[7] or an ebullition of dry
wind [8] or of dry heat [9] ; again, flame is said to be a fleeting, non-
continuous product of the transformation of moist and dry in close
contact.[10] The reason for this distinction between ' fire ' and flame
is obvious, as Zeller says ; for Aristotle could not have made the
outer portion of the terrestrial sphere, contiguous to the aether, to
consist of actual burning flame. According to Aristotle, the stars
are not made of fire (still less all the spaces between them); in
themselves they are not even hot ; their light and heat come from
friction with the air through which they move [notwithstanding
that they are in the aethereal sphere] ; the air in fact becomes fire
through their impact on it ; the stratum of air which lies nearest to
them underneath the aethereal sphere is thus warmed. Especially
is this the case with the sun ; the sun is able to produce heat in
the place where we live because it is not so far off as the fixed
stars and it moves swiftly (the stars, though they move swiftly,
are far off, and the moon, though near to us, moves slowly) ; further,
the motion often causes the fire surrounding the atmosphere to
scatter and rush downwards.[11]

Such phenomena as shooting stars (διάττοντες or διαθέοντες
ἀστέρες) and meteors (of the two kinds called δαλοί and αἶγες) are
next dealt with. These are due to two kinds of exhalation, one
more vaporous (rising from the water on and in the earth), the other

---

[1] *Meteor.* iv. 1, 378 b 10-13, 21-5.
[2] *De gen. et corr.* ii. 2, 329 b 22 sq.   [3] Ibid. c. 8, 334 b 31 sq.
[4] Ibid. c. 3, 330 b 21 ; *Meteor.* ii. 4, 359 b 32, &c.
[5] *Meteor.* i. 3, 340 b 29 ; c. 4, 341 b 14.   [6] Ibid. 341 b 19-21.
[7] Ibid. c. 3, 340 b 23.   [8] Ibid. c. 4, 341 b 21-2.
[9] *De gen. et corr.* ii. 3, 330 b 29.   [10] *Meteor.* ii. 2, 355 a 9.
[11] *De caelo* ii. 7, 289 a 13-35 ; *Meteor.* i. 3, 340 a 1, 341 a 12-36.

dry and smoke-like (rising from the earth); these go upwards, the latter uppermost, the former below it, until, caught in the rotation at the circumference of the sublunary sphere, they take fire. The particular varieties of appearance which they present depend on the shape of the rising exhalations and the inclination at which they rise. Sometimes, however, they are the result, not of motion kindling them, but of heat being squeezed out of air which comes together and is condensed through cold; in this case their motion is like a *throw* (ῥῖψις) rather than a burning, being comparable to kernels or pips of fruits pressed between our fingers and so made to fly to a distance; this is what happens when the star falls downwards, since but for such compelling force that which is hot would naturally always fly upwards. All these phenomena belong to the sublunary sphere.[1] The aurora is regarded as due to the same cause combined with reflection lighting up the air.[2]

Aristotle has two long chapters on comets.[3] He begins, as usual, by reviewing the opinions of earlier philosophers and so clearing the ground. Anaxagoras and Democritus had explained comets as a ' conjunction of the planets when, by reason of coming near, they seem to touch one another'. Some of 'the so-called Pythagoreans' thought that they were one planet, which we only see at long intervals because it does not rise far above the horizon, the case being similar to that of Mercury, which, since it only rises a little above the horizon, makes many appearances which are invisible to us and is actually seen at long intervals only. Hippocrates of Chios and his pupil Aeschylus gave a similar explanation but added a theory about the tail. The tail, they said, does not come from the comet itself, but the comet, as it wanders through space, sometimes takes on a tail ' through our sight being reflected, at the sun, from the moisture attracted by the comet'. Explanations by Hippocrates and Aeschylus follow, of the reasons (1) of the long intervals between the appearances of a comet: the reason in this case being that it is only left behind by the sun very slowly indeed, so that for a long time it remains so close to the sun as not to be visible; (2) of the impossibility of a tail appearing when the comet is between the tropical circles or still further

---

[1] *Meteor.* i. 4, 341 b – 342 a.   [2] Ibid. c. 5, 342 a 34-b 24.
[3] Ibid. cc. 6, 7, 342 b 25 – 345 a 10.

south : in the former position the comet does not attract the moisture to itself because the region is burnt up by the motion of the
sun in it, and, when it is still further south, although there is plenty
of moisture for the comet to attract, a question of angles (only a
small part of the comet's circle being above the horizon) precludes
the sight being reflected at the sun in this case, whether the sun be
near its southern limit or at the summer solstice ; (3) of the comet's
taking a tail when in a northerly position: the reason here being
that a large portion of the comet's circle is above the horizon, and
so the reflection of the sight is physically possible.   Aristotle
states objections, some of which apply to all, and others to some
only, of the above views.   Thus (1) the comet is not a planet,
because all the planets are in the zodiac circle, while comets are
often outside it ; (2) there have often been more than one comet at
one time ; (3) if the tail is due to ' reflection ', and a comet has not
a tail in all positions, it ought sometimes to appear without one ;
but the five planets are all that we ever see, and they are often all
of them visible above the horizon ; and, whether they are all visible,
or some only are visible (the others being too near the sun), comets
are often seen in addition.   (4) It is not true that comets are only
seen in the region towards the north and when the sun is near the
summer solstice; for the great comet which appeared at the time
of the earthquake and tidal wave in Achaea [373/2 B.C.] appeared
in the region where the sun sets at the equinox, and many comets
have been seen in the south.   Again (5) in the archonship of Eucles,
the son of Molon, at Athens [427/6 B.C.], a comet appeared in the
north in the month of Gamelion, when the sun was at the winter
solstice, although, according to the theory, reflection of the sight
would then be impossible.   Aristotle proceeds:

' It is common ground with the thinkers just criticized and the
supporters of the theory of coalescence that some of the fixed
stars, too, take a tail ; on this we must accept the authority of the
Egyptians (for they, too, assert it), and moreover we have ourselves
seen it.   For one of the stars in the haunch of the Dog got a tail,
though only a faint one ; that is to say, when one looked intently
at it, its light was faint, but when one glanced easily at it, it
appeared brighter.
' Moreover, all the comets seen in our time disappeared, without
setting, in the expanse above the horizon, fading from sight by

slow degrees and in such a way that no astral substance, either
one star or more, remained. For instance, the great comet before
mentioned appeared in the winter of the archonship of Astaeus
[373/2 B.C.], in clear and frosty weather, from the beginning of the
evening ; the first day it was not seen because it had set-before the
sun, but on the following day it was visible, being the least distance
behind the sun that allowed of its being seen at all, and setting
directly ; the light of this comet stretched over a third part of the
heaven with a great *leap* as it were (οἷον ἅλμα), so that people
called it a street.   And it went back as far as the belt of Orion and
there dispersed.

' Nevertheless Democritus for one stoutly defended his own theory,
asserting that stars had actually been seen to remain on the disso-
lution of comets.   But in that case it should not have sometimes
happened and sometimes failed to happen ; it should have happened always.   The Egyptians, too, say that conjunctions take
place of planets with one another and of planets with the fixed stars ;
we have, however, ourselves seen the star of Zeus twice meet one of
the stars in the Twins and hide it, without any comet resulting.'

Aristotle adds that this explanation of comets is untenable on
general grounds, since, although stars may seem large or small,
they appear to be indivisible in themselves.   Now, if they were really
indivisible, they would not produce anything bigger by coming in
contact with one another ; therefore similarly, if they only *seem*
indivisible, they cannot *seem* by meeting to produce anything bigger.

Aristotle's own theory of comets explains them as due, much
like meteors, to exhalations rising from below and catching fire
when they meet that other hot and dry substance (also here called
exhalation) which, being the first (i.e. outermost) portion of the
sublunary sphere and in direct contact with the revolution of
the upper (aethereal) part of the heavenly sphere, is carried round
with that revolution and even takes with it part of the contiguous
air.   The necessary conditions for the formation of a comet, as
distinct from a shooting star or meteor, are that the fiery principle
which the motion of the upper heaven sets up in the exhalation
must neither be so very strong as to produce swift and extensive
combustion, nor yet so weak as to be speedily extinguished, but of
moderate strength and moderate extent, and the exhalation itself
must be ' well-tempered ' (εὔκρατος) ; according to the shape of the
kindled exhalation it is a comet proper or the ' bearded ' variety

(πωγωνίας). But two kinds of comets are distinguished. One is produced when the origin of the exhalation is in the sublunary sphere; this is the independent comet (καθ' ἑαυτὸν κομήτης). The other is produced when it is one of the stars, a planet or a fixed star, which causes the exhalation, in which case the star becomes a comet and is followed round in its course by the exhalation, just as haloes are seen to follow the sun and the moon. Comets are thus bodies of vapour in a state of slow combustion, moving either freely or in the wake of a star. Aristotle maintains that his view that comets are formed by fire produced from exhalations in the manner described is confirmed by the fact that in general they are a sign of winds and droughts. When they are dense and there are more of them, the years in which they appear are noticeably dry and windy; when they are fewer and fainter, these characteristics are less pronounced, though there is generally some excess of wind either in respect of duration or of strength. He adds the following remarks on particular cases:

'On the occasion when the (meteoric) stone fell from the air at Aegospotami, it was caught up by a wind and was hurled down in the course of a day;[1] and at that time too a comet appeared from the beginning of the evening. Again, at the time of the great comet [373/2 B.C., see pp. 244, 245 above] the winter was dry and arctic, and the tidal wave was caused by the clashing of contrary winds; for in the bay the north wind prevailed, while outside it a strong south wind blew. Further, during the archonship of Nicomachus at Athens [341/0 B.C.] a comet was seen for a few days in the neighbourhood of the equinoctial circle; it was at the time of this comet, which did not rise with the beginning of the evening, that the great gale at Corinth occurred.'

[1] This appears to be the earliest mention of the meteoric stone of Aegospotami by any writer whose works have survived. The date of the occurrence was apparently in the archonship of Theagenides [468/7 B.C.]. The story that Anaxagoras prophesied that this stone would fall from the sun (Diog. L. ii. 10) was probably invented by way of a picturesque inference from his well-known theory that the fiery aether whirling round the earth snatched stones from the earth and, carrying them round with it, kindled them into stars (Aët. ii. 13. 3; *D.G.* p. 341; *Vorsokratiker*, i², p. 307. 16), and that one of the bodies fixed in the heaven might break away and fall (Diog. L. ii. 12; Plutarch, *Lysander* 12; *Vorsokratiker*, i², pp. 294. 29, 296. 34). Diogenes of Apollonia, too, a contemporary of Anaxagoras, said that along with the visible stars there are also stones carried round, which are invisible, and are accordingly unnamed; 'and these often fall upon the earth and are extinguished like the stone star which made a fiery fall at Aegospotami' (Aët. ii. 13. 9; *D. G.* p. 342; *Vorsokratiker*, i², p. 330. 5–8).

It has been pointed out that Aristotle's account of comets held its ground among the most distinguished astronomers till the time of Newton.[1]

Passing to the subject of the Milky Way,[2] Aristotle again begins with criticisms of earlier views. The first opinion mentioned is that of the Pythagoreans, some of whom said that it was the path of one of the stars which were cast out of their places in the destruction said to have occurred in Phaethon's time; while others said that it was the path formerly described by the sun, so that this region was, so to speak, set on fire by the sun's motion. But, Aristotle replies, if this were so, the zodiac circle should be burnt up too, nay more so, since it is the path not only of the sun but of the planets also. But we see the whole of the zodiac circle at one time or another, half of it being seen in a night; and there is no sign of such a condition except at points where it touches the Milky Way. The remarkable hypothesis of Anaxagoras and Democritus is next controverted; we have already (pp. 83–5) quoted Aristotle's criticisms. Next, a third view is mentioned according to which the Milky Way is 'a reflection of our sight at the sun', just as comets had been declared to be. Aristotle refutes this rather elaborately. (1) If, he says, the eye, the mirror (the sun) and the thing seen (the Milky Way) were all at rest, one and the same part

---

[1] Ideler, *Aristotelis Meteorologica*, vol. i, p. 396. Yet Seneca (*Nat. Quaest.* vii) had much sounder views on comets. He would not admit that they could be due to such fleeting causes as exhalations and rapid motions, as of whirlwinds, igniting them; if this were their cause, how could they be visible for six months at a time (vii. 10. 1)? They are not the effects of sudden combustion at all, but eternal products of nature (22. 1). Nor are they confined to the sublunary sphere, for we see them in the upper heaven among the stars (8. 4). If it is said that they cannot be 'wandering stars' because they do not move in the zodiac circle, the answer is that there is no reason why, in a universe so marvellously constructed, there should not be orbits in other regions than the zodiac which stars or comets may follow (24. 2–3). It is true, he says, that, owing to the infrequency of the appearances of comets, their orbits have not as yet been determined, nay, it has not been possible even to decide whether they keep up a definite succession and duly appear on appointed days. In order to settle these questions, we require a continuous record of the appearances of comets from ancient times onwards (3. 1). When generation after generation of observers have accumulated such records, there will come a time when the mystery will be cleared up; men will some day be found to show 'in what regions comets run their courses, why each of them roams so far away from the others, how large they are and what their nature; let us, for our part, be content with what we have already discovered, and let our posterity in their turn contribute to the sum of truth (25. 7).'   [2] *Meteor*. i. 8, 345 a 11 – 346 b 10.

of the reflection would belong to one and the same point of the mirror ; but if the mirror and the thing seen move at invariable distances from our eye (which is at rest), but at different speeds and distances relatively to one another, it is impossible that the same part of the reflection should always be at the same point of the mirror. Now the latter of the two hypotheses is that which corresponds to the facts, because the stars in the Milky Way and the sun respectively move at invariable distances from us, but at different distances and speeds in relation to one another ; for the Dolphin rises sometimes at midnight, and sometimes at sunrise, but the parts of the Milky Way remain the same in either case ; this could not be so if the Milky Way were a reflection instead of a condition of the actual localities over which it extends. (2) Besides, how can the visual rays be reflected at the sun during the night? Aristotle's own explanation puts the Milky Way on the same footing as the second kind of comets, those in which the separation of the vapour which takes fire on coming into contact with the outer revolution is caused by one of the stars ; the difference is that what in the case of the comet happens with one star takes place in the case of the Milky Way throughout a whole circle of the heaven and the outer revolution. The zodiac circle, owing to the motion in it of the sun and planets, prevents the formation of the exhalations in that neigh-bourhood ; hence most comets are seen outside the tropic circles. The sun and moon do not become comets because they separate out the exhalation too quickly to allow it to accumulate to the necessary extent. The Milky Way, on the other hand, represents the greatest extent of the operation of the process of exhalation ; it forms a great circle and is so placed as to extend far beyond the tropic circles. The space which it occupies is filled with very great and very bright stars, as well as with those which are called ' scat-tered ' ($\sigma\pi o\rho\acute{a}\delta\omega\nu$); this is the reason why the collected exhalations here form a concretion so continuous and so permanent. The cause is indeed indicated by the fact that the brightness is greater in that half of the circle where it is *double*, for it is there that the stars are more numerous and closer together than elsewhere.

XVIII

HERACLIDES OF PONTUS

The Pythagorean hypothesis of the revolution of the earth with the counter-earth, and of the sun, moon, and planets, about the central fire disappeared with the last representatives of the Pythagorean school soon after the time of Plato. The counter-earth was the first part of the system to be abandoned; and it is suggested that this abandonment was due to the extension of the geographical horizon. Discoveries were made both to the east and to the west. Hanno, the Carthaginian, had made his great voyage of discovery beyond the Pillars of Hercules, and on the other (the eastern) side India became part of the known world. It would naturally be expected that, if journeys were made far enough to the east and west, points would be reached from which it should be possible to see the counter-earth, but, as neither the counter-earth nor the central fire proved in fact to be visible, this portion of the Pythagorean system had to be sacrificed.[1]

We hear of a Pythagorean system in which the central fire was not outside the earth but in the centre of the earth itself. Simplicius,[2] in a note upon the passage of Aristotle describing the system of 'the Italian philosophers called Pythagoreans' in which the earth revolves about the central fire and so 'makes day and night', while it has the counter-earth opposite to it, adds that this is the theory of the Pythagoreans as Aristotle understood it, but that those who represented the more genuine Pythagorean doctrine 'describe as fire at the centre the creative force which from the centre gives life to all the earth and warms afresh that part of it which has cooled down. ... They called the earth a star, as being itself too an instrument of time. For the earth is the cause of days and of nights, since it makes day when it is lit up in that part which faces the sun, and it makes

[1] Gomperz, *Griechische Denker*, i³, pp. 97, 98 ; Schiaparelli, *I precursori di Copernico nell' antichità*, pp. 22, 25.
[2] Simplicius on *De caelo*, p. 512. 9-20, Heib.

night throughout the cone formed by its shadow. And the name of counter-earth was given by the Pythagoreans to the moon, just as they also called it "earth in the aether" (αἰθερίαν γῆν), both because it intercepts the sun's light, which is characteristic of the earth, and because it marks a delimitation of the heavenly regions, as the earth limits the portion below the moon.'

It is no doubt attractive to suppose, as Boeckh [1] does, that we have here a later modification of the system of Philolaus. But, as Martin [2] points out and Boeckh [3] admits, the earth in the system described by Simplicius is not in motion but at rest. For Simplicius, so far from implying that the earth rotates, thinks it necessary to explain how the Pythagoreans to whom he refers could, notwithstanding the earth's immobility, call it a 'star' and count it, exactly as Plato does, among the 'instruments of time'. The fact is that the system, except for the detail of the term 'counter-earth' being applied to the moon, agrees with the Platonic system as described in the *Timaeus*, and, as we have seen, there is nothing to suggest that Plato was acquainted with the Philolaic system at all; he was rather basing himself upon the views of Pythagoras and the first Pythagoreans.

A scholiast, writing on the same passage of Aristotle and describing the views of the Pythagoreans in almost the same words as those used by Simplicius, does, however, attribute motion to the earth. They put, he says, the fire at the centre of the earth. 'They said that the earth was a star as being itself too an "instrument". The counter-earth for them meant the moon. . . . And this star [i. e. evidently the earth] *by its motion* (φερόμενον) makes night and the day, because the cone formed by its shadow is night, while day is the illuminated part of it which is in the sun.' [4] The attribution of motion to the earth may be due to a misapprehension by the scholiast, just as Boeckh himself had at first assumed the earth's rotation to be indicated in the passage of Simplicius.

However this may be, if the system of Philolaus be taken, and the central fire be transferred to the centre of the earth (the

---

[1] Boeckh, *Das kosmische System des Platon*, p. 96.
[2] Martin, *Études sur le Timée*, ii, p. 104.   [3] Boeckh, loc. cit.
[4] Scholia in Aristotelem (Brandis), pp. 504 b 42 - 505 a 5.

counter-earth being also eliminated), and if the movements of the
earth, sun, moon, and planets round the centre be retained without
any modification save that which is mathematically involved by the
transfer of the central fire to the centre of the earth, the daily revolution of the earth about the central fire is necessarily transformed
into a rotation of the earth about its own axis in about 24 hours.

All authorities agree that Heraclides of Pontus affirmed the daily
rotation of the earth about its own axis; but the *Doxographi*
associate with this discovery another name, that of 'Ecphantus
the Pythagorean'. Thus we are told of Ecphantus that he asserted
'that the earth, being in the centre of the universe, moves about
its own centre in an eastward direction'.[1] Again, 'Heraclides of
Pontus and Ecphantus the Pythagorean make the earth move, not
in the sense of translation, but by way of turning as on an axle,
like a wheel, from west to east, about its own centre.'[2] Who then
is this Ecphantus, described in another place in Aëtius as Ecphantus
the Syracusan, one of the Pythagoreans? His personality is even
more of a mystery than that of Hicetas. The *Doxographi*, however,
tell us of other doctrines of his; Hippolytus[3] devotes a short
paragraph to him, between paragraphs about Xenophanes and
Hippon, which shows that Theophrastus must have spoken of him
at length. Some of his views were quite original, particularly on
the subject of atoms. Holding that the universe was made up of
indivisible bodies separated by void, he was the first to declare
that the monads of Pythagoras were corporeal; he attributed to
the atoms, besides size and shape, a motive force ($\delta \acute{v} \nu a \mu \iota s$); the
atoms were moved, not by their weight or by percussion, but by
a divine force which he called mind and soul. The universe was
a type of this, and accordingly the divine motive force created it
spherical. Now it is remarkable that Ecphantus's views all agree
with Heraclides' so far as we know them; Heraclides has the same
divine force moving the universe, which he also calls mind and soul;
he has the same theory of atoms, which he calls masses[4] ($\acute{o} \gamma \kappa o \iota$).
And the two hold the same view about the rotation of the earth.

[1] Hippolytus, *Refut.* i. 15 (*D. G.* p. 566; *Vors.* i², p. 265. 35).
[2] Aët. iii. 13. 3 (*D. G.* p. 378; *Vors.* i², p. 266. 5).   [3] Hippolytus, loc. cit.
[4] Galen, *Histor. phil.* 18 (*D. G.* p. 610. 22); Dionysius episcop. ap. Euseb.,
P.E. xiv. 23.   See Otto Voss, *De Heraclidis vita et scriptis*, p. 64; Tannery,
Revue des Études grecques, x, 1897, pp. 134–6.

Zeller observes, in addition, that the remark about the universe being made spherical reminds us of Plato.[1] Just as in the case of Hicetas, the natural conclusion is that the views attributed by the *Doxographi* to Ecphantus were expressed in a dialogue of Heraclides and put into the mouth of Ecphantus represented as a Pythagorean. Theophrastus may then have said something of this sort: ' Heraclides of Pontus has developed the following theories, attributing them to a certain Ecphantus '; and this would account for the *Doxographi* citing the doctrines sometimes by the name of Heraclides, sometimes by the name of Ecphantus.[2]

Heraclides, son of Euthyphron, was born at Heraclea in Pontus, probably not many years later than 388 B.C. He is said to have been wealthy and of ancient family. He went to Athens not later than 364, and there met Speusippus, who introduced him into the school of Plato. Proclus, it is true, denied that he was a pupil of Plato,[3] but this was because Proclus resented his contradiction of the Platonic view of the absolute immobility of the earth in the centre of the universe. Diogenes Laertius,[4] Simplicius,[5] Strabo,[6] and Cicero[7] leave us in no doubt on the subject; and we may also infer his relation to Plato from words of his own quoted elsewhere by Proclus,[8] according to which he was sent by Plato on an expedition to Colophon to collect the poems of Antimachus. Suidas[9] says that, during a journey of Plato to Sicily, Heraclides was left in charge of the school. After the death of Plato in 347, Speusippus was at the head of the school for eight years, and on his death in 338 B.C. Xenocrates was elected his successor, Heraclides and Menedemus, who were also candidates, being beaten by a few votes.[10] Heraclides then returned to his native town, where he seems to have lived till 315 or 310 B.C. While at Athens he is said to have attended the lectures of Aristotle also;[11] but Diogenes' statement that he also 'heard the Pythagoreans'

---

[1] Zeller, i[5], pp. 494, 495. [2] Tannery, loc. cit., p. 136.
[3] Proclus, *in Tim.* 281 E. [4] Diog. L. iii. 46, v. 86.
[5] Simpl. *in Ar. Phys.* iii. 4 (p. 202 b 36), p. 453. 29, Diels.
[6] Strabo, xii. 3. 1, p. 541.
[7] Cic. *De nat. deor.* i. 13. 34; *De legg.* iii. 6. 14; *Tusc. Disp.* v. 3. 8; *De Divin.* i. 23. 46. [8] Proclus, *in Tim.* 28 C.
[9] Suidas, s. v. Ἡρακλείδης. Zeller and Wilamowitz adduce confirmatory evidence. Voss alone disputes the statements; for references see Voss, pp. 11-12.
[10] *Ind. Acad. Hercul.* vi (Voss, p. 7). [11] Sotion in Diog. L. v. 86.

is no doubt incorrect; for by that time the Pythagoreans had left Greece altogether. The words were probably interpolated in the passage of Diogenes by some one who inferred first-hand acquaintance with Pythagorean doctrines on the part of Heraclides from the fact, among others, that he wrote a book 'concerning the Pythagoreans'.[1]

Diogenes Laertius tells us that Heraclides wrote works of the highest class both in matter and style. The remark is followed by a catalogue covering a very wide range of subjects, ethical, grammatical, musical and poetical, rhetorical, historical, with a note that there were geometrical and dialectical treatises as well. His dialogues are classified as (1) those which were by way of comedy, e.g. those on Pleasure and on Prudence, (2) those which were tragic, such as those on Things in Hades and on Piety, and (3) intermediate in character, familiar dialogues between philosophers, soldiers, and statesmen. They were very varied and very persuasive in style, adorned with myth and full of imagination, so original as to make Timaeus describe their author as παραδοξολόγος throughout, while Epicurus and the Epicureans, who attacked his physical theories, spoke of him as 'cramming his books with puerile stories'. There seems to have been more action in his dialogues than in Plato's;[2] his prologues generally had nothing to do with what followed;[3] there were usually a number of characters, and he was fond of introducing as interlocutors personages of ancient times.[4] He was much read and imitated at Rome, e.g. by Varro and Cicero; Cicero, for example, modelled upon Heraclides his dialogue *De republica*. Two of his dialogues at least, those 'On Nature' and 'On the Heavens', may have dealt with astronomy.

He naturally had enemies, who not only impugned his doctrines but took objection to his personality. We are told that he was effeminate in dress and over-corpulent, so that he was called, not Ponticus, but *Pompicus* (Πομπικός); his gait was slow and stately.[5]

Several of the fragments of Heraclides recall passages in Plato. Thus Heraclides represents souls as coming down, for incarnation,

---

[1] Voss, pp. 12–13.
[2] Ibid., pp. 26, 27.
[3] Proclus, *in Plat. Parmenidem*, Book i, *ad fin.*
[4] Voss, p. 22.
[5] Diog. L. v. 86.

from regions in the heaven, which he places in or about the Milky Way [1] (cf. the *Phaedrus* myth).   The universe is a god ; so are the planets, the earth, and the heaven.[2]   Other views of his about the universe and what it contains may also be referred to before we pass to the great discoveries in astronomy on which his fame rests. The universe is infinite ; [3] each star is also a universe or world, suspended in the infinite aether and comprising an earth, an atmosphere and an aether.[4]   The moon is earth surrounded with mist.[5]   Comets are clouds high in air lit up by the fire on high ; he accounts similarly for meteors and the like ; their different forms follow that of the cloud.[6]

We now pass to the first of Heraclides' great discoveries, that of the daily rotation of the earth about its axis.   Besides the passages above quoted, in which ' Ecphantus ' is also credited with the discovery, we have the following clear evidence on the subject :

' He (Aristotle) thought it right to take account of the hypothesis that *both* (i.e. the stars and the heaven as a whole) are at rest— although it would appear impossible to account for their apparent change of position on the assumption that both are at rest—because there have been some, like Heraclides of Pontus and Aristarchus, who supposed that the phenomena can be saved if the heaven and the stars are at rest while the earth moves about the poles of the equinoctial circle from the west (to the east), completing one revolution each day, approximately ; the ' approximately ' is added because of the daily motion of the sun to the extent of one degree. For of course, if the earth did not move at all, as he will later show to be the case, although he here assumes that it does for the sake of argument, it would be impossible for the phenomena to be saved on the supposition that the heaven and the stars are at rest.' [7]

' But Heraclides of Pontus supposed that the earth is in the centre and rotates (lit. ' moves in a circle ') while the heaven is at rest, and thought by this supposition to save the phenomena.' [8]

' Heraclides of Pontus supposed that the earth moves about the

---

[1] Iamblichus in Stobaeus, *Flor.*, p. 378, ed. Wachsmuth.
[2] Cicero, *De nat. deor.* i. 13. 34 (*D. G.* p. 541. 3-13).
[3] Aët. ii. 1. 5 (*D. G.* p. 328 b 4).   [4] Aët. ii. 13. 15 (*D. G.* p. 343).
[5] Aët. ii. 25. 13 (*D. G.* p. 356).   [6] Aët. iii. 2. 5 (*D. G.* pp. 366, 367).
[7] Simplicius on *De caelo* ii. 7 (289 b 1), pp. 444. 31 – 445. 5, Heib.
[8] Ibid. (on c. 13, 293 b 30), p. 519. 9–11, Heib.

centre, while the heaven is at rest, and thought in this way to save the phenomena.'[1]

'This would equally have happened [i. e. the stars would have seemed to be at different distances at different times instead of, as now, appearing to be always at the same distance, whether at rising or at setting or between these times, and the moon would not, when eclipsed, always have been diametrically opposite the sun, but would sometimes have been separated from it by an arc less than a semicircle] if the earth had a motion of translation ; but if the earth rotated about its centre while the heavenly bodies were at rest, as Heraclides of Pontus supposed, then (1), on the hypothesis of rotation towards the west, the stars would have been seen to rise from that side, while (2) on the hypothesis of rotation towards the east, (a) if it so rotated about the poles of the equinoctial circle (the equator), the sun and the other planets would not have risen at different points of the horizon [!], and, (b) if it so rotated about the poles of the zodiac circle, the fixed stars would not always have risen at the same points, as in fact they do ; so that, whether it rotated about the poles of the equinoctial circle or about the poles of the zodiac, how could the translation of the planets in the direct order of the signs have been saved on the assumption of the immobility of the heavens ? '[2]

'How can we, when we are told that the earth is wound round, reasonably make it turn round as well and give this as Plato's view ? Let Heraclides of Pontus, who was not a disciple of Plato, hold this opinion and move the earth round and round (κύκλῳ) ; but Plato made it unmoved.'[3]

The second great advance towards the Copernican system made by Heraclides was his discovery of the fact that Venus and Mercury revolve round the sun as centre. Some of the passages alluding to Heraclides' recognition of this fact import the later doctrine of epicycles ; but it is not difficult to eliminate this anachronism and to arrive at Heraclides' true theory. In some of the references the name of Heraclides is not mentioned. Vitruvius[4] describes the hypothesis thus :

'The stars of Mercury and Venus make their retrograde motions and retardations about the rays of the sun, forming by their courses a wreath or crown about the sun itself as centre. It is also owing to this circling that they linger at their stationary points in the spaces occupied by the signs.'

[1] Schol. in Arist. (Brandis), p. 505 b 46-7.
[2] Simpl. on De caelo ii. 14 (297 a 2), pp. 541. 27 – 542. 2, Heib.
[3] Proclus, in Tim. 281 E.   [4] Vitruvius, De architectura ix. 1 (4). 6.

Next Martianus Capella[1], who drew from Varro's work on astronomy, mentions the same hypothesis, but again without the name of its discoverer.

'For, although Venus and Mercury are seen to rise and set daily, their orbits do not encircle the earth at all, but circle round the sun in a freer motion. In fact, they make the sun the centre of their circles, so that they are sometimes carried above it, at other times below it and nearer to the earth, and Venus diverges from the sun by the breadth of one sign and a half [45°]. But, when they are above the sun, Mercury is the nearer to the earth, and when they are below the sun, Venus is the nearer, as it circles in a greater and wider-spread orbit . . . . .

'The circles of Mercury and Venus I have above described as epicycles. That is, they do not include the round earth within their own orbit, but revolve laterally to it in a certain way.'

Cicero says that the courses of Venus and Mercury 'follow the sun as companions',[2] but has nothing about their revolving round the sun.

It is in Chalcidius[3] that we find the name of Heraclides connected with the revolution of the planets Mercury and Venus round the sun as centre; but, like Adrastus in Theon of Smyrna, he erroneously imputes to Heraclides, as to Plato in the *Timaeus*, the machinery of epicycles. His words are:

'Lastly Heraclides Ponticus, when describing the circle of Lucifer as well as that of the sun, and giving the two circles one centre and one middle, showed how Lucifer is sometimes above, sometimes below the sun. For he says that the position of the sun, the moon, Lucifer, and all the planets, wherever they are, is defined by one line passing from the centre of the earth to that of the particular heavenly body. There will then be one straight line drawn from the centre of the earth showing the position of the sun, and there will equally be two other straight lines to the right and left of it respectively, and distant 50° from it, and 100° degrees from each other, the line nearest to the east showing the position of Lucifer or the Morning Star when it is furthest from the sun and near the eastern regions, a position in virtue of which it then receives the name of the Evening Star, because it appears in the east at evening after the setting of the sun.' . . . . (And so on.)

---

[1] Martianus Capella, *De nuptiis Philologiae et Mercurii*, viii. 880, 882.
[2] Cicero, *Somn. Scip.* c. 4. 2.
[3] Chalcidius, *Timaeus*, c. 110, pp. 176-7, Wrobel.

Chalcidius only mentions Venus in this passage, but he has just previously indicated a similar relation between Mercury and the sun. Reading this passage and the explanation, illustrated by a figure, which follows, together with supplementary particulars given in a passage of Macrobius presently to be mentioned, we can easily realize Chalcidius's conception. According to this we are to suppose a point which revolves uniformly about the earth from west to east in a year. This point is the centre of three concentric circles (epicycles) on which move respectively the sun (on the innermost), Mercury (on the middle circle), and Venus (on the outermost); the sun takes, of course, a year to describe its epicycle.[1] That the epicycle for the sun is wrongly imported into Heraclides' true system is confirmed by the next chapter of Chalcidius, with its illustrative figure, where he imports epicycles into Plato's system also. According to him, Plato used, not one principal circle with three epicycles having as their common centre a point describing that principal circle, but three principal circles, each with one epicycle; two circles, namely a principal circle and an epicycle, being used for each of the three bodies, the sun, Mercury, and Venus. But we know that in Plato's system the sun, Mercury, and Venus described three simple circles of which the earth is the centre. Hence the epicycles must be rejected altogether so far as Plato's system is concerned. Similarly, we must eliminate the sun's epicycle from the account of Heraclides' system, and we must suppose that he regarded Mercury and Venus as simply revolving in concentric circles about the sun.

The same contrast as is drawn by Chalcidius between Heraclides' system and Plato's system, as he represents them respectively, is drawn by Adrastus[2] between two possible theories, the authors of

---

[1] Chalcidius indicates (cc. 81, 109, and 112) that the sun's motion on its epicycle (which is from east to west) is in the contrary sense to the motion (from west to east) of Mercury and Venus on their epicycles respectively (cf. Adrastus in Theon of Smyrna, p. 175, 13-15, who says that the motion of the sun and moon on their epicycles is in the sense of the daily rotation from east to west, while the motion of the five planets on their epicycles is in the opposite sense). The commentators did not fail to see in this fact a possible explanation of Plato's remark that Mercury and Venus have 'the contrary tendency to the sun' (Chalcidius, c. 109, p. 176); and the explanation would be quite satisfactory *if* Plato could be supposed to have been acquainted with the theory of epicycles (cf. pp. 165-9 above).

[2] Adrastus in Theon of Smyrna, pp. 186. 17 - 187. 13.

which he does not specify. The first possibility corresponds to Chalcidius's version of Plato's system ; only Hipparchus's epicycles are, in agreement with Eudoxus's theory of spheres, represented by ' solid ' spheres as distinct from ' hollow '. We are to conceive, in the plane of the ecliptic, three concentric circles with the earth as common centre ; on each circle there moves, in one and the same direction, the centre of an immaterial sphere at such speed that the centre of the earth and these three centres are always in a straight line. As the plane of the ecliptic cuts the three immaterial spheres, this determines three circles which, with Hipparchus, we distinguish from the principal circles as epicycles. The sun moves on the epicycle of the circle nearest the earth, Mercury on that of the next, Venus on that of the outer circle. This is, therefore, precisely the Platonic system as conceived by Chalcidius. The second possibility, says Adrastus, is that the three principal circles may coalesce into one. Thus the three epicycles are reduced to sections of three concentric spheres, and the whole system of these spheres revolves about the earth, their common centre describing a circle about the earth. Here we have Heraclides' system as described by Chalcidius ; but Adrastus's version is better, in that, evidently relying on an older source, he hints that what moves on the main circle is not an immaterial point but the ' true solid sphere of the sun '; that is to say, it is only Mercury and Venus which move on epicycles, i.e. in circles about the sun as centre.[1]

Martin[2] exposed the error of those who inferred from the passage of Macrobius already alluded to that the Egyptians were acquainted with the fact thus stated by Heraclides. Macrobius observes that Cicero, in placing the sun fourth in the order of the planets reckoning from the earth, i.e. after the moon, Venus, and Mercury, followed the order adopted by the Chaldaeans and Archimedes, while

' Plato followed the Egyptians, the parents of all branches of philosophy, who, while placing the sun between the moon and Mercury, yet have detected and enunciated the reason why the sun is believed by some to be above Mercury and above Venus ; for neither are those who hold this view far from the apparent truth.'[3] . . .

[1] Hultsch, ' Das astronomische System des Herakleides von Pontos' in *Jahrb. für class. Philologie*, 1896, pp. 305–16.
[2] Martin, *Études sur le Timée*, ii, pp. 130–3. Cf. Boeckh, *Das kosmische System des Platon*, pp. 142, 143.   [2] Macrobius, *In somn. Scip.* i. 19. 2.

Then, after explaining that Saturn is as far from Jupiter as is indicated by the difference between their periods, 30 years and 12 years respectively, and again, that Jupiter's distance from Mars corresponds to the difference between their periods of 12 and 2 years respectively, he observes that Venus is so much below Mars as corresponds to the shorter period of Venus, one year, while Mercury is so near to Venus, and the sun to Mercury, that they all describe their orbits in one year, more or less, so that, as Cicero says, Venus and Mercury are companions of the sun. There was, therefore, no dispute about the order of the superior planets, Saturn, Jupiter, and Mars, nor about the relative position of the moon as the lowest of all;

'But the proximity of the three others which are the nearest to one another, namely Venus, Mercury, and the sun, has caused uncertainty as regards their order, though only in the minds of others, not of the Egyptians; for the true relation did not escape the penetration of the Egyptians, and it is as follows. The circle on which the sun moves ['circulus, per quem sol discurrit'= the sun's *epicycle*] is lower than, and encircled by, the circle of Mercury; above the circle of Mercury, and including it, is the circle of Venus; hence it is that, when the two planets are describing the upper portions of their circles, they are regarded as placed above the sun, but when they are traversing the lower portions of their circles, the sun is considered to be superior to them.'[1] . . .

Macrobius's main object may have been to put the Egyptians on a level with the Chaldaeans, the oldest cultured Asiatics.[2] But, though the Chaldaeans arranged the planets in an order different from that adopted by Plato, the idea of Mercury and Venus revolving round the sun was certainly not Chaldaean but Greek, and originated with Heraclides. If Macrobius really intended to attribute Heraclides' discovery to the Egyptians, it must be because the theory had perpetuated itself as a tradition of the Alexandrine astronomers anterior to our era.[3] And if the Egyptians had really regarded Mercury and Venus as being in the relation of satellites to the sun, it is not easy to understand why they placed Mercury and Venus above the sun, since they might equally well have placed them below it.

Hultsch explains the evolution of the Heraclides-epicyclic system

---

[1] Macrobius, *In somn. Scip.* i. 19, 5-6.   [2] Hultsch, loc. cit.
[3] Tannery, *Recherches sur l'histoire de l'astronomie ancienne*, pp. 260, 261.

in the following way. The axial rotation of the earth was rejected by Hipparchus. Hence the occasion, for some one living after Hipparchus's time, of modifying Heraclides' system and grafting on to it the theory of epicycles. Or perhaps the post-Hipparchian inventor of the Heraclides-epicyclic blend wished to oppose to some enthusiastic champion of Hipparchus the authority of Heraclides, but could not get rid of epicycles.

The next question which arises is this. Having made Mercury and Venus revolve round the sun as satellites, did Heraclides proceed to draw the same inference with regard to the other, the superior, planets? When it was once laid down that all the five planets alike revolved round the sun, and this hypothesis was combined with that of the revolution of the sun round the earth as centre, the result was the system of Tycho Brahe, with the improvement, already made by Heraclides, of the substitution of the daily rotation of the earth for the daily revolution of the whole system round the earth supposed at rest. Schiaparelli, who added to his first tract, *I precursori di Copernico nell' antichità*, a further extremely elaborate study[1] dealing at length with the above question among others, came to the conclusion that it was probably Heraclides himself who took the further step of regarding all the five planets alike as revolving round the sun, but that, if it was not Heraclides, it was at all events some contemporary of his who did so. This conclusion represents a certain change of view on the part of Schiaparelli after the date of *I precursori*, where he says, 'it appears that Heraclides Ponticus, as the evidence cited indicates, limited to Venus and Mercury the revolution round the sun, and it seems that he retained the earth as the centre of the movements of the superior planets'.[2] Schiaparelli's later view is based upon presumption rather than upon direct evidence, which indeed does not exist. His argument is a *tour de force*, but, although opinions will differ, I for my part think that he trusts too much to the testimony of late writers as to the supposed very early discovery of the machinery of eccentrics and epicycles, and his case does not seem to me to be made out.

---

[1] Schiaparelli, *Origine del sistema planetario eliocentrico presso i Greci*, 1898 (in *Memorie del R. Istituto Lombardo di scienze e lettere*, vol. xviii, pp. 61 sqq.).

[2] Schiaparelli, *I precursori*, pp. 27, 28.

Schiaparelli's arguments are, however, well worthy of consideration, and I will represent them as completely and fairly as I can.
Having hit upon the hypothesis of the revolution of Mercury and
Venus round the sun, and not the earth, as centre, Heraclides had
found a possible explanation of the varying degrees of brightness
shown by the two inferior planets and of the narrow limits of their
deviation from the sun ; he would also easily see that the hypothesis gave a solution of the difficulty of the stationary points and
the retrogradations in the case of these planets. Eudoxus had
tried to solve the latter difficulty by ingenious and elegant combinations of concentric spheres ; but he only succeeded with Jupiter and
Saturn. Callippus went further on the same lines and succeeded
to a certain extent with Mars ; probably, too, he came nearer to
accounting for the movements of Mercury and Venus. The most
formidable objection to the explanation of the planetary movements by means of concentric spheres was the fact that, on this
hypothesis, the distance of each planet from the earth, and consequently its brightness, should be absolutely invariable, whereas
mere ocular observation sufficed to prove that this is not so. This
difficulty was, as we have seen, very early realized ; Polemarchus,
a friend of Eudoxus himself, was aware of it, but tried to make out
that the inequality of the distance was negligible and of no account
in comparison with the advantage of having all the spheres about
one and the same centre ; Aristotle, too, in his *Physical Problems*
(now lost) discussed the same difficulty.[1] The first who tried to get
over the difficulty was Autolycus of Pitane, the author of the tract
On the moving sphere, but even he was not successful.[2] Now Heraclides, departing altogether from the system of spheres, to which
the Aristotelian school doggedly adhered, and adopting a system of
circles more akin to Pythagorean ideas, had suggested a sufficient
explanation with regard to Venus and Mercury; and, as Mars was
seen, equally with Venus, to vary in apparent size and brightness,
it was natural for the same school of thought to try to find an
explanation of the similar phenomena with regard to Mars on *their*
lines as opposed to those which found favour with Aristotle.

Now, with regard to Mars, it would be seen that the times of its

[1] Sosigenes in Simplicius on *De caelo* (293 a 4), p. 505. 21-7, Heib.
[2] Ibid., p. 504. 22-5, Heib.

greatest brightness corresponded with the times when it was in opposition and not in conjunction ; that is to say, it is brightest when it occupies a position in the zodiac opposite to the sun ; it must therefore be nearest the earth at that time, and consequently the centre of its orbit cannot be the centre of the earth, but must be on the straight line joining the earth to the sun. The analogy of Venus and Mercury might then suggest that perhaps Mars, too, might revolve round the sun. I do not attach much importance in this connexion to a passage from Theon of Smyrna quoted by Schiaparelli. Theon, in the passage contrasting two hypotheses (the supposed Platonic and supposed Heraclidean) with regard to the movements of Venus and Mercury, adds :

'And one might suspect that this [the Heraclidean view] repre-sents the truer view of their relative position and order, the effect of it being to make this region the abode of the animating principle in the universe, regarded as a living thing, the sun being as it were the heart of the All in virtue of its great heat and in consequence of its motion, its size, and its connexion with the bodies about it. For in animate beings the centre of the thing, that is, of the animal as animal, is different from the centre of it regarded as a magnitude ; thus with ourselves as men and living beings one centre is the region about the heart, the centre of the vital principle . . . the other is that of the body as a magnitude. . . . Similarly, if we may extend to the greatest, noblest and divine the analogy of the small, insig-nificant and mortal, the centre of the universe as a magnitude is the region about the earth which is cold and destitute of motion ; while in the universe as universe and living thing the region about the sun is the centre of its animating principle, the sun being as it were the heart of the All, which is also, as we are told, the starting-point whence the soul proceeds to permeate the whole body spread over it from the extremities inwards.'[1]

The argument of Theon seems rather to be offered as a plausible defence of the new theory of Venus and Mercury as satellites of the sun, after the event as it were, than as an *a priori* ground for putting forward that hypothesis or for extending it to Mars and the other superior planets.

When the possibility of Mars revolving round the sun came to

---

[1] Theon of Smyrna, pp. 187. 13 – 188. 7.   Cf. Plutarch, *De fac. in orbe lunae,* c. 15, p. 928 B, C ; Macrobius, *In somn. Scip.* i. 20. 1–8.

be considered, it would be at once obvious that the precise hypothesis adopted for Mercury and Venus would not apply, because
the circles described by those planets about the sun are relatively
small circles and are entirely on one side of the earth, whereas the
circle described by Mars comprehends the earth which is inside it.
The next possibility that would present itself would be that the
planet might move uniformly round an *eccentric* circle of some
kind, a circle passing round the earth but with some other point
not the earth as centre. Suppose E is the earth, fixed at the centre
of the universe, QR an eccentric circle with centre O. Draw the
diameter QR through E, O. Then Q represents the perigee of

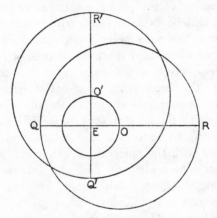

Fig. 12.

a planet moving on the eccentric circle. In opposition, therefore,
Mars will be at Q, and the sun will be opposite to it, i.e. at some
point on ER. If now the oppositions always occurred in the same
place in the zodiac, i.e. in the same direction EQ, this hypothesis
would explain the differences of brightness. But the oppositions
do not always take place in the same direction; they may take
place at any part of the zodiac. Consequently, the direction of
opposition is not constant, as EQ, but the diameter RQ must
move round the centre E in such a way that the *perigeal* point Q
is always opposite to the sun. Therefore Q, *the point of opposition,
revolves round E in the space of a year along the ecliptic in the
direct order of the signs.* Hence O, the centre of the eccentric, also

revolves round E in a year in such a way that it is always in the direction of the sun. We suppose, therefore, that the whole eccentric circle moves bodily round E as centre, as if it were a material disc attached to E as a sort of hinge. If now we suppose Mars to move uniformly round the circumference of the eccentric in the *inverse* order of the signs, completing the circuit from perigee to perigee, or from apogee to apogee, in a time equal to the period of its synodic revolution, the opposition will occur at the right places and the brightness will then be greatest. Further (and this is the most important point) if the distance EO (the 'eccentricity') is chosen in the proper ratio to the radius OR, the irregular movements of the planet, its stationary positions, and its retrogradations will be explained also (this would be clear to any one who was enough of a geometer, though the corresponding facts are easier to see when the hypothesis is that of epicycles). By means of observations it would be possible to deduce the *ratio* of the radius to the 'eccentricity', but not their absolute magnitudes. But the centre O is always in the direction of the sun ; it only remained to fix its distance (EO). The natural thing in the case of Mars would be to make the material sun the centre, just as had been done with the epicycles of Venus and Mercury. The use of ideal points as centres for epicycles and eccentrics was no doubt first thought of, at a later stage, by some of the great mathematicians such as Apollonius.

The next link in Schiaparelli's chain of argument is the fact that the same movement as is represented by movable eccentrics of the sort just described can equally well be represented by means of epicycles, a fact which is proved by Theon of Smyrna and others. Let us then see how the motion of Mars, as above represented by means of a movable eccentric, can be represented by means of an epicycle. Let Figure 13 (A) represent a movable eccentric, E being the earth, S the centre of the eccentric which moves round the circle SS' in the direction shown by the arrow, in such a way that ES is always in the direction of the sun and moves in the direct order of the signs. Let CC' be the eccentric with centre S. Produce ES to meet the eccentric in C, which will then be the position of the apogee of the eccentric. Let the planet be then at the point D describing the circle CC' in the *inverse*

order of the signs. The angle *CSD* or the arc *CD* reckoned from
the apogee in the *inverse* order of the signs will be the *argument
of the anomaly*, or shortly the *anomaly*; the planet will be seen
from the earth in the direction *ED*.

Now [Fig. 13 (B)], on the hypothesis of the epicycle, let Θ be the
centre of the earth. About Θ as centre describe the circle ΣΣ′ equal
to the eccentric circle of the other figure, and draw the radius ΘΣ
parallel (and equal) to *SD* in the other figure. Take Σ as the centre
of the epicycle, and about it describe the circle ΔΔ′ equal to the
circle *SS′* in the other figure. If we produce ΘΣ to *K*, *K* will
be at the moment the apogee of the epicycle. Make the angle

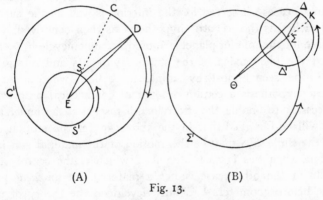

(A)   (B)

Fig. 13.

*K*ΣΔ equal to the anomaly (i.e. the angle *CSD* in the other figure)
but reckoned in the opposite sense (i.e. in the *direct* order of the
signs). Suppose then that the planet is at Δ and seen from the
earth in the direction ΘΔ.

In the triangles *ESD*, ΘΣΔ, *DS* is equal and parallel to ΣΘ,
and the angles *DSE*, ΘΣΔ are equal; therefore *ES*, ΔΣ are
parallel. But *ES*, ΔΣ are also equal; therefore the two sides
ES, *SD* are equal to the two sides ΔΣ, ΣΘ respectively. And
the included angles are equal; therefore the triangles *ESD*, ΔΣΘ
are equal in all respects. And, since the two sides *ES*, ΔΣ are
equal and parallel, and the sides *SD*, ΘΣ are also equal and
parallel, it follows that the third sides *ED*, ΘΔ will be equal and
parallel, i.e. the planet will be seen in the same direction and at
the same distance under either hypothesis.

The conditions necessary in order that this may be true at any instant are two: (1) the radii SD, $\Theta\Sigma$ of the eccentric and the deferent circle respectively must always remain parallel; (2) the anomaly CSD in the eccentric must be equal to the anomaly $K\Sigma\Delta$ in the epicycle, while the anomaly must in the first case be reckoned in the *inverse* order, and in the second case in the *direct* order of the signs. It is evident also that the proof still holds if, instead of making the radii of the two circles in each hypothesis equal, we suppose them proportional only and change the dimensions of either figure as we please.

It is clear why the Greek mathematicians preferred the epicycle hypothesis to the eccentric. It was because the former was applicable to all cases; it served for the inferior as well as the superior planets, whereas the eccentric hypothesis, as then conceived, would not serve for the inferior planets; moreover, the epicycle hypothesis enabled the phenomena of the stationary points and retrogradations to be seen almost by simple inspection, whereas on the eccentric hypothesis a certain amount of geometrical proof would be necessary to enable the effect in this respect to be understood. But it will be observed that in the above figures the motion of S round the circle $S'S$ may be the motion of the material sun in its orbit but, when this is so, the point Σ which is the centre of the epicycle in the other case is not a material but an *ideal* point. Hence, before geometers had fully developed the theory of revolution about ideal points, the *eccentric* hypothesis was the only practicable way of representing the movements of the superior planets, Mars, Jupiter, and Saturn.

Now we infer from a passage of Ptolemy [1] that, while Apollonius understood the theory of epicycles in all its generality, he only knew of the particular class of eccentrics in which the movable centre of the eccentric moves at an angular speed equal to that of the *sun* describing its orbit about the earth. The description by Apollonius of the two hypotheses is in these words:

(1) The epicycle hypothesis: 'Here the epicycle's advance in longitude is in the direct order of the signs round the circle concentric with the zodiac, while the star moves on the epicycle about its centre at a speed equal to that of the anomaly and in the direct

[1] Ptolemy, *Syntaxis* xii. I (vol. ii, pp. 450. 10–17, 451. 6–14, Heib.).

order of the signs in that part of the circumference of the epicycle
which is furthest from the earth.'

(2) The eccentric hypothesis : ' *This is only applicable to the three
planets which can be at any angular distance whatever from the sun*,
and here the centre of the eccentric circle moves about the centre
of the zodiac in the direct order of the signs and *at a speed equal
to that of the sun*, while the star moves on the eccentric about its
centre in the inverse order of the signs and at a speed equal to
that of the anomaly.'

What makes Apollonius say that the eccentric hypothesis is not
applicable to the inferior planets is the fact that, in order to make it
apply to them, we should have to suppose the circle described by the
centre of the eccentric to be greater than the eccentric circle itself.

The object of the passage of Ptolemy is to explain the stationary
points and retrogradations on either hypothesis, and he reproduces
in his own form two propositions which, he says, had been proved
' by other mathematicians as well as by Apollonius of Perga with
reference to one of the anomalies, the anomaly in relation to the
sun.'   It is from the passage in question that it has commonly been
inferred that Apollonius of Perga was the inventor of epicycles.
I agree, however, with Schiaparelli that, if we read the passage
carefully, we shall find that it does not imply this.   It is at least
as easy to infer from the language of Apollonius that, in the case of
the epicycle-hypothesis at all events, he was only stating formally
what was already familiar to those conversant with the subject.

Now the eccentric hypothesis, which is, in the proposition with
regard to it proved by Apollonius, limited to the particular case
of the three superior planets, was evidently generalized at or
before the time of Hipparchus.   This is clear from passages of
Ptolemy and Theon of Smyrna quoted by Schiaparelli.   (1) Ptolemy
says that Hipparchus was the first to point out that it is necessary
to explain how there are two kinds of anomaly in the case of each
of the planets, the *solar* (ἡ παρὰ τὸν ἥλιον ἀνωμαλία) and the
zodiacal, or how the retrogradations of each planet are unequal
and of such and such lengths, whereas all other mathematicians
had based their geometrical proofs on the assumption that the
anomaly and the retrogradation were one and the same respectively.   Hipparchus added that these phenomena were not accounted

for either by eccentric circles, or by circles concentric with the zodiac carrying epicycles, or even by a combination of both hypotheses.[1] (2) 'Hipparchus says it is worthy of investigation by mathematicians why on two hypotheses so different from one another, that of eccentric circles and that of concentric circles with epicycles, the same results appear to follow.'[2] A further allusion to the same remark of Hipparchus shows that the identity of the results following from the two hypotheses was shown with regard to the *sun*,[3] which is the case for which Adrastus proved it.[4] Again, Theon of Smyrna says that ' Hipparchus prefers the hypothesis of the epicycle which he claims as his own, asserting that it is more natural that all the heavenly bodies should be properly balanced, and connected together in the same way, about the centre of the universe; and yet, because he was not sufficiently equipped with physical knowledge, even he did not know for certain which is the natural and therefore true movement of the planets and which the incidental and apparent; but he, too, supposes that the epicycle of each planet moves on the encentric circle and the planet on the epicycle'.[5] (3) In a famous passage where Simplicius reproduces a quotation by Alexander from Geminus or Posidonius (if Geminus was actually copying Posidonius) we read, ' Why do the *sun, moon*, and planets appear to move irregularly? Because, whether we suppose that their circles are eccentric or that they move on epicycles, their apparent irregularity will be saved; and it will be necessary to go further and consider in how many ways these same phenomena are capable of being explained, in order that our theory of the planets may agree with that explanation of the causes which proves admissible.'[6]

The theory of eccentrics had therefore been generalized by Hipparchus's time, but with Apollonius was still limited to the case of the three superior planets. This indicates clearly enough that it was invented for the specific purpose of explaining the movements of Mars, Jupiter, and Saturn about the sun, and for that purpose alone. Who then took this step in the formulation of a system

---

[1] Ptolemy, *Syntaxis* ix. 2 (vol. ii, pp. 210. 19–211. 4, Heib.).
[2] Theon of Smyrna, p. 166. 6–10.   [3] Ibid., p. 185. 13–19.
[4] Ibid., pp. 166. 14–172. 14.   [5] Ibid., p. 188. 15–24.
[6] Simplicius *in Phys.*, p. 292. 15-20, ed. Diels.

which is the same as that of Tycho Brahe? Tannery[1] thinks it was Apollonius, and in that case Apollonius, coming after Aristarchus of Samos, would be exactly the Tycho Brahe of the Copernicus of antiquity.

Schiaparelli, however, as I have said above, will have it that it was not Apollonius, but Heraclides or some contemporary of his, who took the final step towards the Tychonic system. In order to prove this it is necessary to show that epicycles and movable eccentric circles were both in use by Heraclides' time, and Schiaparelli tries to establish this by quotations from Geminus, Proclus, Theon of Smyrna, Chalcidius, and Simplicius; but it is here that he seems to me to fail. The passages cited are as follows.

(1) Geminus: 'It is a fundamental assumption in all astronomy that the sun, the moon, and the five planets move in circular orbits at uniform speed in a sense contrary to that of the universe. For the Pythagoreans, who were the first to apply themselves to investigations of this kind, assumed the movements of the sun, the moon, and the five planets to be circular and uniform. They would not admit, with reference to things divine and eternal, any disorder such as would make them move at one time more swiftly, at one time more slowly, and at another time stand still, as the five planets do at their so-called *stationary points*. For such irregularity of motion would not even be expected of a decent and orderly man in his journeys. With men, of course, the necessities of life are often causes of slowness and swiftness; but with the imperishable stars it is not possible to adduce any cause of swiftness or slowness. Accordingly, they proposed the problem, how the phenomena could be accounted for by means of circular and uniform movements.'[2] Geminus goes on, it is true, to explain why the sun, although moving at uniform speed, describes equal arcs in unequal times, and explains the fact by assuming the sun to move uniformly in an *eccentric* circle, i.e. a circle of which the earth is an internal point but not the centre. But there is nothing to suggest that this was the *Pythagorean* answer to the problem. Geminus says ' *We shall give* the explanation as regards the other

---

[1] Tannery, *Recherches sur l'histoire de l'astronomie ancienne*, c. 14, pp. 245, 253-9.

[2] Geminus, *Isagoge*, c. I. 19-21, p. 10. 2-20, ed. Manitius.

stars in another place ; but *we will show* at once with regard to the
sun how . . . .'

(2) Theon of Smyrna says, quoting Adrastus: [1] 'The apparent
intricacy of the motion of the planets is due to the fact that they
seem to us to be carried through the signs of the zodiac in circles
of their own, being fixed in spheres of their own and moved along
the circles, as Pythagoras was the first to observe, a certain intricate
and irregular movement being thus incidentally grafted on to their
simple and uniform motion, which remains the same.'

(3) Chalcidius says: [2] 'Yet all the planets seem to us to move
unequally and some even to show disordered movements. What
then shall we give as the explanation of this erroneous supposition ?
That mentioned above, which was also known to Pythagoras,
namely that, while they are fixed in their own spheres and so
carried round, they appear, owing to our feebleness of vision, to
describe the circle of the zodiac.'

Schiaparelli adds : 'We cannot attribute any historical value to
this notice unless we admit that by "Pythagoras" are to be understood those same Pythagoreans of whom Geminus speaks. And
it would follow that those Pythagoreans had explained the irregularity of the planetary movements by means of the combination
of two circular movements, one with the earth as centre, the other
having its centre outside the earth (eccentric or epicycle).' But
there is nothing whatever in these passages to suggest eccentrics
or epicycles. Theon follows up his remark by referring to the
combination of movements as explained by Plato in the *Timaeus*,
i. e. the supposition that, while the sun, moon, and planets have
an independent circular movement of their own in the zodiac about
the earth as centre, they also share in the movement of the fixed
stars (the daily rotation about the axis of the universe). The
passage of Chalcidius seems to mean the same thing. Martin
interprets the passages of Geminus and Chalcidius as saying that
Pythagoras denied the irregularity of the movement of the stars
called planets, considering it an optical illusion.[3] Zeller observes
that the passage of Theon indicates that the early Pythagoreans

---

[1] Theon of Smyrna, p. 150. 12–18.
[2] Chalcidius, *Timaeus*, c. 77, 78, pp. 145, 146, ed. Wrobel.
[3] Martin, *Études sur le Timée*, ii, p. 120.

developed the doctrine of Anaximander into a theory of spheres carrying round stars which are made fast to them, and that this is confirmed by the occurrence of the same conception in Parmenides and Plato. Whether all the stars are carried by spheres of their own, i.e. hollow spheres, or only the fixed stars are carried by one sphere, while the planets, as with Plato, are fixed on hoop-like circles, is not clear. But Zeller rejects altogether the view that the Pythagoreans assumed eccentrics and epicycles as not only unsupported by trustworthy evidence but as inconsistent with the whole development of the old astronomy.[1]

But we have not done with the evidence cited by Schiaparelli.

(4) Proclus says[2]: 'The hypotheses of eccentrics and epicycles commended themselves also, so history tells us, to the famous Pythagoreans as being more simple than all others—for it is necessary in dealing with this question, and Pythagoras himself encouraged his disciples, to try to solve the problem by means of the fewest and most simple hypotheses possible.' This passage, as Schiaparelli says, attributes the first idea of movable eccentrics as well as of epicycles to the Pythagoreans. But it has to be considered along with a passage of Simplicius which Schiaparelli regards as the most important notice of all ;

(5) Simplicius says, after speaking of the system of concentric spheres : ' Later astronomers then, rejecting the hypothesis of revolving spheres, mainly because they do not suffice to explain the variations of distance and the irregularity of the movements, dispensed with concentric spheres and assumed eccentrics and epicycles instead—if indeed the hypothesis of eccentric circles was not invented by the Pythagoreans, as some tell us, including Nicomachus and Iamblichus who followed him.'[3] This passage, it is true, may indicate that it was only eccentric circles, and not epicycles also, which the Pythagoreans discovered ; but Schiaparelli regards it as conclusive with reference to movable eccentrics. Unfortunately, he has not allowed for the fact that it was the habit of the neo-Pythagoreans to attribute, so far as possible, *every* discovery to the Pythagoreans, and even to Pythagoras himself. The evidence of Nicomachus would therefore

---

[1] Zeller, i⁵, p. 415 *n.*
[2] Proclus, *Hypotyposis astronomicarum positionum,* c. 1, § 34, p. 18, ed. Manitius.   [3] Simplicius on *De caelo*, p. 507. 9–14, Heib.

be worthless even if it could not easily be accounted for; but, as Hultsch says,[1] the statement is easily explained as a reminiscence of the Pythagorean central fire, for of course in that system each planet moved in a circle about the central fire as centre and, as the earth also moved round the same central fire, the orbit of the planet would be *eccentric* relatively to the earth. The passage of Proclus may be based on the authority of Nicomachus; or it may be a case of a wrong inference, thus: the Pythagoreans sought the simplest hypothesis because they held that that would be the best; the simplest is that of eccentrics and epicycles; therefore the Pythagoreans would naturally think of that hypothesis.

But, even on the assumption that 'the Pythagoreans' are to be credited with the invention of eccentrics and epicycles, the difficulties are great, as Schiaparelli himself saw.[2] Who are the particular Pythagoreans who made the discovery? The problem which, according to Geminus, the Pythagoreans propounded of finding 'how the phenomena could be accounted for by means of circular and uniform motions' is almost identical with that which Sosigenes, on the authority of Eudemus, says that Plato set, 'What are the uniform and ordered movements by the assumption of which the facts about the movements of the planets can be accounted for?'. If now the Pythagoreans had, by Plato's time, discovered the solution by means of movable eccentrics and epicycles, Plato could not have been unaware of the fact, and he would not then have set the problem again in almost the same terms; Plato, however, makes no mention whatever of epicycles or eccentrics. Hence the Pythagoreans in question could not have been the early Pythagoreans or any Pythagoreans up to the time of Philolaus (who was about half a century earlier than Plato); they must therefore be sought among the contemporaries of Plato or in the years immediately after his death; indeed, if the hypothesis had been put forward in his lifetime, we should have expected to find some allusion to it in his writings. We are, therefore, brought down to the period of Philip of Macedon and Alexander the Great. But it was in these reigns that the Pythagorean schools gradually died out, leaving the

---

[1] Hultsch, art. 'Astronomie' in Pauly-Wissowa's *Real-Encyclopädie*, § 14.
[2] Schiaparelli, *Origine del sistema planetario eliocentrico presso i Greci*, pp. 81-2.

name to certain fraternities whose objects were rather ascetic and religious than philosophical;[1] according to Diodorus the last Pythagorean philosophers lived about 366 B.C.[2] Schiaparelli is therefore obliged to assume that, 'if the schools ceased, their doctrines were not entirely lost,' and his whole case for crediting Heraclides or one of his contemporaries with the complete anticipation of the system of Tycho Brahe really rests on this assumption combined with the statement of Diogenes Laertius that Heraclides 'also heard the Pythagoreans'.[3] It is true that Schiaparelli has one other argument, which however seems to be an argument of despair. It is based on the passage, already quoted above (pp. 186-7), in which Aristotle, after speaking of the central fire of the 'so-called Pythagoreans', says :[4] 'And no doubt many others, too, would agree (with the Pythagoreans) that the place in the centre should not be assigned to the earth, if they looked for the truth, not in the observed facts, but in *a priori* arguments. For they hold that it is appropriate to the worthiest object that it should be given the worthiest place. Now fire is worthier than earth . . .' Schiaparelli adds, 'On this passage Boeckh rightly observes that the reference is not to the past, but to opinions held in the time of Aristotle. The Pythagorean doctrines had ceased to be the object of teaching in special schools, but they survived in the opinions of many and in part found favour even in the Academy. From these reflections we draw the conclusion that the first idea of epicycles and of eccentrics was conceived towards the time of Philip or of Alexander, not among the pure Academics, nor in the Lyceum, but among those more independent thinkers who, like Heraclides, without forming a separate school, had remained faithful, at least so far as regards natural philosophy, to Pythagorean ideas, and for that reason could still with some truth be called Pythagoreans, especially by writers of a much later date.' That is to say, Nicomachus must, when claiming the discovery of eccentrics for the Pythagoreans, have been referring to certain persons whom Aristotle expressly distinguishes from that school, his ground for claiming those persons as Pythagoreans being that they were imbued with Pythagorean doctrines. It seems to me

---

[1] Zeller, i[5], pp. 338-42, iii. 2[3], pp. 79 sqq.
[2] Diodorus, xv. 76; Zeller, i[5], p. 339, note 2.   [3] Diog. L. v. 86.
[4] Aristotle, *De caelo* ii. 13, 293 a 27-32.

that, by this desperate suggestion, Schiaparelli practically gives away his case so far as it is based on Nicomachus. But, even if we assume Nicomachus to have been referring to the independent persons who, according to Aristotle, agreed in the theory of a central fire, this does not help Schiaparelli's argument, because in Aristotle's account of those persons' views there is no hint whatever of eccentrics or epicycles.

It is no doubt possible that Heraclides or one of his contemporaries may, in the manner suggested, have arrived at the Tychonic system; but I think that Schiaparelli has failed to establish this, and the probabilities seem to me to be decidedly against it. I judge mainly by the passage of Ptolemy (xii. 1) about the two propositions proved by Apollonius and other geometers. Apollonius was born, probably, 125 years later than Heraclides. Now Heraclides certainly originated a particular hypothesis of epicycles, namely epicycles described by Venus and Mercury about the material sun as centre. By Apollonius's time the hypothesis of epicycles had become quite general, and such a generalization might easily come about in a period of a century and more. But the hypothesis of eccentrics had, by Apollonius's time, advanced only a very short way indeed towards a corresponding generality. Started to explain the movements of the superior planets, the hypothesis originally made the material sun the centre of the eccentric circle, and by Apollonius's time it had been only so far generalized as to allow the sun to be anywhere on the line joining the centre of the earth to the moving centre of the eccentric circle. This represents very little progress for a hundred years ; and the fact suggests that nothing like a hundred years had passed since the first formulation of the hypothesis in its most simple form, corresponding to the first form of the epicycle hypothesis. In other words, the Tychonic system was most probably completed by some one intermediate between Heraclides and Apollonius and nearer to Apollonius than Heraclides, if it was not actually reserved for Apollonius himself. And that there is a fair probability in favour of attributing the step to Apollonius himself seems to me to follow from two considerations. It is *a priori* less likely that the 'great geometer' should merely have proved two geometrical propositions to show the effect of two hypotheses formulated by some of his predecessors, than that he should have attached the propositions to hypotheses, or to a comparison of hypotheses, which he was himself the first to develop ; and the fact that he takes the trouble to mention that the eccentric hypothesis only applies to the case of the three superior planets is more intelligible on the assumption that the hypothesis was at the time a new one, than it would be if the hypothesis had been familiar to mathematicians for some time.

We have lastly to deal with a still greater claim put forward by Schiaparelli on behalf of Heraclides ; this is nothing less than the claim that it was Heraclides, and not Aristarchus of Samos, who first stated as a possibility the Copernican hypothesis. Schiaparelli's argument rests entirely on one passage, a sentence forming part of a quotation from Geminus which Simplicius copied from Alexander and embodied in his commentary on the *Physics* of Aristotle ;[1] and, inasmuch as this passage, as it stands in the MSS., is not only unconfirmed by any other passage in Greek writers, but is in direct conflict with other passages found in Simplicius himself, it calls for the very closest examination. As the context is itself important, I shall give a translation of the whole quotation from Geminus according to the text of Diels ; I shall then discuss the text and the interpretation of the particular sentence relied upon by Schiaparelli. The passage then of Simplicius is as follows :

' Alexander carefully quotes a certain explanation by Geminus taken from his summary of the *Meteorologica* of Posidonius. Geminus's comment, which is inspired by the views of Aristotle, is as follows :

' " It is the business of physical inquiry to consider the substance of the heaven and the stars, their force and quality, their coming into being and their destruction, nay, it is in a position even to prove the facts about their size, shape, and arrangement ; astronomy, on the other hand, does not attempt to speak of anything of this kind, but proves the arrangement of the heavenly bodies by considerations based on the view that the heaven is a real κόσμος, and further, it tells us of the shapes and sizes and distances of the earth, sun, and moon, and of eclipses and conjunctions of the stars, as well as of the quality and extent of their movements. Accordingly, as it is connected with the investigation of quantity, size, and quality of form or shape, it naturally stood in need, in this way, of arithmetic

---

[1] Simplicius, *in Phys.* (ii. 2, 193 b 23), pp. 291. 21 – 292. 31, ed. Diels (1882).

and geometry. The things, then, of which alone astronomy claims to give an account it is able to establish by means of arithmetic and geometry. Now in many cases the astronomer and the physicist will propose to prove the same point, e. g., that the sun is of great size or that the earth is spherical, but they will not proceed by the same road. The physicist will prove each fact by considerations of essence or substance, of force, of its being better that things should be as they are, or of coming into being and change; the astronomer will prove them by the properties of figures or magnitudes, or by the amount of movement and the time that is appropriate to it. Again, the physicist will in many cases reach the cause by looking to creative force; but the astronomer, when he proves facts from external conditions, is not qualified to judge of the cause, as when, for instance, he declares the earth or the stars to be spherical; sometimes he does not even desire to ascertain the cause, as when he discourses about an eclipse; at other times he invents by way of hypothesis, and states certain expedients by the assumption of which the phenomena will be saved. For example, why do the sun, the moon, and the planets appear to move irregularly? We may answer that, if we assume that their orbits are eccentric circles or that the stars describe an epicycle, their apparent irregularity will be saved; and it will be necessary to go further and examine in how many different ways it is possible for these phenomena to be brought about, so that we may bring our theory concerning the planets into agreement with that explanation of the causes which follows an admissible method. *Hence we actually find a certain person, Heraclides of Pontus, coming forward and saying that, even on the assumption that the earth moves in a certain way, while the sun is in a certain way at rest, the apparent irregularity with reference to the sun can be saved.* For it is no part of the business of an astronomer to know what is by nature suited to a position of rest, and what sort of bodies are apt to move, but he introduces hypotheses under which some bodies remain fixed, while others move, and then considers to which hypotheses the phenomena actually observed in the heaven will correspond. But he must go to the physicist for his first principles, namely that the movements of the stars are simple, uniform and ordered, and by means of these principles he will then prove that the rhythmic motion of all alike is in circles, some being turned in parallel circles, others in oblique circles." Such is the account given by Geminus, or Posidonius in Geminus, of the distinction between physics and astronomy, wherein the commentator is inspired by the views of Aristotle.'

The important sentence for our purpose is that which I have italicized, and the above translation of it is a literal rendering of the

reading of the MSS. and of Diels (διὸ καὶ παρελθών τίς φησιν
Ἡρακλείδης ὁ Ποντικός, ὅτι καὶ κινουμένης πως τῆς γῆς κ. τ. ἐ.).
The reading and possible emendations of it will have to be discussed,
but it will be convenient first of all to dispose of a question arising on
the interpretation of the context.   What is meant by 'the apparent
irregularity with reference to the sun (ἡ περὶ τὸν ἥλιον φαινομένη
ἀνωμαλία)'?   Can this be so interpreted as to make it possible to
take the motion of the earth to be rotation about its axis and not a
motion of translation at all?   Boeckh[1] took the πως ('in a certain
way') used of the sun's remaining at rest (as it is also used of the
earth's motion) to signify that the sun is not *quite* at rest; and he
thought that Heraclides meant that the sun and the heaven were
only at rest *so far as the general daily rotation was concerned*, while
the earth rotated on its own axis from west to east in 24 hours, but
that the sun still performed its yearly revolution in the zodiac
circle.   This, however, does not account for the 'apparent *irregularity* or *anomaly* with reference to the sun', which expression could
not possibly be applied to the daily rotation.

Martin[2] and Bergk[3] took the irregularity to be the irregularity
of the sun's own motion in the ecliptic, by virtue of which the sun
seems to go quicker at one time than at another, and the four
seasons differ in length.   But if, as Bergk apparently supposed, the
two hypotheses which are contrasted are (1) the sun moving irregularly as it does and the earth completely devoid of any motion of
translation, (2) the sun completely at rest and the earth with an
irregular motion of translation, it is, as Schiaparelli says, impossible
to get any plausible sense out of the passage.   For the problem of
explaining the irregularity of the sun's motion presents precisely the
same difficulties on the one hypothesis as it does on the other;
the substitution of one hypothesis for the other does not advance
the question in any way, and it explains nothing.   Martin saw this,
and tried another explanation based on the use of the word πως,
'in a certain way'.   The *mean speed* of the sun, says Martin, is one
thing, its *anomaly* is another; the former is accounted for by the

[1] Boeckh, *Das kosmische System des Platon*, pp. 135-40.
[2] Martin in *Mémoires de l'Académie des Inscriptions et Belles-Lettres*, xxx.
2ᵉ partie, 1883, pp. 26 sqq.
[3] Bergk, *Fünf Abhandlungen zur Gesch. der griechischen Philosophie und
Astronomie*, Leipzig, 1883, p. 151.

annual revolution; the latter had to be otherwise accounted for, and one way of accounting for it was that of Callippus, who gave the sun two spheres more than Eudoxus assigned to it. Take now from the sun the *small* movement (of irregularity) *only*, thus leaving it at rest only 'in a certain sense', and give the earth a *small* annual movement sufficient to explain the apparent *anomaly* of the sun. A mere rotation of the earth on its axis would not suffice; the movement must be one of translation in the circumference of a circle, the result of which would be that, for the inhabitants of the earth, the solar anomaly would be the effect of a *parallax*, not daily, but annual, and dependent on the radius of the circle described by the earth in a year. That is, the earth must be supposed to accomplish, on the circumference of a small orbit round the centre of the universe, an annual revolution at a uniform speed from east to west, while the sun accomplishes from west to east its annual revolution about the same centre in a great orbit enveloping that of the earth. Schiaparelli shows the impossibility of this explanation. If we take from the sun only the small *irregularity* of its movement and leave it its mean movement in an enormous circle round the earth, how could any one properly describe this as making the sun '*stationary in a certain sense*', when at the same time the earth, which is made to describe a small orbit, is said to ' *move* in a certain sense'? Moreover, it is inadmissible to suppose that, in Heraclides' time, any one could have assumed that the place in the centre of the universe was occupied by *nothing*, and that both the sun and the earth revolved about an ideal point ; the conception of revolution about an immaterial point appeared later, in the generalized theory of epicycles and eccentrics, and we find no mention of it before Apollonius.

But indeed there is nothing to suggest that Heraclides was aware of the small irregularities of the sun's motion, and it is therefore necessary to find another meaning for the expression ' the apparent irregularity with reference to the sun ' (ἡ περὶ τὸν ἥλιον φαινομένη ἀνωμαλία). I agree with Schiaparelli's view that it must be the same thing as Hipparchus and Ptolemy in the *Syntaxis* commonly describe as ' the irregularity *relatively* to the sun ' (ἡ πρὸς τὸν ἥλιον ἀνωμαλία or ἡ παρὰ τὸν ἥλιον ἀνωμαλία), that is to say, that great inequality in the apparent movements of *the planets*, which alone

was known in the time of Heraclides and which manifests itself
principally in the stationary points and retrogradations. It is true
that in the particular sentence the planets are not mentioned, but
they are mentioned in the sentence of Geminus which immediately
precedes it, and, if our sentence is a quotation of words used by
Heraclides, they no doubt followed upon a similar reference to the
planets by Heraclides.

If then the text as above translated is right, there is no escape from
the conclusion that Heraclides actually put forward the Copernican
hypothesis as a possible means of 'saving the phenomena'. But
it is precisely the text of the sentence referring to Heraclides that
gives rise to the greatest difficulties. The reading of the MSS.
followed in the translation above is διὸ καὶ παρελθών τίς φησιν
Ἡρακλείδης ὁ Ποντικός, ὅτι καὶ κινουμένης πως τῆς γῆς κ.τ.ἑ. Diels [1]
is satisfied with this reading, which, he thinks, renders unnecessary
the many scruples felt by scholars, and the emendation proposed
by Bergk.[2] Gomperz,[3] on the other hand, says that after the most
careful consideration he finds himself compelled to dissent from
Diels' view of the passage. Schiaparelli observes that it is really
impossible to suppose that a historian of sciences such as Geminus
could have used the word τις, and said 'a *certain* Heraclides of
Pontus', in speaking of a philosopher who was celebrated throughout antiquity and whom Cicero, a contemporary of Geminus, read
and spoke of with great respect. This consideration may have
been one of those which induced the editor of the Aldine edition
to insert the word ἔλεγεν before ὅτι, a reading which involves the
punctuation of the passage thus: διὸ καὶ παρελθών τις, φησὶν Ἡρακλείδης ὁ Ποντικός, ἔλεγεν ὅτι. I think there is no doubt that
Boeckh is right in his interpretation of παρελθών as 'having come
forward', which he supports by quoting a number of passages containing the same use of the word. According, therefore, to the
reading of the Aldine edition we have a quotation from one of
Heraclides' dialogues introduced by the parenthetical words in
oratio recta, 'says Heraclides of Pontus,' and the translation will

[1] Diels, 'Über das physikalische System des Straton' in *Berliner Sitzungs-
Berichte*, 1893, p. 18, note 1.
[2] Bergk, op. cit., p. 150.
[3] Gomperz, *Griechische Denker*, i[3], p. 432.

be, 'This explains too why " some one came forward ", as Heraclides of Pontus says, "and said that . . . ." ' Bergk objects that, while παρελθών, 'coming forward,' is used of one who comes forward in a public assembly, it is not, so far as he can find, used of the interlocutors in a dialogue.[1] This is, however, not conclusive, as such expressions marking the interposition of a new speaker may have been common in Heraclides' dialogues ; indeed we gather that there was a great deal of action in them.[2] A more substantial objection is the form of the quotation, the plunging direct, after the words διὸ καί, 'For which reason also,' into the actual words of Heraclides 'some one came forward and said'. This is, it must be admitted, extremely abrupt and awkward ; if Geminus had been quoting in this way, it would have been more natural to put the sentence in a different form, such as 'This is the reason too why, in a dialogue of Heraclides of Pontus, some one came forward and said that . . .'.

Bergk's own suggestion for emendation is to omit the τις, alter παρελθών into προελθών, and write the sentence thus, διὸ καὶ προελθών φησιν· Ἡρακλείδης ὁ Ποντικὸς ἔλεγεν. 'For this reason too, he goes on to say "Heraclides of Pontus said that . . . "' The words διὸ καὶ προελθών φησιν would thus be the words, not of Geminus, from whom the whole passage is quoted, but of Alexander, who is quoting ; these words would therefore come in between one textual citation from Geminus and another. I think this reading has nothing to commend it ; the omission of τις is an objection to it, and the net result is a perfectly unnecessary interposition by Alexander, which moreover spoils the sense ; 'this is the reason, too, why Geminus goes on to say that Heraclides declared . . .' is not so good as 'this is the reason, too, why some one, according to Heraclides of Pontus, said . . .'

I omit a number of suggestions for replacing παρελθών by some other word or words ; they have no authority and, so long as Heraclides of Pontus remains in the sentence either as having himself held the view in question, or as having attributed it to some one else unnamed, they do not really affect the issue.

I now come to Tannery's view of the passage, which is not only

[1] Bergk, op. cit., p. 149.　　　　　[2] Otto Voss, *Heraclides*, p. 27.

that suggested by the ordinary principles of textual criticism, but
furnishes a solution of the puzzle so simple and natural that it
should, as it seems to me, carry conviction to the mind of any
unbiased person.[1]   As Tannery says, from the moment when it is
realized that the insertion of the word ἔλεγεν does not, after all is
said, suffice to remove all difficulties, we are thrown back upon
the text of the MSS. as established by Diels, διὸ καὶ παρελθών τίς
φησιν Ἡρακλείδης ὁ Ποντικός, ὅτι καὶ κινουμένης πως τῆς γῆς κ.τ.έ.,
and we have to consider in what way an error could have crept
into the text.   Now it 'leaps to the eyes' that, if the original text
said simply διὸ καὶ παρελθών τίς φησιν ὅτι καὶ κινουμένης πως τῆς
γῆς κ.τ.έ., it was the easiest thing in the world for a glossarist to
insert in the margin, in explanation of τις, the name of Heraclides
of Pontus, which would then naturally find its way into the text.
If the name is left out, everything is in perfect order.   The passage
in its context is then as follows : 'Why do the sun, moon, and
planets appear to move irregularly ?   We may answer that, if we
assume that their orbits are eccentric circles or that the stars
describe an epicycle, their apparent irregularity will be saved ; and
it will be necessary to go further and examine in how many different
ways it is possible for these phenomena to be brought about,
so that we may bring our theory concerning the planets into
agreement with that explanation of the causes which follows an
admissible method.   This is why one astronomer has actually
suggested that, by assuming the earth to move in a certain way
and the sun to be in a certain way at rest . . .'   Nothing clearer
or more correct could possibly be desired ; the different hypotheses
would then all alike be stated in general terms without the names
of their authors, whereas nothing could be more awkward than
that Geminus, after speaking of the hypotheses of eccentrics and
epicycles in this way, should change the form of statement and
bring in quite abruptly an historical fact about one particular person
by name, or a textual citation from a work of his.   Even Gomperz[2]
admits that it is possible that Ἡρακλείδης ὁ Ποντικός may have
been inserted ' by a (well-informed) reader ' ; but the ' well-informed '

---

[1] Tannery, 'Sur Héraclide du Pont,' in *Revue des Études grecques*, xii, 1899,
pp. 305–11.
[2] Gomperz, loc. cit.

is a pure assumption on his part, due, I think, merely to bias, for how can we possibly pronounce the reader to have been 'well-informed' when there is absolutely no other evidence telling in his favour?

If then, as seems to me inevitable, the words Ἡρακλείδης ὁ Ποντικός are rejected as an interpolation, the view of Schiaparelli based upon the passage must be given up, and there remains no ground for disputing the accuracy of the other definite statement by Aëtius to the effect that 'Heraclides of Pontus and Ecphantus the Pythagorean make the earth move, yet *not* in the sense of translation but with a movement of rotation',[1] confirmed as it is by the sharp distinction drawn in one place by Simplicius between those who supposed the earth to have a motion of translation and Heraclides who supposed it to rotate about its axis.[2]

If it is asked whom Geminus had in mind when using the expression τίς φησιν, we can have no hesitation in answering that it was Aristarchus of Samos, for it is to him that all ancient authorities agree in attributing the suggestion of the heliocentric system.

It is not possible to say at what time the interpolation of the name of Heraclides into the passage took place. There is nothing to show, for instance, whether it was made in the archetype of the MSS. of Simplicius or in the sources from which he drew. As he did not quote Geminus directly, but copied the quotation of Alexander, it is a question whether the gloss is earlier or later than Alexander, or even due to Alexander himself. I agree with Tannery that an annotator of the second or third century of our era, at a period when Heraclides was sufficiently well known through the *Doxographi* as having attributed a movement to the earth, might very well, on reading the first words, κινουμένης πως τῆς γῆς ('if the earth moves in a certain way'), have immediately thought of Heraclides rather than Aristarchus, and have written the name of the former in the margin without looking forward to see what were the words immediately following these. 'In any case,' Tannery concludes, 'the attribution to Heraclides Ponticus of the heliocentric

---

[1] Aët. iii. 13. 3 (*D. G.* p. 378; *Vors.* i², p. 266. 5–7).
[2] Simplicius on *De caelo* ii. 14 (297 a 2), p. 541. 27–9, Heib. See above, p. 255.

system does not in any way rest on the authority of Posidonius or of Geminus ; it is the act of an anonymous annotator of uncertain date, and probably the result of a simple inadvertence only too easy to commit ; it must therefore be considered as null and void.'

It may be added that it is hardly *a priori* surprising that such extensive claims on behalf of Heraclides should prove, on examination, to be in part unsustainable. It was much to discover, as he did, the rotation of the earth about its axis and the fact that Venus and Mercury revolve round the sun like satellites ; it would seem *a priori* almost incredible that the complete Tychonic system should have been evolved in Heraclides' lifetime and 'perhaps' by Heraclides himself, and that he should *also* have suggested the Copernican hypothesis.

XIX

GREEK MONTHS, YEARS, AND CYCLES[1]

ALTHOUGH there is controversy as to whether in the earliest times (e. g. with Homer and Hesiod) the day was supposed to begin with the morning or evening, it may be taken as established that in historic times the day, for the purpose of the calendar, began with the evening, both at Athens and in Greece generally. As regards Athens the fact is stated by Gellius on the authority of Varro, who, in describing the usage of different nations in this respect, said that the Athenians reckoned as one day the whole period from one sunset to the next sunset;[2] the testimony of Pliny[3] and Censorinus[4] is to the same effect. The practice of regarding the day as beginning with the evening is natural with a system of reckoning time by the moon's appearances; for a day would naturally be supposed to begin with the time at which the light of the new moon first became visible, i. e. at evening.

There is no doubt that, from the earliest times, the Greek month (μήν) was lunar, that is, a month based on the moon's apparent motion. But from the first there began to be felt, among the Greeks as among most civilized peoples, a desire to bring the reckoning of time by the moon into correspondence with the seasons of the year, for the sake of regulating the times of sacrifices to the gods which had to be offered at certain periods in the year; hence there was from the beginning a motive for striving after the settlement of a luni-solar year. The luni-solar year thus had a religious origin. This is attested by Geminus, who says:[5]

'The ancients had before them the problem of reckoning the months by the moon, but the years by the sun. For the legal and

---

[1] For the contents of this chapter I am almost entirely indebted to the exhaustive work of F. K. Ginzel, *Handbuch der mathematischen und technischen Chronologie*, vol. ii of which appeared in the nick of time (1911).
[2] Gellius, *Noct. Att.* iii. 2. 2.   [3] Pliny, *N. H.* ii. c. 77, § 188.
[4] Censorinus, *De die natali*, c. 23. 3.
[5] Geminus, *Isagoge*, c. 8, 6–9, p. 102. 8–26, Manitius.

oracular prescription that sacrifices should be offered after the manner of their forefathers was interpreted by all Greeks as meaning that they should keep the years in agreement with the sun and the days and months with the moon. Now reckoning the years according to the sun means performing the same sacrifices to the gods at the same seasons in the year, that is to say, performing the spring sacrifice always in the spring, the summer sacrifice in the summer, and similarly offering the same sacrifices from year to year at the other definite periods of the year when they fell due. For they apprehended that this was welcome and pleasing to the gods. The object in view, then, could not be secured in any other way than by contriving that the solstices and the equinoxes should occur in the same months from year to year. Reckoning the days according to the moon means contriving that the names of the days of the month shall follow the phases of the moon.'

At first the month would be simply regarded as lasting from the first appearance of the thin crescent at any new moon till the next similar first appearance. From this would gradually be evolved a notion of the length of a moon-year. A rough moon-year would be 12 moon-months averaging 29½ days; but it was necessary that a month should contain an exact number of days, and it was therefore natural to take the months as having alternately 29 and 30 days. These 'hollow' and 'full' months are commonly supposed to have been introduced at Athens by Solon (who was archon in 594/3 B.C.), since he is said to have 'taught the Athenians to reckon days by the moon'.[1] But it can hardly be doubted that 'full' and 'hollow' months were in use before Solon's time; Ginzel therefore thinks that Solon's reform was something different. We shall revert to this point later.

At the same time, alongside the 'full' and 'hollow' months of the calendar, popular parlance invented a month of 30 days, as being convenient to reckon with. Hippocrates makes 280 days = 9 months 10 days;[2] Aristotle speaks of 72 days as 1/5th of a year;[3] the riddle of Cleobulus implies 12 months of 30 days each;[4] the original division of the Athenian people into 4 φυλαί, 12 φρατρίαι, and 360 γένη is explained by Philochorus as corresponding to the seasons, months, and days of the year.[5] In the Courts a month

[1] Diog. L. i. 59.   [2] Hippocrates, De carnibus, p. 254.
[3] Aristotle, Hist. an. vi. 20, 574 a 26.   [4] Diog. L. i. 91.
[5] Suidas, s. v. γεννῆται.

was reckoned at 30 days, and wages were reckoned on this basis, e. g. daily pay of 2 drachmae makes for 13 months 780 drachmae $(2 \times 30 \times 13)$.[1] From such indications as these it has been inferred that the Greeks had at one time years of 360 days and 390 days respectively. Indeed, Geminus says that 'the ancients made the months 30 days each, and added the intercalary months in alternate years $(\pi\alpha\rho' \,\dot{\epsilon}\nu\iota\alpha\upsilon\tau\dot{o}\nu)$'.[2] Censorinus has a similar remark; when, he says, the ancient city-states in Greece noticed that, while the sun in its annual course is describing its circle, the new moon sometimes rises thirteen times, and that this often happens in alternate years, they inferred that $12\frac{1}{2}$ months corresponded to the natural year, and they therefore fixed their civil years in such a way that they made years of 12 months and years of 13 months alternate, calling each of such years 'annus vertens' and both years together a great year.[3] Again, Herodotus[4] represents Solon as saying that the 70 years of a man's life mean 25,200 days, without reckoning intercalary months, but, if alternate years are lengthened by a month, there are 35 of these extra months in 70 years, making 1,050 days more and increasing the total number of days to 26,250. But under this system the two-years period (called nevertheless, according to Censorinus, *trieteris* because the intercalation took place 'every third year') would be more than 7 days too long in comparison with the sun, and in 20 years the calendar would be about $2\frac{1}{2}$ months wrong in relation to the seasons. This divergence is so glaring that Ginzel concludes that the system cannot have existed in practice. He suggests, in explanation of Geminus's remark, that Geminus is not to be taken literally, but is in this case merely using popular language (cf. his remark that 90 days = 3 months[5]); he regards Censorinus's story as suspicious because in the following sentence Censorinus says that the next change was to a *pentaëteris* of *four* years each, which involves the supposition that the Greeks of, say, the eighth or ninth century B.C., had already anticipated the Julian system; moreover, Geminus says nothing of a four-years period at all (whether called *tetraëteris* or *pentaëteris*) but passes directly to the *octaëteris* which, according to him, was the *first* period that the ancients constructed.

---

[1] *Corp. Inscr. Att.* ii. 2, no. 834 c, l. 60 (p. 532).   [2] Geminus, *Isagoge*, c. 8. 26.
[3] Censorinus, *De die natali*, c. 18. 2.   [4] Herodotus, i. 32.
[5] Geminus, *Isagoge*, c. 8. 30, p. 112. 7, 10.

On the alternation of 'full' and 'hollow' months an apparently interpolated passage in Geminus says:[1]

'The moon-year has 354 days. Consequently they took the lunar month to be $29\frac{1}{2}$ days and the double month to be 59 days. Hence it is that they have hollow and full months alternately, namely because the two-months period according to the moon is 59 days. Therefore there are in the year six full and six hollow months. This then is the reason why they make the months full and hollow alternately.'

The octaëteris.

Geminus's account of the eight-years cycle follows directly on what he says of the supposed ancient system of alternating years of 12 and 13 months of 30 days each.

'Observation having speedily proved this procedure to be inconsistent with the true facts, inasmuch as the days and the months did not agree with the moon nor the years keep pace with the sun, they sought for a period which should, as regards the years, agree with the sun, and, as regards the months and the days, with the moon, and should contain a whole number of months, a whole number of days, and a whole number of years. The first period they constructed was the period of the *octaëteris* (or eight years) which contains 99 months, of which three are intercalary, 2922 days, and 8 years. And they constructed it in this way. Since the year according to the sun has $365\frac{1}{4}$ days, and the year according to the moon 354 days, they took the excess by which the year according to the sun exceeds the year according to the moon. This is $11\frac{1}{4}$ days. If then we reckon the months in the year according to the moon, we shall fall behind by $11\frac{1}{4}$ days in comparison with the solar year. They inquired therefore how many times this number of days must be multiplied in order to complete a whole number of days and a whole number of months. Now the number $\left[11\frac{1}{4}\right]$ multiplied by 8 makes 90 days, that is, three months. Since then we fall behind by $11\frac{1}{4}$ days in the year in comparison with the sun, it is manifest that in 8 years we shall fall behind by 90 days, that is, by 3 months, in comparison with the sun. Accordingly, in each period of 8 years, three intercalary ($\dot{\epsilon}\mu\beta\dot{o}\lambda\iota\mu\sigma\iota$) months are reckoned, in order that the deficiency which arises in each year in comparison with the sun may be made good, and so, when 8 years have passed from the beginning of the period, the festivals are again brought into accord with the seasons in the year. When this system is followed, the sacrifices will always be offered to the gods at the same seasons of the year.

[1] Geminus, *Isagoge*, c. 8. 34–5, pp. 112. 28 – 114. 7.

' They now disposed the intercalary months in such a way as to spread them as nearly as possible evenly. For we must not wait until the divergence from the observed phenomena amounts to a whole month, nor yet must we get a whole month ahead of the sun's course. Accordingly they decided to introduce the intercalary months in the third, fifth, and eighth years, so that two of the said months were in years following two ordinary years, and only one followed after an interval of one year.[1] But it is a matter of indifference if, while preserving the same disposition of (i.e. intervals between) the intercalary months, you put them in other years.'[2]

Here then we have an account which purports to show how the *octaëteris* was first arrived at, the supposition being that it was based on a solar year of $365\frac{1}{4}$ days. Ginzel, however, thinks it impossible that this can have been the real method, because the evaluation of the solar year at $365\frac{1}{4}$ days could hardly have been known to the Greeks of, say, the 9th and 8th centuries B.C.; this, he thinks, is proved by the erroneous estimates of the length of the solar year which continued to be put forward much later.

Ginzel considers that the *octaëteris* was first evolved as the result of observation of the moon's motion, which was of course easier to approximate to within a reasonable time. The alternation of 6 full with 6 hollow months gives a moon-year of 354 days; but the true moon-year exceeds this by 0·36707 day, and hence, after about $2\frac{3}{4}$ moon-years, a day would have to be added in order to keep the months in harmony with the phases; that is to say, at such intervals, there would have to be a year of 355 days. Now this rate of intercalation corresponds nearly to the addition of 3 days in a period of 8 moon-years, i.e. to a cycle of 8 moon-years in which 5 have 354, and 3 have 355 days, each. (And, as a matter of fact, the same proportion of 5 : 3 serves very roughly to bring the moon-year into agreement with the solar year, for we have only to reckon, in a cycle of 8 solar years, 5 moon-years of 354 days and 3 of 384 days.)[3] Ginzel cites evidence showing that particular years actually had 355 days and 384 days, e.g. Ol. 88, 3 = 355 days, Ol. 88, 4 = 354 days, Ol. 89, 1 = 384 days, and Ol. 89, 2 = 355

---

[1] δι' ἣν αἰτίαν τοὺς ἐμβολίμους μῆνας ἔταξαν ἄγεσθαι ἐν τῷ τρίτῳ ἔτει καὶ πέμπτῳ καὶ ὀγδόῳ, δύο μὲν μῆνας μεταξὺ δύο ἐτῶν πιπτόντων, ἕνα δὲ μεταξὺ ἐνιαυτοῦ ἑνὸς ἀγομένου.

[2] Geminus, *Isagoge* 8. 26-33, pp. 110. 14 – 112. 27.   [3] Ginzel, ii. 330–1.

days.[1] The method by which the *octaëteris* was evolved is, he thinks, something of this sort. Having from observation of the moon constructed an 8-years period containing 5 moon-years of 354 days and 3 intercalated years of 355 days each, making a total of 2,835 days, the Greeks, by further continual observation directed to fixing the duration of the phases exactly, would at last come to notice that, after 8 returns of the sun to the same azimuth-point on the horizon, the phases fell nearly on the same days once more, and also that the sun returned to the same azimuth-point for the eighth time after about 99 lunar months. Now, if the ancients had divided the 2,835 days of 8 moon-years by 96, they would have found the average lunar month to contain $29\frac{17}{32}$ days; and again, if they had multiplied this by 99, they would have obtained $2,923\frac{19}{32}$ or nearly $2,923\frac{1}{2}$ days. But the first inventors of the *octaëteris* certainly did not make the 8 solar years contain $2,923\frac{1}{2}$ days; this, we are told, was a later improvement on the 2,922 days which, according to Geminus, the first *octaëteris* contained. No doubt the first discoverers of it would notice that 99 times $29\frac{1}{2}$ days is $2,920\frac{1}{2}$ days, that is to say, approximately 8 years of 365 days (= 2,920 days). This may have been what led them to construct a luni-solar *octaëteris*. But why did they give it 2,922 days? Ginzel suggests that, as the *octaëteris* was thus shown to be very useful for the purpose of bringing into harmony the motions of the sun and moon, the Greeks would be encouraged to try to obtain a more accurate estimate of the average length of the lunar month. If then, for example, they had assumed $29\frac{16}{30}$ days as the average length, they would have found, at the end of an *octaëteris*, that they were only wrong by 0·3 of a day relatively to the moon, but were nearly two days ahead in relation to the sun.[2] This might perhaps lead them to conjecture that the solar year was a little longer than 365 days; and they may have hit upon $365\frac{1}{4}$ days by a sort of guess. This would give $29\frac{51}{99}$ days as the length of the lunar month. Ginzel thinks that the gradual process by which the Greeks arrived at the 2,922 days may have lasted from the 9th or 8th century into the 7th.[3] This, he suggests, may explain

---

[1] Ginzel, ii. 341-3.
[2] $29\frac{16}{30} \times 99 = 2923\cdot8$ days (against 2923·528, the correct figure); 8 solar years have $8 \times 365\cdot2422 = 2921\cdot938$ days.
[3] Ginzel, ii. 376, 377.

the fact that we find mentions or indications of eight-years periods going back as far as the mythical age. Thus Cadmus passed an 'eternal' (ἀΐδιος) year (i.e. says Ginzel, an 8-year year) in servitude for having slain the dragon of Ares; similarly Apollo served 8 years with Admetus after he killed the dragon Python. The Daphnephoria were celebrated every 8 years; in the procession connected with the celebration an olive staff was carried with a sphere above (the sun), a smaller one below (the moon), and still smaller spheres representing other stars, while 365 purple bands or ribbons were also attached, representing the days of the solar year. The Pythian games were also, at the beginning, eight-yearly. Kingships were offices held for eight years (thus Minos spoke with Zeus, the great God, 'nine-yearly').[1] According to Plutarch the heaven was observed at Sparta by the Ephors on a clear night once in eight years.[2] These cases, however, though showing that 8-years periods were recognized and used in various connexions, scarcely suffice, I think, to prove the existence in such very early times of an accurately measured period of 2,922 days. Ginzel, in arguing for so early a discovery of the *octaëteris* of 2,922 days, departs considerably from the views of earlier authorities on chronology. Boeckh thought that the *octaëteris* was introduced by Solon, and that the first such period actually began with the beginning of the year at the first new moon after the summer solstice in Ol. 46, 3, i.e. 7th July, 594 B.C.[3] As regards the period before Solon, Boeckh went, it is true, so far as to suggest that, as early as 642 B.C., there may have been a rough *octaëteris* in vogue which was not actually fixed or exactly observed; this, however, was only a conjecture. Ideler[4] argued that the *octaëteris* could not be as old as Solon's time (594/3 B.C.) or even as old as Ol. 59 (544–540), because so accurate a conception is in too strong a contrast to what we know of the state of astronomical knowledge in Greece at that time. As regards Solon's reforms, we are told[5] that he prescribed that the day in the

---

[1] *Odyssey* xix. 178, 179.   [2] Plutarch, *Agis*, c. 11.

[3] The practice of beginning the year in the summer (with the month *Hecatombaion*) is proved by Boeckh to have existed during the whole of the fifth century. It was probably much older in Attica; the transition (if the Attic year previously began in the winter) may have taken effect in the time of Solon.

[4] Ideler, *Historische Untersuchungen über die astronomischen Beobachtungen der Alten*, p. 191.

[5] Plutarch, *Solon*, c. 25.

course of which the actual conjunction at the new moon took place should be called ἕνη καὶ νέα, the 'last and new' or 'old-new', and that he called the following day νουμηνία (new moon), which therefore was the first day belonging wholly to the new month. Diogenes Laertius says that Solon taught the Athenians 'to reckon the days according to the moon';[1] and Theodorus Gaza, a late writer, it is true, says that Solon 'ordered everything in connexion with the year generally better'.[2] Boeckh, as already stated, thought that Solon's reform consisted in the introduction of the *octaëteris*. Ginzel, however, holding as he does that the *octaëteris* of 2,922 days was discovered much earlier, considers that Solon's reform had to do with the improvement on this figure by which 99 lunations were found to amount to $2,923\frac{1}{2}$ days, a discovery which led to the formulation of the 16-years and 160-years periods presently to be mentioned; this may be inferred, according to Ginzel, from the fact that the accounts show Solon's object to have been the bringing of the calendar specially into accordance with the *moon*. But it is difficult to accept Ginzel's view of the nature of Solon's reform in the face of another statement as to the authors of the *octaëteris*. Censorinus says:

'This octaëteris is commonly attributed to Eudoxus, but others say that Cleostratus of Tenedos first framed it, and that it was modified afterwards by others who put forward their octaëterides with variations in the intercalations of the months, as did Harpalus, Nauteles, Menestratus, and others also, among whom is Dositheus, who is most generally identified with the octaëteris of Eudoxus.'[3]

Now we know nothing of the date of Cleostratus, except that he came after Anaximander; for Pliny says that Anaximander is credited by tradition with having discovered the obliquity of the zodiac in Ol. 58 (548–544 B. C.), after which (*deinde*) Cleostratus distinguished the signs in it.[4] Thus Cleostratus may have lived soon after 544 B. C. Ginzel seems to admit that Cleostratus was the actual founder ('eigentliche Begründer') of the *octaëteris*.[5] Of Harpalus, who was later than Cleostratus but before Meton (432 B. C.), we only know that he formed a period which brought the moon into agreement with the sun after the latter had revolved

---

[1] Diog. L. i. 59.
[2] Theodorus Gaza, c. 8 and 15.
[3] Censorinus, *De die natali*, 18. 5.
[4] Pliny, *N. H.* ii. c. 8, § 31.
[5] Ginzel, ii, p. 385.

'through nine winters',[1] which statement must, as Ideler says, be due to a misapprehension of the meaning of the words 'nono quoque anno'. According to Censorinus, Harpalus made the solar year consist of 365 days and 13 equinoctial hours.[2] Eudoxus's variation will be mentioned later.

The 16-years and 160-years cycles.

After describing the *octaëteris* of 2,922 days, Geminus proceeds thus:

'If now it had only been necessary for us to keep in agreement with the solar years, it would have sufficed to use the aforesaid period in order to be in agreement with the phenomena. But as we must not only reckon the years according to the sun, but also the days and months according to the moon, they considered how this also could be achieved. Thus the lunar month, accurately measured, having $29\frac{1}{2}$ $\frac{1}{33}$ days, while the octaëteris contains, with the inter-calary months, 99 months in all, they multiplied the $29\frac{1}{2}$ $\frac{1}{33}$ days of the month by the 99 months; the result is $2,923\frac{1}{2}$ days. Therefore in eight solar years there should be reckoned $2,923\frac{1}{2}$ days according to the moon. But the solar year has $365\frac{1}{4}$ days, and eight solar years contain 2922 days, this being the number of days obtained by multiplying by 8 the number of days in the year. Inasmuch then as we found the number of days according to the moon which are contained in the 8 years to be $2,923\frac{1}{2}$, we shall, in each octaëteris, fall behind by $1\frac{1}{2}$ days in comparison with the moon. Therefore in 16 years we shall be behind by 3 days in comparison with the moon. It follows that in each period of 16 years three days have to be added, having regard to the moon's motion, in order that we may reckon the years according to the sun, and the months and days according to the moon. But, when this correction is made, another error supervenes. For the three days according to the moon which are added in the 16 years give, in ten periods of 16 years, an excess (with reference to the sun) of 30 days, that is to say, a month. Consequently, at intervals of 160 years, one of the intercalary months is omitted from ⟨one of⟩ the octaëterides; that is, instead of the three (intercalary) months which fall to be reckoned in the eight years, only two are actually introduced. Hence, when the month is thus eliminated, we start again in agreement with the moon as regards the months and days, and with the sun as regards the years.'[3]

---

[1] Festus Avienus, *Prognost.* 41, quoted by Ideler, op. cit., p. 191.
[2] Censorinus, *De die natali*, 19. 2.
[3] Geminus, *Isagoge*, 8. 36–41, pp. 114. 8 – 116. 15.

This passage explains itself; it is only necessary to add that there is no proof that the 16-years period was actually used. The 160-years period was, however, presupposed in Eudoxus's *octaëteris*, the first of which, according to Boeckh, may have begun in 381 or 373 B. C. (Ol. 99, 4 or Ol. 101, 4) on 22/23 July, the 'first day of Leo', i. e. the day on which the sun entered the sign of Leo; the effect was that, after 20 *octaëterides* and the dropping of 30 days, the beginning of the solar year was again on 'the first of Leo'. In Eudoxus's system, then, the luni-solar reckoning was independent of the solstices.[1] According to the Eudoxus-Papyrus (*Ars Eudoxi*) the intercalary months came in the 3rd, 6th, and 8th years of Eudoxus's *octaëteris*.

Meton's cycle.

Curiously enough, Meton is not mentioned by Geminus as the author of the 19-years cycle; his connexion with it is, however, clearly established by other evidence. Diodorus has the following remark with regard to the year of the archonship of Apseudes (Ol. 86, 4 = 433/2 B. C.).

'In Athens Meton, the son of Pausanias, and famous in astronomy, put forward the so-called 19-years period (ἐννεακαιδεκαετηρίδα); he started (ἀρχὴν ποιησάμενος) from the 13th of the Athenian month Skirophorion.'[2]

Aelian says that Meton discovered the Great Year, and 'reckoned it at 19 years',[3] and also that 'the astronomer Meton erected pillars and noted on them the solstices'. Censorinus, too, says that Meton constructed a Great Year of 19 years, which was accordingly called *enneadecaeteris*.[4] Euctemon, whom Geminus does mention, assisted Meton in the matter of this cycle.

Geminus's account of the cycle shall be quoted in full:

'Accordingly, as the octaëteris was found to be in all respects incorrect, the astronomers Euctemon, Philippus, and Callippus [the phrase is οἱ περὶ Εὐκτήμονα κτέ., as usual] constructed another period, that of 19 years. For they found by observation that in 19 years there were contained 6940 days and 235 months, including the intercalary months, of which, in the 19 years, there are 7. [According to this reckoning the year comes to have $365\frac{5}{19}$ days.]

[1] Boeckh, *Ueber die vierjährigen Sonnenkreise der Alten*, 1863, pp. 159–66.
[2] Diodorus Siculus, xii. 36.   [3] Aelian, *V. H.* x. 7.
[4] Censorinus, *De die natali*, 18. 8.

And of the 235 months they made 110 hollow and 125 full, so that hollow and full months did not always follow one another alternately, but sometimes there would be two full months in succession. For the natural course of the phenomena in regard to the moon admits of this, whereas there was no such thing in the octaëteris. And they included 110 hollow months in the 235 months for the following reason. As there are 235 months in the 19 years, they began by assuming each of the months to have 30 days; this gives 7,050 days. Thus, when all the months are taken at 30 days, the 7,050 days are in excess of the 6,940 days; the difference is ⟨110 days⟩, and accordingly they make 110 months hollow in order to complete, in the 235 months, the 6,940 days of the 19-years period. But, in order that the days to be eliminated might be distributed as evenly as possible, they divided the 6,940 days by 110; this gives 63 days.[1] It is necessary therefore to eliminate the [one] day after intervals of 63 days in this cycle. Thus it is not always the 30th day of the month which is eliminated, but it is the day falling after each interval of 63 days which is called ἐξαιρέσιμος.'[2]

The figure of $365\frac{5}{19}$ days = 365 days $6^h\ 18^m\ 56\cdot9^s$, and is still 30 minutes 11 seconds too long in comparison with the mean tropic year; but the mean lunar month of Meton is 29 days $12^h\ 45^m\ 57\frac{1}{2}^s$, which differs from the true mean lunar month by not quite 1 minute 54 seconds. When Diodorus says that, in putting forward his 19-years cycle, Meton started from the 13th of Skirophorion (which was the 13th of the last month of Apseudes' year = 27th June, 432), he does not mean that the first year of the period began on that date; this would have been contrary to the established practice. The beginning of the first year (the 1st Hekatombaion of that year) would be the day of the first visibility of the new moon next after the summer solstice, i.e. in this case 16th July, 432. The 13th Skirophorion was the day of the solstice, and we have several allusions to Meton's observation of this;[3] presumably, therefore,

---

[1] What should really have been done is to divide 7,050 by 110; this would give 64 as quotient, and the result would be that every 64th day would have to be eliminated, i.e. the day following successive intervals of 63 days. This fact would easily cause 63 to be substituted for the quotient, and this would lead to 6,940 being taken as the number to be divided by 110.

[2] Geminus, *Isagoge*, c. 8. 50-6, pp. 120. 4 - 122. 7.

[3] Philochorus (*Schol. ad Aristoph. Aves* 997) says that, under Apseudes, Meton of Leuconoë erected a *heliotropion* near the wall of the Pnyx, and it was doubtless there that he observed the solstice. Ptolemy says of this observation that it was on the 21st of the Egyptian month Phamenoth in Apseudes' year (*Syntaxis*, iii. 2, vol. i, p. 205, Heib.). This is confirmed by the discovery

Diodorus meant, not that the first year of Meton's cycle began on that day, but that it was on that day that Meton began his *parapegma* (or calendar).[1] Ginzel [2] gives full details of the many divergent views as to the date from which Meton's cycle was actually introduced at Athens. Boeckh put it in Ol. 112, 3 = 330/29 B.C., Unger between Ol. 109, 3 (342/1 B.C.) and Ol. 111, 1 (336/5 B.C.). Schmidt holds that Meton's cycle was introduced in 342 B.C., but in a modified form. The 235 months of the 19-years cycle contained, according to the true mean motion of the moon, 235 × 29.53059 days, or 6,939 days and about $16\frac{1}{2}$ hours. Consequently after 4 cycles there was an excess of four times the difference between 6,940 days and 6,939 days $16\frac{1}{2}$ hours, or an excess of 1 day 6 hours; after 10 cycles an excess of 3 days 3 hours, and so on. The Athenians, therefore, according to Schmidt, struck out one day in the 4th, 7th, 10th, 13th, 16th, 20th, and 23rd cycles, making these cycles 6,939 days each. But, as Ginzel points out, the confusions in the calendar which occurred subsequently tell against the supposition that such a principle as that assumed by Schmidt was steadily followed in Athens from 342 B.C.

Callippus's cycle of 76 years.

Geminus follows up his explanation with regard to the Metonic cycle thus:

' In this cycle [the Metonic] the months appear to be correctly taken, and the intercalary months to be distributed so as to secure agreement with the phenomena; but the length of the year as taken is not in agreement with the phenomena. For the length of the year is admitted, on the basis of observations extending over many years, to contain $365\frac{1}{4}$ days, whereas the year which is obtained from the 19-year period has $365\frac{5}{19}$ days, which number of

of a fragment of a *parapegma* at Miletus which alludes to the same observation of the summer solstice on 13th Skirophorion or 21st Phamenoth, and adds that in the year of . . . ευκτος the solstice fell on 14th Skirophorion or the Egyptian 11th Payni. Diels showed from another fragment that the archon must have been Polykleitos (110/109 B.C.), so that the second observation of the solstice mentioned in the fragment must have been on 27th June, 109, i.e. in the last (19th) year of the 17th Metonic cycle (Ginzel, ii, pp. 423, 424).

[1] The παράπηγμα was a posted record (παραπήγνυμι), a sort of almanac giving, for a series of years, the movements of the sun, the dates of the phases of the moon, the risings and settings of certain stars, besides ἐπισημασίαι or weather indications.

[2] Ginzel, op. cit., ii. 418, 430, 431, 442 sqq.

days exceeds $365\frac{1}{4}$ by $\frac{1}{76}$th of a day. On this ground Callippus and the astronomers of his school corrected this excess of a ⟨fraction of a⟩ day and constructed the 76-years period (ἐκκαιεβδομηκονταετη-ρίδα) out of four periods of 19 years, which contain in all 940 months, including 28 intercalary, and 27,759 days. They adopted the same arrangement of the intercalary months. And this period appears to agree the best of all with the observed phenomena.'[1]

With Meton's year of $365\frac{1}{4}$ $\frac{1}{76}$ days (6,940 divided by 19), four periods of 19 years amount of course to 27,760 days, and the effect of Callippus's change was to reduce this number of days by one. 27,759 days divided by 940 gives, for the mean lunar month, 29 days 12^h 44^m $25\frac{1}{2}^s$, only 22 seconds in excess of the true mean length.

Callippus was probably born about 370 B.C.; he came to Athens about 334 B.C.; the first year of the first of his cycles of 76 years was Ol. 112, 3 = 330/29 B.C., and probably began on the 29th or 28th of June. His cycles never apparently came into practical use, but they were employed by individual astronomers or chronologists for fixing dates; Ptolemy, for example, gives various dates both according to Egyptian reckoning and in terms of Callippic cycles.[2]

Hipparchus's cycle.

It is only necessary to add that yet another improvement was made by Hipparchus about 125 B.C. Ptolemy says of him:

'Again, in his work on intercalary months and days, after premising that the length of the year is, according to Meton and Euctemon, $365\frac{1}{4}$ $\frac{1}{76}$ days, and according to Callippus $365\frac{1}{4}$ days only, he continues in these words: "We find that the number of whole months contained in the 19 years is the same as they make it, but that the year in actual fact contains less by $\frac{1}{300}$th of a day than the odd $\frac{1}{4}$ of a day which they give it, so that in 300 years there is a deficiency, in comparison with Meton's figure, of 5 days, and in comparison with Callippus's figure, of one day." Then, summing up his own views in the course of the enumeration of his own works, he says: "I have also discussed the length of the year in one book, in which I prove that the solar year—that is, the length of time in which the sun passes from a solstice to the same

---

[1] Geminus, *Isagoge*, 8. 57–60, p. 122. 8–23.
[2] Ptolemy, *Syntaxis*, iii. 1, vol. i, p. 196. 6; iv. 11, vol. i, pp. 344. 14, 345. 12, 346. 14; v. 3, vol. i, p. 363. 16; vii. 3, vol. ii, pp. 25. 16, 28. 12, 29. 13, 32. 5.

solstice again, or from an equinox to the same equinox—contains 365 days and $\frac{1}{4}$, less very nearly $\frac{1}{300}$th of a day and night, and not the exact $\frac{1}{4}$ which the mathematicians suppose it to have in addition to the said whole number of days." ' [1]

Censorinus gives Hipparchus's period as 304 years, in which there are 112 intercalary months.[2] Presumably, therefore, Hipparchus took four times Callippus's cycle ($76 \times 4 = 304$) and gave the period 111,035 days instead of 111,036 ($= 27,759 \times 4$). This gives, as the length of the year, 365 days $5^h 55^m 15\cdot8^s$, while $365\frac{1}{4} - \frac{1}{300}$ days $= 365$ days $5^h 55^m 12^s$, the excess over the true mean tropic year being about $6\frac{1}{2}$ minutes. The number of months in the 304 years is $304 \times 12 + 28 \times 4 = 3,760$, whence the mean lunar month is, according to Hipparchus, 29 days $12^h 44^m 2\frac{1}{2}^s$, which is very nearly correct, being less than a second out in comparison with the present accepted figure of $29\cdot53059$ days!

[1] Ptolemy, *Syntaxis*, iii. 3, vol. i, pp. 207. 7 – 208. 2.
[2] Censorinus, *De die natali*, 18. 9.

PART II

ARISTARCHUS OF SAMOS
ON THE SIZES AND DISTANCES OF THE SUN
AND MOON

I

ARISTARCHUS OF SAMOS

WE are told that Aristarchus of Samos was a pupil of Strato of Lampsacus,[1] a natural philosopher of originality,[2] who succeeded Theophrastus as head of the Peripatetic school in 288 or 287 B.C. and held that position for eighteen years. Two other facts enable us to fix Aristarchus's date approximately. In 281/280 B.C. he made an observation of the summer solstice;[3] and the book in which he formulated his heliocentric hypothesis was published before the date of Archimedes' *Psammites* or *Sandreckoner*, a work written before 216 B.C. Aristarchus therefore probably lived *circa* 310–230 B.C., that is, he came about 75 years later than Heraclides and was older than Archimedes by about 25 years.

Aristarchus was called 'the mathematician', doubtless in order to distinguish him from the many other persons of the same name; he is included by Vitruvius among the few great men who possessed an equally profound knowledge of all branches of science, geometry, astronomy, music, &c. 'Men of this type are rare, men such as were, in times past, Aristarchus of Samos, Philolaus and Archytas of Tarentum, Apollonius of Perga, Eratosthenes of Cyrene, Archimedes and Scopinas of Syracuse, who left to

---

[1] Aëtius, i. 15. 5 (*D. G.* p. 313).
[2] Galen, *Histor. Philos.* 3 (*D. G.* p. 601. 1).
[3] Ptolemy, *Syntaxis*, iii. 2 (i, pp. 203, 206, ed. Heib.).

posterity many mechanical and gnomonic appliances which they invented and explained on mathematical (lit. numerical) and natural principles.'[1] That Aristarchus was a very capable geometer is proved by his extant work *On the sizes and distances of the sun and moon*, translated in this volume: in the mechanical line he is credited with the discovery of an improved sun-dial, the so-called σκάφη, which had, not a plane, but a concave hemispherical surface, with a pointer erected vertically in the middle throwing shadows and so enabling the direction and the height of the sun to be read off by means of lines marked on the surface of the hemisphere.[2] He also wrote on vision, light, and colours.[3] His views on the latter subjects were no doubt largely influenced by his master Strato; thus Strato held that colours were emanations from bodies, material molecules, as it were, which imparted to the intervening air the same colour as that possessed by the body,[4] while Aristarchus said that colours are ' shapes or forms stamping the air with impressions like themselves as it were ',[5] that ' colours in darkness have no colouring ',[6] and that light is ' the colour impinging on a substratum '.[7] It does not appear that Strato can be credited with any share in his astronomical discoveries: of Strato we are only told (1) that, like Metrodorus before him, he held that the stars received their light from the sun (Metrodorus alleged this of 'all the fixed stars', and it is not stated that Strato made any limitation);[8] (2) that he held a comet to be 'the light of a star enclosed in a thick cloud, just as happens with λαμπτῆρες (torches) ';[9] (3) that, like Parmenides and Heraclitus, he considered the heaven to be of fire;[10] (4) that he regarded time as 'quantity in (i.e. expressed by) things in motion and at rest ';[11] (5) that he said the divisions of the universe were without limit;[12] and (6) that he maintained that there was no void outside the universe, though there might be within it.[13]

---

[1] Vitruvius, *De architectura*, i. 1. 16.   [2] Ibid. ix. 8 (9). 1.
[3] Aët. i. 15. 5 (*D. G.* p. 313), iv. 13. 8 (*D. G.* pp. 404 and 853).
[4] Aët. iv. 13. 7 (*D. G.* p. 403).
[5] Ibid. iv. 13. 8 (*D. G.* pp. 404 and 853).
[6] Ibid. i. 15. 9 (*D. G.* p. 314).   [7] Ibid. i. 15. 5 (*D. G.* p. 313).
[8] Ibid. ii. 17. 1–2 (*D. G.* p. 346).   [9] Ibid. iii. 2. 4 (*D. G.* p. 366).
[10] Ibid. ii. 11. 4 (*D. G.* p. 340).   [11] Ibid. i. 22. 4 (*D. G.* p. 318).
[12] Epiphanius, *Adv. haeres.* iii. 33 (*D. G.* p. 592).
[13] Aët. i. 18. 4 (*D. G.* p. 316).

The Heliocentric Hypothesis.

There is not the slightest doubt that Aristarchus was the first to put forward the heliocentric hypothesis. Ancient testimony is unanimous on the point, and the first witness is Archimedes, who was a younger contemporary of Aristarchus, so that there was no possibility of a mistake. Copernicus himself admitted that the theory was attributed to Aristarchus, though this does not seem to be generally known. Thus Schiaparelli quotes two passages from Copernicus's work in which he refers to the opinions of the ancients about the motion of the earth. One is in the dedicatory letter to Pope Paul III, where Copernicus mentions that he first found out from Cicero that one Nicetas (i.e. Hicetas) had attributed motion to the earth, and that he afterwards read in Plutarch that certain others held that opinion; he then quotes the *Placita*, according to which 'Philolaus the Pythagorean asserted that the earth moved round the fire in an oblique circle, in the same way as the sun and moon'.[1] The other passage is in Book I, c. 5, where, after an allusion to the views of Heraclides, Ecphantus, and Nicetas (Hicetas), who made the earth rotate about its own axis at the centre of the universe, he goes on to say that it would not be very surprising if any one should attribute to the earth another motion besides rotation, namely revolution in an orbit in space; 'atque etiam (terram) pluribus motibus vagantem et unam ex astris Philolaus Pythagoricus sensisse fertur, Mathematicus non vulgaris.' Here, however, there is no question of the earth revolving round the *sun*, and there is no mention of Aristarchus. But it is a curious fact that Copernicus did mention the theory of Aristarchus in a passage which he afterwards suppressed: 'Credibile est hisce similibusque causis Philolaum mobilitatem terrae sensisse, quod etiam nonnulli Aristarchum Samium ferunt in eadem fuisse sententia.'[2]

I will now quote the whole passage of Archimedes in which the allusion to Aristarchus's heliocentric hypothesis occurs, in order to show the whole context.[3]

---

[1] Ps. Plutarch, *De plac. phil.*=Aët. iii. 13. 2 (*D. G.* p. 378).

[2] *De Revolutionibus Caelestibus*, ed. Thorun., 1873, p. 34 note, quoted in Gomperz, *Griechische Denker*, i³, p. 432.

[3] Archimedes, ed. Heiberg, vol. ii, p. 244 (*Arenarius* I. 4–7); *The Works of Archimedes*, ed. Heath, pp. 221, 222.

'You are aware ['you' being King Gelon] that "universe" is the name given by most astronomers to the sphere, the centre of which is the centre of the earth, while its radius is equal to the straight line between the centre of the sun and the centre of the earth. This is the common account (τὰ γραφόμενα), as you have heard from astronomers. But Aristarchus brought out *a book consisting of certain hypotheses*, wherein it appears, as a consequence of the assumptions made, that the universe is many times greater than the "universe" just mentioned. His hypotheses are that *the fixed stars and the sun remain unmoved, that the earth revolves about the sun in the circumference of a circle, the sun lying in the middle of the orbit*, and that the sphere of the fixed stars, situated about the same centre as the sun, is so great that the circle in which he supposes the earth to revolve bears such a proportion to the distance of the fixed stars as the centre of the sphere bears to its surface. Now it is easy to see that this is impossible; for, since the centre of the sphere has no magnitude, we cannot conceive it to bear any ratio whatever to the surface of the sphere. We must, however, take Aristarchus to mean this: since we conceive the earth to be, as it were, the centre of the universe, the ratio which the earth bears to what we describe as the "universe" is equal to the ratio which the sphere containing the circle in which he supposes the earth to revolve bears to the sphere of the fixed stars. For he adapts the proofs of the phenomena to a hypothesis of this kind, and in particular he appears to suppose the size of the sphere in which he makes the earth move to be equal to what we call the "universe".'

We shall come back to the latter part of this passage; at present we are concerned only with the italicized words. The heliocentric hypothesis is stated in language which leaves no room for dispute as to its meaning. The sun, like the fixed stars, remains unmoved and forms the centre of a circular orbit in which the earth revolves round it;[1] the sphere of the fixed stars has its centre at the

---

[1] There is only one slight awkwardness in the language. The sentence is ὑποτίθεται γὰρ τὰ μὲν ἀπλανέα τῶν ἄστρων καὶ τὸν ἅλιον μένειν ἀκίνητον, τὰν δὲ γᾶν περιφέρεσθαι περὶ τὸν ἅλιον κατὰ κύκλου περιφέρειαν, ὅς ἐστιν ἐν μέσῳ τῷ δρόμῳ κείμενος, and it would be natural to suppose that the relative ὅς would refer to the masculine substantive nearest to it, i.e. κύκλου, 'circle,' rather than τὸν ἅλιον, 'the sun'; but 'which is situated in the middle of the (earth's) *course*' cannot possibly refer to the circle, i.e. to the course itself, and must refer to the sun. The awkwardness suggested to Bergk (*Fünf Abhandlungen*, 1883, p. 162) that Archimedes wrote ὅς ἐστιν ἐν μέσῳ τῷ οὐρανῷ, 'which is in the middle of the *heaven*.' This would enable ὅς to refer to the 'circle', but there seems to be no sufficient ground for changing the reading δρόμῳ.

centre of the sun. But a question arises as to the form in which
Aristarchus's hypotheses were given out. The expression used
by Archimedes is ὑποθεσίων τινῶν ἐξέδωκεν γραφάς, 'put out
γραφαί of certain hypotheses.' I take it in the sense of bringing
out a tract or tracts consisting of or stating certain hypotheses;
for one of the meanings of the word γραφή is a 'writing' or
a written 'description'. Heiberg takes γραφαί in this sense, but
regards ὑποθεσίων as the title of the book ('libros quosdam edidit,
qui hypotheses inscribuntur'[1]). Hultsch,[2] however, takes γραφαί
in its other possible sense of 'drawings' or *figures* constructed
to represent the hypotheses; and Schiaparelli[3] suggests that the
word γραφή here used seems not only to signify a verbal description
but to include also the idea of explanatory drawings. I agree
that it is probable enough that Aristarchus's tract or tracts included
geometrical figures illustrating the hypotheses, but I still think
that the word γραφαί here does not itself mean 'figures' but
means *written statements* of certain hypotheses. This seems to
me clear from the words immediately following γραφάς, namely
ἐν αἷς ἐκ τῶν ὑποκειμένων συμβαίνει κ.τ.έ., '*in which* it results
from the assumptions made that the universe is many times greater
than our "universe." above mentioned'; 'in which' can only refer
to γραφάς or ὑποθεσίων, and it cannot refer to ὑποθεσίων because
what *follows* from the assumptions made cannot be *in* those
assumptions which are nothing but the hypotheses themselves;
therefore 'in which' refers to γραφάς, but a result following from
assumptions does not follow *in* figures illustrating those assumptions but in the course of a description of them or an argument
about them. The words 'in which it results . . .' also show clearly
enough that the tract or tracts did not merely state the hypothesis
but also included some kind of geometrical proof.[4] I need only

[1] Archimedes, ed. Heiberg, vol. ii, p. 245.
[2] Hultsch, art. 'Aristarchus' in Pauly-Wissowa's *Real-Encyclopädie*, ii, p. 875.
[3] Schiaparelli, *Origine del sistema planetario eliocentrico presso i Greci*, p. 95.
[4] Bergk (*Fünf Abhandlungen*, p. 160) thinks that 'γραφάς cannot be taken as
synonymous with γράμματα : this would be a somewhat otiose circumlocution :
but it means the "outline" (Umriss), like καταγραφή. Archimedes chooses this
expression because Aristarchus had rather indicated his hypotheses than worked
them out and established them.' I do not think this inference necessary ;
γραφάς may be quite colourless without being otiose, a sufficient reason for its
insertion being the fact that some word other than ὑποθεσίων is necessary as an

add that there are other cases of the use of γραφή in the sense of 'writing'; cf. an expression in Eutocius, 'I have come across writings (γραφαῖς) of many famous men which give this problem' [that of the two mean proportionals].[1]

Our next evidence is a passage of Plutarch [2]:

'Only do not, my good fellow, enter an action against me for impiety in the style of Cleanthes, who thought it was the duty of Greeks to indict Aristarchus of Samos on the charge of impiety for putting in motion the Hearth of the Universe, this being the effect of his attempt to save the phenomena by supposing the heaven to remain at rest and the earth to revolve in an oblique circle, while it rotates, at the same time, about its own axis.'

Here we have the additional detail that Aristarchus followed Heraclides in attributing to the earth the daily rotation about its axis; Archimedes does not state this in so many words, but it is clearly involved by his remark that Aristarchus supposed that the fixed stars as well as the sun remain unmoved in space. When Plutarch makes Cleanthes say that Aristarchus ought to be indicted for the impiety of 'putting the Hearth of the Universe in motion', he is probably quoting the exact words used by Cleanthes, who doubtless had in mind the passage in Plato's *Phaedrus* where 'Hestia abides alone in the House of the Gods'. A similar expression is quoted by Theon of Smyrna from Dercyllides, who 'says that we must suppose the earth, the Hearth of the House of the Gods according to Plato, to remain fixed, and the planets with the whole embracing heaven to move, and rejects with abhorrence the view of those who have brought to rest the things which move and set in motion the things which by their nature and position are unmoved, such a supposition being contrary to the hypotheses of mathematics'; [3] the allusion here is equally to Aristarchus, though his name is not mentioned. A tract 'Against Aristarchus' is mentioned by Diogenes Laertius among Cleanthes' works; and it was evidently published during Aristarchus's lifetime (Cleanthes died about 232 B.C.).

antecedent to the relative sentence '*in which* it follows from the assumptions made, &c.'

[1] Archimedes, ed. Heiberg, vol. iii, p. 66. 9.
[2] Plutarch, *De facie in orbe lunae*, c. 6, pp. 922 F – 923 A.
[3] Theon of Smyrna, p. 200. 7–12, ed. Hiller.

Other passages bearing on our present subject are the following.

' Aristarchus sets the sun among the fixed stars and holds that the earth moves round the sun's circle (i.e. the ecliptic) and is put in shadow according to its (i.e. the earth's) inclinations.'[1]

One of the two versions of this passage has '*the disc* is put in shadow', and it would appear, as Schiaparelli says, 'that the words "the disc" were interpolated by some person who thought that the passage was an explanation of solar eclipses.' It is indeed placed under the heading 'Concerning the eclipse of the sun'; but this is evidently wrong, for we clearly have here in the concisest form an explanation of the phenomena of the seasons according to the system of Copernicus.[2]

' Yet those who did away with the motion of the universe and were of opinion that it is the earth which moves, as Aristarchus the mathematician held, are not on that account debarred from having a conception of time.'[3]

' Did Plato put the earth in motion, as he did the sun, the moon, and the five planets, which he called the instruments of time on account of their turnings, and was it necessary to conceive that the earth " which is globed about the axis stretched from pole to pole through the whole universe" was not represented as being held together and at rest, but as turning and revolving (στρεφομένην καὶ ἀνειλουμένην), as Aristarchus and Seleucus afterwards maintained that it did, the former stating this as only a hypothesis (ὑποτιθέμενος μόνον), the latter as a definite opinion (καὶ ἀποφαινόμενος)?'[4]

' Seleucus the mathematician, who had written in opposition to the views of Crates, and who himself too affirmed the earth's motion, says that the revolution (περιστροφή) of the moon resists the rotation [and the motion][5] of the earth, and, the air between the two bodies being diverted and falling upon the Atlantic ocean, the sea is correspondingly agitated into waves.'[6]

When Plutarch refers to Aristarchus as only putting forward the double motion of the earth as a *hypothesis*, he must presumably

[1] Aët. ii. 24. 8 (*D. G.* p. 355. 1-5).
[2] Schiaparelli, *I precursori*, p. 50.
[3] Sextus Empiricus, *Adv. Mathematicos*, x. 174, p. 512. 19, Bekker.
[4] Plutarch, *Plat. quaest.* viii. 1, 1006 C.
[5] The Ps. Plutarch version has the words καὶ τῇ κινήσει, 'and the motion,' after αὐτῆς τῇ δίνῃ φησί; Stobaeus omits them, and has τῷ δίνῳ instead of τῇ δίνῃ.
[6] Aët. iii. 17. 9 (*D. G.* p. 383).

be basing himself on nothing more than the word *hypotheses* used by Archimedes, and his remark does not therefore exclude the possibility of Aristarchus having supported his hypothesis by some kind of argument; nor can we infer from Plutarch that Seleucus went much further towards proving it. Plutarch says that Seleucus declared the hypothesis to be true (ἀποφαινόμενος), but it is not clear how he could have attempted to prove it. Schiaparelli suggests that Aristarchus's attitude may perhaps be explained on the basis of the difference between the rôles of the *astronomer* and the *physicist* as distinguished by Geminus in the passage quoted above (pp. 275–6). Aristarchus, as the astronomer and mathematician, would only be concerned to put forward geometrical *hypotheses* capable of accounting for the phenomena; he may have left it to the physicists to say 'which bodies ought from their nature to be at rest and which to move'. But this is only a conjecture.

Seleucus, of Seleucia on the Tigris, is described by Strabo[1] as a Chaldaean or Babylonian; he lived about a century after Aristarchus and may have written about 150 B.C. The last of the above quotations is Aëtius's summary of his explanation of the tides, a subject to which Seleucus had evidently given much attention;[2] in particular, he controverted the views held on this subject by Crates of Mallos, the 'grammarian', who wrote on geography and other things, as well as on Homer. The other explanations of the tides summarized by Aëtius include those of Aristotle and Heraclides, who sought the explanation in the sun, holding that the sun sets up winds, and that these winds, when they blow, cause the high tide and, when they cease, the low tide; Dicaearchus who put the tides down to the direct action of the sun according to its position; Pytheas and Posidonius who connected them with the moon, the former directly, the latter through the setting up of winds; Plato who posited a certain general oscillation of the waters, which pass through a hole in the earth;[3] Timaeus who gave as the reason the unequal flow of rivers from the Celtic mountains into the Atlantic; then, immediately before Seleucus, are mentioned Crates 'the grammarian' and Apollo-

---

[1] Strabo, xvi. 1. 6, i. 1. 9. [2] Cf. Strabo, iii. 5. 9.
[3] Cf. *Phaedo* 111 C sqq.

dorus of Corcyra, the account of whose views is vague enough, the former attributing the tides to 'the counter-movement ($\dot{\alpha}\nu\tau\iota$-$\sigma\pi\alpha\sigma\mu\acute{o}s$) of the sea,'[1] and the latter to 'the refluxes from the Ocean '. When Aëtius adds, in introducing Seleucus's views, that 'he too made the earth move ', we should expect that he had just before mentioned some one else who had done the same.   But Crates adhered to the old view and did not make the earth move ;[2] nor is there anything to suggest that Apollodorus attributed motion to the earth.   Consequently Bergk supposes that, just before the notice of Seleucus's explanation of the tides with reference to the earth's motion, there must have been a notice of a different explanation of them by a person who also attributed motion to the earth, and that, as we know of no other person by name who adopted Aristarchus's views, except Seleucus, the notice which has dropped out must have given a different explanation of the tides by Aristarchus himself.[3]   But, as the motion of the earth referred to in Seleucus's explanation may be rotation only ($\delta\acute{\iota}\nu\eta$ or $\delta\hat{\iota}\nu os$), it seems possible that Heraclides (who made the earth rotate) is the other person referred to in the collection of notices as having 'made the earth move ', although he is mentioned some way back. To judge by Seleucus's explanation of the tides, he would seem to have supposed that the atmosphere about the earth extended as far as the moon and rotated with the earth in 24 hours, and that the resistance of the moon acted upon the rotating atmosphere either by virtue of the relative slowness of the moon's revolution about the earth or of its motion perpendicular to the equator ;[4] Strabo tells us that Seleucus had discovered periodical inequalities in the flux and reflux of the Red Sea which he connected with the position of the moon in the zodiac.[5]

No one after Seleucus is mentioned by name as having accepted the doctrine of Aristarchus, and if other Greek astronomers refer to it, they do so only to denounce it, as witness Dercyllides.[6]   The rotation of the earth is, however, mentioned as a possibility by Seneca.

---

[1] Some details of Crates' views are also given in Strabo, i. 1. 8.

[2] Bergk (*Fünf Abhandlungen*, p. 166) quotes from Strabo, i. 2. 24, the words $\tau\grave{\eta}\nu$ $\pi\acute{\alpha}\rho o\delta o\nu$ $\tau o\hat{\upsilon}$ $\dot{\eta}\lambda\acute{\iota}o\upsilon$.   [3] Bergk, op. cit., p. 167.

[4] Schiaparelli, *I precursori*, p. 36.   [5] Strabo, iii. 5. 9.

[6] Theon of Smyrna, p. 200. 7-12 : see above (p. 304).

'It will be proper to discuss this, in order that we may know whether the universe revolves and the earth stands still, or the universe stands still and the earth rotates. For there have been those who asserted that it is we whom the order of nature causes to move without our being aware of it, and that risings and settings do not occur by virtue of the motion of the heaven, but that we ourselves rise and set. The subject is worthy of consideration, in order that we may know in what conditions we live, whether the abode allotted to us is the most slowly or the most quickly moving, whether God moves everything around us, or ourselves instead.'[1]

Hipparchus, himself a contemporary of Seleucus, reverted to the geocentric system, and it was doubtless his great authority which sealed the fate of the heliocentric hypothesis for so many centuries. The reasons which weighed with Hipparchus were presumably (in addition to the general prejudice in favour of maintaining the earth in the centre of the universe) the facts that the system in which the earth revolved in a circle of which the sun was the exact *centre* failed to 'save the phenomena', and in particular to account for the variations of distance and the irregularities of the motions, which became more and more patent as methods of observation improved; that, on the other hand, the theory of epicycles did suffice to represent the phenomena with considerable accuracy; and that the latter theory could be reconciled with the immobility of the earth.

We revert now to the latter part of the passage quoted above from Archimedes, in which he comments upon the assumption of Aristarchus that the sphere of the fixed stars is so great that the ratio in which the earth's orbit stands to the said sphere is such a ratio as that which the centre of the sphere bears to its surface. If this is taken in a strictly mathematical sense, it means of course that the sphere of the fixed stars is infinite in size, a supposition which would not suit Archimedes' purpose, because he is undertaking to prove that he can evolve a system for expressing large numbers which will enable him to state easily in plain words the number of grains of sand which the whole universe could contain; hence, while he wishes to base his estimate of the maximum size of the universe upon some authoritative statement which will be generally accepted, and takes the statement of Aristarchus as suit-

[1] Seneca, *Nat. Quaest.* vii. 2. 3.

able for his purpose, he is obliged to interpret it in an arbitrary
way which he can only justify by somewhat sophistically pressing
the mathematical point that Aristarchus could not have meant to
assert that the sphere of the fixed stars is actually *infinite* in size
and therefore could not have wished his statement to be taken
quite literally; consequently he suggests that a reasonable interpretation would be to take it as meaning that

(diameter of earth) : (diameter of ' universe ') =
          (diam. of earth's orbit) : (diam. of sphere of fixed stars),

instead of

0 : (surface of sphere of fixed stars) =
          (diam. of earth's orbit): (diam. of sphere of fixed stars),

and he explains that the ' universe ' as commonly conceived by the
astronomers of his time (he refers no doubt to the adherents of
the system of concentric spheres) is a sphere with the earth as
centre and radius equal to the distance of the sun from the earth,
and that Aristarchus seems to regard the sphere containing (as a
great circle) the orbit in which the earth revolves about the sun as
equal to the ' universe ' as commonly conceived, so that the second
and third terms of the first of the above proportions are equal.

While it is clear that Archimedes' interpretation is not justified,
it may be admitted that Aristarchus did not mean his statement to
be taken as a mathematical fact. He clearly meant to assert no
more than that the sphere of the fixed stars is *incomparably* greater
than that containing the earth's orbit as a great circle; and he was
shrewd enough to see that this is necessary in order to reconcile
the apparent immobility of the fixed stars with the motion of
the earth. The actual expression used is similar to what was
evidently a common form of words among astronomers to express the negligibility of the size of the earth in comparison with
larger spheres. Thus, in his own tract *On the sizes and distances
of the sun and moon*, Aristarchus lays down as one of his assump-
tions that ' the earth is in the relation ($\lambda \acute{o} \gamma o \nu$ $\check{\epsilon} \chi \epsilon \iota \nu$) of a point and
centre to the sphere in which the moon moves '. In like manner
Euclid proves, in the first theorem of his *Phaenomena*, that ' the
earth is in the middle of the universe ($\kappa \acute{o} \sigma \mu o s$) and holds the

position (τάξιν) of centre relatively to the universe'. Similarly Geminus[1] describes the earth as 'in the relation of a centre to the sphere of the fixed stars'; Ptolemy[2] says that the earth is not *sensibly* different from a point in relation to the radius of the sphere of the fixed stars; according to Cleomedes[3] the earth is 'in the relation of a centre' to the sphere in which the sun moves, and *a fortiori* to the sphere of the fixed stars, but *not* to the sphere in which the moon moves.

In Aristarchus's extant treatise *On the sizes and distances of the sun and moon* there is no hint of the heliocentric hypothesis, but the sun and moon are supposed to move in circles round the earth as centre. From this we must infer either (1) that the work in question was earlier than the date at which he put forward the hypotheses described by Archimedes, or (2) that, as in the tract the distances of the sun from the earth and of the moon from the earth are alone in question, and therefore it was for the immediate purpose immaterial which hypothesis was taken, Aristarchus thought it better to proceed on the geocentric hypothesis which was familiar to everybody. Schiaparelli[4] suggests that one of the reasons which led Aristarchus to place the sun in the centre of the universe was probably the consideration of the sun's great size in comparison with the earth. Now in the treatise referred to Aristarchus finds the ratio of the diameter of the sun to the diameter of the earth to lie between 19 : 3 and 43 : 6; this makes the volume of the sun something like 300 times the volume of the earth, and, although the principles of dynamics were then unknown, it might even in that day seem absurd to make the body which was so much larger revolve round the smaller.

There is no reason to doubt that, in his heliocentric system, Aristarchus retained the moon as a satellite of the earth revolving round it as a centre; thus even in his system there was one epicycle, that described by the moon about the earth as centre.

[1] Geminus, *Isagoge*, 18. 16, p. 186. 16, ed. Manitius.
[2] Ptolemy, *Syntaxis*, i. 6, p. 20. 5, Heib.
[3] Cleomedes, *De motu circulari*, i. 11.   [4] Schiaparelli, *I precursori*, p. 33.

The apparent diameter of the sun.

Another passage of the *Sand-reckoner* of Archimedes states that
'Aristarchus discovered that the sun's apparent size is about one
720th part of the zodiac circle.'[1]

This, again, is a valuable contribution to our knowledge of
Aristarchus, for in the treatise *On the sizes and distances of the
sun and moon* he makes the apparent diameter not $\frac{1}{720}$th of the
zodiac circle, or $\frac{1}{2}°$, but one-fifteenth part of a sign, that is to say 2°,
which is a gross over-estimate. The nearest estimate to this which
we find recorded appears to be that mentioned by Macrobius,[2] who
describes an experiment madè with a hemispherical dial by marking
the points on which the shadow of the upright needle fell at the
moments respectively when the first ray of the sun as it began to
rise fell on the instrument and when the sun just cleared the horizon
respectively. The result showed that the interval of time was $\frac{1}{9}$th
of an hour, which gave as the apparent diameter of the sun $\frac{1}{216}$th
of 360° or $1\frac{2}{3}°$. Macrobius would apparently have us believe that
this very inaccurate estimate was due to the Egyptians. We have,
however, seen reason to believe that Macrobius probably attributed
to the 'Egyptians' the doctrines of certain Alexandrian astronomers,[3] and in the present case it would seem that we have to do
with an observation very unskilfully made by some even less com-
petent person.[4] The Babylonians had, however, many centuries
before arrived at a much closer approximation; they made the
time which the sun takes to rise $\frac{1}{30}$th of an hour, and, even if
the hour is the double hour (one-twelfth of a day and night), this
gives 1° as the apparent diameter of the sun. How, then, did
Aristarchus in his extant work come to take 2° as the value?
Tannery has an interesting suggestion, which is however perhaps
too ingenious.[5] 'If Aristarchus chose for the apparent diameter
of the sun a value which he knew to be false, it is clear, that his
treatise was mainly intended to give a specimen of calculations

---

[1] Archimedes, ed. Heiberg, ii, p. 248. 19; *The Works of Archimedes*, ed.
Heath, p. 223.

[2] Macrobius, *In somn. Scip.* i. 20. 26–30.   [3] See p. 259 above.

[4] Hultsch, *Poseidonios über die Grösse und Entfernung der Sonne*, p. 43.

[5] Tannery, 'Aristarque de Samos' in *Mém. de la Soc. des sciences phys. et
nat. de Bordeaux*, 2ᵉ sér. v. 1883, p. 241; *Mémoires scientifiques*, ed. Heiberg
and Zeuthen, i, pp. 375-6.

which require to be made on the basis of more exact experimental observations, and to show at the same time that, for the solution of the problem, one of the data could be chosen almost arbitrarily. He secured himself in this way against certain objections which might have been raised. According to the testimony of Macrobius, it seems that in fact the Egyptians had, by observations completely erroneous, fixed the apparent diameter of the sun at $\frac{1}{216}$th of the circumference, i. e. $1\frac{2}{3}°$. Aristarchus seems to have deliberately chosen to assign it a still higher value; but it is beyond question that he was perfectly aware of the consequences of his hypothesis.' Manitius[1] suggests that the 'one-fifteenth part ($\pi\epsilon\nu\tau\epsilon\kappa\alpha\iota\delta\acute{\epsilon}\kappa\alpha\tau\text{o}\nu$ $\mu\acute{\epsilon}\rho\text{o}\varsigma$)' of a sign of the zodiac in Aristarchus's treatise should be altered into 'one-fiftieth part' ($\pi\epsilon\nu\tau\eta\kappa\text{o}\sigma\tau\grave{\text{o}}\nu$ $\mu\acute{\epsilon}\rho\text{o}\varsigma$), which would give the quite acceptable value of $0°$ $36'$. But the propositions in the treatise in which the hypothesis is actually used seem to make it clear that 'one-fifteenth' is what Aristarchus really wrote. Unless therefore we accept Tannery's suggestion, we seem to be thrown back once more on the supposition that the treatise was an early work written before Aristarchus had made the more accurate observation recorded by Archimedes. From the statement of Archimedes that Aristarchus *discovered* ($\epsilon\dot{\upsilon}\rho\eta\kappa\acute{\text{o}}\tau\text{o}\varsigma$) the value of $\frac{1}{720}$th, I think we may infer with safety that Aristarchus was at least the first Greek who had given it, and we have therefore an additional reason for questioning the tradition which credits Thales with the discovery. How Aristarchus obtained his result we are not told, but, seeing that he is credited with the invention of an improved sun-dial ($\sigma\kappa\acute{\alpha}\phi\eta$), it is possible that it was by means of this instrument that he made his observations. Archimedes himself seems to have been the first to think of the better method of using an instrument for measuring angles; by the use of a rough instrument of this kind he made the apparent angular diameter of the sun lie between the limits of $\frac{1}{164}$th and $\frac{1}{200}$th of a right angle. Hipparchus used for the same purpose a more elaborate instrument, his dioptra, the construction of which is indicated by Ptolemy,[2] and is more fully described by Pappus in his commentary on Book V of

---

[1] Proclus, *Hypotyposis*, ed. Manitius, note on p. 292.
[2] Ptolemy, *Syntaxis*, v. 14, p. 417. 2–3 and 20–23, ed. Heib.

Ptolemy, quoted by Theon of Alexandria;[1] Proclus describes it somewhat differently.[2] Though we gather that Hipparchus made many observations of the apparent diameters of the sun and moon,[3] only one actual result is handed down; he found that the diameter of the moon was contained about 650 times in the circle described by it.[4] This would no doubt be the mean of the different observations of the moon at its varying distances; it is of course equivalent to nearly $0°$ $33'$ $14''$. Ptolemy complains that the requisite accuracy could not be secured by the dioptra; he therefore checked the observations as regards the moon by means of 'certain lunar eclipses', and found Hipparchus's values appreciably too high. Ptolemy[5] himself made the apparent diameter of the moon to be (a) at the time when it is furthest from the earth $0°$ $31'$ $20''$, and (b) at its least distance $0°$ $35'$ $20''$. The mean of these figures being $0°$ $33'$ $20''$, and the true values corresponding to Ptolemy's figures being $29'$ $26''$ and $32'$ $51''$, it follows that Hipparchus's mean value is actually nearer the true mean value than Ptolemy's.[6] Aristarchus, as we shall see, took the apparent diameters of the sun and moon to be the same. Sosigenes (2nd c. A.D.) showed that they are not always equal by adverting to the phenomenon of annular eclipses of the sun,[7] and doubtless Hipparchus had observed the differences; Ptolemy found that the apparent diameter of the sun was approximately constant, whenever observed, its value being the same as that of the moon when at its greatest distance, not ('as supposed by earlier astronomers') when at its mean distance.[8] Another estimate of the apparent diameter of the sun, namely $\frac{1}{750}$th of the complete circle described by the sun, or $29'$, is given by Cleomedes as having been obtained by means of a water-clock; he adds that the Egyptians are said to have been the first to discover this method.[9] Yet another valuation appears in

---

[1] Theon, *in Ptolem. magn. construct.* p. 262.
[2] Proclus, *Hypotyposis*, ed. Manitius, pp. 126. 13–128. 13.
[3] Ptolemy, *Syntaxis*, loc. cit.
[4] Ptolemy, *Syntaxis*, iv. 9, p. 327. 1–3, Heib.
[5] Ptolemy, v. 14, p. 421. 3–5; Pappus, ed. Hultsch, vi, p. 556. 17–19.
[6] On the whole of this subject see Hultsch, 'Winkelmessungen durch die Hipparchische Dioptra' in *Abhandlungen zur Gesch. d. Math.* ix (Cantor-Festschrift), 1899, pp. 193–209.
[7] Simplicius on *De caelo*, p. 505. 7–9, Heib.
[8] Ptolemy, *Syntaxis*, v. 14, p. 417. 3–11, Heib.
[9] Cleomedes, *De motu circulari*, ii. 1, pp. 136–8, ed. Ziegler.

Martianus Capella;[1] the diameter of the moon is there estimated as $\frac{1}{600}$th of its orbit or $36'$. This estimate was probably quoted from Varro, and belongs to a period anterior to Hipparchus.[2]

The Year and the Great Year of Aristarchus.

We are told by Censorinus that Aristarchus added $\frac{1}{1623}$rd of a day to Callippus's figure of $365\frac{1}{4}$ days for the solar year,[3] and that he gave 2,484 years as the length of the Great Year, or the period after which the sun, the moon, and the five planets return to the same position in the heavens.[4] Tannery[5] shows that 2,484 years is probably a mistake for 2,434 years, and he gives an explanation, which seems convincing, of the way in which Aristarchus arrived at his figures. They were doubtless derived from the Chaldaean period of 223 lunations and the multiple of this by 3, which was called ἐξελιγμός, a period defined by Geminus as the shortest time containing a whole number of days, a whole number of months (synodic), and a whole number of anomalistic months.[6] The Greeks were by Aristarchus's time fully acquainted with these periods, which were doubtless known through the Chaldaean Berosus, who flourished about 280 B.C., in the time of Alexander the Great, and founded an astronomical school on the island of Cos opposite Miletus. Ptolemy,[7] too, says of the first of the two periods (which he attributes to 'the ancients', not the Chaldaeans specifically) that it was estimated at $6,585\frac{1}{3}$ days, containing 223 lunations, 239 'restorations of anomaly' (i. e. anomalistic months), 242 'restorations of latitude' (i. e. draconitic months, the draconitic month—a term not used by Ptolemy—meaning the period after which the moon returns to the same position with respect to the nodes), and 241 sidereal revolutions *plus* $10\frac{2}{3}°$ which the sun describes in the time in addition to 18 sidereal revolutions. The *exeligmus* then, which was three times this period, consisted of 19,756 days, containing 669 lunations, 717 anomalistic months, 726 draconitic months, and

---

[1] Martianus Capella, *De nuptiis philologiae et Mercurii*, viii. 860.
[2] Tannery, *Recherches sur l'histoire de l'astronomie ancienne*, p. 334.
[3] Censorinus, *De die natali*, c. 19. 2.   [4] Ibid., c. 18. 11.
[5] Tannery, 'La Grande Année d'Aristarque de Samos' in *Mém. de la Soc. des sciences phys. et naturelles de Bordeaux*, 3ᵉ série, iv. 1888, pp. 79-96.
[6] Geminus, *Isagoge*, c. 18, pp. 2co sqq., ed. Manitius.
[7] Ptolemy, *Syntaxis*, iv. 2, pp. 269. 21 – 270. 18, Heib.

723 sidereal revolutions *plus* 32° described by the sun in the period over and above 54 sidereal revolutions.

It follows that the number of days in the sidereal year is

$$\frac{19756}{54+\frac{32}{360}} = \frac{19756}{54+\frac{4}{45}} = \frac{45 \cdot 19756}{2434} = \frac{889020}{2434} = 365\frac{1}{4} + \frac{3}{4868}.$$

Now $\frac{4868}{3} = 1623 - \frac{1}{3}$. Thus, in replacing the complementary $\frac{3}{4868}$ by $\frac{1}{1623}$ Aristarchus followed the fashion of only admitting fractions with unity as numerator, and thereby only neglected the insignificant fraction $\frac{1}{1623.4868}$ or $\frac{1}{7900764}$.

It is clear that Aristarchus multiplied by 45 so as to avoid all fractions, and so arrived at 889,020 days containing 2,434 sidereal years, 30,105 lunations, 32,265 anomalistic months, 32,670 draconitic months, and 32,539 sidereal months.

Tannery gives good reason for thinking that this evaluation of the solar year at $365\frac{1}{4}\frac{1}{1623}$ days was really a sort of argument in a circle and was therefore worthless. The Chaldaean period was obtained from the observation of eclipses ; those which were similar were classified, and it was recognized that they returned at the end of a period estimated at $6,585\frac{1}{3}$ days. If the theory of the sun had been sufficiently established, or if the difference of longitude between the positions of two similar eclipses had been observed and allowance made for the solar anomaly, it would have been possible to evaluate with precision the number of degrees traversed during the period by the sun over and above the whole number of its revolutions. But this precision was beyond the powers of the Chaldaeans, and the estimate of the excess of $10\frac{2}{3}°$ was probably obtained by means of the simple difference between $6585\frac{1}{3}$ days and 18 years of $365\frac{1}{4}$ days or $6,574\frac{1}{2}$ days. This difference is $10\frac{5}{6}$ days, and, if this is turned into degrees by multiplying by $360/365\frac{1}{4}$, we have about $10\frac{2}{3}\frac{1}{91}°$; the complementary fraction $\frac{1}{91}$ would then be neglected as unimportant. Thus Aristarchus's estimate of $365\frac{1}{4}\frac{1}{1623}$ days was valueless, as the Chaldaean period itself depended on a solar year of $365\frac{1}{4}$ days.

The question remaining is whether Aristarchus's Great Year was intended to be the period which brings all the five planets as well as the sun and moon back again to the same places, as appears to be implied by Censorinus, who mentions different estimates of the

Great Year (including Aristarchus's) just after an explanation that 'there is also a year which Aristotle calls the greatest rather than the great year, which is completed by the sun, the moon, and the five planets when they return together to the same sign in which they were once before simultaneously found'.   As Tannery observes, if Aristarchus's Great Year corresponded to an effective determination of the periods of the revolutions of the planets, it would have a particular interest because Aristarchus would have, in accordance with his system, to treat the revolution of Mercury and Venus as heliocentric, whereas in the earlier estimates of Great Years, e.g. that of Oenopides, the revolution of these planets was geocentric and of the same mean duration as that of the sun, so that they could be left out of account.   But, just as we were obliged to conclude that Oenopides could not have maintained that his Great Year of 59 years contained a whole number of the periods of revolution of the several planets, so it seems clear that Aristarchus could hardly have maintained that his Great Year exactly covered an integral number of the periods of revolution of the five planets.   For suppose that his Great Year of 889,020 days is divided by the respective periods of their sidereal revolutions, and that we take the nearest whole numbers to the quotients—say 10,106 for Mercury, 3,950 for Venus, 1,294 for Mars, 206 for Jupiter, 83 for Saturn—the errors as regards the positions at the end of the period would amount, according to Tannery's calculation, to $133°$ for Saturn, $70°$ for Jupiter, $25°$ for Mars, $171°$ for Venus, and $11°$ for Mercury.   This being so, it is difficult to believe that the period of Aristarchus is anything more than a luni-solar cycle.[1]

[1] Tannery, loc. cit., pp. 93-4.

ARISTARCHUS ON THE SIZES AND DISTANCES OF THE SUN AND MOON

History of the Text and Editions.

At the beginning of Book VI of his *Synagoge*, Pappus refers to want of judgement (as to what to include and what to omit) on the part of 'many of those who teach the Treasury of Astronomy (τὸν ἀστρονομούμενον τόπον)'. The marginal note of the contents of the Book, written in the third hand in the oldest MS., says that it contains solutions of difficulties ἐν τῷ μικρῷ ἀστρονομουμένῳ, which words, with τόπῳ understood, indicate that the collection of treatises referred to by Pappus was known as the 'Little Astronomy', as we might say. The collection formed a sort of preliminary course, introductory to what would presumably be regarded as the 'Great Astronomy', the *Syntaxis* of Ptolemy. From Pappus's own references in the course of Book VI we may infer that the Little Astronomy certainly included the following books:

Autolycus, *On the moving sphere* (περὶ κινουμένης σφαίρας).
Euclid, *Optics*,
  „   *Phaenomena.*
Theodosius, *Sphaerica*,
  „   *On days and nights.*
Aristarchus, *On the sizes and distances of the sun and moon.*

No doubt Autolycus's other treatise, *On risings and settings*, Theodosius's *On habitations*, and Hypsicles' ἀναφορικός (*De ascensionibus*) were also included; they duly appear in MSS. containing the whole collection.[1] All these treatises are extant in Greek as well as in Arabic. Not so another important work, the *Sphaerica*

---

[1] Heiberg, *Literargeschichtliche Studien über Euklid*, 1882, p. 152.

of Menelaus, which has only survived in the Arabic and in translations therefrom, but seems to have belonged to the collection, since
Pappus gives four propositions found in Menelaus;[1] this treatise
was important for the study of the *Syntaxis*, as is proved by the
fact that Ptolemy takes for granted certain propositions of
Menelaus.[2]

As regards some of these treatises it is certain that they were by
no means the first or the only works dealing with the same subjects.
Thus Euclid's *Phaenomena* is closely akin to Autolycus's *On the
moving sphere*, and both assume as well known a number of
propositions which are found in Theodosius's *Sphaerica*, a work
much later in date.[3] It is certain therefore that before the date of
Autolycus (latter half of fourth century B.C.) there was in existence
a body of sphaeric geometry; and indeed it would appear to have
contained fully half of the propositions subsequently incorporated
in Theodosius's *Sphaerica*. This early *sphaeric* may have originated with Eudoxus and his school or may have been older still.
Its object was purely astronomical; it did not deal with the geometry
of the sphere as such, still less did it contain anything of the nature
of spherical trigonometry (this deficiency was afterwards made good
by Menelaus's *Sphaerica*); it was designed expressly for such purposes as fixing the sequence of the times of rising and setting of
different heavenly bodies, comparing the durations of the risings
and settings of particular constellations, comparing the apparent
speeds of the motion of the heavenly bodies at different points
in their daily revolution, and so on.[4] Perhaps it may best be

---

[1] A. A. Björnbo, Studien über Menelaos' Sphärik. Beiträge zur Geschichte
der Sphärik und Trigonometrie der Griechen (in *Abhandlungen zur Geschichte
der mathematischen Wissenschaften*, Heft xiv, 1902), pp. 4, 51, 55.

[2] Björnbo, op. cit., p. 51.

[3] On the question of Theodosius's date we know little except that he was
before Menelaus's time. Menelaus made observations in the first year of
Trajan's reign (A.D. 98); and Theodosius, probably of Bithynia, lived before our
era. Vitruvius (first century B.C.) mentions (ix. 8) a Theodosius who invented
a sun-dial for all climates, and he may have been contemporary with Hipparchus
or a little earlier (Tannery, *Recherches sur l'histoire de l'astronomie ancienne*,
pp. 36, 37; Björnbo, op. cit., pp. 64, 65).

[4] The sort of thing may be illustrated by the following enunciations of
propositions:
Autolycus, *On the moving sphere*, 9. ' If in a sphere a great circle oblique to
the axis defines the visible and the invisible (halves) of the sphere [the great
circle is of course the horizon], then of those points which rise at the same time

described as the theoretical equivalent of a material sphere or combination of spheres (such as are said to have been constructed by many astronomers from Anaximander onwards) which should exactly simulate the motions of the heavenly bodies and visualize the order, &c., of the phenomena as they occur. The special necessity for theoretical works of this kind was of course due to the obliquity, with reference to the circle of the equator, of (1) the horizon at any point of the earth's surface, and (2) the plane of the ecliptic in which the independent motions of the sun, moon, and planets were supposed to take place.

We may assume that this mathematical side of astronomy began to be studied very early. We know that Oenopides studied certain geometrical propositions with a view to their application to astronomy; and, whether he brought his knowledge of the zodiac and its twelve signs from Egypt or not, he was apparently the first to state the theory of the oblique movement of the sun.[1] The application of mathematics to astronomy may therefore have begun with Oenopides; but it had evidently made progress by the time of Archytas, Eudoxus's teacher, for Archytas expresses himself, at the beginning of a work *On Mathematics*, thus:

'The mathematicians seem to me to have arrived at correct conclusions, and it is not therefore surprising that they have a true conception of the nature of each individual thing; for, having reached such correct conclusions as regards the nature of the whole universe, they were bound to see in its true light the nature of

those which are nearer the visible pole set later, and of those which set at the same time those which are nearer to the visible pole rise earlier.'

Euclid, *Phaenomena*, 8. 'The signs of the zodiac rise and set in unequal segments of the horizon, those on the equator in the greatest, those next to them in the next smaller, those on the tropic circles in the smallest, and those equidistant from the equator in equal segments.'

Theodosius, *Sphaerica*, iii. 6. 'If the pole of the parallel circles be on the circumference of a great circle and this great circle be cut at right angles by two great circles, one of which is one of the parallel circles [i. e. the equator], while the other is oblique to the parallel circles [say the ecliptic]; if then from the oblique circle equal arcs be cut off adjacent to one another and on the same side of the greatest of the parallel circles [the equator]; and if through the points so determined and the pole great circles be drawn; the arcs which they will intercept between them on the greatest of the parallel circles will be unequal, and the intercept which is nearer to the original great circle will always be greater than that which is more remote from it.'

[1] Tannery, op. cit., p. 33.

particular things as well. Thus they have handed down to us clear knowledge *about the speed of the stars*,[1] *their risings and settings*, and about geometry, arithmetic, and *sphaeric*, and last, not least, about music; for all these branches of knowledge seem to be sisters.'[2]

We must suppose, then, that Theodosius's compilation (long-winded and dull as it is) simply superseded the earlier text-books on *Sphaeric*, which accordingly fell into disuse and so were lost, just as the same fate befell the works of the great Hipparchus as the result of their being superseded by Ptolemy's *Syntaxis*.

Why Euclid's *Optics* was included in the Little Astronomy is not clear. It was a sort of elementary theory of perspective and may have been intended to fore-arm students against the propounders of paradoxes such as that of the Epicureans, who alleged that the heavenly bodies must *be* of the size which they *appear*; it would also serve to justify the assumption of circular movement on the part of the stars about the earth as centre.[3]

It was a fortunate circumstance that Aristarchus's treatise found a place in the collection; for presumably we owe it to this fact that the work has survived, while so many more have perished.

Whether Aristarchus had any predecessors in the mathematical calculation of relative sizes and distances cannot be stated for certain. We hear, indeed, of a book by Philippus of Opus (the editor of the *Laws* of Plato and the author of the *Epinomis*) entitled *On the size of the sun, the moon, and the earth*, which is mentioned by Suidas directly after another work, *On the eclipse of the moon*, attributed to the same author; but we know nothing of the contents of these treatises.

Like the other books included in the Little Astronomy, our treatise passed to Arabia and took its place among the Arabian 'middle' or 'intermediate books', as they were called. It was translated into Arabic by Qusṭā b. Lūqā al-Baʻlabakkī (died about 912), who was also the translator of the three works of Theodosius,

---

[1] In connexion with the remark that the mathematicians had investigated the speed of the stars, it is perhaps worth while to recall that Eudoxus's great theory of concentric spheres was set out in a book *On Speeds*, περὶ ταχῶν (Simplicius on *De caelo*, p. 494. 12, Heib.).

[2] Porphyry, *In Ptolem. Harm.*, p. 236; Nicomachus, *Introd. Arithm.* i. 3. 4, pp. 6. 17 – 7. 2; *Vorsokratiker*, i², p. 258. 4–12.

[3] Tannery, op. cit., p. 36.

Autolycus's *On risings and settings*, and Hypsicles' Ἀναφορικός.[1]
A recension of it, as of all the books contained in the Little
Astronomy, including the *Sphaerica* of Menelaus, which had been
translated by Ishāq b. Ḥunain, was made by Naṣīraddīn aṭ-Ṭūsī,[2]
famous as the editor of Euclid and for an attempt to prove Euclid's
Parallel-Postulate. There are MSS. of this collection, including
of course Aristarchus, in the India Office (743, 744) and in the
Bodleian Library (Nicoll and Pusey, i. 875, i. 895, and ii. 279).

The first published edition of Aristarchus's treatise was a Latin
translation by George Valla, included in a volume which appeared
first in 1488 ('per Anton. de Strata') and again in 1498 ('per
Simonen Papiensem dictum Bevilaquam').[3]

It next appeared in a Latin translation by that admirable and
indefatigable translator Commandinus, under the title:

> *Aristarchi de magnitudinibus et distantiis solis et lunae liber*
> *cum Pappi Alexandrini explicationibus quibusdam a* Federico
> Commandino Urbinate *in latinum conversus et commentariis*
> *illustratus.* Pisauri, 1572.

Commandinus complains of the state of the text, which made the
task of translation difficult, but he does not mention Valla's earlier
translation and was presumably not acquainted with it.

The honour of bringing out the *editio princeps* of the Greek
text belongs to John Wallis. The title-page is as follows:

[1] Suter, *Die Mathematiker und Astronomen der Araber und ihre Werke*
(*Abh. zur Gesch. d. math. Wissenschaften*, x. Heft, 1900), p. 41.

[2] Suter, p. 152.

[3] Fabricius, *Bibliotheca Graeca*, iv. 19, Harles.

ΑΡΙΣΤΑΡΧΟΥ ΣΑΜΙΟΥ

Περὶ μεγεθῶν κỳ ἀποστημ̃ Ἡλίυ κỳ Σελήνης,

ΒΙΒΛΙΟΝ.

ΠΑΠΠΟΥ ΑΛΕΞΑΝΔΡΕΩΣ

Τῦ ᵈ Σωαγωγῆς Βιβλιου Β'

Ἀπόσπασμα.

ARISTARCHI SAMII

De Magnitudinibus & Diſtantiis Solis & Lunæ,

LIBER.

Nunc primum Græce editus cum Federici Commandini *verſione Latina, notiſq; illius & Editoris.*

PAPPI ALEXANDRINI

SECUNDI LIBRI

MATHEMATICÆ COLLECTIONIS,

Fragmentum,

Hactenus Deſideratum.

*E Codice M S. edidit, Latinum fecit,
Notiſque illuſtravit*

JOHANNES WALLIS, S. T. D. Geometriæ
Profeſſor Savilianus ; & *Regalis Societatis*
Londini , Sodalis.

OXONIÆ,

E THEATRO SHELDONIANO,

1688.

The book was reprinted in the collected edition of *Johannis Wallis Opera Mathematica*, 1693-1699, vol. iii, pp. 565-94.

Wallis states in his Preface that he used for the preparation of his text (1) a Greek MS. (which he calls B) belonging to Edward Bernard, Savilian Professor of Astronomy, who had copied it from the Savile MS., and (2) the Savile MS. itself (S). The Savile MS. was copied by Sir Henry Savile himself from another (presumed by Wallis to have been one of the Vatican MSS.), and had (as appeared from notes in the margin) been collated with a second MS. vaguely described as Codex Vetus. Wallis preferred Commandinus's translation to Valla's, and retained the former version intact because it agreed so closely with the Greek MSS. of Savile and Bernard that it seemed to have a common source with them; Wallis also incorporated Commandinus's notes along with his own.

Wallis adds that there are two Selden MSS. in the Bodleian Library containing Aristarchus's treatise in Arabic, and that Bernard had noted in the margin of his MS. (B) anything in the Arabic version which seemed of moment, as well as some things from Valla's translation.

In 1810 there appeared the edition by the Comte de Fortia d'Urban,

> *Histoire d'Aristarque de Samos, suivie de la traduction de son ouvrage sur les distances du Soleil et de la Lune, de l'histoire de ceux qui ont porté le nom d'Aristarque avant Aristarque de Samos, et le commencement de celle des Philosophes qui ont paru avant ce même Aristarque. Par M. de F* * * *.* Paris, 1810.

There follows, as a separate title-page for the work of Aristarchus, Ἀριστάρχου περὶ μεγεθῶν καὶ ἀποστημάτων ἡλίου καὶ σελήνης, followed by the Latin equivalent. Pages 2-87 contain the Greek text along with Commandinus's Latin translation (altered in places). On p. 88 is a note referring to the MSS. used by the editor in preparing the Greek text of the treatise and the scholia. The scholia in Greek and Latin occupy pages 89-199, and are followed by the critical notes, which extend from p. 201 to p. 248. Particulars of the MSS. used will be found in a later paragraph.

This Greek text of Fortia d'Urban was issued prematurely and without any diagrams; an explanation on the subject is contained in the editor's preface to his French translation published thirteen years later,

Traité d'Aristarque de Samos sur les grandeurs et les distances du Soleil et de la Lune, traduit en français pour la première fois, par M. le Comte de Fortia d'Urban. Paris, 1823.

The Preface to this translation, with the omission of an explanation of the lettering in the figures (which is double, to correspond to the Greek text and the Latin and French translations), runs as follows :

'Le texte de l'ouvrage d'Aristarque de Samos, que j'avais revu sur huit manuscrits de la bibliothèque du Roi, et que j'avais fait imprimer en France où il n'avait point encore été publié, avec des scholies absolument inédits, ayant été mis en vente sans mon autorisation, a paru d'une manière presque ridicule. On y trouve citées, à toutes les pages, des planches que j'avais fait graver, mais que des circonstances fâcheuses ont fait disparaître pendant mon séjour en Italie. Je vais tâcher d'y suppléer par la publication de cette traduction qui sera accompagnée de nouvelles planches où j'ai fait graver les lettres grecques pour ceux qui voudront joindre cette traduction au texte . . . Je donnerai d'abord l'ouvrage d'Aristarque de Samos, tel qu'il nous est parvenu; je traduirai ensuite les scholies, suivant ainsi l'ordre observé pour l'impression du texte grec. J'avertis que les démonstrations d'Aristarque s'appuient sur la Géométrie d'Euclide, qu'il suppose connue de ses lecteurs. Paris, 2 avril 1823.'

The French translation is a meritorious and useful book.

There is yet another Greek text, besides those of Wallis and Fortia d'Urban, namely

Ἀριστάρχου Σαμίου βιβλίον περὶ μεγεθῶν καὶ ἀποστημάτων ἡλίου καὶ σελήνης, *mit kritischen Berichtigungen von E. Nizze.* Stralsund, 1856.

This text is, however, untrustworthy, not having been prepared with sufficient care. It was based on the texts of Wallis and Fortia d'Urban without, apparently, any recourse to MSS.

A German translation also exists,

Aristarchus über die Grössen und Entfernungen der Sonne und des Mondes, übersetzt und erläutert von A. Nokk. Freiburg i. B., 1854.

We come now to the MS. authority for our Greek texts. It would appear[1] that our treatise is included in five MSS. in the Vatican, namely Vat. Gr. 204 (10th cent.), 191 and 203 (13th cent.), 192 (14th cent.), and 202 (14th–15th cent.), and in eight at Paris, namely Paris. Gr. 2342 (14th cent.), 2363 (15th cent.), 2364, 2366 (16th cent.), 2386 (16th cent.), 2472 (14th cent.), 2488 (16th cent.), and Suppl. Gr. 12 (16th cent.). There are others at Venice, Marcian. 301 and 304 (15th cent.); at Milan, Ambros. A 101 sup. (14th cent.); at Vienna, Vindobon. Suppl. Gr. 9 (17th cent.); and so on.

The oldest of all these MSS. and by far the best is the beautiful Vaticanus Graecus 204, of the 10th century; indeed it seems to be the ultimate source of all the others, and so much superior that the others can practically be left out of account. This great MS. is described by Menge.[2] Its contents are: fol. 1–36^v Theodosius, *Sphaerica*, i, ii, iii; 37^r–42^v, Autolycus, *On the moving sphere*; 42^v–58^r, *Prolegomena to Euclid's Optics* (τὰ πρὸ τῶν Εὐκλείδου ὀπτικῶν);[3] 58^r–76^v, Euclid's *Phaenomena*; 76^v–82^v, Theodosius, *On habitations*; 83^r–95^r, Theodosius, *On nights and days*; 95^r–108^v, Theodosius, *On days and nights*, ii; 108^v–117^v, Aristarchus, *On the sizes and distances of the sun and moon*; 118^r–132^r, Autolycus, *On risings and settings*, i, ii; 132^v–134^v, Hypsicles, Ἀναφορικός; 135^r–143^v, Euclid's *Catoptrica*; 144^r, figures to the *Catoptrica*; 144^v blank; 145^r–172^r, Eutocius, *Commentary on Books I–III of Apollonius's Conics*; 172^v–194^v, Euclid's *Data*; 195^r–197^r, Marinus, *Commentary on Euclid's Data*; 198^r–205^v, *Scholia to Euclid's Elements*.

The MS. is of parchment, incomplete at the end, and the 206 leaves are preceded by three more, the first of which is empty, the second has a πίναξ, and the third, a sheet of paper fastened in later, contains a Latin index. The first two leaves, containing the beginning of Theodosius's *Sphaerica*, are written by a later hand who

---

[1] I have collected these particulars, except as regards three of the MSS. used by Fortia d'Urban, from the introductions to Heiberg's editions of Euclid and Apollonius in Greek, the same scholar's *Literargeschichtliche Studien über Euklid*, 1882, and *Om Scholierne til Euklids Elementer*, 1888, and from the introductions to one or two other Greek mathematical texts.

[2] Addendum to a review of Hultsch's Autolycus, *Neue Jahrbücher für Philologie*, 1886, pp. 183, 184.

[3] Fol. 42^v–58^r contain Theon's recension of Euclid's *Optics*, with a preface which was apparently written by some pupil of Theon's. It is to this preface that the title refers.

has cleverly imitated the handwriting of the rest of the MS., which is by one hand. The figures, drawn in red, are clear and adequate.[1] Many things in the text are struck out, erased, and changed by different hands. The MS. is rich in old and new scholia. It has on it the stamp of the Bibliothèque Nationale, having been, like the famous Peyrard MS. of Euclid (Vat. Gr. 190), among the MSS. which were taken to Paris in 1808 and restored to the Vatican after the Congress of Vienna.

In settling a text to translate from, I have mainly relied on a photograph of Vat. Gr. 204 together with Wallis's text, though I have had Nizze's text by me and have also consulted Fortia d'Urban's edition of 1810. The occasional references to the Paris MSS. in my critical notes are taken from Fortia d'Urban.[2]

It is not clear from which of the Vatican MSS. Savile copied his own (Wallis's S); it cannot, however, have been Vat. Gr. 204, because (a) nearly all the words and sentences which Wallis supplied, on the basis of Commandinus's translation, in order to fill up gaps in his two MSS., are actually found (either exactly or with no more variation than would naturally be expected between a re-translation into Greek and the original Greek text) in 204, and (b) a scholium from S added by Wallis at the end of Prop. 7 does not appear in 204. Fortia d'Urban suggests, as a possibility, that the MS. of which Wallis had a copy was Paris. 2366, but it seems clear that it cannot have been any of the Paris MSS., and therefore was presumably (as Wallis thought) one of those in the Vatican.[3] There

---

[1] The words used by Menge are 'klar und genau', but I think the figures can hardly be called 'accurate' or 'exact'.

[2] In Fortia d'Urban's critical notes there are several references to the reading of a MS. which he quotes as 2483. But Paris. Gr. 2483 is not included in his list of the MSS. of Aristarchus used by him; and it appears to contain, not Aristarchus, but Nicomachus's *Introductio arithmetica* with scholia (Omont, *Inventaire sommaire des manuscrits grecs de la Bibliothèque Nationale*, ii). It would seem, from internal evidence, that the references should be to Paris. Gr. 2472, not 2483, in these cases.

[3] Fortia d'Urban observes that Paris. 2366 alone omits a sentence in Prop. 1 (πολλῷ ἄρα ἡ ΒΓ τῆς ΒΑ ἐλάσσων ἐστὶν ἢ με΄ μέρος) which Wallis likewise omits, whereas Paris. 2342, 2364, 2488 and Commandinus all have it; hence he thinks that Wallis's MS. may have been a copy of Paris. 2366. But, on the other hand, a sentence in Prop. 13 which is absent from Wallis's text (καὶ ἡ ΒΝ ἐφάπτεται ... λαμπρόν) is, according to Fortia d'Urban, found in all the Paris MSS. except 2342; presumably therefore Paris. 2366 has it. These two cases create a strong presumption that Wallis's MS. was not a copy of any of the Paris MSS.

is apparently no clue to the identity of the 'Codex Vetus' with which S was collated.

We are better informed as to the MSS. used by Fortia d'Urban. He tells us, in the note on p. 88 of the edition of 1810, that they were Codd. Paris. 2342, 2363, 2364, 2366, 2386, 2472, and 2488, and one Vatican MS. The particular Vatican MS. had, he observes, just been brought to Paris; it was therefore presumably Vat. Gr. 204. He does not, however, seem to have collated the latter MS. with sufficient care; for example, he says that some words[1] in the 'setting-out' of Prop. 3 and a whole sentence[2] occurring later in the proposition are wanting in the MS., though, as a matter of fact, they are there in full; when, therefore, on the occasion of the first of these supposed omissions, he says that the Vatican MS. does not seem to him in any way superior to 'our own', he is apparently allowing his patriotism to get the better of his judgement. For the scholia he says that he relied mostly upon Paris. 2342 and 2488; but the scholia in Vat. Gr. 204 seem to correspond exactly. He does not seem to have found in any of his eight MSS. the particular scholium to Prop. 7 taken by Wallis from S; for, while he gives it in his French translation, he says it comes, through Wallis, from S.

---

[1] σελήνης δὲ κέντρον, ὅταν ὁ περιλαμβάνων κῶνος
[2] καὶ διελόντι, ὡς ἡ ΒΓ πρὸς τὴν ΓΑ, οὕτως ἡ ΒΔ πρὸς τὴν ΔΟ.

III

CONTENT OF THE TREATISE

THE style of Aristarchus is thoroughly classical, as befits an able geometer intermediate in date between Euclid and Archimedes, and his demonstrations are worked out with the same rigour as those of his predecessor and successor. The propositions of Euclid's *Elements* are, of course, taken for granted, but other things are tacitly assumed which go beyond what we find in Euclid. Thus the transformations of ratios defined in Eucl. V and indicated by the terms *inversely, alternately, componendo, convertendo,* &c., are regularly and naturally used in dealing with *unequal* ratios, whereas in Euclid they are only used in proportions, i.e. cases of *equality* of ratios. But the propositions of Aristarchus are also of particular mathematical interest because the ratios of the sizes and distances which have to be calculated are really *trigonometrical* ratios, sines, cosines, &c., although at the time of Aristarchus trigonometry had not been invented, while no reasonably close approximation to the value of π, the ratio of the circumference of a circle to its diameter, had been made (it was Archimedes who first obtained the value 22/7). Exact calculation of the trigonometrical ratios being therefore impossible for Aristarchus, he set himself to find upper and lower limits for them, and he succeeded in locating those which emerge in his propositions within tolerably narrow limits, though not always the narrowest within which it would have been possible, even for him, to confine them. In this species of approximation to trigonometry he tacitly assumes propositions comparing the ratio between a greater and a less *angle* in a figure with the ratio between two *straight lines* in the figure, propositions which are formally proved by Ptolemy at the beginning of his *Syntaxis*. Here, again, we have a proof that text-books containing such propositions existed before Aristarchus's time, and probably much earlier, although they have not survived.

The formal assumptions of Aristarchus and their effect.

One of the assumptions or hypotheses at the beginning of the treatise, the grossly excessive estimate of $2°$ for the apparent angular diameter of the moon, has already been discussed (pp. 311, 312 above). We proceed to Hypotheses 4 and 5, giving values for a certain ratio and a certain other angle respectively.

In Hypothesis 5, Aristarchus takes the diameter of the earth's shadow (at the place where the moon passes through it at the time of an eclipse) to be twice that of the moon. The figure 2 for this ratio was presumably based on the observed length of the longest eclipses on record.[1] Hipparchus, as we learn from Ptolemy,[2] made the ratio $2\frac{1}{2}$ for the time when the moon is at its mean distance in the conjunctions; Ptolemy chose the time when the moon is at its greatest distance, and made the ratio insensibly less than $2\frac{3}{5}$ (a little too large).[3]

Tannery[4] shows in an interesting way the connexion between (1) the estimate (Hypothesis 4) that the angular distance between the sun and moon viewed from the earth at the time when the moon appears halved is $87°$, the complement of $3°$, (2) the estimate (Hypothesis 5) of 2 for the ratio of the diameter of the earth's shadow to that of the moon, and (3) the ratio (greater than 18 to 1 and less than 20 to 1) of the diameter of the sun to the diameter of the moon as obtained in Props. 7 and 9 of our treatise.

The diagram overleaf (Fig. 14) will serve to indicate very roughly the relative positions of the sun, the earth, and the moon at the moment during a lunar eclipse when the moon is in the middle of the earth's shadow.

---

[1] Tannery, *Recherches sur l'histoire de l'astronomie ancienne*, p. 225.
[2] Ptolemy, *Syntaxis*, iv. 9, p. 327. 3-4, Heib.
[3] Ibid., v. 14, p. 421. 12-13.
[4] Tannery in *Mémoires de la Société des sciences physiques et naturelles de Bordeaux*, 2ᵉ série, v, 1883, pp. 241-3; *Mémoires scientifiques*, ed. Heiberg and Zeuthen, i, 1912, pp. 376-9.

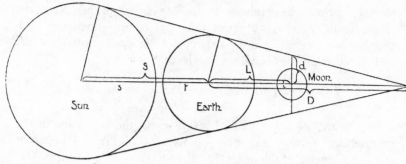

Fig. 14.

Let S be the radius of the sun's orbit,

L .   .   .   moon's orbit,

s the radius of the sun,

l .   .   .   moon,

t .   .   .   earth,

D the distance from the centre of the earth to the vertex of the cone of the earth's shadow,

and d the radius of the earth's shadow at the distance of the moon.

Then we have, approximately, by similar triangles,

$$\frac{D}{S} = \frac{t}{s-t}, \quad \frac{d}{t} = \frac{D-L}{D};$$

whence, if we suppose that $\dfrac{L}{S} = \dfrac{l}{s}$, and put $n = \dfrac{d}{l}$, we easily

derive
$$\frac{t}{l} + \frac{t}{s} = n + 1 \quad . \quad . \quad . \quad . \quad . \quad (1)$$

and
$$\frac{D}{L} = \frac{t}{t-d} = \frac{1}{1 - n\dfrac{l}{t}} \quad . \quad . \quad . \quad (2)$$

Now, since eclipses of the sun occur through the interposition of the moon, $S > L$, so that $s > l$. The ancients knew, too, that the sun is larger than the earth, so that $s > t$. It follows from (1) that $\dfrac{t}{l} > n$, so that the moon is smaller than the earth.

Now suppose δ to be the angle subtended at the centre of the sun by the distance between the moon and the earth at the time when the moon appears halved, i.e. when the earth, sun, and moon form a right-angled triangle with its right angle at the centre of the moon.

Let $x = \dfrac{S}{L} = \dfrac{s}{l} = \dfrac{1}{\sin \delta}$.

We have then from (1), substituting s/x for l,

$$\frac{tx}{s} + \frac{t}{s} = n+1, \text{ or } \frac{s}{t} = \frac{x+1}{n+1},$$

and, substituting lx for s, we have

$$\frac{t}{l} + \frac{t}{lx} = n+1, \text{ or } \frac{t}{l} = \frac{n+1}{x+1}x.$$

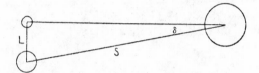

Fig. 15.

Now if $x \left(= \dfrac{s}{l} \right)$ is taken at 19, Aristarchus's mean value, and $n = 2$, these formulae give

$$\frac{s}{l} = 19, \quad \frac{s}{t} = \frac{20}{3} = 6 \cdot \dot{6}, \quad \frac{t}{l} = 2 \cdot 85, \quad \delta = \sin^{-1}\frac{1}{19} = 3° \, 1' \, 1''.$$

Tannery's object is to prove that the method of our treatise was not invented by Aristarchus but by Eudoxus. We know in the first place, from Aristotle, that by the middle of the fourth century mathematical speculations on the sizes and distances of the sun and moon had already begun. Aristotle[1] says:

' Besides, if the facts as shown in the theorems of astronomy are correct, and the size of the sun is greater than that of the earth, while the distance of the stars from the earth is many times greater than the distance of the sun, just as the distance of the sun from the earth is many times greater than that of the moon, the cone marking the convergence of the sun's rays (after passing the earth) will have its vertex not far from the earth, and the earth's shadow, which we call night, will therefore not reach the stars, but all the stars will necessarily be in the view of the sun, and none of them will be blocked out by the earth.'

[1] Arist. *Meteorologica*, i. 8, 345 b 1-9.

Now Eudoxus was the first person to develop scientifically the hypothesis that the sun and moon remain at a constant distance from the earth respectively, and this is the hypothesis of Aristarchus. Further, we are told by Archimedes that Eudoxus had estimated the ratio of the sun's diameter to that of the moon at 9 : 1, Phidias, Archimedes' father, at 12 : 1, and Aristarchus at a figure between 18 : 1 and 20 : 1. Accordingly, on the assumption that Eudoxus and Phidias took $n = 2$ in the above formulae, as Aristarchus did, we can make out the following table :

	$\dfrac{s}{l}$	$\dfrac{s}{t}$	$\dfrac{t}{l}$	δ (calculated value)
Eudoxus	9	3·$\dot{3}$	2·7	6° 22′ 46″
Phidias	12	4·$\dot{3}$	2·76923	4° 46′ 49″
Aristarchus	19 (mean)	6·$\dot{6}$	2·85	3° 1′ 1″

Hence, says Tannery, while Aristarchus took 3° as the value of δ, Eudoxus probably took 6° or $\frac{1}{5}$ of a sign of the zodiac, and Phidias 5° or $\frac{1}{6}$ of a sign. 'I cannot believe that these values were deduced from direct observations of the angular distance. The necessary instruments were in all probability not in existence in the fourth century. But Eudoxus could, on the day of the dichotomy, mark the positions of the sun and the moon in the zodiac, and try to observe at what hour the dichotomy took place. The evaluations involve an error of about twelve hours for Eudoxus, ten for Phidias, and six for Aristarchus. It seems that all of them sought upper limits for δ. It will be noticed that the value of δ especially affects the values of the ratios s/l, s/t; the ratio t/l on the contrary depends mostly on the value of n.'[1] Seeing, however, that the only figures in the above tables which are actually attested are the three in the first column, the 3° of Aristarchus, and the results obtained by Aristarchus on the basis of his assumptions, it seems a highly speculative hypothesis to suppose that Eudoxus started with 6°, and Phidias with 5°, as Aristarchus did with 3°, and then deduced the ratio of the diameter of the sun to that of the moon by precisely Aristarchus's method.

[1] Tannery, *Mémoires de la Société des sciences phys. et nat. de Bordeaux*, 2ᵉ série, v, 1883, pp. 243-4; *Mémoires scientifiques*, ed. Heiberg and Zeuthen, i, p. 379.

Trigonometrical equivalents.

Besides the formal Assumptions laid down at the beginning of the treatise, there lie at the root of Aristarchus's reasoning certain propositions assumed without proof, presumably because they were generally known to mathematicians of the day.   The most general of these propositions are the equivalent of the statements that—

If α is what we call the circular measure of an angle, and α is less than $\frac{1}{2}\pi$, then

(1) The ratio $\sin\alpha/\alpha$ *decreases* as α increases from 0 to $\frac{1}{2}\pi$, but (2) the ratio $\tan\alpha/\alpha$ *increases* as α increases from 0 to $\frac{1}{2}\pi$.

Tannery[1] took pains to set out the trigonometrical equivalents of the particular results obtained by Aristarchus in the several propositions.

If we bear in mind that

$$\sin\frac{\pi}{2} = \tan\frac{\pi}{4} = 1,$$

$$\sin\frac{\pi}{6} = \tfrac{1}{2},$$

$$\tan\frac{\pi}{8} = \frac{1}{\sqrt{2}+1},$$

and if we substitute for $\sqrt{2}$ the approximate value $\frac{7}{5}$ which is assumed by Aristarchus, we can deduce the following inequalities:

(1) If $m > 1$, $\sin\dfrac{\pi}{2m} > \dfrac{1}{m}$,

or   (2) $\cos\dfrac{\pi}{2m} = \sin\left(\dfrac{\pi}{2} - \dfrac{\pi}{2m}\right) > \dfrac{m-1}{m}$,

(3) If $m > 2$, $\sin\dfrac{\pi}{2m} < \tan\dfrac{\pi}{2m} < \dfrac{2}{m}$,

(4) If $m > 3$, $\sin\dfrac{\pi}{2m} > \dfrac{3}{2m}$,

(5) If $m > 4$, $\sin\dfrac{\pi}{2m} < \tan\dfrac{\pi}{2m} < \dfrac{5}{3m}$.

---

[1] Tannery, *Mémoires de la Soc. des sciences phys. et nat. de Bordeaux*, 2ᵉ série, v, 1883, pp. 244 sq.; *Mémoires scientifiques*, i, pp. 380 sqq.

The narrowest limits for $\sin \dfrac{\pi}{2\,m}$ obtained by means of these inequalities are

$$(6) \qquad \frac{5}{3\,m} > \sin \frac{\pi}{2\,m} > \frac{3}{2\,m},$$

whereas, if Aristarchus had known the approximate value $\frac{22}{7}$ for π, he could have obtained the closer upper limit

$$\sin \frac{\pi}{2\,m} < \frac{11}{7\,m}.$$

Now, for example, in Prop. 7, Aristarchus has to find limits for $\sin 3°$, that is to say $\sin \dfrac{\pi}{60}$; thus $m = 30$, and the formula (6) above gives his result

$$\frac{1}{18} > \sin 3° > \frac{1}{20}.$$

In Prop. 4 Aristarchus proves the negligibility of the maximum angle (ϵ) subtended at the centre of the earth by a certain arc (α) on the surface of the moon subtended at the centre of the moon by an angle equal to half the apparent angular diameter of the moon. From the figure of the proposition it is easy to see that, taking the radius of the moon to be unity,

$$\tan \frac{\epsilon}{2} = \frac{\sin \alpha \sin \dfrac{\alpha}{2}}{1 - \sin \alpha \cos \dfrac{\alpha}{2}}.$$

For, if M be the foot of the perpendicular from H on AB,

$$\tan \frac{\epsilon}{2} = \frac{HM}{MA} = \frac{HM}{AB - MB} = \frac{BH \sin \dfrac{\alpha}{2}}{AB - BH \cos \dfrac{\alpha}{2}}$$

$$= \frac{BD \sin \dfrac{\alpha}{2}}{AB - BD \cos \dfrac{\alpha}{2}} = \frac{\sin \alpha \sin \dfrac{\alpha}{2}}{1 - \sin \alpha \cos \dfrac{\alpha}{2}}.$$

This would give, for $\alpha = 1°$, $\epsilon = 0° \ 1' \ 3''$.

What Aristarchus in fact does is to prove that

$$\frac{\epsilon}{\alpha} < \frac{\sin \frac{\epsilon}{2}}{\sin \frac{\alpha}{2}} \text{ i.e. } < \frac{BH}{HA} < \frac{BG}{GA} \text{ or } \frac{BG}{BA-BG} \text{ i.e. } < \frac{\sin \alpha}{1 - \sin \alpha} \cdot$$

Now, if $\alpha = \pi/2m$ $(m > 4)$, formula (5) above would give

$$\frac{2m\epsilon}{\pi} < \frac{5}{3m-5}, \text{ and, if } m = 90, \frac{2\epsilon}{\pi} < \frac{1}{4770}; \epsilon < 0° 1' 8'':$$

but Aristarchus is content with the equivalent of using formula (3) which gives

$$\frac{2\epsilon}{\pi} < \frac{1}{m} \cdot \frac{2}{m-2} \text{ i.e. } < \frac{1}{3960}, \text{ or } \epsilon < 0° 1' 22''.$$

In Prop. 11 Aristarchus uses the equivalent of formulae (3) and (4), proving that

$$\frac{1}{45} > \sin 1° > \frac{1}{60} \cdot$$

Prop. 12 is the equivalent of using formula (2) to prove that

$$1 > \cos 1° > \frac{89}{90}.$$

From formula (2) we deduce

$$\cos^2 \frac{\pi}{2m} > \frac{m^2 - 2m + 1}{m^2} > \frac{m-2}{m};$$

and, for $m = 90$, this gives the equivalent of the first part of Prop. 13, namely

$$1 > \cos^2 1° > \frac{44}{45}.$$

In Prop. 14 Aristarchus determines a lower limit for the ratio L/c, where L is the radius of the moon's orbit and c the distance of the centre of the moon from the centre of the circle of the shadow at the middle of an eclipse. The arithmetical value of the limit depends of course on the particular assumptions which he makes as to the angles subtended at the centre of the earth by the diameter of the moon and by the diameter of the circle of the shadow. If these angles be 2α, 2γ respectively, we see from the figure of Prop. 14 that

$$BR = BM \cos \alpha = L \cos^2 \alpha, \quad BS = L \cos \alpha \cos \gamma, \quad RC = L \sin^2 \alpha.$$

Therefore $SR : RC = L \cos \alpha \, (\cos \alpha - \cos \gamma) : L \sin^2 \alpha$,

and $\qquad CR : CS = L \sin^2 \alpha : L \, (\sin^2 \alpha + \cos^2 \alpha - \cos \alpha \cos \gamma)$
$$= L \sin^2 \alpha : L \, (\mathrm{1} - \cos \alpha \cos \gamma).$$

Now $\qquad BC : CR = (BC : CM) \times (CM : CR)$
$$= (\mathrm{1} : \sin \alpha) \times (\mathrm{1} : \sin \alpha)$$
$$= \mathrm{1} : \sin^2 \alpha.$$

Therefore, *ex aequali*,
$$BC : CS = L : L \, (\mathrm{1} - \cos \alpha \cos \gamma),$$

or $\qquad L : c = \mathrm{1} : (\mathrm{1} - \cos \alpha \cos \gamma)$
$$= \mathrm{1} : (\sin^2 \alpha + \cos^2 \alpha - \cos \alpha \cos \gamma)$$
$$> \mathrm{1} : \{ \sin^2 \alpha + \cos^2 \alpha \, (\mathrm{1} - \cos \gamma) \}.$$

If $\gamma = 2\,\alpha$, as assumed by Aristarchus, this becomes
$$L : c > (\mathrm{1} : \sin^2 \alpha) \, . \, \{ \mathrm{1} : (\mathrm{1} + 2 \cos^2 \alpha) \}.$$

The corresponding inequality obtained by Aristarchus, who assumes that $\alpha = \mathrm{1}°$, is
$$L : c > (45 : \mathrm{1})^2 \, . \, (\mathrm{1} : 3)$$
$$> 675 : \mathrm{1}.$$

The generalized trigonometrical equivalent of Prop. 15 is more complicated and need not be given here. Tannery has an interesting remark, which was however anticipated by Fortia d'Urban,[1] upon one of the arithmetical results obtained by Aristarchus in that proposition. If y be the ratio of the sun's radius to the earth's radius, his result is

$$\frac{y}{y-\mathrm{1}} > \frac{7\mathrm{1}75587 5}{6\mathrm{1}735500}.$$

He replaces this value by $\frac{43}{37}$, merely remarking that ‘ 71755875 has to 61735500 a ratio greater than that which 43 has to 37 ’. It is difficult, says Tannery, not to see in $\frac{43}{37}$ the expression $\mathrm{1} + \frac{1}{6 + \frac{1}{6}}$, which suggests that $\frac{43}{37}$ was obtained by developing $\frac{71755875}{61735500}$ or $\frac{21261}{18292}$ as a continued fraction. ‘We have here an important proof of the employment by the ancients of a method of calculation, the theory of which unquestionably belongs to the moderns, but the first applications of which are too simple not to have originated in very remote times.’

[1] Fortia d'Urban, *Traité d'Aristarque de Samos*, 1823, p. 86, note.

IV

LATER IMPROVEMENTS ON ARISTARCHUS'S CALCULATIONS

WHILE it would not be consistent with the plan of this work to carry the history of Greek astronomy beyond Aristarchus, it will be proper, I think, to conclude this introduction with a few particulars of the improvements which later Greek astronomers made upon Aristarchus's estimates of sizes and distances.

We have already spoken of Aristarchus's assumption of 87° as the angle subtended at the centre of the earth by the line joining the centres of the sun and moon at the time when the moon appears halved. The true value of this angle is 89° 50′, so that Aristarchus's estimate was decidedly inaccurate; no direct estimate of the angle seems to have been made by his successors. Aristarchus himself, as we have seen, afterwards corrected to $\frac{1}{2}$° the estimate of 2° for the apparent angular diameter of the sun and moon alike. His assumption of 2 as the ratio of the diameter of the circle of the earth's shadow to the diameter of the moon was improved upon by Hipparchus and Ptolemy. Hipparchus made it $2\frac{1}{2}$ at the moon's mean distance at the conjunctions;[1] Ptolemy made it at the moon's greatest distance ' inappreciably less than $2\frac{3}{5}$ '.[2]

Coming now to estimates of absolute and relative sizes and distances, we find some data in Archimedes;[3] according to him Eudoxus had declared the diameter of the sun to be nine times the diameter of the moon, and Phidias (Archimedes' father) twelve times; most astronomers, he says, agreed that the earth is greater than the moon, and ' some have tried to prove that the circumference of the earth is about 300,000 stades and not greater '. It seems probable that it was Dicaearchus who (about 300 B.C.) arrived at this value,[4]

[1] Ptolemy, *Syntaxis*, iv. 9, vol. i, p. 327. 3–4, Heib.
[2] Ibid. v. 14, vol. i, p. 421. 12–14, Heib.
[3] Archimedes, *Sand-reckoner* (*Archimedis opera*, ed. Heib., vol. ii, p. 246 sqq): *The Works of Archimedes*, pp. 222, 223.
[4] Berger, *Geschichte der wissenschaftlichen Erdkunde der Griechen*, pp. 370 sqq.

and that it was obtained by taking 24° (1/15th of the whole meridian circle) as the difference of latitude between Syene and Lysi-
machia (on the same meridian), and 20,000 stades as the actual
distance between the two places.[1] Archimedes' own estimates are
scarcely estimates at all; they are intentionally exaggerated, as, his
object being to measure the number of grains of sand that would
fill the universe, he adopts what he considers *maximum* values in
order to be on the safe side.   Thus he says that, whereas Aristarchus tried to prove that the ratio of the diameter of the sun to that
of the moon is between 18 : 1 and 20 : 1, he himself will take the
ratio to be 30 : 1 and not greater, in order that his thesis may be
proved 'beyond all cavil'; in the case of the earth he actually
multiplies the estimate of the perimeter by 10, making it 3,000,000
instead of 300,000 stades.

Before passing on to later writers, it will be convenient to re-
capitulate Aristarchus's figures ; and for brevity I shall use the
letters by which Tannery denotes the various distances and radii,
namely S for the distance of the centre of the sun, L for the
distance of the centre of the moon, from the centre of the earth,
and s, l, t for the radii of the sun, moon, and earth respectively.
Aristarchus's figures then are as follows :

$$L/2l > 22\tfrac{1}{2} \text{ but} < 30 \qquad \text{(Prop. 11)}.$$
$$S/L > 18 \text{ but} < 20 \qquad \text{(Prop. 7)}.$$
$$2s/2t \text{ or } s/t > 6\tfrac{1}{3} \text{ but} < 7\tfrac{1}{6} \qquad \text{(Prop. 15)}.$$
$$2l/2t \text{ or } l/t > \tfrac{19}{60} \text{ but} < \tfrac{43}{108} \qquad \text{(Prop. 17)}.$$

We may with Hultsch,[2] for convenience of comparison with other
calculations, take figures approximating to the mean between the
higher and lower limits; and it will be convenient to express
the various diameters and distances in terms of the diameter of the
earth.   We may say then, roughly, that

$$2l/2t = \tfrac{36}{100} = \tfrac{9}{25} ;$$
$$2s/2t = 6\tfrac{3}{4} ;$$
$$L/2l = 26\tfrac{1}{4} ;$$
$$S/L = 19 :$$

---

[1] Cf. Cleomedes, *De motu circulari*, i. 8, p. 78, Ziegler.
[2] Hultsch, *Poseidonios über die Grösse und Entfernung der Sonne*,
1897, p. 5.

whence

$$L/2t = \tfrac{105 \cdot 9}{4 \cdot 25} = 9\tfrac{9}{20}, \text{ say } 9\tfrac{1}{2};$$
$$S/2t = \tfrac{189}{20} \cdot 19 = 179\tfrac{11}{20}, \text{ say } 180.$$

We are not told what size Aristarchus attributed to the earth, but presumably, like Archimedes, he would have accepted Dicaearchus's estimate of 300,000 stades for its circumference.

Eratosthenes (born about eleven years after Archimedes, say 276 B.C.) is famous for a measurement of the earth based on scientific principles. He found that at noon at the summer solstice the sun threw no shadow at Syene, while at the same hour at Alexandria (which he took to be on the same meridian) it made the gnomon in the *scaphe* cast a shadow showing an angle equal to one-fiftieth of the whole meridian circle; assuming, further, that the sun's rays at Syene and Alexandria are parallel in direction, and that the known distance from Syene to Alexandria is 5,000 stades (doubtless taken as a round figure), Eratosthenes arrived by an easy geometrical proof at 50 times 5,000 or 250,000 stades as the circumference of the earth. This is the figure given by Cleomedes;[1] but Strabo quite definitely says that, according to Eratosthenes, the circumference is 252,000 stades,[2] and this is the figure which is most generally quoted in antiquity. The reason for the discrepancy has been the subject of a good deal of discussion;[3] it is difficult, in view of Cleomedes' circumstantial account, to suppose that 252,000 was the original figure arrived at by Eratosthenes; it seems more likely that Eratosthenes himself corrected 250,000 to 252,000 for some reason, perhaps in order to get a figure divisible by 60 and, incidentally, a round number (700) of stades for one degree. There is some question as to the length of the particular stade used by Eratosthenes, but, if Pliny is right in saying that Eratosthenes made 40 stades equal to the Egyptian σχοῖνος,[4] then, taking the σχοῖνος at 12,000 Royal cubits of 0·525 metres,[5] we get 300 such cubits, or 157·5 metres, as the length of the stade, which is thus equal to 516·73 feet. The circumference of the earth, being 252,000 times this length, works out to about

[1] Cleomedes, *De motu circulari*, i. 10, especially p. 100. 15–23, ed. Ziegler.
[2] Strabo, ii. 5. 7, p. 113 Cas.   [3] Berger, op. cit., pp. 410, 411.
[4] Pliny, *N. H.* xii. c. 13, § 53.
[5] Hultsch, *Griechische u. römische Metrologie* (Berlin, 1882), p. 364. Cf. Tannery, *Recherches sur l'histoire de l'astronomie ancienne*, pp. 109, 110.

24,662 miles, and the diameter of the earth on this basis is about 7,850 miles, only 50 miles shorter than the true polar diameter, a surprisingly close approximation, however much it owes to happy accidents in the calculation.[1]

We have no trustworthy information as to evaluations by Eratosthenes of other dimensions and distances. The *Doxographi*, it is true, say that Eratosthenes made L, the distance of the moon from the earth, to be 78 myriads of stades, and S, the distance of the sun, to be 80,400 myriads of stades[2] (the versions of Stobaeus and Joannes Lydus admit of 408 myriads of stades as an alternative interpretation, but this figure obviously cannot be right). Tannery[3] considers that none of these figures can be correct. He suggests that L was put by Eratosthenes at 278 myriads of stades, not 78; but I am not clear that 78 is wrong. We have seen that, if we take mean figures, Aristarchus made the distance of the moon from the earth to be about $9\frac{1}{2}$ times the earth's diameter. Now $252,000/\pi$, approximately $252,000/3\frac{1}{7}$, is about 80,180, or roughly 8 myriads of stades; $9\frac{1}{2}$ times this is 76 myriads, and Eratosthenes' supposed figure of 780,000 is sufficiently close to this. According to Tannery's conjecture of 2,780,000 stades, the ratio $L/2t$ would be nearly 34·7, which is greater than the values given to it by Hipparchus, Posidonius, and Ptolemy, and also greater than the true value. With regard to Eratosthenes' estimate of S, Tannery points to Macrobius's statement that Eratosthenes said that 'the measure (*mensura*) of the earth multiplied 27 times will make the measure of the sun '.[4] The question here arises whether it is the solid contents of the two bodies or their diameters which are compared. Tannery takes the latter to be the meaning. If this is right, and if Eratosthenes took the value of $\frac{1}{2}°$ for the apparent angular diameter of the sun discovered by Aristarchus, the circumference $2\pi S$ of the sun's orbit would be equal to $27 . 2t . 720$, which, if we put $3\frac{1}{7}$ for π, would give

$$S = 6185\,t = 24,800 \text{ myriads of stades, nearly.}$$

---

[1] Cf. Dreyer, *Planetary Systems*, p. 175.

[2] Aët. ii. 31. 3 (*D. G.* 362–3).

[3] Tannery, 'Aristarque de Samos' in *Mém. de la Soc. des sci. phys. et nat. de Bordeaux*, 2⁰ sér., v, 1883, pp. 254, 255 ; *Mémoires scientifiques*, ed. Heiberg and Zeuthen, i, pp. 391–2.

[4] Macrobius, *In somn. Scip.* i. 20. 9.

But Hultsch[1] shows reason for believing that 'mensura' in the statement of Macrobius means solid content. One ground is the further statement of Macrobius that Posidonius's estimate of the size of the sun in terms of the earth was 'many many times' greater than that of Eratosthenes ('multo multoque saepius', *sc.* 'multiplicata'). But we shall find that Posidonius's figures lead to only about $39\frac{1}{4}$ as the ratio of the diameter of the sun to that of the earth, which is not 'many many times' greater than 27. It seems therefore necessary to conclude, if Macrobius is to be trusted, that according to Eratosthenes s/t was equal to 3, not 27. This would divide the value of S by 9, and $S/2t$ would be equal to $343\frac{1}{2}$ instead of $3092\frac{1}{2}$.

We are much better informed on the subject of Hipparchus's estimates of sizes and distances, thanks to the investigations of Hultsch,[2] who found in the commentaries of Pappus and Theon on chapter 11 of Book V of Ptolemy's *Syntaxis* particulars as to which Ptolemy himself leaves us entirely in the dark. Ptolemy states that there are certain observed facts with regard to the sun and moon which make it possible, when the distance of one of them from the centre of the earth is known, to calculate the distance of the other, and that Hipparchus first found the distance of the sun on certain assumptions as to the solar parallax, and then deduced the distance of the moon. According to the value assumed for the solar parallax (and Ptolemy says that there was doubt as to whether it was the smallest appreciable amount or actually negligible), Hipparchus deduced, of course, different figures for the distance of the moon.[3] Ptolemy does not state these figures, but Pappus supplies the deficiency. Pappus begins by saying that Hipparchus's calculation, depending mainly on the sun, was 'not exact'. Next, he observes that, if the apparent diameter of the sun is taken to be very nearly the same as that of the moon at its greatest distance at the conjunctions, and if we are given the relative sizes of the sun and moon and the distance of one of them, the distance of the other is also given; then, after paraphrasing

---

[1] Hultsch, *Poseidonios über die Grösse und Entfernung der Sonne*, pp. 5, 6.
[2] Hultsch, 'Hipparchos über die Grösse und Entfernung der Sonne' (*Berichte der philologisch-historischen Classe der Kgl. Sächs. Gesellschaft der Wissenschaften zu Leipzig*, 7. Juli 1900).
[3] Ptolemy, *Syntaxis*, v. 11, vol. i, p. 402, Heib.

Ptolemy's remarks above quoted, he proceeds as follows: ' In his first book about sizes and distances Hipparchus starts from this observation: there was an eclipse of the sun which was exactly total in the region about the Hellespont, no portion of the sun being seen, whereas at Alexandria in Egypt about four-fifths only of its diameter was obscured.[1] From the facts thus observed he proves in his first book that, if the radius of the earth be the unit, the least distance of the moon contains 71, and the greatest 83 of these units; the mean therefore contains 77. After proving these propositions, he says at the end of the first book: " In this treatise I have carried the argument to this point. Do not, however, suppose that the theory of the distance of the moon has ever yet been worked out accurately in every respect; for even in this question there is an investigation remaining to be carried out, in the course of which the distance of the moon will be proved to be less than the figure just calculated," so that he himself admits that he is not quite in a position to state the truth about the parallaxes. Then, again, he himself, in the second book about sizes and distances, proves from many considerations that, if we take the radius of the earth as the unit, the least distance of the moon contains 62 of these units, and its mean distance $67\frac{1}{3}$, while the distance of the sun contains 2,490. It is clear from the former figures that the greatest distance of the moon contains $72\frac{2}{3}$ of these units.' The figure of 2,490 for the distance of the sun has to be obtained by a correction of the Greek text. The later MSS. have ς or 90, but one MS. has $\overline{\upsilon\varsigma}$ or 490. The 2,490 is credibly restored by Hultsch on the following grounds. Adrastus [2] and Chalcidius [3] tell us that Hipparchus made the sun nearly 1880 times the size of the earth,[4] and the earth about 27 times the size of the moon. The size means the solid content, and, the cube root of 1880 being approximately $12\frac{1}{3}$, we have approximately

$$t:l:s = 1:\tfrac{1}{3}:12\tfrac{1}{3}$$
$$= 3:1:37.$$

[1] This same eclipse is also mentioned by Cleomedes, *De motu circulari*, ii. 3, pp. 172. 22 and 178. 14, ed. Ziegler.

[2] Theon of Smyrna, p. 197. 8–12, ed. Hiller.

[3] Chalcidius, *Timaeus*, c. 91, p. 161.

[4] A less trustworthy authority, Cleomedes (*De motu circulari*, ii. 1, p. 152. 5–7), mentions a tradition that Hipparchus made the sun 1050 times as large as the earth.

Now the mean distance of the moon is, according to Hipparchus, $67\frac{1}{3}$ times the earth's radius; assuming then that the apparent angular diameter of the sun and moon as seen from the earth is about the same, we find that

$$S = 67\tfrac{1}{3}\, t \,.\, 37 = 2491\tfrac{1}{3}\, t.$$

That is to say, $S = 2490\, t$, nearly. It is clear, therefore, that β has fallen out of the text before $\nu\varsigma$, and the true number arrived at by Hipparchus was 2490.

Thus Hipparchus made the distance of the moon equal, at the mean, to $33\frac{2}{3}$ times the *diameter* of the earth, and the distance of the sun equal to 1,245 times the diameter of the earth. As we said above, Ptolemy does not mention these figures of Hipparchus, much less does he make any use of them. Yet they are remarkable, because not only are they far nearer the truth than Aristarchus's estimates, but the figure of 1,245 for the distance of the sun is much better than that of Ptolemy himself, namely 605 times the earth's diameter, or less than half the figure obtained by Hipparchus. Yet Hipparchus's estimate remained unknown, and Ptolemy's held the field for many centuries; even Copernicus only made the distance of the sun to be equal to 750 times the earth's diameter, and it was not till 1671–3 that a substantial improvement was made, observations of Mars carried out in those years by Richer enabling Cassini to conclude that the sun's parallax was about $9''\cdot5$, corresponding to a distance of the sun from the earth of 87,000,000 miles.[1]

Hultsch shows that the particular solar eclipse referred to by Hipparchus was probably that of 20th November in the year 129 B.C.,[2] and he concludes that the following year (128 B.C.) was the date of Hipparchus's treatise in two books 'On the sizes and distances of the sun and moon'.

Hipparchus, in his *Geography*, definitely accepted the estimate of 252,000 stades obtained by Eratosthenes for the circumference of the earth;[3] if there is any foundation for the statement of Pliny[4] that he added a little less than 26,000 stades to this estimate, making nearly 278,000, the explanation must apparently be that he stated

[1] Berry, *A Short History of Astronomy*, 1898, pp. 205–7.
[2] Cf. Boll, Art. 'Finsternisse' in Pauly-Wissowa's *Real-Encyclopädie*, vi. 2, 1909, p. 2358.
[3] Strabo, ii. 5. 34, p. 132 Cas.   [4] Pliny, *N. H.* ii. c. 108, § 247.

this number as a maximum, allowing for possible errors resulting from Eratosthenes' method;[1] but Berger considers that Pliny's statement is based on a misapprehension.[2]

Posidonius of Rhodes (135–51 B.C.) cannot be reckoned among astronomers in the strict sense of the term, but he dealt with astronomical questions in his work on *Meteorology*, and he wrote a separate tract on the size of the sun.[3] It was presumably in the latter work that he put forward a bold hypothesis as to the distance of the sun, which has the distinction of coming far nearer to the truth than the estimates of Hipparchus and all other ancient writers had done.[4] Cleomedes tells us that Posidonius supposed the circle in which the sun apparently moves round the earth to be 10,000 times the size of a circular section of the earth through its centre. With this hypothesis he combined (says Cleomedes) the assumption which he took from Eratosthenes that at Syene (which is under the summer tropic) and throughout a circle round it with a diameter of 300 stades the upright gnomon throws no shadow (at noon). It follows from this that the diameter of the sun occupies a portion of the sun's circle 3,000,000 stades in length; in other words, the diameter of the sun is 3,000,000 stades.[5] If we only knew the *fraction* of the circumference of the sun's circle occupied by the sun itself, we could calculate the circumference of the earth, and the absolute distance of the centre of the sun from the centre of the earth; but Cleomedes gives us no information on this, and we have to go elsewhere for what we want—in this case to Pliny. Now Pliny says that according to Posidonius there is round the earth a height of not less than 40 stades, which is the region of winds and clouds, and beyond which there is pure air; the distance from the belt of clouds, &c., to the moon is 2,000,000 stades, and the further distance from the moon to the sun is 500,000,000 stades.[6] This would give

$$L - t = 2,000,040 \text{ stades,}$$
$$S - t = 502,000,040 \text{ stades.}$$

[1] Tannery, *Recherches sur l'hist. de l'astronomie ancienne*, p. 116.
[2] Berger, *Gesch. der wissenschaftlichen Erdkunde der Griechen*, pp. 413–14.
[3] Cleomedes, *De motu circulari*, i. 11, p. 118. 4–6.
[4] On the whole of this subject, see Hultsch, 'Poseidonios über die Grösse und Entfernung der Sonne' (*Abh. der Kgl. Gesellschaft der Wissenschaften zu Göttingen, Phil.-hist. Klasse*, Neue Folge, Bd. I, Nr. 5), 1897.
[5] Cleomedes, ii. 1, p. 144. 22–146. 16; ibid. i. 10, pp. 96. 28–98. 5.
[6] Pliny, ii, c. 23, § 85.

Dividing the latter figure by 10,000 we obtain, approximately, for the radius of the earth

$$t = 50,200 \text{ stades.}$$

Hultsch gives reason for thinking that the 500,000,000 stades should be the distance from the centre of the earth to the centre of the sun, not the distance from the moon to the sun; the 40 stades representing the depth of the region of clouds, &c., is clearly negligible; and, as Posidonius dealt in round figures, we may infer that his estimate of the earth's diameter would be 100,000 stades. If now we use the Archimedean approximation of $3\frac{1}{7}$ for π, the circumference of the earth would on this basis be 314,285 stades; but we may, with some probability, suppose that Posidonius would take the round figure of 300,000 stades corresponding to $\pi = 3$, an approximation used by Cleomedes in another place.[1]

On the other hand, Cleomedes gives 240,000 stades as Posidonius's estimate of the earth's circumference based on the following assumptions, (1) that the star Canopus, invisible in Greece, was just seen to graze the horizon at Rhodes as it rose and set again immediately, whereas its meridian altitude at Alexandria was 'a fourth part of a sign, that is, one forty-eighth part of the zodiac circle', (2) that the distance between the two places was considered to be 5,000 stades.[2] The circumference of the earth was thus made out to be 48 times 5,000 or 240,000 stades. But the estimate of the difference of latitude at 1/48th of a great circle, or $7\frac{1}{2}°$, was very far from correct (the true difference of latitude is $5\frac{1}{4}°$ only); indeed the effects of refraction at the horizon would inevitably vitiate the result of such an attempt at measurement of the angle in question as Posidonius was in a position to make. Moreover, the estimate of 5,000 stades for the distance was also incorrect; it was the maximum estimate put upon it by mariners, while some put it at 4,000 only, and Eratosthenes, by observations of the shadows cast by gnomons, found it to be 3,750 stades only.[3] The existence of the latter estimate of the distance between Rhodes and Alexandria seems to account for Strabo's statement that Posidonius favoured ' the latest of the measurements which gave the smallest dimensions to the

[1] Cleomedes, *De motu circulari*, i. 8, p. 78. 22-3.
[2] Ibid. i. 10, pp. 93. 26 – 94. 22.
[3] Strabo, ii. 5. 24, pp. 125-6 Cas.; Berger, *Gesch. der wissenschaftlichen Erdkunde der Griechen*, p. 415.

earth', namely about 180,000 stades;[1] for 180,000 is 48 times 3,750, just as 240,000 is 48 times 5,000.   Now Eratosthenes must presumably have arrived at his distance of 3,750 stades by means of a calculation based on his own estimate of the total circumference of the earth (250,000 or 252,000) and the observed angle representing the difference of the inclination of the shadows thrown by the gnomon at the two places respectively.[2]   We are not told what the angle was, but it can be inferred that it was $5\frac{2}{5}°$ or $5\frac{5}{14}°$, because

$$250,000 \ (252,000) : 3,750 = 360° : 5\frac{2}{5}° \ (5\frac{5}{14}°).$$

It is nothing short of extraordinary that Posidonius should have used the 3,750 stades without a thought of its origin and then calculated the circumference of the earth by combining the 3,750 with an estimate of the corresponding angle which is so grossly erroneous ($7\frac{1}{2}°$).   It may seem not less extraordinary that Ptolemy (following Marinus of Tyre) should have accepted without any argument or question Posidonius's figure of 180,000 stades.   But the explanation doubtless is that Ptolemy's stades were Royal stades of 210 metres (nearly $\frac{1}{7}$th of a Roman mile) instead of Eratosthenes' stades of $157\frac{1}{2}$ metres ; for Ptolemy in his *Geography* says that the length of a degree is 500 stades,[3] whereas Eratosthenes made a degree contain about 700 stades.   Thus, as Ptolemy's stades were to Eratosthenes' as 4 to 3, Ptolemy's estimate of the circumference of the earth would, in stades of Eratosthenes, be 240,000, the same as the estimate attributed by Cleomedes to Posidonius.

As we have seen, Pliny's account of Posidonius's estimates of the distances of the sun and moon leads to about 300,000 stades, and not 240,000, as the circumference of the earth.   What is the explanation of the discrepancy ?   Hultsch takes the 300,000 stades and the assumption that the sun's circle is 10,000 times as large as the circumference of the earth to be part of a calculation of the *minimum* distance of the sun, on the ground that Cleomedes goes on to say that ' it is indeed plausible that the sun's circle is *not less* than 10,000 times the circumference of the earth, seeing that the earth is to it in the relation of a point; but it may also be greater

---

[1] Strabo, ii. 2. 2, p. 95 Cas.   [2] Berger, op. cit., pp. 579, 580.
[3] Ptolemy, *Geography*, vii. 5. 12.

still without our knowing it'.[1] But it is somewhat awkward to suppose with Hultsch that Posidonius is arguing, ' I take the earth to be of the size attributed to it by Dicaearchus, namely 300,000 stades in circumference, *although this figure exceeds the truth* ; but I am satisfied that, even if I take the circumference to be *fully* 300,000 stades, I shall *yet* arrive at an estimate of the sun's distance which is less than the true distance.' The italics are mine, and represent the part of Hultsch's argument which seems to me doubtful. The use of an exaggerated estimate of the earth's circumference with a view to a *minimum* estimate of the sun's distance is so strange that I prefer to suppose that, in the development of the hypothesis about the sun's distance, Posidonius simply used Dicaearchus's figure for the earth's circumference without any *arrière-pensée* at all.

In considering the origin of the bold hypothesis of Posidonius with regard to the sun's distance, it is necessary to refer to the hypotheses of Archimedes with regard to the size of the universe, on which in his *Sand-reckoner* he bases his argument that it is possible to formulate a system for expressing numbers as large as we please, say a number such as the number of the grains of sand which would be required to fill an empty space as large as our ' universe '. For the purpose which he has in view, Archimedes has of course to take what he considers to be outside or maximum measurements. Thus, whereas his predecessors had tried to prove the perimeter of the earth to be 300,000 stades, he will allow it to be as much as ten times that ' and not greater ', viz. 3,000,000 stades. Next, whereas Aristarchus had made the sun between 18 and 20 times as large as the moon, he will take it to be 30 times, but not greater, so that (the earth being greater than the moon) the sun will be less than 30 times the size of the earth. Archimedes proceeds to consider the size of the so-called ' universe ' and of the sun. He has explained that the ' universe ' as commonly understood by astronomers is the sphere which has for its centre the centre of the earth and for its radius the distance between the centre of the earth and the centre of the sun, but that the sphere of the fixed stars is much greater than this so-called ' universe '. Considering now the sun

---

[1] Cleomedes, ii. 1, p. 146. 12–16. The text has μείζονα αὐτὸν ὄντα ἢ πάλιν μείονα, ' it may be greater, or again it may be less '; Hultsch rejects ἢ πάλιν μείονα as a gloss inconsistent with the trend of Cleomedes' argument.

in relation to its orbit, a great circle of the so-called 'universe', Archimedes found by a rough experiment (in confirmation of Aristarchus's discovery that the apparent angular diameter of the sun is $\frac{1}{720}$th of four right angles) that the angle subtended by the sun's diameter is between $\frac{1}{164}$th and $\frac{1}{200}$th part of a right angle, or between $\frac{1}{656}$th and $\frac{1}{800}$th part of four right angles. By means of this result he proves that the diameter of the sun is greater than the side of a chiliagon (or a regular polygon with 1,000 sides) inscribed in its orbit. The proof of this is very interesting because we there see Archimedes abandoning the traditional view that the earth is a point in relation to the sphere in which the sun moves[1] (Aristarchus assumed it to be so in relation even to the *moon's* sphere), and recognizing parallax in the case of the sun, apparently for the first time; for, from the fact that the apparent diameter of the sun, as seen at its rising by an observer on the *surface* of the earth, subtends an angle less than $\frac{1}{656}$th and greater than $\frac{1}{800}$th of four right angles, he proves geometrically that the arc of the sun's orbit subtended by a chord equal to the diameter of the sun subtends at the *centre* of the earth an angle greater than $\frac{1}{812}$th and *a fortiori* greater than $\frac{1}{1000}$th of four right angles.

Now, says Archimedes, since

(perimeter of chiliagon inscribed in sun's orbit)

$< 1,000$ (diam. of sun)
$< 30,000$ (diam. of earth),

while the perimeter of any regular polygon of more than six sides is greater than 3 times the diameter of the circle in which it is described, it follows that

(diameter of sun's orbit) $< 10,000$ (diam. of earth).

Posidonius assumed, not that the diameter of the sun's orbit was *less* than 10,000 times the diameter of the earth, but that it was equal to (or not less than) 10,000 times the earth's diameter. But the origin of his ratio of 10,000 : 1 is sufficiently clear; he took it from Archimedes. Similarly, the combination of the estimate of 300,000 stades for the circumference of the earth with Eratosthenes' assumption that the shadowless circle at Syene was 300

---

[1] Cf. Cleomedes, *De motu circulari*, i. 11, pp. 108–12, ed. Ziegler.

stades in diameter suggests that Posidonius likewise adopted from Archimedes the $\frac{1}{1000}$th part of four right angles as the apparent angular diameter of the sun, being satisfied to take Archimedes' minimum estimate as the actual figure.

It remains to express Posidonius's estimates of the sun's and moon's sizes and distances in terms of the earth's diameter. On the basis of his estimate of 240,000 stades for the circumference of the earth, the earth's diameter, which we will call D, is 240,000/π stades, or about 76,400 stades.

Distance of sun   = 500,000,000 D/76,400 = about 6,545 D.

Diameter of sun   =   3,000,000 D/76,400 = 39¼ D.

Distance of moon =   2,000,000 D/76,400 = 26⅕ D.

Diameter of moon = $\frac{2}{500}$ (diameter of sun) = 0·157 D, nearly.

As Ptolemy gives none of the estimates which Pappus's commentary on the *Syntaxis* quotes from Hipparchus's treatise on the sizes and distances of the sun and moon, it was not unnatural to suppose, as Wolf did,[1] that the elaborate calculations in Ptolemy (v. 13-16) were referable to Hipparchus. This cannot be so as regards the results, as Hultsch has shown by means of Pappus's commentary, though doubtless Ptolemy may have been at least partially indebted to Hipparchus for the methods which he followed. The following are Ptolemy's results:

The mean distance of the moon =   59 times the earth's radius.[2]

„   „   „   „   sun = 1,210   „   „   „

The diameter of the earth = 3⅖ times the diameter of the moon.[3]

„   „   „   sun = 18⅘ „   „   „   „   „

It follows that

the diam. of the sun = about 5½ times the diam. of the earth.

I will conclude with Hultsch's final comparative table[4] of sizes

[1] Wolf, *Geschichte der Astronomie*, pp. 174 sqq.
[2] Ptolemy, *Syntaxis*, v. 15, p. 425. 17-20, Heib.
[3] Ibid., v. 16, p. 426. 12-15, Heib.
[4] Hultsch, *Hipparchos über die Grösse und Entfernung der Sonne*, p. 199.

and distances in terms of the earth's mean diameter ($=1,716$ geographical miles):

	Mean distance of moon from earth	Diameter of moon	Mean distance of sun from earth	Diameter of sun
According to Aristarchus	$9\frac{1}{2}$	$\frac{9}{25} = 0.36$	180	$6\frac{3}{4}$
,, ,, Hipparchus	$33\frac{2}{3}$	$\frac{1}{3} = 0.33$	1245	$12\frac{1}{3}$
,, ,, Posidonius	$26\frac{1}{5}$	$\frac{9}{10} = 0.157$	6545	$39\frac{1}{4}$
,, ,, Ptolemy	$29\frac{1}{2}$	$\frac{5}{17} = 0.29$	605	$5\frac{1}{2}$
In reality	30.2	0.27	11726	108.9

ARISTARCHUS OF SAMOS
ON THE SIZES AND DISTANCES OF THE SUN AND MOON

TEXT, TRANSLATION, AND NOTES

ΑΡΙΣΤΑΡΧΟΥ ΠΕΡΙ ΜΕΓΕΘΩΝ ΚΑΙ ΑΠΟΣΤΗΜΑΤΩΝ ΗΛΙΟΥ ΚΑΙ ΣΕΛΗΝΗΣ

⟨ΥΠΟΘΕΣΕΙΣ⟩

α΄. Τὴν σελήνην παρὰ τοῦ ἡλίου τὸ φῶς λαμβάνειν.

5 β΄. Τὴν γῆν σημείου τε καὶ κέντρου λόγον ἔχειν πρὸς τὴν τῆς σελήνης σφαῖραν.

γ΄. Ὅταν ἡ σελήνη διχότομος ἡμῖν φαίνηται, νεύειν εἰς τὴν ἡμετέραν ὄψιν τὸν διορίζοντα τό τε σκιερὸν καὶ τὸ λαμπρὸν τῆς σελήνης μέγιστον κύκλον.

10 δ΄. Ὅταν ἡ σελήνη διχότομος ἡμῖν φαίνηται, τότε αὐτὴν ἀπέχειν τοῦ ἡλίου ἔλασσον τεταρτημορίου τῷ τοῦ τεταρτημορίου τριακοστῷ.

ε΄. Τὸ τῆς σκιᾶς πλάτος σεληνῶν εἶναι δύο.

ϛ΄. Τὴν σελήνην ὑποτείνειν ὑπὸ πεντεκαιδέκατον μέρος 15 ζῳδίου.

Ἐπιλογίζεται οὖν τὸ τοῦ ἡλίου ἀπόστημα ἀπὸ τῆς γῆς τοῦ τῆς σελήνης ἀποστήματος μεῖζον μὲν ἢ ὀκτωκαιδεκαπλάσιον, ἔλασσον δὲ ἢ εἰκοσαπλάσιον, διὰ τῆς περὶ τὴν διχοτομίαν ὑποθέσεως· τὸν

1. ΑΡΙΣΤΑΡΧΟΥ] ΑΡΙΣΤΑΡΧΟΥ ΣΑΜΙΟΥ W   3. ⟨ΥΠΟΘΕΣΕΙΣ⟩ addidi (cf. ὑποθέσεως l. 18 infra ; ὑποτίθεται Pappus) : ΘΕΣΕΙΣ W   4. τὸ] om. Pappus 8. τε] om. Pappus   12. τριακοστῷ] τριακοστημορίῳ Pappus   16. οὖν] δὴ Pappus 16, 17. τὸ τοῦ ἡλίου . . . ἀποστήματος] τὸ τοῦ ἡλίου ἀπόστημα τοῦ τῆς σελήνης ἀποστήματος πρὸς τὴν γῆν Pappus   18. εἰκοσαπλάσιον] εἰκοσιπλάσιον W   διὰ τῆς . . . ὑποθέσεως] τοῦτο δὲ διὰ τῆς περὶ τὴν διχότομον ὑποθέσεως post l. 1, p. 354 σελήνης διάμετρον posuit Pappus

ARISTARCHUS ON THE SIZES AND DISTANCES OF THE SUN AND MOON

[HYPOTHESES]

1. *That the moon receives its light from the sun.*

2. *That the earth is in the relation of a point and centre to the sphere in which the moon moves.*[1]

3. *That, when the moon appears to us halved, the great circle which divides the dark and the bright portions of the moon is in the direction of our eye.*[2]

4. *That, when the moon appears to us halved, its distance from the sun is then less than a quadrant by one-thirtieth of a quadrant.*[3]

5. *That the breadth of the (earth's) shadow is (that) of two moons.*

6. *That the moon subtends one fifteenth part of a sign of the zodiac.*[4]

We are now in a position to prove the following propositions:—

1. *The distance of the sun from the earth is greater than eighteen times, but less than twenty times, the distance of the moon (from the earth)*; this follows from the hypothesis about the halved moon.

---

[1] Literally 'the sphere of the moon'.

[2] Literally '*verges* towards our eye', the word νεύειν meaning to 'verge' or 'incline'. What is meant is that the plane of the great circle in question passes through the observer's eye or, in other words, that his eye and the great circle are in one plane (cf. Aristarchus's own explanation in the enunciation of Prop. 5).

[3] I. e. is less than 90° by 1/30th of 90° or 3°, and is therefore equal to 87°.

[4] I. e. 1/15th of 30°, or 2°. Archimedes in his *Sand-reckoner* (Archimedes, ed. Heiberg, ii, p. 248, 19) says that Aristarchus 'discovered that the sun appeared to be about 1/720th part of the circle of the zodiac'; that is, Aristarchus discovered (evidently at a date later than that of our treatise) the much more correct value of $\frac{1}{2}$° for the angular diameter of the sun or moon (for he maintained that both had the same angular diameter: cf. Prop. 8). Archimedes himself in the same place describes a rough method of observation by which he inferred that the diameter of the sun was less than 1/164th part, and greater than 1/200th part, of a right angle. Cf. pp. 311-12 *ante*.

αὐτὸν δὲ λόγον ἔχειν τὴν τοῦ ἡλίου διάμετρον πρὸς τὴν τῆς σελήνης διάμετρον· τὴν δὲ τοῦ ἡλίου διάμετρον πρὸς τὴν τῆς γῆς διάμετρον μείζονα μὲν λόγον ἔχειν ἢ ὃν τὰ ιθ πρὸς γ, ἐλάσσονα δὲ ἢ ὃν μγ πρὸς ς, διὰ τοῦ εὑρεθέντος περὶ τὰ ἀποστήματα λόγου, τῆς ⟨τε⟩
5 περὶ τὴν σκιὰν ὑποθέσεως, καὶ τοῦ τὴν σελήνην ὑπὸ πεντεκαιδέκατον μέρος ζῳδίου ὑποτείνειν.

α.

Δύο σφαίρας ἴσας μὲν ὁ αὐτὸς κύλινδρος περιλαμβάνει, ἀνίσους δὲ ὁ αὐτὸς κῶνος τὴν κορυφὴν ἔχων πρὸς τῇ
10 ἐλάσσονι σφαίρᾳ· καὶ ἡ διὰ τῶν κέντρων αὐτῶν ἀγομένη εὐθεῖα ὀρθή ἐστιν πρὸς ἑκάτερον τῶν κύκλων, καθ' ὧν ἐφάπτεται ἡ τοῦ κυλίνδρου ἢ ἡ τοῦ κώνου ἐπιφάνεια τῶν σφαιρῶν.

Ἔστωσαν ἴσαι σφαῖραι, ὧν κέντρα ἔστω τὰ Α, Β σημεῖα, καὶ
15 ἐπιζευχθεῖσα ἡ ΑΒ ἐκβεβλήσθω, καὶ ἐκβεβλήσθω διὰ τοῦ ΑΒ ἐπίπεδον· ποιήσει δὴ τομὰς ἐν ταῖς σφαίραις μεγίστους κύκλους.

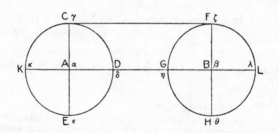

Fig. 16.

ποιείτω οὖν τοὺς ΓΔΕ, ΖΗΘ κύκλους, καὶ ἤχθωσαν ἀπὸ τῶν Α, Β τῇ ΑΒ πρὸς ὀρθὰς αἱ ΓΑΕ, ΖΒΘ, καὶ ἐπεζεύχθω ἡ ΓΖ. καὶ ἐπεὶ

---

1. ἔχειν τήν] ἔχει καὶ ἡ Pappus   διάμετρον] διάμετρος Pappus   3. μείζονα μὲν λόγον ἔχειν] ἐν μείζονι λόγῳ Pappus   τά] om. Pappus   ἐλάσσονα δὲ] ἐν ἐλάσσονι δὲ λόγῳ Pappus   μγ] τὰ μγ Pappus   4. τῆς ⟨τε⟩] ⟨τε⟩ addidi : καὶ τῆς Pappus   6. ὑποτείνειν ante ὑπὸ posuit Pappus   16. δή] δὲ W

2. *The diameter of the sun has the same ratio (as aforesaid) to the diameter of the moon.*[1]

3. *The diameter of the sun has to the diameter of the earth a ratio greater than that which* 19 *has to* 3, *but less than that which* 43 *has to* 6; this follows from the ratio thus discovered between the distances, the hypothesis about the shadow, and the hypothesis that the moon subtends one fifteenth part of a sign of the zodiac.

PROPOSITION I.

Two equal spheres are comprehended by one and the same cylinder, and two unequal spheres by one and the same cone which has its vertex in the direction of the lesser sphere; and the straight line drawn through the centres of the spheres is at right angles to each of the circles in which the surface of the cylinder, or of the cone, touches the spheres.

Let there be equal spheres, and let the points A, B be their centres.

Let AB be joined and produced;
let a plane be carried through AB; this plane will cut the spheres in great circles.[2]

Let the great circles be CDE, FGH.

Let CAE, FBH be drawn from A, B at right angles to AB; and let CF be joined.

---

[1] Pappus gives this second result immediately after the first result, i. e. before the parenthesis 'this follows from the hypothesis . . .'. This arrangement seems at first sight more appropriate, and Nizze alters his text accordingly. But I think it better to follow the above order which is that of the MSS. and Wallis. One consideration which weighs with me is that the second result does not follow from the hypothesis of the halved moon alone; it depends on another assumption also, namely, that the sun and the moon have the same apparent angular diameter (see Prop. 8).

[2] Literally 'it will make, as sections in the spheres, great circles', and then, in the next sentence, 'let it then make the circles CDE, FGH.' In translating these characteristic phrases, which occur very frequently, I wish I could have reproduced the Greek exactly, keeping the word 'sections', but it becomes impossible to do so when the phrase is extended so as to distinguish several sections made by one plane, e.g. one section in one sphere, one section in another sphere, and one section in a cone: Thus 'let it make, as sections, in the spheres, the circles CDE, FGH and, in the cone, the triangle CEK' (Prop. 2) would be intolerable, with or without the multitude of commas, whereas clearness and conciseness is easily secured by saying 'let it cut the spheres in the circles CDE, FGH and the cone in the triangle CEK'.

αἱ ΓΑ, ΖΒ ἴσαι τε καὶ παράλληλοί εἰσιν, καὶ αἱ ΓΖ, ΑΒ ἄρα ἴσαι
τε καὶ παράλληλοί εἰσιν. παραλληλόγραμμον ἄρα ἐστὶν τὸ ΓΖΑΒ,
καὶ αἱ πρὸς τοῖς Γ, Ζ γωνίαι ὀρθαὶ ἔσονται· ὥστε ἡ ΓΖ τῶν ΓΔΕ,
ΖΗΘ κύκλων ἐφάπτεται. ἐὰν δὴ μενούσης τῆς ΑΒ τὸ ΑΖ παραλ-
5 ληλόγραμμον καὶ τὰ ΚΓΔ, ΗΖΛ ἡμικύκλια περιενεχθέντα εἰς τὸ
αὐτὸ πάλιν ἀποκατασταθῇ ὅθεν ἤρξατο φέρεσθαι, τὰ μὲν ΚΓΔ,
ΗΖΛ ἡμικύκλια ἐνεχθήσεται κατὰ τῶν σφαιρῶν, τὸ δὲ ΑΖ παραλληλόγραμμον γεννήσει κύλινδρον, οὗ βάσεις ἔσονται οἱ περὶ διαμέτρους τὰς ΓΕ, ΖΘ κύκλοι, ὀρθοὶ ὄντες πρὸς τὴν ΑΒ, διὰ τὸ ἐν
10 πάσῃ μετακινήσει διαμένειν τὰς ΓΕ, ΘΖ ὀρθὰς τῇ ΑΒ. καὶ
φανερὸν ὅτι ἡ ἐπιφάνεια αὐτοῦ ἐφάπτεται τῶν σφαιρῶν, ἐπειδὴ ἡ ΓΖ
κατὰ πᾶσαν μετακίνησιν ἐφάπτεται τῶν ΚΓΔ, ΗΖΛ ἡμικυκλίων.

Ἔστωσαν δὴ αἱ σφαῖραι πάλιν, ὧν κέντρα ἔστω τὰ Α, Β, ἄνισοι,
καὶ μείζων ἧς κέντρον τὸ Α· λέγω ὅτι τὰς σφαίρας ὁ αὐτὸς κῶνος
15 περιλαμβάνει τὴν κορυφὴν ἔχων πρὸς τῇ ἐλάσσονι σφαίρᾳ.

Ἐπεζεύχθω ἡ ΑΒ, καὶ ἐκβεβλήσθω διὰ τῆς ΑΒ ἐπίπεδον·
ποιήσει δὴ τομὰς ἐν ταῖς σφαίραις κύκλους. ποιείτω τοὺς ΓΔΕ,
ΖΗΘ· μείζων ἄρα ὁ ΓΔΕ κύκλος τοῦ ΗΖΘ κύκλου· ὥστε καὶ ἡ
ἐκ τοῦ κέντρου τοῦ ΓΔΕ κύκλου μείζων ἐστὶ τῆς ἐκ τοῦ κέντρου
20 τοῦ ΖΗΘ κύκλου. δυνατὸν δή ἐστι λαβεῖν τι σημεῖον, ὡς τὸ Κ, ἵν'
ᾖ, ὡς ἡ ἐκ τοῦ κέντρου τοῦ ΓΔΕ κύκλου πρὸς τὴν ἐκ τοῦ κέντρου

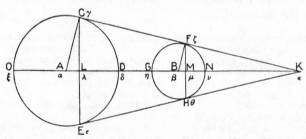

Fig. 17.

τοῦ ΖΗΘ κύκλου, οὕτως ἡ ΑΚ πρὸς τὴν ΚΒ. ἔστω οὖν εἰλημμένον
τὸ Κ σημεῖον, καὶ ἤχθω ἡ ΚΖ ἐφαπτομένη τοῦ ΖΗΘ κύκλου, καὶ
ἐπεζεύχθω ἡ ΖΒ, καὶ διὰ τοῦ Α τῇ ΒΖ παράλληλος ἤχθω ἡ ΑΓ,

6. ἀποκατασταθῇ] ἀποκαταστῇ W   10. ΘΖ] ΖΘ W   11. ἐφάπτεται] ἐφάπτηται W
13. B ad init. Vat. et codd. Paris.   δὴ] δὲ W   17. τομὰς] corr. W : τομὴν
Vat.   18. κύκλος] om. W   HZΘ] ΖΗΘ W   20. τὸ Κ] τὸ ΚΕ Vat.

Then, since CA, FB are equal and parallel, therefore CF, AB are also equal and parallel.

Therefore $CFAB$ is a parallelogram,
and the angles at C, F will be right;
so that CF touches the circles CDE, FGH.

If now, AB remaining fixed, the parallelogram AF and the semicircles KCD, GFL be carried round and again restored to the position from which they started, the semicircles KCD, GFL will move in coincidence with the spheres[1]; and the parallelogram AF will generate a cylinder, the bases of which will be the circles about CE, FH as diameters and at right angles to AB, because, throughout the whole motion, CE, HF remain at right angles to AB.

And it is manifest that the surface of the cylinder touches the spheres,
since CF, throughout the whole motion, touches the semicircles KCD, GFL.

Again, let the spheres be unequal, and let A, B be their centres; let that sphere be greater, the centre of which is A.

I say that the spheres are comprehended by one and the same cone which has its vertex in the direction of the lesser sphere.

Let AB be joined, and let a plane be carried through AB; this plane will cut the spheres in circles.

Let the circles be CDE, FGH;
therefore the circle CDE is greater than the circle GFH; so that the radius of the circle CDE is also greater than the radius of the circle FGH.

Now it is possible to take a point, as K (on AB produced), such that, as the radius of the circle CDE is to the radius of the circle FGH, so is AK to KB.

Let the point K be so taken, and let KF be drawn touching the circle FGH;
let FB be joined, and through A let AC be drawn parallel to BF;

---

[1] The force of κατά here is very difficult to render. The Greek phrase ἐνεχθήσεται κατὰ τῶν σφαιρῶν means 'will be carried, or move, *in* the spheres', that is, the circumferences of the semicircles will pass neither over nor under the surfaces of the spheres, but in coincidence with them throughout, in other words, they will by their revolution *describe* (as we say) the actual surfaces of the spheres.

358 ON THE SIZES AND DISTANCES

καὶ ἐπεζεύχθω ἡ ΓΖ. καὶ ἐπεί ἐστιν, ὡς ἡ ΑΚ πρὸς τὴν ΚΒ, ἡ
ΑΔ πρὸς τὴν ΒΝ, ἴση δὲ ἡ μὲν ΑΔ τῇ ΑΓ, ἡ δὲ ΒΝ τῇ ΒΖ,
ἔστιν ἄρα, ὡς ἡ ΑΚ πρὸς τὴν ΚΒ, ἡ ΑΓ πρὸς τὴν ΒΖ. καὶ ἔστιν
παράλληλος ἡ ΑΓ τῇ ΒΖ· εὐθεῖα ἄρα ἐστὶν ἡ ΓΖΚ. καὶ ἔστιν
5 ὀρθὴ ἡ ὑπὸ τῶν ΚΖΒ· ὀρθὴ ἄρα καὶ ἡ ὑπὸ τῶν ΚΓΑ. ἐφάπτεται
ἄρα ἡ ΚΓ τοῦ ΓΔΕ κύκλου. ἤχθωσαν δὴ αἱ ΓΛ, ΖΜ ἐπὶ τὴν
ΑΒ κάθετοι. ἐὰν δὴ μενούσης τῆς ΚΞ τά τε ΞΓΔ, ΗΖΝ
ἡμικύκλια καὶ τὰ ΚΓΔ, ΚΖΜ τρίγωνα περιενεχθέντα εἰς τὸ αὐτὸ
πάλιν ἀποκατασταθῇ ὅθεν ἤρξατο φέρεσθαι, τὰ μὲν ΞΓΔ, ΗΖΝ
10 ἡμικύκλια ἐνεχθήσεται κατὰ τῶν σφαιρῶν, τὸ δὲ ΚΓΔ τρίγωνον καὶ
τὸ ΚΖΜ γεννήσει κώνους, ὧν βάσεις εἰσὶν οἱ περὶ διαμέτρους τὰς
ΓΕ, ΖΘ κύκλοι, ὀρθοὶ ὄντες πρὸς τὸν ΚΛ ἄξονα· κέντρα δὲ αὐτῶν
τὰ Λ, Μ· καὶ ὁ κῶνος τῶν σφαιρῶν ἐφάψεται κατὰ τὴν ἐπιφάνειαν,
ἐπειδὴ καὶ ἡ ΚΖΓ ἐφάπτεται τῶν ΞΓΔ, ΗΖΝ ἡμικυκλίων κατὰ
15 πᾶσαν μετακίνησιν.

β'.

Ἐὰν σφαῖρα ὑπὸ μείζονος ἑαυτῆς σφαίρας φωτίζηται,
μεῖζον ἡμισφαιρίου φωτισθήσεται.

Σφαῖρα γάρ, ἧς κέντρον τὸ Β, ὑπὸ μείζονος ἑαυτῆς σφαίρας
20 φωτιζέσθω, ἧς κέντρον τὸ Α· λέγω ὅτι τὸ φωτιζόμενον μέρος τῆς
σφαίρας, ἧς κέντρον τὸ Β, μεῖζόν ἐστιν ἡμισφαιρίου.

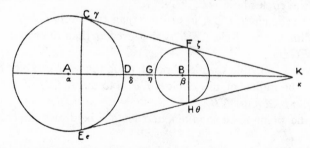

Fig. 18.

Ἐπεὶ γὰρ δύο ἀνίσους σφαίρας ὁ αὐτὸς κῶνος περιλαμβάνει τὴν
κορυφὴν ἔχων πρὸς τῇ ἐλάσσονι σφαίρᾳ, ἔστω ὁ περιλαμβάνων τὰς
σφαίρας κῶνος, καὶ ἐκβεβλήσθω διὰ τοῦ ἄξονος ἐπίπεδον· ποιήσει
25 δὴ τομὰς ἐν μὲν ταῖς σφαίραις κύκλους, ἐν δὲ τῷ κώνῳ τρίγωνον.

8. ΚΓΔ] ΚΓΔ Vat.   9. ἀποκατασταθῇ] ἀποκαταστῇ W   14. ΞΓΔ] ΖΓΔ Vat.
16. β'] Γ Vat.   17. φωτίζηται] φωτίζεται W   22. κῶνος] κόνος Vat.

let *CF* be joined.

Then since, as *AK* is to *KB*, so is *AD* to *BN*,
while *AD* is equal to *AC*, and *BN* to *BF*,
therefore, as *AK* is to *KB*, so is *AC* to *BF*.

And *AC* is parallel to *BF*;
therefore *CFK* is a straight line.

Now the angle *KFB* is right;
therefore the angle *KCA* is also right:
therefore *KC* touches the circle *CDE*.

Let *CL*, *FM* be drawn perpendicular to *AB*.

If now, *KO* remaining fixed, the semicircles *OCD*, *GFN* and the triangles *KCL*, *KFM* be carried round and again restored to the position from which they started, the semicircles *OCD*, *GFN* will move in coincidence with the spheres; and the triangles *KCL* and *KFM* will generate cones, the bases of which are the circles about *CE*, *FH* as diameters and at right angles to the axis *KL*, the centres of the circles being *L*, *M*.

And the cone will touch the spheres along their surface, since *KFC* also touches the semicircles *OCD*, *GFN* throughout the whole motion.

PROPOSITION 2.

If a sphere be illuminated by a sphere greater than itself, the illuminated portion of the former sphere will be greater than a hemisphere.

For let a sphere the centre of which is *B* be illuminated by a sphere greater than itself the centre of which is *A*.

I say that the illuminated portion of the sphere the centre of which is *B* is greater than a hemisphere.

For, since two unequal spheres are comprehended by one and the same cone which has its vertex in the direction of the lesser sphere,   [Prop. 1]
let the cone comprehending the spheres be (drawn), and let a plane be carried through the axis;
this plane will cut the spheres in circles and the cone in a triangle.

ποιείτω οὖν ἐν μὲν ταῖς σφαίραις κύκλους τοὺς ΓΔΕ, ΖΗΘ, ἐν δὲ
τῷ κώνῳ τρίγωνον τὸ ΓΕΚ. φανερὸν δὴ ὅτι τὸ κατὰ τὴν ΖΗΘ
περιφέρειαν τμῆμα τῆς σφαίρας, οὗ βάσις ἐστὶν ὁ περὶ διάμετρον
τὴν ΖΘ κύκλος, φωτιζόμενον μέρος ἐστὶν ὑπὸ τοῦ τμήματος τοῦ
5 κατὰ τὴν ΓΔΕ περιφέρειαν, οὗ βάσις ἐστὶν ὁ περὶ διάμετρον τὴν
ΓΕ κύκλος, ὀρθὸς ὢν πρὸς τὴν ΑΒ εὐθεῖαν· καὶ γὰρ ἡ ΖΗΘ
περιφέρεια φωτίζεται ὑπὸ τῆς ΓΔΕ περιφερείας· ἔσχαται γὰρ
ἀκτῖνές εἰσιν αἱ ΓΖ, ΕΘ· καὶ ἔστιν ἐν τῷ ΖΗΘ τμήματι τὸ
κέντρον τῆς σφαίρας τὸ Β· ὥστε τὸ φωτιζόμενον μέρος τῆς σφαίρας
10 μεῖζόν ἐστιν ἡμισφαιρίου.

γ΄.

Ἐν τῇ σελήνῃ ἐλάχιστος κύκλος διορίζει τό τε σκιερὸν
καὶ τὸ λαμπρόν, ὅταν ὁ περιλαμβάνων κῶνος τόν τε ἥλιον
καὶ τὴν σελήνην τὴν κορυφὴν ἔχῃ πρὸς τῇ ἡμετέρᾳ ὄψει.

15 Ἔστω γὰρ ἡ μὲν ἡμετέρα ὄψις πρὸς τῷ Α, ἡλίου δὲ κέντρον τὸ
Β, σελήνης δὲ κέντρον, ὅταν μὲν ὁ περιλαμβάνων κῶνος τόν τε
ἥλιον καὶ τὴν σελήνην τὴν κορυφὴν ἔχῃ πρὸς τῇ ἡμετέρᾳ ὄψει, τὸ Γ,
ὅταν δὲ μή, τὸ Δ· φανερὸν δὴ ὅτι τὰ Α, Γ, Β ἐπ᾿ εὐθείας ἐστίν.
ἐκβεβλήσθω διὰ τῆς ΑΒ καὶ τοῦ Δ σημείου ἐπίπεδον· ποιήσει δὴ
20 τομάς, ἐν μὲν ταῖς σφαίραις κύκλους, ἐν δὲ τοῖς κώνοις εὐθείας.
ποιείτω δὲ καὶ ἐν τῇ σφαίρᾳ, καθ᾿ ἧς φέρεται τὸ κέντρον τῆς σελήνης,
κύκλον τὸν ΓΔ· τὸ Α ἄρα κέντρον ἐστὶν αὐτοῦ· τοῦτο γὰρ ὑπόκειται·
ἐν δὲ τῷ ἡλίῳ τὸν ΕΖΡ κύκλον, ἐν δὲ τῇ σελήνῃ, ὅταν μὲν ὁ
περιλαμβάνων κῶνος τόν τε ἥλιον καὶ τὴν σελήνην τὴν κορυφὴν ἔχῃ
25 πρὸς τῇ ἡμετέρᾳ ὄψει, κύκλον τὸν ΚΘΛ, ὅταν δὲ μή, τὸν ΜΝΞ,
ἐν δὲ τοῖς κώνοις εὐθείας τὰς ΕΑ, ΑΗ, ΠΟ, ΟΡ, ἄξονας δὲ τοὺς
ΑΒ, ΒΟ. καὶ ἐπεί ἐστιν, ὡς ἡ ἐκ τοῦ κέντρου τοῦ ΕΖΗ κύκλου
πρὸς τὴν ἐκ τοῦ κέντρου τοῦ ΘΚΛ, οὕτως ἡ ἐκ τοῦ κέντρου τοῦ ΕΖΗ
κύκλου πρὸς τὴν ἐκ τοῦ κέντρου τοῦ ΜΝΞ· ἀλλ᾿ ὡς ἡ ἐκ τοῦ

---

4. τὴν ΖΘ] ΖΘ W   11. γ΄] Δ Vat.   15. ἡλίου δὲ] ἡλίου W
16. μὲν] om. W   21. δὲ] δὴ W   25. ΚΘΛ] ΘΚΛ W   26. τοὺς] om. W
27. κύκλου] om. W

Let it cut the spheres in the circles *CDE*, *FGH*, and the cone in the triangle *CEK*.

It is then manifest that the segment of the sphere towards the circumference *FGH*, the base of which is the circle about *FH* as diameter, is the portion illuminated by the segment towards the circumference *CDE*, the base of which is the circle about *CE* as diameter and at right angles to the straight line *AB*;
for the circumference *FGH* is illuminated by the circumference *CDE*, since *CF*, *EH* are the extreme rays.[1]

And the centre *B* of the sphere is within the segment *FGH*; so that the illuminated portion of the sphere is greater than a hemisphere.

PROPOSITION 3.

The circle in the moon which divides the dark and the bright portions is least when the cone comprehending both the sun and the moon has its vertex at our eye.

For let our eye be at *A*, and let *B* be the centre of the sun; let *C* be the centre of the moon when the cone comprehending both the sun and the moon has its vertex at our eye, and, when this is not the case, let *D* be the centre.

It is then manifest that *A*, *C*, *B* are in a straight line.

Let a plane be carried through *AB* and the point *D*; this plane will cut the spheres in circles and the cones in straight lines.

Let the plane also cut the sphere on which the centre of the moon moves in the circle *CD*;
therefore *A* is the centre of this circle, for this is our hypothesis [Hypothesis 2].

Let the plane cut the sun in the circle *EFR*, and the moon, when the cone comprehending both the sun and the moon has its vertex at our eye, in the circle *KHL* and, when this is not the case, in the circle *MNO*;
and let it cut the cones in the straight lines *EA*, *AG*, *QP*, *PR*, the axes being *AB*, *BP*.

Then since, as the radius of the circle *EFG* is to the radius of the circle *HKL*, so is the radius of the circle *EFG* to the radius of the circle *MNO*,

---

[1] In Wallis's figure the letters *F*, *H* are interchanged. With his lettering, the extreme rays should be *CH*, *EF*. I have given *F*, *H* the positions necessary to suit the text, and my figure agrees with that of Vat.

κέντρου τοῦ *EZH* κύκλου πρὸς τὴν ἐκ τοῦ κέντρου τοῦ *ΘΛΚ* κύκλου, οὕτως ἡ *ΒΑ* πρὸς τὴν *ΑΓ*· ὡς δὲ ἡ ἐκ τοῦ κέντρου τοῦ *EZH* κύκλου πρὸς τὴν ἐκ τοῦ κέντρου τοῦ *ΜΝΞ* κύκλου, οὕτως ἐστὶν .ἡ *ΒΟ* πρὸς τὴν *ΟΔ*· καὶ ὡς ἄρα ἡ *ΒΑ* πρὸς τὴν *ΑΓ*, οὕτως ἡ *ΒΟ* πρὸς τὴν 5 *ΟΔ*. καὶ διελόντι, ὡς ἡ *ΒΓ* πρὸς τὴν *ΓΑ*, οὕτως ἡ *ΒΔ* πρὸς τὴν

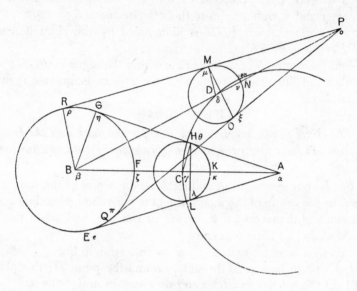

Fig. 19.

ΔΟ, καὶ ἐναλλάξ, ὡς ἡ *ΒΓ* πρὸς τὴν *ΒΔ*, οὕτως ἡ *ΓΑ* πρὸς τὴν *ΔΟ*. καὶ ἔστιν ἐλάσσων ἡ *ΒΓ* τῆς *ΒΔ*· κέντρον γάρ ἐστι τὸ *Α* τοῦ *ΓΔ* κύκλου· ἐλάσσων ἄρα καὶ ἡ *ΑΓ* τῆς *ΔΟ*. καὶ ἔστιν ἴσος ὁ *ΘΚΛ* κύκλος τῷ *ΜΝΞ* κύκλῳ· ἐλάσσων ἄρα ἐστὶν καὶ ἡ *ΘΛ* τῆς *ΜΞ* [, 10 διὰ τὸ λῆμμα]· ὥστε καὶ ὁ περὶ διάμετρον τὴν *ΘΛ* κύκλος γραφόμενος, ὀρθὸς ὢν πρὸς τὴν *ΑΒ*, ἐλάσσων ἐστὶν τοῦ περὶ διάμετρον τὴν *ΜΞ* κύκλου γραφομένου, ὀρθοῦ πρὸς τὴν *ΒΟ*. ἀλλ' ὁ μὲν περὶ διάμετρον τὴν *ΘΛ* κύκλος γραφόμενος, ὀρθὸς ὢν πρὸς τὴν *ΑΒ*, ὁ διορίζων ἐστὶν ἐν τῇ σελήνῃ τό τε σκιερὸν καὶ τὸ λαμπρόν, 15 ὅταν ὁ περιλαμβάνων κῶνος τόν τε ἥλιον καὶ τὴν σελήνην τὴν

while, as the radius of the circle EFG is to the radius of the circle HLK, so is BA to AC,

and, as the radius of the circle EFG is to the radius of the circle MNO, so is BP to PD,

therefore, as BA is to AC, so is BP to PD,

and, *separando*, as BC is to CA, so is BD to DP;

therefore also, alternately, as BC is to BD, so is CA to DP.

And BC is less than BD, for A is the centre of the circle CD; therefore AC is also less than DP.

And the circle HKL is equal to the circle MNO; therefore HL is also less than MO [by the Lemma [1]].

Accordingly the circle drawn about HL as diameter and at right angles to AB is also less than the circle drawn about MO as diameter and at right angles to BP.

But the circle drawn about HL as diameter and at right angles to AB is the circle which divides the dark and the bright portions in the moon when the cone comprehending both the sun and the moon has its vertex at our eye;

---

[1] The promised Lemma (the equivalent of which is stated, rather than proved, in Euclid's *Optics*, 24) does not appear. Some of the MSS. have a scholium containing a rather clumsy proof. A shorter proof is that of Nizze. We can use one circle instead of two equal circles; and we have to prove that, if A, P are points on the radius produced, P being further from the centre (C) than A

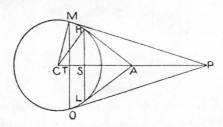

Fig. 20.

is, and if AH, AL be the pair of tangents from A, and PM, PO the pair of tangents from P, then $MO > HL$.

By Eucl. vi. 8 and 17, $CM^2 = CT \cdot CP$, and $CH^2 = CS \cdot CA$; therefore $CT \cdot CP = CS \cdot CA$, or $CA : CP = CT : CS$. But $CA < CP$; therefore $CT < CS$, so that the chord HL is less than the chord MO.

κορυφὴν ἔχῃ πρὸς τῇ ἡμετέρᾳ ὄψει· ὁ δὲ περὶ διάμετρον τὴν ΜΞ
κύκλος, ὀρθὸς ὢν πρὸς τὴν ΒΟ, ὁ διορίζων ἐστὶν ἐν τῇ σελήνῃ τό τε
σκιερὸν καὶ τὸ λαμπρόν, ὅταν ὁ περιλαμβάνων κῶνος τόν τε ἥλιον
καὶ τὴν σελήνην μὴ ἔχῃ τὴν κορυφὴν πρὸς τῇ ἡμετέρᾳ ὄψει· ὥστε
5 ἐλάσσων κύκλος διορίζει ἐν τῇ σελήνῃ τό τε σκιερὸν καὶ τὸ λαμπρόν,
ὅταν ὁ περιλαμβάνων κῶνος τόν τε ἥλιον καὶ τὴν σελήνην τὴν
κορυφὴν ἔχῃ πρὸς τῇ ἡμετέρᾳ ὄψει.

δ΄.

Ὁ διορίζων κύκλος ἐν τῇ σελήνῃ τό τε σκιερὸν καὶ τὸ
10 λαμπρὸν ἀδιάφορός ἐστι τῷ ἐν τῇ σελήνῃ μεγίστῳ κύκλῳ
πρὸς αἴσθησιν.

Ἔστω γὰρ ἡ μὲν ἡμετέρα ὄψις πρὸς τῷ Α, σελήνης δὲ κέντρον τὸ
Β, καὶ ἐπεζεύχθω ἡ ΑΒ, καὶ ἐκβεβλήσθω διὰ τῆς ΑΒ ἐπίπεδον·
ποιήσει δὴ τομὴν ἐν τῇ σφαίρᾳ μέγιστον κύκλον.   ποιείτω τὸν
15 ΕΓΔΖ, ἐν δὲ τῷ κώνῳ εὐθείας τὰς ΑΓ, ΑΔ, ΔΓ· ὁ ἄρα περὶ

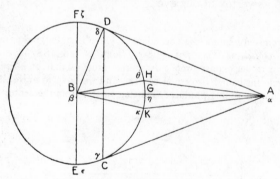

Fig. 21.

διάμετρον τὴν ΓΔ, πρὸς ὀρθὰς ὢν τῇ ΑΒ, ὁ διορίζων ἐστὶν ἐν τῇ
σελήνῃ τό τε σκιερὸν καὶ τὸ λαμπρόν.   λέγω δὴ ὅτι ἀδιάφορός ἐστι
τῷ μεγίστῳ πρὸς τὴν αἴσθησιν.

Ἤχθω γὰρ διὰ τοῦ Β τῇ ΓΔ παράλληλος ἡ ΕΖ, καὶ κείσθω
20 τῆς ΔΖ ἡμίσεια ἑκατέρα τῶν ΗΚ, ΗΘ, καὶ ἐπεζεύχθωσαν αἱ ΚΒ,
ΒΘ, ΚΑ, ΑΘ, ΒΔ.   καὶ ἐπεὶ ὑπόκειται ἡ σελήνη ὑπὸ ιε΄ μέρος

1. τὴν] τὸν Vat.   2. τὴν] τὸν Vat.   3, 4. τόν τε ἥλιον καὶ τὴν σελήνην] om. W
8. δ΄] Ε Vat.   12. τῷ] τὸ W

and the circle about MO as diameter and at right angles to BP is the circle which divides the dark and the bright portions in the moon when the cone comprehending both the sun and the moon has not its vertex at our eye.

Accordingly the circle which divides the dark and the bright portions in the moon is less when the cone comprehending both the sun and the moon has its vertex at our eye.

PROPOSITION 4.

The circle which divides the dark and the bright portions in the moon is not perceptibly different from a great circle in the moon.

For let our eye be at A, and let B be the centre of the moon.

Let AB be joined, and let a plane be carried through AB; this plane will cut the sphere in a great circle.

Let it cut the sphere in the circle $ECDF$ and the cone in the straight lines AC, AD, DC.

Then the circle about CD as diameter and at right angles to AB is the circle which divides the dark and the bright portions in the moon.

I say that it is not perceptibly different from a great circle.

For let EF be drawn through B parallel to CD; let GK, GH both be made (equal to) half of DF; and let KB, BH, KA, AH, BD be joined.

Then since, by hypothesis, the moon subtends a fifteenth part of a sign of the zodiac,

ζῳδίου ὑποτείνουσα, ἡ ἄρα ὑπὸ ΓΑΔ γωνία βέβηκεν ἐπὶ ιε΄ μέρος
ζῳδίου. τὸ δὲ ιε΄ τοῦ ζῳδίου τοῦ τῶν ζῳδίων ὅλου κύκλου ἐστὶν ρπ΄,
ὥστε ἡ ὑπὸ τῶν ΓΑΔ γωνία βέβηκεν ἐπὶ ρπ΄ ὅλου τοῦ κύκλου·
τεσσάρων ἄρα ὀρθῶν ἐστιν ἡ ⟨ὑπὸ⟩ ΓΑΔ ρπ΄. διὰ δὴ τοῦτο ἡ ὑπὸ
5 ΓΑΔ γωνία ἐστὶν με΄ ὀρθῆς· καὶ ἔστιν αὐτῆς ἡμίσεια ἡ ὑπὸ ΒΑΔ
γωνία· ἡ ἄρα ὑπὸ τῶν ΒΑΔ ἡμισείας ὀρθῆς ἐστι ⟨με΄⟩ μέρος. καὶ
ἐπεὶ ὀρθή ἐστιν ἡ ὑπὸ τῶν ΑΔΒ, ἡ ἄρα ὑπὸ τῶν ΒΑΔ γωνία πρὸς
ἥμισυ ὀρθῆς μείζονα λόγον ἔχει ἤπερ ἡ ΒΔ πρὸς τὴν ΔΑ, ὥστε ἡ
ΒΔ τῆς ΔΑ ἐλάσσων ἐστὶν ἢ με΄ μέρος, ὥστε καὶ ἡ ΒΗ τῆς ΒΑ
10 πολλῷ ἐλάσσων ἐστὶν ἢ με΄ μέρος. διελόντι ἡ ΒΗ τῆς ΗΑ
ἐλάσσων ἐστὶν ἢ μδ΄ μέρος, ὥστε καὶ ἡ ΒΘ τῆς ΑΘ πολλῷ

6. ἡμισείας] corr. e μιᾶς, ut videtur, Vat. et Paris. 2342 : μιᾶς F Paris. 2366,
2472 (?), 2488   ⟨με΄⟩ om. Vat. et alii codd.   μέρος] με Paris. 2342 erasis
litteris ρος   10. διελόντι] καὶ διαιρεθέντι W, qui lacunam post 10 ἢ ope
versionis Commandini expleverat

---

[1] This is a particular case of the more general proposition (similarly
assumed by Archimedes in his *Sand-reckoner*) which amounts to the statement
that, if each of the angles α, β is not greater than a right angle, and $\alpha > \beta$, then

$$\frac{\tan\alpha}{\tan\beta} > \frac{\alpha}{\beta}.$$

The proposition is easily proved geometrically (cf. Commandinus on the
passage of the *Sand-reckoner*).

Let BC, BA make with ACD the angles α, β respectively, and let BD be
perpendicular to AD.

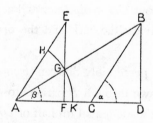

Fig. 22.

Now $\tan\alpha = BD/CD$, $\tan\beta = BD/AD$.
We have therefore to prove that

$$AD : CD > \alpha : \beta.$$

therefore the angle CAD stands on a fifteenth part of a sign.

But a fifteenth part of a sign is 1/180th of the whole circle of the zodiac,

so that the angle CAD stands on 1/180th of the whole circle;

therefore the angle CAD is 1/180th of four right angles.

It follows that the angle CAD is 1/45th of a right angle.

And the angle BAD is half of the angle CAD;

therefore the angle BAD is 1/45th part of half a right angle.

Now, since the angle ADB is right,

the angle BAD has to half a right angle a ratio greater than that which BD has to DA.[1]

Accordingly BD is less than 1/45th part of DA.

Therefore BG is much less[2] than 1/45th part of BA, and, *separando*, BG is less than 1/44th part of GA.

Accordingly BH is also much less than 1/44th part of AH.

Cut off AF equal to CD, and draw FE at right angles to AD and equal to BD. Join AE.

Then $\qquad\qquad \angle EAF = \angle BCD = \alpha.$

Let EF meet AB in G.

Since $AE > AG > AF$, the circle with A as centre and AG as radius will cut AE in H and AF *produced* in K.

Now $\qquad \angle EAG : \angle GAF = $ (sector HAG) : (sector GAK)
$$< \triangle EAG : \triangle GAF$$
$$< EG : GF.$$

Componendo, $\quad \angle EAF : \angle GAF < EF : GF.$

But $\qquad\qquad EF : GF = BD : GF = AD : AF = AD : CD.$

Therefore $\qquad\qquad \alpha : \beta < AD : CD,$

or $\qquad\qquad\qquad AD : CD > \alpha : \beta.$

In the particular application above made by Aristarchus $\alpha = \frac{1}{2}R$, so that $CD = BD$.

In this case therefore $\quad AD : DB > \frac{1}{2}R : \angle BAD,$

or $\qquad\qquad\qquad BD : DA < \angle BAD : \frac{1}{2}R,$

that is to say, $\qquad\qquad \angle BAD : \frac{1}{2}R > BD : DA.$

[2] 'Much less', πολλῷ ἐλάσσων = 'less by much'. πολλῷ μείζων and πολλῷ ἐλάσσων are the traditional expressions used by Euclid and Greek geometers in general for 'a fortiori greater' and 'a fortiori less'. In Euclid the expressions have generally been translated 'much more then is ... greater, or less, than'. But there is no double comparative in the Greek. The idea is that, if a is, let us say, a *little* greater than b, and if c is greater than a, then c must be *much* greater than b.

ἐλάσσων ἐστὶν ἢ μδ´ μέρος. καὶ ἔχει ἡ ΒΘ πρὸς τὴν ΘΑ μείζονα
λόγον ἤπερ ἡ ὑπὸ τῶν ΒΑΘ πρὸς τὴν ὑπὸ τῶν ΑΒΘ· ἡ ἄρα ὑπὸ
τῶν ΒΑΘ τῆς ὑπὸ τῶν ΑΒΘ ἐλάσσων ἐστὶν ἢ μδ´ μέρος. καὶ ἔστιν
τῆς μὲν ὑπὸ τῶν ΒΑΘ διπλῆ ἡ ὑπὸ τῶν ΚΑΘ, τῆς δὲ ὑπὸ τῶν
5 ΑΒΘ διπλῆ ἡ ὑπὸ τῶν ΚΒΘ· ἐλάσσων ἄρα ἐστὶν καὶ ἡ ὑπὸ τῶν
ΚΑΘ τῆς ὑπὸ τῶν ΚΒΘ ἢ τεσσαρακοστοτέταρτον μέρος. ἀλλὰ ἡ
ὑπὸ τῶν ΚΒΘ ἴση ἐστὶ τῇ ὑπὸ τῶν ΔΒΖ, τουτέστιν τῇ ὑπὸ τῶν
ΓΔΒ, τουτέστιν τῇ ὑπὸ τῶν ΒΑΔ· ἡ ἄρα ὑπὸ τῶν ΚΑΘ τῆς ὑπὸ
τῶν ΒΑΔ ἐλάσσων ἐστὶν ἢ μδ´ μέρος. ἡ δὲ ὑπὸ τῶν ΒΑΔ ⟨ἡμισείας⟩
10 ὀρθῆς ἐστιν ⟨με´⟩ μέρος, ὥστε ἡ ὑπὸ τῶν ΚΑΘ ὀρθῆς ἐστιν ἐλάσσων

5, 6. ἐλάσσων . . . ἢ] ⟨ὥστε ἡ ΚΑΘ γωνία τῆς ΚΒΘ γωνίας ἐλάσσων ἐστὶν ἢ⟩ W
9. ⟨ἡμισείας⟩, 10. ⟨με´⟩, supplevit W   10. ⟨τουτέστι τῆς ὀρθῆς ϛ´ μέρος⟩ post μέρος
addidit W

---

[1] This is immediately deducible from a proposition given by Ptolemy
(*Syntaxis*, I. 10, pp. 43–4, ed. Heiberg).

*If two unequal chords are drawn in a circle, the greater has to the lesser
a ratio less than the circumference (standing) on the greater chord has to the
circumference (standing) on the lesser.*

That is, if CB, BA be unequal chords in a circle, and $CB > BA$, then

(chord CB) : (chord BA) < (arc CB) : (arc BA).

Ptolemy's proof is as follows.

Bisect the angle ABC by the straight line BD, meeting the circle again at D.
Join AEC, AD, CD

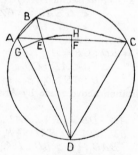

Fig. 23.

Then, since the angle ABC is bisected by BD,

$$CD = AD.$$ [Eucl., iii. 26, 29.]

And $$CE > EA.$$ [Eucl., vi. 3.]

Draw DF perpendicular to AEC.

And BH has to HA a ratio greater than that which the angle BAH has to the angle ABH.[1]

Therefore the angle BAH is less than 1/44th part of the angle ABH.

And the angle KAH is double of the angle BAH,
while the angle KBH is double of the angle ABH;
therefore the angle KAH is also less than 1/44th part of the angle KBH.

But the angle KBH is equal to the angle DBF, that is, to the angle CDB, that is, to the angle BAD.

Therefore the angle KAH is less than 1/44th part of the angle BAD.

But the angle BAD is 1/45th part of half a right angle.

Accordingly the angle KAH is less than 1/396oth of a right angle.[2]

Now, since $DA > DE > DF$, the circle described with D as centre and DE as radius will cut AD between A and D, and will cut DF produced beyond F. Let the circle be drawn.

Since the triangle AED is greater than the sector DEG, and the triangle DEF is less than the sector DEH,

$$\triangle DEF : \triangle DEA < (\text{sector } DEH) : (\text{sector } DEG).$$

Therefore $\qquad FE : EA < \angle FDE : \angle EDA.$ [Eucl., vi. 1 and 33.]

Componendo, $\qquad FA : EA < \angle FDA : \angle EDA.$

Doubling the antecedents, we have

$$CA : AE < \angle CDA : \angle ADE,$$

and, separando, $\qquad CE : EA < \angle CDE : \angle EDA.$

But $\qquad\qquad CE : EA = CB : BA,$

and $\qquad \angle CDE : \angle EDA = (\text{arc } CB) : (\text{arc } BA).$

Therefore $\qquad CB : BA < (\text{arc } CB) : (\text{arc } BA).$

[The proposition is easily seen to be equivalent to the statement that, if α is an angle not greater than a right angle, and β another angle less than α, then

$$\frac{\sin \alpha}{\sin \beta} < \frac{\alpha}{\beta}.]$$

Now, since $\angle CDE = \angle CAB$ and $\angle ADE = \angle ACB$, in the same segments, we have

$$CB : BA < \angle CAB : \angle ACB,$$

or, inversely, $\qquad AB : BC > \angle ACB : \angle BAC,$

which is the property assumed by Aristarchus.

[2] $\frac{1}{2} \cdot \frac{1}{45} \cdot \frac{1}{44} = \frac{1}{3960}.$

ἢ ͵γ λξ'. τὸ δὲ ὑπὸ τηλικαύτης γωνίας ὁρώμενον μέγεθος ἀνεπαίσθητόν ἐστιν τῇ ἡμετέρᾳ ὄψει· καὶ ἔστιν ἴση ἡ ΚΘ περιφέρεια τῇ ΔΖ περιφερείᾳ· ἔτι ἄρα μᾶλλον ἡ ΔΖ περιφέρεια ἀνεπαίσθητός ἐστι τῇ ἡμετέρᾳ ὄψει. ἐὰν γὰρ ἐπιζευχθῇ ἡ ΑΖ, ἡ ὑπὸ τῶν ΖΑΔ
5 γωνία ἐλάσσων ἐστὶ τῆς ὑπὸ τῶν ΚΑΘ. τὸ Δ ἄρα τῷ Ζ τὸ αὐτὸ δόξει εἶναι. διὰ τὰ αὐτὰ δὴ καὶ τὸ Γ τῷ Ε δόξει τὸ αὐτὸ εἶναι· ὥστε καὶ ἡ ΓΔ τῇ ΕΖ ἀνεπαίσθητός ἐστιν. καὶ ὁ διορίζων ἄρα ἐν τῇ σελήνῃ τό τε σκιερὸν καὶ τὸ λαμπρὸν ἀνεπαίσθητός ἐστι τῷ μεγίστῳ.

10   ε'.

Ὅταν ἡ σελήνη διχότομος ἡμῖν φαίνηται, τότε ὁ μέγιστος κύκλος ὁ παρὰ τὸν διορίζοντα ἐν τῇ σελήνῃ τό τε σκιερὸν καὶ τὸ λαμπρὸν νεύει εἰς τὴν ἡμετέραν ὄψιν, τουτέστιν, ὁ παρὰ τὸν διορίζοντα μέγιστος κύκλος καὶ ἡ
15 ἡμετέρα ὄψις ἐν ἑνί εἰσιν ἐπιπέδῳ.

Ἐπεὶ γὰρ διχοτόμου οὔσης τῆς σελήνης φαίνεται ὁ διορίζων τό τε λαμπρὸν καὶ τὸ σκιερὸν τῆς σελήνης κύκλος νεύων εἰς τὴν ἡμετέραν ὄψιν, καὶ αὐτῷ ἀδιάφορος ὁ παρὰ τὸν διορίζοντα μέγιστος κύκλος, ὅταν ἄρα ἡ σελήνη διχότομος ἡμῖν φαίνηται, τότε ὁ μέγιστος κύκλος
20 ὁ παρὰ τὸν διορίζοντα νεύει εἰς τὴν ἡμετέραν ὄψιν.

                              ς'.

Ἡ σελήνη κατώτερον φέρεται τοῦ ἡλίου, καὶ διχότομος οὖσα ἔλασσον τεταρτημορίου ἀπέχει ἀπὸ τοῦ ἡλίου.

Ἔστω γὰρ ἡ ἡμετέρα ὄψις πρὸς τῷ Α, ἡλίου δὲ κέντρον τὸ Β, καὶ
25 ἐπιζευχθεῖσα ἡ ΑΒ ἐκβεβλήσθω, καὶ ἐκβεβλήσθω διὰ τῆς ΑΒ καὶ τοῦ κέντρου τῆς σελήνης διχοτόμου οὔσης ἐπίπεδον· ποιήσει δὴ τομὴν ἐν τῇ σφαίρᾳ, καθ᾽ ἧς φέρεται τὸ κέντρον τοῦ ἡλίου, κύκλον

---

1. ͵γ λξ'] ͵Γ´ρ´ξ' Vat. : ͵γ λξ' μέρος W   7. ἀνεπαίσθητός] sic Vat.   7, 8. καὶ ὁ διορίζων ἄρα ἐν ... ἀνεπαίσθητός ἐστι] ⟨ὁ ἄρα διορίζων κύκλος ἐν ... ἀδιάφορός ἐστι πρὸς αἴσθησιν⟩ supplevit W, qui lacunam in suo codice animadverterat
10. ε'] ς Vat.   13. λαμπρὸν] λαμπρὸν αὐτοῦ W: λαμπρὸν αὐτῆς Nizze   18. ἀδιάφορος] ἀδιάφορός ἐστιν W   19. φαίνηται] WF: φανῆται Vat.
21. ς'] om. Vat.   22. φέρεται] W F Paris. 2364, 2472 (?): φαίνεται Vat. (in ras. sed ν quasi in ρ mutato) Paris. 2366.   24. τῷ] τὸ W

But a magnitude seen under such an angle is imperceptible to our eye.

And the circumference KH is equal to the circumference DF; therefore still more is the circumference DF imperceptible to our eye;

for, if AF be joined, the angle FAD is less than the angle KAH.[1]

Therefore D will seem to be the same with F.

For the same reason, C will also seem to be the same with E.

Accordingly CD is not perceptibly different[2] from EF.

Therefore the circle which divides the dark and the bright portions in the moon is not perceptibly different from a great circle.

PROPOSITION 5.

When the moon appears to us halved, the great circle parallel to the circle which divides the dark and the bright portions in the moon is then in the direction of our eye; that is to say, the great circle parallel to the dividing circle and our eye are in one plane.

For since, when the moon is halved, the circle which divides the bright and the dark portions of the moon is in the direction of our eye [Hypothesis 3], while the great circle parallel to the dividing circle is indistinguishable from it,

therefore, when the moon appears to us halved, the great circle parallel to the dividing circle is then in the direction of our eye.

PROPOSITION 6.

The moon moves (in an orbit) lower than (that of) the sun, and, when it is halved, is distant less than a quadrant from the sun.

For let our eye be at A, and let B be the centre of the sun; let AB be joined and produced, and let a plane be carried through AB and the centre of the moon when halved;

this plane will cut in a great circle the sphere on which the centre of the sun moves.

---

[1] Pappus (pp. 560–8, ed Hultsch) gives an elaborate proof of this proposition depending on two lemmas; the proof, however, in the text as we have it, contains a serious flaw (p. 568. 2–3). But the truth of the assumption in Aristarchus's particular case is so obvious as scarcely to require proof.

[2] ἀνεπαίσθητος is strangely used with dat. as if equivalent to ἀνεπαισθήτως διάφορος or ἀδιάφορος πρὸς αἴσθησιν, 'imperceptibly different from'.

μέγιστον. ποιείτω οὖν τὸν ΓΒΔ κύκλον, καὶ ἀπὸ τοῦ Α τῇ ΑΒ
πρὸς ὀρθὰς ἤχθω ἡ ΓΑΔ· τεταρτημορίου ἄρα ἐστὶν ἡ ΒΔ περιφέρεια. λέγω ὅτι ἡ σελήνη κατώτερον φέρεται τοῦ ἡλίου, καὶ
διχότομος οὖσα ἔλασσον τεταρτημορίου ἀπέχει ἀπὸ τοῦ ἡλίου, τουτ-
5 έστιν, ὅτι τὸ κέντρον ἐστὶν αὐτῆς μεταξὺ τῶν ΒΑ, ΑΔ εὐθειῶν
καὶ τῆς ΔΕΒ περιφερείας.

   Εἰ γὰρ μή, ἔστω τὸ κέντρον αὐτῆς τὸ Ζ μεταξὺ τῶν ΔΑ, ΑΛ
εὐθειῶν, καὶ ἐπεζεύχθω ἡ ΒΖ. ἡ ΒΖ ἄρα ἄξων ἐστὶν τοῦ περι-

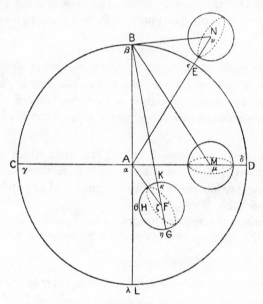

Fig. 24.

λαμβάνοντος κώνου τόν τε ἥλιον καὶ τὴν σελήνην, καὶ γίνεται ἡ
10 ΒΖ ὀρθὴ πρὸς τὸν διορίζοντα ἐν τῇ σελήνῃ τό τε σκιερὸν καὶ τὸ
λαμπρὸν μέγιστον κύκλον. ἔστω οὖν ὁ μέγιστος κύκλος ἐν τῇ
σελήνῃ ὁ παρὰ τὸν διορίζοντα τό τε σκιερὸν καὶ τὸ λαμπρὸν ὁ ΗΘΚ.
καὶ ἐπεὶ διχοτόμου οὔσης τῆς σελήνης ὁ μέγιστος κύκλος ὁ παρὰ
τὸν διορίζοντα ἐν τῇ σελήνῃ τό τε σκιερὸν καὶ τὸ λαμπρὸν καὶ ἡ
15 ἡμετέρα ὄψις ἐν ἑνί εἰσιν ἐπιπέδῳ, ἐπεζεύχθω ἡ ΑΖ· ἡ ΑΖ ἄρα ἐν

1. τὸν] τὸ Vat.   4. ἔλασσον] ἔλαττον Vat.

Let it cut it in the circle CBD; and from A let CAD be drawn at right angles to AB.

Then the circumference BD is that of a quadrant.

I say that the moon moves (in an orbit) lower than (that of) the sun, and, when halved, is distant less than a quadrant from the sun; that is to say, its centre is between the straight lines BA, AD and the circumference DEB.

For, if not, let its centre F be between the straight lines DA, AL, and let BF be joined;

then BF is the axis of the cone which comprehends both the sun and the moon,

and BF is at right angles to the great circle[1] which divides the dark and the bright portions in the moon.

Let the great circle in the moon parallel to the circle which divides the dark and the bright portions be GHK;[2] then since, when the moon is halved, the great circle parallel to the circle which divides the dark and the bright portions in the moon and our eye are in one plane [Prop. 5], let AF be joined.

Therefore AF is in the plane of the circle KGH.

---

[1] It is of course not actually a great circle, but a circle parallel to a great circle, which is however so close to it as to be indistinguishable from a great circle so far as our vision of it is concerned [Prop. 4]. The expression is therefore excusable, as in Hypothesis 3; there is no need to omit μέγιστον from the text as Nizze does.

[2] I have drawn the circle GHK and the other circles representing the sections of the moon as they are drawn in Wallis's figures; but I think the circles in the moon defining the dark and bright portions and, by hypothesis, in the same plane with our eye would be better represented by the dotted circles which I have added to the figure.

τῷ τοῦ *ΚΗΘ* κύκλου ἐστὶν ἐπιπέδῳ. καὶ ἔστιν ἡ *ΒΖ* τῷ *ΚΘΗ*
κύκλῳ πρὸς ὀρθάς, ὥστε καὶ τῇ *ΑΖ*· ὀρθὴ ἄρα ἐστὶν ἡ ὑπὸ *ΒΖΑ*
γωνία. ἀλλὰ καὶ ἀμβλεῖα ἡ ὑπὸ τῶν *ΒΑΖ*· ὅπερ ἀδύνατον. οὐκ
ἄρα τὸ *Ζ* σημεῖον ἐν τῷ ὑπὸ τὴν *ΔΑΔ* γωνίαν τόπῳ ἐστίν.

5 Λέγω ὅτι οὐδὲ ἐπὶ τῆς *ΑΔ*. εἰ γὰρ δυνατόν, ἔστω τὸ *Μ*, καὶ
πάλιν ἐπεζεύχθω ἡ *ΒΜ*, καὶ ἔστω μέγιστος κύκλος ὁ παρὰ τὸν
διορίζοντα, οὗ κέντρον τὸ *Μ*. κατὰ τὰ αὐτὰ δὴ δειχθήσεται ἡ ὑπὸ
ΒΜΑ γωνία ὀρθὴ πρὸς τὸν μέγιστον κύκλον· ἀλλὰ καὶ ἡ ὑπὸ τῶν
ΒΑΜ· ὅπερ ἀδύνατον. οὐκ ἄρα ἐπὶ τῆς *ΑΔ* τὸ κέντρον ἐστὶ τῆς
10 σελήνης διχοτόμου οὔσης· μεταξὺ ἄρα τῶν *ΑΒ*, *ΑΔ* ἐστίν.

Λέγω δὴ ὅτι καὶ ἐντὸς τῆς *ΒΔ* περιφερείας. εἰ γὰρ δυνατόν,
ἔστω ἐκτὸς κατὰ τὸ *Ν*, καὶ τὰ αὐτὰ κατεσκευάσθω. δειχθήσεται δὴ
ἡ ὑπὸ τῶν *ΒΝΑ* γωνία ὀρθή· μείζων ἄρα ἐστὶν ἡ *ΒΑ* τῆς *ΑΝ*.
ἴση δὲ ἡ *ΒΑ* τῇ *ΑΕ*· μείζων ἄρα ἐστὶν καὶ ἡ *ΑΕ* τῆς *ΑΝ*· ὅπερ
15 ἀδύνατον. οὐκ ἄρα τὸ κέντρον τῆς σελήνης διχοτόμου οὔσης ἐκτὸς
ἔσται τῆς *ΒΕΔ* περιφερείας. ὁμοίως δειχθήσεται ὅτι οὐδὲ ἐπʼ
αὐτῆς τῆς *ΒΕΔ* περιφερείας· ἐντὸς ἄρα. ἡ ἄρα σελήνη κατώτερον
φέρεται τοῦ ἡλίου, καὶ διχότομος οὖσα ἔλασσον τεταρτημορίου
ἀπέχει ἀπὸ τοῦ ἡλίου.

1. *ΚΘΗ*] *ΚΗΘ* W   2. ὑπὸ] ὑπὸ ⟨τῶν⟩ W   4. τὴν *ΔΑΔ* γωνίαν]
inusitato sane dicendi more : τὴν ⟨ὑπὸ τῶν⟩ *ΔΑΔ* γωνίαν W, sed dubito an ipse
Aristarchus ὑπὸ τὴν ὑπὸ τῶν scripserit   11. *ΒΔ*] *ΒΕΔ* W   12. κατε-
σκευάσθω] κατασκευάσθω Vat.   13. γωνία] om. W   14. καὶ] om. W
17. ἐντὸς] W F Paris. 2364, 2472 (?) : ἐκτὸς Vat. in ras., Paris. 2363

---

[1] The phrase in the Greek text, κατὰ τὰ αὐτὰ δὴ δειχθήσεται ἡ ὑπὸ *ΒΜΑ* γωνία
ὀρθὴ πρὸς τὸν μέγιστον κύκλον, is strange. Literally this would appear to mean
'In the same way it can be proved that the *angle BMA* is *at right angles* to
the great circle', but this is intolerable. If we took 'the angle *BMA* ' to be
the *plane* of the angle, the expression would be possible, but it would not give
the meaning which is required, namely that the angle *BMA* is a right angle
because *BM* is at right angles to the plane of the circle and therefore to any
straight line in the plane of the circle, such as *AM*, passing through *M*. The

And BF is at right angles to the circle KHG, and therefore to AF; therefore the angle BFA is right.

But the angle BAF is also obtuse: which is impossible.

Therefore the point F is not in the space bounded by the angle DAL.

I say that neither is it on AD.

For, if possible, let it be M; and again let BM be joined, and let the great circle parallel to the dividing circle be taken, its centre being M. •

Then, in the same way as before, it can be proved that the angle BMA [made with the great circle] [1] is right.

But the angle BAM is so also: which is impossible.

Therefore the centre of the moon, when halved, is not on AD.

Therefore it is between AB and AD.

Again, I say that it is also within the circumference BD.

For, if possible, let it be outside, at N;
and let the same construction be made.

It can then be proved that the angle BNA is right; therefore BA is greater than AN.

But BA is equal to AE;
therefore AE is also greater than AN: which is impossible.

Therefore the centre of the moon, when halved, will not be outside the circumference BED.

Similarly it can be proved that neither will it be on the circumference BED itself.

Therefore it will be within.

Therefore, &c.

---

words πρὸς τὸν μέγιστον κύκλον are in fact not wanted, and, if they are retained, cannot be taken with ὀρθή in the sense of 'at right angles to the great circle'; they can only be taken closely with γωνία and as meaning 'towards the great circle', or 'made with the great circle'. But, as the words do not occur in the corresponding passage about the angle BNA lower down, I think they should be struck out, as an interpolation by some one who thought the inference wanted some further explanation but failed to supply it intelligibly.

ζ´.

Τὸ ἀπόστημα ὃ ἀπέχει ὁ ἥλιος ἀπὸ τῆς γῆς τοῦ ἀποστήματος οὗ ἀπέχει ἡ σελήνη ἀπὸ τῆς γῆς μεῖζον μέν
ἐστιν ἢ ὀκτωκαιδεκαπλάσιον, ἔλασσον δὲ ἢ εἰκοσαπλάσιον.

5 Ἔστω γὰρ ἡλίου μὲν κέντρον τὸ Α, γῆς δὲ τὸ Β, καὶ ἐπιζευχθεῖσα
ἡ ΑΒ ἐκβεβλήσθω, σελήνης δὲ κέντρον διχοτόμου οὔσης τὸ Γ, καὶ
ἐκβεβλήσθω διὰ τῆς ΑΒ καὶ τοῦ Γ ἐπίπεδον, καὶ ποιείτω τομὴν ἐν
τῇ σφαίρᾳ, καθ᾽ ἧς φέρεται τὸ κέντρον τοῦ ἡλίου, μέγιστον κύκλον
τὸν ΑΔΕ, καὶ ἐπεζεύχθωσαν αἱ ΑΓ, ΓΒ, καὶ ἐκβεβλήσθω ἡ ΒΓ
10 ἐπὶ τὸ Δ. ἔσται δή, διὰ τὸ τὸ Γ σημεῖον κέντρον εἶναι τῆς σελήνης
διχοτόμου οὔσης, ὀρθὴ ἡ ὑπὸ τῶν ΑΓΒ. ἤχθω δὴ ἀπὸ τοῦ Β τῇ
ΒΑ πρὸς ὀρθὰς ἡ ΒΕ. ἔσται δὴ ἡ ΕΔ περιφέρεια τῆς ΕΔΑ
περιφερείας λ´· ὑπόκειται γάρ, ὅταν ἡ σελήνη διχότομος ἡμῖν φαίνηται, ἀπέχειν ἀπὸ τοῦ ἡλίου ἔλασσον τεταρτημορίου τῷ τοῦ
15 τεταρτημορίου λ´· ὥστε καὶ ἡ ὑπὸ τῶν ΕΒΓ γωνία ὀρθῆς ἐστι λ´.
συμπεπληρώσθω δὴ τὸ ΑΕ παραλληλόγραμμον, καὶ ἐπεζεύχθω ἡ
ΒΖ. ἔσται δὴ ἡ ὑπὸ τῶν ΖΒΕ γωνία ἡμίσεια ὀρθῆς. τετμήσθω
ἡ ὑπὸ τῶν ΖΒΕ γωνία δίχα τῇ ΒΗ εὐθείᾳ· ἡ ἄρα ὑπὸ τῶν ΗΒΕ
γωνία τέταρτον μέρος ἐστὶν ὀρθῆς. ἀλλὰ καὶ ἡ ὑπὸ τῶν ΔΒΕ
20 γωνία λ´ ἐστι μέρος ὀρθῆς· λόγος ἄρα τῆς ὑπὸ τῶν ΗΒΕ γωνίας
πρὸς τὴν ὑπὸ τῶν ΔΒΕ γωνίαν ⟨ἐστὶν⟩ ὃν ⟨ἔχει⟩ τὰ ιε πρὸς τὰ δύο·
οἵων γάρ ἐστιν ὀρθὴ γωνία ξ, τοιούτων ἐστὶν ἡ μὲν ὑπὸ τῶν ΗΒΕ ιε,
ἡ δὲ ὑπὸ τῶν ΔΒΕ δύο. καὶ ἐπεὶ ἡ ΗΕ πρὸς τὴν ΕΘ μείζονα
λόγον ἔχει ἤπερ ἡ ὑπὸ τῶν ΗΒΕ γωνία πρὸς τὴν ὑπὸ τῶν ΔΒΕ

---

3. οὗ] ὃ W F Nizze, sed nihil mutandum   4. εἰκοσαπλάσιον] εἰκοσιπλάσιον
W   6. τὸ Γ] ⟨ἔστω⟩ τὸ Γ Nizze   9. ΒΓ] ΓΒ W   12. ΒΕ] add.
καὶ ἐκβεβλήσθω ἡ ΒΓ ἐπὶ τὸ Δ Vat. Paris. 2364, 2366, 2472 (?)   13. λ´] τριακοστόν W   14. τῷ] om. W   15. λ´] τριακοστῷ W   τῶν] τὴν Vat.
λ´] τριακοστόν W   18. ὑπὸ τῶν (ad init.)] ὑπὸ W   20. λ´] τριακοστόν W
21. γωνίαν] γωνίαν ⟨ἐστὶν⟩ Nizze   ἔχει] om. Vat.   23. ἡ δὲ ὑπὸ τῶν] ἡ δὲ W

PROPOSITION 7.

The distance of the sun from the earth is greater than eighteen times, but less than twenty times, the distance of the moon from the earth.

For let A be the centre of the sun, B that of the earth.

Let AB be joined and produced.

Let C be the centre of the moon when halved;
let a plane be carried through AB and C, and let the section made by it in the sphere on which the centre of the sun moves be the great circle ADE.

Let AC, CB be joined, and let BC be produced to D.

Then, because the point C is the centre of the moon when halved, the angle ACB will be right.

Let BE be drawn from B at right angles to BA ;
then the circumference ED will be one-thirtieth of the circumference EDA ;
for, by hypothesis, when the moon appears to us halved, its distance from the sun is less than a quadrant by one-thirtieth of a quadrant [Hypothesis 4].

Thus the angle EBC is also one-thirtieth of a right angle.

Let the parallelogram AE be completed, and let BF be joined.

Then the angle FBE will be half a right angle.

Let the angle FBE be bisected by the straight line BG ;
therefore the angle GBE is one fourth part of a right angle.

But the angle DBE is also one thirtieth part of a right angle ;
therefore the ratio of the angle GBE to the angle DBE is that which 15 has to 2 :
for, if a right angle be regarded as divided into 60 equal parts, the angle GBE contains 15 of such parts, and the angle DBE contains 2.

Now, since GE has to EH a ratio greater than that which the angle GBE has to the angle DBE,[1]

---

[1] The proposition assumed is again the equivalent of the fact that $\dfrac{\tan \alpha}{\tan \beta} > \dfrac{\alpha}{\beta}$, where each of the angles α, β is not greater than a right angle and $\alpha > \beta$. (Cf. note on pp. 366-7, above.) Let the angles α, β be the angles GBE, HBE respectively in the subjoined figure (Fig. 26). Let GE be perpendicular to BE

γωνίαν, ἡ ἄρα ΗΕ πρὸς τὴν ΕΘ μείζονα λόγον ἔχει ἤπερ τὰ ιε
πρὸς τὰ β. καὶ ἐπεὶ ἴση ἐστὶν ἡ ΒΕ τῇ ΕΖ, καὶ ἔστιν ὀρθὴ ἡ
πρὸς τῷ Ε, τὸ ἄρα ἀπὸ τῆς ΖΒ τοῦ ἀπὸ ΒΕ διπλάσιόν ἐστιν·
ὡς δὲ τὸ ἀπὸ ΖΒ πρὸς τὸ ἀπὸ ΒΕ, οὕτως ἐστὶ τὸ ἀπὸ ΖΗ πρὸς τὸ
5 ἀπὸ ΗΕ· τὸ ἄρα ἀπὸ ΖΗ τοῦ ἀπὸ ΗΕ διπλάσιόν ἐστι. τὰ δὲ μθ
τῶν κε ἐλάσσονά ἐστιν ἢ διπλάσια, ὥστε τὸ ἀπὸ ΖΗ πρὸς τὸ ἀπὸ

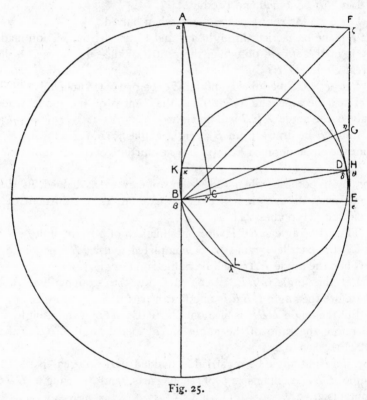

Fig. 25.

ΗΕ μείζονα λόγον ἔχει ἢ ⟨ὃν τὰ⟩ μθ πρὸς κε· καὶ ἡ ΖΗ
ἄρα πρὸς τὴν ΗΕ μείζονα λόγον ἔχει ἢ ⟨ὃν⟩ τὰ ζ πρὸς τὰ ε· καὶ
συνθέντι ἡ ΖΕ ἄρα πρὸς τὴν ΕΗ μείζονα λόγον ἔχει ἢ ὃν τὰ ιβ
10 πρὸς τὰ ε, τουτέστιν, ἢ ὃν ⟨τὰ⟩ λϛ πρὸς τὰ ιε. ἐδείχθη δὲ καὶ ἡ

2. β] δύο W   3. ΒΕ] τῆς ΒΕ W   7. ⟨ὃν τὰ⟩] om. Vat.   κε] τὰ
κε W   8. ⟨ὃν⟩] om. Vat.   9. ἔχει] ἔχουσα W   10. ⟨τὰ⟩]
om. Vat.   δὲ] δὴ W

therefore GE has to EH a ratio greater than that which 15 has to 2.

Next, since BE is equal to EF, and the angle at E is right, therefore the square on FB is double of the square on BE.

But, as the square on FB is to the square on BE, so is the square on FG to the square on GE;

therefore the square on FG is double of the square on GE.

Now 49 is less than double[1] of 25,

so that the square on FG has to the square on GE a ratio greater than that which 49 has to 25;

therefore FG also has to GE a ratio greater than that which 7 has to 5.

Therefore, *componendo*, FE has to EG a ratio greater than that which 12 has to 5, that is, than that which 36 has to 15.

and let it meet BH in H. Let a circle be described with B as centre and BH as radius, meeting BG in P and BE produced in Q.

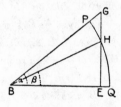

Fig. 26.

Then $\quad\quad \triangle\, GBH : \triangle\, HBE > $ (sector PBH) : (sector HBQ);

therefore $\quad\quad\quad GH : HE > \angle GBH : \angle HBE,$

and, *componendo*, $\quad GE : HE > \angle GBE : \angle HBE.$

[1] Aristarchus here uses the well-known Pythagorean approximation to $\sqrt{2}$, namely $\frac{7}{5}$, one of the first of the successive approximations obtained by the development of the system of 'side-' and 'diagonal-' numbers (as to which see Theon of Smyrna, pp. 43, 44, ed. Hiller, and Proclus, *Comm. in Platonis rempublicam*, ed. Kroll, vol. ii, pp. 24, 25, 27-9, 393-400). The approximation $\frac{7}{5}$ is alluded to by Plato in the *Republic*, 546 C. Plato there speaks of the diagonal of the square, the side of which contains 5 units, and contrasts the 'irrational diameter of 5' (ἄρρητος διάμετρος τῆς πεμπάδος), which is of course $\sqrt{(50)}$, with the 'rational diameter' (ῥητὴ διάμετρος), which is the square root of 50 less a single unit, i.e. the square root of 49.

ΗΕ πρὸς τὴν *ΕΘ* μείζονα λόγον ἔχουσα ἢ ὃν τὰ ιε πρὸς τὰ δύο·
δι' ἴσου ἄρα ἡ *ΖΕ* πρὸς τὴν *ΕΘ* μείζονα λόγον ἔχει ἢ ὃν τὰ λϛ
πρὸς τὰ δύο, τουτέστιν, ἢ ὃν τὰ ιη πρὸς α· ἡ ἄρα *ΖΕ* τῆς *ΕΘ*
μείζων ἐστὶν ἢ ιη. ἡ δὲ *ΖΕ* ἴση ἐστὶν τῇ *ΒΕ*· καὶ ἡ *ΒΕ* ἄρα τῆς
5 *ΕΘ* μείζων ἐστὶν ἢ ιη· πολλῷ ἄρα ἡ *ΒΘ* τῆς *ΘΕ* μείζων ἐστὶν ἢ
ιη. ἀλλ' ὡς ἡ *ΒΘ* πρὸς τὴν *ΘΕ*, οὕτως ἐστὶν ἡ *ΑΒ* πρὸς τὴν *ΒΓ*,
διὰ τὴν ὁμοιότητα τῶν τριγώνων· καὶ ἡ *ΑΒ* ἄρα τῆς *ΒΓ* μείζων
ἐστὶν ἢ ιη. καὶ ἔστιν ἡ μὲν *ΑΒ* τὸ ἀπόστημα ὃ ἀπέχει ὁ ἥλιος ἀπὸ
τῆς γῆς, ἡ δὲ *ΓΒ* τὸ ἀπόστημα ὃ ἀπέχει ἡ σελήνη ἀπὸ τῆς γῆς· τὸ
10 ἄρα ἀπόστημα ὃ ἀπέχει ὁ ἥλιος ἀπὸ τῆς γῆς τοῦ ἀποστήματος, οὗ
ἀπέχει ἡ σελήνη ἀπὸ τῆς γῆς, μεῖζόν ἐστιν ἢ ιη.

Λέγω δὴ ὅτι καὶ ἔλασσον ἢ κ. ἤχθω γὰρ διὰ τοῦ *Δ* τῇ *ΕΒ*
παράλληλος ἡ *ΔΚ*, καὶ περὶ τὸ *ΔΚΒ* τρίγωνον κύκλος γεγράφθω ὁ
ΔΚΒ· ἔσται δὴ αὐτοῦ διάμετρος ἡ *ΔΒ*, διὰ τὸ ὀρθὴν εἶναι τὴν πρὸς
15 τῷ *Κ* γωνίαν. καὶ ἐνηρμόσθω ἡ *ΒΔ* ἑξαγώνου. καὶ ἐπεὶ ἡ ὑπὸ
τῶν *ΔΒΕ* γωνία λ' ἐστιν ὀρθῆς, καὶ ἡ ὑπὸ τῶν *ΒΔΚ* ἄρα λ' ἐστιν
ὀρθῆς· ἡ ἄρα *ΒΚ* περιφέρεια ξ' ἐστιν τοῦ ὅλου κύκλου. ἔστιν δὲ
καὶ ἡ *ΒΔ* ἕκτον μέρος τοῦ ὅλου κύκλου· ἡ ἄρα *ΒΔ* περιφέρεια τῆς
ΒΚ περιφερείας ι ἐστίν. καὶ ἔχει ἡ *ΒΔ* περιφέρεια πρὸς τὴν *ΒΚ*
20 περιφέρειαν μείζονα λόγον ἤπερ ἡ *ΒΔ* εὐθεῖα πρὸς τὴν *ΒΚ* εὐθεῖαν·
ἡ ἄρα *ΒΔ* εὐθεῖα τῆς *ΒΚ* εὐθείας ἐλάσσων ἐστὶν ἢ ι. καὶ ἔστιν
αὐτῆς διπλῆ ἡ *ΒΔ*· ἡ ἄρα *ΒΔ* τῆς *ΒΚ* ἐλάσσων ἐστὶν ἢ κ. ὡς δὲ
ἡ *ΒΔ* πρὸς τὴν *ΒΚ*, ἡ *ΑΒ* πρὸς ⟨τὴν⟩ *ΒΓ*, ὥστε καὶ ἡ *ΑΒ* τῆς
ΒΓ ἐλάσσων ἐστὶν ἢ κ. καὶ ἔστιν ἡ μὲν *ΑΒ* τὸ ἀπόστημα ὃ
25 ἀπέχει ὁ ἥλιος ἀπὸ τῆς γῆς, ἡ δὲ *ΒΓ* τὸ ἀπόστημα ὃ ἀπέχει
ἡ σελήνη ἀπὸ τῆς γῆς· τὸ ἄρα ἀπόστημα ὃ ἀπέχει ὁ ἥλιος ἀπὸ τῆς
γῆς τοῦ ἀποστήματος, οὗ ἀπέχει ἡ σελήνη ἀπὸ τῆς γῆς, ἔλασσόν
ἐστιν ἢ κ. ἐδείχθη δὲ καὶ μεῖζον ἢ ιη.

1. *ΗΕ*] *ΕΗ* W   4, 5, 6. 8. ιη] ὀκτωκαιδεκαπλασίων W   8. τὸ] om. W
10. οὗ] ὁ W F Nizze, sed cf. l. 3, p. 376   11. μεῖζον] μείζων W   ιη] ὀκτωκαιδεκαπλάσιον W   12. κ] εἰκοσιπλάσιον W   τοῦ⟨τὸ⟩ W   13. *ΔΚΒ*]
ΔΒΚ W   15. τῷ] τὸ W   *Κ*] *Γ* Vat.   16. λ' (bis) τριακοστόν W   17. ξ']
ἑξακοστόν W   19, 21. ι] δεκαπλασίων W   22, 24. κ] εἰκοσιπλασίων W
22. ὡς] ὥστε W   23. ἡ *ΑΒ* (prius)] οὕτως ἡ *ΑΒ* W   ⟨τὴν⟩] om. Vat. Paris.
2366, leg. Paris. 2364, 2488   27. οὗ] ὁ W F Nizze, sed cf. l. 3, p. 376
28. κ] εἰκοσιπλάσιον W   μεῖζον] μείζων W Vat.   ιη] ὀκτωκαιδεκαπλάσιον W

But it was also proved that *GE* has to *EH* a ratio greater than that which 15 has to 2;
therefore, *ex aequali*, *FE* has to *EH* a ratio greater than that which 36 has to 2, that is, than that which 18 has to 1;
therefore *FE* is greater than 18 times *EH*.

And *FE* is equal to *BE*;
therefore *BE* is also greater than 18 times *EH*;
therefore *BH* is much greater than 18 times *HE*.

But, as *BH* is to *HE*, so is *AB* to *BC*, because of the similarity of the triangles;
therefore *AB* is also greater than 18 times *BC*.

And *AB* is the distance of the sun from the earth, while *CB* is the distance of the moon from the earth; therefore the distance of the sun from the earth is greater than 18 times the distance of the moon from the earth.

Again, I say that it is also less than 20 times that distance.

For let *DK* be drawn through *D* parallel to *EB*, and about the triangle *DKB* let the circle *DKB* be described; then *DB* will be its diameter, because the angle at *K* is right.

Let *BL*, the side of a hexagon, be fitted into the circle.

Then, since the angle *DBE* is 1/30th of a right angle, the angle *BDK* is also 1/30th of a right angle;
therefore the circumference *BK* is 1/60th of the whole circle.

But *BL* is also one sixth part of the whole circle.

Therefore the circumference *BL* is ten times the circumference *BK*.

And the circumference *BL* has to the circumference *BK* a ratio greater than that which the straight line *BL* has to the straight line *BK*;[1]
therefore the straight line *BL* is less than ten times the straight line *BK*.

And *BD* is double of *BL*;
therefore *BD* is less than 20 times *BK*.

But, as *BD* is to *BK*, so is *AB* to *BC*;
therefore *AB* is also less than 20 times *BC*.

And *AB* is the distance of the sun from the earth,
while *BC* is the distance of the moon from the earth;
therefore the distance of the sun from the earth is less than 20 times the distance of the moon from the earth.

And it was before proved that it is greater than 18 times that distance.

[1] By the proposition proved in Ptolemy's *Syntaxis*, i, 10, pp. 43-4, ed. Heiberg. See, for his proof, the note on pp. 368-9, above.

η'.

Ὅταν ὁ ἥλιος ἐκλείπῃ ὅλος, τότε ὁ αὐτὸς κῶνος περιλαμβάνει τόν τε ἥλιον καὶ τὴν σελήνην, τὴν κορυφὴν
ἔχων πρὸς τῇ ἡμετέρᾳ ὄψει.

5 Ἐπεὶ γάρ, ἐὰν ἐκλείπῃ ὁ ἥλιος, δι' ἐπιπρόσθεσιν τῆς σελήνης
ἐκλείπει, ἐμπίπτοι ἂν ὁ ἥλιος εἰς τὸν κῶνον τὸν περιλαμβάνοντα τὴν
σελήνην τὴν κορυφὴν ἔχοντα πρὸς τῇ ἡμετέρᾳ ὄψει. ἐμπίπτων δὲ
ἤτοι ἐναρμόσει εἰς αὐτόν, ἢ ὑπεραίροι, ἢ ἐλλείποι· εἰ μὲν οὖν
ὑπεραίροι, οὐκ ⟨ἂν⟩ ἐκλείποι ὅλος, ἀλλὰ παραλλάττοι αὐτοῦ τὸ
10 ὑπεραῖρον. εἰ δὲ ἐλλείποι, διαμένοι ἂν ἐκλελοιπὼς ἐν ὅσῳ διεξ-
έρχεται τὸ ἐλλεῖπον. ὅλος δὲ ἐκλείπει καὶ οὐ διαμένει ἐκλελοιπώς·
τοῦτο γὰρ ἐκ τῆς τηρήσεως φανερόν. ὥστε οὔτ' ἂν ὑπεραίροι, οὔτε
ἐλλείποι. ἐναρμόσει ἄρα εἰς τὸν κῶνον, καὶ περιληφθήσεται ὑπὸ
τοῦ κώνου τοῦ περιλαμβάνοντος τὴν σελήνην τὴν κορυφὴν ἔχοντος
15 πρὸς τῇ ἡμετέρᾳ ὄψει.

θ'.

Ἡ τοῦ ἡλίου διάμετρος τῆς διαμέτρου τῆς σελήνης
μείζων μέν ἐστιν ἢ ιη, ἐλάσσων δὲ ἢ κ.

Ἔστω γὰρ ἡ μὲν ἡμετέρα ὄψις πρὸς τῷ Α, ἡλίου δὲ κέντρον τὸ
20 Β, σελήνης δὲ κέντρον τὸ Γ, ὅταν ὁ περιλαμβάνων κῶνος τόν τε
ἥλιον καὶ τὴν σελήνην τὴν κορυφὴν ἔχῃ πρὸς τῇ ἡμετέρᾳ ὄψει,
τουτέστιν, ὅταν τὰ Α, Γ, Β σημεῖα ἐπ' εὐθείας ᾖ, καὶ ἐκβεβλήσθω
διὰ τῆς ΑΓΒ ἐπίπεδον· ποιήσει δὴ τομάς, ἐν μὲν ταῖς σφαίραις

1. η'] om. Vat.   7. πρὸς τῇ ἡμετέρᾳ ὄψει] πρὸς τὴν ἡμετέραν ὄψιν Vat.
8. ἐναρμόσει] ἐναρμώσει Vat.   ἐλλείποι] ἐλλείπει Paris. 2364 : ἐκλείποι F Paris.
2488   9. οὐκ ⟨ἂν⟩ ἐκλείποι] συνεκλείποι Vat. p. m. : οὐκ ἐκλείποι Vat. corr.
(οὐκ supra lineam scripto) F Paris. 2488 : οὐσυνεκλείποι Paris. 2366 : οὐκ ἐκλείπει
Paris. 2342, 2364 : οὐκ ἐλλείπει W Paris.   10. ἐλλείποι] ἐλλείπει W Paris. 2364 :
ἐκλείποι F Paris. 2342, 2488   13. ἐλλείποι] ἐκλείποι F Paris. 2488 : ἐλλείπει
Paris. 2364
16. θ'] H Vat.   18. ιη] ὀκτωκαιδεκαπλασίων W   κ] εἰκοσιπλασίων W
21. ἔχῃ] ἔχει Vat.

PROPOSITION 8.

When the sun is totally eclipsed, the sun and the moon are then comprehended by one and the same cone which has its vertex at our eye.

For since, if the sun is eclipsed, it is eclipsed because the moon is in front of it,
the sun must fall into the cone comprehending the moon and having its vertex at our eye.

And, if it falls into it, either it will exactly fit into it, or it must overlap it or fall short of it.

If now it should overlap it, the sun would not be totally eclipsed, but the portion which overlaps would be unobstructed.[1]

If, however, it should fall short, the sun would remain eclipsed for the time which it takes to pass through the portion by which it falls short.

But it is in fact totally eclipsed and does not remain eclipsed: for this is manifest from observation.[2]

Hence it can neither overlap nor fall short;
therefore it will exactly fit into the cone and will be comprehended by the cone comprehending the moon and having its vertex at our eye.

PROPOSITION 9.

The diameter of the sun is greater than 18 *times, but less than* 20 *times, the diameter of the moon.*

For let our eye be at A, let B be the centre of the sun, and C the centre of the moon when the cone comprehending both the sun and the moon has its vertex at our eye, that is, when the points A, C, B are in a straight line.

Let a plane be carried through ACB;
this plane will cut the spheres in great circles and the cone in straight lines.

---

[1] Gr. παραλλάττοι. As in Euclid, i. 7 and iii. 24, παραλλάττειν means to 'fall beside' or 'awry', to 'miss', to 'pass by without touching'.

[2] It is evident from this that Aristarchus had not observed the phenomenon of an *annular* eclipse of the sun. The first mention of annular eclipses on record appears to be that quoted by Simplicius (on *De caelo*, ii. 12, p. 505, 7-9, Heiberg) from Sosigenes, the teacher of Alexander Aphrodisiensis (end of second century A.D.).

μεγίστους κύκλους, ἐν δὲ τῷ κώνῳ εὐθείας. ποιείτω οὖν ἐν μὲν ταῖς σφαίραις μεγίστους κύκλους τοὺς ΖΗ, ΚΛΘ, ἐν δὲ τῷ κώνῳ εὐθείας τὰς ΑΖΘ, ΑΗΚ, καὶ ἐπεζεύχθωσαν αἱ ΓΗ, ΒΚ. ἔσται

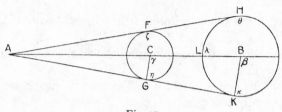

Fig. 27.

δή, ὡς ἡ ΒΑ πρὸς τὴν ΑΓ, ἡ ΒΚ πρὸς ΓΗ. ἡ δὲ ΒΑ τῆς ΑΓ
5 ἐδείχθη μείζων μὲν ἢ ιη, ἐλάσσων δὲ ἢ κ. καὶ ἡ ΒΚ ἄρα τῆς ΓΗ
μείζων μέν ἐστιν ἢ ιη, ἐλάσσων δὲ ἢ κ.

ι'.

Ὁ ἥλιος πρὸς τὴν σελήνην μείζονα μὲν λόγον ἔχει ἢ
ὃν τὰ ϛωλβ πρὸς α, ἐλάσσονα δὲ ἢ ὃν τὰ ͵η πρὸς α.

10 Εστω ἡ μὲν τοῦ ἡλίου διάμετρος ἡ Α, ἡ δὲ τῆς σελήνης ἡ Β.
ἡ Α ἄρα πρὸς τὴν Β μείζονα λόγον ἔχει ἢ ὃν τὰ ιη πρὸς α,
ἐλάσσονα δὲ ἢ ὃν τὰ κ πρὸς α. καὶ ἐπειδὴ ὁ ἀπὸ τῆς Α κύβος πρὸς
τὸν ἀπὸ τῆς Β κύβον γ λόγον ἔχει ἤπερ ἡ Α πρὸς τὴν Β, ἔχει δὲ
καὶ ἡ περὶ διάμετρον τὴν Α σφαῖρα πρὸς τὴν περὶ διάμετρον τὴν Β
15 σφαῖραν γ λόγον ἤπερ ἡ Α πρὸς τὴν Β, ἔστιν ἄρα, ὡς ἡ περὶ
διάμετρον τὴν Α σφαῖρα πρὸς τὴν περὶ διάμετρον τὴν Β σφαῖραν,
οὕτως ὁ ἀπὸ τῆς Α κύβος πρὸς τὸν ἀπὸ τῆς Β κύβον. ὁ δὲ ἀπὸ τῆς
Α κύβος πρὸς *τὸν ἀπὸ τῆς Β κύβον μείζονα λόγον ἔχει ἢ ὃν τὰ
ϛωλβ πρὸς α, ἐλάσσονα δὲ ἢ ὃν τὰ ͵η πρὸς α, ἐπειδὴ ἡ Α πρὸς τὴν
20 Β μείζονα λόγον ἔχει ἢ ὃν τὰ ιη πρὸς α, ἐλάσσονα δὲ ἢ ὃν τὰ κ
πρὸς ἕν· ὥστε ὁ ἥλιος πρὸς τὴν σελήνην μείζονα λόγον ἔχει ἤπερ τὰ
ϛωλβ πρὸς α, ἐλάσσονα δὲ ἢ ὃν τὰ ͵η πρὸς α.

1. εὐθείας] W Paris. 2364: εὐθείαν F Vat. Paris. 2366, 2488   μὲν] om. W
2. τῷ κώνῳ] τοῖς κώνοις Vat. Paris. 2366, 2488   4. ἡ ΒΚ] ⟨οὕτως⟩ ἡ ΒΚ Nizze
ΓΗ] τὴν ΓΗ W   5. ἢ ιη] ηι Vat.   6. ἢ ιη] ιη Vat.
7. ι'] Θ Vat.   13, 15. γ] sic Vat. pro τριπλασίονα: τριπλασίονα W
14. πρὸς τὴν] πρὸς τὴν Β Vat.   21. ἕν] α W

Let it cut the spheres in the great circles FG, KLH, and the cone in the straight lines AFH, AGK,
and let CG, BK be joined.

Then, as BA is to AC, so will BK be to CG.

But it was proved that BA is greater than 18 times, but less than 20 times, AC.   [Prop. 7]

Therefore BK is also greater than 18 times, but less than 20 times, CG.

PROPOSITION 10.

The sun has to the moon a ratio greater than that which 5832 has to 1, but less than that which 8000 has to 1.

Let A be the diameter of the sun, B that of the moon.

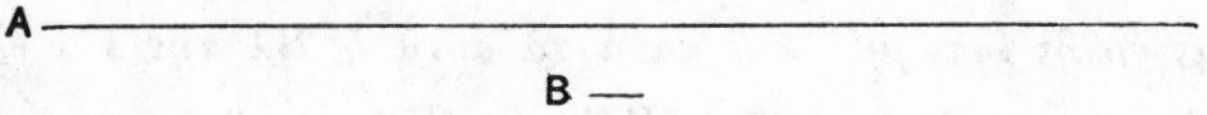

A —————————————————————————————

B —

Fig. 28.

Then A has to B a ratio greater than that which 18 has to 1, but less than that which 20 has to 1.

Now, since the cube on A has to the cube on B the ratio triplicate of that which A has to B,
while the sphere about A as diameter also has to the sphere about B as diameter the ratio triplicate of that which A has to B,
therefore, as the sphere about A as diameter is to the sphere about B as diameter, so is the cube on A to the cube on B.

But the cube on A has to the cube on B a ratio greater than that which 5832 has to 1, but less than that which 8000 has to 1, since A has to B a ratio greater than that which 18 has to 1, but less than that which 20 has to 1.

Accordingly the sun has to the moon a ratio greater than that which 5832 has to 1, but less than that which 8000 has to 1.

ια'.

Ἡ τῆς σελήνης διάμετρος τοῦ ἀποστήματος, οὗ ἀπέχει τὸ κέντρον τῆς σελήνης ἀπὸ τῆς ἡμετέρας ὄψεως, ἐλάσσων μέν ἐστιν ἢ δύο με', μείζων δὲ ἢ λ'.

5 Ἔστω γὰρ ἡ μὲν ἡμετέρα ὄψις πρὸς τῷ Α, σελήνης δὲ κέντρον τὸ Β, ὅταν ὁ περιλαμβάνων κῶνος τόν τε ἥλιον καὶ τὴν σελήνην τὴν κορυφὴν ἔχῃ πρὸς τῇ ἡμετέρᾳ ὄψει. λέγω ὅτι γίγνεται τὰ διὰ τῆς προτάσεως.

Ἐπεζεύχθω γὰρ ἡ ΑΒ, καὶ ἐκβεβλήσθω τὸ διὰ τῆς ΑΒ ἐπίπεδον· 10 ποιήσει δὴ τομὴν ἐν μὲν τῇ σφαίρᾳ κύκλον, ἐν δὲ τῷ κώνῳ εὐθείας. ποιείτω οὖν ἐν μὲν τῇ σφαίρᾳ κύκλον τὸν ΓΕΔ, ἐν δὲ τῷ κώνῳ εὐθείας τὰς ΑΔ, ΑΓ, καὶ ἐπεζεύχθω ἡ ΒΓ, καὶ διήχθω ἐπὶ τὸ Ε. φανερὸν δὴ ἐκ τοῦ προδεδειγμένου ὅτι ἡ ὑπὸ τῶν ΒΑΓ γωνία ἡμισείας ὀρθῆς ἐστι με'· καὶ κατὰ τὰ αὐτὰ ἡ ΒΓ τῆς ΓΑ ἐλάσσων 15 ἐστὶν ἢ με'. πολλῷ ἄρα ἡ ΒΓ τῆς ΒΑ ἐλάσσων ἐστὶν ἢ με' μέρος. καὶ ἔστι τῆς ΒΓ διπλῆ ἡ ΓΕ· ἡ ΓΕ ἄρα τῆς ΑΒ ἐλάσσων ἐστὶν ἢ δύο με'. καὶ ἔστιν ἡ μὲν ΓΕ ἡ τῆς σελήνης διάμετρος, ἡ δὲ ΒΑ τὸ ἀπόστημα ὃ ἀπέχει τὸ κέντρον τῆς σελήνης ἀπὸ τῆς ἡμετέρας ὄψεως· ἡ ἄρα διάμετρος τῆς σελήνης τοῦ ἀποστήματος, οὗ 20 ἀπέχει τὸ κέντρον τῆς σελήνης ἀπὸ τῆς ἡμετέρας ὄψεως, ἐλάσσων ἐστὶν ἢ δύο με'.

Λέγω δὴ ὅτι καὶ μείζων ἐστὶν ἡ ΓΕ τῆς ΒΑ ἢ λ' μέρος. ἐπεζεύχθω γὰρ ἡ ΔΕ καὶ ἡ ΔΓ, καὶ κέντρῳ μὲν τῷ Α, διαστήματι δὲ τῷ ΑΓ, κύκλος γεγράφθω ὁ ΓΔΖ, καὶ ἐνηρμόσθω εἰς τὸν ΓΔΖ 25 κύκλον τῇ ΑΓ ἴση ἡ ΔΖ. καὶ ἐπεὶ ὀρθὴ ἡ ὑπὸ τῶν ΕΔΓ ὀρθῇ τῇ

---

1. ια'] I Vat.   2. οὗ] ὁ W F Nizze, sed nihil mutandum   4. με'] τεσσαρακοστόπεμπτα W   λ'] τριακοστόν W   6. περιλαμβάνων] παραλαμβάνων W
7. ἔχῃ] ἔχει Vat.   γίγνεται] γίνεται W   διὰ] om. W   13. ὑπὸ]
ἀπὸ W   14, 15. με'] τεσσαρακοστόπεμπτον W   14. ΓΑ] ΒΑ W   15–16.
πολλῷ ἄρα . . . με' μέρος] om. W Paris. 2366   17. με'] τεσσαρακοστόπεμπτα W
19. οὗ] ὁ W F Nizze, sed cf. l. 2 supra   21. με'] τεσσαρακοστόπεμπτα W

PROPOSITION 11.

The diameter of the moon is less than 2/45ths, but greater than 1/30th, of the distance of the centre of the moon from our eye.

For let our eye be at A, and let B be the centre of the moon when the cone comprehending both the sun and the moon has its vertex at our eye.

I say that the above proposition is true.

Let AB be joined, and let the plane through AB be drawn; this plane will cut the sphere [i.e. the moon] in a circle and the cone in straight lines.

Let it cut the sphere in the circle CED and the cone in the straight lines AD, AC;
let BC be joined and produced to E.

Then it is manifest from what has before been proved [Prop. 4] that the angle BAC is 1/45th part of half a right angle;

and, in the same way as before, BC is less than 1/45th part of CA; therefore BC is much less than 1/45th part of BA.

And CE is double of BC; therefore CE is less than 2/45ths of AB.

Now CE is the diameter of the moon, while BA is the distance of the centre of the moon from our eye.

Therefore the diameter of the moon is less than

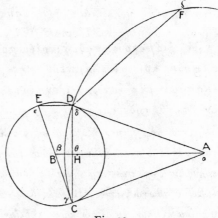

Fig. 29.

2/45ths of the distance of the centre of the moon from our eye.

I say next that CE is also greater than 1/30th part of BA.

For let DE and DC be joined, and with centre A and distance AC let the circle CDF be described; let DF equal to AC be fitted into the circle CDF.

ὑπὸ τῶν ΒΓΑ ἐστὶν ἴση, ἀλλὰ καὶ ἡ ὑπὸ τῶν ΒΑΓ τῇ ὑπὸ τῶν
ΘΓΒ ἐστὶν ἴση, λοιπὴ ἄρα ἡ ὑπὸ τῶν ΔΕΓ λοιπῇ τῇ ὑπὸ τῶν
ΘΒΓ ἐστὶν ἴση· ἰσογώνιον ἄρα ἐστὶν τὸ ΓΔΕ τρίγωνον τῷ ΑΒΓ
τριγώνῳ. ἔστιν ἄρα, ὡς ἡ ΒΑ πρὸς ΑΓ, οὕτως ἡ ΕΓ πρὸς ΓΔ·
5 καὶ ἐναλλάξ, ὡς ἡ ΑΒ πρὸς ΓΕ, οὕτως ἡ ΑΓ πρὸς ΓΔ, τουτέστιν,
ἡ ΔΖ πρὸς ΓΔ. ἀλλ᾽ ἐπεὶ πάλιν ἡ ὑπὸ τῶν ΔΑΓ γωνία με΄ μέρος
ἐστὶν ὀρθῆς, ἡ ΓΔ ἄρα περιφέρεια ρπ΄ μέρος ἐστὶ τοῦ κύκλου· ἡ δὲ
ΔΖ περιφέρεια ἕκτον μέρος ἐστὶν τοῦ ὅλου κύκλου· ὥστε ἡ ΓΔ
περιφέρεια τῆς ΔΖ περιφερείας λ΄ μέρος ἐστίν. καὶ ἔχει ἡ ΓΔ
10 περιφέρεια, ἐλάσσων οὖσα τῆς ΔΖ περιφερείας, πρὸς αὐτὴν τὴν ΔΖ
περιφέρειαν ἐλάσσονα λόγον ἤπερ ἡ ΓΔ εὐθεῖα πρὸς τὴν ΖΔ
εὐθεῖαν· ἡ ἄρα ΓΔ εὐθεῖα τῆς ΔΖ μείζων ἐστὶν ἢ λ΄. ἴση δὲ ἡ
ΖΔ τῇ ΑΓ· ἡ ἄρα ΔΓ τῆς ΓΑ μείζων ἐστὶν ἢ λ΄, ὥστε καὶ ἡ ΓΕ
τῆς ΒΑ μείζων ἐστὶν ἢ λ΄. ἐδείχθη δὲ καὶ ἐλάσσων οὖσα ἢ δύο με΄.

15   ιβ΄.

Ἡ διάμετρος τοῦ διορίζοντος ἐν τῇ σελήνῃ τό τε
σκιερὸν καὶ τὸ λαμπρὸν τῆς διαμέτρου τῆς σελήνης
ἐλάσσων μέν ἐστι, μείζονα δὲ λόγον ἔχει πρὸς αὐτὴν ἢ
ὃν τὰ πθ πρὸς ϛ.

20 Ἔστω γὰρ ἡ μὲν ἡμετέρα ὄψις πρὸς τῷ Α, σελήνης δὲ κέντρον
τὸ Β, ὅταν ὁ περιλαμβάνων κῶνος τόν τε ἥλιον καὶ τὴν σελήνην τὴν
κορυφὴν ἔχῃ πρὸς τῇ ἡμετέρᾳ ὄψει, καὶ ἐπεζεύχθω ἡ ΑΒ, καὶ
ἐκβεβλήσθω διὰ τῆς ΑΒ ἐπίπεδον· ποιήσει δὴ τομὰς ἐν μὲν τῇ
σφαίρᾳ κύκλον, ἐν δὲ τῷ κώνῳ εὐθείας. ποιείτω ⟨ἐν μὲν τῇ σφαίρᾳ
25 κύκλον τὸν ΔΕΓ, ἐν δὲ τῷ κώνῳ εὐθείας⟩ τὰς ΑΔ, ΑΓ, ΓΔ.

---

2. ΘΓΒ] ΕΓΔ W   6. με΄] τεσσαρακοστόπεμπτον W   9. λ΄] τριακοστὸν W
10. περιφέρεια] add. πρὸς τὴν ΔΖ περιφέρειαν Vat.   11. λόγον] λόγον ἔχει Vat.
12, 14. λ΄] τριακοστόν W   12–13. ἴση δὲ ἡ ... ἢ λ΄] om. W   14. με΄] τεσσαρακοστόπεμπτα W
15. ιβ΄] ΙΑ Vat.   21. περιλαμβάνων] παραλαμβάνων W   24–25. ⟨ἐν μὲν ...
εὐθείας⟩ supplevit W : om. codd.

Then, since the right angle EDC is equal to the right angle BCA, while the angle BAC is also equal to the angle HCB, therefore the remaining angle DEC is equal to the remaining angle HBC.

Therefore the triangle CDE is equiangular with the triangle ABC.

Therefore, as BA is to AC, so is EC to CD;

and, alternately, as AB is to CE, so is AC to CD, that is, DF to CD.

But again, since the angle DAC is 1/45th part of a right angle, the circumference CD is 1/180th part of the circle;

and the circumference DF is one sixth part of the whole circle;

thus the circumference CD is 1/30th part of the circumference DF.

And the circumference CD, being less than the circumference DF, has to the circumference DF itself a ratio less than that which the straight line CD has to the straight line FD.[1]

Therefore the straight line CD is greater than 1/30th of DF.

But FD is equal to AC;

therefore DC is greater than 1/30th of CA,

so that CE is also greater than 1/30th of BA [see above].

But it was before proved to be also less than 2/45ths.

PROPOSITION 12.

The diameter of the circle which divides the dark and the bright portions in the moon is less than the diameter of the moon, but has to it a ratio greater than that which 89 *has to* 90.

For let our eye be at A, and let B be the centre of the moon when the cone comprehending both the sun and the moon has its vertex at our eye;

let AB be joined, and let a plane be carried through AB; this plane will cut the sphere [i.e. the moon] in a circle and the cone in straight lines.

Let it cut the sphere in the circle DEC and the cone in the straight lines AD, AC, CD.

---

[1] For, by the proposition proved by Ptolemy (see note on Prop. 4, above),
$$FD : DC < (\text{arc } FD) : (\text{arc } DC),$$
and, by inversion, $\quad (\text{arc } CD) : (\text{arc } DF) < CD : DF.$

ἡ ΓΔ ἄρα διάμετρός ἐστι τοῦ κύκλου τοῦ διορίζοντος ἐν τῇ σελήνῃ
τὸ σκιερὸν καὶ τὸ λαμπρόν.   λέγω δὴ ὅτι ἡ ΓΔ τῆς διαμέτρου τῆς
σελήνης ἐλάσσων μέν ἐστι, μείζονα δὲ λόγον ἔχει ⟨πρὸς αὐτὴν⟩ ἢ ὃν
τὰ πθ πρὸς ϛ.

5 Ὅτι μὲν οὖν ἡ ΓΔ ἐλάσσων ἐστὶ τῆς διαμέτρου τῆς σελήνης,
φανερόν.   λέγω δὴ ὅτι καὶ μείζονα λόγον ἔχει ⟨πρὸς αὐτὴν⟩ ἢ ὃν
τὰ πθ πρὸς ϛ.

Ἤχθω γὰρ διὰ τοῦ Β τῇ ΓΔ παράλληλος ἡ ΖΗ, καὶ ἐπεζεύχθω ἡ ΒΓ. ἔσται δὴ πάλιν κατὰ τὰ αὐτὰ ἡ ὑπὸ τῶν ΔΑΓ
10 γωνία ὀρθῆς μέ μέρος, ἡ δὲ ὑπὸ τῶν ΒΑΓ ὀρθῆς ϛ′ μέρος.   καὶ

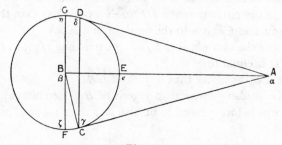

Fig. 30.

ἔστιν ἡ ὑπὸ τῶν ΒΑΓ γωνία ἴση τῇ ὑπὸ τῶν ΓΒΖ· καὶ ἡ ὑπὸ τῶν
ΓΒΖ ἄρα γωνία ὀρθῆς ἐστιν ϛ′, τουτέστιν, τῆς ὑπὸ τῶν ΖΒΕ
γωνίας ϛ′, ὥστε καὶ ἡ ΓΖ περιφέρεια τῆς ΖΓΕ περιφερείας ἐστὶν
ϛ′. ἡ ΓΕ ἄρα περιφέρεια πρὸς τὴν ΕΓΖ περιφέρειαν λόγον ἔχει
15 ὃν τὰ πθ πρὸς ϛ.   καὶ ἔστι τῆς ΓΕ β ἡ ΔΕΓ, τῆς δὲ ΕΓΖ β ἡ
ΗΕΖ· ἡ ἄρα ΔΕΓ περιφέρεια πρὸς τὴν ΗΕΖ περιφέρειαν λόγον
ἔχει ὃν τὰ πθ πρὸς ϛ.   καὶ ἔχει ἡ ΔΓ εὐθεῖα πρὸς ⟨τὴν⟩ ΗΖ
εὐθεῖαν μείζονα λόγον ἤπερ ἡ ΔΕΓ περιφέρεια πρὸς τὴν ΗΕΖ
περιφέρειαν· καὶ ἡ ΔΓ ἄρα εὐθεῖα πρὸς τὴν ΗΖ εὐθεῖαν μείζονα
20 λόγον ἔχει ἢ ὃν τὰ πθ πρὸς ϛ.

2. δὴ] δὲ W   3, 6. ⟨πρὸς αὐτὴν⟩] addidi   10. μέ] τεσσαρακοστόπεμπτον W   τῶν] τὸν Vat.   10, 12, 14. ϛ′] ἐννενηκοστόν W   13. γωνίας] γωνίας,
γωνίας W   15. β bis] διπλῆ W   17. καὶ ἔχει] ἔχει post λόγον (l. 18) posuit W

Therefore CD is a diameter of the circle which divides the dark and the bright portions in the moon.

I say that CD is less than the diameter of the moon, but has to it a ratio greater than that which 89 has to 90.

Now, that CD is less than the diameter of the moon is manifest.

I say, then, that it also has to it a ratio greater than that which 89 has to 90.

For let FG be drawn through B parallel to CD, and let BC be joined.

Then again, in the same way as before, the angle DAC will be 1/45th part of a right angle, and the angle BAC will be 1/90th part of a right angle; but the angle BAC is equal to the angle CBF; therefore the angle CBF is also 1/90th of a right angle, that is, 1/90th of the angle FBE; so that the circumference CF is also 1/90th of the circumference FCE.

Therefore the circumference CE has to the circumference ECF the ratio which 89 has to 90.

Now DEC is double of CE, and GEF double of ECF; therefore the circumference DEC has to the circumference GEF the ratio which 89 has to 90.

And the straight line DC has to the straight line GF a ratio greater than that which the circumference DEC has to the circumference GEF.[1]

Therefore also the straight line DC has to the straight line GF a ratio greater than that which 89 has to 90.

---

[1] By the proposition quoted from Ptolemy, i. 10, pp. 43-4, ed. Heiberg. See note on Props. 4 and 11, above.

ιγ΄.

Ἡ ὑποτείνουσα εὐθεῖα ὑπὸ τὴν ἀπολαμβανομένην ἐν
τῷ σκιάσματι τῆς γῆς περιφέρειαν τοῦ κύκλου, καθ᾿ οὗ
φέρεται τὰ ἄκρα τῆς διαμέτρου τοῦ διορίζοντος ἐν τῇ
5 σελήνῃ τό τε σκιερὸν καὶ τὸ λαμπρόν, τῆς μὲν διαμέτρου
τῆς σελήνης ἐλάσσων ἐστὶν ἢ διπλῆ, μείζονα δὲ λόγον
ἔχει πρὸς αὐτὴν ἢ ὃν τὰ πη πρὸς με, τῆς δὲ τοῦ ἡλίου
διαμέτρου ἐλάσσων μέν ἐστιν ἢ ἔνατον μέρος, μείζονα
δὲ λόγον ἔχει πρὸς αὐτὴν ἢ ὃν κβ πρὸς σκε, πρὸς δὲ τὴν
10 ἀπὸ τοῦ κέντρου τοῦ ἡλίου ἠγμένην πρὸς ὀρθὰς τῷ ἄξονι,
συμβάλλουσαν δὲ ταῖς τοῦ κώνου πλευραῖς, μείζονα λόγον
ἔχει ἢ ὃν τὰ Ϡοθ πρὸς Μ̅ρκε.

Ἔστω γὰρ ἡλίου μὲν κέντρον πρὸς τῷ Α, γῆς δὲ κέντρον τὸ Β,
σελήνης δὲ τὸ Γ, τελείας οὔσης τῆς ἐκλείψεως καὶ πρώτως ὅλης
15 ἐμπεπτωκυίας εἰς τὸ τῆς γῆς σκίασμα, καὶ ἐκβεβλήσθω διὰ τῶν Α,
Β, Γ ἐπίπεδον· ποιήσει δὴ τομὰς ἐν μὲν ταῖς σφαίραις κύκλους, ἐν
δὲ τῷ κώνῳ εὐθείας τῷ περιλαμβάνοντι τόν τε ἥλιον καὶ τὴν γῆν.
ποιείτω ἐν μὲν ταῖς σφαίραις μεγίστους κύκλους τοὺς ΔΕΖ, ΗΘΚ,
ΛΜΝ, ἐν δὲ τῷ σκιάσματι τῆς γῆς κύκλον, καθ᾿ οὗ φέρεται τὰ ἄκρα
20 τῆς διαμέτρου τοῦ διορίζοντος ἐν τῇ σελήνῃ τό τε σκιερὸν καὶ τὸ
λαμπρόν, τὸν ΞΛΝ, ἐν δὲ τῷ κώνῳ εὐθείας τὰς ΔΗΞ, ΖΚΝ·
ἄξων δὲ ἔστω ὁ ΑΒΛ. φανερὸν δὴ ὅτι ὁ ΑΒΛ ἄξων ἐφάπτεται
τοῦ ΛΜΝ κύκλου, διὰ τὸ τὸ σκίασμα τῆς γῆς σεληνῶν εἶναι δύο, καὶ
δίχα διαιρεῖσθαι τὴν ΝΛΞ περιφέρειαν ὑπὸ τοῦ ΑΒΛ ἄξονος, καὶ
25 ἔτι τὴν σελήνην πρώτως ἐμπεπτωκέναι εἰς τὸ τῆς γῆς σκίασμα.
ἐπεζεύχθωσαν δὴ αἱ ΞΝ, ΝΔ, ΒΝ, ΛΞ. ἡ ΔΝ ἄρα ἐστὶν ἡ
διάμετρος τοῦ διορίζοντος ἐν τῇ σελήνῃ τό τε σκιερὸν καὶ τὸ
λαμπρόν, καὶ ἡ ΒΝ ἐφάπτεται τοῦ ΛΝΟΜ κύκλου, διὰ τὸ εἶναι τὸ
Β πρὸς τῇ ἡμετέρᾳ ὄψει, καὶ τὴν ΔΝ διάμετρον τοῦ διορίζοντος ἐν
30 τῇ σελήνῃ τό τε σκιερὸν καὶ τὸ λαμπρόν. καὶ ἐπεὶ αἱ ΞΔ, ΔΝ

1. ιγ΄] ΙΒ Vat.   2. τὴν] om. W   7. με] τὰ με W   8. ἔνατον] ἔνναντον W
14. ἐκλείψεως] ἐκλίψεως Vat.   16. δὴ] δὲ W   18. τοὺς] om. W   19. κύκλον]
κύκλων Vat.   22. ὁ 2°] ἡ W   ἐφάπτεται] ἐφάπτηται W   25. πρώτως] πρῶτως
(ὅλην) Nizze   28–30. καὶ ἡ ΒΝ ἐφάπτεται … λαμπρόν] om. soli, ut videtur, codd.
Savilianus et Paris. 2342   28. ἐφάπτεται] εὐθεῖα ἐφάπτεται W   ΛΝΟΜ] F
Paris. 2364, 2488 : ΛΝΟΝ Vat. : ΛΜΝ W   28–9. εἶναι τὸ Β] τὸ Β σημεῖον
εἶναι W, qui lacunam post l. 28 λαμπρόν ope versionis Commandini expleverat
29. διάμετρον] τὴν διάμετρον εἶναι W

PROPOSITION 13.

The straight line subtending the portion intercepted within the earth's shadow of the circumference of the circle in which the extremities of the diameter of the circle dividing the dark and the bright portions in the moon move is less than double of the diameter of the moon, but has to it a ratio greater than that which 88 has to 45 ; and it is less than 1/9th part of the diameter of the sun, but has to it a ratio greater than that which 22 has to 225.   But it has to the straight line drawn from the centre of the sun at right angles to the axis and meeting the sides of the cone a ratio greater than that which 979 has to 10125.

For let the centre of the sun be at A, let B be the centre of the earth, and C the centre of the moon when the eclipse first becomes total through the moon having fallen wholly within the earth's shadow.

Let a plane be carried through A, B, C ;
this plane will cut the spheres in circles and the cone comprehending both the sun and the earth in straight lines.

Let it cut the spheres in the great circles DEF, GHK, LMN, the earth's shadow in the circle OLN in which the extremities of the diameter of the circle dividing the dark and the bright portions in the moon move, and the cone in the straight lines DGO, FKN.

Let ABL be the axis.

Then it is manifest that the axis ABL touches the circle LMN, because the shadow of the earth is of two moon-breadths, [Hyp. 5] that the circumference NLO is bisected by the axis ABL, and further that the moon has for the first time fallen within the earth's shadow.

Let ON, NL, BN, LO be joined.

Therefore LN is the diameter of the circle dividing the dark and the bright portions in the moon.

And BN touches the circle $LNPM$, because the point B is at our eye, and LN is the diameter of the circle dividing the dark and the bright portions in the moon.

ἴσαι εἰσίν, διπλασίονες ἄρα εἰσὶ τῆς ΛΝ, ὥστε ἡ ΞΝ τῆς ΛΝ ἐλάσσων ἐστὶν ἢ διπλῆ. ἐπεζεύχθωσαν δὴ αἱ ΛΓ, ΓΝ, καὶ διήχθω ἡ ΛΓ ἐπὶ τὸ Ο· πολλῷ ἄρα ἡ ΞΝ τῆς ΛΟ ἐλάσσων ἐστὶν ἢ β. καὶ ἐπεὶ ἡ ΓΛ κάθετός ἐστιν ἐπὶ τὴν ΒΛ, παράλληλος ἄρα ἐστὶν τῇ ΞΝ· ἴση ἄρα ἐστὶν ἡ ὑπὸ τῶν ΛΞΝ τῇ ὑπὸ τῶν ΓΛΝ γωνίᾳ. καὶ ἔστιν ἴση μὲν ἡ ΝΛ τῇ ΛΞ, ἡ δὲ ΛΓ τῇ ΓΝ· ὅμοιον ἄρα ἐστὶν τὸ ΞΝΛ τρίγωνον τῷ ΛΝΓ τριγώνῳ· ἔστιν ἄρα, ὡς ἡ ΞΝ πρὸς τὴν ΝΛ, οὕτως ἡ ΝΛ πρὸς τὴν ΛΓ. ἀλλ' ἡ ΝΛ πρὸς τὴν ΛΓ μείζονα λόγον ἔχει ἢ ὃν τὰ πθ πρὸς τὰ με, τουτέστι, τὸ ἀπὸ ΝΛ πρὸς τὸ ἀπὸ ΛΓ μείζονα λόγον ἔχει ἤπερ τὰ ͵ζϡκα πρὸς τὰ ͵βκε· καὶ τὸ ἀπὸ ΞΝ ἄρα πρὸς τὸ ἀπὸ ΝΛ μείζονα λόγον ἔχει ἤπερ τὰ ͵ζϡκα πρὸς τὰ ͵βκε, καὶ ἡ ΞΝ πρὸς τὴν ΛΟ

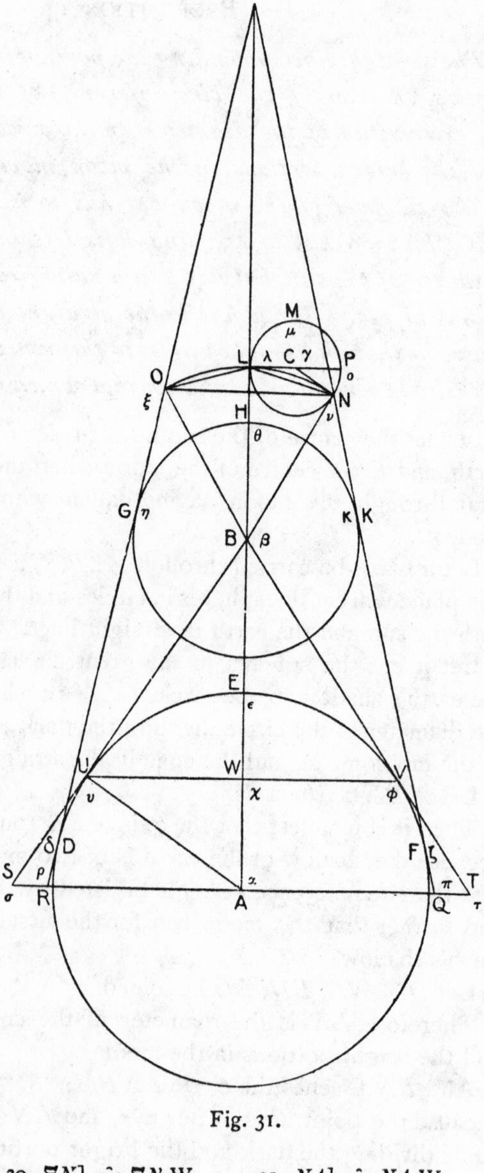

Fig. 31.

8. β] διπλῆ W 30. ΞΝ] τῆς ΞΝ W 31. ΝΛ] τῆς ΝΛ W

Now, since OL, LN are equal, their sum is double of LN, so that ON is less than double of LN.

Let LC, CN be joined; and let LC be carried through to P.

Therefore ON is much less than double of LP.

And, since CL is perpendicular to BL, therefore it is parallel to ON.

Therefore the angle LON is equal to the angle CLN.

And NL is equal to LO, and LC to CN; therefore the triangle ONL is similar to the triangle LNC; therefore, as ON is to NL, so is NL to LC.

But NL has to LC a ratio greater than that which 89 has to 45;[1] that is, the square on NL has to the square on LC a ratio greater than that which 7921 has to 2025.

Therefore the square on ON also has to the square on NL a ratio greater than that which 7921 has to 2025, and (therefore) ON has to LP a ratio greater than that which 7921 has to 4050.[2]

---

[1] For $NL : LP > 89 : 90$, by the preceding proposition.

[2] We have $\qquad ON : NL = NL : LC$;

therefore $\qquad ON : LC = $ (sq. on ON) : (sq. on NL)

$$> 7921 : 2025,$$

whence $\qquad ON : LP > 7921 : 4050.$

μείζονα λόγον ἔχει ἤπερ τὰ ϛ⅄κα πρὸς ͵δν. ἔχει δὲ καὶ τὰ ϛ⅄κα
πρὸς ͵δν μείζονα λόγον ἤπερ τὰ πη πρὸς με· ἡ ΝΞ ἄρα πρὸς ΛΟ
μείζονα λόγον ἔχει ἢ ὃν τὰ πη πρὸς τὰ με. ἡ ἄρα ὑποτείνουσα ὑπὸ
τὴν ἀπολαμβανομένην ἐν τῷ σκιάσματι τῆς γῆς περιφέρειαν τοῦ
5 κύκλου, καθ᾽ οὗ φέρεται τὰ ἄκρα τῆς διαμέτρου τοῦ διορίζοντος ἐν τῇ
σελήνῃ τό τε σκιερὸν καὶ τὸ λαμπρόν, τῆς διαμέτρου τῆς σελήνης
ἐλάσσων μέν ἐστιν ἢ β, μείζονα δὲ λόγον ἔχει ⟨πρὸς αὐτὴν⟩ ἢ ὃν τὰ
πη πρὸς με.

Τῶν αὐτῶν ὑποκειμένων, ἤχθω ἀπὸ τοῦ Α τῇ ΑΒ πρὸς ὀρθὰς
10 ἡ ΠΑΡ· λέγω ὅτι ἡ ΞΝ τῆς διαμέτρου τοῦ ἡλίου ἐλάσσων μέν
ἐστιν ἢ θ′ μέρος, μείζονα δὲ λόγον ἔχει πρὸς αὐτὴν ἢ ὃν τὰ κβ πρὸς
τὰ σκε, πρὸς δὲ τὴν ΠΡ μείζονα λόγον ἔχει ἢ ὃν τὰ ⅄οθ πρὸς
Μ̇ρκε. ἐπεὶ γὰρ ἐδείχθη ἡ ΞΝ τῆς διαμέτρου τῆς σελήνης ἐλάσσων
15 οὖσα ἢ β, ἡ δὲ διάμετρος τῆς σελήνης τῆς διαμέτρου τοῦ ἡλίου
ἐλάσσων ἐστὶν ἢ ιη′ μέρος, ἡ ἄρα ΞΝ τῆς διαμέτρου τοῦ ἡλίου
ἐλάσσων ἐστὶν ἢ θ′ μέρος. πάλιν ἐπεὶ ἡ ΞΝ πρὸς τὴν διάμετρον
τῆς σελήνης μείζονα λόγον ἔχει ἢ ὃν τὰ πη πρὸς τὰ με, ἡ δὲ
διάμετρος τῆς σελήνης πρὸς τὴν τοῦ ἡλίου διάμετρον μείζονα λόγον
ἔχει ἢ ὃν τὰ με πρὸς ⅄· ἐπεὶ γὰρ ἡ τῆς σελήνης διάμετρος πρὸς
20 τὴν τοῦ ἡλίου μείζονα λόγον ἔχει ἢ ὃν α πρὸς κ, καὶ πάντα
τεσσαρακοντάκις καὶ πεντάκις· ἕξει ἄρα ἡ ΞΝ πρὸς τὴν διάμετρον
τοῦ ἡλίου μείζονα λόγον ἢ ὃν τὰ πη πρὸς τὰ ⅄, τουτέστιν, ἢ ὃν
τὰ κβ πρὸς τὰ σκε. ἤχθωσαν δὴ ἀπὸ τοῦ Β τοῦ ΔΕ κύκλου
ἐφαπτόμεναι αἱ ΒΥΣ, ΒΦΤ, καὶ ἐπεζεύχθω ἡ ΥΦ καὶ ἡ ΥΑ.
25 ἔσται δή, ὡς ἡ διάμετρος τοῦ διορίζοντος ἐν τῇ σελήνῃ τό τε σκιερὸν
καὶ τὸ λαμπρὸν πρὸς τὴν διάμετρον τῆς σελήνης, οὕτως ἡ ΥΦ πρὸς
τὴν διάμετρον τοῦ ἡλίου, διὰ τὸ τὸν αὐτὸν κῶνον περιλαμβάνειν τόν

2. ἡ ΝΞ ἄρα] ἄρα ἡ ΝΞ Vat.   3. τὰ με] με W   ὑποτείνουσα]
ἀποτείνουσα Vat.   7. β] διπλῆ W   ⟨πρὸς αὐτὴν⟩] addidi   11, 16. θ′]
ἔννατον W   12. σκε] κε Vat.   ἔχει] ἔχει πρὸς αὐτὴν W   14. β]
διπλασίων W   15. ἢ ιη′] ιη′ Vat.   17. τὰ με] με W   20. α] τὸ α W
21. τεσσαρακοντάκις καὶ πεντάκις] τεσσαρακοντακαιπεντάκις W   22. τὰ ⅄]
⅄ W   23. ΔΕ] ΔΕΖ W

But 7921 also has to 4050 a ratio greater than that which 88 has to 45 ;[1]
therefore NO has to LP a ratio greater than that which 88 has to 45.

Therefore the straight line which subtends the portion intercepted within the earth's shadow of the circumference of the circle in which the extremities of the diameter of the circle dividing the dark and the bright portions in the moon move is less than double of the diameter of the moon, but has to it a ratio greater than that which 88 has to 45.

The same suppositions being made, let QAR be drawn ftom A at right angles to AB.

I say that ON is less than 1/9th part of the diameter of the sun, but has to it a ratio greater than that which 22 has to 225, and has to QR a ratio greater than that which 979 has to 10125.

For, since it was proved that ON is less than double of the diameter of the moon,
while the diameter of the moon is less than 1/18th part of the diameter of the sun,   [Prop. 9]
therefore ON is less than 1/9th part of the diameter of the sun.

Again, since ON has to the diameter of the moon a ratio greater than that which 88 has to 45,
while the diameter of the moon has to the diameter of the sun a ratio greater than that which 45 has to 900:
for, since the diameter of the moon has to the diameter of the sun a ratio greater than that which 1 has to 20, we have only to multiply throughout by 45:
therefore (*ex aequali*) ON has to the diameter of the sun a ratio greater than that which 88 has to 900, that is, than that which 22 has to 225.

Now let BUS, BVT be drawn from B touching the circle DE: and let UV, UA be joined.

Then, as the diameter of the circle dividing the dark and the bright portions in the moon is to the diameter of the moon, so is UV to the diameter of the sun, because the sun and the moon are

---

[1] If we develop $\frac{7921}{4050}$ as a continued fraction, we easily obtain the approximation $1 + \frac{1}{1+} \frac{1}{21+} \frac{1}{2}$, which is in fact $\frac{88}{45}$. See the similar case in Prop. 15, p. 407, and the observation thereon, p. 336 *ad fin.*

τε ἥλιον καὶ τὴν σελήνην τὴν κορυφὴν ἔχοντα πρὸς τῇ ἡμετέρᾳ ὄψει.

ἡ δὲ διάμετρος τοῦ διορίζοντος ἐν τῇ σελήνῃ τό τε σκιερὸν καὶ τὸ λαμπρὸν πρὸς τὴν διάμετρον τῆς σελήνης μείζονα λόγον ἔχει ἢ ὃν τὰ πθ πρὸς τὰ ϛ· καὶ ἡ ΤΦ ἄρα πρὸς τὴν τοῦ ἡλίου διάμετρον μείζονα 5 λόγον ἔχει ἢ ὃν τὰ πθ πρὸς ϛ· καὶ ἡ ΧΤ ἄρα πρὸς τὴν ΥΑ μείζονα λόγον ἔχει ἢ ὃν τὰ πθ πρὸς ϛ. ὡς δὲ ἡ ΧΤ πρὸς τὴν ΥΑ, οὕτως ἡ ΥΑ πρὸς τὴν ΑΣ, διὰ τὸ παραλλήλους εἶναι τὰς ΣΑ, ΥΧ· καὶ ἡ ΥΑ ἄρα πρὸς τὴν ΑΣ μείζονα λόγον ἔχει ἢ ὃν τὰ πθ πρὸς τὰ ϛ· πολλῷ ἄρα ἡ ΥΑ πρὸς τὴν ΑΡ μείζονα λόγον ἔχει ἢ ὃν τὰ πθ πρὸς 10 τὰ ϛ. καὶ τὰ β· ἡ ἄρα διάμετρος τοῦ ἡλίου πρὸς τὴν ΠΡ μείζονα λόγον ἔχει ἢ ὃν τὰ πθ πρὸς τὰ ϛ. ἐδείχθη δὲ καὶ ἡ ΞΝ πρὸς τὴν διάμετρον τοῦ ἡλίου μείζονα λόγον ἔχουσα ἢ ὃν τὰ κβ πρὸς τὰ σκε. δι' ἴσου πολλῷ ἄρα ἡ ΞΝ πρὸς τὴν ΠΡ μείζονα λόγον ἔχει ἢ ⟨ὃν⟩ ὁ συνηγμένος ἔκ τε τῶν κβ καὶ πθ πρὸς τὸν ἐκ τῶν ϛ καὶ σκε, 15 τουτέστιν, τὰ ͵ἀλνη πρὸς τὰ Μ̅σ̅ν̅· καὶ τὰ ἡμίση, τουτέστιν, τὰ ͵αοθ πρὸς τὰ Μ̅ρκε.

ιδ'.

Ἡ ἀπὸ τοῦ κέντρου τῆς γῆς ἐπὶ τὸ κέντρον τῆς σελήνης ἐπιζευγνυμένη εὐθεῖα πρὸς τὴν εὐθεῖαν, ἣν ἀπολαμβάνει 20 ἀπὸ τοῦ ἄξονος πρὸς τῷ κέντρῳ τῆς σελήνης ἡ ὑπὸ τὴν ἐν τῷ σκιάσματι τῆς γῆς ὑποτείνουσα εὐθεῖα, μείζονα λόγον ἔχει ἢ ὃν τὰ χοε πρὸς α.

Ἔστω τὸ αὐτὸ σχῆμα τῷ πρότερον, καὶ ἡ σελήνη οὕτως ἔστω ὥστε τὸ κέντρον αὐτῆς εἶναι ἐπὶ τοῦ ἄξονος τοῦ κώνου τοῦ περι-

---

4. τὰ ϛ] ϛ W   10. β] διπλάσια W   12. τὰ σκε] σκε W
15. Μ̅σ̅ν̅] Μβ.σν W   16. τὰ Μ̅ρ̅κ̅ε] Μα.ρκε W   17. ιδ'] ΙΓ Vat.

comprehended by one and the same cone having its vertex at our eye.[1]

But the diameter of the circle dividing the dark and the bright portions in the moon has to the diameter of the moon a ratio greater than that which 89 has to 90 ;   [Prop. 12]
therefore UV also has to the diameter of the sun a ratio greater than that which 89 has to 90.

Therefore WU also has to UA a ratio greater than that which 89 has to 90.

But, as WU is to UA, so is UA to AS, because SA, UW are parallel ;
therefore UA also has to AS a ratio greater than that which 89 has to 90 ;
therefore UA has to AR a ratio much greater than that which 89 has to 90.

The same is true of the doubles ;
therefore the diameter of the sun has to QR a ratio greater than that which 89 has to 90.

But it was proved [above] that ON has to the diameter of the sun a ratio greater than that which 22 has to 225 ;
therefore, *ex aequali*, ON has to QR a ratio much greater than that which the product of 22 and 89 has to the product of 90 and 225, that is, 1958 to 20250, or, if the halves be taken, 979 to 10125.

PROPOSITION 14.

The straight line joined from the centre of the earth to the centre of the moon has to the straight line cut off from the axis towards the centre of the moon by the straight line subtending the ⟨circumference⟩ within the earth's shadow a ratio greater than that which 675 has to 1.

For let the same figure be drawn as before ;
and let the moon be so placed that its centre is on the axis of the cone comprehending both the sun and the earth ;

---

[1] The proof, which is given by Commandinus, is obvious. The fact cannot be seen from our figure, which, owing to exigency of space, could not be drawn so as to make the angles LBN, UBV equal.

λαμβάνοντος τόν τε ἥλιον καὶ τὴν γῆν, καὶ ἔστω τὸ Γ, μέγιστος δὲ
τῶν ἐν τῇ σφαίρᾳ κύκλος ὁ ΠΟΜ ἐν τῷ αὐτῷ ἐπιπέδῳ ὢν αὐτοῖς,
καὶ ἐπεζεύχθω ἡ ΜΟ· ἡ ΜΟ ἄρα διάμετρός ἐστι τοῦ διορίζοντος ἐν
τῇ σελήνῃ τό τε σκιερὸν καὶ τὸ λαμπρόν. ἐπεζεύχθωσαν δὴ αἱ
5 ΜΒ, ΒΟ, ΛΞ, ΞΒ, ΜΓ· ἐφάπτονται ἄρα τοῦ ΜΟΠ κύκλου αἱ
ΜΒ, ΒΟ, διὰ τὸ τὴν ΟΜ διάμετρον εἶναι τοῦ διορίζοντος ἐν τῇ

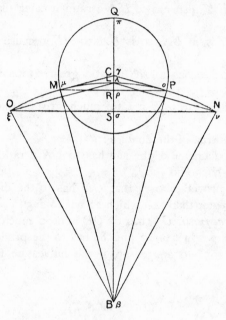

Fig. 32.

σελήνῃ τὸ σκιερὸν καὶ τὸ λαμπρόν. καὶ ἐπεὶ ἴση ἐστὶν ἡ ΞΛ τῇ
ΜΟ· ἑκατέρα γὰρ αὐτῶν διάμετρός ἐστι τοῦ διορίζοντος ἐν τῇ σελήνῃ
τό τε σκιερὸν καὶ τὸ λαμπρόν· ἴση ἄρα καὶ ἡ ΞΜΛ περιφέρεια τῇ
10 ΜΛΟ περιφερείᾳ, καὶ ἡ ΞΜ ἄρα ἴση ἐστὶν τῇ ΛΟ. ἀλλ᾽ ἡ ΛΟ
τῇ ΛΜ ἴση ἐστίν· καὶ ἡ ΞΜ ἄρα ἴση ἐστὶν τῇ ΛΜ. ἔστι δὲ καὶ
ἡ ΞΒ ἴση τῇ ΒΛ, διὰ τὸ τὸ Β σημεῖον κέντρον εἶναι τῆς γῆς, καὶ

2. ἐν τῇ σφαίρᾳ] ἐν τῇ τῆς σελήνης σφαίρᾳ Nizze, suadente F, qui lectionem
cod. Parisiensis 2488 σελήνῃ ante σφαίρᾳ in σελήνης correxit ; mallem ἐν τῇ σελήνῃ
pro ἐν τῇ σφαίρᾳ, sed cf. 1. 14, p. 364; l. 10, p. 386; l. 24, p. 388   4. δὴ] δὲ W
7. τὸ σκιερὸν] τό τε σκιερὸν W   ἐστιν] om. W

let its centre be C, and let the great circle QPM in the sphere [i. e. the moon] be in the same plane with the rest of the figure.[1]

Let MP be joined;
therefore MP is a diameter of the circle which divides the dark and the bright portions in the moon.

Let MB, BP, LO, OB, MC be joined.

Therefore MB, BP touch the circle MPQ,
because PM is a diameter of the circle which divides the dark and the bright portions in the moon.

And, since OL is equal to MP— for each of them is a diameter of the circle which divides the dark and the bright portions in the moon—

therefore the circumference OML is equal to the circumference MLP;
therefore OM is also equal to LP.

But LP is equal to LM;
therefore OM is also equal to LM.

And OB is equal to BL,

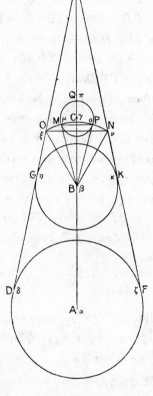

Fig. 33.

because the point B is the centre of the earth, and the earth has

---

[1] Literally 'in the same plane with *them*' (αὐτοῖς), which no doubt means the axis and the sections of the sun and moon made by the plane originally assumed, which also contains the circle in which the diameter of the 'dividing circle' in the moon moves while the moon is passing through the earth's shadow.

⟨τὴν γῆν⟩ σημείου καὶ κέντρου λόγον ἔχειν πρὸς τὴν τῆς σελήνης
σφαῖραν, καὶ τὸν ΜΟΠ κύκλον ἐν τῷ αὐτῷ ἐπιπέδῳ εἶναι· ἡ ἄρα
ΒΜ κάθετός ἐστιν ἐπὶ τὴν ΞΛ. ἔστιν δὲ καὶ ἡ ΓΜ κάθετος ἐπὶ
τὴν ΒΜ· παράλληλος ἄρα ἐστὶν ἡ ΓΜ τῇ ΞΛ. ἔστι δὲ καὶ ἡ
5 ΣΞ τῇ ΜΡ παράλληλος· ὅμοιον ἄρα ἐστὶ τὸ ΛΞΣ τρίγωνον τῷ
ΜΡΓ τριγώνῳ· ἔστιν ἄρα, ὡς ἡ ΣΞ πρὸς τὴν ΜΡ, οὕτως ἡ ΣΛ πρὸς
τὴν ΡΓ. ἀλλ' ἡ ΣΞ τῆς ΜΡ ἐστὶν ἐλάσσων ἢ β, ἐπεὶ καὶ ἡ ΞΝ
τῆς ΜΟ ἐλάσσων ἐστὶν ἢ β· καὶ ἡ ΣΛ ἄρα τῆς ΓΡ ἐλάσσων
ἐστὶν ἢ β· ὥστε ἡ ΣΡ τῆς ΡΓ πολλῷ ἐλάσσων ἐστὶν ἢ β. ἡ ΣΓ
10 ἄρα τῆς ΓΡ ἐλάσσων ἐστὶν ἢ τριπλασίων· ἡ ΓΡ ἄρα πρὸς τὴν ΓΣ
μείζονα λόγον ἔχει ἢ ὃν α πρὸς γ. καὶ ἐπεί ἐστιν, ὡς ἡ ΒΓ πρὸς
ΓΜ, οὕτως ἡ ΓΜ πρὸς τὴν ΓΡ, ἡ δὲ ΒΓ πρὸς τὴν ΓΜ μείζονα
λόγον ἔχει ἢ ὃν με πρὸς α, καὶ ἡ ΓΜ ἄρα πρὸς ΓΡ μείζονα λόγον
ἔχει ἢ ὃν με πρὸς α. ἔχει δὲ καὶ ἡ ΓΡ πρὸς τὴν ΓΣ μείζονα
15 λόγον ἢ ὃν α πρὸς γ· δι' ἴσου ἄρα ἡ ΓΜ πρὸς τὴν ΓΣ μείζονα
λόγον ἔχει ἢ ὃν με πρὸς γ, τουτέστιν, ⟨ἢ⟩ ὃν ιε πρὸς α. ἐδείχθη δὲ
καὶ ἡ ΒΓ πρὸς τὴν ΓΜ μείζονα λόγον ἔχουσα ἢ ὃν με πρὸς α·
δι' ἴσου ἄρα ἡ ΒΓ πρὸς τὴν ΓΣ μείζονα λόγον ἔχει ἢ ὃν τὰ χοε
πρὸς α.

20   ιε'.

Ἡ τοῦ ἡλίου διάμετρος πρὸς τὴν τῆς γῆς διάμετρον
μείζονα λόγον ἔχει ἢ ὃν τὰ ιθ πρὸς γ, ἐλάσσονα δὲ ἢ ὃν
τὰ μγ πρὸς τὰ ς.

Ἔστω γὰρ ἡλίου μὲν κέντρον τὸ Α, γῆς δὲ κέντρον τὸ Β, σελήνης
25 δὲ κέντρον τὸ Γ, τελείας οὔσης τῆς ἐκλείψεως, τουτέστιν, ἵνα τὰ
Α, Β, Γ ἐπ' εὐθείας ᾖ, καὶ ἐκβεβλήσθω διὰ τοῦ ἄξονος ἐπίπεδον,

1. ⟨τὴν γῆν⟩] haec verba prorsus necessaria solus habet Paris. 2364
5. ΛΞΣ] ΛΣΞ W   7, 8, 9. β] διπλασίων W   12. τὴν ΓΡ] ΓΡ W   13. α]
μίαν Vat. Paris. 2366, 2488 : ἕν Paris. 2342, 2364   15. ΓΜ] ΜΓ W   τὴν]
om. W   16. δὲ] δὴ W
20. ιε'] ΙΔ Vat.   23. τὰ ς] ς W

the relation of a point and centre to the sphere in which the moon moves [Hyp. 2], while the circle MPQ is in the same plane ; therefore BM is perpendicular to OL.

But CM is also perpendicular to BM ; therefore CM is parallel to OL.

And SO is also parallel to MR ; therefore the triangle LOS is similar to the triangle MRC.

Therefore, as SO is to MR, so is SL to RC.

But SO is less than double of MR, since ON is also less than double of MP;   [Prop. 13] therefore SL is also less than double of CR, so that SR is much less than double of RC.

Therefore SC is less than triple of CR; therefore CR has to CS a ratio greater than that which 1 has to 3.

And since, as BC is to CM, so is CM to CR, while BC has to CM a ratio greater than that which 45 has to 1,
                                              [see Prop. 11]
therefore CM also has to CR a ratio greater than that which 45 has to 1.

But CR also has to CS a ratio greater than that which 1 has to 3 ; therefore, *ex aequali*, CM has to CS a ratio greater than that which 45 has to 3, that is, than that which 15 has to 1.

And it was proved that BC has to CM a ratio greater than that which 45 has to 1 ; therefore, *ex aequali*, BC has to CS a ratio greater than that which 675 has to 1.

PROPOSITION 15.

The diameter of the sun has to the diameter of the earth a ratio greater than that which 19 has to 3, but less than that which 43 has to 6.

For let A be the centre of the sun, B the centre of the earth, C the centre of the moon when the eclipse is total, so as to secure that A, B, C may be in a straight line.

καὶ ποιείτω τομὰς ἐν μὲν τῷ ἡλίῳ τὸν ΔΕΖ κύκλον, ἐν δὲ τῇ γῇ τὸν
ΗΘΚ, ἐν δὲ τῷ σκιάσματι τὴν ΝΞ περιφέρειαν, ἐν δὲ τῷ κώνῳ
εὐθείας τὰς ΔΜ, ΖΜ, καὶ ἐπεζεύχθω ἡ ΝΞ, καὶ ἀπὸ τοῦ Α τῇ ΑΜ
πρὸς ὀρθὰς ἤχθω ἡ ΟΑΠ. καὶ

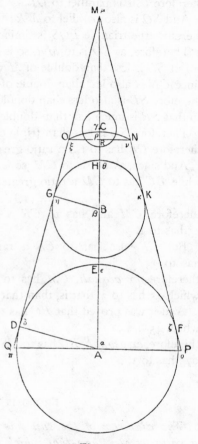

Fig. 34.

5 ἐπεὶ ἡ ΝΞ τῆς διαμέτρου τοῦ
ἡλίου ἐλάσσων ἐστὶν ἢ θ′ μέρος,
ἡ ΟΠ ἄρα πρὸς τὴν ΝΞ πολλῷ
μείζονα λόγον ἔχει ἢ ὃν τὰ θ
πρὸς α· καὶ ἡ ΑΜ ἄρα πρὸς
10 τὴν ΜΡ μείζονα λόγον ἔχει ἢ
ὃν τὰ θ πρὸς α. καὶ ἀνα-
στρέψαντι ἡ ΜΑ πρὸς ΑΡ
ἐλάσσονα λόγον ἔχει ἢ ὃν τὰ
θ πρὸς η. πάλιν ἐπεὶ ἡ ΑΒ
15 τῆς ΒΓ μείζων ἐστὶν ἢ ιη,
πολλῷ ἄρα τῆς ΒΡ μείζων
ἐστὶν ἢ ιη· ἡ ΑΒ ἄρα πρὸς τὴν
ΒΡ μείζονα λόγον ἔχει ἢ ὃν
τὰ ιη πρὸς α. ἀνάπαλιν ἄρα
20 ἡ ΒΡ πρὸς τὴν ΒΑ ἐλάσσονα
λόγον ἔχει ἢ ὃν α πρὸς ιη.
καὶ συνθέντι ἡ ΡΑ ἄρα πρὸς
τὴν ΑΒ ἐλάσσονα λόγον ἔχει
ἢ ὃν τὰ ιθ πρὸς τὰ ιη. ἐδείχθη
25 δὲ καὶ ἡ ΜΑ πρὸς τὴν ΑΡ
ἐλάσσονα λόγον ἔχουσα ἢ ὃν τὰ
θ πρὸς τὰ η· ἕξει ἄρα δι᾽ ἴσου
ἡ ΜΑ πρὸς τὴν ΑΒ ἐλάσσονα
λόγον ἢ ὃν τὰ ροα πρὸς ρμδ,
30 καὶ ὃν τὰ ιθ πρὸς ιϛ· τὰ
γὰρ μέρη τοῖς ὡσαύτως πολλαπλασίοις τὸν αὐτὸν ἔχει λόγον·

6. θ′] ἔννατον W   μέρος] ἡ ἄρα διάμετρος τοῦ ἡλίου μείζονα λόγον ἔχει πρὸς τὴν
ΝΞ ἢ ὃν τὰ θ πρὸς α· καὶ add. W   9. πρὸς α] ἀλλ᾽ ὡς ἡ ΟΠ πρὸς τὴν ΝΞ, τουτέστιν,
ὡς ἡ ΑΟ πρὸς τὴν ΡΝ, οὕτως ἡ ΑΜ πρὸς τὴν ΡΜ, δι᾽ ὁμοιότητα τριγώνων add. W
καί] om. W   10. ΜΡ] ΡΜ W   μείζονα] πολλῷ μείζονα W   14. η] τὰ η W
15, 17. ιη] ὀκτωκαιδεκαπλασίων W   31. ὡσαύτως] ὡσαυτῶι Vat.

Let a plane be carried through the axis,
and let it cut the sun in the circle *DEF*, the earth in *GHK*, the
shadow in the circumference *NO*, and the cone in the straight
lines *DM, FM*.

Let *NO* be joined, and from *A* let *PAQ* be drawn at right
angles to *AM*.

Then, since *NO* is less than 1/9th part of the diameter of the
sun,   [Prop. 13]
therefore *PQ* has to *NO* a ratio much greater than that which
9 has to 1.

Therefore *AM* also has to *MR* a ratio greater than that
which 9 has to 1 ;
and, *convertendo*, *MA* has to *AR* a ratio less than that which
9 has to 8.

Again, since *AB* is greater than 18 times *BC*,   [Prop. 7]
therefore it is much greater than 18 times *BR* ;
therefore *AB* has to *BR* a ratio greater than that which 18
has to 1 ;
therefore, inversely, *BR* has to *BA* a ratio less than that which
1 has to 18 ;
therefore, *componendo*, *RA* has to *AB* a ratio less than that
which 19 has to 18.

But it was proved that *MA* also has to *AR* a ratio less than
that which 9 has to 8 ;
therefore, *ex aequali*, *MA* will have to *AB* a ratio less than
that which 171 has to 144, and therefore less than that which 19 has
to 16 : for parts have the same ratio as the same multiples of
them :

ἀναστρέψαντι ἄρα ἡ ΑΜ πρὸς ΒΜ μείζονα λόγον ἔχει ἢ ὃν τὰ ιθ
πρὸς τὰ γ. ὡς δὲ ἡ ΑΜ πρὸς ΜΒ, οὕτως ἡ διάμετρος τοῦ ΔΕΖ
κύκλου πρὸς τὴν διάμετρον τοῦ ΗΘΚ κύκλου· ἡ ἄρα τοῦ ἡλίου
διάμετρος πρὸς τὴν τῆς γῆς διάμετρον μείζονα λόγον ἔχει ἢ ὃν τὰ ιθ
5 πρὸς γ.

Λέγω δὴ ὅτι ἐλάσσονα λόγον ἔχει ⟨πρὸς αὐτὴν⟩ ἢ ὃν τὰ μγ πρὸς
ϛ. ἐπεὶ γὰρ ἡ ΒΓ πρὸς τὴν ΓΡ μείζονα λόγον ἔχει ἢ ὃν τὰ χοε πρὸς
α, ἀναστρέψαντι ἄρα ἡ ΓΒ πρὸς τὴν ΒΡ ἐλάσσονα λόγον ἔχει ἢ ὃν
τὰ χοε πρὸς τὰ χοδ. ἔχει δὲ καὶ ἡ ΑΒ πρὸς τὴν ΒΓ ἐλάσσονα
10 λόγον ἢ ὃν τὰ κ πρὸς α· ἕξει ἄρα δι' ἴσου ἡ ΑΒ πρὸς τὴν ΒΡ
ἐλάσσονα λόγον ἢ ὃν τὰ Μ̇γφ πρὸς τὰ χοδ, τουτέστιν, ἢ ὃν τὰ
͵ϛψν πρὸς τὰ τλϛ· ἀνάπαλιν ἄρα καὶ συνθέντι ἡ ΡΑ πρὸς τὴν ΑΒ
μείζονα λόγον ἔχει ἢ ὃν τὰ ͵ζπϛ πρὸς ͵ϛψν. καὶ ἐπεὶ ἡ ΝΞ πρὸς
τὴν ΟΠ μείζονα λόγον ἔχει ἢ ⟨ὃν τὰ⟩ ᾿λοθ πρὸς Μ̇ρκε, ἀνάπαλιν
15 ἄρα ἡ ΟΠ πρὸς ΝΞ ἐλάσσονα λόγον ἔχει ἢ ⟨ὃν τὰ⟩ Μ̇ρκε πρὸς
᾿λοθ· ὡς δὲ ἡ ΟΠ πρὸς ΝΞ, οὕτως ἡ ΑΜ πρὸς ΜΡ· καὶ ἡ ΑΜ
ἄρα πρὸς ΜΡ ἐλάσσονα λόγον ἔχει ἢ ⟨ὃν τὰ⟩ Μ̇ρκε πρὸς ᾿λοθ·
ἀναστρέψαντι ἡ ΜΑ ἄρα πρὸς τὴν ΑΡ μείζονα λόγον ἔχει ἢ ὃν τὰ
Μ̇ρκε πρὸς τὰ ͵θρμϛ. ἔχει δὲ καὶ ἡ ΡΑ πρὸς ΑΒ μείζονα λόγον ἢ
20 ὃν τὰ ͵ζπϛ πρὸς τὰ ͵ϛψν· δι' ἴσου ἄρα ἕξει ἡ ΜΑ πρὸς τὴν ΑΒ
μείζονα λόγον ἢ ὃν ὁ περιεχόμενος ἀριθμὸς ὑπὸ τῶν Μ̇ρκε καὶ τῶν
͵ζπϛ πρὸς τὸν περιεχόμενον ἀριθμὸν ὑπό τε τῶν ͵θρμϛ καὶ τῶν
͵ϛψν, τουτέστιν, ὁ Μ̇ϛροε͵εωοε πρὸς Μ̇᾿ϛρογ͵εφ. ἔχει δὲ καὶ ὁ Μ̇ϛροε͵εωοε
πρὸς Μ̇᾿ϛρογ͵εφ μείζονα λόγον ἢ ὃν τὰ μγ πρὸς λζ· καὶ ἡ ΜΑ ἄρα πρὸς
25 τὴν ΑΒ μείζονα λόγον ἔχει ἢ ὃν μγ πρὸς λζ· ἀναστρέψαντι ἄρα ἡ

---

1. ΑΜ] ΑΒ W   6. δὴ] δὲ W   ⟨πρὸς αὐτὴν⟩ addidi   8. ἄρα] ἕξει ἄρα W,
qui lacunam post l. 7 χοε expleverat   ἔχει] om. W   11. Μ̇γφ] Μα͵γφ W
12. τλϛ] τλν Vat.   13. ͵ϛψν] τὰ ͵ϛψν W   14, 15, 17, 19, 21. Μ̇ρκε] Μα͵ρκε W
16. ᾿λοθ] τὰ ᾿λοθ W   17. ᾿λοθ] τὰ ᾿λοθ W   21-2. τῶν ͵ζπϛ] τὸν ͵ζπϛ Vat.
23, 24. Μ̇ϛροε͵εωοε] Μ͵ϛροε καὶ ͵εωοε W, bis   Μ̇᾿ϛρογ͵εφ] Μ͵ϛρογ καὶ ͵εφ W, bis (haud recte)

therefore, *convertendo, AM* has to *BM* a ratio greater than that which 19 has to 3.

But, as *AM* is to *MB*, so is the diameter of the circle *DEF* to the diameter of the circle *GHK*;

therefore the diameter of the sun has to the diameter of the earth a ratio greater than that which 19 has to 3.

Again, I say that it has to it a ratio less than that which 43 has to 6.

For, since *BC* has to *CR* a ratio greater than that which 675 has to 1,   [Prop. 14]

therefore, *convertendo, CB* has to *BR* a ratio less than that which 675 has to 674.

But *AB* also has to *BC* a ratio less than that which 20 has to 1;   [Prop. 7]

therefore, *ex aequali, AB* will have to *BR* a ratio less than that which 13500 has to 674, that is, than that which 6750 has to 337;

therefore, inversely and *componendo, RA* has to *AB* a ratio greater than that which 7087 has to 6750.

Now, since *NO* has to *PQ* a ratio greater than that which 979 has to 10125,   [Prop. 13]

therefore, inversely, *PQ* has to *NO* a ratio less than that which 10125 has to 979.

And, as *PQ* is to *NO*, so is *AM* to *MR*;

therefore *AM* also has to *MR* a ratio less than that which 10125 has to 979;

therefore, *convertendo, MA* has to *AR* a ratio greater than that which 10125 has to 9146.

But *RA* also has to *AB* a ratio greater than that which 7087 has to 6750;

therefore, *ex aequali, MA* will have to *AB* a ratio greater than that which the number representing the product of 10125 and 7087 has to the number representing the product of 9146 and 6750, that is, 71755875 to 61735500.

But 71755875 has to 61735500 a ratio greater than that which 43 has to 37;[1]

therefore *MA* also has to *AB* a ratio greater than that which 43 has to 37;

---

[1] As to this approximation see p. 336 *ad fin.*

AM πρὸς τὴν MB ἐλάσσονα λόγον ἔχει ἢ ὃν τὰ μγ πρὸς ς. ὡς δὲ
ἡ AM πρὸς τὴν BM, οὕτως ἐστὶν ἡ διάμετρος τοῦ ἡλίου πρὸς τὴν
διάμετρον τῆς γῆς· ἡ ἄρα διάμετρος τοῦ ἡλίου πρὸς τὴν διάμετρον
τῆς γῆς ἐλάσσονα λόγον ἔχει ἢ ὃν μγ πρὸς ς. ἐδείχθη δὲ καὶ
5 μείζονα λόγον ἔχουσα ἢ ὃν τὰ ιθ πρὸς τὰ γ.

ις΄.

Ὁ ἥλιος πρὸς τὴν γῆν μείζονα λόγον ἔχει ἢ ὃν ͵ςωνθ
πρὸς κζ, ἐλάσσονα δὲ ἢ ὃν M̅ ,θφζ πρὸς σις.

Ἔστω γὰρ ἡλίου μὲν διάμετρος ἡ A, γῆς δὲ ἡ B. ἀποδείκνυται
10 δὲ ὅτι ἐστίν, ὡς ἡ τοῦ ἡλίου σφαῖρα πρὸς τὴν τῆς γῆς σφαῖραν,
οὕτως ὁ ἀπὸ τῆς διαμέτρου τοῦ ἡλίου κύβος πρὸς τὸν ἀπὸ τῆς
διαμέτρου τῆς γῆς κύβον, ὥσπερ καὶ ἐπὶ τῆς σελήνης, ὥστε ἐπεί
ἐστιν, ὡς ὁ ἀπὸ τῆς A κύβος πρὸς τὸν ἀπὸ τῆς B κύβον, οὕτως
ὁ ἥλιος πρὸς τὴν γῆν, ὁ δὲ ἀπὸ τῆς A κύβος πρὸς τὸν ἀπὸ τῆς
15 B ⟨κύβον⟩ μείζονα λόγον ἔχει ἢ ὃν τὰ ͵ςωνθ πρὸς κζ, ἐλάσσονα δὲ
ἢ ὃν M̅ ,θφζ πρὸς σις· καὶ γὰρ ἡ A πρὸς τὴν B μείζονα λόγον ἔχει
ἢ ὃν ιθ΄ πρὸς γ, ἐλάσσονα δὲ ἢ ὃν μγ πρὸς ς· ὥστε ὁ ἥλιος πρὸς
τὴν γῆν μείζονα λόγον ἔχει ἢ ὃν ͵ςωνθ πρὸς κζ, ἐλάσσονα δὲ ἢ ὃν
M̅ ,θφζ πρὸς σις.

20   ιζ΄.

Ἡ διάμετρος τῆς γῆς πρὸς τὴν διάμετρον τῆς σελήνης
ἐν μείζονι μὲν λόγῳ ἐστὶν ἢ ὃν ⟨ἔχει⟩ ρη πρὸς μγ, ἐν
ἐλάσσονι δὲ ἢ ὃν ξ πρὸς ιθ.

1. τὴν MB] MB W   2. ἡ AM] AM W

6. ις΄] IE Vat.   8. κζ] τὰ κζ W   M̅,θφζ] μυριάδες ζ καὶ ,θφζ W   σις] ις Vat.
et codd. Paris., excepto 2364   9. γῆς δὲ] γῆς W   11. διαμέτρου] διαμέτρου
τῆς W   14. τὸν] τὴν Vat.   15. ⟨κύβον⟩] om. Vat. et codd. Paris.   16. M̅,θφζ]
Μζ,θφζ W   σις] ις Vat.   17. ὥστε] apodosis hic desideratur; exspectaveris
διὰ ταῦτα δὴ ὁ ἥλιος vel ὁ ἥλιος ἄρα   19. M̅,θφζ] μυριάδες ζ καὶ ,θφζ W
20. ιζ΄] ις Vat.   22. ρη] τὰ ρη W

therefore, *convertendo*, AM has to MB a ratio less than that which 43 has to 6.

But, as AM is to BM, so is the diameter of the sun to the diameter of the earth ;

therefore the diameter of the sun has to the diameter of the earth a ratio less than that which 43 has to 6.

And it was before proved that it has to it a ratio greater than that which 19 has to 3.

PROPOSITION 16.

The sun has to the earth a ratio greater than that which 6859 *has to* 27, *but less than that which* 79507 *has to* 216.

For let A be the diameter of the sun, B that of the earth.

Now it is proved that, as the sphere of the sun is to the sphere of the earth, so is the cube on the diameter of the sun to the cube

A————————————————————

B————

Fig. 35.

on the diameter of the earth, just as in the case of the moon [cf. Prop. 10].

Thus, since, as the cube on A is to the cube on B, so is the sun to the earth,

while the cube on A has to the cube on B a ratio greater than that which 6859 has to 27, but less than that which 79507 has to 216:

for A has to B a ratio greater than that which 19 has to 3, but less than that which 43 has to 6:   [Prop. 15]

it follows that the sun has to the earth a ratio greater than that which 6859 has to 27, but less than that which 79507 has to 216.

PROPOSITION 17.

The diameter of the earth is to the diameter of the moon in a ratio greater than that which 108 *has to* 43, *but less than that which* 60 *has to* 19.

Ἔστω γὰρ ἡλίου μὲν διάμετρος ἡ Α, σελήνης δὲ ἡ Β, γῆς δὲ
ἡ Γ. καὶ ἐπεὶ ἡ Α πρὸς τὴν Γ ἐλάσσονα λόγον ἔχει ἢ ὃν τὰ μγ
πρὸς ϛ, ἀνάπαλιν ἄρα ἡ Γ πρὸς τὴν Α μείζονα λόγον ἔχει ἢ ὃν ϛ
πρὸς μγ. ἔχει δὲ καὶ ἡ Α πρὸς τὴν Β μείζονα λόγον ἢ ὃν τὰ
5 ιη πρὸς α· δι' ἴσου ἄρα ἡ Γ πρὸς τὴν Β μείζονα λόγον ἔχει ἢ ὃν

A _____
  ᵃ
        ᵦ B ——
      C ————
        γ

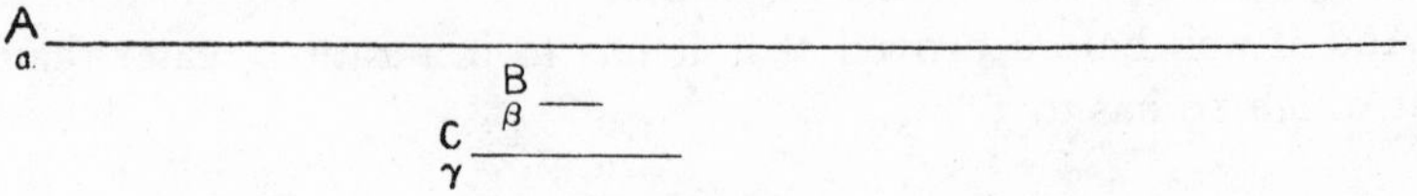

Fig. 36.

τὰ ρη πρὸς τὰ μγ. πάλιν ἐπεὶ ἡ Α πρὸς τὴν Γ μείζονα λόγον ἔχει
ἢ ὃν τὰ ιθ πρὸς τὰ γ, ἀνάπαλιν ἄρα ἡ Γ πρὸς τὴν Α ἐλάσσονα
λόγον ἔχει ἢ ὃν τὰ γ πρὸς τὰ ιθ. ἔχει δὲ ἡ Α πρὸς τὴν Β ἐλάσσονα
λόγον ἢ ὃν τὰ κ πρὸς α· δι' ἴσου ἄρα ἡ Γ πρὸς τὴν Β ἐλάσσονα λόγον
10 ἔχει ἢ ὃν ξ πρὸς ιθ.

ιη΄.

Ἡ γῆ πρὸς τὴν σελήνην ἐν μείζονι μὲν λόγῳ ἐστὶν
ἢ ὃν ⟨ἔχει⟩ M̅ ρκε ̦θψιβ πρὸς M̅ ̦θφϛ ζ, ἐν ἐλάσσονι δὲ ἢ ὃν
M̅ κα ϛ πρὸς ̦ϛωνθ.

15 Ἔστω γὰρ γῆς μὲν διάμετρος ἡ Α, σελήνης δὲ ἡ Β· ἡ Α ἄρα
πρὸς τὴν Β μείζονα λόγον ἔχει ἢ ὃν τὰ ρη πρὸς τὰ μγ, ἐλάσσονα
δὲ ἢ ὃν τὰ ξ πρὸς ιθ· καὶ ὁ ἀπὸ τῆς Α ἄρα κύβος πρὸς τὸν ἀπὸ τῆς
Β κύβον μείζονα λόγον ἔχει ἢ ὃν M̅ ρκε ̦θψιβ πρὸς M̅ ̦θφϛ ζ, ἐλάσσονα
δὲ ἢ ὃν M̅ κα ϛ πρὸς ̦ϛωνθ. ὡς δὲ ὁ ἀπὸ τῆς Α κύβος πρὸς τὸν ἀπὸ
20 τῆς Β κύβον, οὕτως ἐστὶν ἡ γῆ πρὸς τὴν σελήνην· ἡ γῆ ἄρα πρὸς
τὴν σελήνην μείζονα μὲν λόγον ἔχει ἢ ὃν M̅ ρκε ̦θψιβ πρὸς M̅ ̦θφϛ ζ,
ἐλάσσονα δὲ ἢ ὃν M̅ κα ϛ πρὸς ̦ϛωνθ.

1 σελήνης δὲ ἡ Β] σελήνης ἡ Β W   5. ἄρα] γὰρ Vat.   8. ιθ] θ Vat.
ἢ] καὶ ἡ W

11. ιη΄] ΙΖ Vat.   13. ⟨ἔχει⟩ M̅ ρκε ̦θψιβ] ἔχουσι μυριάδες ρκε καὶ ̦θψιβ W
13, 18, 21. M̅ ̦θφϛ ζ] Μζ ̦θφϛ W   14, 19, 22. M̅ ̦ϛ] Μκα ̦ϛ W   16. τὰ μγ]
μγ W   18, 21. M̅ ρκε ̦θψιβ] Μρκε ̦θψιβ W   21. πρὸς] πρὸς μὲν W

For let A be the diameter of the sun, B that of the moon, C that of the earth.

Then, since A has to C a ratio less than that which 43 has to 6,
[Prop. 15]
therefore, inversely, C has to A a ratio greater than that which 6 has to 43.

But A also has to B a ratio greater than that which 18 has to 1 ;
[Prop. 9]
therefore, *ex aequali*, C has to B a ratio greater than that which 108 has to 43.

Again, since A has to C a ratio greater than that which 19 has to 3,
[Prop. 15]
therefore, inversely, C has to A a ratio less than that which 3 has to 19.

But A also has to B a ratio less than that which 20 has to 1 ;
[Prop. 9]
therefore, *ex aequali*, C has to B a ratio less than that which 60 has to 19.

PROPOSITION 18.

The earth is to the moon in a ratio greater than that which 1259712 *has to* 79507, *but less than that which* 216000 *has to* 6859.

For let A be the diameter of the earth, B that of the moon ;
therefore A has to B a ratio greater than that which 108 has to 43, but less than that which 60 has to 19.   [Prop. 17]

Therefore also the cube on A has to the cube on B a ratio

A ——————————

B ——

Fig. 37.

greater than that which 1259712 has to 79507, but less than that which 216000 has to 6859.

But, as the cube on A is to the cube on B, so is the earth to the moon ;
therefore the earth has to the moon a ratio greater than that which 1259712 has to 79507, but less than that which 216000 has to 6859.

COMMENTS OF PAPPUS.[1]

'In his book on sizes and distances Aristarchus lays down these six hypotheses :

1. That the moon receives light from the sun.
2. That the earth is in the relation of a point and centre to the sphere in which the moon moves.[2]
3. That, when the moon appears to us halved, the great circle which divides the dark and the bright portions of the moon is in the direction of our eye.
4. That, when the moon appears to us halved, its distance from the sun is then less than a quadrant by one-thirtieth of a quadrant.[3]
5. That the breadth of the (earth's) shadow is (that) of two moons.
6. That the moon subtends one fifteenth part of a sign of the zodiac.

Now the first, third, and fourth of these hypotheses practically agree with the assumptions of Hipparchus and Ptolemy. For the moon is illuminated by the sun at all times except during an eclipse, when it becomes devoid of light through passing into the shadow which results from the interception of the sun's light by the earth, and which is conical in form; next the (circle) dividing the milk-white portion which owes its colour to the sun shining upon it and the portion which has the ashen colour natural to the moon itself is indistinguishable from a great circle (in the moon) when its positions in relation to the sun cause it to appear halved, at which times (a distance of) very nearly a quadrant on the circle of the zodiac is observed (to separate them) ; and the said dividing circle is in the direction of our eye, for this plane of the circle if produced will in fact pass through our eye in whatever position the moon is when for the first or second time it appears halved.

---

[1] Pappus, vi, pp. 554. 6–560. 10 (Hultsch).
[2] Literally, ' the sphere of the moon.'
[3] Hultsch brackets, as an obvious interpolation, words added here in the Greek text ' instead of (saying) that its distance is 87° : for this is less than a quadrant, or 90°, by 3°, which is 1/30th of 90° '.

But, as regards the remaining hypotheses, the aforesaid mathematicians have taken a different view. For according to them the earth has the relation of a point and centre, not to the sphere in which the moon moves, but to the sphere of the fixed stars, the breadth of the (earth's) shadow is not (that) of two moons, nor does the moon's diameter subtend [1] one fifteenth part of a sign of the zodiac, that is, 2°. According to Hipparchus, on the one hand, the circle described by the moon is measured 650 times by the diameter of the moon, while the (earth's) shadow is measured by it $2\frac{1}{2}$ times at its mean distance in the conjunctions; in Ptolemy's view, on the other hand, the moon's diameter subtends, when the moon is at its greatest distance, a circumference of 0° 31′ 20″, and when at its least distance, of 0° 35′ 20″, while the diameter of the circular section of the shadow is, when the moon is at its greatest distance, 0° 40′ 40″, and when the moon is at its least distance, 0° 46′.

Hence it is that the authors named have come to different conclusions as regards the ratios both of the distances and of the sizes of the sun and moon.

Now Aristarchus, after stating the aforesaid hypotheses, proceeds in a passage which I will quote word for word.[2]

" We are now in a position to prove that the distance of the sun from the earth is greater than 18 times, but less than 20 times, the distance of the moon, and the diameter of the sun also has the same ratio to the diameter of the moon: this follows from the hypothesis about the halved (moon). Again, we can prove that the diameter of the sun is to the diameter of the earth in a greater ratio than that which 19 has to 3, but in a less ratio than that which 43 has to 6: this follows from the ratio thus discovered as regards the distances, from the hypothesis about the shadow and from the hypothesis that the moon subtends one fifteenth part of a sign of the zodiac."

He says " We are in a position to prove that the distances ", &c.,

---

[1] Hultsch brackets, as an interpolation, some clumsy words in the Greek text, the object of which is to qualify 'diameter' and make it mean the diameter of the moon when it is 'at the same mean distance'; there are no such words in Aristarchus.

[2] Gk. λέγων κατὰ λέξιν οὕτως. Although Pappus professes to quote Aristarchus word for word, he shows some slight variations from the text of Aristarchus as we have it; where the changes are for the worse, however, they may be due to copyists rather than to Pappus himself.

implying that he will prove the properties after giving such preliminary lemmas as are of use for the proofs of them. As the result of the whole investigation he concludes that

(1) the sun has to the earth a greater ratio than that which 6859 has to 27, but a less ratio than that which 79507 has to 216;

(2) the diameter of the earth is to the diameter of the moon in a greater ratio than that which 108 has to 43, but in a less (ratio) than that which 60 has to 19; and

(3) the earth is to the moon in a greater ratio than that which 1259712 has to 79507, but in a less (ratio) than that which 216000 has to 6859.

But Ptolemy proved in the fifth book of his Syntaxis[1] that, if the radius of the earth is taken as the unit, the greatest distance of the moon at the conjunctions is $64\frac{10}{60}$ of such units, the greatest distance of the sun 1210, the radius of the moon $\frac{17}{60}\frac{33}{60^2}$, the radius of the sun $5\frac{30}{60}$. Consequently, if the diameter of the moon is taken as the unit, the earth's diameter is $3\frac{2}{5}$ of such units, and the sun's diameter $18\frac{4}{5}$. That is to say, the diameter of the earth is $3\frac{2}{5}$ times the diameter of the moon, while the diameter of the sun is $18\frac{4}{5}$ times the diameter of the moon and $5\frac{1}{2}$ times the diameter of the earth.

From these figures the ratios between the solid contents are manifest, since the cube on 1 is 1 unit, the cube on $3\frac{2}{5}$ is very nearly $39\frac{1}{4}$ of the same units, and the cube on $18\frac{4}{5}$ very nearly $6644\frac{1}{2}$, whence we infer that, if the solid magnitude of the moon is taken as a unit, that of the earth contains $39\frac{1}{4}$ and that of the sun $6644\frac{1}{2}$ of such units; therefore the solid magnitude of the sun is very nearly 170 times greater than that of the earth.'

[1] Ptolemy, *Syntaxis*, v, 14–16, vol. i, pp. 416–427, Heib.

INDEX

A CATALOGUE OF
SELECTED DOVER BOOKS
IN ALL FIELDS OF INTEREST

A CATALOGUE OF SELECTED DOVER
BOOKS IN ALL FIELDS OF INTEREST

CONDITIONED REFLEXES, Ivan P. Pavlov. Full translation of most complete statement of Pavlov's work; cerebral damage, conditioned reflex, experiments with dogs, sleep, similar topics of great importance. 430pp. 5⅜ x 8½. 60614-7 Pa. $4.50

NOTES ON NURSING: WHAT IT IS, AND WHAT IT IS NOT, Florence Nightingale. Outspoken writings by founder of modern nursing. When first published (1860) it played an important role in much needed revolution in nursing. Still stimulating. 140pp. 5⅜ x 8½. 22340-X Pa. $3.00

HARTER'S PICTURE ARCHIVE FOR COLLAGE AND ILLUSTRATION, Jim Harter. Over 300 authentic, rare 19th-century engravings selected by noted collagist for artists, designers, decoupeurs, etc. Machines, people, animals, etc., printed one side of page. 25 scene plates for backgrounds. 6 collages by Harter, Satty, Singer, Evans. Introduction. 192pp. 8⅞ x 11¾. 23659-5 Pa. $5.00

MANUAL OF TRADITIONAL WOOD CARVING, edited by Paul N. Hasluck. Possibly the best book in English on the craft of wood carving. Practical instructions, along with 1,146 working drawings and photographic illustrations. Formerly titled *Cassell's Wood Carving.* 576pp. 6½ x 9¼. 23489-4 Pa. $7.95

THE PRINCIPLES AND PRACTICE OF HAND OR SIMPLE TURNING, John Jacob Holtzapffel. Full coverage of basic lathe techniques—history and development, special apparatus, softwood turning, hardwood turning, metal turning. Many projects—billiard ball, works formed within a sphere, egg cups, ash trays, vases, jardiniers, others—included. 1881 edition. 800 illustrations. 592pp. 6⅛ x 9¼. 23365-0 Clothbd. $15.00

THE JOY OF HANDWEAVING, Osma Tod. Only book you need for hand weaving. Fundamentals, threads, weaves, plus numerous projects for small board-loom, two-harness, tapestry, laid-in, four-harness weaving and more. Over 160 illustrations. 2nd revised edition. 352pp. 6½ x 9¼. 23458-4 Pa. $6.00

THE BOOK OF WOOD CARVING, Charles Marshall Sayers. Still finest book for beginning student in wood sculpture. Noted teacher, craftsman discusses fundamentals, technique; gives 34 designs, over 34 projects for panels, bookends, mirrors, etc. "Absolutely first-rate"—E. J. Tangerman. 33 photos. 118pp. 7¾ x 10⅝. 23654-4 Pa. $3.50

ART FORMS IN NATURE, Ernst Haeckel. Multitude of strangely beautiful natural forms: Radiolaria, Foraminifera, jellyfishes, fungi, turtles, bats, etc. All 100 plates of the 19th-century evolutionist's *Kunstformen der Natur* (1904). 100pp. 9⅜ x 12¼. 22987-4 Pa. $5.00

CHILDREN: A PICTORIAL ARCHIVE FROM NINETEENTH-CENTURY SOURCES, edited by Carol Belanger Grafton. 242 rare, copyright-free wood engravings for artists and designers. Widest such selection available. All illustrations in line. 119pp. 8⅜ x 11¼. 23694-3 Pa. $4.00

WOMEN: A PICTORIAL ARCHIVE FROM NINETEENTH-CENTURY SOURCES, edited by Jim Harter. 391 copyright-free wood engravings for artists and designers selected from rare periodicals. Most extensive such collection available. All illustrations in line. 128pp. 9 x 12. 23703-6 Pa. $4.50

ARABIC ART IN COLOR, Prisse d'Avennes. From the greatest ornamentalists of all time—50 plates in color, rarely seen outside the Near East, rich in suggestion and stimulus. Includes 4 plates on covers. 46pp. 9⅜ x 12¼. 23658-7 Pa. $6.00

AUTHENTIC ALGERIAN CARPET DESIGNS AND MOTIFS, edited by June Beveridge. Algerian carpets are world famous. Dozens of geometrical motifs are charted on grids, color-coded, for weavers, needleworkers, craftsmen, designers. 53 illustrations plus 4 in color. 48pp. 8¼ x 11. (Available in U.S. only) 23650-1 Pa. $1.75

DICTIONARY OF AMERICAN PORTRAITS, edited by Hayward and Blanche Cirker. 4000 important Americans, earliest times to 1905, mostly in clear line. Politicians, writers, soldiers, scientists, inventors, industrialists, Indians, Blacks, women, outlaws, etc. Identificatory information. 756pp. 9¼ x 12¾. 21823-6 Clothbd. $40.00

HOW THE OTHER HALF LIVES, Jacob A. Riis. Journalistic record of filth, degradation, upward drive in New York immigrant slums, shops, around 1900. New edition includes 100 original Riis photos, monuments of early photography. 233pp. 10 x 7⅞. 22012-5 Pa. $7.00

NEW YORK IN THE THIRTIES, Berenice Abbott. Noted photographer's fascinating study of city shows new buildings that have become famous and old sights that have disappeared forever. Insightful commentary. 97 photographs. 97pp. 11⅜ x 10. 22967-X Pa. $5.00

MEN AT WORK, Lewis W. Hine. Famous photographic studies of construction workers, railroad men, factory workers and coal miners. New supplement of 18 photos on Empire State building construction. New introduction by Jonathan L. Doherty. Total of 69 photos. 63pp. 8 x 10¾. 23475-4 Pa. $3.00

THE SENSE OF BEAUTY, George Santayana. Masterfully written discussion of nature of beauty, materials of beauty, form, expression; art, literature, social sciences all involved. 168pp. 5⅜ x 8½. 20238-0 Pa. $3.00

ON THE IMPROVEMENT OF THE UNDERSTANDING, Benedict Spinoza. Also contains *Ethics, Correspondence,* all in excellent R. Elwes translation. Basic works on entry to philosophy, pantheism, exchange of ideas with great contemporaries. 402pp. 5⅜ x 8½. 20250-X Pa. $4.50

THE TRAGIC SENSE OF LIFE, Miguel de Unamuno. Acknowledged masterpiece of existential literature, one of most important books of 20th century. Introduction by Madariaga. 367pp. 5⅜ x 8½.
20257-7 Pa. $4.50

THE GUIDE FOR THE PERPLEXED, Moses Maimonides. Great classic of medieval Judaism attempts to reconcile revealed religion (Pentateuch, commentaries) with Aristotelian philosophy. Important historically, still relevant in problems. Unabridged Friedlander translation. Total of 473pp. 5⅜ x 8½. 20351-4 Pa. $6.00

THE I CHING (THE BOOK OF CHANGES), translated by James Legge. Complete translation of basic text plus appendices by Confucius, and Chinese commentary of most penetrating divination manual ever prepared. Indispensable to study of early Oriental civilizations, to modern inquiring reader. 448pp. 5⅜ x 8½. 21062-6 Pa. $5.00

THE EGYPTIAN BOOK OF THE DEAD, E. A. Wallis Budge. Complete reproduction of Ani's papyrus, finest ever found. Full hieroglyphic text, interlinear transliteration, word for word translation, smooth translation. Basic work, for Egyptology, for modern study of psychic matters. Total of 533pp. 6½ x 9¼. (Available in U.S. only) 21866-X Pa. $5.95

THE GODS OF THE EGYPTIANS, E. A. Wallis Budge. Never excelled for richness, fullness: all gods, goddesses, demons, mythical figures of Ancient Egypt; their legends, rites, incarnations, variations, powers, etc. Many hieroglyphic texts cited. Over 225 illustrations, plus 6 color plates. Total of 988pp. 6⅛ x 9¼. (Available in U.S. only)
22055-9, 22056-7 Pa., Two-vol. set $16.00

THE STANDARD BOOK OF QUILT MAKING AND COLLECTING, Marguerite Ickis. Full information, full-sized patterns for making 46 traditional quilts, also 150 other patterns. Quilted cloths, lame, satin quilts, etc. 483 illustrations. 273pp. 6⅞ x 9⅝. 20582-7 Pa. $4.95

CORAL GARDENS AND THEIR MAGIC, Bronsilaw Malinowski. Classic study of the methods of tilling the soil and of agricultural rites in the Trobriand Islands of Melanesia. Author is one of the most important figures in the field of modern social anthropology. 143 illustrations. Indexes. Total of 911pp. of text. 5⅝ x 8¼. (Available in U.S. only)
23597-1 Pa. $12.95

THE PHILOSOPHY OF HISTORY, Georg W. Hegel. Great classic of Western thought develops concept that history is not chance but a rational process, the evolution of freedom. 457pp. 5⅜ x 8½. 20112-0 Pa. $4.50

LANGUAGE, TRUTH AND LOGIC, Alfred J. Ayer. Famous, clear introduction to Vienna, Cambridge schools of Logical Positivism. Role of philosophy, elimination of metaphysics, nature of analysis, etc. 160pp. 5⅜ x 8½. (Available in U.S. only) 20010-8 Pa. $2.00

A PREFACE TO LOGIC, Morris R. Cohen. Great City College teacher in renowned, easily followed exposition of formal logic, probability, values, logic and world order and similar topics; no previous background needed. 209pp. 5⅜ x 8½. 23517-3 Pa. $3.50

REASON AND NATURE, Morris R. Cohen. Brilliant analysis of reason and its multitudinous ramifications by charismatic teacher. Interdisciplinary, synthesizing work widely praised when it first appeared in 1931. Second (1953) edition. Indexes. 496pp. 5⅜ x 8½. 23633-1 Pa. $6.50

AN ESSAY CONCERNING HUMAN UNDERSTANDING, John Locke. The only complete edition of enormously important classic, with authoritative editorial material by A. C. Fraser. Total of 1176pp. 5⅜ x 8½.
20530-4, 20531-2 Pa., Two-vol. set $16.00

HANDBOOK OF MATHEMATICAL FUNCTIONS WITH FORMULAS, GRAPHS, AND MATHEMATICAL TABLES, edited by Milton Abramowitz and Irene A. Stegun. Vast compendium: 29 sets of tables, some to as high as 20 places. 1,046pp. 8 x 10½. 61272-4 Pa. $14.95

MATHEMATICS FOR THE PHYSICAL SCIENCES, Herbert S. Wilf. Highly acclaimed work offers clear presentations of vector spaces and matrices, orthogonal functions, roots of polynomial equations, conformal mapping, calculus of variations, etc. Knowledge of theory of functions of real and complex variables is assumed. Exercises and solutions. Index. 284pp. 5⅝ x 8¼. 63635-6 Pa. $5.00

THE PRINCIPLE OF RELATIVITY, Albert Einstein et al. Eleven most important original papers on special and general theories. Seven by Einstein, two by Lorentz, one each by Minkowski and Weyl. All translated, unabridged. 216pp. 5⅜ x 8½. 60081-5 Pa. $3.50

THERMODYNAMICS, Enrico Fermi. A classic of modern science. Clear, organized treatment of systems, first and second laws, entropy, thermodynamic potentials, gaseous reactions, dilute solutions, entropy constant. No math beyond calculus required. Problems. 160pp. 5⅜ x 8½.
60361-X Pa. $3.00

ELEMENTARY MECHANICS OF FLUIDS, Hunter Rouse. Classic undergraduate text widely considered to be far better than many later books. Ranges from fluid velocity and acceleration to role of compressibility in fluid motion. Numerous examples, questions, problems. 224 illustrations. 376pp. 5⅝ x 8¼. 63699-2 Pa. $5.00

HISTORY OF BACTERIOLOGY, William Bulloch. The only comprehensive history of bacteriology from the beginnings through the 19th century. Special emphasis is given to biography-Leeuwenhoek, etc. Brief accounts of 350 bacteriologists form a separate section. No clearer, fuller study, suitable to scientists and general readers, has yet been written. 52 illustrations. 448pp. 5⅝ x 8¼. 23761-3 Pa. $6.50

THE COMPLETE NONSENSE OF EDWARD LEAR, Edward Lear. All nonsense limericks, zany alphabets, Owl and Pussycat, songs, nonsense botany, etc., illustrated by Lear. Total of 321pp. 5⅜ x 8½. (Available in U.S. only) 20167-8 Pa. $3.95

INGENIOUS MATHEMATICAL PROBLEMS AND METHODS, Louis A. Graham. Sophisticated material from Graham *Dial*, applied and pure; stresses solution methods. Logic, number theory, networks, inversions, etc. 237pp. 5⅜ x 8½. 20545-2 Pa. $4.50

BEST MATHEMATICAL PUZZLES OF SAM LOYD, edited by Martin Gardner. Bizarre, original, whimsical puzzles by America's greatest puzzler. From fabulously rare *Cyclopedia*, including famous 14-15 puzzles, the Horse of a Different Color, 115 more. Elementary math. 150 illustrations. 167pp. 5⅜ x 8½. 20498-7 Pa. $2.75

THE BASIS OF COMBINATION IN CHESS, J. du Mont. Easy-to-follow, instructive book on elements of combination play, with chapters on each piece and every powerful combination team—two knights, bishop and knight, rook and bishop, etc. 250 diagrams. 218pp. 5⅜ x 8½. (Available in U.S. only) 23644-7 Pa. $3.50

MODERN CHESS STRATEGY, Ludek Pachman. The use of the queen, the active king, exchanges, pawn play, the center, weak squares, etc. Section on rook alone worth price of the book. Stress on the moderns. Often considered the most important book on strategy. 314pp. 5⅜ x 8½. 20290-9 Pa. $4.50

LASKER'S MANUAL OF CHESS, Dr. Emanuel Lasker. Great world champion offers very thorough coverage of all aspects of chess. Combinations, position play, openings, end game, aesthetics of chess, philosophy of struggle, much more. Filled with analyzed games. 390pp. 5⅜ x 8½. 20640-8 Pa. $5.00

500 MASTER GAMES OF CHESS, S. Tartakower, J. du Mont. Vast collection of great chess games from 1798-1938, with much material nowhere else readily available. Fully annotated, arranged by opening for easier study. 664pp. 5⅜ x 8½. 23208-5 Pa. $7.50

A GUIDE TO CHESS ENDINGS, Dr. Max Euwe, David Hooper. One of the finest modern works on chess endings. Thorough analysis of the most frequently encountered endings by former world champion. 331 examples, each with diagram. 248pp. 5⅜ x 8½. 23332-4 Pa. $3.75

TONE POEMS, SERIES II: TILL EULENSPIEGELS LUSTIGE STREICHE, ALSO SPRACH ZARATHUSTRA, AND EIN HELDENLEBEN, Richard Strauss. Three important orchestral works, including very popular *Till Eulenspiegel's Marry Pranks,* reproduced in full score from original editions. Study score. 315pp. 9⅜ x 12¼. (Available in U.S. only)
23755-9 Pa. $8.95

TONE POEMS, SERIES I: DON JUAN, TOD UND VERKLARUNG AND DON QUIXOTE, Richard Strauss. Three of the most often performed and recorded works in entire orchestral repertoire, reproduced in full score from original editions. Study score. 286pp. 9⅜ x 12¼. (Available in U.S. only)
23754-0 Pa. $7.50

11 LATE STRING QUARTETS, Franz Joseph Haydn. The form which Haydn defined and "brought to perfection." *(Grove's)*. 11 string quartets in complete score, his last and his best. The first in a projected series of the complete Haydn string quartets. Reliable modern Eulenberg edition, otherwise difficult to obtain. 320pp. 8⅜ x 11¼. (Available in U.S. only)
23753-2 Pa. $7.50

FOURTH, FIFTH AND SIXTH SYMPHONIES IN FULL SCORE, Peter Ilyitch Tchaikovsky. Complete orchestral scores of Symphony No. 4 in F Minor, Op. 36; Symphony No. 5 in E Minor, Op. 64; Symphony No. 6 in B Minor, "Pathetique," Op. 74. Bretikopf & Hartel eds. Study score. 480pp. 9⅜ x 12¼.
23861-X Pa. $10.95

THE MARRIAGE OF FIGARO: COMPLETE SCORE, Wolfgang A. Mozart. Finest comic opera ever written. Full score, not to be confused with piano renderings. Peters edition. Study score. 448pp. 9⅜ x 12¼. (Available in U.S. only)
23751-6 Pa. $11.95

"IMAGE" ON THE ART AND EVOLUTION OF THE FILM, edited by Marshall Deutelbaum. Pioneering book brings together for first time 38 groundbreaking articles on early silent films from *Image* and 263 illustrations newly shot from rare prints in the collection of the International Museum of Photography. A landmark work. Index. 256pp. 8¼ x 11.
23777-X Pa. $8.95

AROUND-THE-WORLD COOKY BOOK, Lois Lintner Sumption and Marguerite Lintner Ashbrook. 373 cooky and frosting recipes from 28 countries (America, Austria, China, Russia, Italy, etc.) include Viennese kisses, rice wafers, London strips, lady fingers, hony, sugar spice, maple cookies, etc. Clear instructions. All tested. 38 drawings. 182pp. 5⅜ x 8.
23802-4 Pa. $2.50

THE ART NOUVEAU STYLE, edited by Roberta Waddell. 579 rare photographs, not available elsewhere, of works in jewelry, metalwork, glass, ceramics, textiles, architecture and furniture by 175 artists—Mucha, Seguy, Lalique, Tiffany, Gaudin, Hohlwein, Saarinen, and many others. 288pp. 8⅜ x 11¼.
23515-7 Pa. $6.95

THE AMERICAN SENATOR, Anthony Trollope. Little known, long unavailable Trollope novel on a grand scale. Here are humorous comment on American vs. English culture, and stunning portrayal of a heroine/villainess. Superb evocation of Victorian village life. 561pp. 5⅜ x 8½.
23801-6 Pa. $6.00

WAS IT MURDER? James Hilton. The author of *Lost Horizon* and *Goodbye, Mr. Chips* wrote one detective novel (under a pen-name) which was quickly forgotten and virtually lost, even at the height of Hilton's fame. This edition brings it back—a finely crafted public school puzzle resplendent with Hilton's stylish atmosphere. A thoroughly English thriller by the creator of Shangri-la. 252pp. 5⅜ x 8. (Available in U.S. only)
23774-5 Pa. $3.00

CENTRAL PARK: A PHOTOGRAPHIC GUIDE, Victor Laredo and Henry Hope Reed. 121 superb photographs show dramatic views of Central Park: Bethesda Fountain, Cleopatra's Needle, Sheep Meadow, the Blockhouse, plus people engaged in many park activities: ice skating, bike riding, etc. Captions by former Curator of Central Park, Henry Hope Reed, provide historical view, changes, etc. Also photos of N.Y. landmarks on park's periphery. 96pp. 8½ x 11. 23750-8 Pa. $4.50

NANTUCKET IN THE NINETEENTH CENTURY, Clay Lancaster. 180 rare photographs, stereographs, maps, drawings and floor plans recreate unique American island society. Authentic scenes of shipwreck, lighthouses, streets, homes are arranged in geographic sequence to provide walking-tour guide to old Nantucket existing today. Introduction, captions. 160pp. 8⅞ x 11¾. 23747-8 Pa. $6.95

STONE AND MAN: A PHOTOGRAPHIC EXPLORATION, Andreas Feininger. 106 photographs by *Life* photographer Feininger portray man's deep passion for stone through the ages. Stonehenge-like megaliths, fortified towns, sculpted marble and crumbling tenements show textures, beauties, fascination. 128pp. 9¼ x 10¾. 23756-7 Pa. $5.95

CIRCLES, A MATHEMATICAL VIEW, D. Pedoe. Fundamental aspects of college geometry, non-Euclidean geometry, and other branches of mathematics: representing circle by point. Poincare model, isoperimetric property, etc. Stimulating recreational reading. 66 figures. 96pp. 5⅝ x 8¼.
63698-4 Pa. $2.75

THE DISCOVERY OF NEPTUNE, Morton Grosser. Dramatic scientific history of the investigations leading up to the actual discovery of the eighth planet of our solar system. Lucid, well-researched book by well-known historian of science. 172pp. 5⅜ x 8½. 23726-5 Pa. $3.50

THE DEVIL'S DICTIONARY. Ambrose Bierce. Barbed, bitter, brilliant witticisms in the form of a dictionary. Best, most ferocious satire America has produced. 145pp. 5⅜ x 8½. 20487-1 Pa. $2.25

THE CURVES OF LIFE, Theodore A. Cook. Examination of shells, leaves, horns, human body, art, etc., in *"the* classic reference on how the golden ratio applies to spirals and helices in nature . . . . "—Martin Gardner. 426 illustrations. Total of 512pp. 5⅜ x 8½. 23701-X Pa. $5.95

AN ILLUSTRATED FLORA OF THE NORTHERN UNITED STATES AND CANADA, Nathaniel L. Britton, Addison Brown. Encyclopedic work covers 4666 species, ferns on up. Everything. Full botanical information, illustration for each. This earlier edition is preferred by many to more recent revisions. 1913 edition. Over 4000 illustrations, total of 2087pp. 6⅛ x 9¼. 22642-5, 22643-3, 22644-1 Pa., Three-vol. set $25.50

MANUAL OF THE GRASSES OF THE UNITED STATES, A. S. Hitchcock, U.S. Dept. of Agriculture. The basic study of American grasses, both indigenous and escapes, cultivated and wild. Over 1400 species. Full descriptions, information. Over 1100 maps, illustrations. Total of 1051pp. 5⅜ x 8½. 22717-0, 22718-9 Pa., Two-vol. set $15.00

THE CACTACEAE,, Nathaniel L. Britton, John N. Rose. Exhaustive, definitive. Every cactus in the world. Full botanical descriptions. Thorough statement of nomenclatures, habitat, detailed finding keys. The one book needed by every cactus enthusiast. Over 1275 illustrations. Total of 1080pp. 8 x 10¼. 21191-6, 21192-4 Clothbd., Two-vol. set $35.00

AMERICAN MEDICINAL PLANTS, Charles F. Millspaugh. Full descriptions, 180 plants covered: history; physical description; methods of preparation with all chemical constituents extracted; all claimed curative or adverse effects. 180 full-page plates. Classification table. 804pp. 6½ x 9¼. 23034-1 Pa. $12.95

A MODERN HERBAL, Margaret Grieve. Much the fullest, most exact, most useful compilation of herbal material. Gigantic alphabetical encyclopedia, from aconite to zedoary, gives botanical information, medical properties, folklore, economic uses, and much else. Indispensable to serious reader. 161 illustrations. 888pp. 6½ x 9¼. (Available in U.S. only) 22798-7, 22799-5 Pa., Two-vol. set $13.00

THE HERBAL or GENERAL HISTORY OF PLANTS, John Gerard. The 1633 edition revised and enlarged by Thomas Johnson. Containing almost 2850 plant descriptions and 2705 superb illustrations, Gerard's *Herbal* is a monumental work, the book all modern English herbals are derived from, the one herbal every serious enthusiast should have in its entirety. Original editions are worth perhaps $750. 1678pp. 8½ x 12¼. 23147-X Clothbd. $50.00

MANUAL OF THE TREES OF NORTH AMERICA, Charles S. Sargent. The basic survey of every native tree and tree-like shrub, 717 species in all. Extremely full descriptions, information on habitat, growth, locales, economics, etc. Necessary to every serious tree lover. Over 100 finding keys. 783 illustrations. Total of 986pp. 5⅜ x 8½. 20277-1, 20278-X Pa., Two-vol. set $11.00

DRAWINGS OF WILLIAM BLAKE, William Blake. 92 plates from Book of Job, *Divine Comedy, Paradise Lost*, visionary heads, mythological figures, Laocoon, etc. Selection, introduction, commentary by Sir Geoffrey Keynes. 178pp. 8⅛ x 11. 22303-5 Pa. $4.00

ENGRAVINGS OF HOGARTH, William Hogarth. 101 of Hogarth's greatest works: *Rake's Progress, Harlot's Progress, Illustrations for Hudibras, Before and After, Beer Street and Gin Lane*, many more. Full commentary. 256pp. 11 x 13¾. 22479-1 Pa. $12.95

DAUMIER: 120 GREAT LITHOGRAPHS, Honore Daumier. Wide-ranging collection of lithographs by the greatest caricaturist of the 19th century. Concentrates on eternally popular series on lawyers, on married life, on liberated women, etc. Selection, introduction, and notes on plates by Charles F. Ramus. Total of 158pp. 9⅜ x 12¼. 23512-2 Pa. $6.00

DRAWINGS OF MUCHA, Alphonse Maria Mucha. Work reveals drafts-man of highest caliber: studies for famous posters and paintings, render-ings for book illustrations and ads, etc. 70 works, 9 in color; including 6 items not drawings. Introduction. List of illustrations. 72pp. 9⅜ x 12¼. (Available in U.S. only) 23672-2 Pa. $4.00

GIOVANNI BATTISTA PIRANESI: DRAWINGS IN THE PIERPONT MORGAN LIBRARY, Giovanni Battista Piranesi. For first time ever all of Morgan Library's collection, world's largest. 167 illustrations of rare Piranesi drawings—archeological, architectural, decorative and visionary. Essay, detailed list of drawings, chronology, captions. Edited by Felice Stampfle. 144pp. 9⅜ x 12¼. 23714-1 Pa. $7.50

NEW YORK ETCHINGS (1905-1949), John Sloan. All of important American artist's N.Y. life etchings. 67 works include some of his best art; also lively historical record—Greenwich Village, tenement scenes. Edited by Sloan's widow. Introduction and captions. 79pp. 8⅜ x 11¼. 23651-X Pa. $4.00

CHINESE PAINTING AND CALLIGRAPHY: A PICTORIAL SURVEY, Wan-go Weng. 69 fine examples from John M. Crawford's matchless private collection: landscapes, birds, flowers, human figures, etc., plus calligraphy. Every basic form included: hanging scrolls, handscrolls, album leaves, fans, etc. 109 illustrations. Introduction. Captions. 192pp. 8⅞ x 11¾. 23707-9 Pa. $7.95

DRAWINGS OF REMBRANDT, edited by Seymour Slive. Updated Lipp-mann, Hofstede de Groot edition, with definitive scholarly apparatus. All portraits, biblical sketches, landscapes, nudes, Oriental figures, classical studies, together with selection of work by followers. 550 illustrations. Total of 630pp. 9⅛ x 12¼. 21485-0, 21486-9 Pa., Two-vol. set $15.00

THE DISASTERS OF WAR, Francisco Goya. 83 etchings record horrors of Napoleonic wars in Spain and war in general. Reprint of 1st edition, plus 3 additional plates. Introduction by Philip Hofer. 97pp. 9⅜ x 8¼. 21872-4 Pa. $4.00

GEOMETRY, RELATIVITY AND THE FOURTH DIMENSION, Rudolf Rucker. Exposition of fourth dimension, means of visualization, concepts of relativity as Flatland characters continue adventures. Popular, easily followed yet accurate, profound. 141 illustrations. 133pp. 5⅜ x 8½.
23400-2 Pa. $2.75

THE ORIGIN OF LIFE, A. I. Oparin. Modern classic in biochemistry, the first rigorous examination of possible evolution of life from nitrocarbon compounds. Non-technical, easily followed. Total of 295pp. 5⅜ x 8½.
60213-3 Pa. $4.00

PLANETS, STARS AND GALAXIES, A. E. Fanning. Comprehensive introductory survey: the sun, solar system, stars, galaxies, universe, cosmology; quasars, radio stars, etc. 24pp. of photographs. 189pp. 5⅜ x 8½. (Available in U.S. only)
21680-2 Pa. $3.75

THE THIRTEEN BOOKS OF EUCLID'S ELEMENTS, translated with introduction and commentary by Sir Thomas L. Heath. Definitive edition. Textual and linguistic notes, mathematical analysis, 2500 years of critical commentary. Do not confuse with abridged school editions. Total of 1414pp. 5⅜ x 8½.   60088-2, 60089-0, 60090-4 Pa., Three-vol. set $18.50

Prices subject to change without notice.

Available at your book dealer or write for free catalogue to Dept. GI, Dover Publications, Inc., 31 East Second Street, Mineola, N.Y. 11501. Dover publishes more than 175 books each year on science, elementary and advanced mathematics, biology, music, art, literary history, social sciences and other areas.